Media in Global Context
A Reader

Also available in this series

Approaches to Media: A Reader

Edited by Oliver Boyd-Barrett and Chris Newbold

FOUNDATIONS IN MEDIA

General editor: Oliver Boyd-Barrett

Media in Global Context

A Reader

Edited by
Annabelle Sreberny-Mohammadi,
Dwayne Winseck, Jim McKenna
and Oliver Boyd-Barrett

A member of the Hodder Headline Group
LONDON • NEW YORK • SYDNEY • AUCKLAND

First published in Great Britain in 1997 by
Arnold, a member of the Hodder Headline Group
338 Euston Road, London NW1 3BH
175 Fifth Avenue, New York, NY 10010

Distributed exclusively in the USA by
St Martin's Press Inc.,
175 Fifth Avenue,
New York, NY 10010

British Library Cataloguing in Publication Data
A catalogue entry for this book is available from the British Library

Library of Congress Cataloging-in-Publication Data
A catalog entry for this book is available from the Library of Congress

ISBN 0 340 67687 6 (Pb)
ISBN 0 340 67686 8 (Hb)

Produced by Gray Publishing, Tunbridge Wells
Printed and bound in Great Britain by J W Arrowsmith Ltd, Bristol

Contents

General editor's preface   vii

Editors' introduction

Media in global context   ix

Acknowledgements   xxix

Section 1. Conceptualizing the global

1 Mapping the global condition   2
   Roland Robertson
2 Notes on the global ecumene   11
   Ulf Hannerz
3 The globalizing of modernity   19
   Anthony Giddens
4 The theoretical challenge of global society   27
   Martin Shaw
5 Classifying the global system   37
   Leslie Sklair

Section 2. Nation, culture and media

6 The processes: from nationalisms to transnationals   50
   Jesus Martín-Barbero
7 The origins of national consciousness   58
   Benedict Anderson
8 Wishful thinking: cultural politics, media, and collective
   identities in Europe   67
   Philip Schlesinger
9 Broadcasting and new media policies in Taiwan   78
   Sheila Chin
10 National responses and accessibility to STAR TV in Asia   94
   Joseph Man Chan

Section 3. Global media actors

11 The case of the Korean airline tragedy   108
   Laurien Alexandre
12 Hollywood meets Madison Avenue: the commercialization
   of U.S. films   113
   Janet Wasko
13 Global news wholesalers as agents of globalization   131
   Oliver Boyd-Barrett
14 Global television news services   145
   Christopher Paterson

Section 4. Regulating the means of global communication

15 From communication to democratic norms: reflections on the
   normative dimensions of international communication policy   162
   Dwayne Winseck and Marlene Cuthbert

16 Prospects for a global communication infrastructure in the
   21st century: institutional restructuring and network
   development   177
   Richard Hawkins
17 The re-tooling of American hegemony: U.S. foreign
   communication policy from free flow to free trade   194
   Edward A. Comor
18 The European community and the regulation of media
   ownership and control: possibilities for pluralism   207
   Leslie P. Hitchens

Section 5. Challenge and resistance in the global media system

19 Small media and revolutionary change: a new model   220
   Annabelle Sreberny-Mohammadi and Ali Mohammadi
20 Organizing democratic radio: issues in praxis   236
   John L. Hochheimer
21 News, consciousness and social participation: the role of
   women's feature service in world news   248
   Carolyn M. Byerly
22 China turned on (revisited): television, reform and resistance 259
   James Lull

Section 6. Transnational media texts and audiences

23 Global harmonies and local discords: transnational policies
   and practices in the European recording industry   270
   Keith Negus
24 Distinguishing the global, regional and national levels of
   world television   284
   Joseph D. Straubhaar
25 Neighbourly relations? Cross-cultural reception analysis and
   Australian soaps in Britain   299
   Stuart Cunningham and Elizabeth Jacka
26 Finding a place for Islam: Egyptian television serials and the
   national interest   311
   Lila Abu-Lughod
27 Local uses of the media: negotiating culture and identity   323
   Marie Gillespie

Author index   339

Subject index   343

General editor's preface

This volume is one of a series of five readers which aim to provide a comprehensive set of resources for media studies courses. Other volumes of the series address the following themes: approaches to media; media industries and professions; audiences and reception; and media texts. Each volume of the series is intended to stand alone for the benefit of individual students or course organizers of courses at both undergraduate and postgraduate levels in media, journalism and broadcasting, communications, cultural and literary studies and, more generally, of courses in sociology, politics, and literature and education. Taken together, the volumes provide a broad introduction to the study of media, and they cover each of the major issues, topics, themes, approaches and methodologies encountered in the study of media. They are also intended to provide an international inflection both in source and in topic, which is in line with the processes of globalization of the media industries and with world-wide interest in the study of the media.

Oliver Boyd-Barrett

Editors' introduction –
Media in global context

This reader is a compilation of articles that focus on the analysis of communication institutions and processes of media production, circulation, and consumption within a global context. We think that the theorizing around globalization and the empirical issues it opens up could constitute the beginning of a paradigm-shift in international communication. Without embracing the concept wholeheartedly and unreservedly, we feel that it is one of the key constructs being explored across the contemporary social sciences which has, of necessity, repositioned communications at the heart of global affairs. Within international communication, the debates that globalization has precipitated point to a maturation of thinking in the field, a way of pursuing a more fruitful encounter between political economy and cultural studies and of thinking through some of the sterile polarized arguments that have dominated the recent history of international communication scholarship. Hence this volume presents a range of leading research approaches to the study of international communication and offers readers a variety of perspectives on the nature, degree and significance of relationships between concepts of the media and the global.

The debates about globalization, its definitions and dynamics, have stimulated, indeed required, interdisciplinary dialogue across the social sciences to a much greater extent than in the recent past. Hence this collection is multidisciplinary, including scholars from a broad range of fields who provide conceptual frameworks for thinking about globalization and offer ways to analyse and interpret the increasing connections between communications and the processes and experiences of globalization. Giddens and Robertson are social theorists; Sklair offers sociological approaches while Shaw works within international relations; Hannerz and Abu-Lughod are anthropologists, and other contributors 'represent' media studies and cultural studies.

Since much of the debate about globalization has developed after, and as a consequence of, the end of the cold war and the collapse of the Soviet Union, this volume reflects the thinking and lines of argument of the decade of the 1990s. This is a contemporaneous collection, not a collection of key and historic readings but a selection of the most theoretically provocative and empirically intriguing of current work. We have also included material on alternative and minority media, as well as mainstream/malestream media; again, this reveals rather than conceals the cleavages along which current scholarship is split, thus challenging would-be attempts to monopolize the explanatory field and encouraging the consideration of the competing ways of thinking about globalization and communication.

This compilation includes a mixture of previously published and brand new contributions which provide an excellent introduction to the field and its current controversies. As befits a volume interrogating globalization, our authors are international and the empirical loci of the readings do not privilege Western industrial contexts. You will find material on Brazil, China, Egypt, Iran and Taiwan, as well as on Europe and North America.

Globalization and its meanings

Debate about globalization has fed a boom in academic publishing during the 1990s. We incline to the view that the processes which it represents have been in evidence for quite a lot longer than is implied by the manner in which the concept is sometimes used; we would go further and argue that a fascination with some of the dimensions of globalization are also of very long standing, and can be discerned, for example, in much of the excitement which attended the introduction of various new technologies in the nineteenth and early twentieth centuries, including the telegraph, radio, photography and film. This is not to imply that globalization is essentially or even mainly about the media or even that it is necessarily a process that should be associated only with the emergence of industrialization or of modernity in general.

All these are issues which constitute part of the debate about what globalization is and what it signifies. In contemplating the reasons for the intense interest in globalization within social science in the 1990s we suggest that there has been a significant acceleration in the rate at which globalization, in at least some of its manifestations, has become apparent at the level of experience of everyday life. These would include such things as the volume and increasingly international character of the goods that are available for sale to the general public; international tourism and migration, internationalization of ownership, the shared possession and use across national boundaries of cultural icons and media products. Among the latter, the global availability of an increasing range of moving image contents in film and broadcasting, press and magazine coverage and photography, and music is particularly difficult to ignore. Accounting for their extension, the interests they serve, their functions, and the meanings which are invested in them, is a major part of what this volume is about.

As editors we have constructed the volume to explore the links between globalization and media along four principle axes. After investigating the concept in and of itself (Section 1), we have looked for contributions which would explore the connections between globalization and media in relation to national and cultural identity (Section 2), since the theme of globalization suggests either the subversion or supplementation of national cultural identities in favour of alternative, perhaps more localized or more global sources of identity. Sensitive to concerns that the literature on globalization, in its critique of earlier political-economy models of cultural and media imperialism as explanations for transnational cultural processes, has tended to blur the importance and distinctness of agency and cause, we specifically wanted to include chapters that discussed particular media actors (Section 3). We have chosen to focus on actors – the international print and television news agencies – which figured in earlier debates about media imperialism, but here relocated within a perspective of globalization discourse. We have also included the Hollywood film industry and, as an example of the explicit fusion of media and national interest, a case-study of the Voice of America. Our concern with agency is extended in Section 4 to an examination of attempts by national, regional and global institutions to regulate transnational media flows, in recognition that such attempts, whether or not they are considered effective in empowerment or containment, testify to a broad international consensus that transnational media activities and flows are indeed something that need to be regulated or at least, through regulation, to be protected – according to whichever ideological framework is operative. Nonetheless the institutions of formal regulation are mainly represented by national political and commercial elites and reflect their established interests. This confirms the suspicion that rather than seeing globalization as a process that uniformly subverts the national, we should regard nation-states as powerful players in the process of constructing the global: this process of global construction may even consolidate some nation-states while further weakening the already weak.

Efforts to counter what are considered to be the harmful effects of mainstream transnational media, or simply to extend the range of what is on offer beyond that which the mainstream provides, are themselves global in scope, and linked to significantly different articulations of ethnic, gender, political and cultural concerns. These are the subject of Section 5 of the book, which also recognizes that even alternative media, or perhaps especially the alternative media, face considerable challenges at the governing and managerial levels. Section 6 is concerned with media texts and media audiences, especially the texts of transnational media, and the variety of such texts in terms both of origin and genre. Contributions here suggest a greater diversity than the globalization literature might lead us to expect, while (especially ethnographic) studies of audience demonstrate, as is now common in such research, that regardless of the constraints and narrowness of production there is considerable variation in interpretation and usage.

Globalization: competing theoretical approaches

In this introductory chapter we will explore what we see as some of the main features of globalization as it concerns in particular the media and telecommunications. As Section 1 makes clear, debates about globalization cross many disciplines. Giddens firmly situates globalization as a consequence of modernity, whose dynamics radically transform social relations across time and space. More specifically, he argues that globalization occurs in four key domains: the extension of the nation-state system; the global reach of the capitalist economy coupled with the international division of labour; and a global system of military alliances (although we should note that this extract was written prior to 1989 and the collapse of the old military order). Robertson, by contrast, anchors the development of globalizing tendencies in an earlier history than does Giddens. Giddens, outlining a five-phase model in which many more institutions, actors and ideological/cultural elements play a role than in Giddens. Indeed, the two pieces can effectively be read against each other.

Hannerz addresses the assumption common to much globalization discourse, as did theories of cultural and media imperialism before it, that globalization and its culture moves outwards from the 'centre' ('modern'

North and West) towards the periphery in largely one-way flows. He argues that centre-periphery relations are much more complex; cultural flows move in multiple directions, and thus the outcomes are opposite tendencies, both toward what he calls saturation and maturation, toward homogenization *and* heterogenization. This tension or quandary is reflected in many of the contributions later on in the volume. For Shaw the central question is whether a global society is possible. He argues that such a development would be more than just the sum of its parts (global economic relations; global political institutions; a shared globalized culture); it would be based around new forms of identification. By uncoupling the national from the state, he is able to show that 'nations' in fact cross state boundaries and that newer patterns of identification may have quite historical roots. Such a global civil society challenges the state-centric premise of much current social theory, especially of course in international relations.

Sklair analyses various approaches that have been used to classify the emerging world system. Unlike some of the theorizing which is very abstract, often flying way above social reality rather than grounded in it, these approaches are founded on varying kinds of empirical data and valuations of the key dimensions of development. In the end, Sklair is not satisfied with any of them because all remain very state-centric and thus obscure some key dimensions of the world system, such as the capitalist economy which transcends national boundaries, and potential actors on the world stage, like social movements. Thus his selection is mainly to be read as a critique, not as a fully-fledged exposition of his own argument. It provides a backdrop for Sections 3 and 4 of the book which look at transnational actors, and at attempts by them in alliance with nation-states to constitute the global through regulatory systems.

Globalization as the transformation of communicative spaces and social relations

Thinking about the concept of globalization in relation to communication it immediately becomes apparent that the 'spaces' of interaction between people, information, institutions and cultural traditions are being transformed. Broadly speaking, we can suggest that patterns of social interaction and information flows are increasingly occurring across national boundaries to form new bases of political and cultural identity. In contrast to the historical tendency for communication media to be used to *vertically integrate* societies within the contours of the nation-state, emerging patterns of social interaction, political organization and information flows are being supplemented by patterns of transnational, *horizontal integration*.

Communication and the vertical integration of society

In the traditional pattern of the mature industrial societies of the northern hemisphere, one-way flows of communication from a small number of national communication/media institutions – private and/or public – have served to project images and a nationally defined political and cultural agenda down and across social classes and internal cultural boundaries. These practices of 'vertical integration' were sometimes underpinned by universal service mandates designed to make access to the means of communication available to all regardless of where they lived and at a reasonable cost (not only in post, telegraph and telephony, but also in national broadcast systems and, through such devices as postal subsidies and public library services, the press and other reading material). In some countries such measures also served to consolidate linguistic standardization around privileged dialect varieties associated with the political capital and social elite, and the formation of a national political and cultural public sphere which, at its best, mediated and represented the internal diversity of a country.

From an economic point of view, 'vertical integration' shaped an industrial structure that often combined the financing and production of media messages with control over the distribution networks through which such messages flowed. Telecommunication operators also contained forward and backward vertical linkages as they had controlling relations with nation-ally-based equipment manufactures and owned and operated telephone networks and services offered over such networks. The economic dimension of 'vertical integration' was further buttressed by prohibitions against foreign ownership, restrictions on cross-media ownership, and technical standards that erected barriers to the transnational procurement of communications hardware (see the chapter by Richard Hawkins), and sometimes, the contents of communication. Even more generally, this complex of social, political, cultural and economic arrangements and practices was supported by a hierarchical policy process that defined the structural framework and normative goals of the communication system from the top and on behalf of less than well-defined notions of the public interest.

Horizontal patterns of communicative interaction as a supplement to vertical integration

In contrast to the tendency towards vertical integration within nations, one of the key features of globalization is the *transnational horizontal integration* of media structures, processes and audience/media interactions. 'Horizontal' communication here is not being used merely to celebrate new patterns of communicative interaction among people, as for example, in discussions of 'grass-roots communications'. Rather the term refers to a host of processes through which (i) people are being inscribed into transnational patterns of marketing and political communication, (ii) alterations in flows of media products and information that integrate local spaces across national boundaries, (iii) the harmonization of regulatory and legal frameworks and, above all, to (iv) new models of ownership and control in the communications industries that supplement traditional patterns of vertical integration within specific media sectors with forms of horizontal integration of ownership across media sectors, i.e. cable television, broadcasting, telecommunications, publishing, film, etc.

This process of horizontal integration is evidenced by several factors, one of which is the process whereby people are increasingly addressed across national boundaries on the basis of class status and other cultural attributes by marketing, political and cultural agencies alike. Other contributing factors to the increased levels of transnational social interaction are the patterns of information flows made possible by the new technologies of communication, and shifts in the institutional organization – economic, political and legal – of the means of communication.

Several contributors to this volume including Benedict Anderson, Philip Schlesinger, Sheila Chin, Joseph Man Chan and Jesus Martin-Barbero – analyse the effects of these changes on the historical relations between communication, culture and the nation-state. They note the enhanced ability of communications media to escape the boundaries of the nation-state, contributing to new patterns of political action, new forms of economic organization, crises in the power and identities of nation-states, a rejuvenation of non-state based conceptions of cultural identity and new questions about the historical relationship between communication, media and democracy. In consequence there is a confusing array of events and practices that simultaneously point towards the specificity of the 'local' as the container of experience and toward the 'global' dimension of modern life. The difficulty is in conceptualizing the relationship between both, rather than engaging in unqualified celebration of globalization or, conversely, jingoistic worship of the local and tradition (see also Braman and Sreberny-Mohammadi, 1996).

Schlesinger notes that the tendency within the European Union to link communication policy with the use of media for the formation of a 'European cultural identity' is particularly problematic in this respect, as such efforts work with ill-defined assumptions about cultural boundaries and resurrect problematic models of omnipotent media forging a collective consciousness, albeit on a regional rather than a national level. This contrasts with efforts by the European Union to promote local languages and cultures *within* nation-states, or with evidence of local resistance to the consequences of liberalized, transnational markets. From Schlesinger's point of view, this practice only moves state-centric models of public spheres of communication to a higher level of geographical abstraction, and does little to open up the media to greater participation by the citizens of Europe. Conversely, Sheila Chin's chapter on the evolution of cable television in Taiwan shows how attempts to escape the constraints of political cultures by, for example, attempting to access the global satellite facilities of Asia-Sat are restricted by that organization's deference to local government demands and wishes. Joseph Man Chan makes a similar point in response to the Chinese government's ability to bend Star TV's distribution policies to its own ends, in this case with reference to decisions by Star TV not to continue carrying the BBC World Television service.

People, information flows and the new technologies of transnational communication

The attempts of the European Union, Taiwanese cable operators and others to forge new communicative relations across national borders are not unique, and are in fact mirrored by the attempts of advertisers and political and cultural organizations to address people across national boundaries and by the increased transnational flows of information. From the point of view of advertisers, national borders are increasingly irrelevant and, at best, a nuisance, as they attempt to define markets based on class status and desirable psychographic attributes that are independent of national affiliation. Whereas the European Union attempts to move the relations between communication, culture and citizenship to a higher level of geographical *and* political abstraction, advertisers are increasingly using communications media to weld together 'transnational consumption communities'.

Pendakur and Kapur (1995) note how internationally circulated publications, such as *Fortune* and *Business Week*, are celebrating more and more the rise of the middle classes in so-called Third World countries, such as India. While wealthy classes within such countries may be proportionally small, they are numerically quite large. The fact that they increasingly have access to the means of producing and receiving communication, are fluent in English and ideologically predisposed to support capitalism makes them attractive to transnational media operators and advertisers. As a result of these developments larger numbers of people have been integrated into the transnational media system, and media and advertisers have stepped up their efforts to secure international legal protections for 'freedom of commercial speech', along the lines already developed within the United States with a view to harmonizing cultural identities and experiences among those integrated into the transnational media system. In his contribution to this volume, Leslie Sklair writes that these developments form the basis for a 'culture/ideology of consumption' that functions materially to expand the geographical space over which capitalism operates and ideologically to root the legitimacy of global capitalism in the everyday practices of those who consume the goods and values on offer. A similar point is made in the later chapter by Edward Comor. Comor elaborates the relationship of these developments to U.S. efforts to forge and consolidate an international communication policy that extends that country's historical commitment to the 'free flow of information' doctrine.

Transnational communicative interactions are not limited to commercial concerns. Politics and actions by non-governmental organizations (NGOs) and governments alike are increasingly shaped by the use of communication technologies and the transnational flow of information. Thus, as numerous authors have noted, communication media were essential factors linking together people and action across vast areas of geographical space during the disintegration of the eastern-bloc countries, demonstrations for political reform in the People's Republic of China, Thailand, Kenya and elsewhere and around environmental and trade concerns (Jones, 1994; Morumpei, 1996). The articles by Sheila Chin and Joseph Straubhaar in particular indicate the numerous attempts in Taiwan, South and Central America and other areas of the world to deploy communication technologies to extend the patterns of communicative interaction in civil society, on local, national, regional and international levels.

The trends during the 1980s and 1990s towards regulatory liberalization, privatization and commercialization of the media resulted in increased flows of media content and expanded the market for television programming, film and news throughout the world. While this has benefited the U.S. television and film industries – as evidenced by the eight-fold growth in the revenues of Motion Picture Export Association of America (MPEA) companies between 1980 to 1993 – there has been a simultaneous increase of 'cultural exports' from many European countries and some of the less developed countries as well (Straubhaar, 1991; Wasko, 1994). Chapters by Oliver Boyd-Barrett, Chris Paterson, Janet Wasko, and Joseph Straubhaar document these trends as they focus on the increased international scope of major television broadcasters and news agencies. Broadcasters and news agencies such as Reuters, WTN, CNN, the BBC, NBC, CBC, ABC, NewsCorp among others, have established extensive linkages with national and local broadcasting systems – private and public – throughout the world for news feeds, specialized information services and video footage. At one and the same time they represent a highly participative exchange-based co-operative system and yet also a hierarchically organized global network dominated by U.S. and European-based organizations. The structure of global media hierarchies, as both Wasko and Alexandre illustrate, may still parallel hierarchies of global power relations in general.

These developments indicate that a more modest role is being played by public service media in relation to their private sector counterparts. This should not be confused with a general retreat of direct government involve-ment in international communications. Contributions to Sections 3 and 4 demonstrate how governments continue to be involved in international communication on at least two levels. On the one hand, as Richard Hawkins shows, government involvement continues behind the scenes in the arenas of international and regional communication policy. Hawkins suggests that the role of standard setting is becoming increasingly important in developing telecommunications networks world-wide. He notes that, for instance, the International Telecommunications Union (ITU) remains central to such practices, but that the role of this agency is being off-set by the proliferation of regional technical standard-setting committees which reflects the increasing organization of communication networks, information flows and trade in general around hierarchically organized regional blocs.

Hawkins, Winseck and Cuthbert, Comor and Hitchens also note that the role of United Nations-based specialized agencies such as the ITU and the United Nations Education, Scientific and Cultural Organization (UNESCO) in global communications is also supplemented by the increasing reliance on the 'trade in services' regimes unfolding through the North American Free Trade Agreement (NAFTA), the European Community and General Agreement on Trade and Tariffs (GATT)/World Trade Organization (WTO). These authors focus on processes of regulatory liberalization and attempts to incorporate the communication and cultural industries into the far- reaching regional and international agreements typified by the European Community, NAFTA and GATT.

A second and perhaps more ubiquitous and overt form of government participation in global communications is international broadcasting by governments, an area covered by Laurien Alexandre. In this article, Alexandre documents the continued use of international broadcasting by governments in the post cold war period and identifies this as a major element in international relations and efforts to stake out particular visions of a 'New World Order'. Alexandre illustrates her points through the example of the former Soviet Union's downing of Korean Airliner (KAL 007) in the late 1980s.

The essential point here is that governments still perceive international broadcasting, by shortwave for example, as a key part of the efforts to shape the contours of public opinion locally and globally. This reinforces a trend noted earlier by Herbert Schiller (1969) whereby governments in the global system, since at least the Second World War, have used media to circumvent local governments and directly address their citizens.

While international communication scholarship has long documented the dominance of the U.S. in the global media system (see, for example, Schiller, 1969; Sreberny-Mohammadi, *et. al.*, 1985), some of the authors in Section 6 – Lila Abu-Lughod, Keith Negus, Joseph Straubhaar – suggest that the well-documented research from the late 1960s until the mid-1980s demonstrating the 'one-way flow' of television programming, music, news and other forms of communication needs to be revisited and rethought. For example, Straubhaar, in a critique of the idea of globalization as the (primarily U.S.-led) world-wide homogenization of television and the erosion of national and cultural differences, offers evidence indicating that there is by no means a 'one-way flow' of media products from the few to the many. He suggests that the vast demand opened up by regulatory liberalization, commercialization, privatization and new technologies in many national communication systems has not only increased the circulation of Western media products but also opened up more distribution channels for local, national and regional media productions. As a result, several countries during the last 15–20 years have substantially increased the quantity of domestic and regional productions within their national communication systems and served as a source of supply for other regions of the world. In particular, Straubhaar, whilst by no means discounting the idea of globalization altogether, suggests that the 'regionalization' of television into 'geo-cultural' markets linked not only, or even primarily, by geography but also by language and culture, may be a more significant level of analysis. The emergence of new multi-country markets in which audiences may be geographically distant from one another yet remain linked as markets through linguistic and/or other cultural ties is an important development which we can ill-afford to overlook in the discussion or analysis of contemporary flows of media products internationally. The work of Abu-Lughod on Egyptian television serials, and of Negus on the policies and practices of the European recording industry, respectively, offer further evidence of the increasingly complex relations between local, national, regional and international production, distribution and consumption of media texts in a global context.

Such trends towards the structural break-up of the 'one-way flow' of information can be further illustrated by at least two other trends: the proliferation of alternative media and the possibilities opened up by the new telecommunications. With respect to the first trend, *Media in Global Context* includes several articles on the alternative use of media for social and political change. John Hochheimer examines attempts by some groups to organize and operate more democratic forms of radio broadcasting. He suggests that there are a number of costs and constraints that influence any attempt to democratize radio broadcasting, and that no small part of such efforts is confronting the challenges raised once the traditional relations between media producers and consumers are called into question. In their chapter, Annabelle Sreberny-Mohammadi and Ali Mohammadi explore these issues further in relation to radical socio-political change in Iran, and with reference to the utility of low-cost media technologies. Sreberny-Mohammadi and Mohammadi suggest that 'mediated culture has become part of the causal sequence of revolutionary crisis'. Carolyn Byerly addresses similar issues, discussing the potentials and limits of using alternative media to better address the needs and concerns of women.

The discussions of alternative media by Byerly, Hochheimer and Sreberny-Mohammadi and Mohammadi are crucial to understanding media in a global context on at least two accounts. First, although there were efforts in the 1970s and 1980s to promote a New World Information Communication Order with the aim of ameliorating 'inequalities and imbalances of media flow and provision that prompted demands for alternatives at both global and local levels' (Lewis, 1995, p. 5), the connection between these demands and what such alternative practices might look like were under-theorized and undeveloped. The articles included here address this concern by providing a guide for alternative media praxis. Second, they show how such praxis connects the global and the local outside of a state-centric framework, in contrast to 'vertically integrating' national, or regional networks.

The other trend that points towards cracks in the structure of the one-way flow of information are tendencies evident in the flows of information outside the channels offered by forms of mass communication. Here we can refer to the possibilities of telecommunications opening up channels for two-way, interactive communication that deepen the communicative relations within civil society, help to bypass the centralized structures of mass media – private and public – and allow people to communicate across spatial and temporal barriers (Hills, 1993). The declining costs of international telephone calls (while local charges often rise), coupled with the new technologies, has resulted in an enormous upsurge in flows of international telecommunications. According to the Secretary General of the International Telecommunications Union, Pekka Tarjanne, the average telephone subscriber initiates more than 70 minutes of international calls per year (1994, p. 2). For the fortunate few in Sub-Saharan African countries with access to sparse telecommunications networks, the rate of international telephone usage is three times the international average. Thus, in addition to the 'top-down' vertical integration presumed by forms of mass communication, developments in telecommunications suggest that patterns of horizontal communication are beginning to supplement traditional communicative relations on an international basis. Such tendencies are further reinforced by some of the newer forms of communication, such as the Internet and other telecommunications network-based services, although, as will be indicated below, the potential benefits flowing from these developments are far from certain.

The changing global political economy of communications

Underlying these altered geographical spaces of social, communicative and cultural interaction are vast transformations in the global political economy of communication. These transformations are taking place in the ownership and control of the means of communication, the political and legal systems that protect and stabilize the environment in which communication systems operate and the implications that these and the above mentioned changes hold for democratic communication and people's ability to shape the forces impinging on their daily lives.

The transnationalization of media ownership and control: mergers and acquisitions

While the above analysis of people's experience of globalization and international communication suggests that it is extremely difficult to offer a definitive prognosis of the benefits and/or consequences of the changes affecting the media, several contributors to this volume, including Oliver Boyd-Barrett, Edward Comor, Leslie Hitchens, Chris Paterson, Janet Wasko, and Dwayne Winseck and Marlene Cuthbert discuss trends toward the formation of powerful transnational media corporations and to pressures for legal changes that these arrangements are bringing in their wake. The formation of Time Warner in 1989 to build the then world's largest media conglomerate, with over 340,000 employees and branches in the U.S., Australia, Asia, Europe and Latin America and revenues of $10 billion (1989), offered one of the more dramatic illustrations of this trend (Sreberny-Mohammadi, 1996, pp. 123–4). Other examples abound. As a recent report by the Commission of the European Communities notes, between 1990 and 1991 in Europe alone there were 81 different media-related mergers and acquisitions (CEC, 1992, p. 24). Illustrating the tendency for the patterns of ownership and control of media to escape the boundaries of nation-states, the report noted that of the total $103 billion represented by acquisitions in 1990, the value of transactions between Europe, North America and Japan was $20 billion (CEC, 1992, Table VI). From this it is possible to conclude that the structure of media ownership and control is increasingly becoming transnational – although not global, since almost all of the action was within the three areas just mentioned.

The reduction of structural autonomy and some implications for public communication

While interesting in and of themselves, these activities are more important in so far as they indicate an unparalleled, historical process of combination within specific media sectors, between different aspects of the media industries (i.e. broadcasting and press) and between the media industries and industry in general (i.e. electronics, finance, manufacturing, etc.). While mergers and acquisitions have always been a feature of the communications industry, the recent actions are distinctive in terms of *frequency, scope* and *implications for public communication on a global basis*. As Leslie Hitchens notes in her article on the European Commission and the regulation of media ownership and control, the frequency and scope of these mergers and acquisitions have raised significant calls from media critics, independent media producers, citizens' groups and some within the European Union for efforts to regulate levels of media ownership and concentration and to ensure diversity, albeit with little success (as will be indicated below) (CEC, 1992, p. 7).

As the combinations between CBS and Westinghouse and NBC and General Electric, for example, illustrate, mergers and acquisitions have aligned the media industries with enormous corporations whose operations span sensitive areas like nuclear energy, weapons and defence and other areas that blur the lines between corporations and government. This constrains the structural possibilities for media autonomy and for the diverse, even critical, public communications that are necessary for the maintenance and development of democratic societies. As a *Green Paper* by the Commission of European Communities notes, 'autonomy and structural independence among controllers ... constitutes a minimum condition of the diversity of choice offered to the public' (CEC, 1992, p. 19).

The possibility that the reduction of structural autonomy and resultant integration of the media into centres of political and economic power contributes to the instrumental use of the media to shape and limit the range of public communication is not idle speculation. As the critical analysis of these trends offered by several of the authors in *Media in Global Context* illustrate, the reduction of structural autonomy has directly shaped the nature of public communication by: (i) increasing the emphasis on what is commercially viable at the expense of non-profitable forms of media content, (ii) setting local cultural production and access to the media in competition with imported material, (iii) contributing to the loss of cultural specificity as private and public media alike produce for an international market, and (iv) the privatization of censorship as large transnational media corporations display a willingness to jettison sensitive programming to avoid offending local governments as a *quid pro quo* for continued market access.

Chapters by Paterson, Wasko and others illustrate that the range of programme genres has narrowed as the commercialization of media systems throughout the world has progressed. Simply put, in the drive for ratings and commercial success, public and private broadcasters have reduced their commitments – financially and ideologically – to news, public affairs and educational programming in favour of entertainment-based programming. In terms of internal diversity, then, commercialization and competition may have narrowed the range of what is on offer. Second, while the examples introduced by Chin, Straubhaar and others above indicated an increase in the regional production and distribution of information and media content, it has to be asked whether *quantitative* increase necessarily represents a *relative* or a *qualitative* increase. The abundance offered by the emerging communications environment does not necessarily or without regulatory support translate into increased citizens' access to the means of communication or to the generation of unique production and genre styles. Third, increased budget cutbacks in public service media, such as the CBC and Telefilm Canada, have meant an increased reliance on global markets for revenues and international joint ventures, with the result that the content produced simultaneously addresses everyone in general and nobody in particular (Perlmutter, 1993, pp. 21–2). Finally, while media have no doubt played a progressive role in the momentous political transformation of the globe over the last several years, there are some indications that this function sits uncomfortably alongside a willingness of certain transnational media corporations to censor information flows likely to offend local governments.

This has been a long-standing practice, for example, at TV Globo in Brazil (Mader, 1993, pp. 78–82), but is becoming standard practice among private media operating in politically repressive environments where their presence is dependent on local governments. Examples of this include the weak efforts by private media corporations in Turkey to strengthen the 'freedom of expression' provisions addressed in the ongoing process of constitutional reform, the willingness of Murdoch's Star TV, as discussed by Chan, to abandon carriage of the BBC because of news coverage considered hostile by the Chinese government (although reinstated since) and recent statements by the executive officers of the newly formed Disney/ABC network that the new corporation would be willing to avoid political reporting that might be upsetting to governments with less-than-impressive human rights records and far from democratic political systems (Martin, 1995, p. 7).

Power, control, confusion and the new technologies

(i) *Economic and technological convergence in communications.* The above examples of economic convergence indicate a crossing, and in the process a dissolving, of traditional media boundaries. Without a properly conceptualized framework for communications policy, this threatens to extend concentrated control over both the contents and channels found in publishing and broadcasting to telecommunications, where the long-standing common carrier principle separated control of networks from editorial control. Promises are often heard that new telecommunications will decentralize communications production and distribution. In discussing the case of Internet in relation to news-flow, for example, Boyd-Barrett identifies both the opportunities for new market entrants, and the superior resources which existing giants have in exploiting its potential. Thus the processes of restructuring within the communications industries may not be as beneficial for democratic communication as often thought. When we consider the range of activities across the field of communications it becomes apparent that the driving force of technology behind 'media convergence' (or, as some might argue, 'reconvergence') is, at the very least, being strongly influenced and shaped by forces unleashed through economic and legal restructuring. Once it is realized that events are not being driven by some exogenous and inexorable force – technology in this case – space is more available to shape the communications environment to better serve democratic uses of communication.

Comor, Hitchens, Winseck and Cuthbert stress that media (re-)convergence is not solely a by-product of technological innovations and digitization, but rather involves several simultaneous processes. On the one hand, mergers and acquisitions are combining formerly quite distinct, and even new, sectors of the communication industries. The recent *Green Paper* by the Commission of European Communities illustrates the role of economic convergence in bringing together the media across formerly influential technological boundaries. The paper notes that between April 1990 and August 1994 there were a total of 18 different acquisitions or partnerships between telecommunications operators, cable systems, broadcasters and publishers, with a total value of $80.3 billion. Among other things, these activities aligned USWest (telecommunications) with Time Warner (film, publishing, cable tv), combined the activities of MCI (telecommunications) with those of NewsCorp (newspapers, satellite television, terrestrial broadcasting, on-line services), created a partnership between BellSouth, Ameritech and SBC Communications (all telecommunications network and service providers) with Disney/ABC (film, theme parks, broadcasting), and resulted in Rogers/UNITEL (cable tv, television production, broadcasting, telecommunications) acquiring MacLean-Hunter Publishing (publishing, cable tv) (CEC, 1994, p. 27; Jackson, 1992, p. 15; Snoddy, 1995a, p. 20). Such actions are not limited to the so-called Western, industrialized countries but also extend to others, such as Mexico, where the recently privatized TelMex telecommunications operator (now jointly owned by one of the U.S. Regional Bell Operating Companies, France Telecom and Grupo Garso) has just acquired a controlling interest in the country's largest cable network operator, Cablevision (Dombey, 1995, p. 3).

The effect of these activities, notes Hitchens, may be to consolidate control within the communications industry and position companies to take advantage of the much heralded emerging multi-media environment. The examples also illustrate that patterns of vertical integration in the media industries are being supplemented by a more extensive web of horizontal integration. The result is that the patterns of sociological, political and communicative interaction are being mirrored by patterns of economic organization. Such observations ought to caution us against confusing information abundance, horizontal communication and the new technologies with the democratization of communication. They should also sensitize us to the profound questions that recent intra-media, cross-media and inter-industry combinations raise about the nature of communication and power in relation to the new communication infrastructures – integrated broad-band networks, information superhighways, etc. – and about how more democratic forms of communication can be developed that supersede the restrictive forms of control and modes of address found in the more traditional, vertically-arranged press and broadcasting industries.

(ii) *The uses and abuses of technological distinctions as the basis of communications policy/law.* Conceptual confusion and disarray in national communications policy and regulatory frameworks does not shed much light on how more democratic forms of communication might be developed. Imaginings of a more democratic future seem to have devolved almost exclusively to enthusiasts of the new communication and information technologies. Thoroughly ensconced in the technologically determinist visions of an infor-mation society, policy-makers in the U.K., U.S., Canada and elsewhere have either proposed or have successfully removed restrictions on cross-media ownership, partially rescinded the common-carrier principle so that telecommunication operators can provide more traditional media services such as broadcasting (although not in the U.K.) and information services, and shifted from the use of communication policy as a means of shaping the development, organization and uses of communications media toward the general application of competition law. These trends prompt several observations:

Contemporary developments in communication policy/law are simultaneously dissolving technologically specific regulatory practices while strengthening and/or creating others. Although policy-makers often claim to be merely eliminating the antiquated technological distinctions underpinning separate regulatory systems for telecommunications, broadcasting, cable television and publishing that now stand in the way of media convergence (Pool, 1983) the 'regulatory imagination' continues to be severely constrained by technologically-specific concepts. Thus, for example, the European Union proposes to allow for convergence and competition between different communication technologies while at the same time offering guidance on questions of media ownership, control, concentration and diversity that are technologically specific. As Hitchens suggests in her chapter, the European Community's *Green Paper* on pluralism and media concentration offered one of the most illustrative examples of this tendency, discussing the issues almost entirely in relation to terrestrial television and recommending measures for the monitoring of ownership concentration within specific media, or as the Commission calls them, mono-media, sectors.

Such a framework, arguably, resurrects practices frozen in time and is wholly inadequate to the task at hand. While such measures may correct for the effect of mergers and acquisitions on concentration within, say, a national television system, they are oblivious to the effect of such processes *across* dissolving media, political and economic boundaries. Thus, for example, although the acquisition of a television station by BT, AT&T or any other large telecommunications corporation may not adversely effect diversity *within* the television market, it obviously does not increase the range of voices *across* the media. Furthermore, the use of 'technology-specific' measures of ownership and control are unable to address the recent issues raised by Berlusconi's use of his vast media holdings to further his political fortunes or to gauge the impact of the acquisition of NBC by General Electric or CBS by Westinghouse. Obviously such conceptual confusion is not without important sociological and political implications.

Such confusions are not limited to the European Community, but are found in the NAFTA agreement and the recently concluded GATT agreements on telecommunications. NAFTA and GATT draw distinctions between telecommunications and computer services (included in the agreements), on the one hand, and broadcasting, cable television and film (excluded from the agreements), on the other hand (Canada, 1992; TNC, 1993, *Annex on Telecommunications*). Yet, it is unlikely that the technical and economic basis for such practices will persist as single companies, such as the Rogers/UNITEL/Maclean Hunter conglomerate, USWest and Time Warner, etc., offer computer, telecommunications, enhanced network services and video programming over the same technological infrastructure. The reduction of information/communication to a series of ones and zeros through digitization, and the emerging patterns of ownership and control, means that distinctions between data, films, video, or whatever, are useless as regulatory devices. Nonetheless, as the 'technological confusion of the regulatory mind' proceeds apace it is becoming evident that new distinctions are being made between *technological infrastructures* and the *services or contents* being offered over these infrastructures. The former is governed by more extensive regulation, especially that offered by competition law, while the latter tends to fall outside the scope of anything more than remedial public policy efforts. As the NAFTA and GATT agreements indicate, the consequence of this distinction is that many of the new network services offered over telecommunications networks – on-line data bases, Internet services, electronic mail, etc. – are excluded from regulatory attempts to further the public interest or the formation of democratic systems of communication (Winseck, 1996). While these agreements may contribute to increased levels of network competition and form the basis for regional and global trade, they offer little in the way of furthering more global conceptions of communication, citizenship and democracy.

Accompanying the state of 'technological confusion' is a shift from communications policy to competition policy as a basis of guiding the development, organization and uses of the media. Whereas communication policy usually explicitly concerns itself with measures designed to bring about a democratic media and to balance public and commercial interests, competition law aims only to secure the conditions necessary for competition through structural and behavioural regulation and a range of other narrowly defined technical objectives (CEC, 1994). Within the framework of competition law pluralism and access are incidental by-products of competition, objectives that may be over-ridden by more pressing goals of technological innovation, international competitiveness and the formation of common markets (Addy, 1994; CEC, 1994). The outcome of this process is that communication is legally constructed as a commodity like any other, in contrast to the historical link between communication, citizenship and democracy (Keane, 1990), and the economic and legal conditions for technological (re-)convergence solidified.

(iii) *The influence of media (dis-) integration on the social relations of communication.* Other alterations in national, regional and international communications policies and laws have been instrumental in shifting the balance between vertical and horizontal integration in the global political economy of communication. The patterns of mergers and alliances between media firms and between communications hardware and software producers illustrated above have been aided by the removal of restrictions in the U.S. that limited television networks' ability to distribute their own productions. The relaxing of cross-media ownership rules has made it easier to circulate software through all of the available media channels. As Wasko's chapter argues, regulatory changes in the U.S., including the elimination of the Fin/Syn rules and relaxation of cross-ownership restrictions, have allowed major U.S.-based communications conglomerates to enhance their position within the emerging global communications industry, while also consolidating their control at home. A clear expression of the impact of relaxed regulatory restrictions in the U.S. on the structure of the communications industries is the Disney acquisition of ABC, allowing the new Disney/ABC network to exploit the vast Disney library of audio-visual materials as well as the long-standing resources of ABC.

Yet against this tendency to shore up the vertical relations of communication, other recent policy initiatives have pointed in a different direction. Whereas vertical integration is accomplished through control over cultural production, distribution and exhibition, and horizontal integration involves ownership and control across a variety of media – magazines, television, radio, newspapers, cable and telecommunications – there is evidence that production is tending to become 'vertically dis-integrated' as media organizations contract out production to decentralized, independent producers. This practice was pioneered by the public service media during the late 1980s as, for example, the BBC and CBC were directed by their governments, and by the logic of budget cuts, to obtain 25% of their programming from the independent production sector. Such practices have also been adopted by some private sector media, such as the ITV network in the U.K. (Robins and Webster, 1989; Snoddy, 1995b, p. 9). There are indications of similar practices in regard to the international news agencies, as the Boyd-Barrett article shows, in the context of their news-exchange relationships with national or local agencies where in part payment for the delivery of their international service they accept a service of national news. However, these arrangements are of long standing, and counsel the importance of more historically grounded analysis of 'trends' that may be less recent than they at first seem.

What are the effects and implications of these changing relations of information production and distribution? Early on, and coupled with rapidly declining costs of cultural and information production brought about by the new technologies, policies of sub-contracting (vertical dis-integration) mentioned above offered hope that media production and content would be democratized as a wider range of producers and creative talent fed their productions into the media system. However, it appears that this practice has had more ambivalent affects. For example, in Canada, the independent production sector has consisted of production houses already linked with existing private sector broadcasters (Perlmutter, 1993, pp. 23–4). Robins and Webster (1989) also point out that within the U.K. context, vertical dis-integration has primarily served to create concentrated regional pockets of casually employed media producers. They also argue that a secondary effect has been the bypass of labour unions in the media industries, as the independent, casually employed media producers are usually not unionized. Thus, diversification of production has tended to fragment and increase control over the labour force, at the expense of creativity and democratization.

The policies of 'vertical dis-integration', the increasing use of alternative forms of media by activists promoting social and political change throughout the world, and the rapidly declining costs of cultural and information production afforded by the new communication technologies indeed *do* offer enormous potentials for the democratization of communication. However, it is important to realize that the potential for local and alternative forms of media production is confronted by increasing concentration at the national, regional and transnational levels. Thus, local space and alternate media practices continue to be subordinate to and interconnected with the globalization of dominant media corporations. This feature, coupled with the fact that the declining costs of information production have not been matched on the same scale for the distribution of information, means that the possibilities offered by the new technologies and people's struggles to use the media for social and political change are still governed by a set of social relations whereby cultural production remains subordinate to cultural distribution. A video camera is more accessible than a broadcast transmitter, a fax machine, computer and modem remain far cheaper than a tele-communications network, and a photocopier is vastly more affordable than a full-page advertisement in any major newspaper. Until such relations between the production and distribution sides of the communication process are more evenly balanced the prospects for democratic communication will remain elusive.

Media meaning: people, power and the uses, interpretation and effects of media in a global context

The penultimate question emerging from these analyses of the vast transformations influencing the nature of communications media must be about the meaning of these changes for the way people use, interpret and are affected by the media. While such questions are addressed throughout the Reader by its authors, they are specifically pursued by contributors to Sections 5 and 6, in particular Stuart Cunningham and Elizabeth Jacka, Marie Gillespie and James Lull. Together these authors consider the ways in which media content produced in one country is received and interpreted in another; how youth use media; and the ways in which people use media content to resist and challenge attempts to construct and maintain systems of political and ideological orthodoxy.

Lull argues that although the media system in the People's Republic of China is explicitly and structurally aligned with the Communist Party, and is used to extend its monopoly over political and cultural life, the very nature of television and the messages it distributes offers people the chance to explore alternative conceptions of what life could be like. According to Lull, in the spaces taking shape between these 'alternative conceptions of what life could be like' and authorities' attempts to use the media to consolidate power and promote centrally determined visions of modernization, a powerful form of popular culture is emerging that serves to expand the boundaries of freedom, openness and fun in the People's Republic of China. This is influ-enced in part by the quantitatively modest reception of programming from Hong Kong and from the West. These observations caution us against conflating structural control over the means of communication with domina-tion over the experiences that people derive from mediated communication.

In a further reconceptualization of the issue of media power, the anthropologist Conrad Kottak has suggested that it is a mistake to assess the effects of television – negatively or positively – solely in psychological and/or behavioural terms. Rather it is important to consider the processes through which new media are integrated with, and mutually interact and influence, other socio-cultural institutions – the church, family, political systems, educa-tion and myth – to produce new patterns of behaviour, alter everyday conceptions of time and space, and offer new experiences, meanings and a sense of community (Kottak, 1990). From this perspective, the power of media lies not so much in their ability to exercise ideological domination or to impose foreign life-styles, but rather in how they influence and deepen the resources of social interaction and personal experience upon which culture comes to be constructed and lived. The issue then, is not whether or not the media have a powerful influence, but how we conceptualize the nature of influence and the exercise of power. For Gillespie this way of conceptualizing the relationship between media and everyday life is a potent tool for understanding the relationship between media and youth. Such a perspective moves us away from narrow considerations of the effects of, for instance, television on youth, and in particular the relationship between media and violence. Instead, the pertinent questions become those which consider how the contents of television shape the entire conception of what it means to be young and how mediated communication comes to be incorporated in the various styles and practices used by youth to define and evaluate their own concepts of self and to navigate through their relationships with others and the social environment in which they live.

The chapters by Lull, Gillespie and Cunningham and Jacka are important in so far that they draw our attention to the fact that media power is not a one-way street, and needs to be thought of more broadly than the traditional emphasis of much communication scholarship on the effects of media on attitudes, behaviours and opinions. As such, these articles supplement recent attempts to more precisely define the audience and the nature of media effects as traditionally understood (see, for example, Gitlin, 1978; McLeod, Kosicki and Pan, 1991; Ang, 1995; Hay, Grossberg and Wartella, 1996), and remind us that the 'audience' itself is not a concept contained by national borders.

This collection offers expanded definitions of power that point out fruitful lines of inquiry for those trying to understand the relationships between people, power and the uses, interpretations and effects of media in a global context.

References

Addy, G. (1994) *The Competition Act and the Canadian telecommunications industry*. Speech presented to the Institute for International Research, Telecommunications Conference, Toronto, March 29, 1994.

Ang, I. (1995) *Living-room wars – rethinking media audiences for a post-modern world*, Routledge, London.

Braman, S. and Sreberny-Mohammadi, A. (1996) *Globalization, communication and international civil society*, Hampton, U.S.A.

Canada (1992) Canada – USA – Mexico North America Free Trade Agreement. Minister of Supply and Services, Ottawa.

Commission of European Communities (CEC) (1994) Green Paper on the liberalization of telecommunications infrastructure and cable television networks (Part 2), Author, Brussels.

Commission of European Communities (CEC) (1992) *Green Paper on pluralism and media concentration in the internal market*, Author, Brussels.

Dombey, (1995, August 10) Mexican watchdog seen as losing its bite. *Financial Times*, p. 3.

Gitlin, T. (1978) Media sociology: The dominant paradigm. *Theory and society*, 6, pp. 205–53.

Hay, J., Grossberg, L. and Wartella, E. (eds.) (1996) *The audience and its landscape*, Westview Press.

Hills, J. (1993) Telecommunications and democracy: the international experience. *Telecommunications Journal*, Vol. 60, No. 1, pp. 21–9.

Jackson, T. (1995, August 2) Masters of the moving image. *Financial Times*, p. 15.

Jones, A. (1994) Wired world: Communications technology, governance and the democratic uprising. In Comor E. A. (ed.) *The global political economy of communication*, pp. 145–64. St. Martin's, New York.

Keane, J. (1990) *The media and democracy*, Blackwell, London.

Kottak, C.P. (1990) *Prime-time society: an anthropological analysis of television and culture*. Wadsworth Publishing Company, Belmont, CA.

Lewis, P. (1995) Alternative media, Unit 24. In M.A. in Mass Communications, Centre for Mass Communication Research, University of Leicester.

McLeod, J., Kosicki, G. and Pan, Z. (1991) On understanding and misunderstanding media effects. In Curran J. and Gurevitch M. (eds.) *Mass media and society*, Edward Arnold, London, pp. 235–66.

Morumpei, O. R. (1996) The extended pulpit: The church-media alliance in Kenyan politics. In Bailie M., Winseck D. (eds.) (1996/forthcoming) *Democratizing communication?: Comparative perspectives on information and power*, Hampton, New Jersey.

Mader, R. (1993) Television in Brazil. In Dowmunt, T. (ed.) *Channels of resistance: Global television and local empowerment*, British Film Institute, London, pp. 67–89.

Martin, J. (1995, August 7) The news according to Mickey Mouse. *Financial Times*, p. 7.

Pendakur, M. and Kapur, J. (1996) Think globally, program locally: Privatization of Indian national television. In Bailie M. and Winseck D. (eds.) (1997) *Democratizing communication?: Comparative perspectives on information and power*, Hampton, New Jersey.

Perlmutter, T. (1993) Distress signals: A Canadian story – an international lesson. In Dowmunt T. (ed.), *Channels of resistance: Global television and local empowerment*, British Film Institute, London, pp. 16–26.

Pool, I. (1983) *Technologies of freedom*, Oxford, New York.

Schiller, H. (1969) *Mass communications and American empire*, Beacon, Boston.

Snoddy, (1995a, August 10) Radical programme buying plan for ITV. *Financial Times*, p. 9.

Snoddy, (1995b, August 10) NewsCorp and MCI form on-line alliance. *Financial Times*, p. 20.

Sreberny-Mohammadi, A. (1991) The global and local in international communication. In Curran J. and Gurevitch M. (eds.) *Mass media and society*, Edward Arnold, London, pp. 18–38.

Sreberny-Mohammadi, A., *et al.* (1985) *Foreign news in the media: International reporting in 29 countries*. UNESCO, Paris.

Straubhaar, J. D. (1991) Beyond media imperialism: Asymmetrical interdependence and cultural proximity. *Critical studies in mass communication*, Vol. 8, pp. 39–59.

Tarjanne, P. (1994) The missing link: Still missing? Paper presented at the 16th Annual Pacific Telecommunications Conference, Manoa, Hawaii, U.S.A., January 16–20, 1994.

Trade Negotiations Committee (TNC) (1993) *Final Act embodying the results of the Uruguay Round (General Agreement on Trade in Services – Annex on Telecommunications)*. GATT Secretariat, Geneva.

Wasko, J. (1994) Jurassic Park and GATT: Hollywood and Europe – an update. In Corcoran F. and Preston P. (eds.) *Democracy and communication in the new Europe*, Hampton, New Jersey.

Winseck, D. (1996) The shifting contexts of international communication: Possibilities for a New World Information and Communication Order. In Bailie M. and Winseck D. (eds.) (1997) *Democratizing communication?: Comparative perspectives on information and power*, Hampton, New Jersey.

Acknowledgements

Ablex Publishing, New Jersey for the extract from *The Voice of America: From Detente to the Reagan Doctrine*: The case of the Korean airline tragedy, pp. 115–19 © 1988 by L. Alexandre.

Blackwell Publishers and Polity Press for the extract from *Global Society and International Relations: Sociological Concepts and Political Perspectives*: The theoretical challenge of global society, pp. 5–27 © 1994 by M. Shaw.

Johns Hopkins University Press for the extract from *Sociology of the Global System*: Classifying the global system, pp. 10–25 © 1995 by L. Sklair.

Oxford University Press, Oxford for the extract from *Journal of Communication*: National responses and accessibility to STAR TV in Asia, Vol. 44, No. 3, pp. 112–31 © 1994 by M. R. Levy.

Oxford University Press, Oxford for the extract from *Journal of Communication*: Wishful thinking: cultural politics, media and collective identities in Europe, Vol. 43, No. 2, pp. 6–17 © 1993 by P. Schlesinger.

Polity Press, Cambridge for the extract from *Hollywood in the Information Age*: Hollywood meets Madison Avenue: the commercialization of U.S. films, pp. 187–93, 196–209 © 1994 by J. Wasko.

Routledge, London for the extract from *Cultural Studies*: Neighbourly relations? Cross-cultural reception analysis and Australian soaps in Britain, Vol. 8, No. 3, pp. 509–26 © 1994 by S. Cunningham and E. Jacka.

Routledge, London for the extract from *Television, Ethnicity and Cultural Change*: Local uses of the media: negotiating culture and identity, pp. 76, 78–93, 95–104, 106–8 © by M. Gillespie.

Sage, London for the extract from *Communication, Culture and Hegemony: From the Media to Mediations*: The processes: from nationalisms to transnationals (translated by E. Fox and R.A. White), pp. 163–68, 175–78 © 1993 by J. Martín-Barbero.

Sage, London for the extract from *European Journal of Communication*: Global harmonies and local discords: transnational policies and practices in the European recording industry, Vol. 8, No. 3, pp. 295–361© 1993 by K. Negus.

Sage, London for the extract from *Feminism, Multiculturalism, and the Media*: News, consciousness, and social participation: the role of women's feature service in world news, pp. 108–22 © 1995 by Carolyn M. Byerly.

Sage, London for the extract from *Globalization: Social Theory and Global Culture (Theory, Culture & Society Series)*: Mapping the global condition, pp. 50–60, 189–203 © 1992 by R. Robertson.

Sage, London for the extract from *Media, Culture and Society*: Organizing democratic radio: issues in praxis, Vol. 15, No. 3, pp. 473–486 © 1993 by John L. Hochheimer.

Stanford University Press for the extract from *The Consequences of Modernity*: The globalizing of modernity, pp. 63–78, 183 © 1991 by A. Giddens.

University of Chicago Press for the extract from: *Public Culture*: Notes on the global ecumene, Vol. 1, No. 2 © 1989 by U. Hannerz.

University of Chicago Press for the extract from *Public Culture:* Finding a place for Islam: Egyptian television serials and the national interest, Vol. 5, No. 3, pp. 494–512 © 1993 by L. Abu-Lughod.

University of Minnesota Press, Minneapolis MN for extract from *Small Media, Big Revolution: Communication, Culture and the Iranian Revolution*: Small media and revolutionary change: a new model, pp. 19–40 © 1994 by A. Sreberny-Mohammadi and A. Mohammadi.

Section 1

Conceptualizing the global

1

Mapping the global condition

Roland Robertson

From Robertson, R. (1992) *Globalization: Social Theory and Global Culture (Theory, Culture & Society Series)*, Sage, London, pp. 50–60.

We need to enlarge our conception of 'world politics' in such a way as to facilitate systematic discussion, but not conflation, of the relationship between politics in the relatively narrow sense and the broad questions of 'meaning' which can only be grasped by wide-ranging, empirically sensitive interpretations of the global-human condition as a whole. Specifically, I argue that what is often called world politics has in the twentieth century hinged completely upon the issue of the interpretation of and the response to modernity, aspects of which were politically and internationally thematized as the standard of 'civilization' (Gong, 1984) during the late nineteenth and early twentieth centuries with particular reference to the inclusion of non-European (mainly Asian) societies in Eurocentric 'international society' (Bull and Watson, 1984).

Communism and 'democratic capitalism' have constituted alternative forms of acceptance of modernity (Parsons, 1964), although some would now argue that the recent and dramatic ebbing of communism can in part be attributed to its 'attempt to preserve the integrity of the premodern system' (Parsons, 1967, pp. 484–5) by invoking 'socialism' as the central of a series of largely covert gestures of reconciliation . . . toward both the past and the future' (Parsons, 1967, p. 484).[1] On the other hand facism and neo-facism have, in spite of their original claims to the establishment of new societal and international 'orders' (as was explicitly the case with the primary Axis powers of World War II: Germany and Japan), been directly interested in transcending or resolving the problems of modernity. That issue has certainly not disappeared. The world politics of the global debate about modernity has rarely been considered of relevance to the latter and yet it is clear that, for example, conceptions of the past by the major belligerents in World War I illustrated a sharp contrast between 'the temporalities of the nations of each alliance system and underlying causes of resentment and misunderstanding' (Kern, 1983, p. 277), with the nations whose leaders considered themselves to be relatively deprived – notably Germany and Japan – being particularly concerned to confront the problem of modernity in political and military terms.[2] Sociologists and philosophers are familiar with many intellectual developments of the 1920s and 1930s, but these have not been linked to the broad domain of *Realpolitik*. It may well be that the cold war that developed after the defeat of great-power fascism constituted an interruption and partial freezing of the world-cultural politics of modernity and that with the ending of the cold war as conventionally understood those politics will now be resumed in a situation of much greater global complexity, in the interrelated contexts of more intense globalization, the growing political presence of Islam, the discourse of postmodernity and 'the ethnic revival' (Smith, 1981), which itself may be considered as *an aspect of* the contemporary phase of globalization (Lechner, 1984). [. . .]

I maintain that what has come to be called globalization is, in spite of differing conceptions of that theme, best understood as indicating the problem of the form in terms of which the world becomes 'united', but by no means integrated in naive functionalist mode (Robertson and Chirico, 1985). Globalization as a topic is, in other words, a conceptual entry to the problem of 'world order' in the most general sense – but, nevertheless, an entry which has no cognitive matters. It is, moreover, a phenomenon which clearly requires what is conventionally called interdisciplinary treatment. Traditionally the general field of the study of the world as a whole has been approached via the discipline of international relations (or, more diffusely, international studies). That discipline (sometimes regarded as a subdiscipline of political science) was consolidated during particular phases of the overall globalization process and is now being reconstituted in reference to developments in other disciplinary areas, including the humanities (Der Derian and Shapiro, 1989). Indeed, the first concentrated thrust into the study of the world as a whole on the part of sociologists, during the 1960s (discussed in Nettl and Robertson, 1968), was undertaken, as has been seen, mainly in terms of the idea of the sociology of international relations. There can be little doubt that to this day the majority of social scientists still think of 'extra-societal' matters in terms of 'international relations' (including variants thereof, such as transnational relations, non-governmental relations, supranational relations, world politics and so on). Nonetheless that tendency is breaking down, in conjunction with considerable questioning of what Michael Mann (1986) has called the unitary conception of society. While there have been attempts to carve out a new discipline for the study of the world as a whole, including the long-historical making of the contemporary 'world system' (e.g. Bergesen, 1980), my position is that it is not so much that we need a new discipline in order to study the world as a whole but that social theory in the broadest sense – as a perspective which stretches across the social sciences and humanities (Giddens and Turner, 1987, p. 1) and even the natural sciences – should be refocused and expanded so as to make concern with 'the world' a central hermeneutic, and in such a way as to constrain empirical and comparative-historical research in the same direction. [. . .]

In the second half of the 1980s 'globalization' (and its problematic variant, 'internationalization') became a commonly used term in intellectual, business, media and other circles, in the process acquiring a number of meanings, with varying degrees of precision. This has been a source of frustration, but not necessarily a cause for surprise or alarm, to those of us who had sought earlier in the decade to establish a relatively strict definition of globalization as part of an attempt to come to terms systematically with major aspects of contemporary 'meaning and change' (Robertson, 1978). Nevertheless a stream of analysis and research has been developed around the general idea, if not always the actual concept, of globalization. [. . .]

I deal here with relatively recent aspects of globalization, although I want to emphasize as strongly as possible that in doing so I am not suggesting for a moment that moves and thrusts in the direction of global unicity are unique to relatively recent history. I also argue that globalization is intimately related to modernity and modernization, as well as to postmodernity and 'postmodernization' (in so far as the latter pair of motifs have definite analytical purchase). In attempting to justify that proposal I am by no means suggesting that work within the frame of 'the globalization paradigm' should be limited to the relatively recent past. All I am maintaining is that the concept of globalization *per se* is most clearly applicable to a particular series of relatively recent developments concerning *the concrete structuration of the world as a whole*. The term 'structuration' has been deliberately chosen. Although I will shortly consider some aspects of Anthony Giddens's work on 'the global scene,' I cannot address here the general problems which arise from the concept of structuration (Cohen, 1989; Bryant and Jary, 1991). I will say only that if the notion of structuration is to be of assistance to us analytically in the decades ahead it has to be moved out of its quasi-philosophical context, its confinement within the canonical discourses about subjectivity and objectivity, individual and society, and so on (Archer, 1988). It has to be made directly relevant to *the world* in which we live. It has to contribute to the understanding of how the global 'system' has been and continues to be *made*. It has to be focused on the production and reproduction of 'the world' as the most salient plausibility structure of our time (Wuthnow, 1978, p. 65). The same applies to the cultural-agency problematic which Margaret Archer (1988) has recently theorized.

Human history has been replete with ideas concerning the physical structure, the geography, the cosmic location and the spiritual and/or secular significance of the world (Wagar, 1971); movements and organizations concerned with the patterning and/or the unification of the world as a whole have intermittently appeared for at least the last 2000 years; and ideas about the relationship between the universal and the particular have been central to all of the major civilizations. Even something like what has recently been called 'the global–local nexus' (or the 'local–global nexus') was thematized as long ago as the second century BC when Polybius, in his *Universal History*, wrote with reference to the rise of the Roman empire: 'Formerly the things which happened in the world had no connection among themselves . . . But since then all events are united in a common bundle' (Kohn, 1971, p. 121).[3] However, the crucial considerations are that it has not been until relatively recent times that it has been realistically thought that 'humanity is rapidly becoming, physically speaking, a single society' (Hobhouse, 1906, p. 331), and that it has not been until quite recently that considerable numbers of people living on various parts of the planet have spoken and acted in direct reference to the problem of the 'organization' of the entire heliocentric world. It is in relation to this heavily contested problem of the concrete patterning and consciousness of the world, including resistance to globality, that I seek to centre the concept and the discourse of globalization.

The world as a whole could, in theory, have become the reality which it now is in ways and along trajectories other than those that have actually obtained (Lechner, 1989). The world could, in principle, have been rendered as a 'singular system' (Moore, 1966) via the imperial hegemony of a single nation or a 'grand alliance' between two or more dynasties or nations; the victory of 'the universal proletariat'; the global triumph of a particular form of organized religion; the crystallization of 'the world spirit'; the yielding of nationalism to the ideal of 'free trade'; the success of the world-federalist movement; the world-wide triumph of a trading company; or in yet other ways. Some of these have in fact held sway at certain moments in world history. Indeed, in coming to terms analytically with the contemporary circumstance we have to acknowledge that some such possibilities are as old as world history in any meaningful sense of that phrase and have greatly contributed to the existence of the globalized world of the late twentieth century. Moreover, much of world history can be fruitfully considered as sequences of 'miniglobalization,' in the sense that, for example, historic empire formation involved the unification of previously sequestered territories and social entities. There have also been shifts in the opposite direction, as with the deunification of medieval Europe, of which Rosencrance (1986) has spoken – although the rise of the territorial state also promoted imperialism and thus conceptions of the world as a whole. [. . .]

Thus we must return to the question of the actual form of recent and contemporary moves in the direction of global interdependence and global consciousness. In posing the basic question in this way we immediately confront the critical issue of the period during which the move towards the world as a singular system became more or less inexorable. If we think of the history of the world as consisting for a very long time in *the objectiveness* of a variety of different civilizations existing in varying degrees of separation from each other, our main task now is to consider the ways in which the world 'moved' from being merely 'in itself' to the problem or the possibility of its being 'for itself.' Before coming directly to that vital issue I must attend briefly to some basic analytical matters. This I do via the statement of Giddens (1987, pp. 255–93) on 'Nation–States in the Global State System.'

Giddens makes much of the point that 'the development of the sovereignty of the modern state from its beginnings depends upon a reflexively monitored set of relations between states' (Giddens, 1987, p. 263). He argues that the period of treaty making following World War I 'was effectively the first point at which a reflexively monitored system of nation-states came to exist globally' (1987, p. 256). I fully concur with both the emphasis on the importance of the post-World War I period and Giddens's claim that 'if a new and formidably threatening pattern of war was established at this time, so was a new pattern of peace' (1987, p. 256). More generally, Giddens's argument that the development of the modern state has been guided by increasingly global norms concerning its sovereignty is, if not original, of great importance. However, he tends to conflate the issue of the homogenization of the state (in Hegel's sense) – what Giddens calls 'the universal scope of the nation-state' (1987, p. 264) – and the issue of relationships between states.

It is important to make a distinction between the diffusion of expectations concerning the external legitimacy and mode of operation of the state and the development of regulative norms concerning the relationships between states; while readily acknowledging that the issue of the powers and limits of the state has been *empirically* linked to the structuring of the relationships between states and, moreover, that it constitutes a crucial axis of globalization. James Der Derian (1989) has recently drawn attention to an important aspect of that these by indicating the proximity of the formal 'Declaration of the Rights of Man' that sovereignty resides in the nation to Jeremy Bentham's declaration in the same year of 1789 that there was a need for a new word – 'international' – which would 'express, in a more significant way, the branch of law which goes commonly under the name of the *law of nations*' (Bentham, 1948, p. 326).

So while the two issues upon which I have been dwelling via Giddens's analysis undoubtedly have been and remain closely interdependent, it is crucial to keep them analytically apart in order that we may fully appreciate variations in the nature of the empirical connections between them. In sum, the problem of contingency arising from state sovereignty and the development of relational rules between sovereign units is not the same as the issue of the crystallization and diffusion of conceptions of national statehood (Smith, 1979). Nor is it the same as the development and spread of conceptions of the shape and meaning of 'international society' (Gong, 1984). The second set of matters is on a different 'level' than that addressed by Giddens.

My primary reason for emphasizing this matter is that it provides an immediate entry to what I consider the most pressing general problem in the contemporary discussion of globalization. Giddens's analysis is a good example of an attempt to move toward the global circumstance via the conventional concerns of sociological theory. While readily conceding that it was his specific, initial concern to talk about the modern nation state and the internal and external violence with which its development has been bound up, the fact remains that in spite of all of his talk about global matters at the end of his analysis, Giddens is restricted precisely by his having to centre 'the current world system' within a discussion of 'the global *state* system' (Giddens, 1987, pp. 276–7; emphasis added). Even though he eventually separates, in analytical terms, the nation-state system (with the ambiguity I have indicated) as the political aspect of the world system from the 'global information system' (as relating to 'symbolic orders/modes of discourse'); the 'world-capitalist economy' (as the economic dimension of the world system); and the 'world military order' (as concerning 'law/modes of sanction') – along lines reminiscent of approaches of the 1960s (Nettl and Robertson, 1968) and, ironically, of a general Parsonian, functional-imperative approach – Giddens ends up with a 'map' of what he reluctantly calls the world system, which is centred upon his conflated characterization of the rise of the modern state system. [. . .]

A minimal phase model of globalization

I offer here what I call and advocate as a necessarily minimal model of globalization. This model does not make grand assertions about primary factors, major mechanisms, and so on. Rather, it indicates the major constraining tendencies which have been operating in relatively recent history as far as world order and the compression of the world in our time are concerned.

One of the most pressing tasks in this regard is to confront the issue of the undoubted salience of the unitary nation state – more diffusely, the national society – since about the mid-eighteenth century and at the same time to acknowledge its historical uniqueness, in a sense its abnormality (McNeill, 1986). The homogeneous nation state – homogeneous here in the sense of a culturally homogenized, administered citizenry (Anderson, 1983) – is a construction of a particular form of life. That we ourselves have been increasingly subject to its constraints does not mean that for analytical purposes it has to be accepted as *the* departure point for analysing and understanding the world. This is why I argue not merely that national societies should be regarded as constituting but one general reference point for the analysis of the global-human circumstance, but that we have to recognize even more than we do now that the prevalence of the national society in the twentieth century is an aspect of globalization (Robertson, 1989) – that the diffusion of *the idea of* the national society as a form of institutionalized societalism (Lechner, 1989) was central to the accelerated globalization which began to occur just over 100 years ago. I have also argued more specifically that the two other major components of globalization have been, in addition to national systems and the system of international relations, conceptions of individuals and of humankind. It is in terms of the shifting relationships between and the 'upgrading' of these reference points that globalization has occurred in recent centuries. This pattern has certainly been greatly affected by and subject to all sorts of economic, political and other processes and actions; but my task here is to legitimize the need for an overall comprehension of the global circumstance.

I now propose, in skeletal terms, that the temporal-historical path to the present circumstances of a very high degree of global density and complexity can be delineated as follows:

Phase I: The germinal phase lasting in Europe from the early fifteenth until the mid-eighteenth century. Incipient growth of national communities and downplaying of the medieval 'transnational' system. Expanding scope of the Catholic church. Accentuation of concepts of the individual and of ideas about humanity. Heliocentric theory of the world and beginning of modern geography; spread of Gregorian calendar.

Phase II: The incipient phase lasting – mainly in Europe – from the mid-eighteenth century until the 1870s. Sharp shift towards the idea of the homogeneous, unitary state; crystallization of conceptions of formalized inter-national relations, of standardized citizenly individuals and a more concrete conception of humankind. Sharp increases in legal conventions and agencies concerned with international and transnational regulation and communi-cation. International exhibitions. Beginning of problem of 'admission' of non-European societies to 'international society.' Thematization of nation-alism-internationalism issue.

Phase III: The take-off phase lasting from the 1870s until the mid-1920s. 'Take-off' here refers to a period during which the increasingly manifest globalizing tendencies of previous periods and places gave way to a single, inexorable form centred upon the four reference points, and thus constraints, of national societies, generic individuals (but with a masculine bias), a single 'international society,' and an increasingly singular, but not unified conception of humankind. Early thematization of 'the problem of modernity.' Increasingly global conceptions of the 'correct outline' of an 'acceptable' national society; thematization of ideas concerning national and personal identities; inclusion of a number of non-European societies in 'international society'; international formalization and attempted implementation of ideas about humanity. Globalization of immigration restrictions. Very sharp increase in number and speed of global forms of communication. The first 'international novels.' Rise of ecumenical movement. Development of global competitions – for example the Olympics and Nobel prizes. Implementation of world time and near-global adoption of Gregorian calendar. First *world* war.

Phase IV: the struggle-for-hegemony phase Lasting from the mid-1920s until the late-1960s. Disputes and wars about the fragile terms of the dominant globalization process established by the end of the take-off period. Establishment of the League of Nations and then the United Nations. Principle of national independence established. Conflicting conceptions of modernity (Allies v. the Axis), followed by high point of the cold war (conflict within 'the modern project'). Nature of and prospects for humanity sharply focused by the Holocaust and use of the atomic bomb. The crystallization of the Third World.

Phase V: the uncertainty phase Beginning in the late 1960s and displaying crisis tendencies in the early 1990s. Heightening of global consciousness in late 1960s. Moon landing. Accentuation of 'post-materialist' values. End of the cold war and manifest rise of the problem of 'rights' and widespread access to nuclear and thermonuclear weaponry. Number of global institutions and movements greatly increases. Sharp acceleration in means of global communication. Societies increasingly facing problems of multiculturality and polyethnicity. Conceptions of individuals rendered more complex by gender, sexual, ethnic and racial considerations. Civil rights become a global issue. International system more fluid – end of bipolarity. Concern with humankind as a species-community greatly enhanced, particularly via environmental movements. Arising of interest in world civil society and world citizenship, in spite of 'the ethnic revolution.' Consolidation of global media system, including rivalries about such. Islam as a deglobalizing/reglobalizing movement. Earth Summit in Rio de Janeiro.

This is merely an outline, with much detail and more rigorous analysis and interpretation of the shifting relationships between and the relative autonomization of each of the four major components to be worked out. Clearly one of the most important empirical questions has to do with the extent to which the form of globalization which was set firmly in motion during the period 1870–1925 will 'hold' in the coming decades. In more theoretical vein, much more needs to be done to demonstrate the ways in which the selective responses of relevant collective actors, particularly societies, to globalization play a crucial part in the making of the world as a whole. Different forms of societal participation in the globalization process make a crucial difference to its precise form. My main point is that there is

a general autonomy and 'logic' to the globalization process, which operates in *relative* independence of strictly societal and other more conventionally
studied sociocultural processes. The global system is not simply an outcome
of processes of basically intra-societal (*contra* Luhmann, 1982) or even a
development of the inter-state system. Its making has been and continues
to be much more complex than that.

Notes

1. It is of more than passing interest to note that in speaking of communism as a
   radical branch of one of 'the great "reform" movements of postmedieval Western
   history' – socialism – Talcott Parsons said in 1964 that 'it seems a safe prediction
   that Communism will, from its own internal dynamics, evolve in the direction
   of the restoration – or where it has yet not existed, the institution – of political
   democracy' (1964, pp. 396–7). On the other hand, Parsons insisted, problematically,
   that the *internationalism* of communism had made a crucial contribution to world
   order.
2. Ronald Inglehart (1990, p. 33) observes in the course of his empirical analysis of
   culture in advanced industrial societies 'that the publics of the three major Axis
   powers, Germany, Japan, and Italy, all tend to be underachievers in life satisfaction.
   The traumatic discrediting of their social and political systems that accompanied
   their defeat in World War II may have left a legacy of cynicism that their subsequent
   social change and economic success has still not entirely erased.'
3. I owe the precise phrases 'local-global nexus' and 'global-local nexus' to Chadwick
   Alger (1988).

References

Alger, C. (1988) Perceiving, analyzing, and coping with the local-global nexus.
   International Social Science Journal, August, 117.
Anderson, B. (1983) *Imagined Communities*, Verso, London.
Anderson, P. (1984) *In the Tracks of Historical Materialism*, University of Chicago Press,
   Chicago.
Appadurai, A. (1990) Disjuncture and difference in the global culture economy. *Public
   Culture*, Vol. 2, No. 2.
Archer, M. S. (1988) *Culture and Agency: The Place of Culture in Social Theory*, Cambridge
   University Press, Cambridge.
Arendt, H. (1957) Karl Jaspers: citizen of the world. In Schlipp, P. A. (ed.) *The Philosophy
   of Karl Jaspers*, Open Court, La Salle, IL.
Bentham, J. (1948) *The Principles of Morals and Legislation*, Lafner, New York.
Bergesen, A. (1980) From utilitarianism to globology: the shift from the individual
   to the world as a whole as the primordial unit of analysis. In Bergesen, A. (ed.)
   Studies of the modern world-system, Academic Press, New York.
Bryant, C. G. A. and Jary, D. (1991) *Giddens's Theory of Structuration*, Routledge, London.
Bull, H. and Watson, A. (eds.) (1984) *The Expansion of International Society*,
   Clarendon Press, Oxford.
Cohen, I. J. (1989) *Structuration Theory: Anthony Giddens and the Constitution of Social
   Life*, St Martin's Press, New York.
Der Derian, J. (1989) The boundaries of knowledge and power in international
   relations. In Der Derian, J. and Shapiro, M. J. (eds.), *International/Intertextual Relations:
   Postmodern Readings of World Politics*, Lexington Books, Lexington, MA.
Der Derian, J. and Shapiro, J. (eds.) (1989) *International/Intertextual Relations: Postmodern
   Readings of World Politics*, Lexington Books, Lexington, MA.

Giddens, A. (1987) *The Nation-State and Violence*, University of California Press, Berkeley.

Giddens, A. and Turner, J. (1987) Introduction. In Giddens, A. and Turner, J. (eds.), *Social Theory Today*, Stanford University Press, Stanford, CA.

Gong, G. W. (1984) *The Standard of 'Civilization' in International Society*, Clarendon Press, Oxford.

Hobhouse, L. T. (1906) *Morals in Evolution. A Study of Comparative Ethics*, Henry Holt, New York, Vol. I.

Jaspers, K. (1953) *The Origin and Goal of History*, Yale University Press, New Haven, CT.

Inglehart, R. (1990) *Culture Shift in Advanced Industrial Society*, Princeton University Press, Princeton, NJ.

Kern, S. (1983) *The Culture of Time and Space, 1880–1918*, Harvard University Press, Cambridge, MA.

Kohn, H. (1971) Nationalism and internationalism. In Wagar, W. W. (ed.) *History and the Idea of Mankind*, University of New Mexico Press, Albuquerque.

Lechner, F. J. (1984) Ethnicity and revitalization in the modern world system. *Sociological Focus*, Vol. 17, No. 3.

Lechner, F. J. (1989) Cultural aspects of the modern world-system. In Swatos, W. H. (ed.) *Religious Politics in Global and Comparative Perspective*, Greenwood Press, New York.

Lesourne, J. F. (1986) *World Perspectives: A European Assessment*, Gordon & Breach, New York.

Luhmann, N. (1982) *The Differentiation of Society*, Columbia University Press, New York.

Mann, M. (1986) *The Sources of Social Power: Volume 1, A History of Power from the Beginning to AD 1760*, Cambridge University Press, Cambridge.

McNeill, W. H. (1986) *Polyethnicity and National Unity in World History*, University of Toronto Press, Toronto.

Moore, W. E. (1966) Global sociology: the world as a singular system. *American Journal of Sociology*, Vol. 71, No. 5.

Nettl, J. P. and Robertson, R. (1968) *International Systems and the Modernization of Societies: The Formation of National Goals and Attitudes*, Basic Books, New York.

Parsons, T. (1964) Communism and the West: the sociology of conflict. In Etzioni, A. and Etzioni, E. (eds.) *Social Change: Sources, Patterns and Consequences*, Basic Books, New York.

Parsons, T. (1967) *Sociological Theory and Modern Society*, Free Press, New York.

Robertson, R. (1978) *Meaning and Change: Explorations in the Cultural Sociology of Modern Societies*, Basil Blackwell, Oxford.

Robertson, R. (1989) Globalization, politics, and religion. In Beckford, J. A. and Luckmann, T. (eds.) *The Changing Face of Religion*, Sage, London.

Robertson, R. and Chirico, J. (1985) Humanity, globalization and worldwide religious resurgence: a theoretical exploration. *Sociological Analysis*, Vol. 46, No. 3.

Rosencrance, R. (1986) *The Rise of the Trading State: Commerce and Conquest in the Modern World*, Basic Books, New York.

Smith, A. D. (1979) *Nationalism in the Twentieth Century*, New York University Press, New York.

Smith, A. D. (1981) *The Ethnic Revival*, Cambridge University Press, New York.

Wagar, W. W. (ed.) (1971) *History and the Idea of Mankind*, University of New Mexico Press, Albuquerque.

Wallerstein, I. (1987) World-systems analysis. In Giddens, A. and Turner, J. (eds.), *Social Theory Today*, Stanford University Press, Stanford, CA.

Wuthnow, R. (1978) Religious movements and the transition in world order. In Needleman, J. and Baker, G. (eds.), *Understanding the New Religions*, Seabury Press, New York.

2

Notes on the global ecumene

Ulf Hannerz

From Breckenridge, C. A. (ed.) (1989) *Public Culture*, University of
Chicago Press, Chicago, IL, Vol. 1, No. 2, pp. 66–75.

Cultural interrelatedness increasingly reaches across the world. More than
ever, there is now a global ecumene.[1] To grasp this fact, in its wide range
of manifestations and implications, is the largest task now confronting a
macro-anthropology of culture. These notes are devoted to two of the issues
involved: they identify the nature of centre-periphery relationships in cultural
terms, and scrutinize the notion that the world is becoming culturally
homogenized.

Culture and centre-periphery relationships

Until the 1960s or so, acknowledgements of the fact that 'we are all in the
same world' were mostly pieties, with uncertain political and intellectual
implications. Since then, in the social sciences, the globalizing tendency has
usually involved a view of asymmetry; key conceptual pairs have been centre
(or core) and periphery, metropolis and satellite. Asymmetries are present
in the global social organization of meaning as well. But what kind of
asymmetries are they? How closely aligned are the asymmetries of culture
with those of economy, politics, or military might? How do centre-periphery
relationships in the world affect structures of meaning and cultural
expression?

In political and military terms, the world toward the end of the twentieth
century has two superpowers, and whatever freedom of movement other
countries exercise, whether great or small, it ultimately tends to be constrained
by this arrangement. In economic terms, the century has by and large seen
the United States in a dominant position, with a number of lesser powers
grouped around it, varying in ascent or decline. In cultural terms, are there
other powers than these?

The question at least has two sides (which may be to simplify matters).
There is that cultural production in the periphery which is somehow in
response to the political and economic dominance of the centre. Here the
world system as defined in political and/or economic terms is obviously given
cultural recognition of a sort. On the other hand, there is the issue of cultural
diffusion. What defines the centre-periphery relationship here are above
all symmetries of input and scale. When the centre speaks, the periphery
listens, and on the whole does not talk back.

In this case, the cultural centres of the world are not by definition identical with political and economic centres. Are they in practice? Let us consider this in gross terms, as an issue of the overall cultural influence of nations. It can be argued that the centre-periphery relationships of culture are not, at least at any particular point in time, a mere reflection of political and economic power. In the American case, the congruence is undeniable. The general cultural influence of the Soviet Union in the world today, on the other hand, is modest compared with its political and military power. Among the lesser powers, Britain and France may at present be stronger as cultural than as economic and political centres; this is perhaps debatable. Japan, on the whole, keeps a low cultural profile in the world, despite its economic success. Most of what it exports does not seem to be identifiably marked by Japaneseness.

If the global pattern of centre-periphery relationships in culture thus has some degree of separateness, it is easy to see in some instances what is behind a greater cultural influence. To a degree the present cultural influence of Britain and France reflects the fact that the old-style colonial powers could more or less monopolize the centre-periphery cultural flow to their domains. In large parts of the world this still makes London or Paris not just *a* centre but *the* centre. In old settler colonies, historical ties are yet closer, as links of kinship and ancestry also connect the periphery to a specific centre. In Australia, when critics refer to 'the cultural cringe', it is the deference to things English they still have in mind. Language is obviously also a factor which may convert political power into cultural influence, and then conserve the latter. As people go on speaking English, French and Portuguese in postcolonial lands, in postcolonial times, old centre-periphery relationships get a prolonged lease of life. If all this means that the centre-periphery relationships of culture tend to exhibit some lag relative to present and emergent structures of political and economic power, it might also mean that Japan could yet come into greater cultural influence in the world.

One might speculate that people also make different assumptions, in a metacultural fashion, about the nature of the relationship between themselves and their culture. By and large, Americans may not expect that the meanings and the cultural forms they invent are only for themselves; possibly because they have seen at home over the years that practically anybody can become an American. The French may see their culture as a gift to the world. There is a *mission civilisatrice*. The Japanese, on the other hand, – so it is said – find it a strange notion that anyone can 'become Japanese', and they put Japanese culture on exhibit, in the framework of organized international contacts, as a way of displaying irreducible distinctiveness rather than in order to make it spread. (Notably, many of those who engage in introducing aspects of Japanese culture to the world are alien culture brokers.)

Staying with the conception of cultural centres as places where culture is invented and from which it is diffused, however, one cannot be satisfied with only the very generalized picture of the relative standing of a handful of countries as wholes. Too much is missing, and too much is assumed. Countries do not always exercise their influence at the same level across the gamut of cultural expressions. American influence is at present very diverse, but perhaps most conspicuous in science, technology and popular culture; French influence on world culture is rather of the high culture variety, and in fields like upmarket food and fashion; there is widespread interest in the organization and culture of Japanese corporations. In such more specialized ways, places like the Vatican and the Shia holy city of Qom also organize parts of the world into centre-periphery relationships of culture, for certain purposes. As far as symmetries of cultural flow are concerned, there is likewise the notable instance of the Indian film industry, offering entertainment for large parts of the third world.

In this context one should also keep in mind that particularly in such fields as science and technology, the spread of knowledge between nations can be actively prevented, for reasons of economic, political and military advantage. Indeed, there are signs that large-scale restrictive management of knowledge is on the increase. Often it is primarily a part of competitive relationships between centres, but it constrains the cultural flow between centre and periphery as well, maintaining the advantage of the former.

It is another characteristic of the structure of centre-periphery relationships that it has many tiers. Some countries have a strong influence in their regions, due to a well-developed cultural apparatus – Mexico in Latin America, for example, and Egypt in the Arab world. A shared language and cultural tradition can be important in this way, at the same time as a sizeable domestic market for cultural products can give one country an advantageous position in having something to export to the rest of the region. Such regional centres may base their production on meanings and forms wholly internal to the region, or they may operate as cultural brokers, translating influences from their first-tier centres into something more adapted to regional conditions.

World cultural flow, it appears, has a much more intricate organization of diversity than is allowed in a picture of a centre-periphery structure with just a handful of all-purpose centres. A further issue, obviously, if one tries to arrive at a kind of present-day global cultural flow chart, is to what extent the peripheries indeed talk back; which would in large part be a question of the cultural influence of the Third World on the Occident.

Reggae music, swamis, and Latin American novels exemplify the kind of countercurrents that may first enter one's mind; culture coming fully developed, as it were, from periphery to centre, and at the same time culture which the periphery can give away, and keep at the same time. There are indeed instances like these. Yet judging by them alone, however much more desirable one would find it to be able to speak of world culture in terms of equal exchange, the conclusion can at present hardly be avoided that asymmetry rules.

But then there are also other kinds of cultural transfers from periphery to centre, which in themselves exemplify assymetry in other manners. One involves particular embodiments of meaning; objects of art, ritual or other significance, which may not be readily replaceable at the periphery, but which are at one time or other exported, due to the superior economic and political power of the centre, and absorbed by its museums or other collections. Here one may see indeed a tangible impoverishment of the cultures of the periphery – often especially in terms of immediate access to the best in one's cultural heritage, as what is removed is what the centre defines as capital-C culture of the periphery. This is now a field of controversy, with the representatives of the periphery insisting upon the moral right to demand the decommoditization and repatriation of artifacts to their own countries.

There is likewise the kind of periphery-to-centre transfer in which people like anthropologists can come to play a part. Much knowledge concerning the periphery is more available in the centre than in the periphery itself, and especially to the specialists on the periphery from the centre, because of the greater capacity of the centre to organize and analyse knowledge in certain ways. The centre may extract the raw materials for this knowledge, so to speak, from the periphery, but as such, it may at the same time remain there, for again, informants and others need not give up the knowledge that they give away.

Anyway, all this is in gross terms, as a way of beginning to look at cultural management at the most inclusive level. In fact, one does not get very far by talking about the influence of nations, for nations as such, as corporate actors, have only a limited part in the global cultural flow. They may appear in guises such as the USIA, the Fulbright Commission, the British Council, and the Alliance Française, and interact in their own terms in organizations such as UNESCO. Much of the traffic in culture in the world, however, is transnational rather than international. It ignores, subverts and devalues rather than celebrates national boundaries. When we talk about American influence or French influence or Mexican influence, we throw together a great many kinds of asymmetrical relationships, perhaps with a number of symmetrical ones for good measure. A more precise realization of how contemporary world culture is constituted can only result when we take them apart again.

Some questions about alarmism

The forecast that the centre-periphery flow of culture will lead to the disappearance of cultural differences in the world is encountered fairly frequently these days. 'One conclusion still seems unanimously shared,' claims a prominent media researcher; 'the impressive variety of the world's cultural systems is waning due to a process of "cultural synchronization" that is without historical precedent' (Hamelink 1983, p.3). Horror tales are told: 'The incredibly rich local musical tradition of many Third World countries is rapidly disappearing under the onslaught of dawn-to-dusk American pop music.' 'For starving children in the Brazilian city of Recife, to have a Barbie doll seems more important than food.' The prime mover behind this pan-human replication of uniformity is late Western capitalism, equipped with media technology, forever luring more communities into dependency on the fringes of an expanding world-wide consumer society.

The alarmist view of the threat of global cultural homogenization cannot be dismissed out of hand. Yet some questions should be raised which may cast some general light on the problem of the efficacy of the transnational cultural apparatus.

One question is whether the transnational influences must really be seen as wholly deleterious. Current conceptions of cultural imperialism exemplify on the largest imaginable scale the curious fact that according to the economics of culture, to receive may be to lose. In that way, they are a useful antidote to old 'white man's burden' notions of the gifts of culture from centre to periphery as unadulterated benefaction. But perhaps a closer examination allows us to see more shades in the picture. In the areas of scholarship and intellectual life in general, we hardly take a conflict for granted between the transnational flow of culture and local cultural creativity the way we do with popular culture. Without a certain openness to impulses from the outside world, we would even expect science, art and literature to become impoverished. Obviously, for example, Nigerian literary life could hardly exist were it not for the importation of literacy and a range of literary forms. But there would not have been a Nigerian Nobel Prize winner in literature in 1986 if Wole Soyinka had not creatively drawn on both a cosmopolitan literary expertise and an imagination rooted in a Nigerian mythology, and named them into something unique.

Why, then, are we so quick to assume that in this field the relationship between local and imported culture can only be one of competition? Established assumptions about cultural purity and authenticity probably come to the surface here. We imagine that local products are threatened with extinction through the importation of 'cheap foreign junk'. In such references one may detect some hypocrisy, in so far as they imply that all local products are of great intellectual or aesthetic merit, never merely cheap local junk. But we also ignore the possibility that the formal symbol systems of popular culture and the media, and the skills in handling the symbol systems, can be transferred between cultures. As long as there is room for local cultural production as well, this may in itself be helped in its development by the availability of a wider range of models. And at least to the extent that the Nigerian example is anything to go by, it seems to be a dubious assumption that there will never be such room for local production, or that it cannot be created.

It may be objected that such notions of cultural enrichment are not to the point, that even if what is imported is seen as equipment, models and stimuli, it is still destructive in so far as it irreversibly changes local culture. Whatever modifications these imports undergo, however much they are integrated with indigenous culture, they may impose alien formats on it. When literacy comes in, whatever modes of thought may be linked to pure orality are likely to be corrupted. A Nigerian sitcom is still a sitcom. The very shape of popular culture as a social organizational phenomenon, with its great asymmetry in the relationship between performers and audience, might threaten older and more participatory arrangements of cultural expression.

Again this is a serious argument. But there is perhaps only a thin line between a defence of authenticity and an antiquarianism which often turns out to be vicarious. Nigeria, for example, could hardly in this postcolonial era go back completely to its precolonial cultural heritage, for pure tradition, and its collective form of expression, would not serve the contemporary structures of the country and could not match the everyday experiences and desires of many Nigerians today. A popular culture, and a media technology, are now as much necessities in large parts of the Third World as they are in the Occident, and the more realistic hope for continued cultural diversity in the world, with some linkage to local heritage, would rather seem to be for a diversity in motion, one of coexistence as well as creative interaction between the transnational and the indigenous.

Another problem with alarmism tends to be the quality of the evidence for it. Quite frequently it is anecdotal – 'I switched on the television set in my hotel room in Lagos (or Manila, or Tel Aviv, or Geneva), and found that *Dallas* was on.' In a more sophisticated version, it may be pointed out that on one Third World television channel or other, some high percentage of the programming is imported.

To be more completely persuasive, however, arguments about the impact of the transnational cultural flow would have to say something about how the people respond to it. The mere fact that Third World television stations buy a lot of imported programs, for example, often has more to do with the fact that they are cheap than that audiences are necessarily enthralled with them. We may have little idea about how many television sets are on, when they are shown, and much less what is the quality of attention to them.

At least as problematic is the sense that people make of the transnational cultural flow. Even when we refer to it as a 'flow of meaning', we must keep in mind the uncertainties built into the communicative process. If one cannot be too sure of perfect understanding even in a face-to-face interaction in a local context with much cultural redundancy, the difficulties (or the opportunities for innovative interpretations, if one wants to see it another way) multiply where there is largely a one-way cultural flow, between people whose perspectives have been shaped in very different contexts, in places very distant from one another. The meaning of the transnational cultural flow is thus in the eye of the beholder; what he sees we generally know little about.

One intricate issue here is the relationship between different symbolic modes and the global diversity of culture. Do some symbolic forms, in some modes, travel better than others? We know well enough where the barriers of incomprehension are between languages. How is the transnational spread of popular culture affected by varying sensibilities with respect to other modes, particularly the musical and gestural? One may rather facilely explain the popularity of Indian and Hong Kong movies over much of the Third World by referring to the fact that they are cheap (which appeals to distributors) and action-packed (which appeals to somewhat unsophisticated audiences). But the latter point may hide as much as it reveals. What kind, or degree, of precision is there in the audience appreciation of the symbolic forms of another country?[2]

It seems also that the consequences of transnational cultural flow must be understood as they unfold over time. The murderous threat of cultural imperialism is often rhetorically depicted as involving the high-tech culture of the metropolis, with powerful organizational backing, facing a defence-less, small-scale folk culture. Such encounters do perhaps occur. Yet at other times and in other places this is a very ahistorical view. In Nigeria, in the case of popular music but probably with reference to other popular culture forms as well, it seems important that the process by which external borrowings have been absorbed has some time depth. Metropolitan popular music, its genres and its instruments, have filtered into the West African coast societies gradually over the last century, introduced to begin with by modest means. There has been time, then, to absorb such influences, and in turn modify the modifications, and to fit the new popular culture to the evolving national social structure, its audiences and its situations. And this is the local scene which now meets the transnational cultural industries of the late twentieth century.

One can think of two rough scenarios of the long-term effects of transnational cultural flows. I would like to call them the scenarios of saturation and maturation. The former would suggest that as the transnational cultural apparatus unendingly pounds on the sensibilities of the peoples of the periphery, local culture will cumulatively assimilate more and more of the imported meanings and forms, becoming gradually indistinguishable from them. At any one time, what is considered local culture is a little more like transnational imports than what went before it as local culture. This may not sound altogether implausible. The maturation scenario, on the other hand, is based on the possibility that with time, imported cultural items which were at first to some degree in their unaltered, wholly alien forms would with time come to be taken apart, tampered and tinkered with, as people would evolve their own way of using them in a manner more in line with a culture of fundamentally local character.

The two scenarios describe opposing trajectories, but in real life they may well appear interwoven with one another. On the whole, the history of Nigerian popular music seems to have much in common with the maturation scenario. And one can see the reasons why this should be so: developed native musical traditions; an early involvement with foreign cultural imports at a time when the pressure of the transnational cultural apparatus was modest, thus allowing time to adapt; a sizeable market for the local product. Yet this is not to say that the Nigerian market cannot continuously make some room for new music from abroad as well.

The nature of the market is the factor of some importance, not least when one can see the transnational cultural flow as a flow of commodities. Often the importation of culture seems to presume a market which is, as it were, middling poor. Again, when for example Nigerian television stations, and other stations more or less on the periphery, buy programming from the centre, the reason is that they cannot afford to produce their own. On the other hand, they are not poor enough not to be able to import. But the more or less peripheral places can differ in these respects, and can differ also with regard to different kinds of cultural commodities, and can differ over time. Nigeria, the most populous country in Africa, at times quite affluent due to its oil exports, is better equipped than most to engage in cultural import substitution and build up its own internal cultural apparatus. It is also one of those countries which may find some market for its own cultural commodities in its wider region, and eventually to some extent reaches a wider market yet. It has some potential for becoming a centre of sorts in its own right. Smaller national markets may be more dependant on the importation of popular cultural goods from either regional or global centres.

On the other hand, if cultural commodities will only flow transnationally to places where markets exist, there may be places too poor to hold much promise in this regard. As the countries of the periphery are often vulnerable to changes in the relationship of local economies to that of the world, moreover, markets may shift dramatically over time. Small town people who bought imported popular fashions in the marketplace yesterday are perhaps no longer able to do so today; they have other reasons for the import substitution. Quite possibly, if the hold of the centre on the economies of the peripheries is such as to weaken them, at one time or over time, that very fact may also limit its own cultural power over them.

Note

1. Kopytoff (1987, p. 10) defines the ecumene as a 'region of persistent cultural interaction and exchange.'
2. Worth, S. touches upon such problems in his discussion of film anthropology as he asks how cinematic understandings are distributed. Do 'film language' communities have anything to do with language communities; do they relate to the distribution of cognitive styles.

References

Hamelink, Cees T. (1983) *Cultural Autonomy in Global Communications*, Longman, New York.

Kopytoff, Igor (1987) The Internal African Frontier: The Making of African Political Culture. *The African Frontier*, Indiana University Press, Bloomington.

Moore, Wilbert E. (1966) Global Sociology: The World as a Singular System. *American Journal of Sociology*, Vol. 71, pp. 475–82.

Worth, Sol (1981) *Studying Visual Communication*, University of Pennsylvania, Philadelphia.

3

The globalizing of modernity

Anthony Giddens

From Giddens, A. (1991) *The Consequences of Modernity*, Stanford University Press, Stanford, CA, pp. 63–78.

The three sources of the dynamism of modernity are: time–space distanciation, disembedding, and reflexivity. These are not, as such, types of institution, but rather facilitating conditions for the historical transitions referred to earlier. Without them, the tearing away of modernity from traditional orders could not have happened in so radical a way, so rapidly, or across such a world-wide stage. They are involved in, as well as conditioned by, the institutional dimensions of modernity.

The globalizing of modernity

Modernity is inherently globalizing – this is evident in some of the most basic characteristics of modern institutions, including particularly their disembeddedness and reflexivity. But what exactly is globalization, and how might we best conceptualize the phenomenon? The undue reliance which sociologists have placed upon the idea of 'society,' where this means a bounded system, should be replaced by a starting point that concentrates upon analysing how social life is ordered across time and space – the problematic of time–space distanciation. The conceptual framework of time–space distanciation directs our attention to the complex relations between *local involvements* (circumstances of co-presence) and *interaction across distance* (the connections of presence and absence). In the modern era, the level of time–space distanciation is much higher than in any previous period, and the relations between local and distance social forms and events become correspondingly 'stretched.' Globalization refers essentially to that stretching process, in so far as the modes of connection between different social contexts or regions become networked across the earth's surface as a whole.

Globalization can thus be defined as the intensification of world-wide social relations which link distant localities in such a way that local happenings are shaped by events occurring many miles away and vice versa. This is a dialectical process because such local happenings may move in an obverse direction from the very distanciated relations that shape them. *Local transformation* is as much a part of globalization as the lateral extension of social connections across time and space. Thus whoever studies cities today, in any part of the world, is aware that what happens in a local neighbourhood is likely to be influenced by factors – such as world money and commodity markets – operating at an indefinite distance away from that neighbourhood itself. The outcome is not necessarily, or even usually, a generalized set of changes acting in a uniform direction, but consists in mutually opposed tendencies. The increasing prosperity of an urban area in Singapore might be causally related, via a complicated network of global economic ties, to the impoverishment of a neighbourhood in Pittsburgh whose local products are uncompetitive in world markets.

Another example from the very many that could be offered is the rise of local nationalisms in Europe and elsewhere. The development of globalized social relations probably serves to diminish some aspects of nationalist feeling linked to nation-states (or some states) but may be causally involved with the intensifying of more localized nationalist sentiments. In circumstances of accelerating globalization, the nation-state has become 'too small for the big problems of life, and too big for the small problems of life.'[1] At the same time as social relations become laterally stretched and as part of the same process, we see the strengthening of pressures for local autonomy and regional cultural identity.

Two theoretical perspectives

Theorists of international relations characteristically focus upon the development of the nation-state system, analysing its origins in Europe and its subsequent world-wide spread. Nation-states are treated as actors, engaging with one another in the international arena – and with other organizations of a transnational kind (intergovernmental organizations or non-state actors). Although various theoretical positions are represented in this literature, more authors print a rather similar picture in analysing the growth of globalization.[2] Sovereign states, it is presumed, first emerge largely as separate entities, having more or less complete administrative control within their borders. As the European state system matures and later becomes a global nation-state system, patterns of interdependence become increasingly developed. These are not only expressed in the ties states form with one another in the international arena, but in the burgeoning of intergovernmental organizations. These processes mark an overall movement towards 'one world,' although they are continually fractured by war. Nation-states, it is held, are becoming progressively less sovereign than they used to be in terms of control over their own affairs – although few today anticipate in the near future the emergence of the 'world-state' which many in the early part of this century foresaw as a real prospect.

While this view is not altogether wrong, some major reservations have to be expressed. For one thing, it again covers only one overall dimension of globalization as I wish to utilize the concept here – the international co-ordination of states. Regarding states as actors has its uses and makes sense in some contexts. However, most theorists of international relations do not explain *why* this usage makes sense; for it does so only in the case of nation-states, not in that of pre-modern states. The reason is a far greater concentration of administrative power in nation-states than in their precursors, in which it would be relatively meaningless to speak of 'governments' who negotiate with other 'governments' in the name of their respective nations. Moreover, treating states as actors having connections with each other and with other organizations in the international arena makes it difficult to deal with social relations that are not between or outside states, but simply crosscut state divisions.

A further shortcoming of this type of approach concerns its portrayal of the increasing unification of the nation-state system. The sovereign power of modern states was not formed prior to their involvement in the nation-state system, even in the European state system, but developed in conjunction with it. Indeed, the sovereignty of the modern state was from the first *dependent upon the relations between states*, in terms of which each state (in principle if by no means always in practice) recognized the autonomy of others within their own borders. No state, however powerful, held as much sovereign control in practice as was enshrined in legal principle. The history of the past two centuries is thus not one of the progressive loss of sovereignty on the part of the nation-state. Here again we must recognize the dialectical character of globalization and also the influence of processes of uneven development. Loss of autonomy on the part of some states or groups of states has often gone along with an *increase* in that of others, as a result of alliances, wars, or political and economic changes of various sorts. For instance, although the sovereign control of some of the 'classical' Western nations may have diminished as a result of the acceleration of the global division of labour over the past 30 years, that of some Far Eastern countries – in some respects at least – has grown.

Since the stance of world-system theory differs so much from international relations, it is not surprising to find that the two literatures are at arm's distance from one another. Wallerstein's account of the world system makes many contributions, in both theory and empirical analysis.[3] Not least important is the fact that he skirts the sociologists' usual preoccupation with 'societies' in favour of a much more embracing conception of globalized relationships. He also makes a clear differentiation between the modern era and preceding ages in terms of the phenomena with which he is concerned. What he refers to as 'world economies' – networks of economic connections of a geographically extensive sort – have existed prior to modern times, but these were notably different from the world system that has developed over the past three or four centuries. Earlier world economies were usually centred upon large imperial states and never covered more than certain regions in which the power of these states was concentrated. The emergence of capitalism, as Wallerstein analyses it, ushers in a quite different type of order, for the first time genuinely global in its span and based more on economic than political power – the 'world capitalist economy.' The world capitalist economy, which has its origins in the sixteenth and seventeenth centuries, is integrated through commercial and manufacturing connections, not by a political centre. Indeed, there exists a multiplicity of political centres, the nation-states. The modern world system is divided into three components, the core, the semi-periphery, and the periphery, although where these are located regionally shifts over time.

According to Wallerstein, the world-wide reach of capitalism was established quite early on in the modern period: 'Capitalism was from the beginning an affair of the world economy and not of nation-states ... Capital has never allowed its aspirations to be determined by national boundaries.'[4]

Capitalism has been such a fundamental globalizing influence precisely because it is an economic rather than a political order; it has been able to penetrate far-flung areas of the world which the states of its origin could not have brought wholly under their political sway. The colonial administration of distant lands may in some situations have helped to consolidate economic expansion, but it was never the main basis of the spread of capitalistic enterprise globally. In the late twentieth century, where colonialism in its original form has all but disappeared, the world capitalist economy continues to involve massive imbalances between core, semi-periphery, and periphery.

Wallerstein successfully breaks away from some of the limitations of much orthodox sociological thought, most notably the strongly defined tendency to focus upon 'endogeneous models' of social change. But his work has its own shortcomings. He continues to see only one dominant institutional nexus (capitalism) as responsible for modern transformations. World-system theory thus concentrates heavily upon economic influences and finds it difficult satisfactorily to account for just those phenomena made central by the theorists of international relations: the rise of the nation-state and the nation-state system. Moreover, the distinctions between core, semi-periphery, and periphery (themselves perhaps of questionable value), based upon economic criteria, do not allow us to illuminate political or military concentrations of power, which do not align in an exact way to economic differentiations.

I regard the world capitalist economy as one of four dimensions of globalization, following the four-fold classification of the institutions of modernity (see Figure 3.1). The nation-state system is a second dimension; although these are connected in various ways, neither can be explained exhaustively in terms of the other.

If we consider the present day, in what sense can world economic organization be said to be dominated by capitalistic economic mechanisms?

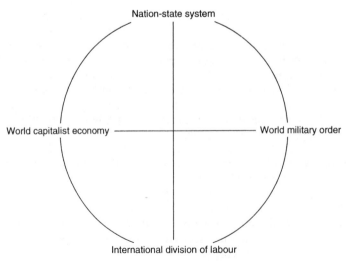

Fig. 3.1.

A number of considerations are relevant to answering this question. The main centres of power in the world economy are capitalist states – states in which capitalist economic enterprise (with the class relations that this implies) is the chief form of production. The domestic and international economic policies of these states involve many forms of regulation of economic activity, but, as noted, their institutional organization maintains an 'insulation' of the economic from the political. This allows wide scope for the global activities of business corporations, which always have a home base within a particular state but may develop many other regional involvements elsewhere.

Business firms, especially the transnational corporations, may wield immense economic power, and have the capacity to influence political policies in their home bases and elsewhere. The biggest transnational companies today have budgets larger than those of all but a few nations. But there are some key respects in which their power cannot rival that of states – especially important here are the factors of territoriality and control of the means of violence. There is no area on the earth's surface, with the partial exception of the polar regions, which is not claimed as the legitimate sphere of control of one state or another. All modern states have a more or less successful monopoly of control of the means of violence within their own territories. No matter how great their economic power, industrial corporations are not military organizations (as some of them were during the colonial period), and they cannot establish themselves as political/legal entities which rule a given territorial area.

If nation-states are the principal 'actors' within the global political order, corporations are the dominant agents within the world economy. In their trading relations with one another, and with states and consumers, companies (manufacturing corporations, financial firms, and banks) depend upon production for profit. Hence the spread of their influence brings in its train a global extension of commodity markets, including money markets. However, even in its beginnings, the capitalist world economy was never just a market for the trading of goods and services. It involved, and involves today, the commodifying of labour power in class relations which separate workers from control of their means of production. This process, of course, is fraught with implications for global inequalities.

All nation-states, capitalist and state socialist, within the 'developed' sectors of the world, are primarily reliant upon industrial production for the generation of the wealth upon which their tax revenues are based. The socialist countries form something of an enclave within the capitalist world economy as a whole, industry being more directly subject to political imperatives. These states are scarcely post-capitalist, but the influence of capitalistic markets upon the distribution of goods and labour power is substantially muted. The pursuit of growth by both Western and East European societies inevitably pushes economic interests to the forefront of the policies which states pursue in the international arena. But it is surely plain to all, save those under the sway of historical materialism, that the material involvements of nation-states are not governed purely by economic considerations, real or perceived. The influence of any particular state within the global political order is strongly conditioned by the level of its wealth (and the connection between this and military strength). However, states derive their power from their sovereign capabilities. They do not operate as economic machines, but as 'actors' jealous of their territorial rights, concerned with the fostering of national cultures, and having strategic geopolitical involvements with other states or alliances of states.

The nation-state system has long participated in that reflexivity characteristic of modernity as a whole. The very existence of sovereignty should be understood as something that is reflexively monitored, for reasons already indicated. Sovereignty is linked to the replacement of 'frontiers' by 'borders' in the early development of the nation-state system: autonomy inside the territory claimed by the state is sanctioned by the recognition of borders by other states. As noted, this is one of the major factors distinguishing the nation-state system from systems of states in the pre-modern era, where few reflexively ordered relations of this kind existed and where the notion of 'international relations' made no sense.

One aspect of the dialectical nature of globalization is the 'push and pull' between tendencies towards centralization inherent in the reflexivity of the system of states on the one hand and the sovereignty of particular states on the other. Thus, concerted action between countries in some respects diminishes the individual sovereignty of the nations involved, yet by combining their power in other ways, it increases their influence within the state system. The same is true of the early congresses which, in conjunction with war, defined and redefined states' borders – and of truly global agencies such as the United Nations (UN). The global influence of the UN (still decisively limited by the fact that it is not territorial and does not have significant access to the means of violence) is not purchased solely by means of a diminution of the sovereignty of nation-states – things are more complicated than this. An obvious example is that of the 'new nations' – autonomous nation-states set up in erstwhile colonized areas. Armed struggle against the colonizing countries was very generally a major factor in persuading the colonizers to retreat. But discussion in the UN played a key role in setting up ex-colonial areas as states with internationally recognized borders. However weak some of the new nations may be economically and militarily, their emergence *as* nation-states (or, in many cases, 'state-nations') marks a net gain in terms of sovereignty, as compared to their previous circumstances.

The third dimension of globalization is the world military order. In specifying its nature, we have to analyse the connections between the industrialization of war, the flow of weaponry and techniques of military organization from some parts of the world to others, and the alliances which states build with one another. Military alliances do not necessarily compromise the monopoly over the means of violence held by a state within its territories, although in some circumstances they certainly can do so.

In tracing the overlaps between military power and the sovereignty of states, we find the same push-and-pull between opposing tendencies noted previously. In the current period, the two most militarily developed states, the United States and the Soviet Union, have built a bipolar system of military alliances of truly global scope. The countries involved in these alliances necessarily accept limitations over their opportunities to forge independent military strategies externally. They may also forfeit complete monopoly of military control within their own territories, in so far as American or Soviet forces stationed there take their orders from abroad. Yet, as a result of the massive destructive power of modern weaponry, almost all states possess military strength far in excess of that of even the largest of pre-modern civilizations. Many economically weak Third World countries are militarily powerful. In an important sense there is no 'Third World' in respect of weaponry, only a 'First World,' since most countries maintain stocks of technologically advanced armaments and have modernized the military in a thoroughgoing way. Even the possession of nuclear weaponry is not confined to the economically advanced states.

The globalizing of military power obviously is not confined to weaponry and alliances between the armed forces of different states – it also concerns war itself. Two world wars attest to the way in which local conflicts became matters of global involvement. In both wars, the participants were drawn from virtually all regions (although the Second World War was a more truly world-wide phenomenon). The only point of holding nuclear weapons – apart from their possible symbolic value in world politics – is to deter others from using them.

While this situation may lead to a suspension of war between the nuclear powers (or so we all must hope), it scarcely prevents them from engaging in military adventures outside their own territorial domains. The two superpowers in particular engage in what might be called 'orchestrated wars' in peripheral areas of military strength. By these I mean military encounters, with the governments of other states or with guerilla movements or both, in which the troops of the superpower are not necessarily even engaged at all, but where that power is a prime organizing influence.

The fourth dimension of globalization concerns industrial development. The most obvious aspect of this is the expansion of the global division of labour, which includes the differentiations between more and less industrialized areas in the world. Modern industry is intrinsically based on divisions of labour, not only on the level of job tasks but on that of regional specialization in terms of type of industry, skills, and the production of raw materials. There has undoubtedly taken place a major expansion of global interdependence in the division of labour since the Second World War. This has helped to bring about shifts in the world-wide distribution of production, including the deindustrialization of some regions in the developed countries and the emergence of the 'newly industrializing countries' in the Third World. It has also undoubtedly served to reduce the internal economic hegemony of many states, particularly those with a high level of industrialization. It is more difficult for the capitalist countries to manage their economies than formerly was the case, given accelerating global economic interdependence. This is almost certainly one of the major reasons for the declining impact of Keynesian economic policies, as applied at the level of the national economy, in current times.

One of the main features of the globalizing implications of industrialism is the worldwide diffusion of machine technologies. The impact of industrialism is plainly not limited to the sphere of production, but affects many aspects of day-to-day life, as well as influencing the generic character of human interaction with the material environment.

Even in states which remain primarily agricultural, modern technology is often applied in such a way as to alter substantially preexisting relations between human social organization and the environment. This is true, for example, of the use of fertilizers or other artificial farming methods, the introduction of modern farming machinery, and so forth. The diffusion of industrialism has created 'one world' in a more negative and threatening sense than that just mentioned – a world in which there are actual or potential ecological changes of a harmful sort that affect everyone on the planet. Yet industrialism has also decisively conditioned our very sense of living in 'one world.' For one of the most important effects of industrialism has been the transformation of technologies of communication.

This comment leads on to a further and quite fundamental aspect of globalization, which lies behind each of the various institutional dimensions that have been mentioned and which might be referred to as cultural globalization. Mechanized technologies of communication have dramatically influenced all aspects of globalization since the first introduction of mechanical printing into Europe. They form an essential element of the reflexivity of modernity and of the discontinuities which have torn the modern away from the traditional.

The point here is not that people are contingently aware of many events, from all over the world, of which previously they would have remained ignorant. It is that the global extension of the institutions of modernity would be impossible were it not for the pooling of knowledge which is represented by the 'news.' This is perhaps less obvious on the level of general cultural awareness than in more specific contexts. For example, the global money markets of today involve direct and simultaneous access to pooled information on the part of individuals spatially widely separated from one another. In conditions of modernity, larger and larger numbers of people live in circumstances in which disembedded institutions, linking local practices with globalized social relations, organize major aspects of day-to-day life.

Notes

1. Bell, Daniel (1987) The World and the United States in 2013. *Daedalus*, 116.
2. See for example Rosenthau, James N. (1980) *The Study of Global Interdependence*, Pinter, London.
3. Wallerstein, Immanual (1974) *The Modern World System*, Academic, New York.
4. Wallerstein, Immanuel (1979) The Rise and Future Demise of the World Capitalist System: Concepts for Comparative Analysis. In Wallerstein, I. (1979) *The Capitalist World Economy*, Cambridge University Press, Cambridge, p. 19.

4

The theoretical challenge of global society

Martin Shaw

From Shaw, M. (1994) *Global Society and International Relations: Sociological Concepts and Political Perspectives*, Polity Press and Blackwell Publishers, Cambridge and Oxford, pp. 5–27.

The world as a single society

The issue of globalization is a radical one for sociology as well as for international relations – and indeed for the social sciences as a whole. It challenges prevailing conceptions, especially many which are implicitly assumed in social theory and analysis, about the very nature of the social, the state and civil society. [. . .]

The term society is used in several senses. The most basic is as a generic term for social relations, which are the essential subject matter of sociology. In this sense, society is the totality or complex of social relations. Since social relations of all kinds are increasingly global, and all forms of social relations everywhere in the world are, at least in some indirect sense, bound into global networks, society in this sense is now necessarily global.

The term is also used, however, and perhaps even more widely, in the sense of *a* society. The assumptions behind such usage is that there are relatively discrete complexes of social relations which can be distinguished from other such complexes and analysed in a largely self-sufficient manner. Note the qualifying adjectives, relatively and largely, for it is a long time since any known area of social life – probably not even the most recently 'discovered' peoples of New Guinea – could be said to be absolutely or wholly separated from wider frameworks of social relations.

There has always been a considerable paradox, and theoretical question-mark, behind most senses in which sociologists have talked of the existence of discrete societies. Such societies have always existed in relation to other societies and have been defined largely by such relationships. In modern times, moreover, societies have been defined by their state institutions and the specific forms of relationships between these. Hence, of course, the assumption by international theorists that inter-state relations can be regarded as largely autonomous from and analytically prior to social relations.

These considerations apply above all to national societies and the way in which they are related to nation-states. National societies, in the modern sense, depend on the existence of nation-states in a system of relations between states. National societies have been state-bounded segmentations of increasingly global social relations. Since there have always been, in modern times, international, transnational and even incipiently global relationships, such segmentations have always been quite arbitrary in some important respects. The ways in which descriptions and analysis have tried to represent them as real – in a more or less absolute or fixed sense – has been patently false, and has reflected the incapacity of much sociology adequately to criticize national ideologies.

The same arguments apply, moreover, even to tribal societies. Such societies have generally existed, over thousands of years, only in relation to other similar societies. Societies, in the sense of discrete human communities, have only been formed through migration, differentiation and mutual contact. The circumstance of a wholly isolated society must be viewed, historically, as a limited exception in which a certain human group temporarily becomes isolated from others. In modern times, moreover, such societies have become increasingly defined by their contact with the Western nation-state system. Even the early anthropological studies, which attempted to define the precolonial forms of social relations, were in fact, as later critiques have established, manifestations of the colonial relationship between tribal societies and Western state-bounded societies.

There is a sense, then, in which the concept of discrete societies was always questionable, when not clearly identified as a partial abstraction from the global complex of social relations.

The national (and corresponding tribal) demarcation of societies work-ed, however, for a certain historical period. From the nineteenth-century heyday of the nation-state, in which classical sociology was largely developed, through the extreme national division of the world in the era of total war, the idea of national society corresponded to immediately comprehensible socio-political realities. The idea was still strong in the mid-twentieth-century 'post-war' condition, in which most modern sociology grew. Although many developments after 1945 were working to undermine this situation, the cold war helped to freeze a certain conception of national society beyond the point at which it could really be sustained in its earlier form.

What is really new in the present situation, most clearly since the end of the cold war, is that, although the idea of discrete national societies retains much resonance, its absolutely supremacy among the ideas of society can no longer hold. This may seem a paradoxical assertion, since the strongest tendency of the years since 1989 has been the reassertion of nationalism. On all sides, people are breaking up multinational states into nation-states, and nation-states into miniature ethnically defined states. Socialism and communism seem to have given way, not to liberalism but to nationalism. And yet the desperation and violence of much of this return to the nation does not speak of an idea whose time has come, but of one which has to been upheld against all the odds.

The new nationalisms are not those of the classic, integrative nation-state, bonding disparate cultures into a single entity, but of the exclusive ethnic group, expelling all those who do not conform. The new nationalisms arise from the disintegration of nation-states and national societies. They reflect both historic pluralism and multi-ethnicity and new patterns formed as a result of recent migration and cultural change. Although ethnic identities seem the most powerful foci, they in fact exist alongside a powerful range of diverse, part-competing, part-overlapping forms of identity, centred on religion, gender, race, class, profession and lifestyle. The virulence of ethnic nationalism reflects its conflict not just with other nationalisms but with ideas of a plural society with multiple identities.

The idea of a national society in the old sense has thus declined as the ideas of a global society and of various more local forms of social identity have grown.

Integration in global society

For some theorists, a society is characterized by normative consensus, reflected in commonly accepted institutions. For others, it is formed simply by the existence of networks of relationships, with mutual expectations, even if the commonality of values and norms among the members is highly limited. The mutual expectations may indeed be of sustained and systematic conflict over values as well as resources.

In this section, we shall explore the sociological meaning of global society, and try to illuminate the issues posed by the dual definitions of society which are on offer.

In order to utilize the dilemma constructively, it is important not to entrench ourselves in the polar positions of 'conflict' and 'consensus' which characterize textbook discussions in sociology. It may indeed be preferable, as a starting point, to examine the *de facto* patterns of social relations, and it is unjustifiable to assume the existence of *de jure* normative consensus as the foundation of society: to this extent the present writer shares the materialist view of the foundation of conflict. As David Lockwood argued, however, in a classic attempt to overcome the polarity, it may be more relevant to see these two approaches as indicating two distinctive dimensions of social cohesion, which can be characterized respectively as 'system' and 'social' integration.[1] The former concerns the extent to which a society's members are factually integrated in social relationships; the latter, the extent to which they are normatively integrated. Lockwood's argument suggests that these are not questions of definition, but empirical issues in the assessment of any given society.

Two versions of 'system' integration may be identified as structuring the sociological debate on globalization. Immanuel Wallerstein's 'world-system' approach analyses the world in terms of the development of global capitalism, in which the division between economic, political and social relationships is seen as artificial. For Wallerstein, globalization is the development of a unified world-system dominated – critics would say excessively – by the socio-economic relationships of capitalism.[2] Wallerstein has recently extended his analysis into the cultural dimension of the world-system, seeing this as dominated by a tension between universalism and particularism (in the form of racism-sexism).[3] This remains, however, a highly simplified view of global society, juxtaposing a one-dimensional view of culture and values with a similar perspective on market relationships.[4]

Anthony Giddens, on the other hand, has proposed a view of globalization which conceptualizes systemic arrangements as multiple and complex.

In Giddens's view, modern society is dominated by knowledge-based abstract systems which co-ordinate human activity, and which enable as well as constrain individual action and choice. For Giddens, the globalization of abstract systems creates opportunities for individuals, as well as crises in which they have constantly to remake their own lives and identities.[5] It is clear from Giddens's view that the increasing integration of systems (plural) does not necessarily imply greater social integration on a global scale. On the contrary, the crises brought about by the failures of or contradictions between the various abstract systems could lead to greater problems of social integration.

Applying the distinction between system and social integration to the developing global society may, therefore, illuminate many of the issues which concern current analysis. Global society clearly exhibits growing system integration, above all at the level of socio-economic relations, but also in the development of cultural and political institutions. What is a great deal more problematic is the development of social integration in the value sense. How far has the growing integration of global systems been accompanied by a genuine emergence of consensus and normative integration? In so far as such developments are occurring, are they confined largely to state, corporate and intellectual elites, or do they involve larger sections, or even all the members of global society?

It is evidently correct to argue that global society, in its existing or likely future form, does not and will not possess either common beliefs and values, or common and accepted institutions, to even the problematic extent to which these have been attributed to national or tribal societies. Indeed it is difficult to argue that global society could ever possess these forms of cohesion in the same ways, or to the same degree, as these more limited societies. This is true because, however fast global integration proceeds, world society seems likely in the foreseeable future (centuries as well as decades) to remain divided between highly differentiated segments. The experience of society in complex multinational states has been that national, ethnic and other divisions remain powerful; it seems inconceivable that these will be less important on the much larger scale of global society, however much global institutions develop. The reverse is more likely to be true, as globalization sharpens existing differences.

Global social integration seems likely, therefore, to remain extremely problematic. Sociologists have, however, analysed cultural developments as one of the main forms of globalization, and such developments pose the issue of integration particularly sharply. A global culture which equates with national cultures may not exist, Featherstone argues, and alleged homogenizing processes ('theories which present cultural imperialism, Americanization and mass consumer culture as a proto-universal culture riding on the back of Western economic and political domination') may have been exaggerated. Nevertheless we can conceptualize global culture, 'in terms of the diversity, variety and richness of popular and local discourses', with an 'image of the globe as a single place, the generative frame of unity within which diversity can take place.'[6]

Anthony Smith, an authority of nationalism, reminds us that the development of global means of communication does not necessarily mean that a common content is shared in all societies.[7] On the contrary, national cultures may maintain or even increase their vibrancy in response to globalizing tendencies. However, a historical perspective such as that proposed by Roland Robertson suggests that the diffusion of nationalism can itself be seen as part of the process of globalization.[8] In his account, the standardization of the nation as the basis for society and state was a facet of the early stages of globalization. By implication, its continuing importance, on which Smith rightly insists, has nevertheless to be seen in the context of the current phase of globalization. Every nationalism is different, but all nationalisms use a common language and symbols – which are global currency. Nationalisms are, as Smith himself suggests, becoming hybrids, exchanging ideas with one another and with other elements in global political discourse. If nations are, in Anderson's term, imagined communities,[9] then one has to be aware of this world-wide intercourse which feeds the way in which nations are imagined.

This discussion suggests that the problem of socio-cultural integration in global society should not be conceptualized in one-dimensional terms. The idea of a simple homogenization is patently inadequate – although homogenizing processes certainly exist – but even diversity can be seen to have integrating aspects. We can, indeed, go further, and argue that the conflictual aspects of diversity, where cultural differentiation is linked to political conflict, can be seen under the rubric of global integration. Conflict sharpens awareness of mutual dependence and promotes the development of common responses and institutions for regulation, which in turn involve cultures of co-operation.

Global society, to put it at its strongest, is no more or less than the entire complex of social relations between human beings on a world scale. As such it is more complete and self-sufficient than just about any other society which has been or could be envisaged. It still represents a partial abstraction relative to the history of human societies, and relative to the natural and living world as a whole. It does not have to be seen as having needs (as in the original functionalist model), as being based on imperatives (such as capital accumulation in the Marxist account of capitalism) or as necessarily entailing a given set of functions and institutions. Its emergence and the social relations, systems and institutions within it can be described under the rubric of historical discontinuity and contingency rather than of functional or historical necessity.

While global society in this sense contains all social relations, not all relations are actually defined at a global level. Global society can also be seen, therefore, as the largest existing, and also the largest possible, framework or context of social relations, but not necessarily the immediately defining context of all social relations. As in all large-scale, complex societies there are many contexts in which relations can be defined, and most are not located in the largest or more general context. Crucial to understanding global society is to comprehend the changing contextualization of social relations, and one of the critical issues is to grasp the extent, forms and processes of globalization. Globalization, indeed, can be seen as the way in which social relations become defined by specifically global contexts.

Global society can be said to exist, in the sense that global relationships are sufficiently strong and established to be defined as the largest context of social relationships as a whole. In an equally if not more important sense, however, it can still be seen very much as an emergent reality.

If global society is still emergent, then this should increase our caution over ascribing to its forms which have characterized previous societies, and draw our attention to its historically specific features. A fundamental feature of global society is the exceptional complexities of its segmentation and differentiation, which subsumes and transforms the complexity of the pre-existing civilizations and national and tribal societies while producing many more from the processes of globalization themselves.

Global society is best understood, therefore, as a diverse social universe in which the unifying forces of modern production, markets, communications and cultural and political modernization interact with many global, regional, national and local segmentations and differentiations. Global society should be understood not as a social system but as a field of social relations in which many specific systems have formed – some of them genuinely global, others incipiently so, and others still restricted to national or local contexts.

Given the segmentation of global society, many of its institutions take a qualitatively different form from those of other societies. The most evident difference between global and national societies is the lack of a centralized state. The contrast here, is, however, a false one, since national societies in modern times exist only by virtue of three conditions: their dependence on particular states, these states' relationships with other states and the segmentation of wider social relations in line with state divisions. These fundamental, structuring facts are overlooked in any comparison which takes national societies as a baseline for global society.

Where national societies have states, global society has a state system. We are so used to thinking of the society–state relationship in a one-to-one sense, in which a single state constitutes the ultimate source of power and authority in a given society, that this concept of state power in global society may seem confusing. The familiar concept of one society, one state is, however, a historically specific one, and to generalize it, and expect any newly identified society to conform to it by definition, is to be guilty of illegitimate generalization.

Interestingly, international relations theorists have characterized the state system as an anarchic one, and in a well-known work Hedley Bull defined 'international society' as an 'anarchic society' comparable with 'primitive' stateless societies.[10] There are problems with this concept of international as opposed to global society. In particular, the definition of it as a 'society' of states to be compared with societies composed of individual human beings raises severe methodological problems. Nevertheless, the idea that a society can be characterized by anarchic relations – that is, by the absence of a clear central authority structure, and in particular of a central state – is clearly valid.

Although we are used to the idea of a society in which economic relations are anarchic (the essence of a market-based economy), the idea of political anarchy is challenging. Yet global society is a society in which anarchy prevails at both these crucial levels of social organization. The economic system of global society is at root that of the global market, co-ordinating an enormously complex division of labour in the production and exchange of commodities.

The political system of global society is basically that of the competitive international system of states, co-ordinating an equally complex diversity of national-state politics. The global cultural system is largely one of diverse, part-competing, part-overlapping, part-distinctive, part-integrated national and sub-national cultures organized around a wide range of principles.

The novel sense in which we talk of a global society at the end of the twentieth century depends, however, on something more than an awareness of these various forms of anarchy (which have characterized the emerging global society for decades if not centuries). Nor is it merely that, as a result of the development of communications, we have a heightened awareness of the anarchic nature of our world. This is important, but what is most significant is that as a result of this heightened awareness we are beginning to experience transformations of systems, institutions and culture. Military, political, economic and cultural crises are increasingly defined as global crises; even relatively limited regional conflicts are seen as global issues. Global society is beginning to be more than the sum of its parts, or, to be more precise, more than a framework for the competition of its parts.

It is in this sense that we should view the development of specifically global institutions (as well as regional and other transnational institutions). The global economic system consists not merely of a global division of labour and global market exchanges, but increasingly also of a variety of global (and regional) economic institutions aiming to regulate these processes. Although such institutions – GATT, IMF, Group of 7, EC, etc. – are dominated by the major Western states, banks and other corporations, they are distinct from any specific state or private interests and operate effectively as global regulators.

The global political system, similarly, consists not merely of an ever-growing number of individual nation-states and alliances or groupings of states. Global (and regional) institutions – above all, with all its defects, the UN – play an increasingly critical role. No matter that such institutions are manipulated by the major Western powers, and that their actions – especially military intervention (as in the Gulf in 1990–1) or non-intervention (as in Bosnia in 1992–3) – depend largely on the interests and policies of these powers, and especially of the United States. These are the developing global political institutions, and not surprisingly they reflect the current realities of global politics.

The global cultural system likewise can be characterized by the growth of global and regional elements. Although no one should doubt the tenacity of particularistic ideas and identities, as of particular economic and political interests, the growth of a common culture is still very striking. It is not just, of course, that means of communication have been transformed and that global communications systems have developed, dominated like most other economic fields by Western corporations with global reach. Nor is it merely that the standard cultural commodities – images, ideas, information – of Hollywood and CNN are globally diffused. More important, although less easily summarized, are the ways that through these processes, intermeshing with economic and political globalization, people are coming to see their lives in terms of common expectations, values and goals. These cultural norms include ideas of standard of living, lifestyle, entitlements to welfare, citizenship rights, democracy, ethnic and linguistic rights, nationhood, gender equality, environmental quality, etc. Many of them have originated in the West but they are increasingly, despite huge differences in their meanings in different social contexts, parts of the ways of life and of political discourse across the world. In this sense, we can talk of the emergence of a global culture, and specifically of global political culture.

A vital issue here is whether we can posit the growth of a global civil society. The concept of civil society forms a pairing with that of the state. In a weak and inclusive sense, civil society denotes society as distinct from the state; in this sense, clearly we can talk of a global civil society, based on the emerging global economy and culture. In a stronger sense, however, writers such as Gramsci have seen civil society in terms of the way in which society outside the state organizes and represents itself, forming both a source of pressure on and, in a certain sense, an extension of the state. Civil society in this sense is constituted by its institutions – classically churches, press, parties, trade unions, etc., but in modern terms also including a variety of communications media and new (no longer directly class-based) social movements and campaigns. The institutions of civil society have historically been national and constituted by the relationship to the nation-state; indeed they may be said to be essential components of the nation. Civil society has been, almost by definition, national.

It is clear that this situation, too, has begun to change in a fundamental way. As an increasing number of issues are being posed in global terms, the common threads weaving together civil societies in many countries have grown ever stronger. Between Western societies, the creation of a common military system during the East–West conflict, and with it of a common economic space, has encouraged the linking of civil societies. Within Western Europe, especially, the development of the European Union at a state level has brought forward – however contradictorily, since there is also societal resistance to European unity – a greater convergence of civil society. Across the former communist world, the collapse of the system revealed the weakness of civil society; while one result is a resurgence of nationalism, there is also an unprecedented opening of civil society to the West. In the rest of the world, there is also a decline of ideas of a Third World, and with it of the programme of national economic independence. There is a greater worldwide recognition of global interdependence, which has been strengthened since 1989.

Does the global linking of civil society amount to the development of global civil society? Clearly such a development must be in its early stages, and yet there are reasons for saying that it has well begun.

Civil society has always been seen as symbiotically linked with the state. Global civil society is coming into existence in an interdependent relationship with the state system, and especially with the developing international state institutions. The development of global civil society can best be understood in terms of a contradictory relationship with the state system. Civil society represents social interests and principles which may well conflict with the dominant interests in the state system. Just as national civil societies may express ideologies which are in contradiction to state interests, so global civil society, in so far as it is constructed around ideas of human rights, for example, may express ideologies which are formally upheld within the state system, but whose consistent application is in contradiction with dominant state interests. Global civil society thus constitutes a source of constant pressures on the state system, although its development is in turn very much dependent on developments in the state system.

The development of global civil society raises the issue of how far global principles of identity are now becoming important. Clearly important groups in all parts of global society are beginning to see membership of this society as a key identifier, alongside nationality and other affiliations. In some parts of the world, other forms of transnational identity are becoming more important – Europeanism, for example, which fairly clearly has close links to globalism, and Islam, which although universal in form is (like most other traditional religions and political ideologies) potentially antithetical to globalism in practice. The strength of globalism and related transnational identifiers is a key sociological test of the emergence of global civil society.

Sociology, international relations and global society

The global society perspective which has been outlined in this chapter constitutes a theoretical challenge to the social sciences as a whole, and to sociology in particular. There is in fact a dual challenge. The challenge to sociology – and by extension to most other social sciences, such as economics, politics, social geography and social history – is to move its level of theoretical and even more of analytical inquiry from the national to the global level, and to recast its categories explicitly in globalist terms.

The challenge to international relations, however, is of a different sort. International relations can be seen as the prime example of a field which is incipiently global, in that its *raison d'être* is to deal with relationships beyond the national level. The challenge to international relations is to move beyond the misplaced abstraction of state relations from the global whole. In the case of international relations, the movement to globalism is from a different starting point, and involves rather different sorts of transformation.

A major part of the paradox of international relations is that inter-state relations have developed further, with stronger institutionalization, than global economic, cultural or social developments. International relations seem therefore to possess a priority – analytical, if not real – over understanding the shifting sands of these other sorts of relationship in global society. International relations has been constructed, as a discipline, on this premise, but now finds it necessary to adjust to the fuller understanding of global society in its widest sense.

Even deeper in the paradox, however, is that international relations theorists have always implicitly recognized the links between state and society. The very name *international* relations implies a concern with relations between nations rather than states. While its intention may be honourable, international relations is a misnomer in so far as the discipline has always really been about relations between states. Its practitioners have generally made the mistake of assuming that states represented nations, and that the interests of the latter are incorporated in the former. When we look at the nation as only one principle of social, cultural and political organization in an increasingly complex global society, the very foundations of the study of international relations are theoretically challenged. The relations between states may remain a legitimate focus of study, but its basis will be recast within a wider globalism.

Notes

1. Lockwood, David (1992) Social integration and system integration. In Zollschan, G. K. and Hirsch, W. (eds.) *Explorations in Social Change*, New York: repr. in Lockwood, D. (1992), *Solidarity and Schism*, Clarendon Press, Oxford, pp. 399–412.
2. Wallerstein, Immanuel (1974) *The Modern World-System*, 3 vols, Academic Press, New York.
3. Wallerstein, Immanuel (1990) Culture as the ideological battleground of the modern world-system. In Featherstone, Mike (ed.) *Global Culture: Nationalism, Globalization and Modernity*, Sage, London, pp. 31–56.
4. See the comments of Boyne, Roy, Culture and the world-system. In Featherstone, *Global Culture*.
5. Giddens, Anthony (1990) *The Consequences of Modernity*, Polity, Cambridge and (1991) *Modernity and Self-Identity*, Polity, Cambridge. These works are discussed more fully later in this book.
6. Featherstone, Mike, Introduction. *Global Culture*, p. 2.
7. Smith, Anthony D. Towards a global culture? In Featherstone (ed.) *Global Culture*, pp. 171–91.
8. Robertson, Roland (1992) Mapping the global condition. In Robertson, *Globalization: Social Theory and Global Culture*, Sage, London pp. 49–60; also in Featherstone, (ed.) *Global Culture*, pp. 15–30.
9. Anderson, Benedict (1979) *Imagined Communities*, Verso, London.
10. Bull, Hedley (1977)*The Anarchic Society*, Macmillan, London.

5

Classifying the global system

Leslie Sklair

From Sklair, L. (1995) *Sociology of the Global System*, Harvester Wheatsheaf, Hemel Hempstead, pp. 10–25.

While the global system is most commonly classified in terms of First, Second and Third Worlds, and these are very convenient and for many purposes useful labels, it is certain that they conceal as much as they reveal. If we are to begin to describe the global system in a more theoretically fruitful manner we will have to look behind these labels. There are at least five main classifications of the global system in current usage and they are all state-centred. These can be roughly characterized as follows:

1. Income-based.
2. Trade-based.
3. Resource-based
4. Quality of life-based.
5. Bloc-based.

Income-based classification

This is the simplest, most widely used, and in some ways the most misleading of the classifications. Economists and economic historians have been interested in measuring poverty and wealth on a per capita basis for some time, and such data have been available for some of the advanced industrial countries for many years. The lack of statistical services in most Third World countries has meant that population figures, let alone GNP per capita figures, have been very sparse and unreliable. This situation improved somewhat in the 1970s, and international agencies have been systematically organizing the collection of such data. Since 1978 the World Bank has been publishing an annual *World Development Report* with a growing number of 'world development indicators' tables (18 tables in 1978, 27 in 1983, 33 in 1988), based for the most part on UN and internal World Bank data sources. This is certainly the most useful, easily accessible and up-to-date compilation of figures. [. . .]

The World Bank ranks all the countries of the world according to their GNP per capita, though countries with populations of less than one million (of whom there were 35 identified in the 1988 Report) are excluded from the main tables. All World Bank financial data are converted into U.S. dollars, and this is, indeed, one serious problem with them. The 1978 Report has 125 countries with GNP per capita figures ranging from $70 (Bhutan) to $15,480 (Kuwait). The countries are divided into six categories as follows:

low-income with GNP per capita up to $250 (34 countries); middle-income over $250 per capital (58 countries); industrialized countries (19); capital surplus oil exporters (three); and centrally-planned economies, communist countries (11). There are several anomalies in this classification. In the first place, while countries listed from 1–92 are in strict GNP per capita order, countries 93, 94 and 95 (South Africa, Ireland and Italy) all have lower per capita figures than 92 (Israel). No fewer than 14 middle-income countries have higher per capita figures than 'industrialized' South Africa, and five of these are 'richer' than Ireland. Further, the per capita figures for the oil exporters and the centrally-planned economies would distribute the countries in these categories fairly widely throughout the list.

By 1983, the categories had changed somewhat, though the anomalies remained. The poorest 34 countries were still identified as low-income economies; the next 60 countries were divided into 39 lower-middle-income and 21 upper-middle-income economies. Four high-income oil exporters, 19 industrial market economies and eight East European non-market economies completed the list of 125 countries. The main differences between the 1978 and the 1983 lists were definitional (the splitting up of the middle-income group) and political (South Africa expelled from the industrial group and relegated to the upper-middle-income group and replaced, incidentally, by Spain; Taiwan expelled altogether from the list and the People's Republic of China integrated into the low-income group at number 21). The two most populous countries in the world. China and India, in the low-income economies group, were also separated out from the rest of this group for averaging purposes; as were oil exporters and oil importers in the middle-income economies group.

By 1988 the total number of countries had risen to 129, split into 39 low-income, 34 lower-middle, 24 upper-middle, four high-income oil exporters, 19 industrial market, and nine centrally-planned economies, renamed 'nonreporting nonmembers' (aptly, as there was little information on them outside the demographic and social indicators tables). Again, a certain amount of category switching had taken place. For example, Hungary, Poland and Romania were inserted into the upper-middle-income group, where their apparent per capita income scores would locate them in any case, whereas Angola, Cuba and North Korea were transplanted from lower-middle-income to nonreporting nonmembers. Further, all the low and middle-income groups were also categorized as 'developing economies' subdivided into oil exporters, exporters of manufactures, highly indebted countries, and sub-Saharan Africa (new sub-categories of great ideological significance), for the purposes of averaging.

It is not only the anomalies in these tables to which I wish to draw attention but the assumptions on which they are based. These assumptions are as follows:

1. GNP per capita can be determined for all of the countries concerned in such a way that meaningful comparisons can be drawn.
2. The per capita income is the basic criterion for drawing comparisons.
3. In some cases other criteria will override the per capita income basis of the classification.

Economists at the World Bank and elsewhere have laboured hard and long to put international data on a sound footing and the 'technical notes' that follow the tables in the reports are full of acknowledgements of the difficulties involved. These difficulties, however, are not simply technical, in the sense of translating one country's GNP or GDP into terms that will bear comparison with those of other countries. They are also a matter of political economy, in the sense that some measures best represent some socio-economic systems while they discriminate against, perhaps by undervaluing the products of, other socio-economic systems or classes of people within a system. A glaring example of this is the neglect of the domestically-consumed products of farmers (particularly women) in the Third World. Such economic activity is excluded from World Bank data.

Women's work in the countries of the Third World is generally rendered 'invisible' by normal national accounting procedures because it usually takes place outside the conventional sphere of wage labour, mostly on the family farm and in the home. This 'invisibility' results in serious understatement of the great economic significance of female labour, especially in the production, collection, preparation and processing of food. Thus, male-dominated organizations like national statistical services and the World Bank, underestimate the real economic activity of Third World countries (see Boserup, 1970).

It is no accident that the global standard used by the World Bank and most other organizations is the U.S. dollar. It is a simple indication that the U.S. economy is the most powerful in the world (despite the fact that it is in relative decline) and that global economic activity does tend to be measured in comparison with the sorts of economic activities with which the United States is mainly involved. Lurking behind these measures, therefore, is a congerie of theories of economic growth and/or development most applicable to the United States and other similar industrial economies.

Income-based classifications on 'developing' and non-market economies are therefore inherently problematic. Where they are used as the basis of inter-country comparisons, which is by far the most common use that is made of them, they predispose the results of such comparisons to certain conclusions which are usually prejudiced by unspoken theory-laden assumptions. However, as long as we are aware of these provisos, and are able to correct the most crass biases at the empirical and conceptual levels, there is clearly a use to which such classifications can be put. For example, the countries of the world can be split into groups according to population as well as per capita income. The logic behind this is obvious. One important basis of comparison between countries is their size, and it is clearly very relevant to an appreciation of the relative levels of economic growth and development achieved by any country, to know roughly among how many people the social product, however large or small, has to be divided. The absolute size of a country is a relatively neglected question in the study of the global system.

If we correlate population categories (1–20 million, 20–50 million, 50–100 million, and 100 million plus) with World Bank GNP per capita categories (roughly lower-, middle-, and higher- income countries) we find that two-thirds of countries are relatively small (up to about 20 million in population) and two-thirds of these are quite poor (GNP per capital of less than $1570), while almost half the relatively rich countries (GNP per capita of more than $8000), have relatively large populations (over 50 million). The only real conclusion that we can draw from such an exercise is that there appears to be no simple relationship between population and the wealth of a nation-state. This might give a little pause to those who dogmatically believe that poverty is a direct consequence of 'overpopulation'.

Trade-based classifications

Though clearly important, income and population size are not the only important characteristics of countries. The structure of the economy and society can be broken down in a variety of ways for a variety of purposes. Those who have investigated the factors that seem to accompany economic growth and development in the second half of the twentieth century have often looked to the historical experiences of the contemporary advanced industrial societies for clues, and they have generally found that patterns of foreign trade are very important. The quantity, value and type of goods and services traditionally exported and imported by most of the contemporary rich nations, indeed, fell into fairly clear patterns. Briefly, they exported manufactured goods and capital, and they imported raw materials. The so-called terms of trade, more accurately labelled 'unequal exchange' (see Edwards, 1985, Ch. 4), ensured that for the most part the prices of raw materials were falling relative to the prices of manufactured goods. A further and central feature of this system of trade was that while those countries exporting manufactures were usually involved in many diverse lines of business, the raw-material exporters were often engaged in the production of one or two major staples. Mono-crop economies are particularly vulnerable to the instabilities in the world market directed, not by the hidden hand of the market, but by the actions of a global collection of profit-maximizing capitalists, usually based in hegemon countries and often acting in unison.

Even those writers who specifically warned against using the historical experiences of contemporary rich countries as a guide for the Third World could not resist drawing some conclusions from the realm of foreign trade. It seemed very obvious, first of all, that a country does not get rich by importing manufactured goods if it can possibly manufacture them itself. This truism was elevated to the status of a theory of and a strategy for development, particularly in Latin America, and became known as 'import substitution industrialization' (ISI). But though they no longer imported some categories of finished products, many Third World manufacturers found they were importing the components, materials and technology for these products instead. When ISI began to fail, or at least brought with it as many problems as it was solving, a new theory and strategy began to emerge, based this time not on imports but on exports. The idea behind this was the mirror image of ISI. What had enriched the rich was not their insulation from imports (rich countries do, in fact, import massively all sorts of goods) but their success in manufactured exports, where higher prices could be commanded than for Third World raw materials. This thinking led to the theory and strategy of 'export-led industrialization' (ELI).

ISI and ELI have been used as complementary and contradictory developmental strategies. Let it suffice to say, at this point, notwithstanding the criticisms that have been made of the assumptions on which both ISI and ELI theories are based, export–import structure is now a key characteristic of the economic growth and by implication developmental prospects of Third World countries. That this should be so is not simply a matter of cognitive theory choice, but also a matter of the economic, political and cultural-ideological interests of theoreticians and practical actors in rich and poor countries. This is not entirely unconnected to another feature of the economies of many Third World countries that has become of great salience in recent years, namely their foreign debt and the effect that servicing that debt, particularly in times of rising and unpredictable interest rates, has on economic and social planning.

Resource-based classifications

No country in the world is entirely self-sufficient in all the materials it uses. Even the largest and most richly resource-endowed countries, such as the United States and the Soviet Union, must import some of the raw materials they use, for example rare metals. The United States is particularly vulnerable in this respect, both because it is lacking in some valuable resources, and because its vast productive machine uses so much of everything. In a book significantly entitled *American Multinationals and American Interests*, Bergson and his colleagues worked out the percentage of key minerals and metals supplied by imports in 1976 (Bergson *et al.*, 1978, Table 5.1). The list includes columbium, sheet mica, strontium (100 per cent); manganese, cobalt, tantalum, chromium (90 per cent plus); asbestos, aluminium, fluorine, bismuth, platinum (80 per cent plus); and tin, mercury, nickel (70 per cent plus). It is no wonder that the United States keep such a large navy patrolling the trade routes of the world. The United States is still resource-dependent to an appreciable degree.

The list leaves out what many consider to be the single most important U.S. import, namely oil. [. . .] The 'U.S. economy is now absolutely dependent on imported oil [and has] sharply increased its dependence on Arab oil imports since 1973' (Gail, 1978, p. 18). This is why the United States pays a good price for half of Mexico's oil.

It is not only the United States that has become dependent on imports of oil. Lucky chance put massive reserves of oil within the national boundaries of some barren and desolate desert kingdoms and political will has, through the organized power of OPEC, turned some of their rulers into the richest men in the world. But however important the possession of oil is for a country, oil exporters such as Nigeria, Mexico and Egypt demonstrate that oil alone is no guarantee of general prosperity. The effect of having to rely on imported oil is of great significance for development. So clear did this become after the 1974 oil crisis, when the upward spiral of oil prices began, that international agencies invented a new category of country: the most seriously affected nations (MSANs), i.e. those countries, mainly in Africa, who could no longer afford to buy oil. Inability to buy oil is widely interpreted to mean inability to sustain even the very low level of industrialization already achieved. Prospects for such countries are extremely bleak.

While it is clearly one very important natural resource on the world stage at present, and for the foreseeable future in the absence of entirely new energy sources, oil is not the only important natural resource. Another is food, and for the hungry it is infinitely more important than oil. Some countries choose to import food items that they could easily grow for themselves because they find it commercially advantageous to grow industrial raw materials for export and to import the food they need, which tends to be less costly relative to their exports. There are few countries which choose to rely on imports of basic cereals (wheat, rice, etc.) if they can avoid it. More or less all the countries in the world which are heavily dependent on cereal imports on a per capita basis are poor countries, or rich countries with relatively little arable land (like Japan).

It would, therefore, be instructive to classify the nations of the world in terms of their oil and cereal resources, as measured by the degree to which they are self-sufficient or seriously dependent on others for their supplies. We must be careful not to speak of oil and cereal *needs* which may be very different from *consumption*. Consumption patterns of the majority of people (not only in the Third World) are ill-matched to their needs because both consumption and needs are generally dictated by transnational practices. When we begin to appreciate more clearly and with great precision how and why so many Third World countries are locked into a global system that is so patently against the interests of the majority of their peoples, we may find one of the keys to the development puzzle, and a valuable clue as to how the global system currently works. A resource-based classification of the nations of the world represents a step towards this goal (see Cole, 1988).

Quality of life

The structure of the economy is clearly the basis on which to build a classification of the countries of the world in terms of their economic growth, or lack of it. Development in the global system implies something more. For many years national and international agencies have been collecting data on some significant social indicators, and it is now possible, with provisos about the nature of the data to make some, albeit rough and preliminary ranking of the nations of the world on the most widely accepted social and welfare criteria. The point of this exercise is to begin to derive a picture of how economic growth and development, as they have been generally defined, are related to the extent that the measures available permit us to draw some conclusions about the relative positions on a world scale of different groups of countries. The social welfare indicators that are most commonly agreed to be of relevance here are the degree of literacy, the distribution of health and educational services, the infant mortality rate and the life expectancy of the population. To this list it would be very desirable to add the status of women and the distribution of income, housing and consumer durables, but there is, as yet, not much reliable information available on these for the poorer countries of the world.

Scholars from various disciplines have been working on these problems since the mid-1940s. The first substantial efforts came from international organizations, particularly United Nations agencies and the OECD (see, for example, UNESCO, 1976). Morris (1979) published a 'Physical Quality of Life Index' but as this was exclusively based on health and educational criteria, it is of limited utility. In an attempt to extend the scope of quality of life methodology, Estes (1988) has constructed an 'Index of Social Progress' based on 44 welfare-relevant social indicators, which includes items normally ignored by economically based measures (like the status of women and children, politics, effects of disasters, cultural diversity, and defence expenditures). The changing distributions between 1970 and 1980 on this index have been calculated for over 100 countries, with some surprising results. For example, some of the countries of East Europe and Costa Rica, rank higher than the United Kingdom and the United States (Estes, 1988).

Gonzalez (1988, Table 4.2), usefully compares four different indexes for a large sample of countries. He finds, not surprisingly, that the two based mainly on economic indicators tend to rank the United States very high (first and second), while the other two, more widely based, classifications rank it lower (sixth and twenty-fourth). This is clearly a very controversial question, and it has been much discussed in the context of the 'basic needs' approach to development. Basic needs theorists argue that it is more fruitful to stress results rather than inputs in order to measure the adequacy of development policy. For example, life expectancy is a better measure of health services than numbers of doctors per person, and calorie supply per capita is a better measure of nutrition than total production of food. Thus, the basic needs approach switches attention from '*how much* is being produced . . . to *what* is being produced, in *what ways*, for *whom* and with what *impact*' (Hicks and Streeton, 1979, p. 577).

In classifying the global system, all measures are theory laden. This is particularly the case for quality of life, for the ways in which quality of life is measured, and specifically the role and definition of basic needs, virtually define our conceptions of development within the global system.

Bloc-based classifications

The final type of classification is one that appears to be less rather than more relevant for the 1990s than previously. This is socio-political blocs. The major bloc-based classification reflects the economic, political and cultural-ideological struggle between capitalism and communism for control over the global system. So important is it, that the decades since the end of the Second World War are commonly referred to as the epoch of the 'cold war' between capitalism and communism.

It is interesting to note that in the 1978 World Bank report some communist countries were given a special category, 'centrally-planned economies'. In the 1983 report this was changed to 'East European non-market economies' and by 1988 the communist countries were either scattered in the 'developing economies' groups or under the anodyne label of 'nonreporting nonmembers'. These changes were partly to handle the massive, though poor, People's Republic of China, incorporated into the 'low-income economies' and the dropping of the geographical reference is a nod of recognition in the direction of the African and Asian and other countries who claim to be socialist.

Irrespective of the decisions of the World Bank classifiers, however, it is an undeniable fact that in the 1990s most hitherto self-proclaimed socialist or communist countries are rapidly coming to an understanding with transnational capitalism, and that the scope and volume of the transnational practices of such states with the states and institutions of the capitalist system have increased dramatically in the last decade. This does not necessarily mean that the socialist or communist countries are 'going capitalist', though it does highlight changing relationships between the global capitalist system and its alternatives.

Communism found its first means of expression in the various international organizations (the *Internationals*) that were established by Marx and Engels and their followers from the 1860s on. However, it is not until the Bolshevik Party, the first communist party to seize state power, ushers in the birth of the Soviet Union that we can realistically speak of a communist bloc. In 1949, the Soviet Union organized the Council for Mutual Economic Aid (Comccon), paralleling the Organization for European Economic Cooperation, which had been formed in 1948 as a framework within which the United States could distribute aid to rebuild the war-shattered West European economies. This body was renamed the Organization for Economic Cooperation and Development (OECD) in 1961, and its membership and functions were extended to promote the global leadership of the capitalist 'Western' democracies. It has the reputation of a 'rich countries' club, though some poorer European countries have now joined.

The most visible public presence of the communist and capitalist blocs, however, is through their military alliances. The Warsaw Pact of East European communist countries is a Soviet-dominated military alliance, established in 1955 in response to the entry of West Germany into U.S.-dominated NATO (North Atlantic Treaty Organization). NATO had been formed after the Second World War in order to tie North America and Western Europe together in a military alliance against the perceived threat of world domination by the Soviet Union. The opposition of these two blocs has had a profound effect on the geopolitics of the global system in the second half of the twentieth century. However, both the Warsaw Pact and NATO have changed since the 1950s, and although their military hegemony, based largely on phenomenal nuclear overkill capacity, remains unsurpassed, other blocs have arisen to challenge them on a variety of strategic issues.

One such alternative bloc, identified by the World Bank and the rest of the world, is the oil exporters, organized through OPEC. They deserve to be listed in this context, as they often operate in unison even if they do not always do so. This idea of collective economic and political action is exactly what is meant when we speak about blocs. There are also several economic unions which operate more or less in a bloc-like manner. Prime amongst these, at the present historical juncture, is the European Community (EC), whose progress towards economic and political integration has been slow, a fact which does not dismay its competitors in world trade. Other economic unions, some short-lived and some longer-lived, in Africa, Asia and the Americas, have had a modicum of influence locally, but none can be said to have had a major influence in global terms. This is largely explained by the realization that most, if not all, of these unions begin from a position of economic and political weakness.

The feeble achievements of the Non-Aligned Movement (NAM) and the Group of 77 confirm this in the political sphere. NAM originated in the Bandung Conference of 1955, where a large number of poor African and Asian countries called for a better economic deal from the rich countries of the world. The Group of 77, named for 77 underdeveloped southern countries, unaligned with either the Soviet or the U.S. camp, came together in 1964 through their common membership of the United Nations (Sauvant, 1981). The Group, now with over 100 members, also presses for a better deal from the rich countries of the world, mainly in the north. The only common interest of these 'southern' countries is their general view that they are being more or less exploited by the rich countries of the 'north'. An expression of this was the call for a 'New International Economic Order'. This produced a torrent of words but little effective action. Such practical failures make it difficult to sustain economic solidarity, political unity or cultural-ideological sympathy.

Blocs are being seen as increasingly irrelevant today largely because the global capitalist system is perceived as increasingly salient. As the countries of the world, irrespective of bloc, appear to become more and more bound up with one another through the extension of transnational practices, some of which are directly identifiable as practices of global capitalism and some of which not, the fact of the global system becomes more and more obvious to ever more people, though the nature of the global system might still appear extremely difficult to grasp.

Conclusion

These five classifications, based on nation-state classifications of income/population, trade, resources, quality of life and blocs, serve different purposes in theory and practice. They can be used, for example, to organize the evidence for and justify morally one or other theory of development or the lack of development. It is very important to be aware of the assumptions that lie behind these classifications and the theories based on them. These theories often guide the practice of those who make and carry out the policies which have led to so little actual economic growth and development in most Third World countries.

These classifications, then, give us a wealth of empirical data, but the result is conceptual confusion and general inconclusiveness when we try to explain anything in terms of such state-centred categories. The tremendous variation in the experiences of First, Second and Third World countries in terms of income, population, foreign trade, resources, quality of life and blocs might lead the faint-hearted to conclude that the global system either does not exist or that it is so hopelessly complex that there is no point in trying to conceptualize it at all. This is precisely the limitation of state-centrist approaches and why all analyses that begin and end with nation-states have such difficulty in finding explanations of what is going on in the global system. To illustrate this point, let us return to the phenomenon that motivates so much research on the global system, namely the gap between rich and poor.

What some writers now term the 'widening gap' between the rich and the poor, both within countries and between the First and the Third Worlds, might tempt us to subscribe pessimistically to the view that the countries of the 'Third World are passive victims of the exercise of First World hegemon countries' power. This view is a direct consequence of the state-centrist approach, and has to be rejected on the grounds that it is theoretically mechanical and empirically false. There are underprivileged individuals and groups in the First World, as well as in the Third and Second Worlds. It is not a geographical accident of birth that determines whether an individual or groups is going to be rich or poor, but a question of class location. Of course, there are relatively as well as absolutely very many more poor people in the Third World than in the First World but this is not only a question of geography but also of transnational class location.

The poor in all countries struggle against the domestic and global forces that oppress them and their resistance takes many forms. Where this involves opposition to those who run the global system in their own interests it will naturally involve transnational practices in the economic, political and cultural-ideological spheres. It is important to recognize how the global capitalist system uses the myth of the nation-state, sometimes in the form of reactionary nationalist ideologies, to deflect criticism and opposition to its hegemonic control of the global system onto the claims of competing nations. Dividing the world up into nation-states, as it is for most practical purposes for most people, is therefore a profoundly ideological strategy. It is not common sense, and the fact that for most people it is one of the fundamental taken-for-granted assumptions of daily life is a measure of the tremendous success and power of the capitalist global system project.

In contrast, ideologies not based on the nation-state tend to be more genuinely transnational in scope. These are of two types, namely those that necessarily exclude outsiders and create an in-group; and those that are inclusively internationalist, and promote the common human characteristics of all who share the planet. A powerful example of the first type is ethnic exclusivism, whose extreme form is found in the fascist idea of 'race pride'. Similarly, some religious fundamentalisms classify all non-believers (generally an ascribed rather than an achieved status) as devilish.

The second type includes the several versions of democratic socialist internationalism (as opposed to bureaucratic communist chauvinism). An integral part of this global project is its feminist goal. Therefore it is best labelled democratic feminist socialism. Its ideal of international comradeship is based on the belief that the survival of humanity is incompatible with capitalist exploitation, imperialism and the patriarchal nation-state. Many tactical and strategic differences separate those who hold these views, particularly between women and men, and between libertarians and those who attach great importance to the construction of organizations and institutions. It is certainly the case that the global capitalist project is a great deal more consistent at this point in time than any democratic feminist socialist project. It is also certainly the case that the global capitalist system has brought to hundreds of millions of people a standard of living that their parents would never have believed possible. In this sense it is a proven success, while democratic feminist socialism is, to most people in the world, an obscure jumble of aspirations. Global capitalism produces the material conditions for socialism, but closes down the political and cultural-ideological space for it.

References

Bergson, C., Horst, T. and Moran, T. (1978) *American Multinationals and American Interests*, Brookings, Washington.

Boserup, E. (1970) *Woman's Role in Economic Development*, St. Martin's Press, New York.

Cole, J. (1988) The global distribution of natural resources. In Norwine and Gonzalez (eds.) (1988), *The Third World: States of Mind and Being*, Unwin Hyman, Boston, Ch. 5.

Edwards, C. (1985) *The Fragmented World*, Methuen.

Eisenstadt, S. (ed.) (1970) *Readings in Social Evolution and Development*, Pergamon, Oxford.

Estes, R. (1988) Toward a 'quality-of-life' index: empirical approaches to assessing human welfare internationally. In Norwine and Gonzalez (eds.) (1988), *The Third World: States of Mind and Being*, Unwin Hyman, Boston, Ch. 3.

Gail, B. (1978) The west's jugular vein: Arab oil. *Armed Forces Journal International*, August, pp. 18–32.

Gonzalez, A. (1988) Indexes of socioeconomic development. In Norwine and Gonzalez (1988), Ch. 4.

Hicks, N. and Streeton, P. (1979) Indicators of development: the search for a basic needs yardstick, *World Development*, July, pp. 567–80.

Morris, M. (1979) *Measuring the Condition of the World's Poor*, Pergamon, Washington.

Norwine, J. and Gonzalez, A. (eds.) (1988) *The Third World: States of mind and being*, Unwin Hyman, Boston.

Sauvant, K. (1981) *The Group of 77*, Oceana, New York.

UNESCO (1976) *The Use of Socio-economic Indicators in Development Planning*, UNESCO, Paris.

Section 2

Nation, culture and media

6

The processes: from nationalisms to transnationals

Jesus Martín-Barbero

From Martín-Barbero, J. (1993) *Communication, Culture and Hegemony: From the Media to Mediations*, (translated by Fox, E. and White, R. A.) Sage, London, pp. 163–8, 175–8.

The mass media in the formation of national cultures

If we are to understand the discontinuities between the state and the nation and the twisted, tortured path by which the masses burst into and became part of Latin American politics we must accept a profound change of perspective regarding the history of the mass media. For, although the social and political demands of the underclasses made themselves heard through the national-popular movements, it was through the discourse of the mass society that the national-popular became a recognizable identity for the great majority of people. With some exceptions, historians of the mass media have studied only the economic structure and the ideological content of the mass media; few have given close attention to the mediations through which the media have acquired a concrete institutional form and become a reflection of the culture. Studies have oscillated between attributing to the media the dynamics of profound historical changes in Latin America or reducing the media to mere passive instruments in the hands of powerful class interests acting with almost absolute autonomy.

If the cultural and political mediations have not been recognized in the history of the mass media, it is without doubt due to the fact that much of the general history leaves out culture or reduces it to high culture in its manifestations of art and literature. In the same way, the political history of Latin American consists of the great moments and important figures and almost never the events and political culture of the popular classes. It was left to an English historian to ask the following kind of questions about Colombian history: 'What was the popular impact of independence? What do we know about the political practices of the illiterate? What do we know about informal communication in politics or how local ideas about national politics are formed?' (see Deas, 1983, p. 151ff.).

To introduce the analysis of the cultural sphere does not mean, however, that we add a new and separate theme, but that we focus on those aspects of the social process that articulate the *meaning* of the economic and the political. This would mean writing the history of the mass media from the perspective of cultural processes as articulators of the communication practices – hegemonic and subaltern – of social movements. Some studies have begun to work from this perspective, and their findings provide a starting point for understanding the mediations from which, for example, information technologies become the media of communication.

The focus on mediations and social movements has shown the necessity of distinguishing two quite different stages in the introduction of media institutions and the constitution of mass culture in Latin America. In the first stage, which stretches from the 1930s to the end of the 1950s, the efficacy and social significance of the mass media do not lie primarily in the industrial organization and the ideological content, but rather in the way the popular masses have appropriated the mass media and the way the masses have recognized their identity in the mass media. Of course, economics and ideology influence how the media functioned, but to discover the meaning and ideology of economic structure we must go deeper to the conflict which in that historical moment gave structure and dynamism to the social movements, namely, the conflict between the masses and the state and the resolution of this conflict in the nationalist populisms and populist nationalisms.

During this first stage, the decisive role of the mass media was their ability to convey the challenge and the appeal of populism, which transformed the mass into the people and the people into the nation.

This appeal came from the state, but it was effective only to the extent that the masses perceived in it some of their basic demands and forms of expression. The function of the *caudillos* and the mass media was to re-semanticize the masses' demands and expressions. This occurred not only in those countries that experienced the 'dramatization' of populism, but also in other countries which, under forms, names and rhythms other than populism, experienced the crisis of hegemony, the birth of nationality and the beginnings of modernity. Film in many countries and radio in virtually all countries gave the people of the different regions and provinces their first taste of nation.[1]

This function of the media is acknowledged, although unfortunately only in the conclusions, by a recent history of radio in Colombia.

> Before the appearance and growth of radio, the country was a patchwork of regions, each separate and isolated. Before 1940, Colombia could very well call itself a country of countries rather than a nation. Hyperbole aside, radio allowed the country to experience an invisible national unity, a cultural identity shared simultaneously by the people of the coast, Antioquia, Pasto, Santander and Bogota. (Pareja, 1984, p. 177)

This observation puts us on the trail of another dimension of the formation of mass culture: transforming the political 'idea' of nationhood into the daily experience and feeling of nationhood.

The second stage in the constitution of mass culture in Latin America began after 1960. When the model of import substitution 'reached the limits of its coexistence with the archaic sectors of society' and the populism could no longer be sustained without radicalizing the first social reforms, the myth and strategies of *development* with its technocratic solutions and encouragement of a consumer society began to replace the worn out populist policies

(Intercom, 1981, p. 21). At this point, the political function of the media was removed and the economic function took over. The state continued to maintain the rhetoric that the air waves were a public, social service – as rhetorical as the social function of property – but, in fact, the state handed over the management of education and culture to the private sector. Ideology became the backbone of a mass discourse whose function was to make the poor dream the same dreams as the rich. As Galeano has said, 'The system spoke a surrealist language'. Not only was the wealth of the land transformed into the poverty of mankind, but scarcity and mankind's basic aspirations were converted into consumerism. The logic of this transformation would not become fully apparent until some years later when the economic crisis of the 1980s revealed the world-wide crisis of capitalism. The crisis could be solved only by making the model and decisions of production transnational and by standardizing, or, at least, pretending to standardize world culture. But by then mass culture would be riddled with new tensions that had their origins in the different national representations of popular culture, the multiplicity, of cultural matrices and the new conflicts and resistances mobilized by transnationalization.

A cinema in the image of the people

Let us begin our analysis of the role of media in the period from 1930 to the late 1950s with that media experience which is the clearest and most easily identifiable expression of Latin American nationalism and mass, popular culture: the cinema of Mexico. According to Edgar Morin, until 1950, film was the backbone of mass culture (1977); and Mexican film performed this function in a special way for the mass culture of Latin America. Film was the centre of gravity of the new culture because

> the Mexican and the Latin American public in general did not experience cinema as a specific artistic or industrial phenomenon. The fundamental reason for the success of film was structural and touched the centre of life. In films this public saw the possibility of experimenting, of adopting new habits and of seeing codes of daily life reiterated and dramatized by the voices they would like to have or hear. They did not go to the movies to dream; they went to learn. Watching the styles and fashions of the actors, the public learned to recognize and transform itself, finding solace, comfort and, secretly, exaltation. (Monsiváis, 1976b, p. 446)[2]

Note carefully this quote because it synthesizes so well our argument. A first interesting aspect is how the great majority of the public perceived and experienced these films. This experience, more than the talent of the actors or the commercial strategies of the entrepreneurs, was responsible for the success of films. Going to the movies was not a purely psychological event, but the point of encounter between the collective lived experience generated by the Revolution and the mediation which, even though it deformed this experience, gave it social legitimacy. Freud has made clear that there is no access to language without passing through the shaping structures of symbolism, and Gramsci has explained that there is no social legitimation without re-semantization through the hegemonic code. Cinema was the living, social mediation that constituted the new cultural experience, and cinema became the first language of the popular urban culture. Beyond the reactionary subject matter and the rigidity of its forms, film connected with the yearnings of the masses to make themselves socially visible. Film became part of the movement to give 'national identity' an image and a voice. People went to the movies more to see themselves in a sequence of images that gave them gestures, faces, manners of speaking and walking, landscapes and colours than to identify with the plots.

In the process of permitting people to see themselves, film formed them into a national body; not in the sense of giving them a nationality but in the way they experienced being a single nation. Along with all of its mystifications and chauvinistic attitudes, film provided an identity for the urban masses which diminished the impact of cultural conflicts and enabled them for the first time to conceive of the country in their own image. Monsiváis sums up to the ambiguity and force of this national image in five verbs: people *recognize* themselves in film with a recognition that is not passive but that *transforms* them; for a people coming from the Revolution, this meant to *pacify* and *resign* oneself, but also to secretly *move upwards*. In other words, it was an experience not only of consolation but of revenge.

Three mechanisms were at work in the new experience of nationalism that film provided. The first was theatrical – film as the dramatic staging and legitimation of peculiarly Mexican models of gestures, linguistic expressions and feeling. It was film which taught the people how to be Mexican in the national sense. The second mechanism was degradation. That is, in order for the people to recognize themselves, it was necessary to place nationhood within their reach. From then on, the national image is one of 'being irresponsible, being filled with filial affection for one's mother, to be an idler, the drunk, the sentimental slob . . . the programmed humiliation of women, the religious fanaticism, the obsessive respect for private property' (Monsiváis, 1976a, p. 86). The third mechanism was modernization. Often the mixture of images contradicted the traditional plots and brought up to date old myths, introduced customs and new models of moral behaviour and gave public access to the new rebelliousness and forms of speaking. 'Without an explicit message, film could not have entered where it did. Without the visible subversion, it could not have found the acceptance it did among a public that was at once so eager and so repressed. Film was the apparent guardian of the traditions it subverted' (Monsiváis, 1983, p. 29). Examples of this are the coherent incoherence which intertwines the bodily expression of Cantinfias with his labyrinthine verbal locutions or the eroticism of prostitutes cutting across a message defending monogamy.

The keys to film's seduction, however, were the melodrama and the stars. The melodrama was the dramatic backbone of all the plots, bringing together social impotency and heroic aspirations, appealing to the popular world from a 'familiar understanding of reality'. The melodrama made it possible for film to weave together national epics and intimate drama, display eroticism under the pretext of condemning incest, and dissolve tragedy in a pool of tears, depoliticizing the social contradictions of daily life. The stars – Maria Félix, Dolores del Rio, Pedro Armendariz, Jorge Negrete, Ninón Sevilla – provided the faces, bodies, voices and tones of expression for a people eager to see and hear themselves. Above and beyond the make-up and the commercial star industry, the movie stars who were truly stars for the people gathered their force from a secret pact that bonded their faces with the desires and obsessions of their publics.

Mexican film had three stages of development. Between 1920 and 1940 movies rewrote the popular legends. Pancho Villa was passed through the traditional models and myths of banditry which made cruelty a form of generosity. The Revolution appeared more as a backdrop than a story-line – the heroic death of the rebel, the assault on the rich hacienda, the march of the soldiers – appear again and again as the scene of the film action. The struggle against injustice was transformed from a fight for an ideal into a fight motivated by loyalty to the leader. This melodramatic transformation stripped the Revolution of its political meaning, but did not become reactionary until the second stage, after the 1930s, when the *ranchero* appeared, making *machismo* the expression of a nationalism that by now had become folklore. This was a *machismo* that was no longer a way that the people could understand and confront death but a compensatory mechanism for social inferiority. *Machismo* becomes the 'excess that redeemed the original sin of poverty . . . a plaintive cry for recognition' (Monsiváis, 1977, p. 31–2).

After the 1940s, Mexican films began to diversify their subject matter. We find now the urban comedy in which the neighbourhood replaced the countryside as the place where the old values found refuge and where the personal relations cut off by the city could be re-created. Other films about the lives of show girls and prostitutes depicted the 'adventures' and eroticism that challenged the traditional family. Both types of films were a bridge between a rural past and an urban present, films in which the city was essentially a place of confusion where memories were lost. In some ways the people projected on to and re-created memories in films that simultaneously degraded and elevated them, capitalizing on their weaknesses and their search for new signs of identity. [. . .]

The birth of the popular mass press

The media which we have examined so far – film, radio and especially music – were born 'popular' precisely because they were accessible to illiterate and uneducated publics. The press, however, also played a role in granting citizenship to the urban masses. This occurred after the changes which dislodged the press from the circle of the literate and learned and tore it loose from the matrix of the dominant culture.

Of all the media the press has the most written history, not only because it is the oldest, but because it is where those who write about history receive cultural acknowledgement. The history of the press looks mainly at the 'serious press'. When it examines the sensationalist press, it does so almost exclusively in economic terms: the growth of circulation and advertising. According to this type of journalism history, it is impossible to speak of politics, much less of culture, when one is dealing with newspapers that are nothing more than a business and scandal-mongering, exploiting the ignorance and low passions of the masses. In contrast to this concept that denies the sensationalist press any political meaning, another type of historical analysis has begun to introduce questions from the sociology of culture and political science. In Europe, this line of research, represented by Raymond Williams and Theodore Zeldin, has acquired a certain importance. In Latin America, Guillermo Sunkel has carried out a pioneering study on the mass popular media in Chile. The subtitle of his recent book reveals the new approach: *A Study of the Relationship between Popular Culture, Mass Culture and Political Culture* (Sunkel, 1985).

Sunkel begins his study with a historical event – the bringing together, beginning in the 1930s, of the life and struggle of the people with the conditions of existence of mass society. This has been accompanied by a profound theoretical reconceptualization of the people in the political culture of the Marxist left. We will leave the analysis of this theoretical and methodological proposal until later and turn now to the map of mediations that shaped the development of the popular mass press in Chile.

A process of political change beginning in the 1920s culminated in 1938 with the formation of the Popular Front and the participation of the parties of the left in the government. During these years the Chilean press changed radically. The workers' press became the left-wing newspapers, and the sensationalist daily papers appeared. The first change was basically a shift in the workers' papers from a purely local setting to an interest in national topics or a presentation of local topics in a national language. This implied at least a potential new group of followers for the left-wing discourse: the mass public. The form of discourse of these newspapers, however, remained within the constraining matrix of the rationalistic enlightenment, performing a function of popular educational formation and political propaganda. The objectives continued to be the education of the populace – raising their political consciousness – and to represent the interests of the masses in relation to the state. But that representation was limited to those issues that the Marxist left considered political or potentially political. Their concept of politics – and therefore of popular representation – did not include other actors than the working class and employers. Such a political press was concerned only with the conflicts that emerged out of the relationships of production – the clash between labour and capital – and only with the factory and labour union. It was a heroic vision that ignored daily life, personal subjectivity and sexuality as well as the cultural practices of the people such as their story telling, their religious customs and the fund of knowledge of the people. All this was ignored or, worse still, stigmatized as sources of alienation and obstacles in political struggle.

Thus, the transformation of the left-wing press was largely the adoption of national-level themes and language as well as a concentration in a smaller number of papers. Of the more than 100 labour newspapers which existed at one time or another between 1900 and 1920 – with their diversity of ideological positions along socialist, anarchist or radical lines – in 1929 only five continued to be published regularly. The official paper of the Communist Party, *El Siglo*, appeared in 1940, culminating a process beginning with the newspaper, *Frente Unico*, which circulated between 1934 and 1936, and *Frente Popular*, from 1936 to 1940.

In the United States and Europe the appearance of the sensationalist press is normally 'explained' as a function of the development of printing technology and the competition between the big newspapers. In Latin America, when the sensationalist press is studied, it is to provide a clear example of the penetration of North American models that, by putting profits ahead of any other criteria, have corrupted the region's tradition of serious journalism. Sunkel looks at the history of the sensationalist press from another angle, and he finds within Chile itself the antecedent press discourses and forms that evolved into the Chilean sensationalist press.

Chile, like many other Latin American countries since the second half of the nineteenth century, has had a great many popular publications which, like the *gacetas* in Argentina (Rivera, 1980a) or the literature of the *cordel* in Brazil (Luyten, 1981), mixed together news, poetry, and popular narratives. In Chile, these were called *liras populares*, and after the First World War they began to gain in news value what they lost in the quality of their poetry. Thus, they began to 'assume the functions of journalism at a historical moment when the experiences of popular culture were on the threshold of mass culture' (Sunkel, 1985, p. 80). In this prototype of popular journalism, written mainly for oral distribution, that is, to be read, declaimed or sung in public places such as the markets, the railway station or in the street, we find the beginnings of the sensationalist press. Already they have the large headlines calling attention to the main story, the prominent graphics illustrating the story, the melodramatization of a discourse gripped by violence and the macabre, and the exaggerated fascination with the stars of sports and entertainment.

From the 1920s, Chile had newspapers that began to adopt and develop the forms of the *liras populares*. In 1922, *Los Tiempos*, already in tabloid form, introduced a new style of journalism. Some years earlier, *Critica* in Argentina had revolutionized journalism, breaking the solemnity and pomposity of the 'serious press' and introducing new elements that explicitly employed manners of popular expression: the graphic reconstruction of the scene of the crime; a short verse commenting on the episode that appeared with the story; a street scene or description of local customs; and a phrase taken from the vocabulary of the thieves (Rivera, 1980b). The Chilean newspaper, *Los Tiempos*, was also characterized by its lively style and use of scandal and humour in reporting the news. *Las Noticias Gráficas* appeared in 1944, presenting itself as 'the paper of the people' and printing the demands of people from the popular classes that were normally not represented or were ignored in the traditional political discourse: the interests of women, the retired people, the world of the jails and the reformatories, the problems of alcoholism and prostitution. This type of press put more emphasis on the police chronicles and took a more irreverent and scandalous tone, with a frequent use of local slang from popular ways of speaking. The new journalism found its best expression in *Clarin*, founded in 1954, where commercial criteria were always tied to and determined by political and cultural criteria. In *Clarin* it was clear that the change in journalistic language was not only a question of attracting the public but of searching out and incorporating other languages circulating at the margins of society. It is in this light that one must interpret the caricature of the forms of speech of different social groups and the transposition of the discourse of crime to political discussion.

The issue of sensationalism calls attention to traces in the discourse of the press of another cultural matrix, much more symbolic and dramatic, which have their origins in the practices and moulds of popular culture. This matrix does not operate on the basis of concepts and generalizations but expresses itself in images and concrete situations. Rejected by the world of official education and serious politics, it survives in the world of the culture industry, and from this base it continues to exercise a powerful appeal to the popular. It is, of course, much easier and less dangerous to continue to reduce sensationalism to a 'bourgeois tool' of manipulation and alienation. It took courage to affirm that 'behind the notion of sensationalism as the commercial exploitation of crime, pornography and vulgar language lies a purist vision of the popular world' (Sunkel, 1985, p. 115). Only by taking this risk, however, was it possible to discover the *cultural* connection between the melodramatic aesthetic and the forms of survival and revenge in the matrix pervading popular cultures. The melodramatic aesthetic dared to violate the rationalistic division between serious and frivolous themes, to treat political events as dramatic events, and break with 'objectivity' by observing the situation from the perspective that appeals to the subjectivity of the readers.

Notes

1. The media built on the groundwork laid by the education system in the provision of this daily experience of nationhood. A key text that provides a general framework for this process and some specific national case studies is Braslavsky and Tedesco, 1982.
2. Monsiváis, 1976b, p. 446. This analysis is based on the work of Monsiváis.

References

Braslavsky, C. and Tedesco, J. C. (1982) Tendencias históricas de la educación popular como expresiones de los proyectos políticos de los estados latino-americanos. Investigaciones Educativas, Mexico.
Deas, M. (1983) La presencia de la política nacional en la vida provinciana, pueblerina y rural de Colombia. In Palacios, M. (ed.) *La Unidad Nacional en América Latina: del Regionalismo a la Nacionalidad*, El Colegio de México, Mexico.
Intercom (1981) Documento básico. In Márquez de Melo, J. (ed.) *Populismo e Comunicacao*, Cortez, São Paulo.
Luyten, J. M. (1981) *A Literature de Cordel em São Paulo*, São Paulo.
Monsiváis, C. (1976a) Cultura urbana y creación intelectual. *Casa de las Américas*, Havana, 116.
Monsiváis, C. (1976b) Notas sobre la cultura mexicana en el siglo XX. In *Historia General de México*, vol. IV, El Colegio de México, Mexico.
Monsiváis, C. (1977) *Amor Perdido*, Era, Mexico.
Monsiváis, C. (1983) La cultura popular en el ámbito urbano. El caso de México, mimeo, Mexico.
Morin, E. (1977) *O Espirito do Tempo, 2: Necrose*, Forense Universitária, Rio de Janeiro.
Pareja, R. (1984) *Historia de la Radio en Colombia*, SC de CS, Bogotá.
Rivera, J. B. (1980a) *El Escritor y la Industria Cultural*, CE de AL, Buenos Aires.
Rivera, J. B. (1980b) *La Forja del Escritor Profesional*, CE de AL, Buenos Aires.
Sunkel, G. (1985) *Razón y Pasión en la Prensa Popula*, ILET, Santiago.

7

The origins of national consciousness

Benedict Anderson

From Anderson, B. (1991) *Imagined Communities: Reflections on the Origin and Spread of Nationalism*, (revised edn), Verso, London, pp. 3–7, 37–46.

Nation, nationality, nationalism – all have proved notoriously difficult to define, let alone to analyse. In contrast to the immense influence that nationalism has exerted on the modern world, plausible theory about it is conspicuously meagre. Hugh Seton-Watson, author of far the best and most comprehensive English-language text on nationalism, and heir to a vast tradition of liberal historiography and social science, sadly observes: 'Thus I am *driven* to the conclusion that no 'scientific definition' of the nation can be devised; yet the phenomenon has existed and exists.'[1] Tom Nairn, author of the path-breaking *The Break-up of Britain*, and heir to the scarcely less vast tradition of Marxist historiography and social science, candidly remarks: 'The theory of nationalism represents Marxism's great historical failure.[2] But even this confession is somewhat misleading, in so far as it can be taken to imply the regrettable outcome of a long, self-conscious search for theoretical clarity. [. . .]

Theorists of nationalism have often been perplexed, not to say irritated, by three paradoxes: (1) The objective modernity of nations to the historian's eye vs. their subjective antiquity in the eyes of nationalists. (2) The formal universality of nationality as a socio-cultural concept – in the modern world everyone can, should, will 'have' a nationality, as he or she 'has' a gender – vs. the irremediable particularity of its concrete manifestations, such that, by definition, 'Greek' nationality is *sui generis*. (3) The 'political' power of nationalisms vs. their philosophical poverty and even incoherence. In other words, unlike most other isms, nationalism has never produced its own grand thinkers: no Hobbeses, Tocquevilles, Marxes, or Webers. This 'emptiness' easily gives rise, among cosmopolitan and polylingual intellectuals, to a certain condescension. Like Gertrude Stein in the face of Oakland, one can rather quickly conclude that there is 'no there there'. It is characteristic that even so sympathetic a student of nationalism as Tom Nairn can nonetheless write that: ''Nationalism' is the pathology of modern developmental history, as inescapable as 'neurosis' in the individual, with much the same essential ambiguity attaching to it, a similar built-in capacity for descent into dementia, rooted in the dilemmas of helplessness thrust upon most of the world (the equivalent of infantilism for societies) and largely incurable.'[3]

Part of the difficulty is that one tends unconsciously to hypostasize the existence of Nationalism-with-a-big-N (rather as one might Age-with-a-capital-A) and then to classify 'it' as *an* ideology. (Note that if everyone has an age, Age is merely an analytical expression.) It would, I think, make things easier if one treated it as if it belonged with 'kinship' and 'religion', rather than with 'liberalism' or 'fascism'.

In an anthropological spirit, then, I propose the following definition of the nation: it is an imagined political community – and imagined as both inherently limited and sovereign.

It is *imagined* because the members of even the smallest nation will never know most of their fellow-members, meet them, or even hear of them, yet in the minds of each lives the image of their communion.[4] Renan referred to this imagining in his suavely back-handed way when he wrote that 'Or l'essence d'une nation est que tous les individus aient beaucoup de choses en commun, et aussi que tous aient oublié bien des choses.'[5] With a certain ferocity Gellner makes a comparable point when he rules that 'Nationalism is not the awakening of nations to self-consciousness: it *invents* nations where they do not exist.'[6] The drawback to this formulation, however, is that Gellner is so anxious to show that nationalism masquerades under false pretences that he assimilates 'invention' to 'fabrication' and 'falsity', rather than to 'imagining' and 'creation'. In this way he implies that 'true' communities exist which can be advantageously juxtaposed to nations. In fact, all communities larger than primordial villages of face-to-face contact (and perhaps even these) are imagined. Communities are to be distinguished, not by their falsity/genuineness, but by the style in which they are imagined. Javanese villagers have always known that they are connected to people they have never seen, but these ties were once imagined particularistically – as indefinitely stretchable nets of kinship and clientship. Until quite recently, the Javanese language had no word meaning the abstraction 'society.' We may today think of the French aristocracy of the *ancien régime* as a class; but surely it was imagined this way only very late.[7] To the question 'Who is the Comte de X?' the normal answer would have been, not 'a member of the aristocracy,' but 'the lord of X,' 'the uncle of the Baronne de Y,' or 'a client of the Duc de Z.'

The nation is imagined as *limited* because even the largest of them, encompassing perhaps a billion living human beings, has finite, if elastic, boundaries, beyond which lie other nations. No nation imagines itself coterminous with mankind. The most messianic nationalities do not dream of a day when all the members of the human race will join their nation in the way that it was possible, in certain epochs, for, say, Christians to dream of a wholly Christian planet.

It is imagined as *sovereign* because the concept was born in an age in which Enlightenment and Revolution were destroying the legitimacy of the divinely-ordained, hierarchical dynastic realm. Coming to maturity at a stage of human history when even the most devout adherents of any universal religion were inescapably confronted with the living *pluralism* of such religions, and the allomorphism between each faith's ontological claims and territorial stretch, nations dream of being free, and, if under God, directly so. The gage and emblem of this freedom is the sovereign state.

Finally, it is imagined as a *community*, because, regardless of the actual inequality and exploitation that may prevail in each, the nation is always conceived as a deep, horizontal comradeship. Ultimately it is this fraternity that makes it possible, over the past two centuries, for so many millions of people, not so much to kill, as willingly to die for such limited imaginings.

These deaths bring us abruptly face to face with the central problem posed by nationalism: what makes the shrunken imaginings of recent history (scarcely more than two centuries) generate such colossal sacrifices? I believe that the beginnings of an answer lie in the cultural roots of nationalism.

At least 20,000,000 books had already been printed by 1500,[8] signalling the onset of Benjamin's 'age of mechanical reproduction.' If manuscript knowledge was scarce and arcane lore, print knowledge lived by reproducibility and dissemination.[9] If, as Febvre and Martin believe, possibly as many as 200,000,000 volumes had been manufactured by 1600, it is no wonder that Francis Bacon believed that print had changed 'the appearance and states of the world.'[10]

[. . .]

One of the earlier forms of capitalist enterprise, book-publishing felt all of capitalism's restless search for markets. The early printers established branches all over Europe: 'in this way a veritable 'international' of publishing houses, which ignored national [sic] frontiers, was created.'[11] And since the years 1500–1550 were a period of exceptional European prosperity, publishing shared in the general boom. 'More than at any other time' it was 'a great industry under the control of wealthy capitalists.'[12] Naturally, 'book-sellers were primarily concerned to make a profit and to sell their products, and consequently they sought out first and foremost those works which were of interest to the largest possible number of their contemporaries.'[13]

The initial market was literate Europe, a wide but thin stratum of Latin-readers. Saturation of this market took about 150 years. The determinative fact about Latin – aside from its sacrality – was that it was a language of bilinguals. Relatively few were born to speak it and even fewer, one imagines, dreamed in it. In the sixteenth century the proportion of bilinguals within the total population of Europe was quite small; very likely no larger than the proportion in the world's population today, and – proletarian internationalism notwithstanding – in the centuries to come. Then and now the bulk of mankind is monoglot. The logic of capitalism thus meant that once the elite Latin market was saturated, the potentially huge markets represented by the monoglot masses would beckon. To be sure, the Counter-Reformation encouraged a temporary resurgence of Latin-publishing, but by the mid-seventeenth century the movement was in decay, and fervently Catholic libraries replete. Meantime, a Europe-wide shortage of money made printers think more and more of peddling cheap editions in the vernaculars.[14]

The revolutionary vernacularizing thrust of capitalism was given further impetus by three extraneous factors, two of which contributed directly to the rise of national consciousness. The first, and ultimately the least important, was a change in the character of Latin itself. Thanks to the labours of the Humanists in reviving the broad literature of pre-Christian antiquity and spreading it through the print-market, a new appreciation of the sophisticated stylistic achievements of the ancients was apparent among the trans-European intelligentsia. The Latin they now aspired to write became more and more Ciceronian, and, by the same token, increasingly removed from ecclesiastical and everyday life. In this way it acquired an esoteric quality quite different from that of Church Latin in mediaeval times. For the older Latin was not arcane because of its subject matter or style, but simply because it was written at all, i.e. because of its status as *text*. Now it became arcane because of what was written, because of the language-in-itself.

Second was the impact of the Reformation, which, at the same time, owed much of its success to print-capitalism. Before the age of print, Rome easily won every war against heresy in Western Europe because it always had better internal lines of communication than its challengers. But when in 1517 Martin Luther nailed his theses to the chapel-door in Wittenberg, they were printed up in German translation, and 'within 15 days [had been] seen in every part of the country.'[15] In the two decades 1520–1540 three times as many books were published in German as in the period 1500–1520, an astonishing transformation to which Luther was absolutely central. His works represented no less than one third of *all* German-language books sold between 1518 and 1525. Between 1522 and 1546, a total of 430 editions (whole or partial) of his biblical translations appeared. 'We have here for the first time a truly mass readership and a popular literature within everybody's reach.'[16] In effect, Luther became the first best-selling author *so known*. Or, to put it another way, the first writer who could 'sell' his *new* books on the basis of his name.[17]

Where Luther led, others quickly followed, opening the colossal religious propaganda war that raged across Europe for the next century. In this titanic 'battle for men's minds', Protestantism was always fundamentally on the offensive, precisely because it knew how to make use of the expanding vernacular print-market being created by capitalism, while the Counter-Reformation defended the citadel of Latin. The emblem for this is the Vatican's *Index Librorum Prohibitorum* – to which there was no Protestant counterpart – a novel catalogue made necessary by the sheer volume of printed subversion. Nothing gives a better sense of this siege mentality than François I's panicked 1535 ban on the printing of *any* books in his realm – on pain of death by hanging! The reason for both the ban and its unenforceability was that by then his realm's eastern borders were ringed with Protestant states and cities producing a massive stream of smugglable print. To take Calvin's Geneva alone: between 1533 and 1540 only 42 editions were published there, but the numbers swelled to 527 between 1550 and 1564, by which latter date no less than 40 separate printing-presses were working overtime.[18]

The coalition between Protestantism and print-capitalism, exploiting cheap popular editions, quickly created large new reading publics – not least among merchants and women, who typically knew little or no Latin – and simul- taneously mobilized them for politico-religious purposes. Inevitably, it was not merely the Church that was shaken to its core. The same earthquake produced Europe's first important non-dynastic, non-city states in the Dutch Republic and the Commonwealth of the Puritans. (François I's panic was as much political as religious.)

Third was the slow, geographically uneven, spread of particular vernac- ulars as instruments of administrative centralization by certain well- positioned would-be absolutist monarchs. Here it is useful to remember that the universality of Latin in mediaeval Western Europe never corresponded to a universal political system. The contrast with Imperial China, where the reach of mandarinal bureaucracy and of painted characters largely coincided, is instructive. In effect, the political fragmentation of Western Europe after the collapse of the Western Empire meant that no sovereign could monopolize Latin and make it his-and-only-his language-of-state, and thus Latin's religious authority never had a true political analogue.

The birth of administrative vernaculars predated both print and the religious upheaval of the sixteenth century, and must therefore be regarded (at least initially) as an independent factor in the erosion of the sacred imagined community. At the same time, nothing suggests that any deep-seated ideological, let alone proto-national, impulses underlay this vernacularization where it occurred. The case of 'England' – on the northwestern periphery of Latin Europe – is here especially enlightening. Prior to the Norman Conquest, the language of the court, literary and administrative, was Anglo-Saxon. For the next century and a half virtually all royal documents were composed in Latin. Between about 1200 and 1350 this state-Latin was superseded by Norman French. In the meantime, a slow fusion between this language of a foreign ruling class and the Anglo-Saxon of the subject population produced Early English. The fusion made it possible for the new language to take its turn, after 1362, as the language of the courts – and for the opening of Parliament. Wycliffe's vernacular *manuscript* Bible followed in 1382.[19] It is essential to bear in mind that this sequence was a series of 'state,' not 'national,' languages; and that the state concerned covered at various times not only today's England and Wales, but also portions of Ireland, Scotland *and France*. Obviously, huge elements of the subject populations knew little or nothing of Latin, Norman French, or Early English.[20] Not till almost a century *after* Early English's political enthronement was London's power swept out of 'France'.

On the Seine, a similar movement took place, if at a slower pace. As Bloch wrily puts it, 'French, that is to say a language which, since it was regarded as merely a corrupt form of Latin, took several centuries to raise itself to literary dignity',[21] only became the official language of the courts of justice in 1539, when François I issued the Edict of Villers-Cotterêts.[22] In other dynastic realms Latin survived much longer – under the Habsburgs well into the nineteenth century. In still others, 'foreign' vernaculars took over: in the eighteenth century the languages of the Romanov court were French and German.[23]

In every instance, the 'choice' of language appears as a gradual, unself-conscious, pragmatic, not to say haphazard development. As such, it was utterly different from the self-conscious language policies pursued by nineteenth-century dynasts confronted with the rise of hostile popular linguistic-nationalisms. [. . .] One clear sign of the difference is that the old administrative languages were *just that*: languages used by and for official-doms for their own inner convenience. There was no idea of systematically imposing the language on the dynasts' various subject populations.[24] Nonetheless, the elevation of these vernaculars to the status of languages-of-power, where, in one sense, they were competitors with Latin (French in Paris, [Early] English in London), made its own contribution to the decline of the imagined community of Christendom.

At bottom, it is likely that the esotericization of Latin, the Reformation, and the haphazard development of administrative vernaculars are significant, in the present context, primarily in a negative sense – in their contributions to the dethronement of Latin. It is quite possible to conceive of the emergence of the new imagined national communities without any one, perhaps all, of them being present. What, in a positive sense, made the new communities imaginable was a half-fortuitous, but explosive, interaction between a system of production and productive relations (capitalism), a technology of communications (print), and the fatality of human linguistic diversity.[25]

The element of fatality is essential. For whatever superhuman feats capitalism was capable of, it found in death and languages two tenacious adversaries.[26] Particular languages can die or be wiped out, but there was and is no possibility of humankind's general linguistic unification. Yet this mutual incomprehensibility was historically of only slight importance until capitalism and print created monoglot mass reading publics.

While it is essential to keep in mind an idea of fatality, in the sense of a *general* condition of irremediable linguistic diversity, it would be a mistake to equate this fatality with that common element in nationalist ideologies which stresses the primordial fatality of *particular* languages and their association with *particular* territorial units. The essential thing is the *interplay* between fatality, technology, and capitalism. In pre-print Europe, and, of course, elsewhere in the world, the diversity of spoken languages, those languages that for their speakers were (and are) the warp and woof of their lives, was immense; so immense, indeed, that had print-capitalism sought to exploit each potential oral vernacular market, it would have remained a capitalism of petty proportions. But these varied idiolects were capable of being assembled, within definite limits, into print-languages far fewer in number. The very arbitrariness of any system of signs for sounds facilitated the assembling process.[27] (At the same time, the more ideographic the signs, the vaster the potential assembling zone. One can detect a sort of descending hierarchy here from algebra through Chinese and English, to the regular syllabaries of French or Indonesian.) Nothing served to 'assemble' related vernaculars more than capitalism, which, within the limits imposed by grammars and syntaxes, created mechanically reproduced print-languages capable of dissemination through the market.[28]

These print-languages laid the bases for national consciousnesses in three distinct ways. First and foremost, they created unified-fields of exchange and communication below Latin and above the spoken vernaculars. Speakers of the huge variety of Frenches, Englishes, or Spanishes, who might find it difficult or even impossible to understand one another in conversation, became capable of comprehending one another via print and paper. In the process, they gradually became aware of the hundreds of thousands, even millions, of people in their particular language-field, and at the same time that *only those* hundreds of thousands, or millions, so belonged. [. . .]

Second, print-capitalism gave a new fixity to language, which in the long run helped to build that image of antiquity so central to the subjective idea of the nation. As Febvre and Martin remind us, the printed book kept a permanent form, capable of virtually infinite reproduction, temporally and spatially. It was no longer subject to the individualizing and 'unconsciously modernizing' habits of monastic scribes. Thus, while twelfth-century French differed markedly from that written by Villon in the fifteenth, the rate of change slowed decisively in the sixteenth. 'By the 17th century languages in Europe had generally assumed their modern forms.'[29] [. . .]

Third, print-capitalism created languages-of-power of a kind different from the older administrative vernaculars. Certain dialects inevitably were 'closer' to each print-language and dominated their final forms. Their disadvantaged cousins, still assimilable to the emerging print-language, lost caste, above all because they were unsuccessful (or only relatively successful) in insisting on their own print-form. 'Northwestern German' became Platt Deutsch, a largely spoken, thus sub-standard, German, because it was assimilable to print-German in a way that Bohemian spoken-Czech was not. High German, the King's English, and, later, Central Thai, were correspondingly elevated to a new politico-cultural eminence. (Hence the struggles in late-twentieth-century Europe by certain 'sub-'nationalities to change their subordinate status by breaking firmly into print – and radio.)

It remains only to emphasize that in their origins, the fixing of print-languages and the differentiation of status between them were largely unself-conscious processes resulting from the explosive interaction between capitalism, technology and human linguistic diversity. But as with so much else in the history of nationalism, once 'there,' they could become formal models to be imitated, and, where expedient, consciously exploited in a Machiavellian spirit. Today, the Thai government actively discourages attempts by foreign missionaries to provide its hill-tribe minorities with their own transcription-systems and to develop publications in their own languages: the same government is largely indifferent to what these minorities *speak*. The fate of the Turkic-speaking peoples in the zones incorporated into today's Turkey, Iran, Iraq, and the USSR is especially exemplary. A family of spoken languages, once everywhere assemblable, thus comprehensible, within an Arabic orthography, has lost that unity as a result of conscious manipulations. To heighten Turkish-Turkey's national consciousness at the expense of any wider Islamic identification, Atatürk imposed compulsory romanization.[30] The Soviet authorities followed suit, first with an anti-Islamic, anti-Persian compulsory romanization, then, in Stalin's 1930s, with a Russifying compulsory Cyrillicization.[31]

We can summarize the conclusions to be drawn from the argument thus far by saying that the convergence of capitalism and print technology on the fatal diversity of human language created the possibility of a new form of imagined community, which in its basic morphology set the stage for the modern nation. The potential stretch of these communities was inherently limited, and, at the same time, bore none but the most fortuitous relationship to existing political boundaries (which were, on the whole, the high-water marks of dynastic expansionisms). [. . .]

Notes

1. See his *Nations and States*, p. 5. Emphasis added.
2. See his (1975) The Modern Janus, *New Left Review*, 94, November–December, p. 3. This essay is included unchanged in *The Break-up of Britain* as Ch. 9 (pp. 329–63).
3. Hobsbawm, Eric (1977) *The Break-up of Britain*, p. 359.

4. Cf. Seton-Watson, *Nations and States*, p. 5: 'All that I can find to say is that a nation exists when a significant number of people in a community consider themselves to form a nation, or behave as if they formed one.' We may translate 'consider themselves' as 'imagine themselves.'

5. Renan, Ernest, Qu'-est-ce qu'une nation? In *Oeuvres Complètes*, 1, p. 892. He adds: 'tout citoyen français doit avoir oublié la Saint-Barthélemy, les massacres du Midi an XIIIe siècle. Il n'y a pas en France dix familles qui puissent fournir la preuve d'une origine franque . . .'

6. Gellner, Ernest, *Thought and Change*, p. 169. Emphasis added.

7. Hobsbawm, for example, 'fixes' it by saying that in 1789 it numbered about 400,000 in a population of 23,000,000. (See his *The Age of Revolution*, p. 78.) But would this statistical picture of the noblesse have been imaginable under the *ancien régime*?

8. The population of that Europe where print was then known was about 100,000,000. Febvre and Martin, *The Coming of the Book*, pp. 248–49.

9. Emblematic is Marco Polo's *Travels*, which remained largely unknown till its first printing in 1559. Polo, *Travels*, p. xiii.

10. Quoted in Eisenstein, 'Some Conjectures,' p. 56.

11. Febvre and Martin, *The Coming of the Book*, p. 122. (The original text, however, speaks simply of 'par-dessus les frontières.' *L'Apparition*, p. 184.)

12. Ibid., p. 187. The original text speaks of 'puissants' (powerful) rather than 'wealthy' capitalists. *L'Apparition*, p. 281.

13. 'Hence the introduction of printing was in this respect a stage on the road to our present society of mass consumption and standardisation.' Ibid., pp. 259–60. (The original text has 'une civilisation de masse et de standardisation,' which may be better rendered 'standardised, mass civilization.' *L'Apparition*, p. 394.)

14. Ibid., p. 195.

15. Ibid., pp. 289–90.

16. Ibid., pp. 291–5.

17. From this point it was only a step to the situation in seventeenth-century France where Corneille, Molière, and La Fontaine could sell their manuscript tragedies and comedies directly to publishers, who bought them as excellent investments in view of their authors' market reputations. Ibid., p. 161.

18. Ibid., pp. 310–15.

19. Seton-Watson, *Nations and States*, pp. 29–29; Bloch, *Feudal Society*, I, p. 75.

20. We should not assume that administrative vernacular unification was immediately or fully achieved. It is unlikely that the Guyenne ruled from London was ever primarily administered in Early English.

21. Bloch, *Feudal Society*, I, p. 98.

22. Seton-Watson, *Nations and States*, p. 48.

23. Ibid., p. 83.

24. An agreeable confirmation of this point is provided by François I, who, as we have seen, banned all printing of books in 1535 and made French the language of his courts four years later!

25. It was not the first 'accident' of its kind. Febvre and Martin note that while a visible bourgeoisie already existed in Europe by the late thirteenth century, paper did not come into general use until the end of the fourteenth. Only paper's smooth plane surface made the mass reproduction of texts and pictures possible – and this did not occur for still another 75 years. But papers was not a European invention. It floated in from another history – China's – through the Islamic world. *The Coming of the Book*, pp. 22, 30, and 45.

26. We still have no giant multinationals in the world of publishing.

27. For a useful discussion of this point, see S. H. Steinberg, *Five Hundred Years of Printing*, chapter 5. That the sign *ough* is pronounced differently in the words

although, bough, lough, rough, cough, and hiccough, shows both the idiolec-
tic variety out of which the now-standard spelling of English emerged, and the
ideographic quality of the final product.
28. I say 'nothing served . . . more than capitalism' advisedly. Both Steinberg and
Eisenstein come close to theomorphizing 'print' *qua* print as the genius of modern
history. Febvre and Martin never forget that behind print stand printers and
publishing firms. It is worth remembering in this context that although printing
was invented first in China, possibly 500 years before its appearance in Europe,
it had no major, let alone revolutionary impact – precisely because of the absence
of capitalism there.
29. *The Coming of the Book*, p. 319. cf. *L'Apparition*, p. 477: 'Au XVIIe siècle, les langes
nationales appraissent un peu partout cristallisées'.
30. Kohn, Hans, *The Age of Nationalism*, p. 108. It is probably only fair to add that
Kemal also hoped thereby to align Turkish nationalism with the modern,
romanized civilization of Western Europe.
31. Seton-Watson, *Nations and States*, p. 317.

References

Bloch, Marc (1961) *Feudal Society*, 2 vols., Manyon, I. A (trans.), University of Chicago
Press, Chicago.
Eistenstein, Elizabeth L. (1968) Some Conjectures about of the Impact of Printing
on Western Society and Thought: A Preliminary Report. *Journal of Modern History*,
Vol. 40, No. 1, March, pp. 1–56.
Fall, Bernard B. (1968) *Hell is a Very Small Place. The Siege of Dien Bien Phu*, Vintage,
New York.
Febvre, Lucien, and Martin, Henri-Jean (1976) *The Coming of the Book. The Impact of
Printing, 1450–1800*, New Left Books, London. [Translation of (1958) *L'Apparition
du Livre*, Albin Michel, Paris.]
Gellner, Ernest (1964) *Thought and Change*, Weidenfeld and Nicholson, London.
Hobsbawm, Eric (1977) Some Reflections on 'The Break-up of Britain'. *New Left Review*,
Vol. 105, September–October, pp. 3–24.
Hobsbawm, Eric (1964) *The Age of Revolution, 1789–1848*, Mentor, New York.
Kohn, Hans (1962) *The Age of Nationalism*, Harper, New York.
Nairn, Tom (1977) *The Break-up of Britain*, New Left Books, London.
Nairn, Tom (1975) The Modern Janus. *New Left Review*, Vol. 94, November–Decem-
ber, pp. 3–29. Reprinted as Ch. 9 in *The Break up of Britain*.
Polo, Marco (1946) *The Travels of Marco Polo*, Marsden, William (ed. and trans.),
Everyman's Library, London and New York.
Renan, Ernest (1947-61) Qu-est-ce qu'une nation? In *Oeuvres Completes*,
Calmann–Lévy, Paris, Vol. 1, pp. 887–906.
Seton-Watson, Hugh (1977) *Nations and States. An Enquiry into the Origins of Nations
and the Politics of Nationalism*, Westview Press, Boulder, Colo.
Steinberg, S. H. (1966) *Five Hundred Years of Printing*, rev. edn, Penguin,
Harmondsworth.

8

Wishful thinking: cultural politics, media, and collective identities in Europe

Philip Schlesinger

From Levy, M. R. (ed.) (1993) *Journal of Communication*, Oxford University Press, New York, Vol. 43, No. 2, pp. 6–17.

Making sense of collective identities in Europe today – and of the part played by communication systems and policies as well as the production and management of culture – is quite a challenge given the rapidity and complexity of contemporary political and economic change. The European continent bears the heavy weight of history. Europe has been the originating site of two world wars, and boundary problems between most of its states and nations have characterized the modern period. It is a highly complex area, too, in respect of the plethora of cultures and languages that play into the construction of political identities. Whereas the U.S. can be imagined as a large market and polity with the vast majority of its population speaking the lingua franca of English, no such image of Europe presently prevails. To try to communicate on the European plane is first and foremost to acknowledge the fact of considerable diversity.

An area of relative stability during the cold war, Europe has now become a moving target. The balance of terror offered us pacification; its removal has unleashed conflict, the Yugoslav ethno-national disputes offering a sobering example of what could be in store for others. Europeans are both observers and participants in the major drama of transformation that continues to evolve after the revolutions of 1989 and the demise of the communist bloc. One key dilemma that we face today lies in the contradictions between the development of civic democracy in the European space and the valorization of the national principle as the prime good. How this is resolved will affect the evolution of civil society and the public sphere, and therefore of the media.

In this article, I take contemporary Europe as my starting point for some reflections on the relevance of communication for analysing the formation of a collective identity. Europe exemplifies in acute form the problem of constructing a collective identity for diverse people amongst whom nationhood and statehood remain key principles of sociocultural and political economic cohesion. Europe therefore illuminates the *limitations* of what we may expect a communication policy to do and causes us to think again about the relations between the social and the communicative.

Some conceptual orientations

The question of identity has become increasingly central to the research agenda of media studies, with more attention being paid to the role that media might play in the cultural constitution of collectivities, most especially nations (Collins, 1990a; Schlesinger, 1991a, 1991b; Tomlinson, 1991).

Characterizing collective identity

Arguably, some of the more general, constitutive features of a collective identity (Melucci, 1989) are as follows:

1. It involves construction and reconstruction of a sense of themselves by self-identifying communities, using the signs provided by their cultures.
2. It is a process of elaboration of collective consciousness, generally involving active strategies of inclusion and exclusion: *We* are defined, in part at least, as being different from how *They* are.
3. The above process extends through time, involving both memory and amnesia, so that the role of versions of history becomes crucial to the self-understanding of a collectivity. Thus, what is understood to be either typically 'national' or 'ethnic' is usually a highly selective account (Fentress and Wickham, 1992; Gellner, 1983; Hobsbawm and Ranger, 1983; Namer, 1987).
4. The same process also extends in space; in Europe, for instance, the paradigm case of collective identity is that of a group located in a specific national territory endowed with meanings. However, in principle, and in fact, we may conceive of collectivities as located otherwise – for instance, as enjoying diasporic identities for which the strict territorial condition does not apply.

It is important to note, therefore, that all constructions of collective identity presuppose assumptions about the origins of a social group, its evolution through time and space, and its arrival at its present destination. Constructing *Europeanness* is especially problematic because it has to emerge from an extensive history of highly conflictual collective identities focused upon the numerous nation-states of the continent (Schlesinger, 1988, 1992). The cold war froze many of the long-standing antagonisms on the European continent. With the partial collapse of the political, economic, and security frameworks that regulated the balance of terror, a major question today is whether the resurgent force of nationalism can be institutionally contained.

After the cold war

It would appear that the tearing down of the Berlin Wall and the subsequent rebirth of nationalism in Europe have marked the end of a particular episode of wishful thinking. One symptom of this tendency has been the proliferation of various euro-formulae that have stressed both the existence of a common culture on the continent and, simultaneously, the desire to construct one. Who now talks, as did Mikhail Gorbachev in the late 1980s, of a 'common

European home'? Ethno-national conflict, racism, and a revived antisemitism have in various ways, and to differing degrees in different states, become more central to the European political agenda. And fears of mass migratory movements from North Africa and Eastern Europe into the more affluent states have fueled conceptions of a (Western) fortress Europe, with strengthened internal policing to regulate the poor, the undesirable, and the potentially disorderly. Consequently, xenophobia (focused upon differences marked by nationality, ethnicity, and race) has become a major issue in Europe (Giorgi, 1992; Hobsbawm, 1992). In the light of this, it is not so surprising that talk of 'European values' sounds rather strained. Moreover, and most relevant for our purposes, the project of creating a *European audiovisual space* – a minimal common cultural currency of the moving image produced by Europeans and addressed to European audiences – is now also placed significantly in question. But we shall return to this later.

The ethno-nationalist revival in Europe, most notably in the East and centre of the continent, but also in different forms in the West, means that, increasingly, claims to collective identity are posed in terms of identities rooted in cultural distinctiveness and that the groups that make such claims think of themselves as nations. This involves the simultaneous invocation of principles of inclusion and exclusion, the drawing of boundaries.

Postmodern delusions

There is an ironic coincidence of this ethno-national surge with the high-water mark of postmodernist thinking about identity. In this latter connection, we can identify two rather questionable postmodernist propositions, which, once challenged, throw into relief just how profoundly inadequate such thinking is.

First, postmodernist thinking lays stress on 'neo-tribalism' (Maffesoli, 1988). The contemporary search for shelter from the uncertainties of ontological insecurity and contingency, so it is held, has led to the formation of 'neo-tribes,' which are formed 'as concepts rather than as integrated social bodies by the multitude of individual acts of self-identification' (Bauman, 1991, p. 249). Social coercion and central state power are replaced by individualized acts of collectivizing will. Such weak social bonds, seemingly chosen as though we were just consumers in the shopping mall of culture, offer us a choice of lifestyles and supposedly endow us with flexible, easily reshaped identities.

Second, current postmodernism tends to emphasize the obsolescence of the classical, sovereign nation-state, the legacy of 19th-century political evolution. The 'reterritorialization' of social power, it is argued, disrupts the older social order organized around the national level. The nation-state in a globalizing world therefore ceases to offer a relevant framework for collective identity. This ostensibly opens up new potential spaces for tolerance of 'the stranger' (Bauman, 1990) and makes the sources of collective identification much more local (Harvey, 1989).

Let us deal with the main objections to each of these lines of argument in turn.

First, contemporary neo-tribalism, rather than being about weak social bonds, is actually about the quest for strong social connections. Contrary to the view that identities can be fashioned in some off-the-shelf manner, ethno-nationalism – the most predominant form of contemporary neo-tribalism – involves a search for community. Arguably, *some* identities are more compelling than others. In short, the grand narrative of the nation is far from dead today; on the contrary, it is undergoing a heady revival. If the right to belong to the national collectivity is narrowly conceived – whether it be in terms of blood, long-term residence, or a dominant religion – this then raises some profound problems for civic, pluralistic, and flexibly inclusive conceptions of democracy. National exclusivity necessarily creates 'minorities' and 'outsiders.'

Second, the nation-state does indeed present us with some problems. There can be no doubt that the world is interdependent in terms of investment flows, migration, communication systems, and so on. Indeed, states are permeable entities and do not exercise unlimited control over their destinies. In Western Europe, for instance, there is supranational pressure on the national state from above (in the form of the European Community with its goals of economic and political integration) and there are in many cases decentralist pressures from below (with sessionalist tendencies in several states). Together with other factors, such as the rolling back of social-welfare democratic ideals, this squeeze from above and below has created problems of national electoral politics, most notably in the lack of a convincing articulation of an alternative to the neo-conservative fetishizing of the market (Balibar, 1991). We could say that this adds up to an identity crisis for the national state. However, it still remains the case that the *nation-state form* persists as the frame of reference for all types of nationalist currents. Thus, the postmodernists, with their dreams of flexi-identities, have it wrong. The nation-state has not been superseded. To be a contemporary European nationalist is either to support the old state or to advocate the creation of a new one.

So, contrary to postmodernist thinking, the elaboration of national identity with the nation-state still offers an appealing grand narrative. Of course, there is a European peculiarity, namely the continuing (perhaps now faltering?) attempt to create a euro-state. This, however, cannot be based upon the classic simplifying nationalist criteria of ethnicity, con-sanguinity, language, or religion. For Europe is simply too diverse. Any eventual euro-state – at least if it were to be democratic – would have to be both civic and pluralistic in character and be premised upon a flexibly inclusive conception of European identity. Quite a tall order.

A European audiovisual space?

As has been noted in passing, high expectations have been held about the potential impact of audiovisual culture in Europe upon the construction of a common European identity.

From economics to culture

The picture can be simply conveyed by some broad brush strokes. In the mid-1980s, the European Commission, the Brussels-based bureaucracy that acts as the administrative machinery for the European Economic Community

(EEC), turned its attention to the question of culture. This was an important departure, as 'European integration' had always had its primary conditions in the creation of a market; the opening up of a single economic space across the member states was seen as the key focus of policy. Now, cultural goods – which, of course, have a dual symbolic and economic nature – were brought into the equation, but still within a framework of thinking dominated by market economics.

In a policy document, *Television Without Frontiers* (Commission of the European Communities, 1984, p. 2), a close link – indeed a causal connection – was drawn between the workings of mass media and the creation of a European identity. In as much as a clear idea was articulated at all, the transmission and consumption of television programs was held to be identity-conferring, although no mechanisms whereby this shaping process might occur were ever specified. Such a view of the role of television is by no means surprising. In the European context, public-service broadcasting and broadcasting controlled more directly by the state have been seen until quite recently as the cultural arm of nation building. Radio and television have been conceived of as providing a focus for the political community, for uniting the nation. Broadcasting, in this perspective, has been perceived as a source of common meanings and of cultural cohesion, providing an agenda for the citizen. It is this essentially *national* conception of television that has been transposed to the *supranational* level. This immediately raises questions about its plausibility in circumstances where no single politico-cultural community is confronted by television, but rather that television faces cultural, linguistic, and political diversity. But such concerns were not being addressed by the advocates of the European audiovisual space.

By the end of the decade, not without complex political bargaining and reservations on the part of several member states, a new starting point had been achieved for giving television its allotted role. In October 1989, the EEC enacted a Television Directive that *inter alia* aimed at standardizing measures relating to the support of television production, advertising rules, the protection of juveniles, and the right to reply. Underlying this, in accordance with the EEC Treaty, was the goal of ensuring that equality of access to market freedom applied to television broadcasting across national frontiers. The Television Directive concerned itself with ensuring that member states did not create national restrictions aimed against the reception and retransmission of programs from other member states. Consequently, the evolution of international law within the EEC has shaped the conditions for legislative action at the national level (Hoffmann–Riem, 1992; Michael, 1990), although the full implications of this still have to work themselves out over time. The tenacity of national media systems in Western Europe and the determining role of national political systems in shaping these remain striking, most especially in respect of the specificity of institutions and the precise balance between regulation and the workings of the market (Blumler, 1992; Dyson, 1990; Østergaard, 1992; and Pohoryles *et al.*, 1990).

Bearing in mind the continuing importance of the national level and the resistances it offers to 'Europeanization,' the European scene could still be seen as a quite specific, and still partial, instance of what has been labelled the 'internationalization of television' (Negrine and Papathanassopoulos, 1991). Both the EEC and the much broader regional grouping, the Council of Europe, have encouraged the development of European television programming via regulatory measures and conventions. Programs have been created that aim at stimulating the production and distribution of audio-visual products. The best known of these in the case of the EEC are the successive MEDIA 92 and MEDIA 95 programs, which have sought to strengthen the European Community's internal market across the component national boundaries. These overarching programs are divided into numerous subprograms that have had some modest impact in creating a European audiovisual market by stimulating new production and in enhancing cross-national collaboration. Nevertheless, this remains exceedingly marginal as a source of production when compared with the extent to which individual European countries import the bulk of their nondomestically produced programming from the U.S. (Mele, 1990). Clearly, this reality has to affect the extent to which the creation of the common *European* audiovisual culture might be envisaged.

The fallacy of distribution

At its most optimistic, then, it has been assumed in official circles that it might be possible to create a common culture through television and cinema production and consumption. A European audiovisual space might thus operate as a kind of public sphere that could confer a European identity upon the various peoples living within it. There has always been a double rationale behind this project. On the one hand, the production of European films and television programs has been conceived of as a kind of cultural defense activity. U.S. television fiction programs and films are widely popular in Europe, as elsewhere, and this popularity has been seen as posing a threat of 'Americanization,' a view most notably articulated in France (Mattelart *et al.*, 1984; Wolton, 1990). The other major logic – indeed, that which has really predominated despite the talk of cultural goals – has been a purely industrial and commercial one: a desire to create a European market. This would allow the development of the hardware to go along with the software and thereby to compete more effectively with Japan (as well as the U.S.) in the international marketplace.

However, bearing in mind the strength of national preferences both for national styles and contents in television consumption patterns, it could fairly be said that the real common currency of the European audiovisual space is actually *American* television's output, for the U.S. produces the moving images that most easily traverse *any* European national barriers. By contrast, European-produced programs apparently offer much more limited scope for audience identification and do not travel too well beyond their national confines or, English-language ones excepted, their language area (Silj, 1992). Europe's cultural diversity, in particular its evidently durable 'linguistic order' (Gifreu and Corominas, 1991), means that audiovisual products are diversely consumed and interpreted. It has been observed that the 'robustness of European states and their languages makes it extremely unlikely that further political integration will be accompanied by language unification' (De Swaan,

1991, p. 321), which suggests that current consumption patterns are likely to persist. The question of language is at the heart of sociocultural resistance to homogenization and is a major factor in explaining the failure to succeed in creating a pan-European televisual market via direct broadcast satellite (Collins, 1990b). Cultural differences have had economic consequences manifested in quite distinctive consumption patterns for products in different European countries. It is not surprising that from pan-European aspirations, satellite operators have moved into distributing television either by national markets or by homogeneous language areas, notably the English, German, and Scandinavian (Richeri, 1992). The conditions for the easy passage of European films and television programs from one European country to another have not yet been attained. These presuppose an openness to forms of cultural exchange in which knowing about proximate others is valued and, moreover, may be experienced as popular entertainment.

What these observations suggest, then, is that there is something inherently improbable about asking people to consume television as if they already had a European imagination. We could term this the *fallacy of distribution*, according to which it is supposed that distributing the same cultural product leads to an identity of interpretation on the part of those who consume it. But this is really the crudest determinism, for the availability of particular audiovisual texts does not define what is made of them in the context of reception, especially when they are absorbed through different cultural and linguistic frameworks. The empirical evidence from reception studies rather suggests the pertinence of cross-national variation in the viewing process (Liebes and Katz, 1990) as well as the shaping impact of discourses rooted in class, gender, ethnicity, and social experience (Schlesinger *et al.*, 1992). The proposed enlargement of the EEC is likely to complicate the European case even further, especially as currently the assertion of national difference is more apparent than support for the common culture.

Indeed, since the idea of a European audiovisual space was first formulated in the 1980s, the European scene has been quite transformed by the ending of the cold war. The making, if only in part, of a common European culture and identity via transborder flows of European-made television seems today an almost naive aspiration (Robins and Morley, 1992). It presupposed precisely the stability of the contending ideological blocs that conferred an external pressure upon the EEC and which thereby reinforced a sense of collective purpose. In December 1991, the draft Treaty on European Union was presented to the European Council at Maastricht, and this contained federal aspirations for the EEC. Since that time, the drive toward political union has slackened, and perhaps even gone into reverse. Certainly, writing in the mid-autumn of 1992, it is the present crisis of European institutions that is most striking to this observer. The EEC, which has been the focus of the aspiration to *become European* on the part of the former states of the Eastern bloc, may itself be in decline, with potentially far-reaching consequences.

In the early 1990s, the reunification of Germany and its growing preponderance in the EEC and beyond it, the uncertain future of the successor states to the Soviet Union and former Soviet bloc, and the bloody disintegration of Yugoslavia impose new conditions upon any thinking about what Europe now is and what it could be.

This clearly relates to the emergent question of national communication policy in postcommunist Europe. Looking ahead, it seems plausible to assume, as authoritarian nationalism becomes more pronounced in this area, that the cultural dependency inherent in foreign ownership and control of media and telecommunication systems is likely to become increasingly salient (Mansell, 1992; Splichal, 1992). If that is so, the chances of constituting an international – in this case, wider European – public and cultural space in which a common overarching identity may be elaborated look rather slim.

The problem of cultural management

Plainly, the analysis of the prospects of audiovisual culture in Europe directs attention to the anterior sociopolitical conditions within which communication occurs. The example discussed above exposes the limitations of what might be called a rationalist approach to cultural management in the supranational context. What has been presupposed by the attempt to create an audiovisual space is a set of quite specific conditions: (a) that a sector of cultural activity can be transformed by policy means, (b) that the means and ends of cultural policy can be adequately identified and acted upon, (c) that the space within which policy action is to take place is bounded and relatively predictable, and (d) that a viable balance between state intervention and the operations of the market might be achieved.

These assumptions characteristically underline the media policy process at the level of the nation-state, and there is an inherent uncertainty about achieving specified goals even within that relatively predictable framework. Add the complicating condition of the diversity of a supranational Europe in which questions about the precise extent of the politico-cultural boundaries remain on the agenda because of new accessions, and it is easy to see how difficult large-scale cultural management may be.

Culture represents a particular problem for a supranational project because existing nation-states often (if not invariably) constitute strong foci of cultural identification for their populations. 'Europe' does not constitute such a focus in its own right. We can illustrate the point simply by noting the difference between thinking of oneself as a 'European' (a label once synonymous with that of being a white colonizer of nonwhite peoples' territories) and of one's being 'a member of the (as yet nonexistent) European nation.'

There is one possible solution to the lack of a common European culture and that is to take to the cultural high road. Some have argued for the existence of European 'core values.' A typical shopping list could include democracy, private property, the market, Roman law, renaissance humanism, Christianity, individualism, and rationalism (Smith, 1991). To take this line, though, does raise a theoretical question: How could such values articulate with one another to produce a new collective identity? How, moreover, might their variable distribution across Europe's state and nations affect the possibility of creating an overarching framework for 'Europeans'?

Such questions lead to another. If it be accepted that collectivities are constituted by processes of inclusion and exclusion, where are the lines of incontestable Europeanness to be drawn? One powerful strand of argument has excluded Russia and (except Greece) the area of orthodox Christianity more generally (e.g., Dahrendorf, 1990). In yet another exclusionary move, the identification of Europeanness with Christianity of whatever ilk – a view classically stated by T. S. Eliot (1948, pp. 122–124) almost half a century ago – has raised some quite different questions about who belongs, most particularly about the status of Muslims within Europe. Needless to say, this may also inform contemporary antisemitism in continuity with earlier manifestations this century. Thus far, however, this issue has emerged most sharply on the nationalist right in relation to the position of the Muslim minorities inside European states, but it has also been on the agenda in the shape of a long-standing ambivalence concerning the admission of (Muslim) Turkey to the EEC. In this connection, it has been argued that the Western media have played a major role in offering both a distorted view of the Muslim world to the West and vice versa and that consequently urgent cultural mediation is sorely needed (Ahmed, 1992).

Alongside such macro boundary constructions, resurgent etho-nationalism offers a major source of potential resistance to Europeanization. Separatist or strongly regionalist currents are alive in various states in the West – in Catalonia and the Basque Country in Spain, in Scotland in the U.K., in Belgium, and in Northern Italy. In East and Central Europe, Yugoslavia represents the exemplary case of bloodletting, but major ethnic and national tensions (often leading to armed violence, as, for example, in the Caucasus and in Central Asia) together with resurgent antisemitism are widespread throughout the postcommunist world.

Currently, therefore, a perspective on collective identities in Europe suggests that we confront a paradoxical situation on the continent. The process of European integration is contributing to crises of national identity at the state level. At the same time nationality is being reaffirmed as the value for collectiveness both by Western neo-nationalists and by the leadership of East and Central European states and the successor states of the Soviet Union. Statehood remains the inescapable building-block of European integration. It is precisely this, which represents the attraction for national separatists intent upon leaving their existing states and then 'joining Europe,' that is likely to make national culture so crucially important. Yet, the proliferation of states can only make the project of European integration more difficult. Indeed, new accessions from among the European Free Trade Area (EFTA) countries and the postcommunist states could well reinforce the national separatist temptation for existing nations without states already inside the EEC, since statehood offers the crucial lever for the exercise of power and influence. And that in turn could only further complicate the role of audiovisual communication within and between states, for the magnetic pull of the nationalist project seems inescapable.

References

Ahmed, A. S. (1992) *Postmodernism and Islam: Predicament and promise*, Routledge, London.
Balibar, E. (1991) Es gibt keine Staat in Europa [There is no state in Europe]: Racism and politics in Europe today. *New Left Review*, Vol. 186, pp. 5–19.
Bauman, Z. (1990) Modernity and ambivalence. *Theory, Culture and Society*, Vol. 7, No. 2–3, pp. 239–60.

Bauman, Z. (1991) *Modernity and ambivalence*, Polity Press, Cambridge.

Blumler, J. G. (ed.) (1992) *Television and the public interest: Vulnerable values in West European broadcasting*, Sage, London.

Collins, R. (1990a) *Culture, communication and national identity: The Case of Canadian television*, University of Toronto Press, Toronto.

Collins, R. (1990b) *Television: Policy and culture*, Unwin Hyman, London.

Commission of the European Communities (1984) *Television without frontiers: Green paper on the establishment of the common market for broadcasting, especially by satellite and cable* (COM, 84, 300 Final), CEC, Brussels.

Dahrendorf, R. (1990) *Reflections on the revolutions in Europe. In a letter intended to have been sent to a gentleman in Warsaw*, Chatto and Windus, London.

De Swaan, A. (1991) Notes on the emerging global language system: Regional, national and supernational. *Media, Culture and Society*, Vol. 13, No. 3, pp. 309–23.

Dyson, K. (1990) Les politiques audiovisuelles européennes: Les leçons des années 80 [European broadcasting policies: Lessons from the 80s]. *Médiaspouvoirs*, Vol. 20, pp. 95–104.

Eliot, T. S. (1948) *Notes towards the definition of culture*, Faber and Faber, London.

Fentress, J. and Wickham, C. (1992) *Social memory: New perspectives on the past*, Blackwell, Oxford.

Gellner, E. (1983) *Nations and nationalism*, Blackwell, Oxford.

Gifreu, J. and Corominas, M. (eds.) (1991) *Construir l'espai Català de comuniciõ* [Constructing and Catalan communicative space], Centre d'Investigaciò de la Comunicaciõ, Barcelona.

Giorgi, L. (1992) Constructing the xenophobic subject. *Innovation*, Vol. 5, No. 2, pp. 25–39.

Harvey, D. (1989) *The condition of postmodernity*, Blackwell, Oxford.

Hobsbawm, E. (1992) Nationalism and ethnicity. *Intermedia*, Vol. 20, No. 4–5, pp. 13–15.

Hobsbawm, E. and Ranger, T. (1983) *The invention of tradition*, Cambridge University Press, Cambridge.

Hoffman-Riem, W. (1992) Trends in the development of broadcasting law in Western Europe. *European Journal of Communication*, Vol. 7, No. 2, pp. 147–171.

Liebes, T. and Katz, E. (1990) *The export of meaning: Cross-cultural readings of DALLAS*, Oxford University Press, New York.

Maffesoli, M. (1988) *Le temps des tribus: Le déclin de l'individualisme* [The time of the tribes: The decline of individualism], Méridiens Klincksieck, Paris.

Mansell, R. (1992) The West looks east: Reformulating telecommunication strategies. *Innovation*, Vol. 5, No. 1, pp. 67–86.

Mattelart, A., Delcourot, X. and Mattelart, M. (1984) *International image markets: In search of an alternative perspective*, Comedia, London.

Mele, M. (1990) Ilmercato europeo dei programmi audiovisivi [The European broadcasting market]. In Rath, C. D., Davis, H. H., Gargon, F., Bettetini, G. and Grasso A. (eds.), *Le Televisioni in Europa* [Television in Europe], Edizioni della Fondazione Giovanni Agnelli, Turin, pp. 331–61.

Melucci, A. (1989) *Nomads of the present: Social movements and individual needs in contemporary society*, Hutchinson Radius, London.

Michael, J. (1990) Regulating communications media: From the discretion of sound chaps to the arguments of lawyers. In Ferguson, M. (ed.), *Public communication: The new imperatives. Future directions for media research*, Sage, London, pp. 44–60.

Namer, G. (1987) *Mémoire et société* [Memory and society], Méridiens Klincksieck, Paris.

Negrine, R. and Papathanassopoulos, S. (1991) The internationalization of television. *European Journal of Communication*, Vol. 6, No. 1, pp. 9–32.

Østergaard, B. S. (ed.) (1992) *The media in Western Europe: The Euromedia handbook*, Sage, London.

Pohoryles, R., Schlesinger, P. and Wuggenig, U. (eds.) (1990) *Media structures in a changing Europe*, ICCR, Vienna.

Richeri, G. (1992) Televisione e nuove tecnologie: Satelliti e cavi nell'evoluzione europea [Television and new technologies: Satellite and cable in the evolution of Europe]. In A. Silj (ed.), *La nuova televisione in Europa, Vol. I. Realità nazionali e televisione senza frontiere* [Europe's new television: National realities and television without frontiers], Gruppo Fininvest, Milan, pp. 77–121.

Robins, K. and Morley, D. (1992) What kind of identity for Europe? *Intermedia*, Vol. 20, No. 4–5, 23–24.

Schlesinger, P. (1988) Kollektive Identitäten, Freunde, Feinde [Collective identities, friends, enemies]. *Innovation*, Vol. 1, No. 1, pp. 102–15.

Schlesinger, P. (1991a) *Media, state and nation: Political violence and collective identities*, Sage, London.

Schlesinger, P. (1991b) Media, the political order and national identity. *Media, Culture and Society*, Vol. 13, No. 3, pp. 297–308.

Schlesinger, P. (1992) 'Europeanness' – A new cultural battlefield? *Innovation*, Vol. 5, No. 2, pp. 11–23.

Schlesinger, P., Dobash, R. E., Dobash, R. P. and Weaver, C. K. (1992) *Women viewing violence*, BFI Publishing, London.

Silj, A. (1992) Mercati nazionali e mercato europeo [National markets and the European market]. In Silj, A. (ed.). *La nuova televisione in Europa, Vol. I, Realità nazionali e televisione senza frontiere* [Europe's new television: National realities and television without frontiers], Gruppo Fininvest, Milan, pp. 3–47.

Smith, A. D. (1991) *National identity*. Penguin, Harmondsworth.

Splichal, S. (1992) Le transfert de l'économie de l'information vers l'Europe de l'Est. Rêve ou cauchemar? [Transferring the information economy to Eastern Europe. Dream or nightmare?]. *Réseaux*, Vol. 53, pp. 75–88.

Tomlinson, J. (1991) *Cultural imperialism*, Pinter Publishers, London.

Wolton, D. (1990) *Eloge du grand public: Une théorie critique de la télévision* [In praise of the public: A critical theory of television], Flammarion, Paris.

9

Broadcasting and new media policies in Taiwan

Sheila Chin

Centre for Mass Communication Research, University of Leicester (1995).

The 1990s have proved to be a very important decade for the Taiwanese broadcasting system. The traditionally dominant position of television broadcasting is facing challenges from cable and satellite television. As a result, viewers now exercise far greater choice with respect to the channels and programmes that they can legally view. The introduction of new media technologies and practices is quickly subordinating the role of government broadcasting policy to a series of rear-guard and reactive policies. These new policies include the regulation of new media, the launching of public television, and the partial deregulation of traditional media.

The Taiwanese broadcasting system in historical context

After the government of the Republic of China (ROC) relocated to Taiwan in 1949, only four radio companies controlling 10 radio stations existed (including those transferred from the China): two military owned stations, one private station and seven Kuomintang-based BCC outlets (the largest radio station network owned by the KMT – the only executive party at that time) (*Radio and Television Yearbook*, 1990, p. 10). Afterwards, 14 new radio companies were established from 1950 to 1960 – the golden decade of radio broadcasting in Taiwan. After the introduction of the first television broadcasting station in 1962, the growth of radio slowed considerably. Although the number of radio companies had grown to 33 by 1992, and the number of radio stations to 192, this rate of growth was considerably slower than during the 1950s. The vast number of these stations – 137 – were controlled by the government (30.7%), KMT (24.4%), and military (16.1%), while the remainder were privately owned (28.6%) (Cheng, 1988, p. 35).

The first television station, Taiwan Television Enterprise (TTV), was established on 10 October, 1962. The second television station, China Television Company (CTV), was established in 1968 and began broadcasting on 10 October, 1969. The third television station, Chinese Television System (CTS), was an expanded and renamed station that had taken over from the previous Educational Television Station (ETV). CTS began broadcasting on 31 October 1971 (*Radio and Television Yearbook*, 1976, p. 11; Wen, 1987; Sun, 1992). Until recently, these three stations provided the foundation for the Taiwanese television broadcasting system. Essentially, they operated as the equivalent of three networks, serving the entire country, since there were no strictly local television stations until 1995.

The development of television stations was based heavily on political considerations. When the People's Republic of China (PRC) inaugurated their television broadcasting service in 1958, the government found the urgent need for a television service. Although television was valued as a symbol of modernization and a tool to unify the country, the relative lack of resources and haste that went into setting up the system resulted in a television system that was, somewhat paradoxically, overly dependent on advertising and incapable of generating the confidence of entrepreneurs. A well thought out policy and legal environment for television had to wait until 1976, when the government proposed the *Broadcasting and Television Law*.

Up to 1992, TTV was owned by six Taiwan provincial government banks (48.95%), several Japanese companies (Fuji, Hitachi, NEC, and Toshiba) (19.58%), and domestic private investors (31.07%) (*Radio and Television Yearbook*, 1976, p. 11; Wen, 1987; Sun, 1992). When TTV was established, the government sought out technological and financial support from the United States and Japan. The former rejected to join, but the latter considered the potential market for television sets in Taiwan significant enough to warrant its investment (Hsueh, 1988, p. 33).

As for CTV and CTS, CTV was owned by BCC and KMT-affiliated enterprises, such as Cheng-Chung Bookstore, Central Daily News, the Central Motion Picture Company, and the Hwa-Shia Investing Company. Together these companies held 68.23% of the company's shares, while private radio stations held 7.77% of the shares and other private investors the remaining 24%. The Ministry of National Defence (MND) and three military affiliate enterprises held the vast majority of shares in CTS (76.06%, while the Ministry of Education (MOE) possessed 10.39% of the shares and other private investors controlled 13.55% (Wen, 1987; Sun, 1992).

From the capital structure of the three television stations it is clear that TTV, CTV and CTS have been securely controlled by the government, KMT, and military. Such control is reinforced by the fact that the general managers of TTV, CTV, and CTS are all appointed by the government and that the boards of the three television stations are, essentially, a 'club of retired high-ranking KMT officials and generals of MND' (Wang, 1993, p. 108). Even the private investors in television stations must have special relationships with the government or the military. Owing to these arrangements, it is impossible for the three television stations to challenge the government or executive party. All have invested in television strictly on the basis of expected profits (Lee, 1987, p. 188).

The government's desire for a docile media system and private investors' purely instrumental view of television have produced a highly profitable, but crass, commercial television system incapable of meeting any reasonable standards of programming quality. Political news is done neither fairly nor with respect to views that might differ from those of the government. Programming in regional dialects has been reduced to facilitate the standardization of the Chinese language around the official Mandarin dialect, suppressing the possibility of a multi-cultural society and causing conflict between people speaking different dialects. Moreover, programming typically neglects special interests and programming for children in favour of, for example, imported Japanese drama programmes that are often shown during prime time.

This approach to broadcasting triggered much animosity towards the system and efforts to decentralize it in favour of different voices, public television that better attends to minority interests, and cable television and satellite television services that offer people more viewing choices. The poor quality of the conventional television system created widespread pressures for greater importation of foreign broadcasting services, the deregulation of broadcasting systems within the country, the development of cable television stations and the establishment of public television.

The fight for open skies

The fight for a reorganized media system was initiated by the opposition Democratic Progressive Party (DPP), mainly through their support of the illegal television broadcasting operations of the Green Television Station, cable television broadcasting (CATV) and efforts to block CTV broadcast signals. The objectives of the DPP was to push the government to decentralize electronic media.

Green television station

In the late 1980s, the DPP legislators often physically fought with the KMT legislators during efforts to pass or reject special bills. Whenever the three television stations showed the scene of fighting, the DPP members always complained they were not fairly reported in the news coverage. In order to balance television coverage, the DPP produced videotapes to show their view of events in the Legislative Yuan and tried to propagate their allegations by other means.

In the summer of 1987, one of the KMT legislators, Jaw, Shau-Kong, applied for four types of broadcasting licenses: AM radio, FM radio, television and cable television. At the same time a DPP legislator, Kong, Ning-Hsiang, applied for three licenses: FM radio, television and cable television (*Independence Evening Post*, 28 July 1987, p. 3). The Government Information Office (GIO) rejected both of their applications by saying that no extra broadcasting channels were available, while indicating that the government was studying the possibilities for granting cable television licenses.

Just prior to the 1989 election, Hwang, Hsin-Chieh, the former DPP chairman, applied for a license to operate a television station. The answer from the GIO was once again that there were no extra channels available. Finally, the DPP lost its patience. On 30 November 1989 – two days before the election – the DPP smuggled television transmission equipment into the country from abroad and established the illegal 'Green Television Station' to broadcast a two-hour programme to introduce its candidates (*United Daily News*, 1 December 1989, p. 3).

When the government ordered the local police to crack down on the illegal television station, Yu, Ching, the Taipei county magistrate who happened to be the DPP candidate whose offices were being used to house the television transmitters, refused to let the GIO official and police confiscate the equipment. Yu's lawyer, Chang, Jung-Chian argued that the government's monopoly over the country's three television stations afforded it ample opportunities to express its views and that there was therefore no reason to seek to limit Yu's freedom of expression. He also alleged that the *Broadcasting and Television Law* was against the constitution. Since the event occurred before the election, the government was reluctant to confront the DPP. As a result, the GIO only reiterated provisions of the *Broadcasting and Television Law* preventing anyone from installing stations, boosters, antennas, or transmitters to broadcast programmes without a license. However, such admonitions did not deter the DPP, who shortly afterwards smuggled transmitters from abroad and put them into three mobile cars to avoid confiscation by the police. Ultimately, however, this initiative proved futile as the weak signals were blocked by surrounding buildings (*Liberty Times*, 27 March 1989, p. 3).

Unrelenting, the DPP tried other methods; this time the facilities of the regional satellite broadcaster, AsiaSat, were sought. Despite agreeing to pay the required deposit and annual lease fees, AsiaSat refused to carry the DPP's broadcasts on the grounds that it does not do business with those unable to obtain approval from their government (*United Daily News*, 13 September 1990, p. 3; *United Daily News*, 25 September 1990, p. 39).

TDCATV (Taiwan Democratic Cable Television)

After the failed attempts to establish the Green Television Station and to use AsiaSat facilities, the DPP decided to try cable television facilities. The first TDCATV network was established in Chung-Her, an area in Taipei county, on 28 February 1990. As soon as the first Democratic Cable Television Station was established, other stations sprouted up all over the island. By 15 October 1990 there were 24 Democratic Cable Television Stations organized under the auspices of the 'League of Taiwan Democratic Cable Television' (TDCATV). Co-production centres were established to unify the political programmes of these networks in an effort to make them more influential (*Independence Morning Post*, 16 October 1990, p. 45). Aware that providing an exclusive schedule of political programmes would turn away viewers, TDCATV also carried video and satellite programming typically offered by other cable operators.

The coalition

Not surprisingly, the government and the GIO were not pleased with the spread of the 'Fourth Channel stations'. While the 'condition' of Fourth Channel cable network operators and some dissidents within the DPP publicly threatened to continue broadcasting and to jam the signals from CTV and TTV, their efforts were curtailed through pressure applied by the national intelligence agency. Nonetheless, the 'coalition' continued to argue that it was fighting against the government's unfair monopoly over broadcasting. Such a position was supported by professors Ching, Jei-Cheng, Weng, Hsio-Chi, and Kuo, Li-Hsi of the National Cheng-Chi University, who suggested that the 'coalition' was reasonably responding to the 'systematic violence of the government' (*The Great China News*, 14 January 1992, p. 3). Meanwhile, DPP legislators Peng, Pai-Sien and Chen, Shei-Pien backed the coalition in the legislature by pushing the government to release more television channels (*The Great China News*, 15 January 1992, p. 3).

The boom of cable television: CATV and fourth channels

Taiwanese cable television originated from regular Common Antennas Television (CATV) systems and the activities of 'Fourth Channels' set up by cable television pirates and political opposition. The 'Fourth Channel' is a term coined by the general public to describe the fact that the illegal TDCATV system offered programming alternatives to the three official television stations.

When TTV was established in 1962 reception was poor due to the mountainous and rugged terrain stretching across the middle of the island. Thus, as had been the case notably in the United States and Canada, the original impulse for cable television in Taiwan came from businessmen setting up CATV systems to improve signal reception to areas poorly served by over-the-air broadcasting. According to Michael Kwan, in 1969 Hua Lien, on the east coast of Taiwan, became the first city to possess a CATV system.

Since the *Broadcasting and Television Law* of 1976 did not deal with CATV, CATV remained virtually unregulated until 1979 when the GIO announced measures for the installation and operations of CATV systems. These measures permitted businessmen to set up CATV to improve television reception, but banned receiving programmes other than those of the three authorized television stations. While the outlines of the technical, economic and regulatory framework were beginning to emerge, the spread of CATV remained relatively minor, serving only 400,000 households by 1991 (Sung, 1991, p. 106).

The first over-the-air 'Fourth Channel' television station, according to Michael Kwan, emerged around 1970 in Taipei. Unlike the operators of CATV, the operators of Fourth Channel broadcasting outlets were not illegal until the *Cable Law* was passed by the Legislative Yuan on 16 July 1993 (*Central Daily News International Edition*, 17 July 1993, p. 2). According to research done in 1991, there were more than 200 'Fourth Channel' stations, 600,000 household subscribers, and four million viewers with revenues of more than three billion NT dollars.

In the early stages of CATV and Fourth Channel development, the two systems co-existed rather harmoniously due to agreements that gave the former exclusive responsibility for transmitting television programmes while the latter would only air video programmes. Both agreed that co-operation rather than competition would suit their respective interests, at least that was the agreement until foreign satellite television made it possible for CATV systems to carry 50–60 channels of programming. Afterwards the CATV systems typically loaded their networks with at least the three authorized television stations, 21 satellite channels, one UHF Open University channel, five (two Chinese, two Western and one Japanese) film/video channels, two stock market information channels, two Parliament channels, one to three shopping channels, one religious channel, one cartoon channel, one KTV channel, one programme schedule service and other entertainment services. The merging of television programming and video services on the CATV systems meant that the earlier harmony between CATV and Fourth Channels were over (Wen, 1993, p. 473).

By 1979 the government began to worry about the challenge to existing television stations, video shops and movie industry from CATV networks. In response, the GIO made its first crackdown on illegal cable television stations. Yet, the efforts of the government to bring these networks to heel were met with a greater resolve amongst the illegal cable operators to set up even more networks. Government enforcement of its broadcasting law was impeded by the fact that the many of the illegal cable operations were aligned with the DPP. For its part, the government lacked the resolve to turn the crisis in media law into a full-scale political confrontation. Similarly, enforcement agencies feared that confiscation might affect their next budgets, as DPP legislators took revenge on the agencies through their influence over budget allocations. Thus, despite the fact that the illegal cable operations were violating Article 45 (1) of the *Broadcasting and Television Law*, the threat of political confrontation and an administrative crisis seriously constrained enforcement of the media law.

The government's difficulties were further confounded by the fact that any actions against illegal cable operators would raise the ire of those subscribing to these systems. On 15 May 1990, a survey of 1143 people showed that 55% of persons thought it was necessary to establish one or two more television stations (*Min Sheng Pao*, 15 May 1990, p. 10). On October 2 1990, the day after the government crackdown on TDCATV's Capital Channel, a *United Daily News* interview of 671 people showed that only 40% of people agreed with the government's methods for controlling the illegal operators, 14% disagreed and a clear majority (62%) wanted the government to permit cable television (27 October 1990, p. 3).

Of course this widespread support begs questions about why cable television is so popular. Wen, Shui-Chi (1993, pp. 461–3) suggests that there are five reasons that explain people's enthusiastic embrace of cable television:

1. *individual demand*: people expect multiple sources of news, information and entertainment programming.
2. *the technology factor*: from 1970 to 1990, Taiwanese technology had progressed to a stage where it was possible to domestically produce coaxial cable, amplifiers, and the other hardware that cable television needs. The appearance of the videotape and satellite television programmes provided a plentiful source of software to fill the expanding capacity of the hardware.
3. *the economic factor*: when cable television emerged, the national income was enough to buy colour television but not enough to buy video recorders. The reasonable installation fee (gradually reduced from 2500 NT dollars to none) and monthly fee (gradually increasing from 400 to 600 NT dollars) was attractive to most household subscribers.
4. *the statutory factor*: there was no statue to regulate cable television stations for more than 20 years.

5. *the underground economy*: the Taiwanese pirate videotape factories supplied American and Japanese movies, sex videos and recent releases to cable television stations at a low price, allowing CATV systems to expand their market at a low cost.

This latter factor not only challenged the authority of the government, but enraged the Motion Picture Export Association of America (MPEAA) – a consortium of nine U.S. film distributors that markets and distributes films for the Hollywood majors. The MPEAA condemned the illegal cable television stations for broadcasting pirate videotapes and impairing their profits. Under the pressure of the film industry, American Trade Representatives strongly lobbied for a new legal regime for cable and a government crackdown on illegal cable television. These issues rose to the top of the agenda during Taiwan-American Copyright and Patent Protection Negotiations in March 1991.

Feeling the danger of crisis, some 70 Fourth Channel operators established 'the Cable Television Association' in 1990 to protect their interests. One year later, their members had increased to more than 170. Some Fourth Channel operators announced that they would mobilize their members island wide to support the anti-pirating movement. They also proposed that participants pay the copyright fees for the programmes they carried and 300,000 NT dollars deposit to guarantee that they would not broadcast pornographic videotapes (*China Times*, 1 September 1990, p. 38). In addition, some operators even began to produce and/or broadcast public interest programmes on their channels to improve their image (*United Daily News*, 8 December 1990, p. 3).

The passing of the Cable Law

Under the pressure from the DPP, the operators, and the American officials, the *Cable Law* was finally passed on July 16 1993 which banned cross-media ownership, foreign investment, and established the 'one area five systems' rule. The main points of the new law are:

1. The main cable television network is established by the Ministry of Communications (MOC), but operators own and operate local networks (Article 4).
2. The Cable Television Review Commission will be responsible for licensing and supervising the management of cable systems (Article 8).
3. The Review Commission consists of 13–15 commissioners, 11 of whom are scholars, specialists or representatives of the MOC and GIO. No more than one-half of the commissioners can belong to the same party (Article 9).
4. The commissioners of the Committee are nominated by the Premier and appointed by the Legislative Yuan. Each Commissioners' term is a minimum of three years and not more than six years (Article 10).
5. Foreigners cannot own and operate cable television networks. The directors of the board and the general manager from other non-cable, media enterprises cannot act as directors or managers of a cable television station (Article 20).

6. The maximum numbers of cable television stations in each area cannot be more than five. The MOC will study and announce the number of areas to be served at a later date (Article 27).
7. The amount of domestic programmes carried by cable television stations should not be less than 20% (Article 36).
8. Advertisements should be broadcast before or after the programme. Advertisements can be inserted once for programmes longer than 60 minutes in length. The total quantity of the advertisement should not be more than 10% of the length of the programmes (Article 38).
9. The operators should set aside 2% of their revenues for use by local governments in cultural construction initiatives and 1% to support public television (Article 44).
10. There are no capital limitations on cable television operators and cross-media ownership is permitted (*Central Daily News International Edition*, 17 July 1993, p. 2).

Since the establishment of a cable television station is capital intensive – around 200 million NT dollars – it is likely that most cable systems will be controlled by large companies or conglomerates. As such, there will be a strong tendency for small cable television operators to either integrate with big operators or to be forced out of existence by them. Even though the *Cable Law* allows up to five cable systems in any given area, it is unlikely that more than one or two systems will be able to withstand the monopolistic/oligopolistic forces of the industry. Thus, although the *Cable Law* brings a degree of stability to the uncertainties, even illegalities, of the Taiwanese cable industries, it is uncertain how many of the 26 cable systems licensed in 1995 will survive the monopolistic tendencies characteristic of the cable industry (*Central Daily New International Edition*, 5 May 1995, p. 7).

The struggle of public television

Somewhat surprisingly given the trends of deregulation and regulatory liberalization elsewhere in the world, one of the important outcomes of attempts to liberalize the media environment in Taiwan has been the establishment of the Broadcasting Development Fund for Chinese Public Television (CPTV). When the Cable Law Review Commission was formed in March 1990, the GIO set as one of its goals the use of some revenues from the cable industries to fund the development of public television. Over the course of the following year, members of Public Television Commission were selected by the GIO, the former representative to Singapore, Wang, Hsiao-Hsian, appointed as the Secretary General of the Commission, and a draft *Public Television Law* submitted to the Executive Yuan (Wen, 1993, p. 490).

The original idea for public television had been forwarded by the former Premier, Sun, Yun-Hsuan, in 1980, as a means of producing and distributing social education programmes (*United Daily News*, 7 February 1980, p. 4). Shortly afterwards, in 1982, the Ministry of Education and GIO were invited by the Executive Yuan to discuss the basic project of public television. Originally, it was proposed that the three official television stations would provide a half hour of public television programming during the day time and again at night as an interim step on the way to a full scale public television operation (Lee, 1987, p. 289). The first public television programme was broadcast on 20 May 1984, but a fully operational public television station was not established until 10 years later due to budgetary constraints.

Although the three television stations agreed to the government's proposal, and even offered to increase the amount of public television programming from 9–15 hours per week, the allocation of such programming to off-peak times was not very appropriate. The three television stations also sought permission to broadcast advertisements before and after public programmes to make up for 'losses' incurred by carrying the public programmes. Furthermore, the three television stations could change or cancel the time allocated to public programmes when and where they deemed it necessary. Thus, it was quite obvious that these arrangements were not very satisfactory and that any real commitment to public, educational television would have to be through a station purposely designed to serve these goals (*Broadcasting and Television Industry Development Foundation Report*, 1988, pp. 12–3).

Because public television did not have its own station and budget, the government was able to exercise an enormous amount of control through its control of the budget. For instance, in the financial year of 1989 the public television budget was 210.9 million NT dollars, 83.44% of the budget came from the government, 12.9%, from the Broadcasting Development Fund, and the rest from revenues or donations. Such financial arrangements made it very clear that 'public television' was just another form of 'government television', wedded as tightly to the GIO and centres of political and administrative power as traditional broadcasters. These tidy arrangements have been thoroughly criticized by communication scholars and others throughout Taiwan, and are in large measure responsible for the inability to stabilize the legal status of the public broadcaster. However, it now appears that a full-fledged Public Television Station and accompanying legal framework will be put into place sometime in 1996.

The deregulation of satellite broadcasting and the development of satellite projects

The emergence of satellite broadcasting flows has not been stimulated solely by indigenous demands for a better television structure, but mainly by new technology initiatives from Japan and Hong Kong. Although Taiwanese television first used satellite technology after obtaining retransmission rights for the 1969 Apollo XII Moon Trip, a long time passed before the technology became a regular part of the Taiwanese media landscape.

Within the Asian region, it was Japan's Direct Broadcasting Satellite (DBS), BS-2A, launched in 1984, that first broke the link between the terrestrial broadcasting systems and national borders, as it extended television signals to distant areas and covered South Korea and Taiwan with its footprint. While the Koreans took great offence at this action on the grounds of national and cultural sovereignty, Taiwan officials were more sanguine in their response noting that linguistic and economic barriers meant that most people would not have access to the Japanese DBS system. Nonetheless, largely for symbolic reasons, the Taiwanese government banned the import, sale and letting of receiving hardware (Lee, 1985, pp. 1–2).

While the government expected that language and economic factors would erect barriers to DBS reception, there are at least four factors that undermined these assumptions. First, rises in income and the relative ease of buying illegally imported dishes meant that receiving dishes dotted the landscape. Second, the illegal but well organized cable television stations, coupled with people's desire for more programming choices, meant that satellite viewing spread like wild fire. Third, although the Japanese language did prove to be a barrier to Taiwanese audiences, many programs such as MTV, sports and geographic channels meant that programs were less tightly tied to language and more to a visual aesthetic. Even language proved less of a barrier than anticipated, since the historical experience of Japanese colonization left a residue of Japanese language capabilities among a sizeable portion of the Taiwanese population. Finally, President Lee, Teng Hui offered a relatively open and democratic environment which had many positive influences on the media landscape (Yang, 1991, p. 38).

In addition, there were many indications that President Lee was keenly interested in satellite technology, a factor which obviously meant a relatively liberal attitude with respect to the direction of satellite policy. Lee even intimated to close officials that Taiwan would soon have its own satellite. As a further step toward the full embrace of satellite technology, the Ministry of Communications (MOC) lifted restrictions on the ownership and installation of KU band dishes – nick-named the 'small ear' – in November of 1988 (Hsiung, 1989, p. 2). By this time the deregulation of satellites was well under way. Capping of the march toward satellite communications, the National Science Council (NSC) and MOC both announced that Taiwan would soon launch its own satellite (*China Times*, 12 December 1990, p. 3; 28 March 1991, p. 17). Thus, in a remarkably short period of time the government had moved from prohibiting the technology to promoting it.

However, the policy was not yet one of completely open skies. Since C band dishes – nick-named the 'middle ear' or 'big ear' according to their size – could receive five channels from China, the government was reluctant to legalize them. The government argued this was necessary to prevent people from receiving classified national secrets and endangering national security. Ironically, government agencies, such as Ministry of Foreign Affairs and the GIO, private hotels, and even the three television stations, all installed illegal dishes to receive satellite programmes. Yet, after the government allowed individual citizens to visit China in 1987, there was no reason to prohibit people from watching the Chinese programmes via satellite. As such, the 'Provisional Articles' (1991) and the 'Methods of Regulating Telecommunications during Periods of Mobilisation and Pacification of Insurrection' (1973) governing the use of C-band reception dishes were abolished. While the new 1992 regulations prohibit private citizens from owning C-band dishes, institutions, groups, and tourist hotels can apply for the installation of C-band dishes (*China Evening Times*, 1 August 1992, p. 1).

According to the MOC in August 1992, Taiwan was under the footprint of DFHZ-A1, A2, A3, GORIZONT-A3, PALAPA-B2, AsiaSat-1, INTELSAT-

F3, and BS-3B. With a C-band dish and authorized decoder, Taiwanese viewers could receive 26 channels (*China Evening Times*, 1 August 1992, p. 1). Channels are increasing all the time, but those currently available include well-known satellite television channels such as NHK I and II, Wowow (Japan), CCTV (China), ABC, CBS, NSC, CNN, ESPN (U.S.A.), five channels from Star TV (H.K.), two channels of TV3S (H.K. and Taiwan), and other channels from Indonesia, Malaysia, Australia and Russia, etc.

As for the satellite project proposed by MOC and NSC, unfortunately they have had a bumpy start. According to the MOC, the Taiwanese government could establish a private joint company with American based Pacific Satellite Holding Incorporated in Papua New Guinea. This new company would be called the 'Pacific Satellite Corporation'. Taiwan would have 30% of the shares and an exclusive ground station. In addition, after the company launched its first satellites, Taiwan could have four transponders for communications use. However, after two years' negotiation, the Taiwanese ministry of Foreign Affairs found that Pacific Satellite Holding Incorporated was nothing but a 'paper company' (*China Times*, 28 March 1991, p. 17). This fact shattered the hope of MOC to lead the development of satellite technology, which was subsequently turned over to the NSC.

As for the NSC, there were different problems. According to a project proposed in May 1988 to the Executive Yuan, the NSC was asking for 10 billion NT dollars to launch a low orbit satellite within five years for scientific use. The project would be under the charge of foreign satellite companies and Taiwanese engineers, with the hope that the NSC would acquire satellite technology through the co-operative venture. The project immediately resulted in serious debate in the Legislative Yuan (Li, 1990, pp. 26–30). Since the NSC did not have complete research before it proposed the project, there were suspicions among legislators that President Lee Teng Hui was behind the scheme and that the real motives behind the scheme were less than transparent (Yang, 1991, pp. 38–40). After significant public opposition to the project and the refusal of the American government to transfer satellite technology to Taiwan, the project was quashed (*China Times*, 17 October 1990, p. 1).

Taiwan's policy towards satellite communications was further hastened along at the beginning of the 1990s by the regional broadcasting initiatives of the new Hong Kong-based Star TV. The popularity of the regional broadcaster worried many scholars about the political cultural implications of over-reliance on foreign satellite broadcasting. These political and cultural concerns dove-tailed auspiciously with revised NSC plans to chart an independent path for Taiwan in the area of satellite technology. According to a revised NSC plan, Taiwan would develop three satellites – one for scientific use and two for communications purposes – over 15 years, utilize a larger budget of 13.6 billion NT and obtain the assistance of a U.S. company for the launching of the satellites. This coalescing of scientific with political, cultural and economic considerations proved compelling, as the Executive Yuan and the Legislative Yuan offered their approval to the projects (*China Times*, 12 December 1990, p. 3; *United Daily News*, 15 April 1992, p. 1; *Central Daily News International Edition*, 30 April 1995, p. 7, *Central Daily News International Edition*, 2 July 1995, p. 7, *Central Daily News International Edition*, 14 July 1995, p. 7).

In another project, Taiwan and Singapore have agreed to spend 215 million dollars to launch a communication satellite in 1997. The satellite will provide for radio and television broadcasting and the establishment of one terrestrial receiving station each in Taiwan and Singapore (*Central Daily News International Edition*, 2 June 1995, p. 15). This project stems from Taiwan's unique status as a country and the People's Republic of China (PRC). Because of this unique situation, most Western countries very carefully consider the reactions of the PRC before entering into weapons and technology transfers to Taiwan. Without recognition in the United Nations, or the international body governing the distribution of orbital and spectrum resources used for satellite communications, the International Telecommunications Union, it is impossible for Taiwan to develop a fully independent satellite program. It is for this reason that Taiwan has had to co-operate with Singapore or the United States on the above mentioned and other satellite projects.

These factors, as well as some of the internal political conditions of the country noted above, mean that it has been very difficult for Taiwan to develop a comprehensive communication policy, especially with respect to satellites. However, a variety of economic and other factors have forced the government to respond. Domestic television operators were initially hopeful that the government would regulate the reception of satellite signals, while obviously cable and satellite operators sought different regulatory responses. To date, the most interesting response has been the commissioning of Fu Jin University to research the state of satellite law internationally, a task that was completed in 1994 and expected to inform the development of a draft Satellite Law to be introduced by 1997. In the meantime, commercial pressures have pushed the MOC to open up the uplink of programming transmission in early 1995 (*The Great China News*, 12 December 1993, p. 1; *Central Daily News International Edition*, 19 December 1994, p. 3; *Central Daily News International Edition*, 15 February 1995, p. 6).

The deregulation of broadcasting systems

After establishing new regulatory regimes for the new electronic media of cable and satellite television, the government began to liberalize its policies towards traditional broadcasting systems. As a first step, on 1 September 1994 the GIO announced that it would accept applications for community, local and national radio stations. The GIO's decision was significantly tied to the upcoming elections for positions of governor of Taiwan and for the position of mayor in the cities of Taipei and Kaoshiung. At the time of its decision there were around 40 illegal radio stations broadcasting in support of the DPP, New Party and a variety of independent candidates. After 45 years of illegal radio broadcasting in Taiwan, the primary goal of the GIO was to bring many of the stations under the umbrella of a legitimate legal regime while eliminating the others. Through this policy, the 'GIO issued 46 community radio station licences and 24 local radio station licences. As a result, there are now 103 radio stations . . . In addition, there are still 53 vacancies for community radio stations, 28 vacancies for local radio stations, six vacancies for FM radio stations, and one vacancy for a national radio station. In the future, there will be 191 radio stations in Taiwan if all the vacancies are fulfilled' (*Central Daily News International Edition*, 1 January 1995, p. 7).

Since the government had provided a legal channel for application, GIO strongly warned illegal operators that it would confiscate their equipment and stop their broadcasts. The announcement immediately acquired support, especially among the illegal radio stations operated by the New Party. The numbers of illegal radio stations decreased from 40 to 30 and their broadcasting time shrank from 24 hours to three or five hours a day (*Central Daily News International Edition*, 1 January 1995, p. 7).

At the same time, the GIO also considered deregulating television. Shortly after announcing its new radio policy, the GIO was informed by the MOC that the MND would release several channels for television broadcasting during 1994 and 1995. The GIO decided to use these channels to establish two national television stations and six local television stations in the north, middle, south, Ilan, Hualien, and Taitung regions – a policy that would establish local television broadcasting in Taiwan for the first time. An application for a fourth national television station by the People's Television Station was accepted by the GIO at the beginning of 1994. Though it has deep relations with DPP, its General Manager E. M. Ho, the former deputy General Manager in TTV, alleged that it would run the television station independently. The application process for the remaining national television station was to begin in September 1995. The six local television stations will be established later after a period of public consultations (*United Evening News*, 22 August 1994, p. 1; *Central Daily News International Edition*, 4 June 1995, p. 7; *Central Daily News International Edition*, 18 June 1995, p. 3; *Central Daily News International Edition*, 6 July 1995, p. 3).

Conclusion

After a long period of fighting and evolution, the government has loosened its grip over the electronic media. As a result, a new media environment is taking root in Taiwan on the basis of 103 radio stations, 88 vacant radio frequencies awaiting licensing, five terrestrial television stations (including the existing three television stations and the two new planned television stations), one public television which does not operate yet, more than 300 cable television stations which have been in the process of licensing since mid-1995 and more than 10 domestic satellite television stations.

It is clear that media deregulation (radio and television) and regulation of cable and satellite are the consequence of what was originally a very unhealthy media system. These changes have also been triggered by external circumstances and political considerations, driven mainly by the explosion in broadcasting by satellite communication in the Asian region. The features of the Taiwanese response to these developments that seem to stand out most are:

1. Like most countries, Taiwanese media regulations always lag behind developments in communications technology, with the government typically adopting reactive and rearguard policies that do little more than confirm what already exists.

2. The tradition of top down media policy has been destabilized and ultimately undermined by the DPP, new media and cable and satellite operators whose interests usually do not correspond with those of the government.
3. After years of struggle, the major victors in the battle over communication policy in Taiwan are the opposition DPP, applicants for the new national, local and cable television and radio licenses, and citizens who are now afforded more choice.
4. Unlike the usual pattern of regulatory liberalization and commercialization eroding the public service media, in Taiwan these forces have given birth to public television, although it is clear that the private sector media will continue to dominate the Taiwan's media landscape.

To most audiences, cable television, satellite television, and public television are but different variations of the same thing. For most, more commercial channels will mainly mean more of the same programming fare rather than a real expansion in the range of choices available. The real challenge lying ahead is to use public television, cable and satellite services to serve the interests of local areas, interests not well reflected in the traditional commercial media as well as the goal of linguistic and cultural diversity.

Rather than further expanding the quantitative flow of information through increased availability of hardware, as proposed by the communications satellite project, the real task is to use the media to make a qualitative difference in the types of information available, the interests represented and the development of alternative forms of small-scale and/or point to point communications. In order to achieve such goals, a comprehensive, forward-looking communications policy is needed that doesn't merely react to new technologies but serves the development of not only point-to-multipoint services, such as broadcasting, distribution of services to cable system, broadcast data network and video teleconferencing, but also multipoint-to-point services, such as credit card verification, field office to home office communications, remote data collection, and monitoring.

Note

1. The VCR was introduced by Sony in 1976 at a price of $1500 (U.S.). Then, one U.S. dollar equalled 40 NT dollars, making the price of the VCR about 60,000 NT dollars in 1976. Given this price there were only 961 VCRs in the entire country during 1976 (Wang and Chung, 1988, p. 210).

References

Books:

Broadcasting and Television Industry Development Foundation Report: I (1988) Broadcasting and Television Industry Development Foundation, Taipei.
Chang, Li. (1990) *R.O.C. Public Television Research*, Unpublished MA Thesis, the Graduate School of Journalism of Culture University.
Cheng, Jei-Cheng (1988) *Examine Communication Media*, Commonwealth Magazine, Taipei.

Chi, Ching-Yao (1986) R.O.C. Public Television Development. In *Radio and Television Magazine*, Vol. 50, October.

Feng, Chien-San (1993) Public Television. In Jeng, Jui-Cheng (ed.) *Media Deregulation*, the report of Cheng-Hsueh, Taipei.

Hsueh, Cheng-Hsiung (1988) *Media Dominance: Examine Taiwanese Television News*, Unpublished MA Thesis: the Graduate School of Sociology of Taiwan University.

Lee, Chin-Chuan (1987) *Media Imperialism*, Jiu-Ta, Taipei.

Lee, Tsung-Li (1985) *The Study of the R.O.C.'s Policy in Reaction to Japanese DBS*, Unpublished MA Thesis: the Graduate School of Journalism of Fu Hsin Kang College.

Li, H. L. (1990) When Will the Satellite be Launched? In *Business Weekly*, 16 April, pp. 26–30.

Liu, Yu-Li (1992) *Scarcity of Spectrum, Political Access, and Broadcast Autonomy: the Open Broadcasting Channel Debate in Taiwan*, Unpublished Ph.D. dissertation: Indiana University.

Peng, Bonnie (1994) The Regulation of New Media in Taiwan. In *Asian Journal of Communication*, Vol. 4, No. 2, pp. 97–110.

Radio and Television Yearbook (1976) Radio and Television Magazine, Taipei.

Radio and Television Yearbook (1990) Radio and Television Magazine, Taipei.

Sun, Pu-Yuan (1992) Who are the Three Private Shareholders in CTS? In *Wealth Magazine*, Vol. 118, January.

Sung, Mei-Chin (1991) *Excellence Magazine*, October, pp. 106–9.

Wang, G. (1993) Satellite television and the future of broadcast television in the Asia Pacific. Paper presented at the Conference on Communication, Technology and Development: Alternatives for Asia, AMIC, Kuala Lumpar, Malaysia, June 25–27, 1993.

Wen, Man-Ying (1987) Facing the General Managers of the Three Domestic Television Stations. In *Global Views Monthly*, April.

Wen, Shiu-Chi (1993) Taiwanese Illegal Media. In Jeng, Jui-Cheng (ed.) *Media Deregulation*, the Report of Cheng-Hsueh, Taipei.

Williamson, Mark (1988) Broadcasting by Satellite: Some Technical Considerations. In Negrine, Ralph (ed.) *Satellite Broadcasting: the Politics and Implications of the New Media*, Routledge, London, pp. 23–48.

Yang, Chin-Chih (1991) *The Role of Satellite Communications for National Development in Developing Countries: the Case of Taiwan*, Unpublished MA thesis: the Centre for Mass Communication Research, University of Leicester.

Newspapers and periodicals:

Central Daily News International Edition, 17 July 1993, p. 2.
Central Daily News International Edition, 19 December 1994, p. 3.
Central Daily News International Edition, 1 January 1995, p. 7.
Central Daily News International Edition, 15 February 1995, p. 6.
Central Daily News International Edition, 30 April 1995, p. 7.
Central Daily News International Edition, 5 May 1995, p. 7.
Central Daily News International Edition, 2 June 1995, p. 7.
Central Daily News International Edition, 4 June 1995, p. 7.
Central Daily News International Edition, 18 June 1995, p. 3.
Central Daily News International Edition, 20 June 1995, p. 3.
Central Daily News International Edition, 2 July 1995, p. 7.
Central Daily News International Edition, 6 July 1995, p. 3.
Central Daily News International Edition, 10 July 1995, p. 7.
Central Daily News International Edition, 14 July 1995, p. 7.

China Times, 1 September 1990, p. 38.
China Times, 17 October 1990, p. 1.
China Times, 12 December 1990, p. 3.
China Times, 28 March 1991, p. 17.
China Times, 7 July 1993, p. 30.
China Times, 13 July 1993, p. 1.
China Evening Times, 1 August 1992, p. 1.
Independence Evening Post, 28 July 1987, p. 3.
Independence Morning Post, 16 October 1990, p. 4.
Liberty Times, 27 March 1989, p. 3.
Min Sheng Pao, 15 May 1990, p. 10.
Min Sheng Pao, 15 January 1992, p. 10.
The Great China News, 14 January 1992, p. 3.
The Great China News, 15 January 1992, p. 3.
The Great China News, 12 December 1993, p. 1.
United Daily News, 7 February 1980, p. 4.
United Daily News, 27 October 1990, p. 3.
United Daily News, 1 December 1989, p. 3.
United Daily News, 13 September 1990, p. 3.
United Daily News, 25 September 1990, p. 3.
United Daily News, 8 December 1990, p. 3.
United Daily News, 15 April 1992, p. 1.
United Evening News, 22 August 1994, p. 1.

10

National responses and accessibility to STAR TV in Asia

Joseph Man Chan

From Levy, M. R. (ed.) (1994) *Journal of Communication*, Oxford University Press, New York, Vol. 44, No. 3, pp. 112–31.

AsiaSat 1, launched in April 1990, provided the first privately owned satellite communication network covering all of Asia. The satellite is owned by Hong Kong's Hutchison Whampoa conglomerate, Britain's Cable and Wireless, and China's CITIC Technology Corporation. STAR TV, initially a 50:50 joint venture between Hutchison Whampoa and its chairman Ka-shing Li, sold 64% of its stakes to Rupert Murdoch's News Corp. in July 1993. Leasing 12 transponders from AsiaSat 1, STAR TV was granted a license by the Hong Kong government in December 1990.

Based in Hong Kong, STAR TV launched its free-to-air service in October 1991. The northern and southern footprints of AsiaSat 1 cover 38 nations, from Egypt to Japan and from Indonesia to Siberia, capturing a potential audience of 2.7 billion, half of the world's population. STAR TV initially aimed to attract the top five per cent of this enormous audience: the well-educated, the wealthy, the professional, and the English-speaking (Fredenburg, 1991).

[. . .]

STAR TV offers a total of five channels, including thematic channels of music videos (MTV), sports, news (BBC World Service Television), and family entertainment, as well as a channel of broadcasts in Mandarin Chinese, all running on a 24-hour basis. With the exception of the Chinese channel (which broadcasts programs produced in Hong Kong, Japan, Taiwan, China, and elsewhere), the other four channels carry mainly Western programs obtained through contractual suppliers or the international market. The English BBC news channel is the only one that provides partial translation into Mandarin. The aforementioned five channels are full STAR TV services. Its southern beam carries an additional affiliated channel, the ZEE TV, a Hindi general entertainment service set up by an Indian partnership of STAR TV. [. . .]

From STAR TV's debut in late 1991 until November 1993, the number of households that can receive its signal has increased to more than 40 million, with the majority concentrated in the People's Republic of China, India, and Taiwan. Table 10.1 sums up the state of penetration and the national responses in selected countries. [. . .]

Table 10.1. Penetration and regulation of STAR TV in selected counties in Asia as of November 1993

Country	STAR TV-capable households (% of total TV households)	Mode of control/Dish reception	Network (cable or MMDS)
People's Republic of China	30,363,000 (22%)	Dish may legally receive AsiaSat 1 signals with license.	Not legal or illegal, controlled by administrative rules; rudimentary cable TV widespread; cable systems growing fast; carriage of STAR TV quite common in both.
Hong Kong	331,000 (21%)	Both TVRO and SMATV are legal.	Pay-TV by MMDS introduced in late 1993; carriage of STAR TV to be worked out.
India	7,278,000 (25%)	License required.	Rudimentary cable TV; illegal but widespread, carrying STAR TV.
Indonesia	50,000 (< 1%)	TVRO legal; license needed for SMATV. Data unavailable.	No cable TV; license needed for SMATV.
Israel	621,000 (49%)		Cable TV legal; carrying STAR TV.
Japan	Very limited	TVRO and SMATV legal for Ku-band;	Cable TV legal but not carrying STAR TV. C-band undefined.
Malaysia	Very limited	Restricted to royalty and VIPs.	Subscription TV being set up by government.
Pakistan	77,000 (4%)	License required but policy is widely ignored.	Rudimentary cable TV growing, some carrying STAR TV.
Philippines	187,000 (5%)	Regulation nonexistent.	Cable TV legal, carrying STAR TV.
Singapore	Very limited	Legal only for financial institutions.	Subscription TV legal, but not carrying STAR TV.
South Korea	184,000 (2%)	TVRO and SMATV allowed.	Cable TV being set up by government.
Taiwan	2,376,000 (46%)	C-band dish reception legalized in August 1992.	Cable TV used to be illegal but widespread and carrying STAR TV; legalized in August 1993.
Thailand	143,000 (2%)	TVRO legal, license required; SMATV allowed in hotels and condominiums.	MMDS network legal in Bangkok only.

Sources: Compiled from STAR TV (1993, 1994); Scott (1990, 1991); Ingelbrecht (1992); and staff (*Asiaweek*) (1991b). The penetration figures are based on surveys, direct counts, and projections by Frank Small & Associates Marketing and Research Consultants, Hong Kong.
Note: Total STAR TV-capable households in the above surveyed countries: 41,610,000.

It should be noticed that the penetration figures reported in Table 10.1 represent only the number of households that are able to receive STAR TV. Viewership figures, such as television ratings and shares are not available. [. . .]

Although queries can be raised over the accuracy of such projections, because of limited sample areas and the huge size of the projected regions, the penetration figures should give a rough indication of accessibility to STAR TV in different countries and provide some basis for comparing accessibility across nations.

[. . .]

An examination of Table 10.1 leads us to categorize the national responses to STAR TV in Asia into four main types: virtual suppression, regulated openness, illegal openness and suppressive openness. The demarcation criteria are the nature of national policy on satellite television and the state of policy implementation. An analysis of each type follows.

Virtual suppression

This response is exemplified by Singapore and Malaysia, where reception of STAR TV is legally banned for ideological, cultural, and political reasons. Only the very privileged are allowed access. In the case of Malaysia, only the royalty and the most powerful people in society are able to freely access STAR TV. The ban is imposed for fear that uncontrolled information from outside may disrupt social, racial, and religious harmony. In Singapore, only financial institutions can set up TVROs to receive STAR TV and other satellite television services. This exemption is made to maintain the competitiveness of Singapore as a financial centre in spite of the government's perceived interest in maintaining tight ideological control.

Regulated openness

Hong Kong and the Philippines belong to this ideal type, as do, to a greater or lesser degree, Thailand, South Korea, Israel, Indonesia, and Japan. These countries open themselves up to STAR TV but retain control over redistribution by SMATV, cable network, or other media, thus establishing a compromise that allows entry of STAR TV but at the same time maintains some control over the signal's distribution. In the long run, this policy is likely to be the one most preferred by governments in Asia. In the case of Hong Kong, STAR TV can currently be received by TVRO and SMATV. While the Philippines has no regulations controlling TVRO and SMATV, it allows the operation of cable television networks that can carry STAR TV. MTV is also rebroadcast through a UHF channel in Manila.

Illegal openness

This response is represented by Taiwan and India, which have surfaced as two of STAR TV's largest markets. In these countries, STAR TV is easily accessible through SMATV or cable networks that proliferate in spite of legal restrictions. [. . .]

Although Taiwan finally legalized dish reception to C-band satellite signals in August 1992 after years of illegal practice, the redistribution of STAR TV by cable network remains a violation of a law that prohibits the establishment of cable networks altogether. Periodic crackdowns by the government on underground networks have had only temporary dampening effects. When an underground channel has reached a critical penetration, the government cannot help but acquiesce to reality. With the passage in August 1993 of a new law governing cable television, STAR TV will be carried by the new cable networks being formed, thus repositioning Taiwan in a state of regulated openness.

A similar situation exists in India, where dish reception is legal with licenses, but cable redistribution is technically illegal. By the archaic Indian Telegraph Act of 1885, it is against the law to dig across a road to lay cables without the permission of the Telecom Commission. To bypass the law, the cable operators in India run their lines over the streets by means of branches and lamp posts. Hampered by a lack both of resources and of the will to police the phenomenal growth of such rudimentary networks, the Telecom Commission is reported to have shown signs of resignation (Pratrap, 1991).

Suppressive openness

While suppressive openness sounds like a contradiction in terms, it may be seen as a halfway point between virtual suppression and illegal openness in terms of the relative social difficulty one has to overcome in order to access STAR TV. While suppressive openness shares with virtual suppression the intention to fend off foreign ideology, it lacks the latter's effective control, resulting in a subdued form of illegal openness.

China, the largest potential market of STAR TV, is the major representative of this mode of control. For fear of ideological influence from the West, China generally forbids the reception of all external television. However, STAR TV is known to have been picked up by dishes that belong to collectives and by rudimentary and elaborate cable networks, registering a total penetration of more than 30 million households by late 1993.

A factor that contributes to this phenomenal penetration is the relaxation of social control resulting from the sociopolitical and economic reforms since the late 1970s. Added to this relaxed control is China's huge size and population, which make it difficult for the central authorities to monitor the reception of satellite television. The launching of AsiaSat 1 has unintentionally provided a pretext for some Chinese institutions to receive STAR TV. This is because AsiaSat 1 is also beaming signals for a television station shared by the Chinese provinces of Yunnan and Guizhou. [. . .] Since it is legal, with the proper license, to receive AsiaSat 1 signals, institutions and some cable networks can therefore access STAR TV while claiming to be tuning in to provincial television.[1] Even some related government agencies are split over the issue of banning dish reception because of differing vested interests. While the propaganda departments are for ideological control, the technical departments that manufacture the dishes advocate a more liberal reception policy (Wang, 1993). Meanwhile, more Chinese provinces and cities are setting up subscription television, which may provide a long-term redistribution network for STAR TV. For instance, a cable network in Wuhan, a joint venture between Hong Kong and mainland China, offers all but the news channel of STAR TV.

All these factors are conducive to transforming China from a state of suppressive openness to one of illegal openness. [. . .] Redistribution has been interrupted only when the Chinese Communist Party has waged occasional ideological campaigns. By 1993, watching Hong Kong television had become so commonplace and widespread in Guangdong that major Hong Kong broadcasters sponsored ratings research in the province. The ratings reports indicate that Hong Kong television attracts more viewers in the Chinese cities and counties near Hong Kong than does Chinese television (Chan, 1994).

Major determinants of STAR TV accessibility

[. . .]

Regulation policy

Broadcasting regulation is the most decisive factor affecting accessibility to satellite television. Certainly not all Asian nations have the same restrictive controls over satellite television; some are more open than others, resulting in the four types of control identified above. But it is accurate to say that most Asian governments cite 'cultural invasion' and 'social stability' as reasons for the control of foreign satellite television. They are afraid that alien values and outside information may erode traditional and indigenous culture and disrupt racial, religious, and political harmony in their societies. In addition, they often have a vested interest in maintaining the status quo of the television industry, which is generally heavily regulated, with ownership and control monopolized by the state. For some governments, broadcast television is an important source of revenue, as well as an agent of sociopolitical control. Even in the few Asian nations where terrestrial broadcasters are commercially owned, these broadcasters tend to pressure their governments to shield them from competition from the sky. The logical measure for these governments is to manage information by restricting its inflow through satellite television. [. . .]

Competition from terrestrial television

In countries where satellite reception is forbidden, the impact of terrestrial television on accessibility to satellite television is not manifest because of its protected status. While good terrestrial television tends to suppress the demand for alternative programming, be it from satellite television or from other sources, unsatisfactory terrestrial television opens a potential market for satellite television.

In contrast, in an open country the competitiveness of terrestrial television is the crucial factor in determining whether people will tune in to satellite television. Terrestrial broadcast television often enjoys the loyalty of an audience that tends to prefer its locally oriented programming to that of satellite television, which tends to please a wider audience with the lowest-common-denominator approach.

In an open market like Europe, the success or failure of satellite television, according to Collins (1990), depends largely on its ability to deliver TV programming that has an equal or superior cost-benefit ratio to competing terrestrial services. Viewers will turn to non-home productions only when they find foreign programs to be of higher technical quality, more interesting content, and greater variety. In Asia, where local programming is generally of low quality and limited choice, STAR TV often commands a more competitive position. In many countries, STAR TV is meeting a market demand rather than having to create one. [. . .]

Technological innovations

Breakthrough in satellite transmission and reception technology are conducive to increased accessibility to satellite television. Compression technology, for example, will greatly increase the channel capacity of AsiaSat 1. In addition, transmission of STAR TV programs with multiple soundtracks is now technologically feasible. Each transponder can be rigged to carry up to six audio tracks. Up to now, the heavy cost incurred in dubbing or simultaneous interpretation has prevented STAR TV from offering extensive multilingual service. Only brief hourly segments of the BBC news channel are translated into Mandarin. STAR TV will overcome the language and cultural barriers more successfully if it can offer dubbing or simultaneous interpretation on a greater scale.

When dishes measuring one foot or smaller are available for receiving signals from STAR TV, policing will become virtually impossible. The trend toward a lowered reception cost will lead to the growth of satellite television. As shown in Table 10.1, penetration is high where STAR TV can be redistributed through a cable or other kind of network. The programming demands of the cable networks currently mushrooming in Asia will finance the proliferation of satellite television.

Linguistic barriers

Language diversity poses a barrier to the spread of a regional satellite television like STAR TV, particularly in Asia where a wide range of languages exists. Excluding STAR TV's associate Hindi channel, STAR TV has one Mandarin-language channel and four English-language channels, one of which, the BBC World Service Television, carries partial Chinese translation. Sports and music channels broadcast in English do not require advanced linguistic skills on the part of the audience. However, language comprehension is essential to channels offering dramas, movies, and information. English is emerging as the language of the rich and the educated in Asia and throughout the world (Findahl, 1989), and this is clearly the most important factor in STAR TV's choice of English as its major broadcasting language. However, to wide and deepen its penetration, STAR TV needs to overcome this barrier by providing multilingual channels. [. . .]

It should be noted that Mandarin Chinese is spoken by more people than any other language in the world. About half of the population served by STAR TV is Chinese. Concentrated on the mainland and scattered in other Asian countries, the Chinese constitute the largest potential audience.

Recognizing this, STAR TV dedicated one of its channels to Mandarin-language programming. Once the language barrier is overcome, limitations of accessibility in China can be attributed mainly to the state's restrictive policies. Satellite television programming directed at a specific language group greatly enhances competitiveness with terrestrial television, as evidenced by the success of STAR TV's Mandarin channel in Taiwan.

The prohibitive effect of the linguistic barrier is evidenced by cases like Indonesia. Thailand, and South Korea. In these countries, satellite reception methods such as TVRO, SMATV, or MMDS are generally allowed. However, the penetration of STAR TV is insignificant in each country. This situation is linked to the fact that only a small proportion of each country's population understands English or Mandarin, the languages now used by STAR TV. [. . .]

Programming and cultural gaps

The programming of satellite television in relation to program types, quality, variety, language, and schedule all affects its competitive position in the range of media choices in a nation. Although STAR TV tends to fill its channels with low-cost programs acquired through the international market, these products are quite competitive for reasons mentioned earlier. If STAR TV wants to compete with the strong terrestrial programming in places like Japan and Hong Kong, it will need to upgrade its existing free programs or offer specialized subscription television services.

Cultural differences among nations call for different censorship standards that set the parameters for satellite television's programming policies. Asia is noted for its diversity in religion, creeds, and codes of behaviour. In Singapore, for instance, even magazines like *Cosmopolitan* have been banned for advocating 'promiscuous' values in the last decade; televised permissiveness has been strictly forbidden (Stewart, 1992). For similar reasons, the government of Pakistan restricts the screening of any programming that could be seen as titillating, including even fashion models' walk on the runway (Staff, 1991a). In contrast, this author has noted that kissing and fondling are allowed on Japanese and Hong Kong television.

STAR TV tries not to violate the national regulations, creeds, and beliefs of various countries or to show any ideological or political bias. [. . .]

Undoubtedly, this tension creates constraints over its programming policy. A case in point is the decision of STAR TV's MTV channel not to screen Madonna's video 'Erotica' as its American counterpart did in late hours. As D. Atyeo, chief of STAR TV's MTV, explained: '[Erotica] is obviously designed to shock and outrage, and we're here to entertain. When you're dealing with a wide range of religions, cultures and beliefs it's hard to see not offending someone and we're very conscious of this' (Dykes, 1992, p. 25). [. . .]

In the short run, STAR TV has to take the cultural gaps among nations into consideration when making programming policies. In the long run, cultural differences will be less of a problem as cultural homogenization, especially among the Asian middle class, intensifies. How this cultural homogenization may occur is discussed further in the conclusion.

Financing

Accessibility to satellite television is linked indirectly to its financing, upon which its very survival and competitiveness are based. The two major sources of revenue for satellite television are regional or global advertising and subscriptions. With the increasing integration of the world economy and the growth of multinational advertising agencies, global campaigns for some universal products are emerging. Boyle (1992) has observed that some universal products have detected 'a worldwide convergence of consumer psychographics that is happening in tandem with the building of the infrastructure of the global electronic village' (p. 143). This scenario represents a somewhat futuristic view of global marketing.

[. . .]

Writing in 1990 on the advertising finance of satellite television in Europe, Collins passed the verdict that 'no trans-national advertising market exists' (1990, p. 5). The picture began to look less gloomy when British Sky Broadcasting finally began to make a modest profit in 1992 (Nott, 1992). Despite STAR TV's success in securing commitments for US$100 million worth of advertising for 1992 and 1993, advertisers are reportedly 'slow to warm to the concept of a regional free-to-air broadcaster, particularly one that is unable to give precise viewership figures' (Schaffer, 1992, p. 15).

Subscription will be an alternative source of revenue for STAR TV when its plans of setting up pay-TV channels are implemented. It has to overcome the cost barriers and the difficulty in collecting subscriptions efficiently over the vast region of Asia. Until then, it will have to depend on advertising as its major source of revenue.

The overall health of a satellite television's financial condition depends on its investment controls as well. It is reported that STAR TV has managed to maintain a relatively low initial investment and operating cost through revenue-sharing joint ventures with program suppliers. According to one account, STAR TV 'has secured cheap programming through arrangements with MTV, the BBC, Prime Sports Network of Denver and Hong Kong's ATV. Apart from a small down payment, STAR will pay nothing for a program until it starts making money. As a result, the annual operating costs of the five channels are said to total only US$80 million' (Taylor, 1992, p. 60). Innovative business arrangements such as these are vital to reducing costs, particularly at a time when advertising and subscription income is meager.

National affluence

The affluence of a nation is positively related to the growth of its middle class, the availability of advertising revenue, and the affordability of satellite television reception, all of which are conducive to an increased accessibility to satellite television. Asian countries vary widely in their state of economic development, ranging from poor Bangladesh and Mongolia to affluent Japan and Hong Kong. The major target markets of STAR TV are in the Far East and South East, which since the 1980s has been the fastest growing area in the world. In tandem with economic growth has been the gradual formation of an educated and affluent middle class. While this middle class may be small as a proportion of the population, the sheer size of the base population has rendered it huge in absolute numbers, thus creating a lucrative market for STAR TV and other satellite television services. Dissatisfied with what are often regarded as 'dull' programs on state-run television, this middle class tends to look for alternative programming in videos and from the sky. [. . .]

Interplay of factors

All the factors described above interact and combine to determine the final accessibility of STAR TV in a country. In those countries that decide to fend off satellite television for ideological or political reasons, STAR TV is limited to an insignificant number of elite institutions and individuals. It will take time for factors like technological innovations, economic affluence, and audience demand to loosen a tight regulatory grip.
[. . .]

The interplay of all these factors is well illustrated by the case of Taiwan, which, as mentioned earlier, shows a form of illegal openness to satellite television. Officially, the Mandarin-language channel of STAR TV is targeted at all overseas Chinese in Asia. Taiwan has emerged as an important Chinese market as a result of the tight control over access that exists elsewhere. STAR TV constructs its Chinese programming package from a mix of productions from Hong Kong, mainland China, Taiwan, Japan, and elsewhere. The remarkable penetration of STAR TV in Taiwan can be attributed partly to the competitiveness of STAR TV's programs over those of the three local, government-controlled stations. This success is also a result of STAR TV's scheduling of entertainment programs during a late prime-time slot when the local stations are required by law to broadcast 'educational' or 'public affairs' programs generally regarded as boring (Fang, 1992). Currently about one-half of Taiwanese households are STAR TV-capable and Taiwan-based advertising is growing rapidly. It will be interesting to see how the terrestrial broadcasters will react to this erosion of their audience share.

Hong Kong, the home base of STAR TV, provides an illustration of the basic forces at work in a different setting (Lau, 1992; Lee, 1992). In the course of making policy on satellite television, the terrestrial television broadcasters of Hong Kong, like their counterparts elsewhere, demanded that policy regulators should protect them from competition from the sky. At the same time, the potential operators of subscription television in Hong Kong put pressure on the government not to let STAR TV undermine its develop-ment. In response to these cross pressures, the Hong Kong government granted the license to STAR TV in 1990 with two conditions attached: the first was that STAR TV, during its first three years of service, could not broadcast in Cantonese, the dialect spoken in Hong Kong. The second was that STAR TV could not charge subscription fees for its service until 1993. [. . .]

In 1993, STAR TV was scheduled to start broadcasting in Cantonese on music, sports, and news channels and to launch four subscription channels. In order to protect the subscription network started in the same year,

Cantonese was again banned on STAR TV's planned pay channels for the first three years of operation. In addition, the government intended to require that the operator of the subscription network must carry STAR TV's pay channels. Indeed, Wharf Cable, operator of the subscription network, had agreed to be the sole distributor of STAR TV when it received the license in 1993. All these regulatory moves represent compromises made among diverging social forces. The case of Hong Kong shows the importance of the interactions among language, regulation, technology, local broadcasters, and network operators in defining the environment of STAR TV.

There are signs indicating that China will move from a state of suppressive openness into one of illegal openness. As mentioned earlier, relaxed social control during the reform years and the difficulty in enforcing administrative or legal restrictions in a large and populous country are conducive to the emergence of a state of illegal openness. Given the Chinese government's deep concern for ideological control, it is unlikely that accessibility to STAR TV on the mainland will increase steadily or without setbacks. The evolutionary path is likely to be interrupted by occasional crackdowns, to be followed by a growth spurt each time, until the audience size reaches a point beyond effective policing. Indeed, in early 1994 Beijing has been trying to tighten control over unauthorized reception of foreign satellite television. How effective this restrictive policy will be and how long it will last remain to be seen.

[. . .]

Implications for the internationalization of television

The development of satellite television is part of the general process of the internationalization of television, which includes program trades, diffusion of program formats, joint ventures, and the like (Chan, 1994; Negrine and Papathanassopoulos, 1991). Internationalization as such has raised concerns about the erosion and domination of indigenous cultures by an alien one. In much of the world, the perception of a threat of 'cultural imperialism' is particularly strong when satellite television's programming originates in the West.

While the bulk of STAR TV's existing programs are made in the West, it broadcasts a variety of Asian programs as well. STAR TV is popularizing some Asian anchors, artists, singers, and productions. Blending Western programs with regional elements has been noted as a programming trend (Wang, 1993). Consequently, cultural homogenization resulting from STAR TV is taking place not only at the global level but also at the regional level. As if in tandem with the growing economic integration among Asian nations, a regional identity and consciousness is in the making.

Whether cultural homogenization at the regional level is less undesirable than at the global level and whether cultural homogenization at any level at all is undesirable are value questions that should be dealt with elsewhere. It should be noted that while STAR TV may not be the cultural integrator of Asia, it has indeed initiated a long process of cultural integration at the regional level by making the same television programs, Asian or Western, available to Asians across national boundaries.

[. . .] The advent of STAR TV will increase the pressure toward the general trend of deregulation in broadcasting, thereby lessening the role of government broadcasters. Indeed, it will become very difficult, if not impossible, to police the reception of satellite television when technological advances further miniaturize the required dish. [. . .] A pragmatic response by nations would be to establish controls over the redistribution of satellite television and to increase the competitiveness of local television by upgrading its quality and increasing its variety. As Hoffman-Riem (1988) has maintained, the solution is not in impairing 'the flow of information and making society inaccessible for new media, but by safeguarding an independent communication infrastructure and fostering the ability to respond to externally conveyed communication in such a way that national interests are preserved' (p. 269). [. . .]

Breakdown of the prior consent principle

STAR TV has set an Asian precedent that potentially defies the 'prior consent' principle that the World Administrative Radio Conference and the United Nations adopted for controlling signal spillovers. By this principle, direct television broadcasting should not cross national boundaries without the prior consent of the affected countries (Fisher, 1990; Lau, 1992). While some countries still find the impact of STAR TV to be too insignificant for serious concern, others have adopted either an open or restricted policy toward it.

So far, no country has asked the Hong Kong government to limit the coverage of STAR TV by appealing to the prior consent principle; nor has any nation raised the issue of the possible infringement of information sovereignty. Japan is reported to have 'serious concern' over STAR TV's broadcasting into the country (Hughes, 1991). However, an official at Japan's Ministry of Posts and Telecommunications has stated that his government realizes that it is impossible to penalize STAR TV in any meaningful way. In effect, this leaves regulation of the international flow of information via STAR TV in the hands of national governments and information ministries rather than through international negotiations. If the virtually mute response to STAR TV on the international level continues, it will serve as a tacit recognition of the breakdown of the prior consent principle.

What facilitates the tacit recognition of this breakdown is interesting. Three plausible reasons come to mind:

1. Hong Kong, STAR TV's home state, is too small and too apolitical a city to prompt an outcry of 'cultural invasion.' Other Asian states with histories of imperial reigns would not so easily escape such a charge. If Japan were the country of origin of STAR TV, the responses from its Asian neighbours, particularly those who were victims of past Japanese military activity, would likely be similar to the South Korean government's hostile reaction to the spillover of Japan's NHK. Indeed, the acquisition of STAR TV in 1993 by a Western media giant like News Corp. has already aroused anti-imperialist sentiments among some government officials in Malaysia, China, India, and other countries.

2. Generally, the impact of STAR TV on national media-cultural systems has not yet been strongly felt, and so its suppression or control is not high on most governments' priority lists. [. . .]
3. Some governments realize that technological advance will soon make it almost impossible to enforce legal restrictions on satellite television reception. [. . .]

Emerging systems

To some nations, STAR TV is a threat; to others, it represents a challenge. While it is unrealistic to place hope in getting the host country of satellite television to abide by the prior consent principle, a protective policy can only buy time for terrestrial television. The pressure from regional satellite television will increase as STAR TV expands its influence and when other competing satellite television services emerge. In fact, several consortia – including one formed by Hong Kong's TVBI, Turner Broadcasting System, Australian Broadcasting, ESPN, and Home Box Office – are planning to broadcast television throughout Asia (Davies, 1993; Heath, 1993). Time does not appear to be on the side of the affected nations, which should seize this moment to shape their television industry in such a way that it will be able to compete and to grow internationally. This aim is not unachievable: domestic programs have always proven to be preferable to imported ones when they are comparable in other aspects.

Note

1. A Chinese rule, announced in mid-1990 by the Ministries of Radio, Television and Film, Public Security and National Security and passed by the State Department, requires that dish owners obtain permits effective from January 1 1991 (Gu *et al.*, 1992; Hughes, 1992).

References

Boyle, M. (1992) *The future of television,* NTC Business Books, Lincolnwood, IL.

Chan, J. M. (1994) Media internationalization in China: Processes and tensions. *Journal of Communication*, Vol. 44, No. 3, pp. 70–88.

Collins, R. (1990) *Satellite television in Western Europe*, John Libbey, London.

Davies, S. (1993, July 12) Big guns line up for a broadcast bonanza. *South China Morning Post*, p. 17.

Dykes, J. (1992, October 9) The Madonna MTV will not show. *South China Morning Post*, p. 25.

Fang, J. S. (1992, October 30) STAR TV has penetrated Taiwanese households. *Hong Kong Economic Journal*.

Findahl, O. (1989) Language in the age of satellite television. *European Journal of Communication*, Vol. 4, No. 2, pp. 133–59.

Fisher, D. (1990) *Prior consent to international direct broadcasting*, Kluwer Academic, Boston.

Fredenburg, P. (1991, October) Challenges for STAR TV. *Asian Business*, p. 12.

Gu, B., Luo, R., Lai, P., Lao, G., Tan, Z., Zhou, P. and Xia, T. (1992, April 26) Satellite television will eventually penetrate the bamboo curtain. *China Times Weekly (Asia)*, pp. 50–51.

Heath, R. (1993, June 16) Battle for viewers begins as News Corp. buys TVB stake. *South China Morning Post*, p. 1.

Hoffmann-Riem, W. (1988) International regulation of direct satellite broadcasting: Illusions and alternatives. *European Journal of Communication*, Vol. 3, No. 3, pp. 247–74.

Hughes, O. (1991, December 10) Japanese concern at satellite broadcasts. *South China Morning Post*, p. 7.

Hughes, O. (1992, January 21) Beijing pulls plug on hotel's satellite TV. *South China Morning Post*, p. 1.

Ingelbrecht, N. (1992, February) Asia switches on the set. *Asian Business*, pp. 38–41.

Lau, T. Y. (1992) From cable television to direct-broadcast satellite: Emerging policy issues in the Asia-Pacific region. *Telecommunications Policy*, Vol. 16, 7, 576–90.

Lee, P. (1992) Media and communications. In Cheng, J. and Kwong, P. (eds.) *The Other Hong Kong Report*, Chinese University of Hong Kong Press, Hong Kong, pp. 383–403.

Negrine, R. and Papathanassopoulos, S. (1991) The internationalization of television. *European Journal of Communication*, Vol. 6, No. 1, 9–32.

Nott, S. (1992, March 15) Boost from Britain for STAR TV. *South China Morning Post (The Guide)*, p. 4.

Pratrap, A. (1991, October 21) Challenge or threat. *Time (International)*, p. 51.

Shaffer, Bretigne (1992, May) Broadcast wars still inconclusive. *Asian Advertising and Marketing*, pp. 13–16.

Staff (1991a, October 25) When screens go blank. *Asiaweek*, p. 61.

Staff (1991b, October 25) Tuning in the world. *Asiaweek*, pp. 60–62.

Stewart, L. (1992, October 22) Singapore decides not to frighten the horses. *South China Morning Post*, p. 19.

Taylor, M. (1992, March 5) Celestial vision. *Far Eastern Economic Review*, pp. 59–60.

Wang, G, (1993) *Satellite television and the future of broadcast television in the Asia Pacific*. Paper presented at the Conference on Communication, Technology and Development: Alternatives for Asia, AMIC, Kuala Lumpur, Malaysia, June 25–27 1993.

Section 3

Global media actors

11

The case of the Korean airline tragedy

Laurien Alexandre

From Alexandre L. (1988) *The Voice of America: From Detente to the Reagan Doctrine*, Ablex Publishing, New Jersey, pp. 115–19.

The case of the KAL

Perhaps one of the most enlightening examples of U.S. disinformation was the manner in which the Reagan administration's public diplomacy apparatus covered the 1983 Korean Airline tragedy. The superjet Korean commercial liner (KAL 007) carrying 269 passengers was shot down by a Soviet interceptor plane after intruding deeply into Soviet airspace over the strategic Sahkalin Islands on the last day of August 1983. The U.S. government immediately launched into a full scale offensive, filling domestic and foreign airwaves with its account of the tragic events – that the airliner had strayed into Soviet territory unbeknownst to U.S. intelligence, that the place was shot down without warning by Soviet pilots, and that the Soviets knew it to be a civilian passenger airliner. The Soviet government, which unforgiveably waited a full six days before admitting its pilot's involvement, has continued to articulate the position that KAL 007 and an accompanying reconaissance plane were on an intelligence-gathering mission for the United States.

The American government orchestrated a partial exposition of that night's events, an orchestration which found uncritical reception in the nation's media. Perhaps the full and complete story will never be known, but it has become increasingly clear over time that the nation's official public diplomacy agency, the USIA and its massive broadcasting arm, the VOA, took up the crusade to absolutely discredit the Soviet Union with righteous vigour. An international anti-Soviet campaign began almost immediately. It was a simple story to tell – good versus evil, God-fearing opposing godless, truth over deceit – the stuff of prime-time drama and government disinformation. The President talked of 'acts of barbarism, born of a society that wantonly disregards individual rights and the value of human life.'[1] Congress adopted a motion accusing the USSR of 'one of the most infamous and reprehensible acts in history.'

During the days and weeks following the incident, high-ranking officials from the State Department, USIA, VOA, and the NSC met on a daily basis to develop and disseminate a global campaign designed to prove the Soviet's premeditated culpability and to refute all implications of U.S. wrongdoing.[2] The NSC's Special Planning Group on Public Diplomacy

(SPGPD), with its action officer Walter Raymond, Jr., a longtime CIA operative who had been assigned to the NSC on the strong recommendation of William Casey, played a major role in getting the propaganda operation off the ground.[3]

The USIA established a task force after the plane's downing. As stated in the 13-page report entitled *Soviet Destruction of KAL: September 1–6 1983* (and subsequent report for September 7–13), the three objectives of the planning group were: (a) 'to reinforce the impact of world reaction by emphasizing the human and multinational dimensions' (b) 'to inform peoples without ready access to commercial media via VOA,' and (c) 'to stimulate continuing international attention to the issues raised by the tragedy which concern all nations.' The task force fulfilled these objectives by successfully placing government spokespeople on domestic and foreign media outlets, by vigilantly preparing assessments of world press reaction for policy makers here and abroad, by distributing hundreds of wireless transmissions to U.S. missions around the world, and by a constant barrage of partial facts over the international airwaves. During the first weeks, six members of the task force worked around the clock to secretly prepare an audio-visual translation of the Soviet pilot's air-to-ground conversation for UN presentation on September 6th – a translation whose version was as conspicuously edited as Nixon's 18 minutes. USIA head Charles Wick called this 'one of the finest hours of VOA.'[4]

While the VOA is but one small component of the enormous public diplomacy apparatus, its role in the KAL campaign was significant. A liaison between the State Department's Korean Working Group and the VOA was established for daily consultation. Policy directives for VOA's play of unfolding events drew from both White House and State sources. Sophisticated materials refuting Soviet accounts of the tragedy were developed for VOA use in features, editorials, and news programming.

VOA transmitters were boosted far beyond normal capabilities. Two days after the downing, 56 additional hours were added to VOA's Soviet Union broadcasts. By week's end, it had increased to 90 additional weekly hours including 17 hours daily in Russian alone. The justification used for such an onslaught was that the VOA was 'giving the world thirsty for truth the knowledge of what happened.'[5] So tremendous was the burden placed on VOA transmitting facilities that Voice engineers warned that sustaining the massive effort for more than a week could cause major equipment failure. Every technical resource was pushed to its limit because, as stated by one top VOA news manager, 'this was the biggest story of the year, perhaps the decade.'[6]

To tell the very big story, the VOA used two of the oldest techniques in the propaganda handbook, sustained repetition and emotional manipulation. Among other special programming, VOA broadcast heart-wrenching stories of victim's families compiled by a stringer in Seoul and repeatedly aired by the Korean language service. The airliner story became the 'Must Lead' item on each newscast in all 42 languages during every on-air hour. For the first week following the downing, extensive use was made of statements and comments by senior U.S. officials who repeatedly voiced the official American line. The VOA frequently rebroadcast substantial excerpts from an interview it conducted with the U.S. Ambassador to the Soviet Union, Arthur Hartman. Secretary of State Schultz's day-after speech was fully translated into Russian and Ukranian and within minutes was broadcast and then repeatedly aired over the next few days. President Reagan's September 5th speech to the nation was carried in full in Worldwide English, Russian, Ukranian, Georgian, Polish and Chinese, while the other 37 languages carried extensive excerpts of the talk. Reagan's September 10th radio address, where he accused the Soviet Union of 'stonewalling the world' and 'mobilizing their entire government behind a massive cover-up,'[7] was carried live in Worldwide English and translated in full by all other 41 language services.

It was truly an effective use of the international airwaves for broadcasting of the American point of view, precisely the task of the VOA and the public diplomacy apparatus in general. The Voice's programming time was filled with the testimony of experts who could be used to corroborate the American perspective. One VOA correspondent was flown out to interview a Soviet defector military pilot now living in the United States, but when Victor Belenko made mention that Soviet pilots were not taught to visually recognize commercial from military aircraft, a statement which would have given some degree of substantiation to Soviet claims that their pilot did not know KAL 007 was a commercial flight, the VOA thought fast. The radio insured absolute Soviet culpability by pointing out that the Soviet Union knew the schedule of every commercial plane that flew near 'the strategic area the Russians still hold from the Japanese.'[8] This counter claim would seem to hold little weight when one realizes that the KAL 007 had flown several hundred miles off course. Undaunted by such discrepancies, news officials said that the incident not only showed the inhumaneness with which the Soviets approached the situation, but 'it also showed that they are just plain not very good at what they do.'[9]

Daily three-minute VOA editorials preached the official government position with the enthusiastic rhetoric of this administration. VOA editorials were – and are – played once an hour following the newscast in every language. In low priority foreign language desks which are only on-air for an hour or less, the editorials are aired once daily. In high priority broadcasts to Eastern Europe and the Soviet Union, the editorials are repeated as often as 10 times a day. Although written by VOA policy officers, the editorials have direct daily input from the State Department. In the first weeks following the shootdown, the interagency task force insisted on the repetition of harsh official commentary. Editorials completely incriminating the Soviet Union for cold-blooded, premeditated murder appeared virtually on a daily basis. One of the earliest editorials said, 'It should come as no surprise that the Soviet rulers, who are not accountable to their own people for what they do, are now having difficulty accounting to the world for their destruction . . . It raises grave doubts about the place of the Soviet Union in the community of civilized nations.'[10] Another noted that 'International bullies are much like individual bullies; the best way to deal with them is to stand up to them.'[11]

Standing up to the 'international bully' is exactly what Ronald Reagan said he was doing when he asked for and received from Congress more defence allocations that September. It was also precisely the ammunition he needed to request more money for increased public diplomacy activities, particularly appropriations for VOA. 'The truth is mankind's best hope for a better world. That's why in times like this, few assets are more important than the Voice of America and Radio Liberty,' said the president, as 'our primary means of getting truth to the Russian people.'[12]

But Reagan's truth is very partial business. In the case of KAL 007, American public diplomats saw it as something we had and the Russians did not. Their 'brutal disregard' for humanity and truth was juxtaposed with America's commitment to the truthful dissemination of an objective and comprehensive accounting of the events. But VOA's efforts failed to include any information which was damaging to the official U.S. account, a version which according to scholar David Pearson was 'neither credible or complete.'[13] As Seymour Hersh noted in his *The Target is Destroyed*, 'There is a frightening irony in all this: the president of the United States, relying on information that was wholly inaccurate and misleading, was accusing the other side of telling lies, and was perceived as being moderate in so doing.'[14] As an example, at the very time that a report was delivered to the White House which concluded that identification of the KAL 007 would have been extremely difficult for the Russian pilot, a high-ranking VOA news manager told this author that the Russians showed callous disregard for humanity when they '*knowingly* shot down the commercial airliner.'[15]

To cite another example of the use of the partial release of KAL 007 facts, official American accounts have continued to charge that the Soviet pilot failed to warn the Korean plane before it was shot down. The USIA-prepared audio-visual translation would have us believe this interpretation of events. Yet, despite information which now indicates that the Russian pilot did indeed follow internationally-accepted interception procedures and warned the Korean craft, which then took unexplained evasive action, VOA editorials continued to present the case for absolute Soviet indifference and failure to abide by global regulations. Said one editorial a full year after the downing, 'Only one country knew the plane was off course. Soviet authorities tracked the plane for over two hours . . . Soviet authorities ordered the fighter pilot to fire. Two missiles were launched and the Soviet pilot reported, 'Target is destroyed.'[16]

In its practice of partial coverage and insistent on complete Soviet culpability, the USIA continues to disinform the world's people. There is no question that the Soviet Union downed the KAL 007 and its first accounts of the tragic events were riddled with inconsistencies and evasiveness. But the Reagan administration and its public diplomacy channels, publicly devoted to the comprehensive and truthful dissemination of information, have remained silent on many of the issues subsequently raised, questions such as whether or not the airliner was part of a spy mission, questions such as when did the United States know of the plane's location and why didn't it inform the craft of possible impending danger. 'We cannot control the paranoia,' said David Pearson, 'of a Soviet society that shoots when in doubt, whether on orders from above or on impulse from below. We can and should, however, take responsibility for our own contribution to this tragedy and the tensions, fears and international disorder that it has promoted.'[17] Instead of diminishing this crisis state of the world, highly effective U.S. disinformation has increased East-West suspicion and distrust.

Notes

1. Parenti, Michael (1986) *Inviting Reality*, St. Martin's Press, New York, p. 56.
2. U.S. Congress, Senate, Committee on Foreign Relations, *USIA: Recent Developments*, Hearings Before the Committee on Foreign Relations, 98th Cong., 1st sess., 22 September 1983, report entitled 'Soviet Destruction of KAL Flight Chronology of USIA Activities, Sept. 1–6, 1983' and 'Sept. 7–19,' pp. 6–13, 19–20. All following quotes in text are from this report.
3. Hersh, Seymour (1986) *The Target is Destroyed*, Random House, New York, pp. 137–8.
4. U.S. Congress, Senate, Committee on Foreign Relations. *USIA: Recent Developments*, p. 22.
5. Ibid.
6. Interview with Edward de Fontaine, VOA deputy news director, Washington, 7 October 1983.
7. Irwin, Don, World Being Stonewalled, Reagan Says. *Los Angeles Times*, 11 September 1983, p. 1, 26.
8. Interview with de Fontaine.
9. Ibid.
10. VOA editorial, 9 October 1983.
11. VOA editorial, 1 September 1984.
12. Irwin, p. 1, 26.
13. Pearson, David, KAL 007: What the U.S. Knew and When We Knew It. *The Nation*, August 18–25, p. 205. Pearson amplified his arguments more completely in *The Nation's* anniversary issue 'KAL 007: Unanswered Questions' August 17–24, 1985.
14. Hersh, p. 131.
15. Interview with de Fontaine. On January 13, 1988 a *Los Angeles Times* (p. 1) story, 'Soviets May Have Erred on KAL Jet,' reported on a recently declassified intelligence document which indicated that U.S. officials knew one day after the downing that the Soviets were unaware it was a civilian airliner. At that very time, Reagan told Congressional leaders that the U.S. had 'definite proof that they intentionally shot down that unarmed civilian plane.'
16. VOA editorial, 1 September 1984.
17. Pearson, David p. 124.

12

Hollywood meets Madison Avenue: the commercialization of U.S. films

Janet Wasko

From Wasko, J. (1994) *Hollywood in the Information Age*, Polity Press, Cambridge, pp. 187–93, 196–209.

Hollywood motion pictures have long been recognized as commodities. Yet, these days motion pictures also are the vehicles for even further commercial activity in the form of advertising and merchandising.

It is as difficult to ignore the brand-name products scattered throughout a typical Hollywood blockbuster, as it is to avoid the ever-present tie-in campaigns featured at supermarkets and quick-food outlets. Meanwhile, there is a proliferation of toys, games and other merchandise based on Hollywood films. While there are numerous studies of movie advertising, few have considered the implications of the growing trend of advertising within films and merchandising activities which surround them.[1]

This chapter examines the growth of advertising and marketing in and around Hollywood films and argues that these marketing strategies have become more deliberate and carefully co-ordinated than in the past. These developments, furthermore, enhance the commodification of culture and promote a consumer society. The chapter will consider product advertising, tie-in campaigns, and licensing and merchandising activities. The creative, economic and cultural implications of these developments will then be discussed.

Product advertising

The notion that U.S. films stimulate demand for U.S. products has long been acknowledged.[2] By the 1920s fashions seen in films were being promoted by stars and retail establishments and the cigarette industry was lobbying performers to smoke on screen.[3] Placement of name brand products within major motion pictures is not a new phenomenon; just one example is Joan Crawford drinking Jack Daniels whiskey in the 1945 production, *Mildred Pierce*.[4]

However, in these earlier times product placement was a much more casual, even haphazard endeavour. Property masters would call the local Jack Daniels distributor and ask for some product to be used in the film, or simply go to the store and buy the product themselves. The Jack Daniels distributor would more than likely send a couple of cases so that the property master would not only have enough product for the film but plenty left over to spread among the cast and crew, thus engendering a measure of goodwill toward the company.

Today the system of product placement is much more deliberate and sophisticated. Indeed, the vast majority of Fortune 500 companies are involved in product placement activities,[5] and the process has become an industry in and of itself. There now exist somewhere between 15 and 30 companies whose sole purpose is to secure placement for their clients' products.[6] Jack Daniels itself employs a product placement firm.

This section will explore the recent trend of product advertising in the Hollywood film industry and argues that as Hollywood continues to search for additional sources of revenue, the commodification of the film industry will continue to accelerate. This process has manifested itself not only in terms of product placements within films, but in such practices as advertising on videos and within motion picture theatres. Each of these areas will be analysed separately, but it should be remembered that they are tied by a common thread. When considered as a whole, evidence indicates that the Hollywood film industry is rapidly becoming a major advertising medium.

Product placement

Arranging the appearance or mention of specific brand names in motion pictures has become a multimillion dollar business. Firms charge clients fees ranging from \$5000 to 250,000 for guaranteed placement in a contracted number of films with escalation clauses for particularly extensive or prominent appearances.[7] Some companies (e.g. Coca-Cola, Pepsi, Anheuser-Busch) have formed their own in-house divisions dedicated specifically to product placement and/or Hollywood advertising activities.

Product placement firms and corporate in-house divisions typically review 400–500 movie screenplays per year looking for opportunities. One such company, Creative Film Promotions, utilizes a computer program to search scripts for product placement ideas. On average the firm claims the computer will discover at least 50 potential placements in a given screenplay; for example, adding a dresser with a client's brand of clock radio and cosmetics whenever a script reads 'INTERIOR: BEDROOM.'[8]

Such efforts have resulted in significant product placements in Hollywood films. The Pepsi-Cola Entertainment Marketing Group (Pepsi's in-house placement division) reported placing the Pepsi trademark in approximately 70 feature films in 1989, while another private firm, Entertainment Marketing Group, placed products in 150 films the same year.[9] Another firm, Associated Film Promotions, claims to have placed clients in more than 175 features.[10] It has been estimated that current movies contain, on average, 30–40 minutes of screen time given over to product plugs.[11] This translates to approximately one-third of a typical movie containing product advertisements.

Why the current growth in product placement activity? From Hollywood's point of view, product placement means added revenues. On the other hand, product placement equals effective advertising for corporate sponsors. According to Twentieth Century Fox Licensing and Merchandising

Corporation (Fox's subsidiary responsible for product placement), the studio will charge anywhere from $20,000 to $100,000 or more for a product appearance in a major motion picture.[12] If one assumes 20–50 potential promotional opportunities per film, it follows that a producer could easily realize well in excess of one million dollars from product placements in a given production. The amount charged for placement is directly correlated with the level of prominence the product achieves in the film. If the product merely appears in the background, the fee is significantly lower than if the product is actually handled by the movie's star.[13] Verbal mention of a product, as in the film *Wall Street*, where Martin Sheen's character yelled to the waitress, 'Get this kid a Molson Light,' also pushes the fee higher.[14]

One result of the acceleration of this type of activity is that placements have become standard operating procedure; simply part of the negotiation that can reduce the cost of production.[15] Negotiations do not always revolve around a straight cash fee, however. Often placement deals involve product, equipment and its maintenance, or advertising commitments. Paramount's *Days of Thunder*, in which star Tom Cruise drives a neon Chevy Lumina stock car named for Coca-Cola Company's Mellow Yellow soft drink, serves as an appropriate example. The placement agreement provided that General Motors would not only provide the necessary car(s), but also mechanics to make sure they operated properly. In addition, both Chevy and Coca-Cola committed themselves to extensive promotional campaigns tied to the movie. Such media expenditures can literally add tens of millions of dollars to a movie's promotional budget.[16] Joe Allegro, co-owner of the Entertainment Marketing Group, estimates that of the placements his firm secures approximately one-half are for cash and the remaining 50 per cent are for media or equipment.[17]

Meanwhile, corporate marketing departments are equally enthusiastic about product placements. In an era of generally rising media costs, motion pictures with their new afterlife of videocassettes and pay television are increasingly attractive from a cost standpoint. If a movie grosses $50 million, the advertiser has reached an audience of 13.7 million in theatre viewers.[18] The industry generally assumes that if a movie grosses $50 million, it will likely sell 200,000 videocassettes. If the movie grosses over $50 million, it could easily sell 300,000 videos. It is further assumed that a top feature film will be rented five or more times per week, thus adding an additional (over theatre) 25–30 million impressions per placement. And when pay cable and network TV are added into the equation, the cost to advertisers is literally pennies per thousand.[19] In addition, advertisers feel as though they are reaching an otherwise hard-to-reach audience: the 12–24-year-old market.[20]

But most convincing is evidence that movie placement works. The most cited example is Hershey Company's Reese's Pieces, when sales levitated 85 per cent after *E.T.: The Extra Terrestrial*. Another case is little-known Mumford High School in Detroit, which sold $1 million worth of T-shirts after Eddie Murphy appeared in one in *Beverly Hills Cop*.[21] Patrick Denin, marketing co-ordinator for the movie *Rocky V*, asserts that product placements 'are more credible than endorsements because they portray someone using a product in everyday life.'[22] A critical factor here is product *usage* as compared to the mere appearance of a product in the film. Research by one product placement firm found that nearly 60 per cent of respondents recalled (3–5 day delayed recall) Sylvester Stallone eating Wheaties in the movie *Rocky III*. However, only one per cent remembered a quick shot of a William Grant and Sons Glenfiddich scotch bottle.[23]

It seems reasonable to assume that such findings will provide impetus for advertisers to further intrude into the creative process. Sandra Locke, the director of the film *Impulse*, relates such a conflict. During one scene, a TV set was supposed to be blaring a commercial, which was contracted to be on screen. Locke says her view of the scene did not accommodate the commercial on screen, so she asked if audio placement would be sufficient, i.e. allowing the audience to hear but not see the commercial. She was told that if the TV with the commercial did not appear on screen, 'we don't get the money.'[24] In reality, product placers increasingly view themselves as agents for products and, therefore, view their function as getting 'parts' for their clients. If obvious opportunities for placement are not available, then placers are wont to rewrite scripts to fit in product plugs. 'I'm part screenwriter,' says placer Larry Dorn, 'I'm a creative artist.'[25] Associated Film Promotions claims it had a salad-making scene added to the film *North Dallas Forty*, simply and specifically to promote Bertolli salad oil.[26] Another example is the use of Mumm's champagne in *Moonstruck*; originally another brand of champagne was to be used.

Lois Sheinfield has suggested the following:

> The movie industry may not realize the legal problems attendant upon this 'valuable resource' [corporate America] and the commercialization of film. Take for example a movie version of Macbeth. What if Lady M tries to get the damned spot out with a can of Ajax? If Ajax is Kovoloff's client and has to be presented in a positive manner, then naturally the Lady will get the spot out. Well, that's a problem. No matter that Shakespeare didn't want her to get the spot out. He's dead and can't complain. The problem is Truth in Advertising. Can Ajax get out a blood spot on the brain? Aye, there's the rub![27]

Such anecdotes point out the very real danger of product placements dictating production content. Peggy Charren, president of Action for Children's TV, says, 'It has gotten to the point where it (product placement) influences the story, where they'll say, 'Let's do this instead of that, so we can make 20 deals.' It affects the content of editorial speech. That's one reason you're likely to see films set only in the present instead of historical subjects. You can't make Marie Antoinette eat Domino's Pizza.'[28]

Movie producers generally argue that they choose subjects of interest and then listen to product placement appeals. Further, they argue that product placements do not unduly influence artistic interpretation and point out that placements often end up on the cutting room floor. Finally, it is suggested that such placements allow an element of reality by providing real products in realistic settings. A product placement firm executive explained that, 'They used to go to great lengths not to have a known product name in the movies. But now, a generic name would detract from a scene. Unless you wanted it to look camp, like *Repo Man*, with all those cans that said 'Food.''[29]

Recent developments and knowledge of the intricacies of the system challenge these disclaimers. First, while it may be true that topics are contemplated without regard to product placements, it also seems increasingly likely that in an age of rising production costs consideration of potential revenues will be analysed before the undertaking of any project. While it can be stated that a topic matter, in the abstract, may be beyond the purview of advertisers, can the same be said of the presentation in terms of individual scenes?

Second, the efficacy of the 'cutting room floor' argument has recently become considerably more tenuous. Black and Decker has filed a $150,000 lawsuit naming Twentieth Century Fox and Krown-Young and Rubicam as defendants. The basis of the suit is breach of promise, in that a Black and Decker drill did not appear in the movie *Die Hard 2*.[30] If other manufacturers pursue this course of action, and given the quantity of expenditures that often support product placement, and it seems inevitable that they will, then producers may be much less inclined to leave placements on the cutting room floor.

An additional permutation is the fact that product placement firms represent more than one branded product, leading to family deals where for a given amount of money the entire family, or some subdivision thereof, is placed in a film. Reality, in this case, has nothing to do with the vision of director or producer but rather with what products happen to be represented by a given placement firm.

In addition to recommending products and creating scenes to depict those products, script screeners also function to warn their clients of possible negative consequences for their products. Thus warned that a product is going to be used in a manner that may reflect adversely on the firm, corporations have a chance to lobby a producer to make changes or threaten a lawsuit before the film reaches the theatres.

The level of intrusion by advertisers into motion pictures has come under scrutiny by both citizen and legislative bodies. The concern of many is that product placement is a form of advertising that is largely unregulated. Congress is looking at placements by the cigarette industry with the intent of banning such 'paid advertisements' in feature films.[31] Meanwhile, the Center for the Study of Commercialization, sponsored by the Center for Science in the Public Interest, a consumer advocacy group, has gone even farther and advocated the use of subtitles to identify every paid appearance or mention of a product or brand in a movie.[32] The group recently filed a petition with the Federal Trade Commission to declare product placements 'an unfair business practice and require on-screen disclosure of products advertised in films.'[33]

Certainly this practice has not been restricted solely to motion pictures. A recent survey by *Advertising Age* found 818 'free plugs' over a 24-hour period on the three networks.[34] There is even a case of a product placement within a novel.[35] But for motion pictures, the phenomenon is becoming more and more entrenched. As president of marketing for Walt Disney Pictures, Bob Levin, recently observed, 'I believe it's a long-term relationship that's now going to exist [between] the movie industry and product marketers.'[36] [...]

Tie-ins

'Joint promotions can help defray the cost of marketing a movie . . . and they
help us reach broader demographics. With joint consumer product promotions,
we can touch an audience that we don't normally reach with traditional movie
advertising.' Jan Kean, national director of promotions for Orion Pictures
Corporation.

The boundary between what constitutes a tie-in and merchandising is at
best indistinct. In this text, tie-ins will be considered as promotional campaigns tied to specific films, but associated with products not in the movie
per se, nor based on characters or objects in the movie. Thus, the availability
of a 'special edition Rambo knife' selling for $2250 falls under the category
of merchandising, whereas the inclusion of a 60 second Pizza Hut commercial
and coupon book good for $20 in food and Pepsi products at Pizza Hut
restaurants on the *Teenage Mutant Ninja Turtles* videocassette constitutes a
tie-in.[37] While it is true that the Turtles are renowned for their voracious
appetite for pizza, Domino's Pizza, through a product placement deal, is
the one that appears in the movie. The tie-in between pizza and the Ninja
Turtles is a logical one, but instances of such things are not always as clear-
cut. For instance, in order to promote the introduction of Paul Newman's
salad dressing to its outlets, Burger King offered the videocassette of his
film *Absence of Malice* to customers at a reduced price when they purchased
salads.[38]

With so many promotional activities associated with a film, sometimes
it becomes unclear who is promoting who or what is promoting what. To
gain a clearer understanding of what is involved, a more in-depth look at
specific instances is warranted. It is recognized that these are high profile,
big budget examples. But rather than being aberrations from the norm, these
examples are actually in the vanguard of tie-in practices and thus serve more
as models than brief one-offs to be discounted.

'Willow'

George Lucas' film *Willow*, about a race of little people, sparked off a rash
of tie-in activity. It is estimated that over $50 million in marketing tie-ins
was riding on this one feature. Quaker Oats Co. alone committed $26 million
in promotional programs. Other companies involved included General
Foods, Hunt-Wesson, Kraft, Wendy's International, Tonka Toys, Parker
Brothers, and Random House.

While the advertising budget of the distributor, MGM/UA Communications, was in excess of $6 million, Lucas Film Ltd. promised a further $20
million in advertising and promotional support for its licensees. But these
figures pale in comparison with the accumulative amounts coming from
these licensees. Not only are the amounts of money being thrown around
impressive, but the number of products tied to the film are equally over-
whelming. Although the biggest media budgets were tied to Quaker's
children's cereals (such as Cap'n Crunch and Oh's), the promotion also was
extended to adult brands, including Aunt Jemima pancake mix, Rice-A-Roni
side dishes and Quaker 100% Natural Cereal. The Quaker promotion kicked

off on June 12 1988, with a free standing insert (FSI) including coupons for free milk and a *Willow* spoon-and-dish premium. A second FSI offered $6 in coupons, plus other *Willow* premiums for consumers purchasing a variety of Quaker brands. In addition, these tie-ins were the focus of a five-week flight of TV spots for Cap'n Crunch.

Kraft Inc.'s multibrand cheese promotion – its biggest of the year – kicked off with a national FSI on May 22nd offering *Willow* products. Kraft's involvement included virtually all of its cheese products group: Cheez Whiz, Cracker Barrel, Kraft Singles, 100 per cent Natural Cheeses, Philadelphia Brand cream cheese and Velveeta. The latter contained free *Willow* tickets in packages during May and June.

Meanwhile, Wendy's spent an estimated $5 million on a children's meal promotion tied to the film, and featured *Willow* magic cups with heat-sensitive decals depicting scenes from the film. This was backed by network TV and print advertising support. Beatrice Hunt-Wesson ran a back-to-school promotion for Peter Pan peanut butter tied to the film, while Dow Chemical Co.'s Ziploc brand had in-pack character trading cards in its sandwich bags. In addition, children were able to get free school folders at Dow's in-store displays. General Foods Corporation's Jell-o brand sponsored a give-away of two million *Willow* activity books in support of the Children's Miracle Network fund-raising telethon. Finally, there were toy tie-ins through Tonka Corporation, a board game from Parker Brothers and book versions for both adults and children from Ballantine Books.[39]

Although *Willow* did not materialize into the anticipated box-office smash, Quaker exceeded its promotion objectives by 50 per cent.[40] Thus for Quaker, at least, the tie-ins clearly worked, despite the movie's limited success at the box-office.

It is apparent, then, that most of the tie-ins came from companies which had no literal connection with the movie – after all, no one in the film actually eats any Velveeta cheese (on screen, that is). The benefit to these companies comes from their association with a potentially successful movie which gives their essentially dull products (in terms of image) the chance to be thought of as part and parcel of a world of mystery and wonder. The purchaser can be involved in the fantasy world of *Willow* through the cards, figures, cereal bowls, etc., offered by these manufacturers.

For the movie, these kinds of tie-ins mean additional (free) TV and print advertising, point-of-sale advertising in every major supermarket in the country (which would be difficult to arrange without such tie-ins) and the chance to be associated with 'good' promotional campaigns which tie themselves in turn to charitable causes (as in the case of Jell-o or freebies for the kids associated with back-to-school as in the case of Hunt-Wesson and Dow Chemical).

'Oliver & Company' and 'Land Before Time'

When we look at the release and marketing strategy for two other films that hit the screens in late 1988, the complexity and interdependency of marketing tie-ins becomes clearer. *Oliver & Company* (Disney) had exclusive promotional tie-ins with Sears, Roebuck and Co. and McDonald's Corporation.

Land Before Time (Universal/Amblin) went with J. C. Penney, Pizza Hut, and Dow Chemical Company. The unusual situation of two major animated features from major distributors scheduled for Christmas release meant that advertising and promotional tie-ins were even more crucial than normal. Because of the need to successfully break into the lucrative Christmas market, neither studio took any chances.

Marketing consultant for Universal and Amblin Entertainment, Martin Levy, acknowledged that they were doing somewhat more in their overall marketing effort because of competition from the Disney movie. Besides the tie-ins, Universal sent about 40,000 dinosaur 'education kits' to schools across the country. In each kit were activities such as running twine out 30 feet to better understand how big the prehistoric beasts really were (note: another example of 'good' marketing through schools, similar to the *Willow* examples). As one might expect, Universal was not solely concerned with the children's education, and thus each kit also included photos from the movies and a one-sheet display poster.

The campaigns by both sides were informed by the tremendous success that Universal had had with *An American Tail* (1987). Although the film was pitted against a re-release of Disney's *Cinderella*, it grossed $48 million at the box-office, breaking records for the initial release of an animated feature. And, as of November 1988, *An American Tail* had sold over one million videocassettes. This success has been credited to one of the industry's most extensive merchandising and promotional deals (at that time) with Sears and McDonald's. Noting this phenomenon, Disney wasted no time in snapping up exclusive merchandising deals with Sears and McDonald's, starting with *Oliver & Company*. The deal was no doubt helped by the successful campaign run by Disney in the summer of 1988, with limited merchandising deals set up with McDonald's and Coca-Cola for Spielberg's *Who Framed Roger Rabbit?* McDonald's and Coca-Cola spent $12 million and $10 million respectively on campaigns associated with the movie.[41]

The marketing strategy employed by Universal for *Land Before Time*, however, serves as a model for this type of enterprise, although obviously there are variations depending on the company involved. As Levy explains, 'the first thing you do is establish the film.' The $12 million campaign – featuring the slogan, 'Here's the new one from the creators of *An American Tail*' – was a straightforward appeal and contained no mention of merchandise. The bulk of the advertisements were on network, spot and cable TV, targeting young women with children. After the movie broke, the advertising baton was passed to partners J. C. Penney and Pizza Hut. Penney's, which had $50 million worth of everything from plush animals and kids' clothing to sheets and wrapping paper tied up in the promotion, supported the licensing deal with a $6 million corporate advertising budget. This included two weeks of national TV and five holiday pre-prints, including an eight-page newspaper insert with a *Land Before Time* pop-up. The advertisements included movie clips for in-store advertising, for which Penney's created jungle-like shops to house dinosaur merchandise themed to the movie. In this jungle environment Penney's ran a videotape of select scenes from the film and listed local theatres showing it. Pizza Hut, for their part, spent an estimated $10 million, including four weeks of TV, direct mail and print. The only restrictions placed were that no advertisements were to break until November 16, two days before the movie's release. Thus, there was a tightly organized advertising campaign from early November through Christmas. In January, Dow Chemical stepped in with Ziploc bag advertisements touting its exclusive *Land Before Time* plastic glass promotion. Universal sustained its own campaign during this period, but as Levy notes, 'the biggest bulk of TV was from them [the tie-in partners] not us and that is why we developed the spots with them so carefully'.[42]

The exact nature and extent of co-operation between the tie-in partners and the studios certainly varies, according to the film and the participants. When Universal planned to release *An American Tail*, they were forced to change the release date (which in many cases, is of crucial importance) by Sears and McDonald's, who felt that the licensing risk was too great if they were given only a few weeks to sell their wares during the all-important Christmas season. Thus, instead of breaking the film when children's Christmas vacations started in mid-December, the release date was brought forward to mid-November. Although in the past, movie companies had been reluctant to share plots and character developments before release (Disney, in particular, still holds off from this), Amblin, although known for its secrecy in the past, gave the *Land Before Time* script to Penney's and Pizza Hut about a year before release on a confidential basis.

More examples could be cited, but the nature and extent of tie-ins for big budget films, particularly those aimed at children, is essentially the same. As Belinda Hulin-Salkin notes,

> Consumer promotions have gone Hollywood. In the continuing quest to cut through the media clutter – and rise above eroding network television ratings – marketers increasingly have set their sight on what may be the last captive media audience in America: moviegoers. And as film industry executives place more and more emphasis on bottom-line results, these partners are now welcomed onto movie sets with air kisses and open arms. The days when film makers could afford to snub tie-in proposals from manufacturers are clearly over.[43]

But lest one think that all we have here is a flurry of merchandisers beating down the doors of Hollywood in order to tie their products to the latest hot movie, this is indeed a two-way flow. Pamela Ellis-Simons notes that 'movie studios, fully realizing how much an extra $20 million or so in advertising can help their film, are now courting marketers with the lure of exclusive deals. Overfield (Penney's) reports that several studios have already come to Penney's about future tie-ins.'[44]

Some films released during the summer of 1990 were reported to have received $30–40 million in tie-in revenue, with the 'Dick Tracy Crimestopper Game' promotion by McDonald's purported to be the largest movie tie-in ever at $40 million. However, 1991's big summer movies boasted only 'modest' support averaging around $10–15 million per film.[45]

Clearly the situation is beneficial to all parties involved. No budget-conscious studio could pass up the chance for the extra advertising clout that tie-ins can furnish. However, it is unclear to what extent the desire for this extra exposure influences the studios' conduct or the content of the films. Marketers will not be willing to invest or promote films that they do not feel can guarantee a return. Stung by past failures, such as *Howard the Duck*, marketers will wish more and closer involvement with the studios, as indicated with *Land Before Time*. Thus, it would seem that only the safest of commodities will be the recipients of the tie-in goldmine, and consequently variety and innovation may be pushed aside. Moreover, as we noted with the involvement of Disney with Sears and McDonald's, some of the most lucrative outlets have already been tied to exclusive contracts, further restricting the ability of other studios to exploit the potential of these symbiotic relationships should they so desire.

Since 1988 the studios have intensified their marketing strategies of videos, as well, incorporating techniques similar to packaged-goods companies. Tie-ins with beverages and packaged foods mean valuable display placements in supermarkets, convenience stores and restaurants. An example is Disney's 1989 holiday campaign, which included cross-promotion of its videos with Coca-Cola, Procter and Gamble and McDonald's. Other studios made similar arrangements with other companies, allowing their products to be seen much more widely than in video rental stores.[46]

In a new merchandising wrinkle, Paramount Pictures announced a tie-in arrangement with Kmart, which would promote all of its summer films during 1991. The promotion – entitled 'Passport to Summer Entertainment' – involved scratch and win cards redeemable for prizes at the stores. While not unusual in itself, it marked the first time a complete list of summer films would be tied to a single promotional partner.[47]

Meanwhile, *Advertising Age* reported that home video marketers spent $85 million during the second half of 1991 to market movies to children. Distributors aligned with promotional partners to share the costs. For example, Fox Video's *Home Alone* was backed with a $25 million promotional campaign shared by Pepsi-Cola and American Airlines, while New Line Home Video, Burger King and Nabisco devoted $20 million to promoting the video release of *Teenage Mutant Ninja Turtles II*.[48]

Merchandising and licensing

> Merchandising! We put the picture's name on everything. Merchandising, merchandising, that's where the real money from the movie is made.
> (Just Plain) Yoghurt, played by Mel Brooks, in *Space Balls*.

> Warner Communications – Licensing the World.
> Seen on a shopping bag carried by a woman in San Francisco airport.

The distinction between tie-ins and merchandise is often blurred, as some merchandise is produced for tie-ins. This study will consider merchandise as commodities based on movie themes, characters or images which are designed, produced and marketed for direct sale, and not connected to other products or services (as with tie-ins).

Licensing has been described as a 'legal mechanism by which one party legally obligates itself to pay the holder of a copyright or trademark a specific royalty in order to use a name, likeness or image.'[49] Thus, licensing is the legal act – the process of selling or buying property rights to produce commodities using specific copyrighted properties. On the other hand, merchandising can be thought of as the mechanical act of making or selling a product based on a copyrightable product.

There is an extremely wide variety of movie-based merchandise, including items based on a specific movie, character or theme, or ongoing movie characters and themes. While there has been a strong emphasis on children's toys, games and other items (lunch boxes, school supplies, etc.), other movie-based merchandise includes home furnishings (clocks, towels, bedding, mugs, telephones), clothing, jewellery, stationary items, print material (novelizations, trading cards, posters, etc.), food (especially cereals and candy), and decorations (such as Christmas ornaments).

Other more unusual, less mass-produced items sometimes accompany (or follow) movie releases, including 'art objects' such as prints, sculptures, ceramic figures, and animation sets (an example is the set of five Bugs Bunny animation cells available from the Warner collection at $3250). Other examples would be a replica of Rambo's knife ($2250), Bugs Bunny greetings calls (1-900-VIP-BUGS), and *Gone with the Wind* wine.[50]

Other merchandise is based on the celebrity status of Hollywood stars. While successful actors and actresses in the 1940s started independent film companies, celebrities of the 1980s pitched their own brand of salad dressing (Paul Newman), line of clothing (Brooke Shields), or perfume and cologne (Elizabeth Taylor). Though not based on characters or themes from specific films, these items draw on the status of the film star to sell products, and thus should be considered Hollywood-related merchandise.

In addition to specific film- or character-based merchandise, some of the larger entertainment companies now offer generic movie or studio merchandise. Examples include Warner Brothers hats, jackets, and mugs, miniature movie clapper boards, and mock Academy Awards. These items are sold through the studios' catalogues or 'entertainment stores,' such as Suncoast Motion Picture Company. The Hollywood Chamber of Commerce has joined in, marketing trading cards based on stars featured on Hollywood Boulevard's 'Walk of Fame,' Thus, Hollywood increasingly has been selling itself in merchandisable forms.

While movie-based merchandising can be viewed as part of the proliferation of commercialization in Hollywood, this type of activity is part of a larger merchandising and licensing trend. Licensed products represented $66.5 billion in retail sales in 1990.[51] TV programs and characters – especially those aimed at children – are an obvious and prevalent form of merchandising, while sports teams and players, rock stars, and musical groups have long histories of licensing and merchandising activities.[52] For instance, the growing phenomenon of sports cards dates back to the 1880s, when tobacco companies included baseball heroes in packets of tobacco.[53] These days products are based on well-known images, brands and even companies, e.g. Coca-Cola clothes, Harley-Davidson sunglasses. Even non-commercial organizations in the U.S.A. are now offering merchandise, such as the products available from public broadcast stations. *Signals* is a catalogue published by the WGBH Education Foundation, which offers videos of PBS series, plus T-shirts, mugs, books, jewellery and other educational, comic, or 'tasteful' items, sometimes, but not always, connected to PBS programming.

Movie-based merchandise is especially motivated by the proliferation of such activities, as well as the massive, co-ordinated merchandising campaigns – often started months before a film's release – associated with a few blockbuster films. This merchandising bonanza represents sizable profits. Sales of merchandise licensed from movies and stage shows in 1985 brought in $3.5 billion, although only $2.2 billion was received in 1987.[54]

Some recent examples include *Batman*, which grossed $250 million and earned $50 million in licensing fees, *Rambo III*, which involved 50 licensing agreements for more than 75 products,[55] and *The Jetsons*, which also attracted 50 licenses. Meanwhile, the *Star Trek* television series and films have generated a $500 million merchandising bonanza for the 35 companies which produce various products.[56] Merchandising successes have not only featured cuddly, heroic characters: Freddy Krueger of *Nightmare on Elm Street* has generated more than $3 million in licensing fees for Freddy posters, T-shirts, and other items.[57]

Universal's *Jurassic Park* may represent the ultimate model (at this point in time) for blockbuster merchandising/tie-in/product placement activities. The dino-tale made over $50 million at the box-office during the first weekend of release in June 1993, and reached $750 million in gross world-wide revenues before the year ended.

But that was only half the story. As one reporter announced, the feature film 'has unleashed a wave of dinosaur-mania across the U.S.'[58] More accurately, Universal Pictures and producer/director Steven Spielberg unleashed a wave of Jurassic Park products, playing into the already-existing interest in dinosaurs and prehistoric creatures. The film was accompanied by over 1000 products identified as official Jurassic Park merchandise, distributed by 100 official Jurassic Park manufacturers around the world. The products included the usual: T-shirts, toothbrushes, and school supplies. Also available were $15 boxer shorts with images of velociraptors, a $1 Jurassic Park jawbreaker ('take eons to eat') and a line of 30 toys (featuring 'Dino Damage') from Kenner. The tie-in included McDonald's and Toys-R-Us, which distributed free Jurassic Park boxes including sample products and coupons.

Interestingly, the film itself was a tie-in, with the Jurassic Park logo in the film repeated on official Jurassic Park merchandise, plus a scene in the film featuring the park's gift store displaying Jurassic Park merchandise – the same merchandise available outside the movie. Thus, Universal and Spielberg neatly combined Jurassic Park merchandising, product placement and tie-in activities into one process.

The recent proliferation of movie merchandising may be related to the current upswing in general merchandising, as well as an increase in animated features and the re-release and remakes of films with readily identifiable, on-going characters and themes. But while these recent developments may reflect a new stage in Hollywood's commodification of entertainment, merchandising is not really a new game in Tinseltown.

Until the 1960s and 1970s, relatively little merchandising activity took place in Hollywood, except for Disney. For the Disney company, merchandising started almost simultaneously with the tremendous success of Mickey Mouse's *Steamboat Willie*. Although various histories claim that Walt Disney was not necessarily interested in licensing his characters, merchandising activities still provided needed revenue to continue producing expensive animated films.[59] In 1929 the company was offered $300 to put Mickey Mouse on writing tablets, and by January 1930, Mickey appeared in a comic strip distributed by King Features (Hearst-owned). During the 1930s, the George Borgfeldt Co. was authorized to handle the licensing of Mickey and Minnie products, which included handkerchiefs, drums, rubber balls and other toys. But in 1932, Herman 'Kay' Kayman took over and began to flood the market with Disney products. 'Mickey's likeness soon appeared on everything from soap to ice-cream cones to Cartier diamond bracelets ($1250).'[60]

During the depths of the depression, the Disney merchandising bonanza supposedly saved the Lionel Co. with the sale of 253,000 Mickey Mouse handcars and the Ingersoll Waterbury Co. with the sale of 2.5 million Mickey Mouse watches. By 1934, annual profits on films and merchandise brought in over $600,000 for the Disney company. Mickey is still claimed to be the most popular licensed character in the world today, appearing on more than 7500 items, not including publications.[61] (More on Disney later in this section.)

But the Disney company has been the exception, rather than the rule. While the motion picture industry may have been relatively slow to pick up on merchandising activities, television was less hesitant. Since the 1950s, there have been numerous examples of licensing and merchandising successes from children's shows to westerns to action adventure programs But the current phase of film-based licensing can be traced back to the merchandising successes of *Star Wars* and *E.T.* in the 1970s.

According to one industry source, '[e]ntertainment licensing is a very small and closely knit community.'[62] The *owners* of licensable properties are most often the major entertainment corporations which distribute a wide range of entertainment commodities and hold copyrights and trademarks for movie-based characters and themes. Special licensing divisions often are organized to handle these properties (and those owned by others, as well), e.g. Warner's Licensing Corporation of America (LCA) and Disney's Consumer Products division. But even smaller successful film producers sometimes are involved in licensing, as represented by Lucasfilm Licensing.

Licensees include a wide array of individuals, companies, and firms which buy the rights to produce merchandise based on a copyrighted character or image. Larger companies usually do their own research before licensing a character or product, although information is available (for a price) from *research companies* such as Marketing Evaluations/TVQ, which measures consumer attitudes toward celebrities, brand names, and cartoon characters.[63] *Retailers* are those companies which offer the products for sale to the public. Five *trade magazines* covering the licensing industry have started since 1979, thus indicating the rapid growth of the merchandising business.

Licensees usually pay royalties based on a fixed percentage (typically 5–15%) on the wholesale or retail selling price of the licensee's products.[64] Other promotional deals involve a fee, ranging from $25,000 for an average film to $100,000 for a major film or sequel. In addition 'the marketer pays royalties or a per cent of premium sales (the average is 6% or 7% of the manufacturer's selling price).'[65] Another source explains that most licensers add an 8–15% fee on top of the normal price of a licensed product.[66]

While there are sometimes complications over the sharing of ancillary rights, creative control (i.e. how a character is used), or quality standards for products,[67] the arrangements often are advantageous for all parties concerned.

The benefits for studios are the increased profits – 'easy dollars . . . all bottom line and very clean.'[68] Such revenues also contribute to production costs, which continue to rise dramatically for Hollywood productions. In addition, merchandising typically helps to promote a film, especially when linked to other activities, thus creating synergy within a corporation. It is even claimed that for some films, merchandising is necessary for success at the box-office. A recent example was the weak release of *Teenage Mutant Ninja Turtles* in Japan, which was blamed on the lack of merchandising back-up.[69]

For merchandisers, the obvious advantage is to be linked to a successful movie. 'A film has the potential to be a big event that will produce a product to break out of the pack,' explains James Pisors, director of licensing and entertainment for Tonka Toy Co.[70]

However, it seems that Hollywood wants the toymakers more than the toymakers want Hollywood, as indicated by the toy industry's $16 billion retail revenue in 1989 (three times the revenues received at the box-office for Hollywood films).[71] Products based on a movie can be considered risky for merchandisers, as they often have short lifespans connected to the box-office release of the film.[72] Some toy companies are not even interested in this type of merchandise, noting that '[a]s soon as the movie is pulled from release, the corresponding property usually becomes ancient history on toy shelves and unless it's timed for Christmas it isn't worth the financial exposure.'[73]

Licensees may have to take further risks initially by sinking money into a film that is not completed (or sometimes not even started). There also is criticism that movie companies put 'too much emphasis on box-office at the expense of merchandise.'[74] Thus, some conclude that 'the risk of a licensing failure falls mostly to the manufacturer of the product, not to the company selling its name.'[75]

At worst, a studio may need to change a release date, especially to coincide with the lucrative Christmas season.[76] But for the most part, licensing represents an attractive proposition to movie makers who can offer merchandisable properties.

But what is merchandisable? And why do some products succeed while others fail? As one industry insider notes, '[t]he licensed property *per se* is relatively insignificant . . . for the most part it doesn't matter whether it's a film or TV character or a toy or a hot new band. It can be anything from a rock to a raisin.'[77] Another industry executive offered advice for television, which also seems applicable to film: 'A program must have a sense of adventure and create an environment which the child or adult can relate to on many plateaux. In other words, the situation must develop into *toyetic applications* – characters which have a personality that can be easily transferred to dolls and playset environments' (emphasis added).[78]

However, there seem to be as many examples of merchandising failures as there are of successes. Some are connected to unsuccessful (in terms of box-office) films, like *Howard the Duck*. When the film flopped in 1986, LJN

Toys was reported to have written down $1 million.[79] Other films have been successful at the box-office, but not in terms of merchandising (i.e. *Jaws, Back to the Future, Who Framed Roger Rabbit?, Rambo, First Blood: Part II*).

The editor of *Toy and Hobby World*, Larry Carlat, has suggested four basic reasons for these 'bombs.'[80] The first element is timing. Carlat notes that there is a 'merchandising window of opportunity' during which the movie is doing well at the box-office. There also are seasonal variations, with summer and Christmas as the hottest marketing periods of the year for both movies and merchandise. Another tricky timing problem is co-ordinating merchandise availability with the film's opening. While *Batman's* pre-exposure campaign seemingly worked well, the strategy used for *Dick Tracy* (merchandise mostly timed with the film's release) may have contributed to the disappointing performance of Tracy merchandise, at least according to many merchandisers. (The Disney company seemed to be quite pleased, however, as discussed in the case study to follow.)

Another factor suggested by Carlat is competition, as he argues that there are only a few 'hot licenses' at any one time. However, one successful film may start a 'feeding frenzy,' during which symbiotic relationships are formed. He notes that '[i]n entertainment licensing, everyone feeds off each other, at least until the consumer can't stomach it anymore.' In addition, Carlat points out that movie licensing is streaky or cyclical, as indicated, for instance, by contrasting the total sales from 1985 ($3.5 billion) and 1987 ($2.2 billion).

Some companies are trying to overcome this problem by focusing on characters or images that endure. An example is *The Simpsons*. Although originally a television-based merchandising phenomenon, the Fox strategy of 'playing licensing for the long haul' also translates to movie-based properties. Al Ovadia, vice-president of licensing and merchandising for Twentieth Century Fox, explains that '[w]e're really looking five years down the line . . . We're not just putting their pictures on a T-shirt. We're trying to sell the whole attitude.'[81]

The final factor mentioned by Carlat is the kiss of death to merchandisers – no market demand. Although there are many merchandising success stories, there also is the real difficulty of translating film fantasy to popular products. One way of overcoming part of this problem is creating merchandise not dependent on people seeing a film,[82] or not directly linking the merchandise to a specific film. The main problem, however, is the creation of merchandise that consumers are interested in buying, whether or not they have actually seen the films on which the products are based.

Copied or pirated merchandise is another issue which might be added to Carlat's list, but mostly pertains to successful merchandising efforts which attract imitators and copyright infringers.[83] Obviously, the companies involved in licensing are strong supporters of stringent copyright and trademark protection.

Notes

1. Haralovich, M. B. (1985) Film Advertising, the Film Industry, and the Pin-up: The Industry's Accommodations to Social Forces in the 1940s. In Austin, Bruce A. (ed.) *Current Research in Film: Audiences, Economics, and Law*, Ablex

Publishing, Norwood, NJ, Vol. 1; Staiger, Janet (1990, Spring) Announcing Wares, Winning Patrons, Voicing Ideals: Thinking about the History and Theory of Film Advertising. *Cinema Journal*, Vol. 29, No. 3; Gaines, Jane and Herzog, Charlotte (eds.) (1990) *Fabrications: Costume and the Female Body*, Routledge/New York American Film Institute Readers.

2. See Guback, Thomas H. (1976) Hollywood's International Market. In Balio, Tino *The American Film Industry*, University of Wisconsin Press, Madison, Wisc.
3. Staiger, 'Announcing Wares.'
4. Spillman, S. Marketers Race to Leave Their Brand on Films. *Advertising Age*, 1 July 1985.
5. Kalish, D. Now Showing: Products! *Marketing and Media*, 23 August 1988.
6. Spillman, 'Marketers Race'; Lang, N. A. You Oughta Be in Pictures. *Beverage World*, April 1990.
7. Lang, 'You Oughta Be in Pictures'; Sheinfeld, Lois P. Dangerous Liaisons. *Film Comment*, September/October 1989, p. 70.
8. Hajdu, D. Commercials on Cassette. *Video Review*, December 1988.
9. Lang, 'You Oughta Be in Pictures'; Fleming, Michael, Product Pluggola Padding Pic Producers' Budgets. *Variety*, 9 May 1990.
10. Sheinfeld, 'Dangerous Liaisons,' p. 71.
11. Hajdu, 'Commercials on Cassette.'
12. Ibid.
13. Kalish, 'Now Showing: Products!'
14. Lang, 'You Oughta Be in Pictures.'
15. The Ad Line is Increasingly Becoming the Thing for Costly Features. *Variety*, 4 April 1990.
16. Magiera, Marcy, Coming Attractions: Movie Tie-Ins Galore. *Advertising Age*, 28 May 1990.
17. Fleming, Michael, Turtles, Toons and Toys 'R' In. *Variety*, 18 April 1990.
18. Ibid.
19. Kalish, 'Now Showing: Products!'
20. Sheinfeld, 'Dangerous Liaisons,' p. 71.
21. Spillman, 'Marketers Race.'
22. Loro, L. and Magiera, Marcy, Philly Products Angle for Ringside in 'Rocky V'. *Advertising Age*, 5 February 1990.
23. Spillman, 'Marketers Race.'
24. The Ad Line is Increasingly Becoming the Thing. *Variety*.
25. Hajdu, 'Commercials on Cassette.'
26. Ibid.
27. Sheinfeld, 'Dangerous Liaisons,' pp. 70–2.
28. Fleming, 'Turtles, Toons and Toys.'
29. Silbert, Jon, When Screens Become Billboards. *American Film*, May 1989.
30. Simpsons' Suit Cites Oregonians. *Register-Guard*, 14 June 1990.
31. Colford, S. W. Tobacco Critic Opens New Front. *Advertising Age*, 27 March 1989; Lallande, A. The Capital Cutting Room. *Marketing and Media Decisions*, 23 August 1989.
32. CSPI Calls for Movie Subtitles Identifying Paid Products. *Broadcasting*, 3 April 1989.
33. Rothenberg, R. Movies Become Another Vehicle for Advertisers. *Register-Guard*, 23 June 1991.
34. Lang, 'You Oughta Be in Pictures.'
35. Lallande, 'The Capital Cutting Room.'
36. Magiera, Marcy, Madison Avenue Hits Hollywood. *Advertising Age*, 10 December 1990.
37. Magiera, Marcy, Pizza Hut Ties In with Turtles Video. *Advertising Age*, 30 July 1990.

38. Peters, J. Studios Split on Videos as Premiums. *Variety*, 13 June 1990.
39. Fitzgerald, K. and Leisse-Erickson, J. 'Willow' Stirs Promo Frenzy. *Advertising Age*, 16 May 1988.
40. Ellis-Simons, Pamela, Screen Gems? *Marketing and Media Decisions*, 23 November 1988.
41. Grover, Ronald, Hitching a Ride on Hollywood's Hot Streak. *Business Week*, 11 July 1988.
42. Ellis-Simons, 'Screen Gems?'
43. Hulin-Salkin, B. Movie Tie-ins. *Incentive*, June 1989.
44. Ellis-Simons, 'Screen Gems?'
45. Magiera, Marcy, Hollywood Cools Off Summer Film Tie-ins. *Advertising Age*, 15 April 1991.
46. Mayer, I. Good-bye, Easy Growth. *Channels/Field Guide 1989*.
47. Magiera, 'Hollywood Cools Off.'
48. Magiera, Marcy, Videos Aim $85M at Kids. *Advertising Age*, 17 June 1991, p. 16.
49. Borden, Lester J. 'Merchandising and Distribution Techniques of Programmes,' paper presented at New Dimensions in Television meeting Venice, Italy, March 1981.
50. Cebrzynski, G. I Didn't See the Movie, But I Drank the Wine. *Marketing News*, 16 April 1990, p. 4.
51. Johnson, Jay L. Licensing: A $65.5 Billion Industry. *Discount Merchandiser*, June 1991, pp. 36–41, 76–8.
52. For example, the National Basketball Association reported receiving over $1 billion from licensing activities in 1991, while just one player – Michael Jordan – was to receive $21.2 million from his product endorsements during 1992. 'Morning Briefings,' *Register-Guard*, 30 January 1992. See also Wasko, Janet and Phillips, Mark, Teal's the 'Deal in Sports Merchandising.' *Oregon Sports News*, Spring 1993, pp. 48–51.
53. Williams, Pete, Recession Hits Foundation of House of Cards. *USA Today Baseball Weekly*, 2 January 1992, p. 24.
54. Ellis-Simons, 'Screen Gems?'
55. Fleming, 'Product Pluggola.'
56. Blickstein, Jay, Trek Merchandise Sales Beaming Up. *Variety*, 2 December 1991, p. 54.
57. Nightmare Called Freddy Becomes Toymaker Dream. *Register-Guard*, 7 September 1989.
58. Fox, David, 'Jurassic' Stomps Record. *Los Angeles Times*, 15 June 1993.
59. See Schickel, Richard (1968) *The Disney Version*, Avon Books, New York.
60. Solomon, Charles (1989) *Enchanted Drawings*, Alfred A. Knopf, New York.
61. Ibid.
62. Carlat, Larry, Bombs Away. *Variety*, 30 May 1990.
63. See "Dick Tracy' Seen as Risky Business.' *Variety*, 30 May 1990.
64. Carlat, Larry, How It Really Works. *Variety*, 30 May 1990; The Walt Disney Company, Form 10K, 1990.
65. Ellis-Simons, 'Screen Gems?'
66. Johnson, 'Licensing.'
67. See Fleming, 'Product Pluggola.'
68. Borden, 'Merchandising and Distribution Techniques.'
69. Alexander, Garth, No Toys in Tokyo Puts 'Turtles' in the Soup. *Variety*, 15 April 1991.
70. Grover, 'Hitching a Ride.'
71. Fleming, 'Product Pluggola.'
72. See Forkan, James P. Licensees Hope for Movie Magic. *Advertising Age*, 22 February, 1988.

73. ''Dick Tracy','' *Variety*.
74. Ibid.
75. Day, Kathleen Being Famous Pays in Licensing Game. *Los Angeles Times*, 6 October 1985.
76. Ellis-Simons, 'Screen Gems?'
77. Carlat, 'How It Really Works.'
78. Borden, 'Merchandising and Distribution Techniques.'
79. Grover, 'Hitching a Ride.'
80. Carlat, 'Bombs Away.'
81. Will the Summer Stifle 'Simpsons' Sizzle? *Variety*, 30 May 1990.
82. Ellis-Simons, 'Screen Gems?'
83. See 'Simpsons' Suit Cites Oregonians. *Register-Guard*, 14 June 1991; and the following discussion of Disney.

13

Global news wholesalers as agents of globalization*

Oliver Boyd-Barrett

Centre for Mass Communication Research, University of Leicester (1996).

Introduction

Traditionally, news agencies reported news and sold news to other media. They were 'wholesalers'. Major agencies like Reuters (U.K.) and Associated Press (AP)(U.S.A.) established international reporting networks and distributed news to media and non-media clients around the world. Clients included national agencies: these traded, in unequal exchange, their national news for the international coverage of the global agencies. National agencies then compiled news wires combining national and international news to domestic clients, who also drew on the services of local agencies for news of particular cities or specialist subjects.

News agencies give clients access to a wider and more dependable range of (mainly) global political, economic and sports news, through text, news photography, video and electronic networks than any single client could provide unilaterally. The small number of elite media outlets who maintain international reporters typically field up to a handful or two in a few

*This chapter draws from interview data with news agency sources carried out by the author as part of a larger project still in progress in Hong Kong, Jerusalem, London, Madrid, and New York, in the period November 1995 to April 1996. These interviews focus mainly on bureau chief and senior executive perceptions of significant changes in the global news business since 1980. For hard data I have supplemented these with the Annual Reports of Reuters Holdings PLC (1992-5). Earlier historical data covering the period 1830-1980 is drawn mostly from the author's previous publications: see Boyd-Barrett (1980), Boyd-Barrett and Palmer (1981) and Boyd-Barrett (1985); references to regional news agencies are mainly drawn from Boyd-Barrett and Thussu (1992). Other sources on the earlier history of news agencies, especially sources which have been published since the author's (1980) study include Read's (1992) history of Reuters, Fenby (1986), on the international agencies generally, Rantanen (1990) and Rantanen and Vartanova (1995) on Russian and East European news agencies, Palmer in Tunstall and Palmer (1991) on Agence France Presse. For recent hard data on the television news agencies I have drawn liberally from Carla Brooks Johnstone (1995) and to a lesser extent from Friedland (1992) and Paterson (1994) on the global video agencies generally, and the work of Cohen *et al.* (1996) on Eurovision. With T. Rantanen the author is editing a collection of articles on national and international news agencies in the context of globalization (Sage, forthcoming).

major capitals or crisis locations. The major agencies, by contrast, sustain many hundreds globally. They are the first, often unaccredited sources of intelligence for 'breaking' news stories for media, finance and governmental clients, a bedrock to which clients may add more personalized coverage or commentary.

In liberal democracies their role is problematic: they subvert the surface appearance of source diversity in 'retail' media. Where links have been established between news agencies and other interests (political or commercial) such concerns have intensified.

For governments involved in their ownership or sponsorship (today's major global agencies are independent of government, with the partial exception of Agence France Press (AFP)), the news agencies were vehicles for dissemination of state information and propaganda to national and international audiences, and for intervention in incoming and outgoing flows of information. What they did not control or finance, they could attempt to manipulate. Conversely, global agencies could subvert state information policies of other powers: e.g. 1890s efforts of the cartel, (Reuters, Havas and Wolff) to maintain Wolff as monopoly supplier of international news to the Imperial Russian Telegraph Agency and of Russian news to the rest of the world, at a time when the Russian government desired greater Russian control over news in order to promote a favourable international image and attract external investment (Rantanen, 1990).

'Third World' critics within the non-aligned movement (NAM) bitterly criticized Western-based global agencies during the 1970s New World Information and Communication Order (NWICO) debates. Newly-independent ex-colonies discovered that continuing economic dependence effectively limited their political autonomy. Barriers were not just material but also ideological, relating to how developing countries were perceived by Western governments and investors. Identification of significant countries, events and opinions were thought to be influenced by the global agencies who could boost or undermine a nation's construction of national image, with economic as well as political consequences. Bolstered by their own governments' ideology of 'free flow', the Western-based agencies saw themselves as champions of truth and objectivity; threatened by claims for a free and *balanced* flow, their respective Western governments (U.S.A. and U.K.) withdrew support from the forum (UNESCO) through which such claims had been advanced – a measure of the significance attached by major sources of state and economic power to the transnational machineries of image formation.

I am arguing that agencies contribute both to processes of national consolidation and to globalization, simultaneously. They were the first transnational media systems. They were adept transnational business operators. In operation and in content they developed a modern global consciousness, contributing transnational information, gathered at speed, to political and economic elites directly or through media. They helped formulate the concept of news as about events, elite people, elite nations, their international conflicts and interests. They exploited the political and economic currency of news as a commodity affecting the value of other commodities. They forged domestic and transnational links between state, capital, media and civil society: state and capital provided patronage and revenue, in order to secure information and to influence the information which agencies fed to public media.

News agencies offer laboratories for a convergence of political economy (1970s) and cultural studies (1980s) approaches to media research within a discourse of globalization (1990s) neither underplaying diversity of production or of reception while sensitive to media texts as commodities of often highly concentrated global economic power. While in practice political economy approaches to agencies have prevailed, globalization discourse contextualizes and potentially supersedes previous debates about media as international actors, from a discourse of media as agents of *propaganda* (1920s–1930s) through to the *free-flow* doctrine of post World War II (1940s–1950s), to dependency and *media imperialism* theory (1960s–1970s) underpinning the NWICO debates, to the *new world order* of capital freedom and reader autonomy of the 1980s and finally to *globalization* in the 1990s. The encounter with globalization will compel a more rounded attention to issues of political-economy, culture, identity and meaning.

I will examine transformations and continuities in agency activity over the two decades since my 1980 study, with a view to relating these to current globalization theory.

Defining characteristics

Some 20 years ago I identified (Boyd-Barrett, 1978; 1980, pp. 22–28) a global news system at the heart of which were the 'Big 4' Western-based news agencies (at that time – Agence France Press (AFP), Associated Press (AP), Reuters, United Press International (UPI)). Within this closely integrated, hierarchical but symbiotic system the major agencies – which from 1859 to 1934 had carved up the world into exclusive territories of influence – loosely depended, in addition to their own reporters, on exclusive alliances with national agencies for a routine supply of news of national territories and which, in turn, depended on the major agencies for an exclusive supply of international news. This sustained national agencies' (sometimes fragile) monopoly control over domestic media markets. Sometimes national governments insisted on this arrangement. Many national agencies were established with the assistance, direct or indirect, of global agencies.

The sustained influence of the 'Big 4' I ascribed – subject to a number of important qualifications – to a unique blend of characteristics, principal among which were: *long heritage*, origination in the world's *imperial capitals*, intimate ties with the world's *'advanced nations'*, wealthy domestic markets to finance transnational forays, *independence of government*, selling services on a commercial, *contractual basis*, allowing some scope for *client media participation*, exhibiting strong tendencies towards *diversification of services* but, so far as news was concerned, selling a *broadly similar product* – 'spot news' – in a *competitive environment*. I also noted that they were *technological innovators*. They were dominant partners in *two-way relationships with national agencies*.

How has this model stood up to the events of the past 20 years? Of the original 'Big 4' one has virtually withdrawn. UPI, barely surviving a succession of economic and takeover crises since the 1980s, is currently owned

(1996) by Saudi-based Middle East Broadcasting Corporation. Its reporting and sales activities have been considerably reduced.

Are there significant new players? In the sphere of print general news agency journalism I would say not, at least at the top. The momentous collapse of the Soviet Union, however, led to the partial eclipse of government agency TASS (once 'number five' in reporting strength, perhaps, but not in sales) in favour of a private agency, Interfax. In the sphere of wholesale financial news for non-media clients, Reuters remains dominant on world markets; leading competitors include Dow Jones (strongest financial agency in the U.S.A.), Knight-Ridder and Bloomberg.

There has been considerable change among the television news agencies. The 1970s television news market was dominated by Visnews, owned by Reuters in partnership with the BBC and NBC; and by UPITN, jointly owned by UPI and the U.K.'s Independent Television News (ITN). Other sources included news co-operatives run by public service broadcasters such as the Eurovision News Exchange. The Visnews/UPITN duopoly was threatened by the appearance of Ted Turner's CNNI (now part of Telecommunications Inc., and Time-Warner), especially during the Gulf War which boosted global awareness of CNNI. CNNI could undermine established 'wholesalers' by feeding direct to a world-wide audience in a 'retail' operation distributed by satellite and cable. Yet despite its own reporting (20 non-U.S. international bureaux) and exchange relationships with 200 broadcasters, CNNI continues to buy wholesale services, especially Reuters Television, WTN and APTV. Both CNNI success, and dramatic expansion in number of television channels brought about by digitization, compression, and deregulation, stimulates global competition.

Main players in the mid-1990s video news 'wholesale' market, providing raw material in natural sound with textual back-up, are APTV, Reuters, and WTN. It is very uncertain whether the market is large enough to support more than two profitable global television news agencies. Major 'retail' global broadcasters include CNNI, BBC World Service Television (WSTV) and the Murdoch channels (BSkyB in Europe, Fox in the U.S. and STAR TV in Asia).

Reuters acquired total control of Visnews in 1992, and renamed it Reuters Television. For some viewers this 'wholesale' service has a 'retail' feel via satellite channels such as BSkyB (Europe), Fox in the U.S., and up to 1996, 'Tele Noticias' in the Americas and Spain. Withdrawal from 'Tele Noticias' suggests that for Reuters such 'retail' activity in this market competes unhelpfully with its 'wholesale' clients. Reuters Television distributes to 200 broadcasters and affiliates in 84 countries. By buying into ITN (18% of shares, acquired in 1993) Reuters has a stake in its main 'competitor', WTN. This happened after the BBC, once part-owner of Visnews with Reuters, established BBC World Television for satellite distribution in 1992.

WTN originated from UPITN and is now a partnership of ABC (80% in 1994), ITN (U.K.)(10%), and Nine Network (Sydney, Australia)(10%). ABC, part of the Capital Cities Corporation, is now owned by Disney. WTN, with 15 principal bureaux and camera crews in almost 90 sites, relies substantially on ABC's 215 U.S. affiliate stations for U.S. coverage and on ITN for U.K. coverage. WTN supplies to the BBC in place of Reuters.

Other (wholesale) players include Eurovision, and Eurovision's Asian equivalent, Asiavision. Eurovision and Asiavision, representing public service television stations in their respective regions under the auspices of EBU and ABU, continue to run complex news-exchange networks, supplying video for regional stations, but dependent on Reuters, WTN, APTV and other agencies for almost 50% of output. Other retail players in the global market include NBC, CBS, (U.S.A.), and Televisa's ECO (Mexico). Companies such as Microsoft are gearing up for the supply of multi-media news services by Internet: Microsoft announced in 1995 a deal with NBC for a 24-hour cable news channel and an interactive news service on the Internet. Meanwhile, Reuters augments its sales of news and information services both to Internet providers and to private electronic 'Intranets', taking account of GATT deregulation facilitating such networks, in a move that will become more significant in decades ahead.

To these may be added a wave of financial television news services either for direct electronic feed to computer screens in financial institutions, brokerage houses, banks, currency dealers and other market traders, or for satellite and cable television. These include Reuters Financial Television, and Bloomberg Information Network for direct feed to client computer screens; CNNfn., Dow Jones' European Business News and its sister channel, Asia Business News, and NBC's CNBC for satellite broadcasts. Reuters has established television 'studios' in the offices of key informants in leading source institutions for instant relay of statements and commentary.

Arguably there has been a significant increase in the number of major players in international news. If this entails an increase in source diversity it should be a cause for celebration. If, on the other hand, it confirms to retail news media the economic futility of sustaining independent international news operations ('downsizing' has been a significant theme throughout the communications companies in the 1990s), then there has been no increase in diversity, and possibly a reduction (see Winseck 1992, and Paterson, 1994).

Arrival of new players has implications for the 'long heritage' which I claimed for the major agencies in 1980. Some but not all the actors have indeed been around for a long time. But new providers reinforce an Anglo-American tradition of news dominance, and perhaps the swing to European dominance, argued by Tunstall (1992), may have reversed back in favour of the U.S.A.

Once distinctive institutions with a perceived 'public service' function, how far are agencies absorbed within the global struggle of multi-media conglomerates? Not much. AP is an independent co-operative of daily U.S. newspapers. AFP is directed by the French state, media and journalists, but has joined forces with Bloomberg for supply of economic news outside the U.S.A. Reuters is a publicly owned company: some shareholders may be more influential than others (e.g. News International in the 1980s), but the Reuter Trust prohibits ownership of 30% or more of the company by any one interest, group or faction.

Identification with the world's (ex)-imperial capitals and advanced nations still helps account for the agencies' strength. Links to national media and power elites secured privileged access to domestic sources, building agency credibility for world markets. They secured similar access in those developing nations incorporated within the global economy and needing access to global news networks for information and influence.

Established advantages inflate the scale of investment required of new market entrants, who from day one must be capable of gathering and distributing their own news globally, at maximum possible speed and accuracy. New market entry is rare: Associated Press (a junior member of the cartel which then pushed itself to full equivalency, busting the cartel in 1934) is the only successful 20th century example. The shift to video news provides new opportunities linked to changing technology and skills, and yet of the new players at least two are directly owned by print news agencies. Internet (and, more particularly, Intranets), may enhance entry opportunities but existing giants are the first to move in.

Location at the heart of an ex 'imperial' or 'advanced' power is not a sufficient condition for the development of a global agency. The association of Reuters with London, and of Havas (later AFP) with Paris, helped provide European and global communication links (telegraphic cable, radio, then telephonic cable – until the advent of satellite) and access to power-brokers of the 19th and 20th centuries. But while Germany was an imperial power no German news agency achieved truly world-wide status after the demise of Wolff in World War I (although DPA is certainly one of the strongest national agencies). The United States, with a few exceptions, was not a (major) territorial imperialist yet spawned AP, UPI and INS, and various television and financial news agencies (including Dow Jones Telerate, Knight-Ridder, Bloomberg) and is home for leading syndicates such as the New York Times News Service, Washington Post–Los Angeles Times news service. Amongst other 'advanced countries' are some, like Italy or Japan, which were once imperial and which attempted to reinforce imperial power through news agency networks. They were either outmanoeuvred by the established cartel or were disadvantaged by language. The Spanish agency, EFE, is, however, an increasingly influential player in news flows between Spanish-speaking countries.

Countries in the newly-industrialized world may have the economic power to finance a global agency but no entrepreneurs seem inclined to try: a realistic assessment of the risks or expectation of a meagre return? There are safer and more lucrative ways of making money. The real money is not so much in news but in what can be done with a global news network through diversification.

A prosperous, media-wealthy domestic market appears to be a necessary if not sufficient condition for a global agency. Associated Press membership includes most major U.S. dailies, and is the most subscribed source of text, photo and audio news for U.S. newspapers and broadcasters. Strong domestic market reflects population size and per capita wealth, in turn attracting advertisers who thus indirectly finance news agency subscriptions. Market size in itself is only part of the story: co-operative solidarity in the case of AP is also important – a sounder base than the more conventionally commercial UPI. The AP experience confirms the view that domestic market monopoly may be necessary to sustain global activity.

Reuters had a similar advantage until 1984 when it became a publicly-floated company on the London stock exchange: previously it was a limited liability company owned by the Press Association, (U.K. national news agency), on behalf of the provincial press, and the Newspaper Publishers' Association for the national press. As with AP, this vertical link with the U.K. press consolidated a domestic market whose leading media thus had a stake in Reuters' success. The U.K. is the single most important client country for Reuters, accounting for 16% of total revenues in 1995 (reflecting London's strength as an international financial centre), but the U.K. market is less important to Reuters than the U.S.A. to Associated Press or France to AFP, whose home markets account for four-fifths of revenues. The domestic French market is important on account of government subventions to AFP. While declining in relative importance they account for over half AFP's revenues, in the form of controlled prices for state client subscriptions. For Reuters the equivalent economic base is (Western) Europe, then Asia. In 1995 revenues from Europe, the Middle East and Africa accounted for 54.57% of the total, of which most was European; Asia/Pacific accounted for 18%, followed by the U.S.A. at 15.4%. We can still conclude that a wealthy domestic clientele continues to be important to the survival of major print news agencies.

Do market disparities have implications for service? This was an issue behind NWICO concerns about alleged failure of global agencies to satisfy Third World information needs despite significant trends towards 'regionalization' of agency services at the time, including Arabic language services (Reuters, AFP) for the Middle East, and customized services for African and South American regions. Biases persist with respect to which countries and regions receive most coverage and prominence (the Soviet Union and Eastern Europe getting very little attention, relatively, until the emergence of Solidarity in 1970s Poland). Recent scarcity of content analysis studies limits current discussion. Widespread application of electronic storage and retrieval and increases in news volume obscure the issue by giving freedom of menu choice. The most problematic aspects of bias in agency news may be less geopolitical and more to do with such factors as narrowness of topic range (mainly international and major national economics, politics, military affairs, international and major internal conflict, sport); concentration on elites; prominence of official sources; and application of conventional western news criteria (e.g. favouring conflict over stability, event rather than process).

Domestic markets are less important for video agencies, which are all offshoots of well-established enterprises. They build on parent infrastructures of bureaux, staff, communications networks, source and client links. AP's bid to prepare itself for multi-media delivery, APTV, is not at present distributed within the U.S.; CNNI grew out of CNN in the U.S.; BBC World Service Television draws from an integrated BBC news network which includes the U.K. government-funded listening station at Caversham which monitors foreign broadcasting and radio-transmitted agency services, particularly from (ex-) communist countries, for its electronic Monitor service to client media – of largely unremarked importance for Reuters (a 'wholesale' service for wholesalers). Reuters Television developed out of Visnews: it shares the same basic newsroom in London as the agency's general and financial news services (although the anticipated advantages of such integration have not materialized); increasingly, Reuters reporters have multimedia skills, and there are economies of scale in shared use of bureaux space and communications. Reuters still retains a special relationship with NBC, whose 40% shares in Visnews it bought out in 1992, and which is a supplier of U.S. news. WTN draws on parental ABC–ITN U.S.–U.K. operations. Eurovision is dependent on large public service television networks across Europe.

Video news services are secondary creations of established media, generating revenue from operations which parent companies would maintain in any case. Global text agencies are not usually affiliated with a single retail media corporation, although UPI was a creation of Scripps and INS was founded by Hearst.

Twenty years ago I said the agencies were non-governmental. I argued that AFP's state ties were not in the same league as the Soviet TASS, Chinese Xin Hua or many national agencies of developing countries which reported directly to government ministries, and that AFP was less implicated than its predecessor, Havas. I did not predict that French governments in the 1990s would still try to block senior appointments they disliked. Reuters had been a beneficiary of covert state aid, even post-World War II (e.g. through subsidy to a Reuter's partner, the Arab News Agency, in the Middle East), but I considered that the financial news services now provided a basis for independence. In fact secret government subvention continued into the 1970s through underwriting of subscriptions from BBC World Service radio and subsidization of Reuters (unsuccessful) creation of a Latin American co-operative, LATIN (Read, 1992). The video agencies have no direct link with governments; BBC WSTV is financed from sale of advertising space and toll charges from cable companies, unlike its domestic broadcast services (financed by licence fee) or World Services radio (financed by government) – but early losses may have been covered from state sources (Friedland, 1992). Political independence helps determine whether agencies are perceived to be tolerably credible; evidence suggesting otherwise is damaging.

Evidence of client participation is mixed. AP's membership structure is intact; members and associate members are consulted in its running. But this applies principally to domestic members. UPI's development of international client consultation in the 1980s is largely aborted. AFP involves newspapers, state ministries and journalists on its governing body, privileging the influence of domestic clients. Reuters client links follow conventional good practice The agency encourages regular contact of Reuters staff with (non-media financial news) clients, nurturing sensitivity to client need, providing support and advice. This may off-set client resentment against the company's market power, and runs counter to earlier insistence on distance between reporters and sources to preserve reporting integrity. Such a principle, arguably, was misplaced; it may be more important for reporters to be aware of what information clients want, and how it should be presented.

Diversification continues to be extremely important. The importance of Reuters economic services was clear in the 1970s, but few could have predicted the scale of profits in the early 1980s which inspired its newspaper owners to realize their long-dormant investments through public flotation in 1984. Success of financial and interactive services (accounting for 94% of all 1995 revenues) provide a surer foundation for all coverage than could have been provided by media clients alone and have provided the basis for improvement in media sales and services. Media clients account for only 6% of revenues, but absolute revenues from media quadrupled 1985–1991. Two decades saw a three-fold increase in bureaux numbers and a six-fold increase in personnel, with massive investment in new technology of benefit for general news as for financial news clients: services that increase speed, broaden band-width, provide historical data services, software packages for data manipulation, a global photo service delivering several times the number of news pictures at several times the speed than was available 20 years before (Reuters had no photographic operation until it took over UPI's non-U.S. photo service in 1984), and of course a television news service. The financial television news service alone had over 8000 customers by 1995.

This marriage of journalism with capitalism may enhance credibility; the agency is less vulnerable to political pressures or to machinations of large media shareholders. Financial markets have a voracious appetite for credible analysis and data on which rest market decisions governing astronomical sums. There is an almost infinite range of issues carrying implications for finance. Does this have implications for the range of Reuters general news? Given the increase in news volumes it is unlikely that in absolute terms there is any topic which is less reported on today. There may be a more subtle danger: the rise to power of employees who have not been immersed in the hustling world of general news, and who lack the kind of imagination which can identify stories in the most unpromising of contexts.

Reuters' revenue multiplied some 40 times since 1977 to a 1995 total of £2703 million. Revenues from media services grew approximately 16 times. In 1977 Reuters and AP were on a level but by 1993 Reuters had 10 times the turnover. Media services revenue alone was equivalent to more than half of AP's total revenues. In the 1960s, Reuters economic services accounted for 30–50% of total revenue. This increased to 85% in 1980 and 94% in 1995. In 1980 there were 13,000 clients; in 1995 there were 327,000 customer screens across 154 countries. In 1977 there were 350 editorial staff out of 2377 personnel operating from 60 bureaux world-wide; by 1995 this had grown to 1863 journalistic staff out of 14,347 personnel operating from 143 editorial bureaux and a total of 207 offices in 90 countries. (AP in 1993 had 144 domestic U.S. bureaux and 92 international bureaux). Reuters' top executives each earned between £340,000 and £650,000 in salary and benefits in 1995.

Reuters' principal services are (a) *information products*, accounting for 69% of revenues, delivering prices, datafeeds and data-analysis software tools covering currencies, stocks, bonds, futures, options and other instruments; (b) *transaction products* which enable traders to deal from their keyboards in such markets as foreign exchange, futures and options, and securities, accounting for 31% of revenues and (c) *media products*, accounting for 6% of revenues, delivering news in text, television, still pictures, sound and graphics to newspapers, broadcasters, electronic briefing and online services.

AFP also has economic news services (partnering with Bloomberg), and a newsphoto service. AP entered video news with APTV in 1994, in addition to its text and voice services for press and broadcasting clients. All agencies are exploring Internet possibilities. Reuters Television and WTN offer supplementary services, including ready-for-air programmes, privately commissioned programmes and archive services, international crewing, and sale of advertising time. Several agencies offer communications services for other companies. WTN, for example, in a joint-venture with British Aerospace Communications, provides fixed and mobile links and video conferencing.

Core activities need to be seen to be free of external influence or corruption from other interests. AP cannot within the terms of its not-for-profit constitution engage in commercial activity that does not centre on news reporting and news distribution. All major players are principally engaged in production of a similar product – spot news, their defining activity (even feature services link exclusively with recent or anticipated spot-news events). The picture is clouded by links with larger corporations in the case of the video agencies (e.g. WTN and Disney; CNNI and Time Warner) although such corporations are still principally *media* conglomerates.

Agencies operate in a strongly competitive climate. This is most true of video agencies, but can the potential market support the current number? I have alluded to the decline in number of major global text agencies from four to three. North American agencies still perform more strongly than the European on South American markets *pace* the presence there of the Spanish national agency, EFE. Reuters and AFP still dominate as news suppliers within Anglophone and Francophone regions of Africa respectively. Reuters has been active in exploitation of the new markets of ex-Soviet Russia and Eastern Europe. Asia is a particularly mixed situation. Reuters is the leading financial news agency globally but it too faces competition from Bloomberg, Knight-Ridder, Dow Jones Telerate (associated with the Wall Street Journal), especially in the U.S. market where Reuters considers its progress has been disappointing. Reuters' strength rests on comprehensiveness of its services, which can be accessed on a single screen (not necessarily a Reuters terminal) including general news and financial television reports, together with sophisticated data manipulation and historical data services; for many years it has successfully acted as an electronic dealing forum for money markets, a principle now extended to equities, advertising and similar ventures. In money markets it could be argued that Reuters has contributed to a global infrastructure that among other things permits the occasional destabilization of national currencies.

Intensifying competition is the growth in number of distribution channels, including Internet and multi-media. In principle Internet should facilitate access to new market entrants, drawing on the access to a range of news sources which Internet makes possible. Internet is increasingly an important destination for news announcements from institutional news sources, and some leading newspapers employ journalists to surf the Internet for stories. It increasingly seems wasteful to send a reporter to cover, say, a sports event when the result of that event is provided over the Internet perhaps even before it is made available to the reporter. But of course, sports reporters do not attend events merely to report results; they report on players, the state of the pitch, the weather and all kinds of incidental circumstances than can contribute to the 'story'; increasingly, reporters will be called upon to make their reports in any of the principal modes of print, photography, voice and television.

The global agencies originate most of their own news coverage; they can deliver their news faster and more reliably through their own communications networks – differences of mere seconds have huge implications for financial news markets prepared to pay substantial sums for those seconds and to ensure security of the information that is conveyed. Existing agencies are also well positioned to provide news services to the Internet, reaping money from the gateway services (Reuters is part-owner of at least one of these and provides services to several), and private networks, in relation to the number of 'hits' and the sale of advertising space on news pages (further evidence of new links between advertising and news agencies, not seen since the days of the pre-war French agency, Havas).

The agencies are exploiters of global communications technology; innovativeness is driven by competition to be fastest at lowest cost. The technology connection has characterized the business from applications of pigeon and Morse telegraphy, through to Reuters' ownership of extensive international cable networks, and later adaptations of Marconi's invention of the wireless. Computerization of the global networks, with journalists inputting text direct to screens was well advanced by the mid-1970s, followed by application of satellite technology in the late 1970s. There is significant R&D investment in customer hardware, software packages, electronic photographic composition and dissemination. This is hardly to be wondered at: Reuters networks alone have been said to rival the Pentagon's.

With the onset of the 'information superhighway', there develops a possibility, no stronger than that, that the rest of the world may catch up with the agencies, reducing their competitive technological advantage. While there may not be many global providers, the world is replete with other media, and alternative sources: newspapers, magazines, television channels, electronic providers. But few of these are strong on international news; what they do cover often comes from news agencies or other – normally Western-based – media like Time, Newsweek, etc., which in turn also subscribe to the news agencies.

News agencies and the globalization debate

I have reviewed the principal characteristics of global agencies; I have noted significant changes, notably the decline in number of leading print news agencies, but an increase in television news agencies. But I have argued that the overall picture seems to be more of the same. Concern about news agencies within academe was always associated with the dominance-dependency model and the NWICO debates which it fed: news agencies were surprisingly prominent in that debate. Foisted on the newly-developing world as a 'development' concept in the 1950s by UNESCO (improving 'free flow' of information, contributing to democracy and economic growth) news agencies acquired a bad name when it was realized that they represented very junior members of a global system dominated by Western giants. Unable to control their external image, developing nations had even less control over other people's representations of them. This model comes close to the cultural or media imperialism position which I espoused at that time; for all the defects of that model, and there are many, the global news system conforms well to many features of it.

The globalization thesis has sometimes been advanced as a model more finely attuned to complexity and to the patterns of difference and variety across and within nations and cultures (Tomlinson, 1991). A common approach (Tunstall, 1977; Sinclair *et. al.*, 1996) is to focus on regional patterns of production. But appreciation of complexity should not be at the expense of identifying global patterns of media concentration, and gross inequalities of access to mass audiences which they entail; if we are looking for patterns among the factors determining the range of media products available we are quickly drawn to major sources of national and global financial and political power. It is not uninteresting that Mexico's Televisa exports telenovelas to the rest of South America, or that Brazil's TV Globo sells telenovelas to Italy or to Russia. But we have to set the scale of their activity against that of Hollywood, for example, in terms of global dollars and titles, and what those dollars are then used for by the handful of media conglomerates that dominate transcultural media flows, bearing in mind that media imperialism was argued to be multi-dimensional (Boyd-Barrett, 1977), having to do with the design of communications technology, ways of organizing media systems, professional values and the content itself. Yes, we need to study how audiences take meaning from those products; but no matter how many different meanings they may take it does not eliminate concern about *whose* voices, representations, or stories make it to mainstream media and whose do not. Media conglomerates may no longer be exclusively American; boards of directors may include Japanese, Dutch, or Brazilians. This does not make them one iota more answerable, democratic, responsible, imaginative, or less recklessly preoccupied with personal and institutional profit.

In the major news agencies we confront a number of paradoxes; some are driven by profit, to satisfy their shareholders; others by an ethic of service to satisfy news appetites of their newspaper owners. All are global; they command the global news system; they are American and Western European in origin. They are committed to professional ideologies of independence and objectivity which offer a protective shield against complete penetration by commercialism.

The agencies are of general value to the assessment of the globalization thesis. They are a salutary reminder that international media activity was well-established by the mid-19th century, well organized and disciplined on international markets, and also commodified. There is nothing new about media acting as global agents or about media promoting globalization.

News agencies are a part of modernization, and link it with globalization: they respond to the same processes that generated newspapers, and to the needs of newspapers for a stable, reliable and relatively cheap source of international news. We do not need to assume globalization is a product of modernization. Globalization relates back to the diffusion and intercourse of ancient civilizations and cultures through military organization, population control, construction of roads, linguistic and literary practices, etc. What changes is the *form* of globalization. News agencies represent communication appropriate to the informational and relational needs of state, capital and civic society in modernity.

As global actors agencies emerge from modernity (*viz* industrialization, universal rationality, nationalism), and reinforce it through construction of global identities. Global agencies consolidated information networks within national boundaries through support for national agencies, contributing to the rationalization of communication between state and people and discourses about nation and state. They contributed to internationalization, constructing influential international news agendas that acted upon retail media, governments and finance. They developed and exploited technologies to improve global communications networks. They brought the global to the local and incorporated the local within the global in their day-to-day news gathering and news-dissemination, selling international news to national and local media and using local and national media as sources of news for global distribution. Reuters and other financial agencies have facilitated global financial transactions, and have even created the means (Reuters transaction services) to conduct international negotiations in equities, money markets and certain commodities. They provide the data which enable news commentators to think globally by picking up on parallel processes in different nation states and relating these to actors and events at global level.

Western in origin, global agencies are nourished by the Western news ideologies which they themselves constructed in the second half of the nineteenth century in response to telegraphic economics (Shaw, 1967), the rise of 'curiosity' journalism as exemplified by Dickens' 'Household Words' and Northcliffe's 'Titbits', and the positivistic fact-privileging influence of scientism (Schudson, 1978), and infected by small town values that helped to determine what was not 'normal' (and therefore interesting) (Gans, 1979). Study of news agencies confirms that globalization is Westernization. Agencies themselves inflected globalization as Westernization when taking Western-interests-as-norm (e.g. in their cold-war coverage, and in their skewed global maps privileging news from Western Europe, the United States and theatres of activity elsewhere which had direct relevance to western concerns) and promoted western values of news, business and politics. They confirm globalization as a process simultaneously economic, political and cultural: it has to do with belief systems which have been commodified within a political-economic dynamic.

News agencies contribute to the homogenization of global culture in form and in source, while greatly multiplying the texts available within these standardized discourses. They contribute to the development of local forms which they then incorporate as contributors and as clients.

New global culture is not the product of an equal contribution of all who are party to it or exposed to it and is equal only in as much as all parties have equal chances to take whatever meanings they want from it (if we want to assume that users have equal access to the texts, that they are equally skilled in making such meanings, or that they have been taught, through the structure of such discourse itself, *how* to make and take meanings). Global culture is not the product of equal choice; few are consulted in its manufacture. Study of news agencies is a reminder not to overlook the concrete structures through which the global culture is constructed. It tells us that globalization is neither anarchic nor random; it is the outcome of cultural agencies whose operations can be traced systematically.

References

Boyd-Barrett, Oliver and Thussu, D. K. (1992) *Contra-flow in Global News*, John Libbey, London.

Boyd-Barrett, Oliver (1985) Assessment of News Agency and Foreign Broadcast Monitoring Services as Information Sources, HATO, The Hague.

Boyd-Barrett, Oliver and Palmer, Michael (1981) *Le Trafic des Nouvelles*, Alain Moreau, Paris.

Boyd-Barrett, Oliver (1980) *The International News Agencies*, Constable, London.

Boyd-Barrett, Oliver (1978) *World Wide News Agencies: Development, organization, competition, markets and product; a study of Agence France Presse, Associated Press, Reuters and United Press to 1975*, PhD thesis, Open University.

Boyd-Barrett, Oliver (1977) Media Imperialism: Towards an International Framework for the Analysis of Media Systems. In Gurevitch *et al.* (eds.) *Mass Communication and Society*, pp. 116–35.

Cohen, A., Levy, M., Roeh, I., Gurevitch, M. (1996) *Global Newsrooms, Local Audiences. A Study of the Eurovision News Exchange*, John Libbey, London.

Fenby, Jonathan (1986) *The International News Services, A Twentieth Century Fund Report*, Schocker Books, New York.

Friedland (1992) *Covering the World. International Television News Services*, Twentieth Century Fund, New York.

Gans, H. (1979) *Deciding What's News*, Vintage Books, New York.

Johnston, Carla Brooks (1995) *Winning the Global TV News Game*, Focal Press, Boston.

Palmer, Michael (1991) Agence France Press. In Tunstall J. and Palmer M., (eds.) *Media Moguls*, Routledge, London.

Paterson (1994) Concentration and Competition Among Global Television News Agencies: Implications for Coverage of the Developing World, Paper presented at the *MacBride Round Table*, Honolulu, Hawaii.

Rantanen, Terhi (1990) *Foreign News in Imperial Russia*, Suomalainen Tiedeakatemia, Helsinki.

Rantanen, Terhi and Vartanova, Elena (1995) New Agencies in Post-Communist Russia. From State Monopoly to State Dominance. *European Journal of Communication*, Vol. 10, No. 2, pp. 207–20.

Read, Donald (1992) *The Power of News, the History of Reuters*, Oxford University Press.

Reuters Holdings PLC, *Annual Report*, 1992–5, Reuters, London.

Shaw, Donald L. (1967) News Bias and the Telegraph. *Journalism Quarterly*, Vol. 44, No. 1, pp. 3–12.

Schudson, M. (1978) *Discovering the News: A Social History of the News*, Basic Books Inc., New York.

Sinclair, J., Jacka E. and Cunningham, S. (1996) *New Patterns in Global Television*, Oxford University Press.

Tomlinson, J. (1991) *Cultural Imperialism*, Pinter, London.

Tunstall, J. (1977) *The Media are American*, Constable, London.

Tunstall, Jeremy (1992) Europe as a World News Leader. *Journal of Communication*, Vol. 42, No. 3, pp. 84–9.

Winseck, Dwayne (1992) Gulf war in the global village: CNN, Democracy and the information age. In Wasko J. and Mosco V. (eds.) *Democratic Communication in the Information Age*, Garamond, Toronto.

14

Global television news services

Christopher Paterson

Georgia State University, U.S.A. (1996)

Television news, an international cultural product born of that most successful of global growth industries, information, is quite suddenly found proliferating. Although CNN has exported television news from Atlanta to the world since 1984, it was rarely seen outside of expensive Western hotels until the 1990's, when it was joined by a host of domestic and international competitors. The internationalization of television news, while unquestionably a crucial aspect of the processes generally lumped together as 'globalization', seems paradoxically to be the least well examined, yet most alluded to, aspect of the globalization phenomena.

Scholars and journalists alike recount *ad nauseam* how the reassuring drone of CNN seems to be everywhere they are (which may say more about these correspondents than the global reach and influence of CNN). Speculation is rife as to the impact of China's exposure to the satellite television news of the BBC. Scholars have noted with fascination, but little explication, that TV news junkies are being cultivated by major communications conglomerates in the furthest reaches of Africa and Latin America, and that Europe has yet to reach the point of news saturation, despite the plethora of news channels available to most viewers. Many countries to which Western TV news is a newcomer promote its spread one day, and furiously condemn and censor it the next.

Rarely are these curious processes concerning the internationalization of television news detailed and contextualized (Ferguson, 1992). Instead, they are all too often used as anecdotal examples of a much broader conception of the globalization of communications, a conception related much more to the spread and impacts upon culture of entertainment products, such as television serials, films, and music. Yet the seat of the globalization of television news is London (Clarke, 1995), not Hollywood, the political implications of television news flow are profound, and while there is certainly increasing integration of television news into the activities of the major global communications conglomerates, that integration is in its infancy. (As of this writing, for example, it seems the Disney Corporation has yet to discover that it owns the second largest provider of international television news pictures; they've developed no synergistic global television news strategy.)

Beyond cataloguing these trends, this article interrogates some of their inevitably multitudinous implications. Does the availability of more television news expand knowledge and promote dialogue through its diversity, or stifle intelligent discourse through the commodification and homogenization of crucial information? Is there more information from more perspectives or more information from fewer perspectives? In global television news, things are not always as they seem. Often, more is less.

News wholesale concentration

The ability of evening television news programmes to instantly produce dramatic pictures from news events anytime, anywhere in the world can be dazzling. How do they do it? Firstly, the 'news' is what the broadcaster chooses to put into the programme (always mindful of what is in a competitor's programme – where competition exists, which now, is almost everywhere). There are few unillustrated stories, at least in part, because stories without illustration are less likely to be chosen as news for television.[1] Secondly, illustration to accommodate the needs of most broadcasters, most of the time, is commercially available at considerably less expense and effort than broadcasters might encounter attempting to illustrate their international stories on their own. The few sources for those international images have much to do with the sameness, the homogeneity of international television news stories; they account for why different broadcasters tend to carry the same few international stories each day (out of a presumably infinite pool of potential stories), and why those stories tend to look very much alike from broadcaster to broadcaster (Malik, 1992; Cohen, 1996).

Broadcasters generally feel an obligation to provide news from outside of their own locality or national borders, but rarely are willing to allocate the resources to discover and gather such news on their own. Most leave this task to just a few important, but largely unknown, public and commercial TV news providers. Wire services and newspaper syndicates provide information from remote corners of the globe, but television stories require video images that are professionally produced and compelling. From most of the world, only a few companies now provide this. These are the organizations which operate at the 'wholesale' level of international television.

The wholesalers of TV news visuals, sounds, and textual information operate at a level of the industry traditionally hidden from the television audience (lest your favourite broadcaster lose the limelight in which they thrive). International examples are Reuters Television, Worldwide Television News (WTN), and Associated Press Television (APTV), and in Europe, the public news exchange mechanism Eurovision, in the United States, the commercial TV news co-operative Conus.[2] Other regional news exchanges serve the Arab World (Arabvision) and East Asia (Asiavision), though these contribute less to global news flow.

Organizations at the second tier are 'packagers' and distributors of news constructed from the raw material of the first tier. These 'retailers' are primarily the television networks and their surrogate newsfeed operations providing news to affiliates. As in other information industries, they can be seen as simply adding value to existing information, and reselling it. CNN overlaps into both tiers, and some other global players such as Reuters are attempting to do so.[3]

With other major communications conglomerates, these few players have come to dominate international television news flow, providing news programs or source material world-wide. This two tier structure has become more relevant in the last decade due to industrial realignments and cutbacks by broadcast networks involving the downsizing of news divisions (Dominick, 1988; Waite, 1992), leading to greater dependence by the second tier upon the first. Thus, this structure is not well described in earlier studies of television news.

The roots of the television news agencies stretch back over four decades. The Fox Movietone newsreel company operated with UPI, then combined with the international newsfilm operations of Britain's ITN into UPITN in 1967, and finally transformed into Worldwide Television News in 1985 after years of financial turmoil. Another newsreel company, the British Commonwealth International Film Agency (BCIFA), became Visnews in 1964, then partially owned by Reuters. In late 1992 Reuters bought out the remaining shares in Visnews from then co-owners NBC and BBC, and the company became Reuters Television. By seizing control of the largest video news agency from broadcasters, that buyout destroyed television news alliances which stretched back to the earliest days of broadcasting, and sent a shockwave through a TV news industry gradually being taken over by media conglomerates grounded in print. The Associated Press entered the television news agency business in 1994 to finally break the three decade old Reuters/WTN duopoly.

The television news agencies gather audio-visuals and story information continuously from well over 50 bureaux, a far larger number of stringers, and from client television stations world-wide. The largest, Reuters Television, claims 70 world-wide bureaux and over 260 client broadcasters in 85 countries. They also pull stories from the European Broadcasting Union (EBU) and other co-operative exchanges. They then edit together their own story packages consisting of video and 'natural sound', and satellite them to client broadcasters in any of several daily satellite feeds (and through Eurovision, making it a highly competitive 'marketplace' for the agencies).

Some audio commentary and electronic text are also provided to clients, providing information to accompany the visuals, and occasionally finished stories that a broadcaster can put right on the air are offered. Clients pay the agencies from tens of thousands of dollars to several millions of dollars yearly, depending upon a variety of factors including the size of the station's audience, the number and type of news feeds received, and the amount of stories the station contributes to the agency.

Among the British and American networks (the most influential of news agency clients) the affiliations are as follows: The most popular American newscast, that of Disney's American Broadcasting Company (ABC), receives WTN footage as majority owner of WTN.[4] NBC subscribes to Reuters. CBS has switched from WTN to Reuters and back to WTN (and has for some time syndicated a small amount of their video internationally as CBS International).

CNN produces much of its own international material, but also subscribes to all three agencies. The BBC has a long-standing alliance with Reuters, but is now shifting to WTN and APTV. ITN shifted recently from longtime supplier WTN (which ITN owns a piece of) to Reuters (which owns a piece of ITN), and may now shift back. News Corporation's Sky depends entirely on Reuters for international coverage. Strict copyright rules are observed to ensure that no station broadcasts and no agency distributes news video which they haven't paid for or produced themselves.

There is little empirical data about the amount of agency video actually used by broadcasters; even the television news agencies themselves rarely generate such data.[5] The Eurovision news exchange (EVN) is the major source of international images for European broadcasters,[6] and a major source for broadcasters throughout the rest of the world. Hjarvard (1995a) found 66.5% of Eurovision items came from WTN and Visnews during a survey period in 1990, but Eurovision figures for 1994 show 48.3% of all items were from agencies.[7] My own analysis demonstrates how this number can skyrocket during international crises: during a constructed week in early August 1995, during the Bosnian civil war, the major morning satellite feed of Eurovision, EVNO, consisted of 84% news agency items, not untypical in 1995.

Barring major shifts in ownership or corporate policy, for the next several years these agencies are likely to remain the dominant providers of international television news, especially for news which does not originate from the traditionally well covered news-elite countries of the world; places where few broadcasters bother with regular coverage of their own (e.g. Wallis and Baran, 1990). The dominance of these few Anglo-American conglomerates in the production of these influential and ideological products – television news images – has been ignored in studies of TV news. And the process of news selection and production within these companies is virtually unknown.[8]

TV agency as agenda-setter

A British TV news editor stated in 1986,

> The role of the agencies is a crucial thing which the domestic British audience has no idea exists, but it is the major force in deciding what ends up on television screens from abroad.[9]

More importantly, international images are selected by a remarkably few senior editors within the few news wholesale organizations. APTV, Reuters, and WTN have been the focus of my research involving extended ethnographic analysis of news production in each of their London newsrooms. Reuters Television (and previously, Visnews) and WTN, had previously maintained a long tradition of secrecy, so the manner in which global television news is determined and produced had never been thoroughly described as is only possible with an extended qualitative analysis.

My project hypothesizes that since television is the major force in shaping how Europe and America see the world, and is becoming so in the rest of the industrialized world and much of the developing world, then images selected by these few television journalists of similar training and background,[10] are absolutely crucial determinants of how people world-wide perceive other nations and global issues. It is important, therefore, to understand how these journalists see the world and shape our image of it.

Television news agencies traditionally argue that the images and information they provide are ideologically neutral products, to which any subscribing broadcaster may add their own narrative spin. In other words, television journalists do not tend to view their occupation as 'constructing reality' (i.e. Tuchman, 1978; Schlesinger, 1987). From its inception, the motto of Visnews photographers was 'We don't take sides, we just take pictures' (Read, 1992). Ignored or denied is the fact that the story chosen, the images and sounds selected, and the information sent to clients with the story significantly affect the way the television viewer will understand it, and ultimately, perceive the world.

In an analysis of Eurovision, Cohen, *et al.* (1996), find considerable commonalty in the images used by broadcasters world-wide, due to the pervasiveness of the few common sources discussed here, but are supportive of this 'neutral image' thesis. However, a considerable body of theory suggests that news images themselves do convey meanings which cannot be, or routinely are not, substantially altered, or 'localized' by the broadcaster of those images (i.e. Hall, 1988, 1992; Golding and Elliot, 1979). The images of the world, especially of non-elite, usually developing countries, distributed by television news agencies (often the only images available) may be crucial determinants of popular perceptions.

The news agency role is critical for additional reasons. To a considerable degree, news agencies set the agenda for what international stories broadcasters choose to carry in their newscasts. This is done through the choice of stories they distribute to clients, the amount of visuals provided, and the nature and amount of accompanying audio and textual information provided with that video. The basic 'agenda setting' hypothesis (McCombs, 1981, 1988; McCombs and Shaw, 1972) that mass media play a role in determining the degree of attention the public, or other media, pay to certain issues, emerges as an important one regarding the relationship between the wholesale and retail levels of international television news.

Various examples of cases involving television news agencies setting the press agenda are revealed in my research. But it is also important to note that my observational research reveals significant agenda setting of the TV news agency agenda by other media: the process works both ways. London TV news agency journalists are highly dependent on the BBC and on popular and elite London newspapers that shape their view of what should be covered and how.

Two timely and potent cases deserve brief mention: that of coverage of the civil war in the former Yugoslavia,[10] and a recent African crisis. Both examples are based largely upon my direct observation of agency news production during these crises. Television news plays a substantial role in shaping public perception of international crises, particularly in industrialized nations where dependence upon television news for information is strongest. The public is especially dependant upon the story provided by television news in moments of rapidly developing international crisis, when other media cannot provide information with either the speed or excitement provided by television. In international crisis television news workers are under extreme pressure to understand a story sufficiently to tell it, and then to tell it visually as they understand it. This tautology is problematic for several reasons. They must comprehend a story, or believe they do, with little information, and must then craft a brief visual version of the story. If the story is non-visual, or if the most relevant visuals are unattainable, they must improvise to provide visual evidence of the crisis they perceive. The story of the 'crisis' emerges from many influences far removed from considered journalism.

In recent years war coverage has made up a substantial portion of news agency output, and has diverted their resources from the developing world or less conflictual, more process oriented, stories such as economics or politics in non-western countries.[11] Quantifying these influences, however, is problematic. War coverage may be defined in many ways: it may be scenes from the battle front in Bosnia, or it may be a UN Security Council meeting in New York where Bosnia is one item on the agenda. Similarly, the diversion of resources to war coverage also resists quantification, for staff (and equipment) movements are very difficult to track within international news gatherers, and subject to constant change.

During late 1995, agency concentration on the wars in Bosnia, and to a far lesser degree, Chechnia, was considerable, comprising the vast major- ity of agency contributions to Eurovision. Dependance by broadcasters upon the agencies for this kind of coverage was apparent from the high level of agency material being accepted by Eurovision during my study period: upwards of 90% on many days, when the percentage has historically been closer to 50% or 60%. The agencies have devoted massive resources to covering the wars of the former Yugoslavia, sometimes putting close to a hundred staff and freelance workers in the area.[12]

Without constant TV news agency coverage there would still have been a war in Bosnia, but little of it would exist in the global consciousness, so little would it matter on the world stage. At least two agency photographers were killed, and many others injured. It is well that no more journalists sacrificed their lives, for the media of the world had little intention of showing the reality of a terrible war, and the news audiences of the world, when they made their voices heard at all, tended to agree.[13]

Major broadcasters in Bosnia came and went – some few, like the BBC – stuck it out for the duration. The print press was more fickle; the presence of a print reporter at the battle front carries little weight with readers. But news agencies could not leave, for their mandate was to be where no one in their right mind would, to provide a never ending stream of accurate information and exceptional pictures from a war which permitted neither. But that unique position, that privileged place as chronicler of the war, embraced a paradox. For the war was what the news agencies – print and television – told their clients it was; few other international journalists were there to argue. The war was what the agencies, with all the pressures upon them that have so little to do with classical definitions of news (and more to do with economics, competition, politics of access, quality of visuals, etc.), could report it to be.

There's the rub: the war news agencies manufactured for the world was the very war they covered. News agencies could report only a small portion of the Bosnian civil war, those portions involving dramatic events occurring within the reach of agency journalists. But that war, the war of singular, seemingly unconnected dramas in a few locations, became the war known to the world, the war the world reacted to, and thus, the war the journalists themselves would continue to focus their efforts upon despite the knowledge of a much larger, much more complex, all but unknown war underway just out of their reach.[14] International television news agencies created the dominant image of the Bosnian civil war, an image highly distorted by the structural constraints inherent in television news agency coverage routines. Further, the coverage shaped by those constraints has had an ongoing agenda-setting impact across all media, making the distorted image (i.e. focus on Sarajevo, Serbs as sole aggressors), the guide for coverage by all media.

As in the case of war coverage, the world is especially dependent upon the TV news wholesalers for coverage of news from developing countries and remote regions. The role of major international TV news providers in the making, or unmaking, of a major international story (or news personality) can also be directly tied to their decision to allocate resources to such stories. Without the pictures and logistical support provided by such companies, the world's television broadcasters can provide their viewers with little coverage. There is evidence that television coverage occasionally drives Western policy responses, which in turn drive further press interest in such stories (Gowing, 1994). The story of the Rwandan refugee crisis in 1994 provides an interesting example.

To the global news brokers, what constitutes the news out of Africa? Mort Rosenblum (1993) phrases the question powerfully:

> During 1992, for example, the number of children who died worldwide for lack of simple attention – a little food, a measles shot – surpassed five million. Most were Africans. That is as if every four minutes for an entire year, a school bus full of kids plunged over the north rim of the Grand Canyon. If that began to happen, in Arizona, someone would put up a railing. Why is Africa different?

The sheer number of lives at stake is clearly a minor factor in the selection of news from Africa. In the summer of 1994, as Rwandan refugees by the hundreds of thousands fled into Goma, Zaire, aid agencies sounded the alarm that a humanitarian disaster of unprecedented proportions loomed. For days, television kept virtually silent, despite no shortage of information on the crisis and its implications (I stress, information, not pictures).[15]

Suddenly, the world's television newscasts came alive with news of the Goma tragedy, far too late to influence governments to try to reverse the exodus or to get supplies in place before people began to die. In a sad echo of the Ethiopian famine a decade earlier, wealthy governments soon reacted to pressure from the compelling television coverage, and moved to provide assistance. In the meantime, similar, albeit smaller disasters unfolded in other parts of Africa, with no attention from the rest of the world. So what key event made Goma so suddenly and thoroughly newsworthy, when it had until then been a non-story for TV?

The creation of a Goma television story (for the global TV audience) was the result of a decision in the Geneva headquarters of the European Broadcasting Union, where news managers had received a sufficient number of requests for coverage from member broadcasters to decide to allocate certain costly resources, in this case, a 'flyaway' satellite dish and the technicians to go with it, to the Goma story. Until then no other major TV news service had been willing to allocate such resources, despite the magnitude of the story and the difficulty in getting news pictures out by other means. For one television news agency, the cost of sending their own live transmission equipment at the end of a busy news month, when they were already over budget, influenced their decision to sit back and see what other first tier services, like the EBU, would do.

When the Goma flyaway went online vivid pictures became available of the Goma camps minutes after they were shot, and reporters from around the world converged on Goma because the ability to reach their audience live, at relatively little cost, had now been provided. And when the EBU decided that the flyaway should fly away to another world hotspot, with it went the story of Goma's refugees. Medium became the message in Goma, as the realities of modern television news overshadowed the realities of the Rwandan tragedy, and reinforced the confusing world of fleeting and incomprehensible disaster that is the world's image of Africa.

This case demonstrates how technological factors involving resource allocation combined with an accumulation of demand for visuals of what had, up until then, been a mostly non visual story (and thus for TV, a nonstory). Such instances are common. Television tells stories best when it can illustrate them with exciting and graphic pictures, but such pictures cost more to provide from Africa than they do from Chicago or London.

In developing world coverage, the issues are harder to illustrate and the costs are higher than anywhere else, and often so are risks to personnel and equipment, so the benefit of coverage must be concurrently higher as well. As the Goma story illustrates, rarely do the providers of international television visuals find the benefit sufficient. Exceptions generally exist only where costs have already been subsidized and facilitated through the prior existence of reliable satellite facilities, a measure of security, and a comfortable pillow for a reporter's head. Such has been the case with South Africa (South Africa's neighbours were deemed not to have these attributes)(Paterson, 1992), or Somalia, where coverage facilitated by the public relations expertise of the U.S. military ensured that the right story would make it home (Ottosen, 1994).

The coverage decisions of the international television news agencies are based largely upon client interest, what their rival company is doing, and the costs of allocating resources to areas which are expensive to provide coverage from. Do economic and technological considerations prevail in determining developing world coverage, or do the gatekeepers possess ethnocentric biases which decrease the priority given to covering poor countries and dark people? Or, do the international services simply respond to the will of international broadcasters? There is not enough data on these aspects of international news to answer these questions, but by identifying the key players and understanding the system in which they operate, we can at least ask more appropriate questions.

News retail explosion

The retail level of international television news has seen parallel trends toward globalism and regionalism, both trends spurred by CNN and by the availability of international coverage from the commercial sources just described. The BBC (World Television) and Time-Warner's CNN (International) now broadcast globally. News Corporation's Sky TV, STAR TV, and Fox News broadcast through much of the world and are merging into a single news network to challenge CNN. Other satellite channels, with more soon to come, provide a wide range of news services in areas that previously had little or no television news.

Despite the proliferation of services, few have shown a profit for their corporate owners. Only CNN does so at the retail level (Westcott, 1995a), and WTN (barely), at the wholesale level. One recent trend is proving profitable: Regional financial news networks such as C-NBC, the Asia Business Channel, Bloomberg, and Reuters Financial Television are growing rapidly. C-NBC claims now to reach over 65 countries through various satellite channels. National public broadcasters are in decline world-wide, the result of many forces, including comparison by their audiences to these slick, and timely, global commercial services. NHK[16] and Deutsche Welle, like the BBC, are building global news networks. Television news has moved from being mostly a publicly owned service to being mostly a privately owned service.

During the 1990's, much of Europe has been swept by a wave of new television news channels. Following on the heels of CNN's growth in popularity on European satellite and cable TV was a European attempt to provide a European flavour to news: Euronews. The problem has been defining European flavour. Euronews, owned by several European public broadcasting organizations and a French media conglomerate, broadcasts news video only, without news anchors, voiced over in five different languages. It has been criticized for an inability to please its diverse audience, and for its impersonal approach to news presentation. Euronews' principal source is Eurovision, which in turn takes international stories from WTN and Reuters and AP. Euronews also takes a direct feeds from the two larger agencies.[17]

The two major British broadcasters are considering pan-European news channels of their own. The third British newscaster, Sky News, already has a European news service reaching over 33 countries.[18] But if these developments in pan-European news broadcasting exemplify internationalization, the 'counter-tendencies to the process of internationalization' which Negrine and Papathanassopoulos (1991) hypothesize are also emerging. These are primarily the cultural and linguistic barriers to transnational broadcasting which abound in the European television market. The result has been the rapid development of several single language news channels, aimed at specific regional or national audiences (see also Garitaonandia, 1993). (Though notably, the global services deliver the news in English, contributing to English becoming a global 'lingua franca', as put by Schiller (1991)).

Major examples are the German language channels VOX, owned by News Corporation, and N-TV, owned by Time-Warner and German investors. VOX takes its international news from Reuters.[19] N-TV's international news comes from Reuters[20] and from CNN, whose principal international sources are Reuters and WTN. In partnership with ABC, the French broadcaster TF1 and pay television operator Canal Plus have proposed a French language satellite news channel. International news would be provided by WTN, although TF1 and Canal Plus are also Reuters subscribers.[21]

The point here is that the channels proliferate, but the sources stay the same (and so to, it seems, do the owners). Malik (1992) demonstrated the worldwide congruence in international television news coverage:

> what our pages show is that the power of the exchange systems and the TV news agencies is much greater than the public generally feel or know.

His data showed the same video, of the same stories, from the same sources, running in roughly the same position in newscasts all over the world on the evening of his survey. The recent trends in European television news suggest further homogenization of international news, despite the increase in news channels.

News homogenization

The proliferation of television news is ultimately insignificant, and in fact, illusory, if the original source of most international news material is all the same: News Corporation, Reuters, and their ideologically identical sometimes competitors, sometimes allies, in London. The player I identify as the most influential purveyor of international news, Reuters, is closely allied to Rupert Murdoch, handling international television news coverage for News Corporation. Reuters is reported to be the third largest media conglomerate in the world (*Sunday Times*, 13 March 1994), and owns a piece of ITN, which in turn owns a piece of WTN. Since Reuters, WTN, and ITN are with AP, CNN and the BBC the most significant international television news gathering services, and since Murdoch is building his own global news network, the potential influence of a Reuters/Murdoch alliance in international television news production is enormous.[22]

The impact of commercialization and concentration of control over international television news is beyond the scope of this article, but past examples give cause to worry. The commercialization of American network news division, and their move into 'infotainment', has been well chronicled. Reuters and WTN privilege more profitable enterprises like contract production and satellite distribution for corporations and governments, and sports and entertainment 'news', in the allocation of their resources. Such influences on resource allocation within a news department have editorial consequences. At NBC, more blatant corporate influence in the news division's product have been demonstrated (Husseini, 1994). Rupert Murdoch is widely believed to have used his print and broadcast news holding in Britain to bolster Thatcher and Thatcherism (Bagdikian, 1989), thus his growing influence on the global news agenda bears watching. He has promised, for example, that his new global news network will give a different view of Cuba than does CNN, whose 'Bureau Chief and democracy consultant (is) Fidel Castro' (Murdoch, 1996).

Television news has been widely ignored in the globalization literature due, in part, to rapid change in the industry and the difficulty to determine its effect. But TV news is also being seen less as a special case – a form of television which provides a needed socio-political function – than as just another global cultural product. With the producers of the source material for international television news and the owners of regional and global television becoming increasingly concentrated, the content of international television news is becoming increasingly homogeneous and diversity in the 'marketplace of ideas' is diminished. When considered in conjunction with other trends of globalization – broadcast privatization, deregulation, increasing commercialization and consumerism – the potential threat to cultural and ideological plurality and thereby, local and national identify, is vast.

Conclusions

Where do local audiences fit into the globalization of TV news? The manner in which I have described international television news here privileges the concept of news flow, in this case, from few sources to many national, regional, and global broadcasters. But as Kavoori (1994) points out, privileging flow often results in the neglect of meaning. We are left with a sense of what the audience receives, but little sense of their sense of it all. In all the discourse on the globalization of television news, the relationship between text and audience, and the particularities of such global media products, are all but ignored.

The culturally specific particularities of the reception of global media products must be properly analyzed on their own terms, and not unquestioningly identified with the nation and/or culture native to their ownership. Should Rupert Murdoch implement a global news network of his own would it be Australian, American, or English? It would more likely be a uniquely international product, produced in a great many places. CNNI is such a text now, even if its producers remain predominantly American and borrow heavily from American broadcast traditions.

New and innovative analytic paradigms are required to assess the interaction of text and audience, with care taken to avoid the outdated media imperialism paradigm lurking in many contemporary critiques of news globalization. Global conglomerates create global products for an imaginary global audience. What does this mean to the very real consumers of these alien genres, audiences who may be used to a very different style of information presentation from their public broadcaster?[23]

The trend at the wholesale tier of international television news is to try to be a diversified, multi-media news agency cum all purpose TV production company. Reuters and Associated Press have the backing of deep corporate pockets to continue in the marginally profitable field of television news gathering, providing they don't spend too much from doing it. Disney Corporation's commitment to stepchild WTN's future is far from certain.

Broadcasters, too, will continue to diversify. Large broadcasters are increasingly marketing their produced news products to smaller broadcasters around the world. For example, NBC markets a European version of its successful domestic 'Dateline' program, combining elements of the domestic program with specially produced international material (Westcott, 1995a). The wholesale/retail distinction may become less significant as all players offer their news products directly to subscribing computer users, the form of (multi-)media consumption predicted to eventually displace television. For now, the homogeneity of international television news sources is a concern. Despite the increasing number of news services, ownership is highly concentrated, and broadcasters are becoming increasingly dependant upon a few news providers to supply the international images they use on the air; use to shape our global reality.

Notes

1. Many studies of television newsrooms have reported that the availability of visual images is an important factor in determining whether a foreign news story is included in a newscast (Golding and Elliott, 1979; Molina, 1990; Schlesinger, 1987; and others). Molina notes that at Mexico's Televisa,

   > Television stories whose visual element is available through any of the news exchanges stand a better chance of being included in the programme's agenda than those where only text is available.

   As put by Cohen, *et al.* (1996).

   > . . . in many instances a (European broadcast) service decides to present a story only because it has footage available.

2. 'Conus' is a clever use of the satellite industry's abbreviation of 'continental United States'. Conus was started in 1984 to link, and enable shared use of, the satellite news gathering resources of local television stations (and encourage their investment in this technology). CNN and the American broadcast networks also operate news exchanges for their affiliated stations.
3. CNN is a global broadcaster and a global provider of news pictures. Its pictures and finished stories may be used by broadcasters around the world with whom it has an exchange agreement, and many do so, especially on fast breaking stories where CNN has the only exciting coverage (such was the case in the first days of the Gulf War). However, since CNN pictures are edited for a CNN story, and are usually accompanied by CNN narration, broadcasters prefer raw video from news agencies or news co-operatives when it is available. CNN has speculated about globally syndicating the raw video it shoots, but has declined to do so to avoid going into competition with its principle suppliers, the three television news agencies.
4. Specifically, Disney owns Capital Cities, which owns ABC, which owns 80% of WTN.
5. Broadcasters are often reluctant to admit just how much purchased material they use, preferring to leave their audience with the impression that they are doing all of their own international coverage.
6. In their recent large study of Eurovision, Cohen *et al.* (1996) find Eurovision member broadcasters make up between 35% and 100% of their foreign coverage from Eurovision. Larger broadcasters with resources beyond Eurovision (subscriptions to agency satellite feeds and their own international bureaux) are less likely to depend on it.
7. EBU data from Cohen *et al.* (1996).
8. Not coincidentally, this is the subject of this author's research.
9. Channel 4 News Editor Richard Purvis, in Harrison and Palmer, 1986, p. 73.

10. At the time of my research in each London television news agency newsroom, only white skinned journalists were employed, journalists are almost exclusively British, American, or Australian, and senior editorial posts are exclusively male. My interviews addressed professional and educational histories, which were similarly uniform.

11. The various wars of the ex-Yugoslavia commenced in 1992 and continue at the time of this writing, although the Dayton Peace Accords and outside military intervention are succeeding in bringing peace to the region for the moment.

12. For example, I have recorded numerous cases of the limited news agency resources based in Africa being relocated to other world hotspots – the Gulf War, the fall of Eastern Europe, the ex-Yugoslavia wars – for months on end. This doesn't mean an agency won't still cover an African story, but it does mean they are less likely to do so, since with fewer of their own resources nearby the story will cost more to cover.

13. See, for example, Westcott, Tim (1995b) War Stories: The Agencies, Television Business International, November.

14. See, for example, BBC correspondent Martin Bell (1995), who describes letters from the British viewing public to the BBC, urging less display of war violence and carnage. British broadcasters enacted strict censorship of violent footage to avoid regulation; war was thus made tolerable.

15. Bell (1995) describes his nagging frustration at being unable to get to the war out of reach of television. For analysis of when TV does and does not affect policy, see Gowing, Nik (1994) Real Time Television Coverage of Armed Conflicts, John F. Kennedy School Working Paper, Cambridge, Massachusetts.

16. The following account of television coverage of Goma results from ethnographic research by the author with certain providers of international television news. This dish was operated by the BBC for the EBU, according to Craig Covault, Satellite Earth Stations, *Aviation Week and Space Technology*, Vol. 141, No. 10, pp. 120, via LexisNexis.

17. Westcott, Tim (1995a) Getting Mighty Crowded. *Television Business International*, November.

18. Reuters internal document, May 1993 and Le Journal de Geneve (via Nexis/Lexis) August 23 1993.

19. Satellite TV Finance (via Nexis/Lexis), April 29 1993, and Reuter European Business Report (via Nexis/Lexis) September 1 1993.

20. Reuters internal document, May 1993.

21. Ibid.

22. Satellite TV Finance (via Nexis/Lexis), March 4 1993 and Reuters internal document, May 1993.

23. In 1995, the British trade journal Broadcast (17 February, 15) ominously editorialized:

> Reuters Television has taken a step away from its agency roots by climbing into bed with Rupert Murdoch. Although it will still act as a supplier, it is inextricably linked to Murdoch's empire. We can only wait to see if the Fox and Sky deals are followed by one with Star TV – it would seem logical, given Murdoch's desire for a news service spanning the globe. But where will Reuters TV move from here? Putting TV reporters in its bureaux and working closely with a single organization puts it in the position of a pseudo-broadcaster.

APTV includes this passage in their promotional material sent to Reuters clients.

24. Recent doctoral dissertations which begin to examine these global news reception issues include Dillinger (1995), Helland (1995), Kavoori (1994).

References and further reading

Auletta, Ken (1993) Raiding the Global Village, *New Yorker*, August 2, pp. 25–30.
Bagdikian, Ben (1989) The Lords of the Global Village Nation, June 12.
Bell, Martin (1995) *In Harm's Way*, Hamish Hamilton, London.
Boyd-Barrett, O. (1980) *The International News Agencies*, Constable, London.
Broadcast (1995) 17 February, 15.
Broadcasting and Cable Special Report – News Services: Filling Changing Needs and Niches, May 31, 1993, 27–44.
Clarke, Steve (1995) London: International News Capital Variety, December 18.
Cohen, A., Levy, M., Roeh, I., Gurevitch, M. (1996) *Global Newsrooms, Local Audiences: A Study of the Eurovision News Exchange*, John Libbey, London.
Covault, Craig, Satellite Earth Stations, Aviation Week and Space Technology, Vol. 141, No. 10, pp. 120, via Lexis/Nexis.
Dillinger, Brent (1995) *Finnish Views of CNN Television News: A Critical Cross-Cultural Analysis of the American Commercial Discourse Style*, University of Vaasa.
Dominick, J. R. (1988) The Impact of Budget Cuts on CBS News, *Journalism Quarterly*, Summer, Vol. 65, No. 2, pp. 469–473.
Fenby, Jonathan (1986) *The International News Services, A Twentieth Century Fund Report*, Schocken Books, New York.
Ferguson, Marjorie (1992) Mythology about Globalization. *European Journal of Communication*, Vol. 7, pp. 69–93.
Freedom Forum Media Studies Center (1993) The Media and Foreign Policy in the Post-Cold War World Briefing Paper, Columbia University, New York.
Friedland, Louis (1992) Converging the World: International Television News Services Paper for the Twentieth Century Fund.
Galtung, J. and Ruge, M. (1970) The Structure of Foreign News in Tunstall, Jeremy (ed.) *Media Sociology*, Constable, London.
Garitaonandia, Carmelo (1993) Regional Television in Europe. *European Journal of Communication*, Vol. 8, pp. 277–94.
Golding, Peter and Elliott, Philip (1979) *Making the News*, Longman, NY.
Gowing, Nik (1994) Real Time Television Coverage of Armed Conflicts, John F. Kennedy School Working Paper, Cambridge, MA.
Hall, Stuart (1988) The Rediscovery of 'Ideology': Return of the Repressed in Media Studies. In Gurevitch M., Bennett T., Curran J., and Woollacott J. (eds.) *Culture, Society, and the Media*, Routledge, London, pp. 56–90.
Hall, Stuart (1992) Encoding, decoding in During, Simon (ed.) *The Cultural Studies Reader*, Routledge, London, pp. 90–103.
Harrison, Paul and Palmer, Robin (1986) News Out of Africa: Biafra to Band Aid, Hilary Shipman, London.
Heinderyckx, Francois (1993) Television News Programmes in Western Europe: A Comparative Study. *European Journal of Communication*, Vol. 8, pp. 425–50.
Helland, Knut (1995) Public Service and Commercial News, University of Bergen.
Hjarvard, Stig (1993) Pan-European Television News: Towards A European Political Public-Sphere. In Drummond, P., Paterson, R. and Willis, J. (eds.) *National Identity and Europe: The Television Revolution*, British Film Institute, London.
Hjarvard, Stig (1994) The Global Spread of a European Model: The Experiences of Regional News Exchange Networks Using a Public Model of Cooperation. Paper for the IAMCR conference in Seoul, Korea.
Hjarvard, Stig (1995a) *Internationale TV-nyheder. En historisk analyse af det europeiske system for udveksling af internationale TV-nyheder*, Akademisk Forlag, Copenhagen.
Hjarvard, Stig (1995b) TV News Flow Studies Revisited. *Electronic Journal of Communication*, Vol. 5, No. 2 and 3, pp. 24–38.

Husseini, Sam (1994) Felons on the Air: Does GE's Ownership of NBC Violate the Law? *Extra!* Nov./Dec.

Johnston, Carla Brooks (1995) *Winning the Global TV News Game*, Focal Press, Boston.

Kavoori, Anandam P. (1994) Globalization, Media Audiences and Television News: A Comparative Study of American, British, Israeli, German and French Audiences, University of Maryland.

Lansipuro, Yrjo (1987) Asiavision News Exchange. *Intermedia*, Vol. 15, No. 1, pp. 22–7.

Larson, James (1984) Television's Window on the World: International Affairs Coverage on the U.S. Networks Ablex, Norwood, NJ.

Le Journal de Geneve (via Nexis/Lexis), August 23 1993.

Malik, Rex (1992) The Global News Agenda. *Intermedia*, 20/1.

McCombs, Maxwell E. (1981) The Agenda Setting Approach in Nimmo, Dan O. and Sanders, Keith R., (eds) *Handbook of Political Communication*, Sage, Beverly Hills, pp. 121–40.

McCombs, Maxwell E. (1988) Setting the Agenda: The Evolution of Agenda-Setting Research. Paper presented at SOMMATIE X. Veldhoven, The Netherlands, April.

McCombs, Maxwell E. and Shaw, Donald C. (1972) The Agenda Setting Function of Mass Media. *Public Opinion Quarterly*, Vol. 36, pp. 176–87.

McManus, John (1994) *Market-Driven Journalism*, Sage, Thousand Oaks, CA.

Melnik, Stefan (1981) *Eurovision News and The International Flow of Information: History, Problems and Perspectives 1960–1980*, Studienverlag, Dr. N. Brockmeyer, Bochum.

Molina, Gabriel Gonzalez (1990) The Production of Mexican Television News: The Supremacy of Corporate Rationale, University of Leicester.

Murdoch, Rupert (1996) Transcript of address to the National Association of Broadcasters, April 15.

Murdock Graham (1982) Large Corporations and the Control of the Communications Industries. In Gurevitch, M. *et al.* (eds) *Culture, Society, and the Media*, Macmillan, London.

Musa, Mohammed (1990) News Agencies, Transnationalization and the New Order Media. *Culture and Society*, Vol. 12, pp. 325–42.

Negrine, R. and Papathanassopoulos, S. (1991) The Internationalization of Television. *European Journal of Communication*, Vol. 6, pp. 9–32.

Ottosen, Rune (1994) Rambo in Somalia: A Critical Look at the Media Coverage of Operation Restore Hope. Paper for the 6th MacBride Round Table, Honolulu.

Paterson, Christopher (1992) Television News from the Frontline States. In Hawk, Beverly (ed.) *Africa's Media Image*, Praeger, New York.

Paterson, Christopher (1994) More Channels, Fewer Perspectives: International Television News Provider Concentration, Paper presented at the British Film Institute's European Film and Television Studies Conference, London.

Read, Donald (1992) *The Power of News: The History of Reuters, 1849–1989*, Oxford University Press, Oxford.

Reuter European Business Report (via Nexis/Lexis), September 1 1993.

Rosenblum, Mort (1993) *Who Stole the News?* John Wiley, New York.

Satellite TV Finance, April 29 1993: July 8 1993 (via Nexis/Lexis).

Schlesinger, Philip (1987) *Putting 'Reality' Together: BBC News*, 2nd edn, Routledge, London.

Schlesinger, Philip (1991) Media, the Political Order and National Identity. *Media, Culture, and Society*, Vol. 13, pp. 297–308.

Shoemaker, P. and Reese, S. (1991) *Mediating the Message: Theories of Influence on Mass Media Content*, Longman, New York.

Shoemaker, P., Danielian, L., Brendlinger, N. (1991) Deviant Acts, Risky Business and U.S. Interests: The Newsworthiness of World Events. *Journalism Quarterly*, Winter, pp. 781–95.

Sreberny-Mohammadi, A., Stevenson, R., Nordenstreng, K. (1984) The World of News Study. *Journal of Communications*, Winter, pp. 120–142.

Tuchman, Gaye (1978) *Making News: A Study in the Construction of Reality*, Free Press, NY.

Tunstall, J. and Palmer, M. (1991) *Media Moguls*, Routledge, London.

Vanden Heuvel, Jon (1993) For the Media, a Brave (and Scary) New World. *Media Studies Journal*, Fall, Vol. 7–4, pp. 11–19.

Waite, Teresa L. (1992) As Networks Stay Home, Two Agencies Roam the World, *New York Times*, March 8, 5.

Wallis, Roger and Baran, Stanley (1990) *The Known World of Broadcast News*, Routledge, London.

Weaver, J. B., Porter, C. J. and Evans, M. E. (1984) Patterns of Foreign Coverage in U.S. Network TV: A Ten Year Analysis. *Journalism Quarterly*, Vol. 61, No. 2, pp. 356–63.

Westcott, Tim (1995a) Getting Mighty Crowded, *Television Business International*, November.

Westcott, Tim (1995b) War Stories: The Agencies, *Television Business International*, November.

Westerstahl, J. and Johansson, F. (1994) Foreign News: News Values and Ideologies. *European Journal of Communication*, Vol. 9, pp. 71–89.

Section 4

Regulating the means of global communication

15

From communication to democratic norms: reflections on the normative dimensions of international communication policy

Dwayne Winseck and Marlene Cuthbert

From Hamelink, C. (ed.) (1997) *Gazette*, Vol. 59, No. 1, pp. 1–20.

Introduction

This paper analyses recent international communication policies, especially the North American Free Trade Agreement (NAFTA) and the General Agreement on Trade and Tariffs (GATT). Our purpose is to consider the implications of recent regional and international policies for attempts to promote global communications equity through UNESCO and the ITU (International Telecommunications Union). We argue that by shielding information/communication policy from public participation, and by shifting international communication policy out of UNESCO and the ITU, NAFTA and GATT institutionalize a transnational politics of 'limited democracy' (Cox, 1992).

In contrast to these trends, we offer an alternative conception of democracy and normative principles that might be applicable to the analysis of international communication. We address this question by working out a theory of *Pragmatic Democracy* on the basis of George Herbert Mead's (1968) concept of 'universal communication', and offer a more substantive theory of *Communicative Democracy* constructed on the basis of C. Wright Mills' (1939, 1956) notion of 'public communication' and Jurgen Habermas' (1992, 1989a, 1989b) theories of the 'public sphere' and the 'ideal speech situation'. These three theories – *Limited/Technical Democracy, Pragmatic Democracy* and *Communicative Democracy* – are compared across several measures and used as the basis for a critique of NAFTA and GATT Annexes on Telecommunications and Information Services (Canada, 1992; TNC, 1993).

Communication policy as state organized industrial policy

Several scholars point to the isolation of communication research from communication policy (Hamelink, 1993; Noam, 1993) and to an inverse correlation between public access to communication policy proceedings and the incorporation of information technologies and services into strategies of industrial and competition policy. This is true nationally and inter-nationally. Recent policies within Canada, the European Union, and the United States specifically argue for the development of new 'information superhighways' based on private financing, commercial operating criteria and for only very narrowly tailored public service responsibilities to be assigned to network and information service providers (CRTC, 1995; Bangemann, 1994; U.S., 1994). The ITU also accepts these criteria, and furthermore, has encouraged all countries to attract foreign investment and to remove regulatory measures that restrict the convergence of the media industries as a means of stimulating the development of a global information infrastructure (Tarjanne, 1994).

Accompanying these trends has been the enhanced status of the private sector in the ITU, for example, not only as part of national delegations, but also directly in the ITU's policy planning committees, technical standards committee and in other activities (Winseck, 1996). In contrast, there are no similar arrangements for the constituents of national and international civil society to participate in these affairs. As Johan Galtung recently explained, international geopolitics are well suited to participation by nation-states and transnational corporations, but no such thing as a similarly organized civil society operates in international organizations such as UNESCO or the ITU (1994, p. 25).

Thus, one of the principle tensions of the nascent global political economy is the gap between the limited democracy of corporatist planning, on the one hand, and the potential for the democratization of society and com-munication on the other by involving citizens groups in the international communications policy process. It is this tension that causes us to suggest that contemporary approaches to policy, not only for communication but in general, promote a global political economy based on '*limited democracy*'. In contrast to these developments, however, other social and political theorists suggest that the globalization of modernity is creating demands for power, knowledge and authority to be legitimated through forms of public communication and situated within the institutional structures of democ-racy. These theorists – for example Anthony Giddens (1994), Robert Cox (1992) and David Held (1992) – suggest that a primary dialectic within the globaliza-tion of modernity exists between, on the one hand, the transnational diffusion of democratic values, reflexive approaches to knowledge/power, the rise of a transnational middle class and communication technologies, etc., and on the other hand, attempts among those with power to keep politics, econom-ics, technology and culture within the domain of 'limited democracy'.

The three faces of democracy: implications for international communication policy

In this section we trace these antinomies to existing tensions between the '*technical*' and '*communicative*' dimensions of democracy (Winseck, 1997). Our principle argument will be that the first concept has historically dominated the theory and praxis of democracy and that it will, if democracy prevails at all within the domain of international communication policy, set the parameters of 'limited democracy' in the international community. In contrast, the communicative dimension offers a more expansive concept of democracy, a concept that is in fact rooted in the very structure and history of communication. We draw from writings by George Herbert Mead, C. Wright Mills and Jurgen Habermas to develop these ideas about communication, policy and democracy.

The technical dimension of democracy: representation and limits

While democracy is often thought to be a very expansive concept, in practice it now mainly refers to the periodic right to vote, the ability of citizens to change the political leadership, participation through/as representation, rule by expert systems and policy agencies, and the institutional separation of the economy, government, legal system and civil society on the basis of formalized rules/laws and functionally-based competencies (Huntington, 1993; Held, 1987; Hayek, 1986; Weber, 1946). This theory of democracy also separates private from public interests, attempting to expand the boundaries of the former while tightly circumscribing the scope of the latter. Another crucial feature of representative democracies is a political and legal framework based on 'general rules . . . equally applicable to all citizens' (Hayek, 1986, p. 24).

The technical view of democracy privileges *stable* forms of *representative government*, which are derived from clear distinctions between a concept of participation rooted in periodical voting and representation, on the one hand, and the actual day to day governance of societies, on the other. On the first side of the distinction is the domain of the people, while on the other side of the divide are the rulers and experts who carry out governance and policy-making on a day to day basis. From this view, democracy, by nature, must be *limited democracy*. Otherwise, excesses of participation will interfere with governing, political stability, the economic functions of private markets and the liberties of others (Hayek, 1986; Huntington, 1993). This view underlies communications policy agencies, such as the Federal Communications Commissions (FCC), the Canadian Radio-television and Telecommunication Commission (CRTC), or the ITU, that function primarily as expert-based policy-making systems that mediate the competing aims of various industry participants and the State, as well as *represent* the public interest as they understand it.

From the 'limited democracy' perspective, communication systems are privately financed so as to secure autonomy from state interference; based on a set of negative freedoms clearly delineated in a constitution so that people do not confuse the realm of the possible with what is actually on offer, and representative social relations. Representative media contain clear distinctions between the majority of people who receive and consume information and a smaller class of media professionals who represent the public interest and mediate the relations between the state, economy and civil society (Galtung, 1994; Pye, 1966). Communications media also organize public opinion which serves to legitimate power and authority, and thus the media help to displace coercive social and political relations enforced through the state's monopoly control over the means of violence (Weber, 1946, pp. 92–5; Keane, 1991; Habermas, 1989a, p. 215). In general this view sees media systems as representative institutions rather than participatory spheres of public communication. The recent history of international communication policy and the New World Information and Communication Order (NWICO) have been primarily about whether this model of media organization could be applied to the developing countries, or whether other more equitable and participatory forms of media could be envisioned and implemented.

George Herbert Mead and the foundations of 'pragmatic' and 'communicative democracy'

In contrast to the above view, others have offered more expansive views of democracy that are not so much rule-based and 'rule-maintaining', as they are 'rule-altering' and transformative (Beck, 1994). George Herbert Mead, C. Wright Mills and Jurgen Habermas suggest that the basic structures of this more expansive conception of democracy are already imminent in the most fundamental technology of human communication: language. Essentially, Habermas and Mead set out the provocative thesis that the very basic presuppositions of language – equality, reciprocity, sincerity and truth – are also the basic presuppositions of democracy. Read retrospectively, Habermas' writings on communicative action (1992, 1989a) and the public sphere (1989b) suggest that the history of democracy is the history of struggles to represent these basic presuppositions in sociological form, i.e. the Athenian Agora, the bourgeois public sphere, constitutional protections for freedom of communications, and contemporary attempts to realize more expansive concepts of communication rights and to democratize the institutional structures of communications media. Of course the NWICO that so influenced the ITU, UNESCO and international communication policy since the early 1970s can also be viewed through this prism.

According to Habermas, while representative democracy is undoubtedly an historical advance over all that preceded it, and the technical dimensions of democracy are essential for securing individual freedoms, these characteristics do not exhaust the potentials of democracy. For Habermas, democracy means that the rules and goals of society are shaped through spheres of public communication. In turn, public communication must be open to all, directed toward the discovery of public rather than private interests, and driven by the force of argumentation, not power (the *communicative* dimension of democracy) (Habermas, 1989a, p. 215, 1989b).

The communicative dimension of democracy is not only crucial to the legitimation of power and authority, but, as Mead and Mills have pointed out, to the cultivation of 'democratic minds'. According to Mead, Mills and Habermas, non-distorted communication is fundamental to the socio-psychological development of the democratic spirit. For these authors, communication provides the medium through which individuals can assume the perspective of another individual and to reflexively shape their actions in relation to this other, not on the basis of power, but understanding, tolerance and perspective (Mead, 1968, pp. 200–6; Mills, 1939, pp. 427–30; Habermas, 1992, 1989a). As such, communication mediates the intentions of the individual with specific contexts of action and provides the medium of reflexive discourse about identity, social interaction and the environment in which one lives.

Linked to the new communication technologies, reflexivity, empathy and discourses about society and social change could occur among publics no longer separated by time and space. Mead saw this as *potentially* contributing to the development of the socio-psychological and public conditions necessary for a 'universal' democratic culture. Communication technologies were possibly liberatory, not in nature, not in and of themselves, but because of their potential to amplify the essentially democratic aspects of language – reciprocity, equality, sincerity and truth. The crucial question was whether or not communications technologies would harness and amplify the emancipatory potentials of language, or themselves be harnessed to the imperative of commerce, power and strategy in mass, industrial societies (Mead, 1968, pp. 21–3; Mills, 1956).

These themes of communication, reflexivity, democracy and emancipation have become increasingly prominent in the writings of Habermas (1989a), and there are interesting affinities between Mead's ideas and those of Anthony Giddens (1994) and David Held (1992) who note that Mead's views of 'reflexive modernity' are animating contemporary discourses about globalization, modernity and democracy.

Yet Mead's ideas need to be approached with some trepidation. One limit to Mead's understanding of communication is that he never really escaped the normative constraints on the imagination set by views of 'systems complexity' and 'limited democracy'. While Mead's views extend beyond the 'technical dimensions' of democracy introduced above to anticipate the role of people in *transforming* and improving society, he never went beyond seeing 'public communication' as specialist-lead discourses about the relationships between technology and society. Consistent with the pragmatist school of which he was a part, Mead's theory situated specialist/expert systems as representative mediators of the public good. Thus, even the universalist presuppositions he claimed to find in language and other forms of communication were, in the end, subordinated to the prevailing views of representative and technocratic democracy. This reflected an even larger problem within Mead's theoretical framework: the lack of attention given to how the universalist conception of communication assumed by Mead is consistently segmented and shaped by tradition, class, and certain modes of thought (i.e. instrumental rationality) and experience (Mills, 1939, p. 430; Habermas, 1989a, pp. 165–170, 1992).

Jurgen Habermas, C. W. Mills and a theory of communicative democracy

In the hands of Mills and Habermas, the theoretical shortcomings of Mead's idealized concept of 'universal communication' are turned into theoretical virtues. For both theorists, the concept of 'universal communication' supplies the animating normative standpoint of a critical theory of communication with an emancipatory intent. Through the concepts of 'universal communication', 'the ideal speech situation', the 'public sphere' and 'public communication', Habermas and Mills found a theoretical ideal anchored in the material realities of the everyday world from which they could launch their critique of existing patterns and institutionalized forms of communication and make proposals for alternative media systems.

C. W. Mills (1956) offered the concept of 'public communication' as a means of adeptly extending Mead's concept of universal communication in light of the systems of 'mass communication' taking hold within the United States and elsewhere.

Mills' concept of public communication offers a powerful framework for the critical analysis of existing communication systems and for thinking about what kind of systems could be created in the future. His ideas about public communication not only anticipate important aspects found in Habermas' concept of the public sphere, but go beyond certain tendencies of the public sphere concept to become trapped within the narrow confines of 'negative freedoms' – a point to which we return below. According to Mills, in a democratic communication system:

> (1) [v]irtually as many people express opinions as receive them. (2) . . . [T]here is a chance to immediately and effectively answer back any opinion expressed in public. Opinion formed by such discussion (3) readily finds an outlet in effective action, even against – if necessary – the prevailing system of authority. And (4) authoritative institutions do not penetrate the public, which is thus more or less autonomous in its operation (1956, p. 326).

The strength of this particular framework is that it is *universal* in its reach, enhances the *possibilities for people to actively shape* the societies in which they live, and goes beyond, but does not abandon, *negative freedoms*. While existing communication systems hardly approximate such criteria, Mills 'communicatively-grounded' standpoint offers a powerful framework for the critical analysis of communication, technology, policy and society – nationally, regionally and internationally. By thinking of language, power and media within the context of other 'authoritative institutions' and within one coherent analytical framework, Mills' writings offer a critical theory of communication distinct from the 'limited democracy' perspective introduced above, as well as the pragmatic orientation of Mead.

The 'ideal speech situation' and the 'public sphere' are as prominent and important to Habermas' writings, as the concept of 'universal communication' is to Mead's, and the theory of 'public communication' to the writings of Mills (Habermas, 1992, 1989a, 1989b). In essence, Habermas' position is that the public sphere is the sociological and institutionalized expression of the democratic and emancipatory potentials of language/communication. Given this, the public sphere institutionalizes a powerful normative rule of democracy: the universal right to communicate as a basic feature of social existence. According to Habermas, it is these empirical and normative aspects of communication that suggests communication as a primary mechanism of social and political organization.

Central to the public sphere concept is the idea that it is open to all, based on universality and the principle of non-excludibility. Under the pressure of this principle, communication becomes the quintessential public good, open to all and considered to be a cornerstone of modernity and democracy. To the extent that the conditions of the public sphere are met – open to all, directed by truth and sincerity rather than power and strategy and concerned with the public good – relations between the state and civil society approximate the presuppositions of democratic theory. It is through the public sphere that the state and civil society in democratic societies become linked on the basis of communication, legitimacy and public opinion rather than coercion, manipulation, tradition, capital or bureaucratic principles associated with efficiency and objectivity (Habermas, 1989b).

In contrast to Mead, Habermas draws on the tradition of critical theory to show how the potentials of communication are systematically distorted by, on the one hand, the growth of the bureaucratic state, and on the other hand, by the rise of large industrial combines in the economy in general and media in particular. With the rise of the state as a dominant communicative actor, public opinion has become a resource to be managed by strategic interests rather than something to be formed out of the exchange of private opinion and the use of reason in public (Habermas, 1989b, pp. 181–235). Of course this is consistent with Mead's view that social institutions are reshaped through communicative interaction. However, in Habermas' hands these patterns of communication are expressions of power and domination rather than the benevolent expression of public communication suggested by Mead's under-theorized notions of power, technology and institutions.

Thus, Habermas' critical communication theory of society recognizes that civil society and communication have been radically transformed through the instrumentalization of politics/policy within the corporatist state, by vast economic inequalities and the rise of the modern corporation. Mirroring developments in the political economy in general the commercialization of the communication media has redirected the constituents of the public sphere from citizens to commercial interests. As communication media have become sites primarily for economic accumulation rather than the formation of public opinion, the nature of access has been skewed away from those with something to say towards those with something to sell. While this has increased product diversity, ideological diversity has withered (Golding and Murdock, 1991, pp. 23–9). While public knowledge is potentially a means of enlightenment, under these conditions of 'distorted communication' it tends towards control.

The relevance of communicative democracy as a normative guide for international communication policy: a critique

Although we believe that theories of communicative democracy offer a significant advance over the perspectives of 'limited' and 'representative' democracy, it is important to note that they are not entirely appropriate to the study of international communication policy. This stems from an over-reliance on negative concepts of communication freedoms, the lack of institutional spheres of public communication between civil society and capital, and the fact that the work of Mead, Mills and Habermas was never designed with international applications in mind.

By limiting his critique of the rise and fall of the public sphere to negative concepts of communication freedoms, Habermas fails to recognize that Western models of democracy and communication freedoms have always lacked an institutionalized sphere of communication between civil society and capital on a similar magnitude to that existing between civil society and the state. In this regard, C. W. Mills' (1956) stress on public communication is more enlightening than Habermas's concept of the public sphere, as the earlier quote indicates. Galtung observes that while the major constituents of modernity include the state, civil society and capital, only communicative relations between the state and civil society are constitutionally protected (1994, p. 8). The United States Supreme Court recently illustrated this theoretical point when it ruled that while the Constitution prohibits the state from abridging people's right to free speech, it contains no similar measure to protect citizens against actions taken by private corporations that abridge their right to free speech (Chief Justice Antonin Scalia, cited in Gregg, 1989, p. 80). Subsequent decisions have done the same, arguing that policies preventing simultaneous corporate control over the channels *and* contents of communication 'deprive telephone companies of the editorial judgement, control and discretion that are the essence of their First Amendment rights' (US Court of Appeals (4th Circuit), 1993, p. 12).

Finally, with its historical roots in the nation-state, the applicability of the public sphere to the international plane has been restricted to a limited right to communicate, multilateralism and parliamentary procedures of representative democracy in the UN and its agencies (Galtung, 1994, p. 25). On this score, we need to turn to David Held's recent attempts (1992) to offer a transnational theory of democracy, and to Anthony Giddens (1994), who proposes the concept of 'reflexive modernization' as the motor of globalization. These concepts complement those of Mead, Mills and Habermas. Together these complementary concepts outline a critical theory of globalization simultaneously grasping the contours and *meaning* of the emerging transnational political economy of communication. In order to further such discussions, Table 1 summarizes and compares the three views on democracy introduced here.

The normative assumptions of the telecommunication and information sections of NAFTA and GATT

From our brief critique of Habermas' attempts to formulate a critical communication theory of society, several tensions are made apparent, for instance, between the right to communicate and property rights, between the concept of negative freedoms evident in the idea of the public sphere and the limited notion of a positive right to communicate in the *Universal Declaration of Human Rights* and, finally, in the ambiguous role of the state in adjudicating between these competing rights. As Keane observes, the state in Western democratic theory has always been torn between competing demands to protect the supremacy of property rights versus its obligations to promote the conditions supportive of equality, liberty and general well-being (1991, pp. 165–70).

Like their counterparts at the national level, the actions and structure of most international institutions bear the traces of these contradictions. This is most evident in the ITU and UNESCO in their uncertain allegiance to, and structuring of, the competing principles evident in the 'free flow of information' doctrine versus the 'free and balanced flow of information' position, copyright law versus the conception of information as a public good, and technological interconnectivity versus national sovereignty issues,

Table 15.1. The three faces of communication and democracy

Type of democracy	Limited democracy	Pragmatic democracy	Communicative democracy
Orientation to rules	High	Moderate	Low
Value given to social change	Low	Moderate (within rep. democracy)	High (fundamental to democracy)
Citizen participation	Limited, representative and periodical	Regular but elite guided	Extensive communicative interaction
View of technology	Neutral/evolutionary	Malleable and possibly liberating	Expression of power
Orientation to power	Limited/state-centric	Conciliatory	Focus of critique
Nature of rights/freedoms	Negative freedoms	Mixed negative and positive freedoms (social contract)	Mixed (equitably distributed and realized in praxis)
Value given to economic change	High super-ordinate	Resigned	Subordinate to reflexive praxis
Understanding of communication	Commodity/entertain political knowledge, watchdog, representative	Empathy/reciprocity/SocPsych develop, integration, mediated participation	Legitimization/mediation of power/emancipation, participatory
Orientation to knowledge	Specialists/experts	Expert but public mediation	Reflexive and critical

for example. The difference between these institutions and emerging ones concerned with international communication policy, such as NAFTA and GATT, is that the former have yet to resolve the 'democratic dilemma', while the latter have decisively intervened in favour of a limited set of negative freedoms, property rights over communication rights, a narrowly defined range of public goods and a role for the state in creating and protecting markets rather than in promoting ill-defined notions of the public interest.

Traditional institutions of international communication policy such as the ITU, UNESCO and INTELSAT, are obviously not entirely commensurate with the concept of the 'public sphere'. However, at least from the early 1970s until midway through the 1980s, these organizations were somewhat universal in nature and at least open to expert-based discussions of the link between communication and human values. In this sense they approximated Mead's ideal of pragmatic democracy. Commitments to pragmatic democracy were evident in references to communication as a human right, principles of universal inclusion, re – sentative parliamentary democracy based on the principle of one nation, one vote and their concepts of multilateralism. In marked difference to the narrow trade emphasis of today's international communication policy initiatives, the United Nations adopted Article 19 of the *Universal Declaration of Human Rights* in 1948. Similar to the concerns raised by Galtung and Mills above, references to people's rights to 'receive' as well as to 'impart' information 'regardless of frontiers' indicate the extent to which Article 19 eschewed narrow definitions of communication rights in favour of a balance between negative and positive freedoms. According to Article 19

> . . . Everyone has the right to freedom of opinion and expression; this right includes freedom to hold opinions *without interference* and to see, receive an impart information and ideas through any media *regardless of frontiers* (emphasis added).

Other evidence of some concern by these international institutions for normative considerations include efforts to meet the 'special needs of the developing countries' by ITU assistance in technology transfers, providing guaranteed access to communication resources held in common (i.e. the radio spectrum and orbital slots for certain forms of satellite communication) and regular monitoring of the global status of communication equity, as in the MacBride Report of 1980, the Maitland Report of 1984 and further reports in 1994 (Winseck and Cuthbert, 1991). Coupled with INTELSAT's use of cross-subsidies and the ITU's adoption of accounting procedures that were favourable to the developing countries, these measures represented a type of global social contract.

Obviously, however, the commitment to the universal view of communication has varied historically and has been tempered by the fact that the primary social actors involved in these institutions have been nation-states and the private sector. During the 1980s the international community was faced with the choice of expanding beyond a form of pragmatic democracy or narrowing the scope of democratic possibilities even further. Essentially the choice was between maintaining the status quo, adopting a more expansive concept of communicative democracy or regressing behind the norms established during the 1970s and early 1980s towards forms of even more 'limited democracy'. The outcome to this 'democratic dilemma' was by no means pre-determined and easily resolvable.

On the one hand, policy recommendations coming from the ITU sponsored *Maitland Report* (1984) and the 1988 ITU World Administrative Telephone and Telecommunications Conference (WATTC) suggested that an expanded social contract for international communication was still possible. The Maitland Commission advocated extending basic telephone service into the furthest reaches of the Third World and spawned interesting discussions about digital broadband telecommunications being developed and implemented on a reasonably equitable basis. These latter discussions were far more critically-oriented and attuned to the socio-economic realities of most of the world's countries than the current mind-numbing discussions about global information infrastructures that simply universalize U.S.-bred policy discourses. The *Maitland Report* also led to the development of the Centre for Telecommunications Development, a venture intended to offer practical financial and technical assistance to developing countries undertaking telecommunications network development projects (ITU, 1984; Gore, 1994; Vincent, 1997).

Within this same context, the ITU became a key site of extensive and protracted debates about the scope of international, public-interest style regulation *vis-à-vis* the new communication technologies and information services. The debate was most prominent leading up to and during the ITU's 1988 WATTC. European and Third World countries argued for an expansive interpretation of the public interest, in contrast to proposals from the U.K., Japan, Australia and North America to exempt the new so-called enhanced services from ITU regulatory policy (Mansell *et al.*, 1990, pp. 57–8). The outcomes of the debates had ambivalent consequences for future attempts to expand the historical links between communication, citizenship and the public interest or democracy at the international level: on the one hand WATTC adopted a regulatory framework for the so-called enhanced services. On the other, those wishing to sign bilateral and multi-lateral agreements involving enhanced services could exempt themselves from the relevant ITU regulations.

Beyond the ambivalent outcomes of debates over international communication policy in the ITU and UNESCO, other international agreements on the horizon served to eviscerate the relationship between communication and human values altogether. For example, efforts to bring telecommunications and information services into international trade agreements proceeded through NAFTA and GATT.

The incorporation of telecommunication and information services entirely within a 'trade in services' framework emasculates advances made during the 1970s and 1980s towards equity in global communication. Both agreements restore a truncated policy discourse limited to issues of technological inter-connectivity, reinstate the 'first come, first serve' regulatory regime and expand the 'free flow of information' doctrine central to U.S. international communication policy. The 'free flow of information' doctrine is expanded as the agreements remove restrictions on foreign investment in private telecommunication networks and situate most of the new technologies and information services outside the purview of national regulatory regimes, and thus the possibility of public interventions. NAFTA and GATT also augment the 'free flow of communication' doctrine by allowing for unrestricted cross-national investments in private communication networks, extending the protection offered under conventional international copyright regimes for traditional media, television and film, and by extending 'intellectual property' protections to new forms of information, such as databases and genetic biological/information (Canada, 1992, Ch. 13, Article 1302(2); TNC, 1993, *Annex on Telecommunications*, Article 5). Furthermore, unlike the NAFTA's 'cultural industries' exemption clause, under GATT countries can trade film and television programming as goods and services (Kakabadse, 1995, pp. 75–6).

These legal protections overcome the historical and inherent properties of communication that have identified them with concepts of citizenship, defined them as a public good or treated them within the boundaries of the nation-state. For example, information has often been defined as a classic public good since it is not used up during consumption and its value rapidly approaches zero as costs to reproduce another copy of a film, video cassette or book, or attach someone to the public telecommunication network, diminish. In contrast to the public good properties of information, and the universal aspects of communication and the public sphere identified by Habermas, Mills and Mead, NAFTA and GATT establish restrictive legal regimes based on the exclusionary principles of private property.

Viewed in this light we can see NAFTA and GATT as decisively shifting communication and information out of the public sphere and into the private domain. By codifying a uniform relationship between the public and private sectors of the nation's party to the agreements, NAFTA and GATT eliminate thorny policital and cultural questions raised earlier in this article, as well as questions that arise from our comparative analysis of theories of democracy. Remarking on these historical shifts within the context of international communication policy, Winseck (1996) has noted

> that the contemporary initiatives generated by NAFTA and GATT are not guided by principles of national sovereignty, public participation, local cultural conditions and autonomy. Instead, the formalization of regulatory regimes is guided by generic definitions relating to transparency, technical standards, the separation of regulatory, political and operating authority and the establishment of a narrow range of public communication services. As a consequence, regulation no longer serves as an instrument of the public interest but rather for the organization of commercial markets and the protection of capital accumulation.

In essence, NAFTA and GATT meet all the criteria of technical democracy, but very few of the criteria of pragmatic and/or communicative democracy. It is probably of little surprise to those familiar with the history of the ITU and UNESCO, and the hostility of the U.S. and a few others to the power of the postcolonial countries to form blocks and significantly affect the policy agendas and outcomes of these agencies, that new policy frameworks would emerge to displace the role of the ITU and UNESCO. It was precisely the limited support that these two institutions gave to the New World Information and Communication Order (NWICO) that precipitated the exit of the U.S., Britain and Singapore from UNESCO in 1984 and 1985, and raised threats of similar action in regard to the ITU (Hills, 1993, p. 9).

NAFTA and GATT resolve these tensions by shifting international communication policy out of the ITU and UNESCO and into new arenas without any regulatory tradition in international communication. In effect, NAFTA and GATT are the *tabula rasa* upon which the future of international communications policy is being written free of the meddlesome history of pragmatic democracy and universal multilateralism that prevailed in UNESCO and the ITU.

Conclusion

Commenting on the new international telecommunications policy regime, U.S. delegate to the ITU's 1992 WATTC, George B. Helman, noted that 'for the first time since the evolution of NWICO, no extraneous political issues were raised . . . [and] . . . there was no serious North-South cleavage' (cited in Vincent, 1997). Yet, despite these comments and other superficial appearances, Helman was mistaken.

The issues are not, as Helman and other proponents of treating communication/information services within the context of trade policy tend to argue, about whether or not there will be a politics of communications policy. Instead, the central issue is: What kind of politics of communication will prevail and what normative anchors will underwrite the prevailing system of politics, definitions of democracy and legitimations of power?

At one side of the spectrum, the politics of limited democracy reinforces the corporatist tendency to steer and mediate relations between society, technology, communication and power from above – all the while obscuring the normative dimension of these issues behind the veil of so called objective technical considerations, formal rules and systems complexity. But this does not mean that these agreements are devoid of normative content. Any system of politics is essentially an argument about which concept of the 'good life' should prevail (Aristotle) and what strategies are necessary to achieve the desired state of affairs (Machiavelli). In this instance, the formalization of rules on a world-wide basis, the rebalancing of private and public interests and the expansion of the 'free flow of information' doctrine are entirely commensurate with a certain view of democracy. Indeed, the expanded free flow of information doctrine simultaneously enlarges communication technology and information services markets while expanding the scope of citizen's rights to obtain vast amounts of information, and to communicate with others across national borders, free from state interference. Viewed in this way, NAFTA and GATT are a boon for liberal democracy. However, by *shielding* the new technologies and information services from citizen's interventions, international communications policies *institutionalize* the biases of 'limited democracy' against possibilities for more extensive citizen participation in public affairs, social change and the communicative generation of norms to guide the new technologies.

In contrast, a political and normatively-driven view of how things could be seeks to further sociologically/institutionally/legally entrench the democratic and emancipatory foundations of language – equality, reciprocity, sincerity and truth – in the 'electronic public spheres' of the emerging 'transnational information society.' While this position appears increasingly unlikely, perhaps solace can be taken in the fact that its normative anchors are literally right under our noses instead of dependant on balances of power and strategies that are here today and gone tomorrow. In contrast, limited democracy rest on intractable contradictions between private and public interests, property versus communication rights, freedom of speech versus the right to communicate, and so on. These tensions cannot be settled on the basis of any fundamental normative claim or rational basis, but rather, hang on the changing material, ideological and power dynamics of the day. It appears to us that efforts to amplify the constituents of language commensurate with people's needs and the potentials of the new information technologies offer far surer footings for democratic communication in the 'global information age.'

References

Bangemann, M. (1994) *Europe and the global information society*, European Council, Brussels.

Beck, U. (1994) The reinvention of politics. In Beck U., Giddens A. and Lash S. (eds.) *Reflexive modernisation: politics, tradition and aesthetics in the modern social order*, Polity, Cambridge, pp. 1–55.

Canada (1992) *Canada – U.S. – Mexico North American Free Trade Agreement*, Westlaw, US.

CRTC (1995) *Competition and culture on Canada's information highway*, Minister of A Supply and Services, Ottawa.

Cox, R. (1992) Global perestroika. In Miliband R. and Panitch L. (eds.) *The socialist register*, Merlin London, pp. 26–43.

Galtung, J. (1994) *State, capital and civil society: A problem of communication.* (Paper presented to the 6th Annual MacBride Roundtable at the University of Hawaii – Manoa, January 20–23, 1994.)

Giddens, A. (1994) Living in a post-industrial society. In Beck U., Giddens A. and Lash S. (eds.) *Reflexive modernization: Politics, tradition and aesthetics in the modern social order*, Polity, Cambridge, pp. 56–109.

Golding, P. and Murdock, G. (1991) Culture, communications, and political economy. In Corran, J. and Gurevitch, M. (eds.) *Mass media and society*, Edward Arnold, London, pp. 15–33.

Gore, United States Vice-President A. (1994) Global Information Infrastructure. Speech to the International Telecommunications Union, Buenos Aires, Argentina, March 21.

Gregg, R. (1989) A political economy of dial-a-porn. *Studies in Communication and Culture,* Vol. 1, pp. 72–90.

Habermas, J. (1992) *Postmetaphysical thinking*, Massachussetts, Institute of Technology, Cambridge, MA.

Habermas, J. (1989a) *Jurgen Habermas on society and politics*, Beacon Press, Boston.

Habermas, J. (1989b) *The structural transformation of the public sphere*, Massachussetts Institute of Technology, Cambridge, MA.

Hayek, F. (1986) Economic freedom and representative government. In Donald I. and Hall S. (eds.) *Politics and ideology*, St. Edmunds, Great Britain, pp. 23–6.

Hamelink, C. (1993) *IAMCR Newsletter*, Vol. 2, No. 3.

Held, D. (1992) Democracy: From city states to a cosmopolitan order? *Political studies*, Vol. 60, pp. 3–34.

Held, D. (1987) *Models of democracy*, Stanford University, Stanford, CA.

Hills, J. (1993) US hegemony and GATT. *Media development*, Vol. 2, pp. 8–12.

Huntington, S. (1993) *The third wave*, University of Oklahoma, London.

ITU (1994) Report on the state of world telecommunications. *ITU Newsletter*, No. 1, pp. 9–12.

ITU (1984) *The Maitland Report*, Author, Geneva.

Kakabadse, M. A. (1995) The WTO and the commodification of cultural products. *Media Asia*, Vol. 22, No. 2, pp. 71–7.

Keane, J. (1991) *The media and democracy*, Polity, Cambridge.

Mansell, R., Holmes, P. and Morgan, K. (1990) European integration and telecommunications. *Prometheus*. Vol. 8, No. 1, pp. 50–66.

Mead, G. H. (1910/1968) *Mind, self and society*, Morris C. W. (ed.) University of Chicago, Chicago.

Mills, C. W. (1956) *The power elite*, Oxford University, New York.

Mills, C. W. (1939) *Power, politics and people*, Oxford University, New York.

Noam, E. (1993) Reconnecting communications studies with communications policy. *Journal of Communication*, Vol. 43, No. 3, pp. 199–206.

Pye, L. (1966) *Aspects of political development*, Little Brown and Co, Boston.

Tarjanne, P. (Secretary-General, ITU) (1994) Regulating the international information infrastructure, International Organizations Server, Internet.

Trade Negotiations Committee (TNC) (1993) *Final Act embodying the results of the Uruguay Round (General Agreement on Trade in Services – Annex on Telecommunications)*, Gatt Secretariat, Geneva.

United Nations (1948) *Universal Declaration of Human Rights*, Author, Geneva.

United States (1994) Administration 'White Paper' on Communications Act reforms, Government Printing Office, Washington, DC.

United States Court of Appeals (4th Circuit) (1993) The Chesapeake and Potomac Telephone Company of Virginia, *et. al.* v. United States of America and National Cable Television Association (nos. 93–240, 93–241). Internet Bell Atlantic Gopher Server.

Vincent, R. C. (1997) The New World Information and Communication Order (NWICO) in the context of the Information Superhighway. In Bailie, M. and Winseck, D. (eds.) *Democratizing Communication?: Comparative perspectives on information and power*. Hampton Press: Cresskill, NJ, pp. 375–404.

Weber, M. (1946) From *Max Weber: Essays in Sociology*, Gerth H. H. and Mills C. W. (eds.) Oxford, New York.

Winseck, D. (1996) Expanding the 'free flow of communication' doctrine. In Vincent, R., Nordenstreng, K. and Traber, M. (eds.) *Towards equity in global communication*, Hampton Press.

Winseck, D. (1997) The shifting contexts of international communication. In Bailie M. and Winseck D. (eds.) *Democratizing communication?: Comparative perspectives on information and power*, Hampton Press, Cresskill, NJ.

Winseck, D. and Cuthbert, M. (1991) Space WARC: A new regulatory environment for communication satellites? *Gazette*, Vol. 47, pp. 195–203.

16

Prospects for a global communication infrastructure in the 21st century: institutional restructuring and network development

Richard Hawkins

Science Policy Research Unit, University of Sussex, U.K. (1995).

The premise is now widely accepted that the primary locus of much economic activity is shifting from the national to the global arena. Analysts point to the rise of 'global business', and seek to describe the characteristics of the 'stateless corporation', an entity that is presumed to bear no special allegiance to any particular nation state. In turn, the prospect of economic globalization generates speculation about political globalization. Many political as well as economic problems are now perceived to be global in origin, thus suggesting that only 'global solutions' to these problems would be optimal, or even possible.

It is very significant that underpinning every vision of a globalized economy, and to a large extent driving these visions along, is the assumption that a seamless, global network infrastructure will be developed that will be capable of supporting a wide spectrum of electronic communication and information services in both public and private environments. This is the 'global information infrastructure' or 'information superhighway' as envisaged by many current political and industrial initiatives in the U.S., Europe and Japan. Indeed, without this network infrastructure, it would be difficult to envisage how any of the characteristics of global socio-economic structures as described by theorists and visionaries could be operationalized.

Nevertheless, the superficial attractiveness of the 'global network' concept has tended to overshadow the fact that it is still basically actions initiated by a small group of companies, based in a remarkably small number of countries, that determine the world-wide conditions for network development and use. By 1994, of the approximately US$ 96 billion in revenues generated by the 16 largest developers of telecommunication equipment, about 70 per cent was generated by only seven firms based in just six countries (the U.S., Germany, Canada, France, Sweden and Japan). Of this total, European firms generated about 60 per cent, U.S. firms about 30 per cent, and Japanese firms about 10 per cent (ITU, 1994). Similarly, recent figures on the top 100 computer firms show that of just under US$ 280 billion in revenues generated by these firms, nearly 60 per cent was generated by firms based in the U.S., Japan, and in just five European countries (OECD, 1992). In this case, however, European firms produced only 14 per cent of the total revenues in this group, whereas the U.S. generated 61 per cent and Japan 25 per cent. Likewise, the US and Japan currently share better than 50 per cent of the nearly US$ 100 billion world-wide market for semiconductors (Electronics Times, 1995).

Clearly, R&D and production capabilities in the information and communication technology (ICT) sectors are heavily concentrated in the G7 countries. This is by no means an indication, however, that the ICT 'super-states' are necessarily closer to achieving the internationally harmonized teams of network interconnection and interoperation that would be required to support a global information and communication infrastructure. Indeed, throughout the G7 countries, this kind of transparency remains the exception rather than the rule (only the U.S. and Canada have harmonized technical infrastructures, but even here the administrative infrastructures remain very different). Moreover, as will be shown below, the institutional mechanisms for negotiating the technical and administrative agreements necessary to provide and sustain a global information and communication infrastructure appear to be fragmenting at the international level rather than consolidating.

Are we faced with a paradox? Is the institutional structure incongruent with a network development logic that is clearly directed at global integra-tion? Perhaps. More likely, however, we are simply failing to interpret predictions about the nature and extent of 'globalized' ICT infrastructures in the context of their historical background, and of currently observable phenomena.

The main objective of this chapter is not to question the probability or feasi-bility of the 'global network' as such, although these questions could and should be asked. The objective is rather to examine the prospect for globaliza-tion in terms of some principal factors in the evolution of relationships between the dominant corporate and political actors involved in planning, building and managing the information and communication infrastructure. A further objective is to explore the implications of these relationships for non-G7 countries, particularly those referred to as the 'middle-ranking' economies – countries with high potential for economic growth but still faced with suboptimal productive and distributive capabilities.

The paper argues that the 'global' dimension of the information and communication infrastructure is developing around regional power centres, and that 'globalism' should really be conceptualized in terms of interregional relationships rather than fully multilateral ones. Evidence for this is drawn primarily from analysis of the structural changes that are occurring in the institutional mechanisms for negotiating the technical and administrative agreements necessary to build and sustain internationally operational ICT infrastructures.

Behind the global vision

Before we can consider the prospect of global communication networks, we have to ask the question 'What does 'globalization' actually mean?' More than 25 years ago, Kindleberger pointed the way to a global paradigm by predicting the imminent demise of the nation state as the primary economic unit (Kindleberger, 1969). More recently, Reich (1990) proposed that many corporations were becoming 'globalized' in the sense that, increasingly, they appeared to bear little allegiance to any particular nation state, and that they were distributing their activities flexibly amongst their international subsidiaries in order to maximize material, human, and financial resources.

Nevertheless, the term 'globalization' is inherently problematic. It can be taken merely to refer to the development of international markets for goods and services produced in the first instance in structures dominated by national economies. Most cited examples of globalization turn out to be little more than this. The problem is how to extrapolate from international economic integration to 'globalization' as such. In the minds of most analysts, 'globalization' involves more than the kind of 'shallow' economic integration that results from increased cross-border flows of goods and services. Rather, it is perceived to involve the kind of 'deep' economic integration that results from the distribution of shares, at the production level, in the international division of labour (UNCTAD, 1994; Mittleman, 1994). Seen in this light, and especially where questions of the international distribution of research and development (R&D) capabilities are concerned, the evidence for globalization is far from conclusive.

While agreeing with the premise that there are increasing international interdependencies in world commerce, Dunning nevertheless draws the conclusion that although trade and investment might become less dependent upon traditional notions of comparative advantage, the 'locational attractions' of particular countries in this new commercial environment would be determined by conditions created by both industry *and* government (Dunning, 1989, pp. 2–6). In other words, the role of the state in international commerce is not disappearing, but merely transforming from a primarily protective function to one of facilitation in the provision of infrastructural conditions conducive to attracting enterprise. Hu (1992), on the other hand, used corporate data to illustrate the substantial financial, legal, and organizational ties that still exist between multinational firms and their 'home' states. Moreover, Hu illustrated that the material benefits bestowed by multinational firms upon their 'host' states are generally of a substantially lesser order than those accruing to their 'home' states, and that there are no *prima facie* reasons for multinational firms to wish to alter these arrangements.

Presumably, if the system of world production is truly globalizing, there should be some *general* indications that R&D capability is diffusing as a result of the spread of multinational enterprises. One of the few available general indicators of innovation activity is patenting. Patel and Pavitt (1991) have used U.S. patent data to show that large international manufacturing firms appear to engage in minimal technical innovation activity through their foreign subsidiaries, indicating that multinational firms have yet to show signs of moving significant amounts of R&D activity into their 'host' states. In an examination of the patenting behaviour of telecommunication equipment manufacturers, moreover, Schmoch and Schnöring (1994) detect only a low level trend to foreign distribution of R&D.[1]

On the other hand, Ruggie (1993) has insisted that just because the mechanisms for truly global forms of political organization and economic activity cannot yet be shown conclusively to exist, it should nevertheless not be assumed that they can never exist. Ruggie proposes that a 'post-modern' political structure could well evolve which is not based upon national institutional forms. Transnational 'microeconomic links', for example might create 'non-territorial' economic regions (Ruggie, 1993, p. 172). Contained in Ruggie's proposition, however, is the implicit assumption of a functioning global communication infrastructure that is not under the overall control of national institutions. In an important sense, Ruggie's argument stands or falls on the strength of the case (which he does not make) that such communication systems can actually exist.

Another stream of analysis suggests that globalization should be defined in terms of the process by which cross-border production and distribution links can be governed (UNCTAD, 1994, Haggard, 1995). From this scenario, a kind of global *realpolitik* emerges, in which no assumptions are made that the distribution of benefits from global forms of organization will be wide or equitable. Quite the contrary, the objective of globalization could well be to further concentrate control over productive resources among a small group of economically powerful states (Chesnais, 1994). Furthermore, as a governance paradigm imposed by a group of already dominant state and corporate structures, globalization could result in the accentuation of local differences, and in the strengthening of regional political and trade *blocs* (Streeten, 1991; Mittleman, 1994).

These debates are highly complex and cannot be resolved here. Suffice it to say that the dangers are clear of proceeding on the assumption that the nation state or nationally-based corporate structures will soon disappear as organizing forces in political and economic relationships. In considering the prospects for a global communication infrastructure, we must be sure to make clear distinctions between 'globalization' in terms of the actual extension of innovative, productive, wealth creating capabilities, and 'globalization' in terms of mere marketing strategies for the increased international distribution of existing products and services.

The globalization issue goes well beyond considerations of whether a qualitatively different international information and communication infrastructure is imminent, and how it might look. The terms on which interaction with any such infrastructure might be effected must also be scrutinized. There is a reasonable body of evidence (see Bell and Pavitt, 1993), that successful technological accumulation is a function of the ability of the accumulator to link the importation of technology with the development of indigenous skills and the creation of opportunities for further innovation at the local level. The over-riding question for most of the world is 'Can there be equitable distribution of the benefits of a global network infrastructure if there is no corresponding distribution of the capability to control its evolution and determine conditions of access and use?'

Based upon the nature and extent of existing indigenous national capabilities in ICT, there are essentially three (not entirely exclusive) national scenarios for the accumulation of information and communication network technologies and services:

Group 'A' countries in which a substantially comprehensive and independent R&D, productive, administrative, and distributive capacity in the ICT sectors is already firmly established.

Group 'B' countries in which the national position in ICT is not independently sustainable or comprehensive, but in which there is a substantial enough level of active indigenous technical and industrial expertise in the ICT area to support degrees of independent R&D activity, the proactive development of limited forms of manufacturing activity, and independent marketing and trading arrangements.

Group 'C' countries in which access to new network technologies and services is normally achieved by 'buying-in' the technology and expertise, or by engaging in limited joint-venture activities with firms based in Group A and Group B countries.

It is important to note that this classification does not have to illustrate a 'developed/developing' country polarization, although in practise this usually exists. For our immediate purposes, however, the gap between Group A countries and Group C countries will be considered in the admittedly abstract terms of ICT capabilities, and not in terms of general levels of development. It could be argued, for example, that Canada and Sweden – both highly developed economies – are nevertheless Group B countries in terms of ICT in that their national capabilities are highly concentrated in selected areas. Likewise, small but otherwise comparatively affluent economies like Iceland or Luxembourg fall into Group C. It is nonetheless important to stress that the majority of countries fall into Groups B and C, and that the vast majority fall into Group C. Moreover, the major differences in the general levels of development clearly produce a major gap between the starting positions of Group B countries like Canada or Sweden, and those of newly industrializing countries that are nominally in the same group.

The significance and dynamics of regions in infrastructural development

The 'globalized' network environment remains a rather abstract concept. At present, the political and economic space between nation states and visions of a global community is occupied by *regional* structures. The actual direction and momentum of international network infrastructure development can be illustrated in much more concrete terms by focusing on the nature of international co-operation and competition as expressed in regional and interregional relationships.

The European Union (EU) is the only functioning example of a regional economic and political structure built upon a comprehensive set of formal international agreements between a relatively large number of states. Other regional entities are either formed around a much looser set of institutional ties, or are otherwise limited in scope to specific issue areas – like trade and commerce. Whatever political goals there may be in the relationship between regional partners is left unspecified.

A notable aspect of regional structures, however, is that although there may be high degrees of economic, political and technical parity between some of the partners, regionalization tends to appear as a 'cluster' of states in various stages of economic development. These clusters are formed either around a small group of dominant economies, as with Germany, the U.K. and France in the European Union, and the United States and Japan in the Asia-Pacific Economic Cooperative (APEC), or around a single dominant economy, as with the United States in the North American Free Trade Agreement (NAFTA).

In examining the dynamics of network development, however, we are concerned with '*technological* regions'. These can be defined as collections of formal and/or informal international alliances formed to promote, consolidate and co-ordinate ICT-related activities within relatively discrete orbits of economic and political influence (see Hawkins, 1992, p. 340). In this sense, 'regionalism' has less to do with geography than with building and sustaining mechanisms for the transfer, application, and control of technology within more-or-less definable spheres of international interaction. This form of regionalism is related closely to the patterns of international relations encouraged by regional economic and political institutions as just described, but it does not follow these patterns exclusively.

The trend towards technological regionalization can be shown most directly by examining changes in the international mechanism for setting technical standards. In terms of planning for 'global' networking environments, standards are particularly necessary both to ensure the integrity of existing network architecture as technology evolves, and to provide for the incorporation of new technical architectures into the network. Particularly in telecommunication, the wholesale restructuring of the standardization mechanism along regional lines has paralleled a number of significant realignments among public and private sector actors that have important implications for the way in which network infrastructures will develop.

Virtually since its inception, the International Telecommunication Union (ITU) has assumed ultimate responsibility for issuing the international technical 'recommendations' upon which the interconnection and interoperability of the global telecommunication system has depended. During roughly the past 10 years, however, there has been a steady progression away from centralized international standards-setting in the ITU, and towards a regionalized structure.

Today, substantial responsibility for defining standards has migrated to the U.S. T1 committee, the Japanese Telecommunications Technology Committee (TTA) and the European Telecommunications Standards Institute (ETSI). The diffusion of responsibility was partly a practical move in the wake of the break-up of AT&T, and subsequent liberalization pressures in the European and Japanese telecommunication markets, to ensure that existing levels of technical integrity in the network would be maintained in a more competitive market environment. It was also partly a result of the increasing complexity and quantity of the work-load in standardization and an expression of dissatisfaction with the responsiveness of the ITU standards-making mechanism in the light of quickly developing technologies, and differing industrial and political priorities in the U.S., Europe and Japan (Hawkins, 1992).

In terms of institutional alignments, however, the regional diffusion of standards-making powers indicates a more general migration of control over this critical element in international network development, from the traditional 'club' of national monopoly public network operators (PTO) to a number of other actors. Regional standards bodies were the first to offer full direct participatory rights to all entities with material interests in telecommunication. In the first instance, this was particularly significant for telecommunication equipment manufacturers who were in the process of re-examining the nature of their established vertical ties with national PTOs. Prospects for entry into formerly closed and potentially lucrative markets in the U.S., Japan and the EU had become especially attractive to these firms, particularly given the increasing R&D costs of digital network technologies. Being able to influence standardization independently of the priorities of specific national PTOs became an important element in establishing new export orientations in many of these firms.

Regionalization has been a less generally obvious phenomenon in the computer sector, but no less significant. Although computer interconnection standards have had an international public focus in the Joint Technical Committee (JTC-1) of the International Organization for Standardization (ISO) and the International Electrotechnical Commission (IEC), they have retained a substantially national focus in terms of practical applications. Moreover, most of the input into international and national standardization efforts has been from countries that tend in any case to be at the centre of regional structures. This has been most visible in Europe where a regional focus has been established through the European Standardization Committee (CEN) in conjunction with policy support from the European Commission. In the computer industry generally, however, centralized international initiatives like JTC-1 are being eroded steadily by private, specialized industry consortia, most of which have primarily national and regional orientations. Furthermore, often for very pragmatic reasons, the historically strong support from European and North American governments for international standards has recently shown significant signs of weakening (Sweeney and Mendler, 1994; Carver, 1992).

There are also significant regional implications in that computer vendors are becoming involved directly in regional telecommunication standards bodies. Although the ITU and ISO frequently reference each other's standards, there is still very little direct co-operation between these two bodies. The advent of regional telecommunication standards bodies with open participatory criteria has for the first time provided an institutional window for computer vendors and other non-traditional actors in the telecommunication sector to exert direct influence on the telecommunication standardization process and thus, potentially, to influence the whole scope of public and private network development. It has also potentially opened up an avenue for the technical agreements forged in the burgeoning consortia community to influence the shape of the basic network infrastructure.

The relationship between the regional standards bodies and the ITU is presented officially as one of the orderly and rational distribution of resources and responsibilities. Since 1989, a series of standards summits have been organized, ostensibly with the purpose of co-ordinating standards work, although there is no general evidence that projects are more co-ordinated now than they were in the era before the summits were convened. It is significant, however, that participation in the interregional discussions, which, in the original configuration, was restricted to T1, ETSI, TTC and ITU, is now opening up to include independent national delegations from a number of economically and technically advanced countries that do not wish to be identified exclusively with either T1, ETSI or TTC. Canada and Australia, for example, are participating in this way (ECSA 1992; Iida 1993). Thus, although the regional bodies began life primarily with an industry rather than a public sector orientation, it is now becoming more-and-more difficult to determine when and where national interests are being vested in the regional bodies as opposed to their traditional place in the ITU.

National objectives in planning the 'global' network

Throughout the history of the telecommunication system, technical arrangements have gone hand-in-hand with administrative and governance systems at both domestic and international levels (Headrick, 1991). How, then, will national interests be expressed in regional and interregional contexts? Will certain forms of regionalism acquire advantages over others?

To begin to address these questions, it must first be noted that the whole concept of 'infrastructure' is now very different from what it was before the era of digital network technologies. Mansell, for example, argues that the network infrastructure has evolved conceptually from being primarily a conduit for the exchange of messages, to being an aggregation of network-based services, specialized in varying degrees, and held together by network 'intelligence' as operationalized in software (Mansell, 1990, 1993). In other words, the contemporary 'infrastructure' is now far more modular in aspect, holding out the prospect that the supply and control of individual modules could be effected through far more flexible supplier/operator arrangements than in the past.

In so far as an international form of governance is possible over this new environment, it must deal with the issues of where in the network the controlling and enabling intelligence will reside, and who will have owner-ship rights under what circumstances. It must also make determinations of how the development, deployment and use of this intelligence is or is not compatible with the public interest.

The common assumption among policy-makers is that these problems will be addressed by international standards and administrative agreements, and that these will open up the world-wide trade in network equipment and services and lower the cost of market entry for domestic firms. As we have just seen, however, there are now many questions about the exact meaning of 'international' as applied to these standards and agreements. At best, and for the foreseeable future, the term may actually refer to regional agreements, or to regional and national versions of ITU recommendations.

Although ITU technical and administrative recommendations have been accepted as international standards for well over a century, the practice of applying localized 'versions' of these recommendations has thwarted the creation of an internationally harmonized global infrastructure. Europe, for example, remains substantially a patchwork of idiosyncratic network infrastructures, despite nominal conformance to ITU recommendations, and in the face of intense recent political and commercial pressure to harmonize these networks more fully. Similar patchworks are common throughout the world, especially among countries that are net importers of communication technology. Moreover, this pattern was replicated in the migration to digital technologies. By the mid-1980s, for example, the world market was laden with more than half-a-dozen incompatible digital switching systems. Equipment manufacturers encouraged 'lock-in' to their evolving digital product lines by introducing leading edge technologies into developing markets at prices that were not always initially commensurate with their R&D and production costs (Antonielli, 1991).

By the end of the 1980s the European Union had established itself as a virtual 'test-bed' for the development of a truly transparent and technically harmonized regional information and communication infrastructure. It was reckoned in many quarters, both inside and outside the EU, that if indeed such a network could be established, the resulting size of a single European firms in overcoming national barriers to network interconnection and interoperation, would give European technology suppliers a significant 'momentum' advantage in opening up new international markets.

The U.S. responded to the European initiatives, however, and defined its own regional focus in the Americas by an entirely different route. In the Latin American countries, there were many long-standing technical links to European supply firms, particularly Ericsson, Siemens and Alcatel (Hobday, 1990, pp. 169–76). However, the European presence in Latin American telecommunication left in its wake an infrastructural patchwork much akin to that in Europe, thus opening up an opportunity for U.S. interests to co-ordinate the future development of this infrastructure through a pan-American standardization initiative.

Intriguingly, the institutional framework chosen for this initiative was the Organization of American States (OAS). Notwithstanding its independent organizational status, the OAS is a long established mechanism by which the U.S. has pursued its foreign policy in the region (Slater, 1967). In advance of the 1992 ITU Americas Regional Telecommunication Development Conference in Acapulco, Mexico, the Committee of the Inter-American Telecommunications Conference (CITEL), an organ of the OAS, formulated a plan of action for regional telecommunication development that focused substantially upon the harmonization of the ICT infrastructure in the Americas (ATSS, 1992b). In the event, the Acapulco conference named CITEL to act as the official institutional focus of future telecommunication developments in the Americas region.

Subsequently, T1 convened the Americas Telecommunications Standards Symposium in Orlando, Florida, which produced further commitments to facilitate interoperable networks and services in the Americas through the OAS/CITEL mechanism (ATSS, 1992a). The institutional framework for realizing these technical aims, however, was the existing U.S. standardization mechanism, and the entire initiative was geared to support the broader U.S. and Canadian aim of increasing general levels of economic activity between countries of North, Central, and South America (ATSS, 1992a).

As applied to the whole of the Americas region, the OAS/CITEL initiative is still in the formative stages. However, the basic concepts of this initiative also inform the telecommunication agreements in NAFTA, which is much closer to being an operational trading framework. With respect to the U.S. and Canada, most of the NAFTA provisions reflect the *status quo*. For Mexico, however, they could portend fundamental changes. Although the Mexican public network is largely configured around European technology and according to European versions of ITU standards, U.S. firms in the industrialized US/Mexico border area operate private networks using U.S. network equipment and standards. NAFTA stipulates that Mexico must remove restrictions on service provision by U.S. and Canadian firms (Shefrin, 1993). Eventually, therefore, Mexico may have little choice but to develop its future network infrastructure around standards that are most easily accessible as embedded in U.S. and Canadian products.

The above case has relatively mature characteristics, but other extended regional relationships, led by European and Japanese interests, also show signs of developing. What the situation in the Americas illustrates, however, is that a regional technical profile configured with flexible institutional links that are somewhat at arms-length from formal political agenda, may have more optimal characteristics for the diffusion of technical and commercial influence than the European paradigm based upon formal alliances between a large number of countries.

In relations with national and regional entities outside of its immediate sphere of influence, the U.S. can act simultaneously as the centre of a region and as an independent state, an option that Europe does not have to anything like the same extent. A statement from a recent study of the U.S. experience with regional dynamics in the recent World Administrative Radio Conference is both revealing and potentially important to countries seeking to position themselves with respect to regional structuring:

'. . . the fluid state of alliances presents the United States with an important opportunity to encourage the formation of other blocks of countries, either on a regional basis or perhaps based on a particular special interest, that could support US positions. The United States would not necessarily have to be an official member of such alternative alliances for them to prove useful . . . the United States should cultivate alliances, both with members of the Western Hemisphere (sic) and with individual countries or other regional or international organizations that share US concerns, in order to promote US interests' (U.S. Congress, 1993 p. 25).

Just how the ITU might be able to hold the 'centre' should the interregional interests clash is becoming unclear. The ITU appears now to be concentrating upon the 'development' issues in terms of facilitating the financial aspects of infrastructure development. In its support in principle of private sector financial initiatives like WorldTel (Cutts, 1993), and its provision for the loosening of restrictions on direct and independent participation in ITU affairs by individual companies, the message is being conveyed that the ITU would now prefer to leave development decisions up to the suppliers and their potential customers in the developing an newly industrializing world. Given the poor record of other approaches to this problem in the past, it will be interesting to monitor the progress of this new regime.

In summary, for the foreseeable future, the technical and administrative environment for information and communication networks appears to encompass three basic elements:

1. Dominant centres of regional influence, primarily structured around formal and informal technological and trade alliances between Group A countries.
2. A global telecommunication governance system base upon varieties of technological and regulatory 'quasi-diplomacy' carried out between regionally-oriented commercial and political entities.
3. Incidences of 'articulation' between regions, involving interregional trade in equipment and services.

If, as this chapter argues, present indications do not favour a 'globalizing' scenario, neither do they necessarily favour 'balkanization'. As dominant telecommunication powers strive to gain access to each other's domestic and export markets, all of which remain to some extent 'protected' by incompatible standards, a sensible strategy involves both 'exposure' *and* 'entrenchment'. As we move into the next century, the most likely pattern for major equipment suppliers and service providers is for them to concentrate their efforts upon building regional infrastructures and operating in regional markets. Although the international trade structure is becoming organized into regional blocs, however, trade *between* the blocs is still linked to bilateral relationships between individual states and not between regions as such. Moreover, regional markets may not be sufficient to sustain the costs of new R&D, particularly for multinational firms like Ericsson or Nortel with relatively small markets in their home countries. We must consider, therefore, that although technical regions are not necessarily bounded by physical geography, historical technical and economic ties between individual countries can still be important determinants of regional structures.

Pressures will certainly emerge at the peripheries of these regions, and, in such an environment, it is imperative that all of the actors become engaged in monitoring, borrowing and adapting technological approaches that become standardized in the other regions. This is already evident in the significant amount of cross-membership that is occurring between regional technical bodies. It is also evident in the increasing incidences of 'cross-regional' adoption where industry in one region opts for technology developed or improved in other regions.

Interregional articulation – exploiting the seams

It remains for us to construct a sketch of the current geo-political terrain for telecommunication and information networks, and to suggest some options for the strategic exploitation of this terrain in terms of the development of national ICT innovation and networking capabilities.

Although the U.S., the European Union, and Japan are to varying extents the dominant *regional centres*, there is still a certain amount of market encroachment between these large blocs. In some cases, as, for example, with the importation of Asian-made semiconductors into the U.S. and

Europe, encroachment is very significant. Moreover, countries like the U.S., Canada, and Mexico are part of both the Americas and the Asia-Pacific regions.

The terrain begins to look even more challenging, however, when we consider that there are also a number of *sub-regions* – areas that are not yet fully incorporated into any of the three main regional groupings because of the state of market development in these areas, and/or for political and cultural reasons. Figure 16.1 shows the influence of the regional centres in both their three primary regional ICT orbits and in the five regional sub-orbits that seem most immediately to suggest themselves.[2]

The figure illustrates that regionalization should not be conceptualized solely in terms of three monolithic entities, but in terms of a highly dynamic process of interregional articulation involving countries that do not necessarily have exclusive ties to any particular regional centre. A potentially misleading aspect of the figure is the appearance of European dominance in the sub-regional markets. This is largely the result of historical factors, mostly connected to the dominant presence of European telecommunication equipment supply companies in former European colonies. Thus, much of the current European presence in these markets is related to the installed

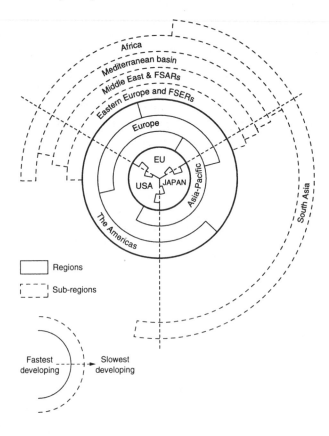

Fig. 16.1.

base of equipment. The U.S. and Japan have smaller portions of these markets, but the market segments they exploit – including their segments of the European regional market – are typically the high growth segments like semiconductors, and specialized private network equipment.

Sub-regions might also become organized as 'clusters' of states orbiting around selected dominant partners. However, dominant actors in the sub-regions are unlikely to be able to sustain their positions unless they have especially close ties to one or more of the principal regional centres. *Dominance in a sub-regional context could depend upon the ability to 'broker' the positions and aspirations of sub-regional states with the productive capacity of more than one of the principle regional centres.*

Indeed, there is ample historical precedent for this brokerage role. To give but one example, Canada has long maintained a 'diplomatic' profile in the international technical institutions (like the ITU and ISO) that is disproportionate to the size of its economy. One of the principal reasons for this prominence was a widely shared perception in the rest of the world that Canada was in a position to play the role of technological intermediary between the dominant position of the U.S. and the needs of the developing world (Salter and Hawkins, 1990). The Canadian role of 'broker' is still in evidence, even if in the NAFTA era it is much more identifiably linked to U.S. priorities. The Telecommunications Standards Advisory Council of Canada, for example, prepared and put forward much of the draft material subsequently adopted in the resolutions of the Americas Telecommunications Standards Symposium (ATSS, 1992a).

Within the three major regional groupings, new prototype broker states show signs of emerging. Brazil, for example, could eventually play this role in Latin America. Not only does Brazil have investment in its telecommunication sector from Europe, Japan and the U.S., but it has also developed a sophisticated indigenous R&D and production capability in digital telecommunication technology (Hobday, 1990). A similar situation might apply with Singapore and/or Korea in the Asia-Pacific/South Asia areas.

These prototypes are also beginning to appear in the sub-regions. India, for example, might play a broker role in the South Asia sub-region. Although the general level of ICT infrastructural development is uneven, India possesses high technical capabilities and experience with foreign ICT investment from across the regional spectrum. Likewise, the Republic of South Africa is a strong candidate to assume a major brokerage role in the development of the communication infrastructure in sub-Saharan Africa, especially given the historical control patterns exerted by the RSA over existing communication systems in this region. It has often been said that Africa is the only area of the world with no indigenous 'technology engine', in the form of a technically advanced state with technology export potential. The new political regime in the RSA may augur well for the creation of such an engine.

Tied institutionally to both the European and American orbits, Turkey has already assumed a broker role in the Middle East and in the former Soviet Asian republics. Turkey has developed a considerable indigenous telecommunication expertise through a long-standing relationship with Canada's Nortel (Yücel, 1993), and Turkish investment in its domestic telecommunication infrastructure since 1985 has been as high as 1% of GNP per annum, some 85% of this amount financed internally (World Bank, 1993). The Turkish network is approximately 50% digital, a higher proportion than in many OECD countries. Turkey has also begun to export domestically produced digital exchange technologies to the central Asian republics of the former Soviet Union, thus re-establishing trade links that, in many cases, have existed for millennia.

The 'wild card' in this scenario is of course China. Any allocation of 'sub-regional' status to a country comprising one-fifth of the world's population and a rapidly expanding technological and commercial capability in virtually all industrial sectors, is in some sense spurious. We are faced with the prospect that China may eventually become the primary economic focus of the Asia-Pacific/South Asian region. At the same time, China has displayed a reluctance to become definitively associated with any of the existing regional structures, and even though the COCOM export control regime has been abandoned, restrictions remain on the export of many U.S. and European telecommunication technologies to China. On the other hand, since 1993, a Memorandum of Understanding has existed between China and AT&T with respect to the development of the Chinese telecommunication system (Warwick, 1994).

Taking Canada as an historical example and Brazil, Singapore, India, South Africa and Turkey as potential prototypes, a number of initial conditions suggest themselves from which new 'broker states' might emerge.

Irrespective of the actual shape and extent of economic and political alliances, there is an international perception and economic independence.

• There is a long history of commercial and cultural presence in specific developing markets.
• There are historical disjunctions of technical, political and trade ties – i.e. broker states have significant ties to more than one regional centre.
• There is a high potential for the development of indigenous technological capability relative to the actual size or present sophistication of its domestic markets.
• There is extensive experience with inward investment in R&D and manufacturing capability.

Conclusion

'Global' aspirations are being expressed in terms of an interregional rather than a fully multilateral interface, thus giving already dominant interests more manageable commercial and technical bases from which to pursue their international objectives. The capacity to control the terms on which the technical infrastructure for future information and communication systems is deployed and accessed is in no small measure dependent upon the ability to select and support appropriate areas for the development of indigenous innovative capacity, and to form technological alliances in regional and sub-regional structures. To accomplish these aims in less developed countries, the idea of 'locational advantage' must be understood in the widest sense. It must incorporate historical trade and cultural links within selected sub-regional orbits, indigenous specialized technical capabilities, and the accumulation of experience dealing with foreign firms.

The sub-regions illustrated in Figure 16.1 are significant in 'global' terms, in that they constitute a good portion of the current expansion market for the ICT products – particularly public network equipment – manufactured by firms in the major regional centres. By acting in concert, the countries in these sub-regional groupings may be able to exert positive influence upon the major international suppliers of ICT goods and services, by linking technology acquisition to the provision of specific functional interconnection and interoperation requirements.

On the available evidence, however, there appears to be no general pattern of globalization in terms of the distribution of control over the production and use of infrastructural technologies for information and communication systems. In spite of their cultivation of a global image, the information technology and telecommunication industries look set to remain tied to a select number of highly developed national markets and political structures.

Note

1. Findings such as these have been criticized on the grounds that patent data analysis is not a good enough measure of R&D activity. Intriguingly, however, Patel (1994) has subsequently shown that there is nevertheless a significant correlation between the results of patent data analysis and the few other available indicators of internationalized R&D activity. The data used for correlation purposes were those collected by the U.S. National Science Foundation on self-financed foreign R&D expenditure by U.S. firms.
2. The chart is based upon a very rough approximation, compiled from a number of miscellaneous data sources, of the share of the ICT equipment and services markets held by each of the three regional centres as compared to each other. It is by no means an indication of the relative value of these market shares, nor is it a depiction of trends in market acquisition. It is also only a reasonably accurate description as of about 1993–94 – there are more recent signs, for example, that the African and South Asian sub regions may be trading places.

References

Americas Telecommunications Standards Symposium (ATSS) (1992a) 'Meeting Report', in the Official Report of the Americas Telecommunications Standards Symposium, Orlando, Florida, April 13–15.

Americas Telecommunications Standards Symposium (1992b) 'Attachment 5', Official Report of the Americas Telecommunications Standards Symposium, Orlando, Florida, April 13–15.

Antonelli, C. (1991) *The Diffusion of Advanced Telecommunications in Developing Countries*, OECD, Paris.

Bell, M. and Pavitt, K. (1993) Technological Accumulation in Developing Countries In Summers, L. H. and Shah, S. (eds.) *Proceedings of the World Bank Annual Conference on Development Economics 1992*, World Bank, Washington DC, pp. 257–82.

Carver, B. (1992) Open Government. *Network*, May, pp. 81–9.

Chesnais, F. (1994) *La Mondialisation de Capital*, Syros, Paris.

Cutts, P. (1993) ITU plans a global coalition to fund the developing world. *Telecom Markets*, August 5, pp. 6–7.

Dunning, J. H. (1989) Governments, Economic Organisation and International

Competitiveness, University of Reading, Dept. of Economics, Discussion papers in international investment and business studies, series B, Vol II, No. 130.

ECSA (1992) Final Report of the 3rd Interregional Telecommunications Standards Conference, Tokyo, 5–6 November 1992, Washington, Exchange Carriers Standards Association, mimeo.

Electronics Times (1995), 12 January, p. 1.

Haggard, S. (1995) *Developing Nations and the Politics of Global Integration*, The Brookings Institution, Washington.

Hawkins (1992) The doctrine of regionalism: a new dimension for international standardization in telecommunication. *Telecommunications Policy*, May/June, pp. 339–53.

Headrick, D. (1991) *The Invisible Weapon: Telecommunications and International Politics, 1851–1945*, Oxford University Press, New York.

Hobday, M. (1990) *Telecommunications in Developing Countries: The Challenge from Brazil*, Routledge, London.

Hu, Yao-Su (1992) Global or stateless firms are national firms with international operations. *California Management Review*, Winter, pp. 107–26.

Iida, T. (1993) Changing standardization environment prompts changes in ITSC. *New Breeze*, Winter, pp. 23–5.

ITU (1994) *World Telecommunication Development Report*, International Telecommunication Union, Geneva, p. 22.

Kindleberger, C. (1969) *American Business Abroad*, Yale University Press, New Haven.

Mansell, R. (1990) Rethinking the Telecommunication Infrastructure: The New Black Box. *Research Policy*, Vol. 19, pp. 501–15.

Mansell, R. (1993) *The New Telecommunications: A Political Economy of Network Evolution*, Sage, London.

Mittleman, J. H. (1994) The Globalisation Challenge: Surviving at the Margins. *Third World Quarterly*, Vol. 15, No. 3, 1994, pp. 427–43.

OECD (1992) *OECD Information Technology Outlook*, Organisation for Economic Cooperation and Development, Paris.

Patel, P. (1994) Localised Production of Technology for Global Markets. *Cambridge Journal of Economics* (forthcoming).

Patel, P. and Pavitt, K. (1991) Large Firms in the Production of the World's Technology: an Important Case of 'Non-Globalisation'. *Journal of International Business Studies*, Vol. 22, No. 1, pp. 1–22.

Reich, R. (1990) Who is Us? *Harvard Business Review*, January/February, pp. 53–64.

Ruggie, J. G. (1993) Territoriality and Beyond: Problematizing Modernity in International Relations. *International Organization*, Vol. 47, No. 1, Winter, pp. 139–74.

Salter, L. and Hawkins, R. (1990) *The Standards Environment for Communications and Information Technologies. Volume One: A Guide*, Communications Canada, Ottawa.

Schmoch, U. and Schnöring, T. (1994) Technological strategies of telecommunications equipment manufacturers: A patent analysis. *Telecommunications Policy*, July, pp. 397–413.

Shefrin, I. A. (1993) The North American Free Trade Agreement: telecommunication in perspective. *Telecommunications Policy*, January/February, pp. 14–26.

Slater, J. (1967) *The OAS and United States Foreign Policy*, Ohio State University Press, Columbus.

Streeten, P. (1991) Global Prospects in an Interdependent World. *World Development*, Vol. 19, No. 1, pp. 123–33.

Sweeney, T. and Mendler, C. (1994) TCP/IP: It's Official. *Communications Week International*, 27 June, pp. 1, 40.

UNCTAD (1994) *World Investment Report 1994*, United Nations Commission on Trade and Development, Geneva, p. 118.

U.S. Congress, Office of Technology Assessment (1993) *The World Administrative Radio*

Conference: Technology and Policy Considerations, OTA-TCT-549, US Government Printing Office, Washington, May.

Warwick, W. (1994) A review of AT&T's business history in China: The Memorandum of Understanding in Context. *Telecommunications Policy*, April, pp. 265–74.

World Bank (1993) *Turkey: Informatics and Economic Modernization*, World Bank, Washington.

Yücel, F. (1993) An option for Turkey to gain its information technology, paper presented at the OECD/Tübitak Conference on the Changing Role of Governments in Introducing New IT, Ankara 27–28 September.

17

The re-tooling of American hegemony: U.S. foreign communication policy from free flow to free trade

Edward A. Comor

School of International Service, American University, Washington, DC.

This chapter presents an abbreviated history and analysis of contemporary United States foreign communication policy developments. It traces the often problematic but ultimately successful efforts of U.S. officials to secure America's long-standing free flow of information aspirations through the institutionalization of free trade. More significantly, however, in the following pages I redress commonplace assumptions that contemporary international communication-based developments presage a decline in the powers of nation states.

Rather than its relative *decline*, I believe that what is underway is a shift in the *form* in which the nation state relates to transnational developments. While it is widely recognized that the United States 'remains the political and military guarantor of disciplinary neo-liberalism',[1] recent trade-based agreements constitute the legal bases for much more. In the following pages, I argue that for the foreseeable future the American state will remain the complex mediator of global communication and information developments. More than just the expression of new technological applications and a growing international service sector, these developments constitute the prerequisites for the re-tooling of U.S. international hegemony. The nation state thus remains the primary nodal point through which capitalism continues to evolve. As such, states also constitute the essential sites through which its global development may be promoted, reformed or resisted.

The state as the mediator of globalization

The American state recently has been restructured in ways that have prioritized international free flow of information developments through the ascendancy of international and trade-related offices. The complex forces underlying this structural shift from domestic to global economic priorities have reflected and involved a realignment of dominant class relationships, both in the United States and overseas. The international political economist whose theoretical work best elaborates this is Robert W. Cox. Resisting the temptation to simplify late-twentieth century developments as a period in which global forces have supersceded national, Cox understands that the state has acted and continues to act as the complex mediator of a changing political-economic landscape. This contemporary history, according to Cox, has involved the emergence of government and state actors legitimizing the neo-liberal reordering of domestic and international relations.[2] Unfortunately, what remains underdeveloped in his work are the details of how state agents have mediated the inter-corporate and intra-state conflicts that have emerged in conjunction with globalization developments. As a result of the political-economic tranformations characterizing contemporary capitalism, new private and public sector interests have arisen to challenge long-standing national and international status quos.

Despite the fact that structural disparities and outright conflicts are underplayed in the work of Cox (in large part a result of his tendency to focus on complex capital-labour relationships rather than the organizational and institutional nodal points that directly shape these relations), this has been a sin of research neglect rather than of theoretical omission. While production and class relations are central to Cox's methodology, 'other factors enter into the formation or nonformation of real historical classes'. These, Cox explains, include 'agencies of collective action that can evoke and channel class consciousness'.[3]

The theoretical perspectives developed by Robert Cox provide students of international communications with important insights. Beyond the typical Marxist emphasis on capital-labour relations, Cox understands this relationship to be dynamic and directly conditioned by the organizations and institutions that mediate them. These mediations, usually involving various private and public sector organizations and institutions, directly influence the intellectual capacities of individual and organized agents. To some extent, the widespread establishment of such mediated relations over time constitute what can be called historical structures. In these constructions, Cox understands the state to be a central agent, consecrating dominant forms of production both institutionally and ideologically. 'How the state does this,' writes Cox, 'has to be explained because it in turn explains the structuring of power within society.'[4]

Informed by this fundamental but, in the age of globalization, often overlooked emphasis on the role of the state, I believe that an analysis of U.S. micro/domestic processes in the context of macro (national and international) developments reveals at least the potential for the hegemonic renewal of the United States in the international political economy. Given that the American state has acted as the mediator among and on behalf of mostly U.S.-based corporations in restructuring the contemporary world order, more attention to domestic structures and struggles not only remains analytically relevant, it is strategically essential.

America's free flow of information crisis

In recent years, American private and public sector interests have come to recognize that future U.S. hegemonic capacities depend on the internationalization of liberal ideals and consumerist practices. This understanding has evolved in the context of a more general recognition that U.S.-based corporations hold dominant world positions in most information-based commodity activities. These industries – those primarily engaged in the production and dissemination of copyrighted materials, including news-papers, periodicals, book publishing, broadcasting, cable television, audio recordings, motion pictures, advertising, computer software, and data processing – in real value-added terms, grew from $93.8 billion (U.S.) in 1977 to $206.6 (U.S.) billion in 1991.[5] Already in 1986, American-based companies were responsible for over 43 per cent of world revenues in this sector. This dominance was particularly strong in information-based services where U.S. corporations generated 47 per cent of global revenues.[6] Not only was the United States the world's largest services exporter, it also held the largest services trade surplus.[7] Reflecting this growing economic significance was an emerging consciousness among state personnel of the substantive importance of information and communication activities.

As the theoretical perspective outlined in the previous section indicates, this emerging political-economic recognition did not necessarily mean that U.S.-based interests could mobilize the American state to successfully reform international institutions and, through these, also reform market access and remuneration policies of foreign governments. This is not to say that American state officials were not consistent advocates of the free flow of information (which, of course, they had been since 1945). Rather, like all bureaucratic monoliths, it would take an extraordinary effort to restructure the American state in a way that would make the free flow of information a foreign policy priority. Either the various offices that for many years had been responsible for foreign communication policy had to be co-ordinated or a single agency had to emerge that would become the effective champion of free flow. Although the United States was the *provocateur par excellence* of post-1945 international communications, the development of this kind of effective U.S. policy structure has taken form only recently. While America's much discussed free flow of information principles have consistently provided U.S. officials with a shared perspective and approach, the ability – and even desirability – of pursuing a set of clear and consistent policy goals has emerged only in the contemporary free trade era.

Rather than the co-ordination of existing departments and agencies responsible for aspects of foreign communication policy (such as special-ized offices in the Department of State, the Department of Commerce, the United States Information Agency, the Federal Communications Commis-sion (FCC), and many others), the ascendancy of the Office of the United States Trade Representative (USTR) and its contemporary focus on international services and intellectual property rights now has established a comprehensive and relatively coherent foreign communication policy. Beyond the free flow of information and its many legal barriers and enforcement problems, the free trade of information-based services has emerged to serve the pressing needs of U.S. *and* many foreign based transnational corporations (TNCs). But again, it is important to point out that this was not an unproblematic development.

In the early-1980s, in response to an emerging discrepancy between international legal-political communication superstructures and domestic service sector capacities, U.S.-based TNCs orchestrated a global elite-targeted 'consciousness raising' campaign. Led by financial services corporations, several American executives recognized that the United States was unlikely to change foreign attitudes toward information-based services through a unilateral attempt to reform existing international institutions. American Express Vice President Joan Edelman Spero, for instance, wrote that to be successful, Americans had to convince foreign governments that a free flow of information was in their long-term economic interests also. This, she believed, would be possible only through a concerted effort to promote the righteousness of neo-liberal trade ideals concerning information-based activities.[8]

Compelling this emerging corporate activism was a policy vacuum in Washington. In foreign communication policy, given both the U.S. constitutional separation of powers and the growing dependency of domestic corporate activities on international communications, the legal supremacy of the executive branch in foreign policy generated intra-state conflicts. Moreover, private sector dominance over a broad range of communication and information activities for many years had been institutionalized through commercially-oriented judicial interpretations of the First Amendment.[9] In the United States, therefore, an activist state has been structurally inhibited while inter-agency (and to some extent intra-agency) conflict has been perpetuated in part due to the enormous economic stakes involved in most communication-related policy decisions.[10]

At the very time that an increasing number of U.S.-based corporations needed a stable international free flow of information regime, the U.S. public sector thus lacked the means to redress what had become an international legal impasse. Specifically, decades of conflict between American and foreign officials on free flow versus prior consent principles – an ultimately unresolvable debate in international law – stymied the aspirations of dominant U.S. corporations to establish unrestricted international market access and remuneration rights. Faced with the reality of its relative economic decline, and unable to modify the legal supremacy of the nation state's authority to control information flows within its borders (as represented by the principle of 'prior consent'), U.S. officials faced a foreign communication policy crisis in the mid-1980s. In order to take advantage of its historical opportunity to dominate foreign markets in the future information economy, and to provide American capitalism with an opportunity to reassert its post-1945 international position, a secure and comprehensive transnational communication regime was needed but remained structurally unobtainable.

Strategic steps toward the reassertion of hegemony

An outgrowth of this legal impasse was the withdrawal of the United States from the United Nations Educational, Scientific and Cultural Organization (UNESCO) in 1984. Although a range of reasons were given for this action (from UNESCO's political corruption to its financial incompetence), the more substantive reasons likely involved its status as a key nodal point of the New World Information and Communication Order (NWICO) – a movement led by mostly less developed countries (LDCs) using the UN system as a forum in which to modify LDC information and communication development prospects through protectionist measures and public sector subsidies. But beyond this potential to limit U.S. corporate freedoms (most vocally represented by the American Newspaper Publishers Association and its influential mass media membership), the Reagan administration attack on the NWICO is only fully comprehensible when seen in the context of Reagan's initiation of the so-called second cold war and the related Reagan doctrine which considered Third World 'progressives' to be the explicit or implicit agents of Soviet Union-based worldwide anti-American activities.

Remarkably, the White House orchestrated withdrawal from UNESCO was opposed by career State Department officials, the Central Intelligence Agency, and even some Reagan appointees mandated to monitor UNESCO. For White House officials and those appointees holding foreign policy offices, UNESCO was commonly seen as the 'Grenada' of international institutions – widespread attacks and a subsequent withdrawal sought not only to undermine the NWICO's core mediator, it also sought to intimidate other international organizations and institutions whose activities threatened U.S. efforts to reassert its hegemony.[11]

European, Japanese and Canadian-based TNC executives became the primary targets of American corporate efforts to modify the perspectives of foreign governments. As service providers, some of these foreign corporations presumably would be opposed to U.S. competition in their domestic markets. To counter this, U.S.-based TNCs promoted the realization that foreign corporations also are service *consumers* and emphasized the potential benefits available once their access to U.S. advertising, consultancy, financial and other relatively advanced services are established.[12] U.S. private sector interests thus pushed ahead of American state officials in efforts to modify how foreigners perceive both free flow and free trade. In this project, U.S.-based TNCs forged a strategic network of elite relations through which their interests could be identified, formulated and promoted.[13] American state officials followed this lead by beginning the process of reconceptualizing the free flow of information to involve free trade issues.[14]

By the mid-1980s, just prior to the start of U.S.-Canadian free trade negotiations, a complex overlapping of U.S. trade policy with foreign communication policy had emerged. It is likely that efforts by the Reagan administration to discipline less developed countries (LDCs) through its withdrawal from UNESCO (and U.S. threats to replace the International Telecommunications Union (ITU) with a private sector-based organization), while fueled by neo-conservative zealotry, more fundamentally was driven by the economic and policy crisis at hand. The relative decline of the U.S. economy, the recognition that its information-based service corporations constituted its most competitive international sector, and the sudden recognition that the long-standing international law-based free flow of information effort had run its strategic course, all converged on Washington where a policy vacuum enabled the free trade 'solution' to blossom.

In the context of aggressive efforts by American officials to redress international resistance to free flow through free trade, as early as 1987 an ITU legal symposium examined international telecommunication issues *as trade issues* in order to co-ordinate these concerns with those emerging in the GATT. In part, this GATTization of the ITU was a response to suggestions that the technical regulations set by the ITU since the nineteenth century now should be evaluated as *trade* facilitators or impediments. In 1988, the ITU's World Administrative Telegraph and Telephone Conference formally recognized that future telecommunication services regimes should be negotiated as trade regimes.[15]

The mediating role of the American state was crucial in this institutional transformation. Suggestions from some U.S. private and public sector officials to American state agencies that if the ITU failed to actively promote a free trade agenda an international telecommunications regime based on private sector proprietary standards should be considered as an alternative to the Union constituted an unlikely but nevertheless important threat to ITU officials – particularly in light of the Reagan administration's withdrawal from UNESCO.[16] In 1989, ITU Secretary General Butler came to believe that the survival of the Union required it to co-operate with the GATT process. ITU procedures – traditionally dominated by nation-state officials and interested hardware manufacturers – subsequently were opened up to corporate officials as well as industrial and scientific organizations in order to incorporate the interests of telecommunication distributors and users directly into the regulatory process. In 1989, a High-Level Committee was established to review the ITU's mandate and activities and to recommend structural reforms. Its report, completed in 1991, recommended the inclusion, for the first time, of officials from transnational corporations to act as advisors on LDC development and investment strategies. Jonathan Solomon, the Director of Corporate Business Development at the British-based TNC Cable & Wireless, called these recommendations and the ITU's institutional 'corporate restructuring' the beginning of its new role as 'the world tele-communication systems integrator'.[17] Butler's successor, Pekka Tarjanne, has carried forward these reforms, expressing a belief that technological and transnational corporate pressures will compel the ITU to reform itself so as not to be a barrier to the changes taking place in the international economy. Telecommunications, according to Tarjanne, are to be considered as 'tools for trade'.[18]

The institutionalization of free trade

The services issue-as-trade issue equation placed the USTR in the role of America's central foreign communication policy agent. Recognizing that other countries would need to be pulled toward the re-conceptualization of communication and information issues as trade issues (rather than just being 'pushed' into it), the Reagan White House, with Congressional support, instructed the USTR to pursue bilateral service and intellectual property rights agreements. Through the establishment of trade treaties with Israel and Canada, and industry-specific deals with Japan and the European Community (EC), precedents and standards were set for future GATT negotiations. These agreements also would compel GATT members to take part in multi-lateral negotiations or face potential exclusion from the U.S. market.

The GATT Uruguay Round negotiations were completed at the end of 1993. Last moment resistance by France resulted in the temporary exclusion of its television and film industries. While the Clinton administration was berated by the Motion Picture Association of America and related interests for this and other exemptions, the more general provisions in the agreement on services, telecommunications and intellectual property (when viewed in the context of developments involving digital technologies, fibre optics and telesatellites), undoubtedly will facilitate the rapid transnationalization of most information-based commodity activities. Through digitalized transmissions, the ability of nation state officials to make distinctions between the cross-border flow of a Hollywood film and a financial transaction is virtually erased.

Unlike the apparent exclusion of so-called culture industries in the Canada-U.S. Free Trade Agreement (where, in the words of one commentator, Canada gained 'the freedom of the mouse facing the snake, not daring to move any more'[19]), and in light of the ever-present U.S. threat to apply unilateral retaliatory measures, the EC agreed only to apply general GATT provisions to its audio-visual sector. Under the most favoured nation provision of the new services agreement, for example, the EC listed some audio-visual sector activities under its allowed exemptions. These exemptions are valid for a maximum of 10 years. However, because a progressive liberalization of these activities must begin before this decade-long exemption ends, the Europeans have relatively little time to develop the regional production and distribution capacities needed to compete in a digitalized international free trade environment.[20]

Implications

The reception of West European television and radio signals in Eastern Europe, the distribution of mostly pirated U.S.-produced videos, and the long-standing activities of the Voice of America, Radio Liberty and Radio Free Europe, are now rightly or wrongly cited as important components facilitating the end of the cold war. The mushrooming availability of in-home communication technologies and other forces facilitating the expansion of transnational information activities will generate, it now is commonly believed, ongoing demands for democracy and consumerism.[21] Moreover, the recent re-emergence, at least in some Washington circles, of terms like 'radical perestroika', reflect an emerging belief among policy makers that exposure to corporate-produced information and entertainment itself undermines popular support in foreign countries for apparently anti-capitalist (and, to some extent, anti-American) policy developments. But whatever the role of electronic communications in the collapse of communism, its importance in relation to the concerns of this chapter are twofold. First, the end of the Soviet bloc represented the opening up of new expansion opportunities for capitalism – a particularly important opportunity given the perpetual economic crises facing most LDCs. And second, the dissolution of *the* political counter-weight to international capitalism meant that the capacity of LDCs and other nation states to oppose U.S.-led efforts to establish a universal free trade in services and a requisite intellectual property rights regime would be weakened.

Not only did the U.S. market remain the world's most lucrative (thus compelling LDCs to seek open access), the end of the Soviet bloc removed a significant obstacle from U.S. reform aspirations in a range of international organizations and institutions. Capitalism, in effect, became the only game in town, and the implications of this for American negotiators became obvious. According to one of the USTR's North American Free Trade Agreement negotiators, 'we [U.S. trade officials] have gotten a lot further away from counting beans and pairs of shoes...[to explicitly focusing on] the overall environment that creates our competitiveness.'[22]

American-based TNCs directly involved in information-based products and services, such as IBM, AT&T, Disney and others have long promoted the assumption that communication technologies will facilitate the development of new economic opportunities leading to greater national wealth. In recent years, virtually every sector of the international economy has been influenced by technological change directly involving the convergence of computers and telecommunications. Through the application of digital and compression technologies, a broad range of integration opportunities continue to unfold. To survive, TNCs must undertake ongoing modifications involving massive investments and efforts to control the environments in which production, distribution and consumption take place. The monetary and non-monetary costs that these entail involve and further stimulate the pursuit of market stability and predictability. This, in turn, encourages collusion rather than competition on an increasingly global scale.[23]

As transnational communication systems become essential tools in the globalization of marketing and consumption, the commercial, short-term and acritical biases generated among publics through their use will contribute to the weakening capacities of the world's social-economic peripheries to mount sustained counter-hegemonic challenges. The producers and distributors of information-based products and services making new forms of information available to mass consumers seek little more than the sensual engagement of audiences. More generally, when information becomes increasingly thought of as a commodity and treated as such, national and international laws and regulations treat publics as consumers rather than as citizens. And while virtually all that is sellable will be made available to the consumer possessing adequate monetary and non-monetary resources, there exists little substantive evidence to indicate that most of the world will not remain marginalized and/or 'massified' as a result of this 'information revolution'. From this perspective – one that focuses on human intellectual and organizational capacities rather than legal and/or technological opportunities – non-elite or 'have-not' individuals and groups stand little chance of developing and practicing the critical and creative intellectual capacities required to take advantage, both politically and economically, of the so-called information revolution.

The institutionalization of a virtually universal and enforceable free trade in services and information property rights regime through the mediation efforts of the United States has facilitated three important but often neglected historical developments. *First,* the kind of information needed to facilitate far-reaching political reforms and/or the economic development of the 'less developed' is becoming more available to those who can already afford to pay for it. Contrariwise, those individuals, collectivities and states who need this kind of information not only are less able to afford it, their time also is being colonized with sensually-engaging (rather than intellectually-provocative) 'infotainment' services. *Second,* the free flow/free trade regime will further stimulate the kinds of technological and legal developments desired by large-scale corporations seeking to take full advantage of existing information economy opportunities. Because of the extraordinary costs involved in establishing secure marketplace positions in these activities, relatively few opportunities are likely to emerge for the world's less wealthy and less knowledgeable – including those who aspire to challenge the dominant positions of the already powerful. And *third,* the developments outlined in this section constitute conditions on which the American hegemonic project can be reinvigorated. This third point is discussed in the conclusion below.

Conclusion: free flow/free trade and U.S. hegemony

Because the ideals of individualism, competition, and equality under the law are to some degree promulgated through everyday interactions in the capitalist marketplace, the workplace, and through the ownership and use of household and portable 'personal' technologies, the atomistic worldview of liberalism constitutes both a reflection of predominant conceptions of reality and day-to-day practices. Liberalism therefore reflects not only a particular kind of 'common sense', for many people it also constitutes, quite literally, 'the way it is'. Both its ongoing practice and conceptualization thus accommodate social fragmentation over mass organization – the latter constituting the precondition for the development of a widespread, sustainable and 'realistic' counter-hegemonic movement.

Aspects of the work of Robert Cox complement this perspective. In its broadest use, the concept of hegemony refers to a process of political, economic, military and cultural predominance involving relations among classes, states and international institutions. As Stephen Gill writes, 'hegemony is not simply a form of direct ideological domination. Hegemony is won in the context of a political struggle and its central goal is to obtain political legitimacy for the arrangements preferred by the dominant class.'[24] More specifically, the concept represents a process that involves the capacity to engage in and dominate institutional developments and, when necessary, control the form of mediated compromises.

It is through predominant and far-reaching social-economic nodal points – such as institutions, organizations and technologies – that hegemony is structurally expressed and potentially challenged. As shown in this chapter, the American state continues to act as a core mediator in the process of forging and reforming these institutions, organizations and technologies. Given the centrality of the United States in this era of globalization, the American state constitutes the essential site through which to reorganize the domestic *and* international conditions through which hegemony is established, maintained and perhaps challenged.

While the dominant position of the United States in the world economy has been reinforced through the GATT Uruguay Round agreement and related international communication-based reforms, the doors that these developments have opened for U.S.-based corporations could presage problems for the American and, indeed, the international political economy. The globalization of information-based commodity activities now, for example, is directly affecting the form in which the United States deals with international financial crises. Due to the rapid growth in the volume, rapidity and subsequent volatility of financial market activities, U.S. mediated reforms of the GATT and the ITU already are conditioning challenges to the structural capacities of existing American state agencies. The decision made by President Clinton in 1995 to exercise executive branch authority in response to the collapse of the Mexican peso – foregoing the two or three weeks needed to attain congressional approval for a federal loan plan – reflects the temporal problematic of democratic debate. In facilitating the free flow of information in general, and electronically-based economic activities in particular, the old Hollywood adage 'Time is Money' is taking on an extraordinary new meaning. This brings to the surface a contradiction that is inherent in the form in which U.S.-capital relations take place: the inflexible characteristics of the American state (and, to varying degrees, all nation state structures) will compel continuing tension, frequent crises, and ongoing change. Again, state-capitalist relations, while changing, remain interdependent. As such, the role of the state remains a core problematic even in this age of globalization. As Leo Panitch puts it, 'capitalism has not escaped the state but rather ... the state has, as always, been a fundamental constitutive element in the very process of extension of capitalism in our time'.[25]

According to Robert Cox, the state constitutes the core nodal point in contemporary globalization activities. This recognition not only underlines the domestic and structural complexities of globalization – involving, for example, the necessary but often difficult restructuring of states in response to global and/or domestic forces – it directs our attention towards the importance of consent in its successful implementation. The death of the NWICO, the collapse of communism, and the GATTization of international communications have converged on the eve of the twenty-first century in large part through the mediation and consensus-building activities of the American state. While the principle of national sovereignty remains supreme in international law, digital and miniature technologies nevertheless are making national borders increasingly porous to information. Moreover, the Uruguay Round agreement provides information producers and distributors with new mechanisms through which they can demand both market access *and* remuneration for their transnational services.

Because relatively expensive specialized information services themselves often are prerequisites to the development of the intellectual capacities required to access and comprehend specialized (and expensive) services, the economic capacity to utilize many information-based commodities is directly related to pre-existing intellectual and/or organizational capacities.[26] In general, what can be termed the commoditization of information is reinforcing domestic and global social-economic disparities despite the presence of apparently more accessible communication technologies and their assumed liberalizing implications.[27]

Through the ascendancy of free trade, the world's masses and peripheries are more likely to become acritical consumers than effective political and economic employers of information resources. As argued above, the American state, as the core nodal point through which these developments have been facilitated and future crises redressed, continues to constitute the crucial site for policy activism and democratic resistance. Ironically, however, most Americans remain caged in a liberal-consumerist myopia or entrenched in some form of isolationist dogma. As for the world's peripheries, they still hold a structural position through which U.S. and international policies can be affected – most still live in nation states whose mobilization now constitutes the only feasible form of *mass* resistance to the global developments outlined above. However, in an era in which the 'common sense' of globalization promotes the assumption that the days of the nation state are irrevocably numbered, this form of mass mobilization is becoming a more and more distant alternative in our collective imaginations.

Assumptions regarding the necessity of formulating counter-hegemonic challenges at a global level – while correctly focusing on the role of cultural capacities in redressing dominant neo-liberal 'common sense' assumptions – appear misguided. Not only does the mounting of a Gramscian 'war of position' at the global level remain a far more difficult task than at the national level, for the foreseeable future it is of secondary importance given the history of U.S. foreign communication policy presented in this chapter.

Notes

1. Gill, Stephen R. Neo-Liberalism and the Shift Towards a U.S.-Centered Transnational Hegemony In Henk, Overbeek (ed.), *Restructuring Hegemony in the Global Political Economy*, Routledge, London, p. 278.
2. See Cox, Robert W., (1991) The Global Political Economy and Social Choice. In Drache, Daniel and Gertler, Meric S., (eds.) *The New Era of Global Competition, State Policy and Market Power*, McGill-Queen's University Press, Montreal and Kingston, esp. p. 337 and p. 343.
3. Cox, Robert W., (1987) *Production, Power, and World Order*, Columbia University Press, New York, p. 2.
4. Ibid, p. 5.
5. As measured in relation to national Gross Domestic Product (GDP), these industries constituted 2.2 percent of U.S. GDP in 1977 and 3.55 percent in 1991. If industries producing and disseminating a product that is only partially copyrighted are included, such as architectural services; industries that distribute copyrighted materials, such as libraries; and related industries that produce and maintain equipment used exclusively for copyrighted materials, such as computer and television manufacturers, the scale and relative importance of these activities increase substantially. Employment in these industries rose from 1.5 million jobs in 1977 to 2.9 million in 1991. Also from 1977 to 1991, employment in information-based industries grew by an average of 4.5 per cent each year, while employment in the U.S. economy as a whole grew at an average rate of 1.6 per cent. See Siwek, Stephen E. and Furchtgott-Roth, Harold, (1993) *Copyright Industries in the U.S. Economy, 1993 Perspective*, International Intellectual Property Alliance, Washington, DC, pp. 8–10.
6. UNESCO *World Communication Report*, (1989) UNESCO, Paris, p. 83.
7. While from 1987 to 1992 the U.S trade surplus in services increased almost fourfold, reaching $60.6 billion (U.S.) in 1992, the U.S. trade deficit in goods was reduced from –$159.5 billion in 1987 to –$96.2 billion in 1992. As a result of the services surplus, in 1987 the U.S. trade deficit was lowered by eight per cent,

and in 1990 services exports reduced this by 36 per cent. In 1992, the U.S. trade deficit was reduced by 63 per cent as a result of America's relative strength in services. See Coalition of Service Industries (1993) *The Service Economy*, Vol. 7, July, No. 3, p. 13.

8. Spero, Joan Edelman, (1982) Information: the Policy Void. In *Foreign Policy*, Fall, No. 48, p. 155.
9. Horwitz, Robert, (1991)The First Amendment Meets Some New Technologies. In *Theory and Society*, February, Vol. 20, No. 1, pp. 21–72.
10. Tunstall, Jeremy, (1986) *Communications Deregulation*, Basil Blackwell, Oxford, pp. 198–9.
11. On this history, see Preston, William Jr., Herman, Edward S. and Schiller, Herbert I., (1989) *Hope & Folly*, The United States and UNESCO 1945–1985, University of Minnesota Press, Minneapolis,. On the second cold war and the Reagan Doctrine, see Halliday, Fred (1983) *The Making of the Second Cold War*, Verso, London and McMahan, Jeff, (1985) *Reagan and the World*, Monthly Review, New York.
12. Drake, William J. and Nicolaidis, Kalypso, (1992) Ideas, Interests, and Institutionalization: 'Trade in Services' and the Uruguay Round. In *International Organization*, Winter, Vol. 46, No. 1, p. 49.
13. Sauvant, Karl P., (1986) *International Transactions in Services: The Politics of Transborder Data Flows*, Westview, Boulder, p. 199.
14. For example see U S. Department of Commerce, 'Long-Range Goals in International Telecommunications and Information'. National Telecommunications and Information Administration (Unpublished 1983), and Jane Bortnick, 'International Telecommunications and Information Policy: Selected Issues for the 1980s'. Report prepared for the U S. Senate, Committee on Foreign Affairs (Unpublished 1983).
15. Woodrow, R. Brian, (1991) Tilting Towards a Trade Regime, The ITU and the Uruguay Round Services Negotiations. In *Telecommunications Policy*, August, Vol. 15, No. 4, p. 331.
16. Ibid, pp. 329 and 334.
17. Solomon, Jonathan, (1991) The ITU in a Time of Change. In *Telecommunications Policy*, August, Vol. 15, No.4, p. 375.
18. Woodrow, R. Brian, Tilting Towards a Trade Regime, p. 333.
19. Falkenberg, K. F., The Audio Visual Sector in the Uruguay Round (Unpublished memo: 18/19 November 1994), p. 243. On the cultural protection clause in the U.S.–Canada Free Trade Agreement, see Comor, Edward, (1991) The Department of Communications Under the Free Trade Regime. In *Canadian Journal of Communication*, Vol. 16, No. 2.
20. Falkenberg, K. F., The Audio Visual Sector in the Uruguay Round, pp. 244–5. The Motion Picture Association of America estimates that this 10 year exemption will deny U.S. film and television producers up to $6.4 billion (U.S.) in foreign revenues. Figure in letter from Bonnie Richardson, Director of Federal Affairs, Motion Picture Export Association of America, to Donna R. Koehneke, Secretary of the International Trade Commission, 2 May 1994, p. 2 (unpublished).
21. See U.S. Department of Commerce, (1991) Comprehensive Study of the Globalization of Mass Media Firms. Notice of Inquiry issued by National Telecommunications and Information Administration, February, pp. 51–9.
22. Personal Interview with Emory, Simon, Deputy Assistant United States Trade Representative, Office of the United States Trade Representative, Washington D.C., 9 September 1992.
23. Melody, William H., (1994) The Information Society: Implications for Economic Institutions and Market Theory. In Comor, Edward A. (ed.), *The Global Political Economy of Communication, Hegemony, Telecommunication and the Information Economy*, Macmillan and St. Martin's, London and New York.

24. Gill, Stephen, (1990) *American Hegemony and the Trilateral Commission*, Cambridge University Press, Cambridge, p. 118.
25. Panitch, Leo, (1994) Globalization and the State. In Miliband, Ralph and Panitch, Leo (eds.) *Socialist Register 1994*, The Merlin Press, London, p. 87.
26. Murdock, Graham, and Golding, Peter, (1989) Information Poverty and Political Inequality: Citizenship in the Age of Privatized Communications. In *Journal of Communication*, Summer, Vol. 39, No. 3.
27. Parker, Ian, (1988) Economic Dimensions of 21st-Century Canadian Cultural Strategy. In Parker, Hutcheson John and Crawley, Patrick (eds.) *The Strategy of Canadian Culture in the 21st Century*, TopCat Communications, Toronto, p. 224.

18

The European community and the regulation of media ownership and control: possibilities for pluralism

Leslie P. Hitchens

University of Warwick, Coventry, U.K. (1995).

Introduction

Traditionally the regulation of television broadcasting was able to be conducted along relatively clear lines. It was possible to determine what fell within the sphere of broadcasting, whilst regulation could be contained within national boundaries. Technological developments, particularly the introduction of satellite and cable broadcasting, contributed to a change in the traditional patterns of regulation. Within the media context, television has been one of the most closely regulated forms within Europe. In some countries, public broadcasting has been the only source, whilst in others, such as the U.K., the pattern has been a dual one of public and private broadcasting. Even the latter model has been subjected to close regulatory control in relation to structure and to content. The onset of cable and satellite posed dilemmas then for national regulatory systems which were used to exert close control over what could be broadcast, and by whom, within their borders. Satellite, in particular, did not respect national borders. Attempts by member states within the European Community (also referred to as the 'EC') to try to prevent cross-border broadcasting, were pre-empted by the European Court of Justice which, in a series of judgments, ruled that broadcasting constituted a service under the EC Treaty and, therefore, Article 59 guaranteed the service of transfrontier broadcasting freedom of movement.[1] The outcome was the introduction of a directive for the harmonization of programme and advertising rules for television broadcasting.[2] The Television without Frontiers Directive was designed to contribute to the completion of the internal market: harmonization would enable unhindered reception by one member state of television broadcasts originating in another member state. The Television Directive has not been without controversy. There have been concerns about the legality of some of its provisions, particularly the quota for a certain proportion of European broadcasts, as well as doubts as to whether the EC was the most appropriate forum for this type of regulation. The Council of Europe with its wider European membership and more cultural-specific mandate has seemed the more appropriate forum.[3] Nevertheless the Television Directive is still in place and is currently being revised.

Transfrontier broadcasting has also ensured that the issue of media owner-ship and control has come within the sights of the European Community, although, as yet, there has been no specific regulation. The changing nature of media technology and the changing patterns within the media indus-try, which are causing a move from national to transnational ownership, make a move from national regulation to regulation at a supra-national level a logical step. Of course, there is a clear case, as with the Television Directive, for arguing that the Community is not the most logical site for such regula-tion, given that it represents only a small number of European countries, and not necessarily those which, geographically and linguistically, are from the most natural grouping. Nevertheless, it is within this forum that the current moves towards regulation of media ownership are likely to occur.

It will be argued in this chapter that regulation of media ownership by the Community will be handicapped by three specific issues. The first is the question of whether the EC has the competence to legislate to protect pluralism. To the extent that the Community lacks competence to design regulation specifically for this purpose, then it will be argued that legislation proposed by the Community will be compromised and its potential effectiveness reduced. This is an issue that presents its own inherent difficulties, but which also has a pervading influence on the other issues which this article will consider. The second issue is the impact of converging technologies. Because of technological developments it is no longer possible to view broadcasting as a discrete sector. Convergence of the computer, telecommunications and broadcasting sectors mean that one can no longer clearly distinguish between these sectors on the basis of their ability to deliver data, voice or video. However, the European Commission's examination of media ownership has done exactly that, and it is difficult to be confident that any proposed legislation will take a different perspective. The result is that EC legislation may try to regulate a media environment which is disappearing. The third issue which is likely to limit Community efforts regulating media ownership is the Community's commitment to the implementation on the information society.[4] The informa-tion society, and, in particular, the expansion of the telecommunications industry, is seen as crucial for the future of the Community's economic viability and competitiveness. The same technological developments which are collapsing the traditional boundaries between broadcasting and telecommunications are enabling the multimedia revolution. The danger is that the Community's commitment to developing the right conditions for the expansion of the information society sector will prevent the Community creating a coherent regulatory framework which takes into account the convergence of technologies.

Background

The issue of whether to introduce Community legislation regulating media ownership has been under discussion for at least four years. Much of this has centred around a Green Paper, published by the European Commis-sion, at the end of 1992, *Pluralism and Media Concentration in the Internal Market, An Assessment of the need for Community action*.[5] The purpose of the Green

Paper was to analyse the issue of concentration in the media (television, radio and press) and the need for action, and to suggest possible courses of action. After publication of the Green Paper the Commission instigated a wide consultation process. This resulted in the production in 1994 of a report by the Commission, *Follow-up to the Consultation Process relating to the Green Paper on 'Pluralism and Media Concentration in the Internal Market'.*[6] This, in turn, launched a further round of consultations, and it is from this that the Commission is expected to report and to propose a draft directive. The initiative for the Green Paper arose, in particular, out of concerns expressed by the European Parliament. In a resolution of 15th February 1990,[7] the European parliament had requested the Commission to '. . . put forward proposals for establishing a special legislative framework on media mergers and takeovers . . .'. The Parliament again expressed its concern in 1992, passing a further resolution, *Resolution on media concentration and diversity of opinions.*[8] In both cases, the Parliament's concern was the need to protect freedom of expression and to encourage pluralism and a diversity of opinion.

The move in Europe over the past decade away from a public broadcasting model to a dual system of public and private broadcasters has produced considerable merger and acquisitions activity. Between 1989–1990, 81 mergers and acquisitions within the EC were announced in the media industry: 37 affected television.[9] In 1990 there were approximately 57 mergers and acquisitions in the EC, compared with 20 in the United States, and 6 in the rest of the world (mainly Japan). However, the value of the American and Japanese transactions was far greater.[10] It was the degree of this merger activity and concern about media concentration which led to the European Parliament's calls for action. There had previously been some consideration of this issue by the Commission in its statement on audio-visual policy[11], but this was brief and, essentially, referred only to the need for further consideration. However, it had recognized that Community competition law might not be sufficient to deal with media concentration.[12]

The first issue: the competence of the community

As mentioned, one of the difficulties surrounding European Community regulation of media ownership is the competence of the EC to legislate in this area. This is an issue which dominates the Green Paper. Safeguarding pluralism is not a matter which falls expressly within the Community's portfolio, although the Commission does acknowledge that the EC should not act in a way which is detrimental to the pursuit of pluralism.[13] Although the Commission acknowledges that protection of pluralism is of fundamental importance, it assesses the need for action within the context of completion of the internal market. Thus, the question for the Commission is converted. It is not what is the most appropriate form of regulation to ensure pluralism, but does regulation of media ownership and control interfere with the internal market? This produces a tension which will pervade attempts to regulate in this area, and which will have an impact on the form of such regulation.

The Green Paper's assessment of the issue made, *inter alia*, two main conclusions.[14] The first was that the Commission did not consider it had any role to play in purely safeguarding pluralism. Member states were able to protect pluralism even where the situation had a Community dimension. However, there was concern that national laws promoting pluralist objectives could interfere with the operation of the internal market. The second conclusion was a recognition that general competition law was not necessarily appropriate for this area. A merger might have implications for pluralism, but unless it also had some anti-competitive impact, it would not come under competition law scrutiny. One difficulty in relying on competition law will be the issue of what constitutes the market. For example, in the case of a multimedia merger where, say, a company owning a newspaper acquires a company holding a television licence, the market might be defined as the television market and not the media market which includes both television and newspapers. Hence, no competition question might arise, but the merger could raise serious concerns for pluralism.

Although the Commission was primarily concerned about the operation of the internal market, it did consider also the effect of media concentration on pluralism. Concluding that the number of media controllers would be the most relevant measure (compared with the number of channels or titles, or diversity of content) for assessing diversity, the Green Paper also stated that '. . . autonomy and structural independence among controllers . . . constitutes a minimum condition of the diversity of choice offered to the public'.[15] An evaluation of the level of media concentration was provided by an economic study commissioned by the European Commission.[16] The results of the economic study showed that media mergers tended to take place within the home country, so that there were few cross-border mergers[17], although it predicted that more cross-border activity would develop by the larger media groups.[18] The economic study also suggested that cross-border activity might be undertaken by cash rich non-media companies such as water distribution companies. The study named companies such as CGE and Lyonnaise des Eaux (water distribution companies) as potential actors.[19] Although this trend was noted by the Green Paper no further consideration was given to it. However, economic groupings of media and non-media activities can raise issues of importance for media pluralism particularly in the areas of promotion of group interests and the dissemination of information. In 1988, Fininvest, the Italian media group, acquired a department store chain. Shortly afterwards, a programme of cross-promotion began, whereby Fininvest's television stations carried daily slots featuring the department store.[20] More recently Berlusconi showed his willingness to use his media interests to promote his political election campaign. Alan Bond, the former Australian entrepreneur, whose interests included breweries, mining and media threatened to use his television interests against a business competitor, the AMP Society, if it continued to oppose him in relation to other commercial interests.[21] In Britain, the use by Lonrho PLC of its press interests in the battle between Lonrho and the Al Fayed brothers is another example.[22]

An attempt to reconcile the need to promote pluralism with the Community's economic objectives was made by the Commission. It predicted that the realization of the internal market would create opportunities for media companies which, in turn, would promote pluralism.[23] It also concluded that promotion of the Community's industrial policy, by strengthening Community industry and competitiveness, would contribute to the maintenance of pluralism.[24] This is an approach which is often advocated. Yet it rests on two assumptions which may not necessarily follow. The first assumption is that if competition goals are pursued a multiplicity of operators will follow. However, experience indicates that this might not be so: increased competition for markets has generally resulted in concentration within the broadcasting and newspaper industries.[25] Secondly, it rests on the assumption that an increase in the number of media operators will produce increased diversity. However, there is no necessary reason why this should be so. Media operate in a commercial and business context and it is only the commercially viable who will have access to the outlets. Increasing the number of outlets will only provide increased access to '. . . those least likely to criticize the prevailing distribution of wealth and power.'[26] The move towards transnational horizontal mergers may only exacerbate this tendency. Reliance on a competitive environment to foster pluralism may be too simplistic. The Community also has an obligation to protect fundamental rights within the structure and objectives of the Community.[27] However, this obligation does not impose a duty to adopt express pluralist measures. Instead, it is seen as an obligation and competitiveness through industrial policy, and promoting the expansion of the audio-visual industry through audio-visual policy.[28] The Green Paper admitted that the nature of these objectives might differ from an objective of promotion of pluralism. Relying, however, on the view that increased competition could promote pluralism, it did not see these objectives as inevitably conflicting.

Whilst the Green Paper admitted that Community competition law was not wholly suitable for the protection of pluralism, it did not see that this created a need for specific Community action. Such action could be dealt with at the national level.[29] The Green Paper was, however, concerned about the effect of national anti-concentration measures on the internal market, and identified several difficulties. Such laws might restrict free movement of services where there was a risk of circumvention; restrict the right of establishment; restrict or distort competition; create legal uncertainty regarding circumvention; or hinder access to media activity.[30] For example, if the grant or renewal of a licence was difficult under one set of laws, circumvention might occur. This is a particular risk where the form of media is satellite or cable broadcasting.[31] It could also drain investment from areas where ownership restrictions are more stringent.[32] Certain forms of anti-concentration measures, such as limitation of interest to a specified percentage, were thought likely to discourage foreign investment. In the Commission's view, this could discourage investment by foreign operators because of the likely fragmentation of capital.[33] The Green Paper concluded that there might be a need for action at Community level to ensure, not primarily the maintenance of pluralism, but, because of the obstacles, the proper functioning of the single market.[34] Thus, the Green Paper's final position is that intervention may be necessary for the protection of the internal market.[35] The Green Paper did not advocate a particular course of action, but put forward three options. The first was that no action be taken.[36]

The second option was to introduce some form of co-operative action to ensure greater transparency of media ownership and control, whilst the third option was to introduce Community legislation which would eliminate differences between national restrictions on media ownership.[37] This could be in the form of a harmonizing directive or a Council regulation.[38]

The Commission had concluded that the problems and obstacles for the internal market associated with a lack of supra-national regulation were potential rather than actual. Yet some of the responses received during the consultation period illustrated a different picture. The responses covered a variety of interest groups such as public organizations, media corporations, regulatory bodies and trade union groups. Many of the responses were predictable although some of the U.K. media companies considered that action was necessary because of the problems of circumvention, citing their experience of British Sky Broadcasting ('BSkyB'). The European Group of the International Federation of Journalists ('EGIFJ') cited examples, in Denmark and Germany, of national laws being circumvented because the media operator had been able to move to another member state and then transmit back to the home state.[39] This was an issue which the Commission had not considered to be a major problem, although it was probably the most frequently raised issue amongst the responses. The EGIFJ also referred to what it considered as the dangers of media concentration, both multimedia and mixed industry, and cited examples in the U.K. (News Corporation), Spain, Germany and France.[40] Fininvest argued that whilst markets should be opened up this would not be achieved by Community regulation:[41] 'Before setting limits to ownership or creation of television networks, a positive approach would insist on action to create the greatest possible space for freedom of enterprise and freedom of thought'.[42] BSkyB, the subject of complaint by other media groups making responses, also thought that action at Community level was inappropriate, but that any regulation introduced should be based on the most liberal regime operating within the EC.[43] Predictably, those advocating no change tended to be those media groups which had benefited from liberal national laws whilst those advocating regulation were generally those groups which perceived injustice in the way that the current national laws operated.

Other responses thought that the Commission lacked sufficient clarity about its aims and the types of controls which would be appropriate, and, hence, that the case for Community action level was not made out.[44] This illustrates the dilemma faced by the Commission in that it was assessing the regulations controlling pluralism whilst, at the same time, having to advocate such regulation in the context of protection of the internal market. The Green Paper leaves major issues unconsidered and undiscussed; in particular, little thought appears to have been given as to how such regulation might operate.[45] Whilst it acknowledges a concern about pluralism, it is not clear what role this plays in the paper's final conclusions and what place it will have in the Community's pursuit of the internal market. What is clear, however, is that any proposed regulation will be primarily for the purpose of ensuring the operation of the internal market. Protection of pluralism will be a subsidiary issue.

The second issue – the changing media environment

It has been noted that the impetus for the Green Paper was in part the increasing degree of merger activity within the European Community. Since then, however, it would probably be reasonable to conclude that this activity has increased and that the nature of that activity has changed. What one can now observe is that not only is there considerable merger activity, but also, in the advent of the multimedia revolution, the development of strategic alliances particularly within the broadcasting and telecommunications sectors. There is clearly a trend for media, computer and telecommunications operators to combine together in order to ensure a place within the multi-media world. Thus, one of America's largest telecommunications companies, MCI Communications (in which British Telecom has a 20% shareholding), invested in Murdoch's News Corporation with the intention of establishing a joint venture to merge the latter's news and entertainment resources with MCI's telecommunication networks.[46] Mergers between news and entertainment groups and between programme production and distribution have also been evident. The ABC network and Walt Disney Company merger, the Time Warner and Turner Broadcasting merger and Viacom's takeover of Blockbuster and Paramount all provide evidence of this. The increasing move from media-related vertical mergers to horizontal mergers adds a new dimension to the Commission's study of this area.

Despite being aware of these trends, its deliberations have tended to focus on monomedia and cross-media restrictions. This focus, together with the likelihood that Community regulation will be driven by internal market concerns, results in a lack of coherent strategy dealing with current media activity. Much current national regulation of ownership and control tends to distinguish between terrestrial and satellite broadcasting with the focus very much on terrestrial television as the dominant medium. To what extent Community proposals for regulation would change this pattern is as yet unclear but, certainly, if regulation of media ownership is to be comprehensive it should address the relationship between terrestrial television and non-terrestrial broadcasting, particularly with the advent of digital transmission.

More importantly, the Green Paper seems to have viewed broadcasting as existing in isolation. The technological developments are obscuring the divisions between broadcasting, telecommunications and computer communications, and if regulation of media ownership is to be effective it must take this development into account. The approach which comes through is that the EC is continuing to plan for regulation as if broadcasting and telecommunications were still two quite distinct sectors, so that broadcasting will be covered by specific regulatory control whilst telecommunications will be left to general competition law. Whilst the follow-up paper does acknowledge that the new technologies must be taken into account, this appears to refer only to such technologies as satellite broadcasting, so there is no certainty that there will be any attempt to bring broadcasting and telecommunications into a coherent regulatory framework affecting ownership. This seems even less likely when one takes into account the Community's commitment to the information society. In the light of the convergence of technology, the

Commission has made no attempt to address the question of how to define 'broadcasting': to ask what should now be the subject of special regulatory treatment. It may no longer be simply enough to ask 'who has control of a television licence', the relevant questions may also be who has control of the access technology, the programme catalogues, the programme production companies, and the telephone networks.

The third issue – the information society

One issue which makes it especially unlikely that the Community will address the type of questions for regulation, which it has been suggested might arise from the converging technologies, is the Community's commitment to the implementation of the information society. The development of the information society lies in the same technological developments which are making so complex the issue of regulation of media ownership. The economic importance of the information society was recognized some time ago by a Commission White Paper addressing questions of competitiveness and employment in the Community.[47] Particularly significant here is the place of the telecommunications industry, which is seen as a rapidly growing industry, and especially relevant for the EC's economic position compared with the United States and Japan.

Pivotal in setting out the policy of the Community on the information society is the Bangemann Report, which was the result of considerations by the High-Level Group under the chairmanship of Martin Bangemann.[48] The group had been requested to identify the measures needed for the development of the information society structure. The report is important in setting down the principles which will shape the information society, most central of which is a commitment to the market mechanism as the means of launching the information society.[49] Also significant is the recognition that the entertainment media is important for stimulating the domestic multimedia market which might otherwise be resistant to the initial costs of the required equipment.[50] This is important because it shows that the media has a very clear economic role in the information society's establishment. Given the perceived economic importance of the information society to the future of the Community, it is unlikely that the regulation of media ownership will be allowed to interfere with this drive. Some hint of this is given in the Bangemann Report. Although it states that the issue of regulation of media ownership must be addressed, there is a strong inference that it views the issue only in terms of the traditional concept of 'media'. The purpose of such regulation is also made clear. Although acknowledging the need to protect pluralism, regulation must be to remove the potential for current national rules: to '. . . impede companies from taking advantage of the opportunities offered by the internal market, especially in multimedia, and [which] could put them in jeopardy *vis-à-vis* non-European competitors'.[51] In the same way, the Commission's Acting Plan setting out the steps for the implementation of the information society concentrates on issues relating to telecommunications. It again stresses the need for regulation of media ownership at the European level, but makes no attempt to consider this in the context of the information society and the impact of changing technologies.[52]

The likely submergence of media ownership regulation to the economic demands of the information society is evidenced by the attitude taken in the Follow-up Paper. Its purpose, it will be recalled, was to report on the consultation period and to assess the current position. The publication of the Green Paper predated the White Paper, the Bangemann Report and the Action Plan, but the Follow-up Paper was published after these. The Follow-up Paper acknowledged that its assessment was taking place '. . . at a turning point in the history of the media sector in Europe . . .'.[53] This was an acknowledgement of the impact of changing technologies and the Community's commitment to the implementation of the information society. The consultations conducted after the Green Paper indicated to the Commission that there was majority support for some form of change in the regulatory system affecting media ownership. However, what was less clear was whether regulation should take place at national or EC level, and the form it should take.[54] What is interesting, in the Commission's assessment of the situation is that, whilst the importance of preserving pluralism is acknowledged, the real impetus for introducing a regulatory framework at the European level is the recognition that obstacles created by the patchwork of national legislation are hindering the opportunities for media operators to expand within the internal market.[55] This concern is exacerbated by the changing nature of the media market, so that the problems of the current regulatory patchwork are felt to be more acute because they might limit the opportunities for media and other operators to take advantage of the transformation of traditionally separate markets such as computers, broadcasting and telecommunications into the integrated information society market.

The Commission was also concerned that the changing nature of the media market was contributing to increased national regulation, so that the situation is likely to become even more complex.[56] The following statement reflects the tensions facing Community policy: '[t]his [the national regulatory patchwork] limits the opportunities for media companies to make the most of the growth potential of the Internal Market, and hence to play a more active part in promoting pluralism.'[57] The implication is that if a coherent regulatory system is introduced, it will enable more media operators to enter the market, and this will in turn promote pluralism. Reasons have already been suggested as to why creating a more competitive market will not necessarily contribute to greater diversity. But, apart from this, the statement is telling in that it betrays the real purpose of a European regulatory system for media ownership. The intention will be to create the system most likely to facilitate industry development, but consistent still with some pluralist-protecting measure. This seems to indicate that there will be strong pressure from the media industry to impose as light a regulatory framework as possible at the European level in order to assist the development of the multimedia industry. Such pressure will be difficult to resist given, also, that the competence of the Community to take action in this area does not include specifically a competence to regulate for pluralism. The Follow-up Paper also launched a second round of consultation for the purpose of deciding whether there should be Community action, and the scope for such action.[58] The Follow-up Paper is concerned that without coherent European level regulation, media operators will not be able to take advantage of the new technologies, and, in the face of globalization of the media industry, will not be able to compete internationally.[59] Indeed, the Commission assessed this as the fall-out of preserving the status quo, or not taking any action at the Community level.[60]

Conclusion

If EC regulation of media ownership is eventually introduced (and this could be a very slow process), the type of regulation adopted is, as this article has suggested, going to be constrained by the constitutional objectives by which the Community is bound. Whereas regulation of media ownership and control usually exists for the protection of pluralism, within the Community context, such regulation would be for the purpose of pursuing primarily economic objectives. This must surely result in a distortion of the regulatory design. This is one difficulty affecting Community regulation of media ownership. The impact of this difficulty, however, is exacerbated by the other issues discussed in this article. Whether deliberate or otherwise, the Commission consistently seems to ignore the impact of the convergence of the broadcasting, telecommunications and computer technologies for the regulation of media ownership. This will certainly influence the effectiveness of any legislation for this area. One could not accuse the Commission of being ignorant of such developments, because it is these very developments which are fuelling the concerted Community activity which is occurring in the establishment of the information society. The economic importance which the Community attaches to the information society, and the role which the media sector will be called upon to play to assist in the former's establishment, will almost certainly ensure that European regulation of media ownership, when introduced, will be designed to interfere as little as possible with the economic concerns of the European Community and its members. The issues raised in this article, together, are likely to ensure that protection of pluralism will become little more than a gesture, if, and when, European regulation of media ownership is introduced.

Notes

1. See *Italy v. Saachi* [1974] ECR 409; *Procureur du Roi v. Debauve* [1980] ECR 833; and *Coditel v. Cine Vog Films* [1980] ECR 881.
2. Council Directive of 3 October 1989 on the co-ordination of certain provisions laid down by law, regulation or administrative action in Member States concerning the pursuit of television broadcasting activities [1995] OJL298/23. Referred to in this article as the 'Television without Frontiers Directive' or the 'Television Directive'.
3. For a discussion of some of the legality issues over the Directive, see de Witte, B., (1995) The European Content Requirement in the EC Television Directive – Five Years After. In Barendt, E. M. (ed.), *The Yearbook of Media and Entertainment Law 1995*, Clarendon Press, p. 101. The Council of Europe adopted a Convention on Transfrontier Television some months after the Directive. It is in similar terms to the Television Directive, but for EC member states the Directive takes precedence. For an examination of the Convention and its relationship to the Directive, see Barendt, E. M., (1993) *Broadcasting Law A Comparative Study*, Clarendon Press, chapter X.

4. Terms like 'information society', 'multimedia revolution' and 'information superhighway' tend to be used interchangeably but the European Commission has expressly adopted the term 'information society' to describe the communications and information revolution: European Commission Information Society Project Office (1995) *Introduction to the Information Society: The European Way*, 3. For a discussion of the implications of the EC's commitment to the information society see Hitchens, L. P., (1996) Identifying European Community Audio-Visual Policy in the Dawn of the Information Society. In Barendt, E. M. (ed.), *The Yearbook of Media and Entertainment Law 1996*, Clarendon Press.

5. COM(92)480 final, 23 December 1992. Referred to in this article as the 'Green Paper'. For a detailed discussion of the Green Paper see (1994) 57 MLR 585.

6. COM(94)353 final, 5 October 1994. Referred to in this article as the 'Follow-up Paper'.

7. OJ No C 68, 19 March 1990, 137 at 138.

8. OJ No C 284, 2 November 1992, 44 at 46.

9. Booz-Allen and Hamilton, *Study on Pluralism and Concentration in Media – Economic Evaluation*, Final Report, 6 February 1992 ('the Economic Study'), 4.34. Media industry here included cinema and video.

10. *Id*, 4.35.

11. European Commission, *Communication from the Commission to the Council and Parliament on audiovisual policy*, 21 February 1990, COM(90) 78 final, 21.

12. *Ibid*.

13. *Supra* n 5, 7.

14. *Id*, 7–9.

15. *Id*, 19. The Commission considered that whilst diversity of content would be the most logical measure the complexity of analysis was too great and also lent itself to subjectivity.

16. *Supra* n 9.

17. *Supra* n 5, 24.

18. *Id*, 15.

19. *Ibid*. The development of mixed conglomerates is a trend which has been noted elsewhere: see Murdock (1990) Redrawing the Map of the Communications Industries: Concentration and Ownership in the Era of Privatization. In Ferguson (ed), *Public Communication the New Imperatives*, Sage, London, 1 and 4 and see Barendt E. M., (1993) *Broadcasting Law A Comparative Study*, Clarendon Press, 124.

20. Murdock, *id*, 8.

21. Australian Broadcasting Tribunal *The Bond Inquiry, Decision on Facts*, 7 April 1989, pp. 30–3. On another occasion, Bond, whilst doing business in Chile, expressed a wish to the then president, General Pinochet, to send a television crew to Chile to show the success of the Chilean government: Tiffen, The Revolution in Australian Media Ownership 1986–1987. *Working Papers in Australian Studies*, no. 36, p. 9.

22. For other examples see Murdock, *supra* n 19, 8.

23. *Supra* n 5, 59.

24. *Supra* n 5, 60.

25. Barendt, *supra* n 19, 122.

26. Murdock and Golding (1977) Capitalism, Communication and Class Relations. In Curran *et al.* (eds.) *Mass Communications and Society*, Edward Arnold, London, 12 and 37.

27. *Supra* n 5, 61.

28. *Supra* n 5, 62.

29. *Supra* n 5, 87–8.

30. *Supra* n 5, 88–98.

31. *Supra* n 5, 89.
32. *Supra* n 5, 93.
33. Whilst one can appreciate the view that such a restriction is more likely to deter operators, from countries where such restrictions do not apply, it is not entirely clear why a restriction of say 25% should be seen as being of a size likely to act as a disincentive to investment. In a large listed public company with a wide spread of shareholding 25% (and less) would be a very significant holding and may enable management influence or control.
34. *Supra* n 5, 99.
35. *Ibid.*
36. *Supra* n 5, 113–4.
37. *Supra* n 5, 115–7.
38. *Supra* n 5, 117. There was also a suggestion of establishing a regulatory body to help implement the directive, but there seems to be little support for this idea and it is expected that it will not be pursued when the draft directive is published.
39. European Group of the International Federation of Journalists (1993) *An Action programme for the Media in Europe*, 31 March 1993, 8–9.
40. *Id*, 6.
41. Fininvest Comunicazioni, *Considerations on the advisability of action at EC level on ownership and control of concentrations in the communications sector*, March 1993, 1.
42. *Id*, 22.
43. British Sky Broadcasting Limited, *The European Commission's Green Paper on Pluralism and Media Concentration in the Internal Market: An Assessment of the Need for Community Action*, April 1993, 12.
44. Independent Television Commission, *Comments by the Independent Television Commission on the Commission of the European Communities Green Paper on Pluralism and Media Concentration in the Internal Market*, 16 April 1993, 5.
45. The only attention to this appears to be a list of possible areas for regulation: *supra* n 5, 108.
46. *The Sunday Times*, 14 May 1995, p. 3.
47. *Growth, Competitiveness, Employment: The Challenges and Ways Forward into the 21st Century*, COM(93)700 final, 5 December 1993.
48. *Europe and the Global Information Society: Recommendations to the European Council* (26 May 1994).
49. *Id*, 3.
50. *Id*, 9–10.
51. *Id*, 19.
52. *Communication from the Commission to the Council and the European Parliament and to the Economic and Social Committee and the Committee of Regions, Europe's Way to the Information Society: An Action Plan*, COM(94)347 final, 7.
53. *Supra* n 6, 4.
54. *Supra* n 6, 5.
55. *Ibid.*
56. *Supra* n 6, 5 and 20.
57. *Supra* n 6, 5.
58. *Supra* n 6, 6.
59. *Supra* n 6, 20.
60. *Supra* n 6, 30–1.

Section 5

Challenge and resistance in the global media system

19

Small media and revolutionary change: a new model

Annabelle Sreberny-Mohammadi and Ali Mohammadi

From Sreberny-Mohammadi, A. and Mohammadi, A. (1994) *Small Media, Big Revolution: Communication, Culture and the Iranian Revolution,* University of Minnesota Press, Minneapolis, MN, pp. 19–40.

The particular dynamics of the Iranian revolution, and the many unexpected political experiences of the past few decades, suggest a need and give us the basis for a new model of contemporary revolutionary mobilization that is significantly different from previous dynamics of revolutionary upheaval. Mediated culture has become part of the causal sequence of revolutionary crisis, as well as central to revolutionary process. [. . .]

All revolutionary processes are political processes, whether or not there are underlying economic causes and/or demands. Thus all revolutions are also communicative processes, including the articulation of sometimes-competing ideologies and demands, the development of leaders and followers, the circulation of information, the exhortations to participation and mobilization. Popular mythology might think of the storming of the Bastille as the revolutionary act, but in fact much of the politicizing and argumentation, the reading and writing, the persuading and criticizing, that went before were as much if not more 'political' than the final dramatic acts of violence. Revolution has rarely been thought of in communications terms. For example, only recently, with the flourish of publishing that not only celebrates but also rethinks the French Revolution of 1789, have media forms and communicative networks been set at the centre of its analysis. Darnton and Roche (1989, p. xii) write that historians have generally 'treated the printed word as a record of what happened instead of an ingredient in the happening. But the printing press helped shape the events it recorded. It was an active force in history . . . we have never attempted to understand how the dominant means of communication in the most powerful country of the West contributed to the first great revolution of modern times.'

In the contemporary world, media are part of political problems and part of the solutions, essential elements of repressive political structures as well as vehicles for their overthrow. [. . .] At issue is how certain forms of media can function to support popular mobilization, particularly within repressive contexts.

The problem of defining 'small media'

'Small media' has become a popular rubric for various kinds of mediated alternatives to state-run broadcasting systems, but the definition of non-mass media has never been very precise. From Schramm's (1972) attempts to define 'big' and 'little' media, to definitions of 'group media' (*Media Development*, 1981), 'community media' (Wade, 1981; Byram, 1981), or 'radical' media (Downing, 1984), what has been crucial is a notion of these media as participatory, public phenomena, controlled neither by big states nor big corporations. Thus the distinction between 'big' and 'small' cannot depend on particular kinds of technologies or even on their putative audiences, but rather on the manner of use of all technologies. Even broadcast media could have a different shape, as suggested by Brecht (1930) over 60 years ago:

> Radio should be converted from a distribution system to a communication system. Radio could be the most wonderful public communication system imaginable, a gigantic system of channels – could be, that is, if it were capable not only of transmitting but of receiving, or making the listener not only hear but also speak, not of isolating him, but of connecting him. This means that radio would have to give up being a purveyor and organise the listener as purveyor.

This is an activist model for the 'emancipatory use' of the media (Enzensberger, 1970), which focuses on popular involvement rather than on professional production, on horizontal rather than vertical communication, and on active participation in meaning-making rather than the passive absorption of mass-mediated culture and values. Of course, in Western democracies locally based and organized, non-profit, participatory forms are many and various. They include local/free newspapers, community radio and television channels, citizens' video, community computers, and so on (Downing, 1984; Jankowski *et al.*, 1992). Such media projects are developed by pressure groups, political organizations, counterculture *aficionados*, and local communities and minority groups.

These alternative, participatory media forms not only satisfy demands for different contents, catering to tastes, interests, and orientations not catered to by mass-media output and sometimes challenging that output, but are also vehicles for direct participation in the mediated communications process and for the extension of the voices of groups and ideas otherwise not heard. The very existence of this non-mass-media environment is a measure of the vibrancy of a democratic society. Downing (1984, p. 2) stresses the importance of self-managed dissonant media, which 'have posed a genuine alternative to the media patterns of both West and East.'

The kind of media use described might be covered under Fathi's (1979) rubric of 'public communication.' This shifts focus to an autonomous sphere of activity independent of the state, the popular production of messages, a public coming into being and voicing its own 'opinion' in opposition to state-orchestrated voices; to the use of channels and technologies that are readily accessible and available; and to messages that are in the main produced and distributed freely as opposed to private/corporate production for profit or control by state organizations. Jankowski *et al.* (1992) call such media 'the people's voice,' although 'people's voices' might be more apt. [. . .]

Alternate channels and political challenge

[. . .] In the contemporary development of popular movements against strong states we face a new model of revolutionary mobilization. Its mode of participation is extensive – mass – but low level; its ideology is populist and profoundly antistatist. Indeed, that ingredient provides the glue for the populist solidarity that is rapidly manifest. Most groups in the society become convinced that the first and necessary step in change is the removal or fundamental alteration of the existing state structure. In Iran, because the royalist despotism of the Shah was associated with Western neocolonialism and dependency, anti-Westernism was a key ideological notion.

The forms of organization are creative and spontaneous, based on a mix of small media and traditional networks rather than on formal parties or organized unions. The dynamic is predominantly urban. Recent events saw mass demonstrations in Beijing, East Berlin, Bucharest, Budapest, and Prague – not in the outlying countryside. Leading activists and major participants were students and intellectuals (as in Iran, the People's Republic of China, Czechoslovakia, and Romania), not the peasantry. In the cases of Iran, the Philippines, and Poland, religious organizations and religious leadership also were significant. Although members of the urban working class participated in the mass demonstrations and rallies, their organizations were not central to the process; it was really only in Poland that an older form of political organization, a trade union, evolved into the more encompassing structure of Solidarity and came to play the crucial role in a struggle that lasted much longer than many of the more precipitous events of 1989. These movements suggest new forms of populist solidarity to achieve major political change, at least temporarily, although many of these tenuous coalitions splinter as soon as the immediate shared goal is achieved.

In all these recent movements, the distribution of various kinds of small media and the ability to produce and disseminate messages, often through electronic means, was key. Thus, these movements reflect a certain level of economic development and spread of consumer durables, even within contexts of otherwise extreme economic dislocation and shortages, as in Poland and Romania. Often, this communications hardware has been smuggled in illegally, against existing state regulations. This process may also simply involve the shift in use of ordinary media from predominantly entertainment purposes to function as centres of political persuasion and mobilization. These situations reflected strong states with elaborate forces of coercion and persuasion, and powerful, centrally controlled mass media, with almost no possibilities for alternative political mobilization. The final dynamic of populist mobilization in these circumstances was comparatively brief yet immensely powerful, often fueled rather than quashed by regime violence against the participants.

Small media and revolutionary mobilization

In this section we will suggest some problematics that a model of small media needs to address to help elucidate and explain their crucial role in political mobilization in repressive contexts.

Small Media as Political Public Space
The wall is the voice of a people shouting.
Omar Cabezas
(quoted in Mattelart, 1986, p. 37)

The essence of repressive societies is that political activity is severely restricted, and as part of that restriction comes a control over public communication. [...] In Iran, a royalist dictatorship created the single political party, the mass media were state-controlled, and the secret police, SAVAK, monitored all public activity. One-party systems have sometimes been thought of as highly 'mobilized,' yet a more accurate analysis reveals a cadre of highly mobilized and motivated people, the party members (who often constituted not more than 15 per cent of the population), and the rest of the population. In Iran, the level of political mobilization was very low until the Shah changed strategy in the mid-1970s and developed a single party and attempted a popular mobilization, which backfired. In such big-state, big-media environments, the possibilities for the more familiar elements of democratic participatory political organization, such as political groups and parties, unions and interest groups with their regular and open meetings, and an independent political press or electronic media, were utterly circumscribed.

As Barrington Moore (1978, p. 482) argued, 'for any social and moral transformation to get under way there appears to be one prerequisite that underlies all . . . *social and cultural space* within the prevailing order.' In Iran, however, a public sphere of autonomous, citizen-directed, participatory debate functioning independently of the state appeared not to exist. This sphere is essentially a communicative environment in which people can freely voice opinion, gather to debate, and create politics. Yet political resistance developed, somewhere in the interstices and crevices of such systems. But where? Here the potential for small media to act as a resource of resistance, a tool of revolutionary mobilization, exists in the carving out and occupation of such oppositional 'space.'

As potential sites of struggle, as carriers of already-familiar forms of communication and symbol systems, as structures that are embedded in everyday life and very hard to control, small media and cultural resistance offer fertile ground. Media function as a 'virtual space' that temporarily connects people through the use of shared printed material, visual slogans, or electronic broadcasts. In situations where people are disallowed somatic solidarity – to physically assemble, demonstrate, march – small media can help to foster an imaginative social solidarity, often as the precursor for actual physical mobilization. Thus they are vitally important resources for mobilization (Tilly, 1978).

[. . .] In Eastern Europe as in the Soviet Union, the counterpoint to state surveillance and state-run media was the powerful networks of samizdat and *magnetizdat*. Occasional, small circulation and clumsily produced materials were, in this highly censored context, of direct political significance in developing a public sphere. 'Books, irregularly appearing periodicals, almost illegible newssheets, retyped lectures, 'public' gatherings of 80 people squashed inside a single apartment, 'public' lectures attended by 120 people: these are potent reconstructions of an oppositional public realm' (Downing, 1984, p. 308).

Sometimes the reclaiming of actual public space is more overt. As Rothschuh Villanueva and Cabezas show for Nicaragua (in Mattelart, 1986), various indigenous forms of cultural expression became part of the popular cultural opposition. Walls of city streets became the canvas of a political movement, the means of communication of the masses as well as ways for organized political groups to communicate with the masses, providing a voice for the people. [. . .] Similarly, in Iran city walls revealed the ongoing struggle with tatters of posters, whitewash over old slogans, and ever-new slogans, a public dance of speaking and silencing. Public space potentially heralded a public sphere.

In Iran no public sphere existed. The royalist dictatorship controlled directly or indirectly all forms of expression while SAVAK, the security organization, surveilled all public life. No autonomous political parties, independent labour unions, or interest groups were allowed. Such control sounds like a state socialist or fascist regime, but even those regimes are typically far more politically mobilized than was Iran. The royalist dictatorship was a particularly repressive form of authoritarian system, and there appeared to be no space within which any kind of oppositional, popular movement could launch itself.

Yet the dynamics of recent movements and the role of small media suggest we have operated with a far too narrow definition of the 'political public sphere,' using this term in a very formalist and delimited manner and often obscuring the relationships between communication, culture, and politics. The apparent 'lack' of formal organizations such as parties and unions, and the apparent 'lack' of public opinion because little measurement of opinion existed are taken as the absence of politics. But politics in Iran has always been more fluid, more informal, and more invisible than the organized politics of the established democracies, revealing another blind spot of a narrowly Western optic. There have always been informal political circles (*dowreh*) and gatherings of known individuals based on familiarity and trust developed over time (Bill, 1972; Zonis, 1971), but there was little sense in the public arena that such political groups were growing, articulate, or effective.

In Iran, as in Poland, the Philippines, and elsewhere, public 'space' could also be found within the religious networks. The religious leadership often possessed far more extensive and far more culturally appropriate resources for mobilization than did the secular intelligentsia. The resources of the religious leadership in Iran included a nationwide network of physical spaces – the mosques – that were points of public assembly, the only such network not penetrated by the state.

Small media: technologies for political survival

In Iran, new technologies of communication also helped to open up a potential public sphere of dissent. Small media such as audiotapes became electronic extensions of the religious institutions and its political discourse, and photocopied leaflets were the preferred weapon of the secular groupings, giving voice to what was to become an enormous popular movement.

The argument that political mobilization depends on developing political resources, usually some form of public communication, is not new. What is significant is that at certain moments, and more and more with the spread of certain technologies, control is impossible, even within the most repressive, security-oriented states. This is so for two main reasons: the nature of new communications technologies, and the development of international communications systems and international reception of messages. It is increasingly difficult even for the most repressive regime to control political communications. [. . .]

Certain technologies carry within themselves the means for reproduction, making control an even more difficult task. Key to the success of some recent movements or to the longevity of others has been the technical fact that contemporary small media – particularly audio and videocassettes, xerography, personal computers, and fax machines – are the source of multiple points of production and distribution. Audiocassette systems, video recording, and polaroid photography, for example, require no independent processing techniques but contain within the hardware the possibility of instant production and reproduction of messages. Anyone can reproduce such messages, and indeed the dynamics of movements depend precisely on each participant's making additional copies and spreading them around. Thus, Soviet samizdat would be typed and retyped in multiple copies to the extent of carbon-copy legibility by anyone who could do so. In Poland the underground network was created by KOR (Committee for Workers' Self-Defense) with signed communiqués that publicized the struggles of workers and intellectuals, and carried the exhortation that 'by disseminating this bulletin you are acting within your rights, and playing a part in their defense. Read it, copy it, and pass it on' (quoted in Downing, 1984, p. 326). Xerography not only makes light of such tedious work but also offers an advance over various printing processes because it produces instant and virtually untraceable copy (absent the most sophisticated forensic science) from potentially multiple sources so that the loss of one machine does not imply the demise of an entire movement. The good old days when smashing the printing press meant the end of radical agitation are long gone. The networking of personal computers and on-line information systems offer similar possibilities of uncontrollable multipoint production and dissemination of messages. Unfortunately the political right has jumped to use such channels, as the use of computer networks by racist groups in the U.S. and the circulation of anti-Semitic computer games in Austria attest.

In Poland, the opposition movement graduated from the classic samizdat method of reproduction based on typewriter and carbon copies to the recycling of antiquated duplicators, photocopiers, and offset lithography to create the technological tools of the underground network. Cassette tapes of the Gdansk negotiations circulated through factories. The political police spent a considerable part of its time trying to repress this growing underground small-media movement, and even a year after martial law had been imposed its squads seized over a million leaflets, silenced 11 radio transmitters, found 380 printing shops, and confiscated nearly 500 typewriters (C. Civic, quoted by Downing, 1984, p. 327). Independent media work still continued, however. Within the Polish context, these self-managed media created new spaces for public argument and debate, independent of the power structure, and proved to be important first steps in the giant movement that ensued. As Downing notes, 'no alternative communication channel should be written off simply because it is small' (p. 345). [. . .]

In Iran it was interesting to see how the function of certain technologies shifted from one of bureaucratic control to one of political participation. Before the popular movement developed, the use of photocopy machines even for university teaching was heavily controlled. The simplest reproduction of a diagram or set of figures for classroom use was a major procedure in universities, requiring multiple signatures and often taking so long that the need had passed by the time permission was granted. Come the movement, and a sea change occurred! The photocopy machine at Iran Communications and Development Institute (ICDI), for example, where Annabelle worked, became the hub of activity; its operator was a key political actor in the evolving moment, and the different fellow travellers of various political factions would vie for access to the machine. Other researchers who worked at ICDI during the revolution have noted the same phenomenon (Green, 1982).

Small media in the global context

Another factor that profoundly complicates the issue of 'control' of the national environment is the spread of international communications, which has collapsed global space, promoted an immense speedup of historical processes, and eroded the container effects of national boundaries (Giddens, 1990). [. . .]

One of the most notable elements of the 1989 events, as with the Iranian movement, was the comparatively open access that international television and press crews had to the sites of political activity. The main televisual news agencies, Visnews and UPITN, and the television networks such as CNN and others, sell their news footage to many other stations, so that the dramatic live coverage of the unfolding movements centering on Tianamen Square, around the Brandenburg Gate, in Wenceslas Square, in Budapest and in Bucharest, would be seen throughout the world. This truly was revolution while the whole world was watching. [. . .]

By the 1980s, with much of the globe caught in a snare of underwater cables and fiber optics, satellite footprints and shortwave transmissions, telecommunications, fax, and mail, national boundaries are porous. Many people living within strong states are able to pick up foreign media messages at the turn of a dial. [. . .]

International communications can play complex roles in domestic political upheavals. First, it has profoundly altered the nature of political exile. Exiled political activists no longer wait for events to change so that they can return home, but instead can propagandize to change conditions from outside their country, a deterritorialization of politics (Shain, 1989; Sreberny-Mohammadi and Mohammadi, 1987). There is considerable international clandestine radio broadcasting (Soley, 1987), as well as the documented beginnings of exile videography: Polish exiles in Paris smuggled videotapes *into* Poland, and Czech activists smuggled tapes of illegal demonstrations and state-orchestrated violence *out* of the country. Members of the Iranian exile community, both before and after the revolution, produced an enormous amount of political literature and broadcasting, altering the new environment in which they sojourned as much as they attempted to alter conditions back 'home'.

Not only do exiles send materials home, but as political actors they can try to mobilize international public opinion to take up their case in international public forums such as the United Nations. A large part of the function of groups such as Amnesty International and Human Rights Watch is to alert international public opinion about rights violations within specific countries and to mobilize resources to effect change. Iranian secular middle-class political groups tried hard to utilize various international channels to mobilize international public opinion in their favour, and achieved some modicum of success.

Occasionally, such international communication actually benefits or links political elements *within* a nation who otherwise cannot communicate or even know of each other's existence. Here, the international linkage becomes a necessary intermediate stage in what is really domestic political communication. [. . .]

Beyond the organization of exile communication for political purposes, international news carriers are crucial to the provision of information and imagery world-wide, made even faster with the use of satellites. Sometimes such channels provide information that is kept restricted within the society in question, and states attempt to block their penetration through jamming or preventing the purchase of shortwave receiving equipment. The detailed coverage of major stories by Western international broadcasters, such as the BBC and the Voice of America, Deutsche Welle, Radio Monte Carlo, and Israeli radio, has made them primary information sources in many political upheavals, often listened to on shortwave behind drawn curtains. In Iran, international media attention appeared to validate the 'historical importance' of the events at hand. [. . .] Among ordinary people, the reputation of international broadcasters was high, to the extent that a Tehrani electronics salesman in the north of the city told us in 1979 that people came to purchase 'a radio BBC'! Revolutions are national political phenomena fought on specific pieces of real estate, but global communications flows allow, and even foster, the 'deterritorialization' of politics in terms of the possible separation of political actors from their specific 'sphere of influence' (see the special edition of *Third World Quarterly* on 'The Politics of Exile,' 1987).

Small media as the catalyst for political participation

The connection between communications and participation is poorly developed. The basic mass-media model of vertical message transference sees the audience only as a group of message consumers (accredited with varying degrees of selectivity, and so forth). Yet the proliferation of new media, the lowering of costs, the differentiation of the audience into taste cultures, and new models of the active audience offer opportunities for communications participation so that the erstwhile 'passive' audience can actively produce not only meaning but messages. Much of this is not new in the West, where community radio, local publishing ventures, and a host of pressure groups using a variety of channels exist. What certain technological developments offer, however, is the potential for developing and renewing participation in societies with state surveillance and limited possibilities for independent political participation, even inside authoritarian states. In such contexts, to communicate is to act politically, with the implication that simple definitions of participation or its lack may well be outdated.

The relation between communications and politics is symbiotic, and it is impossible to separate the issue of participation in the political process from participation in the communications process. [. . .]

These outlooks appear to work within a narrow definition of the 'political' that does not accord well with the Iranian experience, or with the Chinese, East European, and many other contexts. Under such repressive states, the ideological and cultural spheres cannot have any autonomous development but are orchestrated by the state, as is the process of economic development. Thus the 'political' is not a neatly delimited sphere to which specifically political demands may be made. The very lack of development of institutions of participation encouraged the strengthening of preexisting collective identities and the politicization of cultural practices and rituals.

Political communication has been far too preoccupied with that most visible of participatory activities, voting. But not all systems have voting procedures, and all political systems have participation. Even passivity is meaningful. In Iran, the Shah promoted a strong self-deceptive tendency to believe that all was well (i.e. *qui tacit, consentit*) induced by the failure of those around him to provide the full facts about social discontent to his attention, partly because he made it clear that he did not like to hear bad news (Graham, 1978). The outward appearance of submission is no proof of the inward acceptance of oppression, however. That the Shah was psychologically affected by the depth of popular hostility that became evident in 1977–78 seems to be a factor in his irresolution about responses to the political opposition.

At the popular level, once the pervasive silence was shattered by the speaking out of intellectuals and professionals who were not immediately pounced on by SAVAK, and then by the first demonstrations, the collective fear of reprisals and feelings of powerlessness were rapidly dissolved. Fear was sometimes transformed into its opposite, a desire for martyrdom. The contagion effect spread and the surveillance structure of the once-absolute state fell asunder. Communication acts were in themselves political moments of involvement and daring, and the public process of communicating that such events had occurred required further involvement. We shall examine the welter of leaflets that were circulated, the calligraphic graffiti, the stencil images of urban guerillas, and the posters. Each of these represented an individual or group become political participant. In a context that had allowed no autonomous political participation for decades, the exhilaration of involvement and the visible and audible breaches in the wall of public silence were critical initial steps in the formation of the mass popular movement. Indeed, one interesting aspect of the mobilization is the shift between intellectual initiation of the process and the subsequent mass takeover and leadership, that is, the extent to which the previously mass 'spectators' became even more 'gladiatorial' than the secular activists (Milbrath and Goel, 1977) and were ready to encounter and battle with the military forces of the state.

There is a tension between this claim we are making about the 'spontaneity' of participation, and its orchestration by the clergy. The Iranian popular movement cannot be seen simply as a voluntaristic process of a developing public opinion, although there were sizeable segments of the Iranian population who had been waiting for the chance to act and for whom the fracturing of state power suddenly offered undreamed-of opportunities. For most ordinary Iranians, involvement was provoked by the combination of the coercive power of primordial identity, the continued social status of the *ulema*, religious leaders, and their political rhetoric. The Shah, on the few state occasions when it could be controlled, provoked participation through fear, fear of reprisal and of involvement with SAVAK. With the clergy and Khomeini, participation was orchestrated through the politicization of a deep-rooted cultural identity and the compulsion of religious duty – an ideology, leadership, and ethos accepted as compelling by a crowd of believers in the absence of alternatives, and a deeply coercive process.

The Iranian movement, much like the movements of Poland, the Philippines, and even Nicaragua, can be characterized by massive, low-level participation that cut across clear social-class divisions, evident in such actions as participation in mass demonstrations and the shouting of antiregime slogans from urban rooftops. The political culture of mistrust (Zonis, 1971) and private grumbling was rapidly transformed into an immensely powerful collective movement of strangers.

Small media and indigenous culture

One way in which cross-class solidarity was effected in Iran was in the repoliticizing of familiar traditional popular culture. In authoritarian systems, with severe repression of the political sphere, popular culture almost inevitably becomes the locus of political opposition, the venting of oppositional sentiments, the developing of critiques, and the playing out of alternative visions. As we have already argued, even if the existence of some delimited formal sphere called the 'political' is lacking, that does not mean that politics does not exist, but rather that it is not in actuality separated from the broader sociocultural milieu in which competition for symbolic meaning occurs. Separating culture from politics is difficult, and, in processes of political change, many indigenous cultural resources may be mobilized and developed to create a cultural resistance with political impact against would-be hegemonic regimes.

Obviously these processes can take many forms by utilizing traditional channels and by combining the use of modern small-media technologies with traditional cultural forms (music, poetry, and so on). [. . .]

The themes of indigenous cultural identity and its erosion by external cultural elements, and the deleterious effects of Western culture may function as popular rhetorical tropes that help to build a mass movement against some external power. [. . .]

The performing arts, puppeteers, and other traditional cultural forms have also been involved with political mobilization. These forms acted as vehicles of expression of protest, dissent, and reform in India, so that 'these native media of 'sung communication' and 'enacted information' proved more than a match to the Government-controlled mass media during the many political and social campaigns launched by Gandhiji' (Ranganath, 1980). Bassets (in Mattelart and Seigelaub, 1983) describes the variety of clandestine communications developed under and against Franco's dictatorship, from typewritten letters to clandestine press agencies, from the underground political press to anonymous poetry or simply the symbolic painting of letters on walls (P for protest, A for amnesty, L for liberty). [. . .]

The repoliticization of popular culture as a mode of generating solidarity appears quite common, although in different contexts different media and different genres will be invoked. Popular culture takes many forms, and cultural resistance and opposition are not necessarily revolutionary. Popular culture can be highly politicized, and entertainment can be a powerful vehicle for political gathering and mobilization. The showing of an underground video in a private house in Poland or Czechoslovakia, the semi-public viewing of 'critical' films, and the production and distribution of an opposition leaflet all create a symbolic space that serves to redefine the political. Participation in such events and the acceptance and reading of such material are forms of political action in and of themselves, carried out in defiance of and at possible risk from the state. [. . .] Repressive states understand well the potential power of popular culture to undermine them, hence the widespread repression and censorship regularly reported in *Index to Censorship* (Article 19) and by Amnesty International.

Much of the power of the small media used in Iran was due to their integration of the culturally familiar, their embeddedness in the extant public (as opposed to regime-dominated) cultural frameworks of the society. Yet because of regime censorship no well-developed national-popular culture had emerged inside Iran other than a traditional religious culture. There was a limited reading public, so novels had limited circulation; film was popular, yet the cinema-going public was essentially young and male. Only perhaps in music did traditional forms and instrumentation blend with Westernized forms to create a truly new and popular cultural form, continued in exile in California (Naficy, 1993).

Small media and religious networks: a crucial linkage

Various aspects of preexisting popular culture may be built upon, but the key element in many recent movements was religion. Religious networks functioned as a site for an oppositional public sphere, religious thematics were reconstituted as political rhetoric, and religious leaders emerged as political figures. In the Philippines, Nicaragua, and South Africa, religious perspectives, religious leaders, and religious space have constituted crucial elements of the popular mobilization. The Polish experience with the growth of Solidarity reflects perhaps the closest similarities to the Iranian situation. These include the importance of the church as an alternative public space and guarantor of culture and values in a centrally administered environment; the building of cross-class coalitions with a church base; the skepticism about the official media; and the initiation of an alternative media network (Liu, 1982). In Poland as in Iran, it was not just a random element of traditional, indigenous culture that served as the basis of popular mobilization but religious culture, which provided the nexus of authority, popular cultural practices, and experimental solidarity able to mobilize a previously nonparticipatory people. As Zubaida (1987, p. 145) notes, 'religion is . . . the sphere of social solidarities based on common belonging, with specific institutions and rituals of worship, which identifies the believers and separates them from the practitioners of other faiths . . . in situations of communal competition or conflict, individuals respond according to communal solidarity, in which the religious component is essential.' The comparative evidence suggests that this is not a phenomenon limited to Islam and Iran – see Tiryakian (1988) on Nicaragua and Poland, for example – but rather it is to be understood within the context of the weak political development of civil society in autocratic states. That this religious unity may be a temporary phenomenon, with deeper social rifts and ethnic antagonisms subsequently reexposed – as after the Islamic revolution – is not to dispute the temporary community-binding powers of religion.

Thus it is religion as habitus, the daily lived practices of a culture, that creates ties of affect, of meaning, of shared experience. And though the Iranian movement does not involve competition with other religious communities, it does involve competition with more modern ideologies of nationalism and class analysis, none of which had the rootedness or emotional resonance of Islam. Even the most skilled politician with a secular rhetoric began with enormous disadvantages in the emergent political culture of Iran in the 1970s. [. . .]

In contexts where the political public sphere and civil society are poorly developed and secular debate highly circumscribed, religious identity provides a kind of latent political solidarity, taken for granted or dormant until called upon, then readily mobilized against alternate visions of the collectivity. But religion in the politicized discourse of the Iranian revolution offered even more potent dynamics of mobilization. Religious tradition provided a discourse of religious duty, of compulsion to act, that was readily adopted by the religious leadership. Thus, far from a simple voluntaristic choice to act, strong elements of social coercion were built into the relationship between religious leadership and its mass following in Iran. Furthermore, as in many religious traditions, the very repetitive interaction between religious leaders and followings enabled the former to develop an oral language honed on frequent interactions with a predominantly nonliterate audience that was accessible and familiar, and played on deeply valued identities and outlooks. In comparison, the would-be secular leaders in Iran were poorly equipped at every level, having to invent their political organizations, rhetoric, and practice almost from scratch in 1977.

Forms of small media and social authority

We want to avoid a narrow, deterministic technological logic that privileges the power of media or that would argue simply that small media make revolutions, but at the same time it is necessary to recognize that the form of media itself affects the nature of the communication and the response. This is particularly significant for political processes where the use of different forms of media can create different kinds of relations between sender and receiver, leader and followers.

Oral/aural culture was rooted in the constant interchange of communally possessed knowledge, unlike the individualized speculation more characteristic of writing. Oral culture is thus essentially authoritarian, not interested in the new but desirous of fostering and preserving the old, the traditional, by saying it repeatedly. Ong (1967) argues that oral culture has a penchant for citing authorities to claim contact with the communal heritage and for negotiating the complexities of everyday life, and often is marked by the daily relevance of prayer and religious ceremony. Religious knowledge possesses authority not only as the received 'word of God' but because it is community-binding, a 'tribal possession,' and of necessity authoritarian. Cultural maintenance and group continuity are one and the same, and support an accepted pattern of authority.

The weak development of print forms and the severe control of them, coupled with state support for electronic broadcasting, created in Iran, as in other parts of the Third World, a powerful secondary orality (Ong, 1982). Like primary orality, secondary orality has a mystique of participation, fosters a communal sense, concentrates on the present moment, and uses formulas. As we have already argued, immediate oral communication plays on the ethos of the speaker, the rhetoric of the religious opposition implicitly invoking its already-considerable social authority. Secondary orality plays on and elaborates the already-established ethos of the now-mediated speaker. Thus cassettes of Khomeini's speeches carried not only the 'word' of the political message (which argued that it was the duty of all believers to mobilize to defend their faith) but also the 'voice' of the sender, an already-admired charismatic figure, and became an immensely powerful form of communication experienced in countless Iranian living rooms.

The discursive reconstruction of collective memory/identity

In this chapter we have focused on the evolution or reconstitution of an oppositional public sphere comprised of small-media technologies and the extant religious network, re-creating the social space and structures for political work. We have suggested how religious identity in particular could be built on as a cultural identity that readily promoted solidarity, and how religious figures possessed a spoken language easily understandable by illiterate populations. Perhaps one of the final elements in the puzzle of political change is the actual discourse of revolution, how alternative identities and political goals were constructed in language to frame revolutionary ideology. The articulation of such discourse includes a sense of collective memory, a rewriting of collective identity, and the politicization of 'tradition.' [. . .]

In Iran, there were a number of competing versions of 'collective memory' including that of the royalist state and also those of the opposition. The Shah actively promoted the notion of 2500 years of Persian monarchy, of which he was the pinnacle, symbolized most ostentatiously by his own corona-tion at Persepolis in 1971. This was, of course, a quite discontinuous tradition with no single bloodline, his own father having established a new dynasty after an interregnum in the 1920s. This version of history skirted over questions of political legitimacy or possibilities for republican structures, and ignored the changing physical boundaries of the entity called Persia/Iran or the difference between the ancient empires of Persia and the modern state of Iran.

Secular opposition groups borrowed both national and international 'spirits of the past' to reconstruct their tradition. Many articulated a line of political struggle from the constitutional movement at the turn of the century, the Jangali movement in the north that established the first revolutionary republic on Iranian soil, through Mossadeq and his nationalist-democratic movement, to the development and role of modern political groupings such as the *Tudeh*, *Fedai'i*, and *Mojahedin*. Some also called into play international proletarian struggles and global revolutions, orienting the Iranian movement toward a world revolutionary tradition. In Tehran in 1979 it was easier to buy cassettes of Cuban, Algerian, and Chinese revolutionary music than a dozen eggs. [. . .]

The religious elements could call upon a known and valued current communal identity, with a clearly demarcated past, heroes, and key events, to reconstitute a collective identity capable of challenging both the national identity of the royal despotism and the alternative identities proposed by the secular opposition. Although Shiism is not a monolithic unity, with both quietistic and radical interpretations and traditions, and deep internal lines of conflict, for popular consumption at a moment of political rupture a rather unified rhetoric was articulated, spearheaded by Khomeini. It was a time-binding, community-binding discourse of religious identity that, when coupled with the social spaces and social authority of its articulators, was a hard ideology to challenge or ignore. [. . .] In the politicization of memory and cultural tradition, both are changed. No longer can tradition be lived innocently and naively. In its active mobilization as a resource in an ideological struggle against an opposing cultural and political reality, tradition itself is irrevocably altered, undergoing the process of retraditionalization that has already been discussed.

Summary

This alternative model of popular communication for mobilization that focuses on small media or grass-roots media, on cultural resistance and popular empowerment, is enjoying quite a vogue. Communication as people's power (*Media Development*, 1988; Jankowski *et al.*, 1992; Dowmunt, 1993) appeals to our optimism and our desire to know that change is possible, that people can take control of their own lives, that both the models of development and dependency underestimated the traditional cultural resources that the Third World and other peoples possess.

But we must be wary of creating a new 'myth of small media' to replace the 'myth of the mighty media,' to use Shinar's (1980) label, as the new reigning model. What can be important and exciting about this new line of thinking is that it takes the existing cultural frames seriously, as well as acknowledging the complex set of reactions and interactions that develop between big media and small, between the state and the people, between the national and international contexts; it is often rather naive, however, about social structure and class differences, and operates with too-simple dichotomies such as state and people. Although for limited periods of time a situation may indeed take on that colouring, when the dust settles it is usually clear that certain interests win over others. Notions of solidarity, populism, even indigenous culture, may be useful rhetorical tropes in political struggle – and in academic analysis – but may come to cover over, rather than uncover, problematic questions.

The story of the Iranian revolution is presented in our book (Sreberny-Mohammadi and Mohammadi, 1994) as a case study of one particular revolutionary situation in which regime hegemony utilizing big media was successfully confronted by political and cultural resistance based on small media. The specifics of the Iranian case and its particular conjunctions of forces must be acknowledged, as well as the operation of many other forces beyond the communicative and cultural.

Bibliography

Bill, James (1972) *The Politics of Iran: Groups, Classes and Modernization*, Merrill, Columbus, Ohio.

Brecht, Bertolt (1979–80) Radio as a Means of Communication: A Talk on the Functions of Radio (1930), trans. Hood, Stuart. *Screen*, Vol. 20, No. 3/4, Winter.

Byram, Martin (1981) People's Participation Demands Change. *Media Development*, Vol. 27.

Darnton, Robert and Roche, Daniel (eds.) *Revolution in Print: The Press in France, 1775–1800*, University of California Press, Berkeley, 1989.

Downing, John (1984) *Radical Media*, South End Press, Boston.

Dowmunt, Tony (ed.) (1993) *Channels of Resistance*, BFI, London.

Enzensberger, Hans Magnus (1970) Constituents of a Theory of the Media. *New Left Review*, Vol. 64, November–December.

Fathi, Asghar (1979) The Role of the Islamic Pulpit. *Journal of Communication*, Vol. 29, No. 3, Summer, pp. 102–5.

Giddens, Anthony (1990) *The Consequences of Modernity*, Stanford University Press, Stanford.

Graham, Robert (1978) *Iran: The Illusion of Power*, Croom Helm, London.

Green, Jerrold (1982) *Revolution in Iran*, Praeger, New York.

Jankowski, Nick, Prehn, Ole and Stappers, James. (1992) *The People's Voice: Local Radio and Television in Europe*, John Libbey, London.

Liu, Michael Tien-Lung (1982) Explaining the Revolutionary Outcomes in Iran and Poland. *Theory and Society*, Vol. 17, No. 2, March.

Mattelart, Armand, (ed.) (1986) *Communicating in Popular Nicaragua*, International General, New York.

Mattelart, Armand and Siegelaub, Seth (eds.) (1983) *Communication and Class Struggle. Vol. 2: Liberation, Socialism*, International General, Paris.

Media Development (1981) Special issue on 'Group Communication in Different Cultures', Vol. 27, No. 2.

Media Development 'Communication: People's Power' (theme issue) (1988) Vol. 35, No. 1.

Milbrath, L. W. and Goel, M. L. (1977) *Political Participation*, Rand McNally, New York.

Moore, Barrington, Jr. (1978) *Injustice: The Social Bases of Obedience and Revolt*, Macmillan, London.
Naficy, Hamid. (1993) The Development of an Islamic Cinema in Iran. In *Third World Affairs 1987*, Third World Foundation, London, pp. 447–63.
Ong, Walter (1967) *The Presence of the Word*, University of Minnesota Press, Minneapolis.
Ong, Walter (1982) *Orality and Literacy*, Routledge, London.
Ranganath, H. K. (1980) Not a Thing of the Past: Functional and Cultural Status of Traditional Media in India. *International Commission for the Study of Communications Problems*, 92, UNESCO.
Schramm, Wilbur (1972) *Big Media. Little Media*. Information Center on Instructional Technology, Washington, D.C.
Shain, Yossi (1989) *The Frontier of Loyalty: Political Exile in the Age of Nation State*, Westview Press, Boulder, CO.
Shinar, Dov (1980) The 'Myth of the Mighty Media': Communication Networks in Processes of Social Change. Unpublished paper.
Soley, Lawrence (1987) *Clandestine Radio Broadcasting*, Praeger, New York.
Sreberny-Mohammadi, Annabelle and Mohammadi, Ali (1987) Post-revolutionary Iranian Exiles: A Study in Impotence. *Third World Quarterly*, special issue on 'The Politics of Exile', Vol. 9, No. 1, January, pp. 108–29.
Sreberny-Mohammadi, Annabelle and Mohammadi, Ali (1994) *Small Media, Big Revolution: Communication, Culture and the Iranian Revolution*, University of Minnesota, Minneapolis, MN.
Tilly, Charles (1978) *From Mobilization to Revolution*, Addison-Wesley, Reading, MA.
Tiryakian, Edward (1988) From Durkheim to Managua: Revolutions as Religious Revivals. In Alexander, Jeffrey C. (ed.) *Durkheimian Sociology: Cultural Studies*, Cambridge University Press, Cambridge.
Wade, Graham (1981) Community Video: A Radical Alternative. *Media Development*, Vol. 27.
Zonis, Marvin (1971) *The Political Elite of Iran*, Princeton University Press, Princeton.
Zubaida, Sami (1987) Components of Popular Culture in the Middle East. In Stauth, Georg and Zubaida, Sami (eds.) *Mass Culture, Popular Culture, and Social Life in the Middle East*, Westview Press, Boulder, CO.

20

Organizing democratic radio: issues in praxis

John L. Hochheimer

From Corner, J. and Schlesinger, P. (eds) (1993) *Media, Culture and Society*, Sage, London, Vol. 15, No. 3, pp. 473–86.

> Democracy . . . is the understanding by all the community of the information that will enable them to make a decision. The reception of that information depends on the full information being presented and on that information being comprehensively received . . . And if one doesn't understand this information, then no truly democratic decision can be taken . . .
>
> Information is often provided in a language not understood, comprising the codifying jargons of various specialized vocabularies of the various disciplines of the many technologies influencing how we conduct our lives . . . when democratic decisions on these matters have to be taken, that's where media workers interface with the democratic process. (Sapper, 1983, p. 116)

From their inception, the media of electronic communication have been structured to benefit the interest of political, military and economic power, as constituted within the control of the few. It was the development of radio[1] that set the foundation for the relationships between the media and their audiences which exist to this day. This was no less true in Great Britain or in Germany prior to 1914 (Hood, 1979–80) than it was in the U.S. after the outbreak of the First World War (Barnouw, 1966; Douglas, 1987).

Following the war, as governments and industry moved to consolidate their control of the medium, and the ways in which its utilization might be conceptualized, radical practitioners and scholars speculated on ways in which control of the medium might also be shared with listeners. Among these, Walter Benjamin spent several years attempting to develop radio forms in which listeners exercised greater control over form and content. During the Weimar years, he wrote about 80 radio plays (*Hörspiele*) for Radio Berlin and the station in Frankfurt am Main. He was particularly interested in transforming radio into a truly two-way form of communication from what he called a 'one-way street' (Schiller-Lerg, 1984). Bertolt Brecht, too, wrote essays and Hörspiele in the 1920s and 1930s in which he tried to develop 'art for radio and radio for art', bringing listeners into more direct responsibility for production and programme choice (Hood, 1979–80, p. 21).[2] Writing after emigrating to New York, Theodor Adorno (1939), constructed an extensive memorandum speculating about the uses and forms of 'Music in Radio', and the ways in which listeners could become more actively engaged with the medium.

The idea of more democratically-constituted radio is now being adapted to the realities of the last decade of the century where locally-based communications media are at a crossroads. While interest in building more community-oriented media appears to be increasing (Lewis and Booth, 1989), pressures to maintain gains, as well as to ensure continued access for and to all who want or need it, are evident too.

Where such newly conceptualized media come into being, and as more people become involved with producing information for themselves, inevitable problems need to be addressed. This chapter describes a number of these problems, pointing out where pitfalls may occur, and suggests areas to examine for solutions.

Ideally, management of a community radio station, for example, would comprise a democratic structure. Yet, inherent in the difficulties of attempting to establish and maintain democratically-based media is the problem of what constitutes a 'communicative democracy' and how to realize one in practice (Jakubowicz, 1990b). There are few, if any, guides for where to begin and what signs to look for along the way. The literature on how to organize a station, and how to maintain the station once it has begun to function, is scant.[3]

While Barlow (1988, p. 81) argues that the democratic structure of community radio in the U.S. has, despite its shortcomings, encouraged 'active citizen participation and a healthy diversity of opinion', White (1984, p. 1) maintains that 'the democratization of communication is often a voyage into uncharted and hostile waters'.

In trying to address this problem, Skogerbo (1988) stresses that democratization of communication should be understood from three separate, yet often intertwined, perspectives: (1) as the extension of the democratic society, (2) as means to increase pluralism through the media, and (3) as democratically organized institutions in which responsibility and decision-making is diffused rather than centralized. Drawing on the works of Berrigan (1977) and Jouet (1977), Jankowski (1988) argues that access is the *sine qua non* of democratic media participation. The issues centre on power and control: which communities should be given access to the air? Who speaks for these communities? And whose interests are served by these decisions (Hochheimer, 1988a)?

But these issues remain to be resolved for people interested in establishing a new means of democratic community communications systems. There are few, if any, guidelines from the experiences of others upon which to determine the relative likelihood of success. A part of the problem is that most studies have been undertaken by community activists and/or critical scholars who have little experience in the organization of alternative station structures.

The media can only be as democratic, free and pluralistic as the society within which they exist. The media of mass communication can hardly be considered autonomous actors, either in Western capitalist societies (Jakubowicz, 1990b), or in the newly emerging countries of Eastern Europe (Vreg, 1990). Further, borrowing from Stuart Hall (1989), there is no way the planning, implementation and operation of communication systems can proceed without understanding their linkage to positions and structures of power.

No model exists to suit all situations. All the experiences from the past can do is to point the ways towards better futures. The issues faced by planners can be seen as constituting four core areas to be addressed. These areas correspond to inevitable problems which must be dealt with directly in the evolution of the communicative project.

Imagine that a group wants to start an alternative, democratically constituted radio station. Imagine further that the people involved have boundless energy and interest in providing members of their community with access to the microphones of the station. The problems immediately begin:

1. Who serves whom? Is the function of the station to serve its constituent community segments? Or do the communities act as resources for the station to present to society as a whole?

The station can be conceptualized either as a conduit for views emanating from the community, or it can be seen as a source of information for the community. Community segments either come to the station in order to communicate among themselves or between other segments in society.

The management of the station must constantly assess for whom the station is functioning. Hein (1988), for example, demonstrates that, in the interest of meaningful participation by members of the community, a station should be set up to serve as a community resource for the people in the community. The people who help to set up the station can do so as a training mechanism for people in the local community who, it is expected, will take over the operation of the station as they see fit.

This, however, may work best in a homogeneous community, such as the one Hein describes in Ecuador.[4] Schulman (1985), in describing the establishment of a community station for the people of East Harlem, New York, finds the populations to be served are much more heterogeneous, so that identifying key population segments becomes more difficult.

Ultimately, the station is conceptualized and operates either as a centre *of* the community, or as a centre *for* the community. Small stations in homogeneous areas see themselves as centres of the community, in that they act as channels for many community members to share information between themselves. The station is as much a part of the local political/cultural network as are dances, community meetings, local government or markets. Staffing is by members of various community groups, making the stations *of* the community. Examples exist in places like Bolivia (O'Connor, 1990), Sitka. Alaska (McClear, 1982); Ecuador (Hein, 1988), the Pine Ridge, South Dakota. Indian reservation (Widlok, 1989) and Nicaragua (White, 1988).

Stations *for* the community are those who have a regularly paid staff. Volunteers come from the community, but the primary interaction between station and community is between sender and audience. These seem to work better in more heterogeneous locales and in places with larger populations. Examples of such stations exist in places like Vancouver, BC (Widlok, 1981; von dem Bussche, 1984; Lewis and Booth, 1989), Berkeley, CA (Barlow, 1988) and in New York City (Schulman, 1988).

2. Who speaks for which community interest? Who decides what are legitimate voices to be heard? Which points of view are the most compelling? What happens when ideas and technical skills are at odds? How are community views solicited, encouraged? In other words, to what degree does/can the station bring its audiences into the process of programme production for themselves?

Not everyone wants to speak, nor does everyone wish to be heard. 'A universal desire to communicate to the masses' is a fallacy without much supporting evidence (Jakubowicz, 1990b). While Brecht's oft-cited dictum (1940/1983) foreseeing a dialogic radio system[5] was supplemented by Walter Benjamin's attempts at actualizing true two-way communication through radio (Schiller-Lerg, 1984, pp. 414–18), we cannot assume that all people are equally engaged with the medium, nor do they have the time, motivation or desire to be so.

What about those who do wish to be heard? Station planners often try to make access feasible, yet problems remain. Should the station be the conduit for all who come before the microphones? Or does the station exercise some form of gatekeeping? Frequently, those who come to the station to be heard not only are drawn from the more disaffected parts of society (who certainly need channels of expression in a system dominated by the powerful), but they are also those who have the easiest means of access to the station, because of access to transport, time off from work or proximity.

Jakubowicz (1990b) argues that truly 'free, equal, unhindered' mass communications are unachievable at the societal level primarily because such a system would not allow for meaningful feedback between participants in communication. He suggests (following White, 1984) that 'segments' of society should be in a position to introduce arguments, information, elements of culture, etc., so that they can be heard/seen/read by all other segments of society. No segment of society should be restrained from addressing other segments of society, and no segment should be excluded from hearing all others. Over time, ideally, all points of view can be heard.

This assumes, of course, the existence of democratic arrangements within society, as both Vreg (1990) and Jakubowicz (1990b) note. Yet, even within ostensibly democratic societies, there remain a variety of problems. How many 'segments' of society can be identified? By whom? Who speaks for which segment? Conventional ways of thinking about societal segmentation (using race, gender, age, religion, union affiliation, socio-economic status, class and now sexual orientation) may prove inadequate. If we are to go beyond these categories, who will be capable and authorized to decide the basis for new classifications? Obviously, each society will present unique problems.

3. Conversely, what happens when power, or people, become entrenched? When the interests, needs, skills, political agendas of newcomers are at odds with those of the founders? How do these differences get worked out?

Even assuming equitable differentiation of segments is possible, the next problem is, who speaks for each segment? Must elections be held? Are there power blocs within communities who have determined who traditional spokespersons are? Should these be the most articulate people and/or the ones with the most technical expertise? Or should they be drawn from the ranks of those with the most disposable time? Should spokespersons be rotated to allow a wide variety of people the opportunity to participate?

Research over the past decade had found that those most active in programme production are most likely to be most active in the community, the middle class and centrally located in local networks (Prehn, 1981; Browne, 1988; Jankowski and Mol, 1988; Skogerbo, 1988; Jakubowicz, 1990a).

Once people begin to participate, frequently they see themselves as the most knowledgeable spokespeople from the community segment they serve. If other people within that segment also want to participate, decisions need to be made concerning how access can be equitably distributed.

Quite often, the original participants do not receive the newcomers with equanimity; instead, there may be resentment at the attempts of the newcomers to change 'our' station. Thus, factional in-fighting can be an issue even within a given segment. Molnar (1990), for example, shows that a new generation of broadcasters may come to a community station with a different set of perspectives and political priorities from those who originally set it up. Consequently, the problem of mediation among segments and between generations at a station must be a matter of continuing concern.

4. How can decisions be made within a democratically-constituted hierarchy? Who decides? Who authorizes, empowers and checks on those authorized to decide? What happens when power is diffused?

This may be the most critical set of issues. Those who come to participate in community radio generally do so, in part, as a rejection of the structure, philosophy and programming of more mainstream, traditional media (Barlow, 1988). A part of what is rejected is what is seen as a hierarchical, non-democratic structure of mainstream station operations. Indeed, as Barbrook (1985) maintains, it challenges the division between broadcasters and receivers within society.

Jakubowicz (1990b) argues for a representative communicative democracy in which all segments of society can own or control their own media, or have adequate access to the media, so that they can communicate with each other and with all segments of society. Decision-making in the management of communication

> should take place in conditions of equality, autonomy and adequate represen-
> tation. If these conditions are met in the way the media are organized and run,
> and in social communication itself, then representative communicative
> democracy has a chance of satisfying most of the expectations of the democratic-
> minded society.

While Jouet's (1977) notion of self-management may mean that the public ultimately has *no* meaningful input to station decision-making (see Jakubowicz, 1990b), how can the structure of alternative media be created? Can stations, as organizational structures, combine parts of direct and representative democracy, as described by Downing (1984)? Or is Jakubowicz's (1990b) diffused 'representative participatory communicative democracy' the way to go?

Community radio stations differ from traditional, mainstream stations not only in their world-view, broadcast policies and content. They also differ in their structure. A commercial broadcaster has the leverage to hire and fire, to determine income and to coerce workers to act in ways deemed important by the management.

Alternative media which fashion themselves as 'democratic media organizations' bear little resemblance to their more formally-structured siblings. Yet they need some kind of structure to maintain themselves.[6] They can be seen to be based on Max Weber's 'value-rational' orientation to social action, in that commitment to the goals of the organization is made for its own sake, independently of the prospects of success for the organization (Weber, 1968, p. 24). Even within such 'collectivist-democratic' organizations, which attempt to reject the formal bureaucracies inherent to commercial media, authority and structure are, nonetheless, important.

These alternative organizations can be differentiated from bureaucratic organizations along at least eight dimensions: authority, rules, social control, social relations, recruitment and advancement, incentive structure, social stratification and differentiation. Each is discussed in terms of a representative participatory communicative democratic structure as described by Jakubowicz (1990b). Following the description of the ideal will be an evaluation of the strengths and shortcomings of this approach.

Authority is the central issue in the structure of the station. All members of the station have the rights to have full and equal input to decision-making. Decisions are reached through a process of consensus, since only the authority of the whole is seen to have moral weight. Only group decisions are seen to be legitimate and binding on the whole.

Areas of authority may be delegated, but only by consensus. Areas of authority are carefully circumscribed, and they are subject to recall by the whole group.

In a community radio station, authority is given by the various segments in the community to their representatives in the station.[7] These, in turn, decide consensually what decisions need be made.

Rules and formality are kept to a minimum and such stations function more often in an *ad hoc* manner. This minimizes predictability in station operations but allows for the introduction of more participation from members of the community with differing value bases.

Social control consists of the means of power exercised by those in authority. Since authority is diffuse and rules are few, so too are the means of social control less formalistic than in bureaucratic organizations. In such collectivist organizations, control is maintained primarily by personalized and moralistic appeals for the good of everyone. Compliance is chiefly normative, asking that a person act a certain way 'in the interests of equality', or 'for the good of the community'. Especially important is that such appeals carry more force the more homogeneous is the group which operates the station. The more heterogeneous the operation, the more difficult are appeals to common norms, since these are fewer.

Social relations between members of the station are key elements as well. Community stations strive toward the construction of an ideal community within the station itself where interpersonal relationships are of vital importance. Over time the station may tend to resemble the world outside, especially where a heterogeneous set of segments is each interested in the station's goals and operations.

Friendship and socio-political values appear to be the main criteria for *recruitment and advancement* in the community station. Those who can work well with others are those who can advance the best. With work being low paid (and often voluntary), with hours at the station taking away time from more lucrative employment, few seek to make a career of their work here. The attributes that make for the best recruits are: articulation skills, ability to organize and mobilize others, political values, self-direction, ability to work under pressure, friendship, commitment to the organization's goals and relevant experience (Rothschild-Whitt, 1979, p. 515).

The *incentive structure* in a community station must be primarily value fulfilment, since money and other forms of remuneration are in short supply. The work is often a labour of love and low salaries (or continued work for no pay when the organization is low on funds) come with the territory. Values of community structure, doing good in the world and working to some greater long-term goal are often given as incentives by workers in collectivist organizations. Often, members live and work and eat together to help keep costs down.[8]

Control over their work is another reason why people are attracted to such stations. They can produce the programmes they think the community wants and needs to hear. They can explore music, information, styles, discussions available nowhere else. They have the time to experiment with new ideas, unconventional political views, alternative lifestyles, etc. (Barlow, 1988).

Community stations seek to maintain an egalitarian structure, thus minimizing *social stratification* within the organization. Pay is roughly equivalent, or is within a narrow range. Task sharing, dress, job rotation, workplace structure and decision-making are kept as egalitarian as possible.

Differentiation is purposefully kept to a minimum. The division of labour that differentiates management from labour, or administration from performance, is kept as small as practicable. This is accomplished by three means: role rotation, teamwork or task-sharing, and the diffusion of specialized knowledge through internal education. The creation of a volunteers' manual for the community radio station in East Harlem, for example, was a major task for the integration of new members as well as the reduction of differentiation among older ones. People in leading positions in certain tasks may be required to be followers in others, thus diffusing the hierarchy throughout the organization (see Schulman, 1985).

The eight criteria are, of course, ideals which do not and cannot exist in their totality. There are also costs and constraints to constituting a community radio station in this manner. A few of these are: time, homogeneity, emotional intensity, non-democratic individuals, environmental constraints, individual differences and limited resources.

As Rothschild-Whitt reminds us, democracy takes *time*. Morale may be higher, more innovative ideas can come from more points of view, more segments may be represented but, due to the diffuse structure, decision-making can often be a ponderously slow beast, driving the most committed participants to distraction.

Typically, there are programming, business, political, community outreach and 'people' meetings, resulting in scarce time remaining for the central task of the organization, which is putting programming on the air. The group needs to decide what is vital and what is not, what can be dispensed with occasionally. A premium should be placed on delegating to sub-groups that can be accountable to the whole.

A balance must be struck between everyone having input into all decisions and streamlining in the interests of time and saving energy. But who decides, and how these decisions are made, is crucial.

Homogeneity helps to streamline decision-making, but only at the cost of decreasing the diversity of the groups. Unified action among diverse people with divergent interests and goals can only be achieved through consensus and that takes time and compromise. To groups who feel they have compromised everywhere else, and that the community radio station is the sole outlet for them to 'tell it like it is', homogeneity of opinion and action may be elusive goals.

Many collectivist organizations are staffed by people from similar backgrounds (such as those with sufficient free time, or who have independent means of support); the desire to truly represent all segments of the community may, therefore, also remain elusive. In order to streamline the operation, the station may seek out others of like opinion; this, too, stifles the heterogeneity the station needs to remain a legitimate channel for open communications. While homogeneity may allow for easier consensus-building, it can also stifle the social *raison d'etre* of the station, losing its legitimacy in the ears of its audience and supporters.

Emotional intensity can tear the fabric of the station apart. People who come to the community radio station are generally those who have been displaced or neglected or ignored by the more mainstream media. Now that they have been given access and voice to discuss the issues most important to them, they may be inclined to be territorial about their time on the air. Further, in the heterogeneous environment, they tend to see those with other motivations as representing the oppressive majority. Confrontation may be endemic, stress may accompany every decision because turf is so jealously guarded.

People often use several coping mechanisms to deal with the level of emotional rancour which is possible. Criticism may be taken as personal invective, differences of opinion may be suppressed for fear of opening old wounds, open participation is avoided to minimize conflict. Further, conflict is difficult to accept when consensus is being attempted, because unanimity is required. Also, face-to-face meetings tend to bring latent tensions out into the open. Furthermore, the pressures and tensions of being a minority-group member (however designated) tend to remove the ability of many to sustain democratic spirit and behaviour for very long. They have long recognized the contradiction between the proclamation that living in a democracy is the means by which people can take greater control over their own lives, while in reality they are denied the means by which they can see this control demonstrated or by which they can put such control into practice (Hochheimer, 1992). Thus, as Rothschild-Whit points out:

In the face of these behavior-shaping institutions, it is very difficult to sustain collectivist personalities. It is asking, in effect, that people shift gears, that they learn to act one way inside their collective, and another way outside. In this sense, the difficulty of creating and sustaining collectivist attributes and behavior patterns results from a cultural disjuncture. It derives from the fact that alternative work organizations are as yet isolated examples of collectivism in an otherwise capitalist-bureaucratic context (1979, p. 522).

While there are some recent examples of how this may be overcome (cf. Schulman, 1985; Hochheimer, 1988a), the problems remain for those who plan to create viable alternative radio stations.

Conclusion

As practice and research in community radio moves into its next phase of development, practitioners, activists and scholars need to take greater heed of the problems posed by attempting to create 'democratic media'. This article has been an attempt not so much to be prescriptive, but rather to advise on what problems need to be faced directly when planning and constructing community radio.

The tenure of KPFA in Berkeley (now in its fifth decade, see Barlow, 1988; Lewis and Booth, 1989), suggests that people may respond actively and creatively in the right conditions. There is an abundance of community segments under-served by existing media; urban and rural poor, children, people with AIDS, displaced workers, elderly people, etc., who need to become involved in creating information for themselves.[9]

While the media of communication can be no more democratic and egalitarian than those who create them, they can help point the way for more democratic community praxis in the future. The challenges and practical experiences spelled out by Brecht, Benjamin and Adorno, await renewed exploration.

Notes

1. As opposed to its forbear, wireless telegraphy (see Douglas, 1987).
2. Hood argues that Brecht saw these as two separate issues, which are subsumed in the broader issues of how anyone could exploit radio or art at all. '(A)rt and radio should be placed at the disposal of pedagogic aims . . . the possibility of such direct pedagogic exploitation of art seems unattainable today because the state is not interested in educating youth for collectivism' (cited in Hood, 1979–80, p. 21).
3. Both Schulman (1985) and Hein (1988) describe theoretical and functional problems of establishing and maintaining stations.
4. Alan O'Connor notes (1991, personal correspondence) that even within a relatively 'homogeneous' community there may be severe cleavages along political, religious and generational lines. Among the Otovalo Indians investigated by Hein (1988), there are sharp differences between political factions within the community. Among the Bolivian miners O'Connor (1990) studied, there are divisions within the union leadership.
5. 'Radio should be converted from a distribution system to a communication system. Radio could be the most wonderful public communication system imaginable,

a gigantic system of channels – could be, that is, if it were capable not only of transmitting but of receiving, of making the listener not only hear but also speak, not of isolating him but of connecting him. This means that radio would have to give up being a purveyor and organize the listener as purveyor . . . [Radio] alone can organize the great discussion between industry and consumers about the standardization of objects of daily use, the debates over the rise in the price of bread, the disputes in local government. If you should think this is utopian then I would ask you to consider why it is utopian' (Brecht, 1940/1983, p. 169).

6. This section of the paper borrows heavily from the work done by Joyce Rothschild-Whitt (1979), and from those whose work follows in this tradition.
7. In the U.S., this authority must be overseen by a governing body to which a licence is granted by the Federal Communications Commission. Other countries have different formal, sanctioned means of authority. This excludes radio pirates, which are answerable primarily to the activists who operate them.
8. And play and, often, sleep together to keep morale up.
9. See Hochheimer (1988b) for examples of working with one such group – displaced farm families.

References

Adorno, Theodor W. (1939) *Memorandum: Music in Radio*, Princeton Radio Research Project, Princeton, NJ.

Barbrook, Richard (1985) Community Radio in Britain, *Radical Science Journal*, Vol. 16, pp. 71–2.

Barlow, William (1988) Community Radio in the US: The Struggle for a Democratic Medium. *Media, Culture and Society*, Vol. 10, No. 1, pp. 81–105.

Barnouw, Erik (1966) *A Tower in Babel: A History of Broadcasting in the United States to 1933*, Oxford University Press, New York.

Berrigan, Frances (ed.) (1977) *Access: Some Western Models of Community Media*, UNESCO, Paris.

Brecht, Bertolt (1940/1983) Radio as a Means of Communication: A Talk on the Function of Radio. In Mattleart, Armand and Siegelaub, Seth (eds.) *Communication and Class Struggle*, Vol. 2: *Liberation, Socialism*, International General, New York, pp. 169–71.

Browne, Duncan R. (1988) What's Local About Local Radio. *RTV Theory and Practice*, Special Issue 3, pp. 122–44.

Douglas, Susan J. (1987) *Inventing American Broadcasting 1899–1922*, Johns Hopkins University Press, Baltimore, MD.

Downing, John D. H. (1984) *Radical Media: The Political Experience of Alternative Communication*, South End Press, Boston.

Hall, Stuart (1989) Ideology and Communication Theory. In Dervin, Brenda, Grossberg, Lawrence O'Keefe, B. J. and Wartella, Ellen (eds.) *Rethinking Communication. Vol. 1*, Sage Publications, Newbury Park, CA.

Hein, Kurt John (1988) *Radio Baha'i Ecuador: A Baha'i Development Project*, George Ronald, Oxford.

Hochheimer, John L. (1988a) Community Radio in the United States: Whom Does it Serve? *RTV Theory and Practice*, Special Issue 3, pp. 160–84.

Hochheimer, John L. (1988b) Community Support for Farm Crisis Intervention: Developing Support Through Communication, *Proceedings of the 16th Biennial Congress of the International Association for Mass Communication Research*, Vol. 2, pp. 1767–92.

Hochheimer, John L. (1990) Journalism Pedagogy for the Non-poor: Towards Liberatory Praxis for Middle-class Students. In Splichal, Slavko, Hochheimer, John and

Jakubowicz, Karol (eds.) *Democratization and the Media: An East–West Dialogue*, Faculty of Sociology, Political Science and Journalism, University of Ljubljana, Trieste, pp. 173–85.

Hood, Stuart (1979–80) Brecht on Radio. *Screen*, Vol. 20, No. 314, pp. 16–23.

Jakubowicz, Karol (1990a) Solidarity and Media Reform. *European Journal of Communication*, Vol. 5, pp. 333–53.

Jakubowicz, Karol (1990b) Stuck in a Groove: Why the 60s Approach to Communication Democratization Will No Longer Do. Paper presented to the Biennial Congress of the International Association for Mass Communication Research, Bled, Yugoslavia (August).

Jankowski, Nicholas W. (1988) *Community Television in Amsterdam*, unpublished doctoral dissertation, University of Amsterdam.

Jankowski, Nicholas W. and Mol, Anne-Lieke (1988) Democratization of Communication and Local Radio in the Netherlands. *RTV Theory and Practice*, Special Issue 3, pp. 97–121.

Jouet, Josiane (1977) *Community Media and Development: Problems of Adaptation*, UNESCO, Paris.

Lewis, Peter M. and Booth, Jerry (1989) *The Invisible Medium: Public, Commercial, and Community Radio*, Macmillan, London.

McClear, Richard (1982) General Manager, KCAW-FM (Raven Radio), Interview, July.

Molnar, Helen (1990) Public Radio Broadcasting: The Democratisation of the Australian Media. Paper presented to the Working Group on Community Radio and Television, Biennial Congress of the International Association for Mass Communication Research, Bled, Yugoslavia (August).

O'Connor, Alan (1990) The Miners' Radio Stations in Bolivia: A Culture of Resistance. *Journal of Communication*, Vol. 40, No. 1, pp. 102–10.

O'Connor, Alan (1991) Personal correspondence.

Prehn, Ole (1981) *Lokal-TV* (Local Television), Aalborg Universitetsforlag, Aalborg.

Rothschild-Whitt, Joyce (1979) The Collectivist Organization: An Alternative to Rational-Bureaucratic Models. *American Sociological Review*, Vol. 44, (August), pp. 509–27.

Sapper, Alan (1983) Media Workers in the First Line of Democracy. In Mosco, Vincent and Wasko, Janet (eds.) *The Critical Communications Review, Vol 1: Labor, the Working Class, and the Media*. Ablex Pub, Corp, Norwood, NJ, pp. 115–27.

Schiller-Lerg, Sabine (1984) *Walter Benjamin und der Rundfunk* (Walter Benjamin and Radio), K. G. Saur, Munich.

Schulman, Mark (1985) *Neighborhood Radio as Community Communication*, unpublished doctoral dissertation, The Union Graduate School.

Schulman, Mark (1988) Radio and Cultural Identity: Community and Communication in Harlem, USA. *RTV Theory and Practice*, Special Issue 3, pp. 185–214.

Skogerbo, Eli (1988) Demokratisperspektiv pa lokalfjernsyn (A Democratic Perspective on Local Television), Report No. 2, Department of Media and Communication, University of Oslo.

von dem Bussche, Yvonne (1984) Freies Radio in der Praxis [The Practice of Free Radio]: Co-op Radio Vancouver. *Medium*, Vol. 14, No. 3, pp. 7–11.

Vreg, France (1990) Dilemmas of Communication Pluralism in Social Systems. In Splichal, Slavko, Hochheimer, John and Jakubowicz, Karol (eds.) *Democratization and the Media: An East–West Dialogue*, Faculty of Sociology, Political Science and Journalism, University of Ljubljana, Trieste, pp. 10–19.

Weber, Max (1968) *Economy and Society*, Roth, Guenther and Wittich, Claus (eds.) Bedminster Press, New York.

White, Robert A. (1984) The Need for New Strategies of Research on the Democratisation of Communication. Paper presented to the Annual Conference of the International Communication Association, San Francisco, May.

White, Robert A. (1988) Participatory Radio in Sandinista Nicaragua. Paper presented to the Biennial Congress of the International Association for Mass Communication Research, Barcelona.

Widlok, Peter (1981) Sprachrohr für Minderheiten [Communicator for Minorities]: Vancouver Co-operative Radio. *Medium*, Vol. 11, No. 10, pp. 28–32.

Widlok, Peter (1989) Indianerradio in den USA [Indian Radio in the USA]: KILI-FM in South Dakota. *Rundfunk und Fernsehen*, Vol. 37, No. 4, pp. 511–23.

21

News, consciousness, and social participation: the role of women's feature service in world news

Carolyn M. Byerly

From Valdivia, A. (ed.) (1995) *Feminism, Multiculturalism, and the Media*, Sage, London, pp. 108–22.

News and women

News, in all of its various forms, has historically underrepresented and misrepresented women. Through the late 1970s, world news routinely ignored women's problems and accomplishments as subjects for serious coverage in most countries. Even as women's rights movements in the 1960s and 1970s helped to expand women's roles in the public spheres of paid workforces and politics, news coverage ignored or trivialized their gains. One content analysis of international wire services in the late 1970s revealed that only 1.5% of major wire service news was about women (Gallagher, 1981).

Development news, which has been defined as news concerned with economic, political, and social change and with historical and other factors bringing those about (Giffard *et al.*, 1991), has also ignored women through the years (Anand, 1992; Giffard *et al.*, 1991). Development news (or journalism) has been practised primarily in developing nations of the Third World, where it has been believed that traditional Western news, with its focus on singular events and oddities, is less useful than news that can forge a coherent picture of a particular nation and its relations to other nations. The informational needs of the news audience, emphasis on self-reliant development, and advances in socioeconomic structures (such as land reform and new educational programs) are major themes of development news (Giffard, 1984).

Some recent research has shown that through the years, there has been little improvement in either the quantity or quality of news and other information about women in the world's media. Mohanty's (1991) cross-cultural survey found that prevailing news values still define most women and their problems as un-newsworthy and, when women are included, their portrayals are predictably sexual or confined to the private sphere of home. Rakow and Kranich (1991) suggest that news is essentially 'a masculine narrative in which women function not as speaking subjects but as signs' (p. 9). The authors add that 'Any improvement in women's treatment in news will require not simply more coverage of women or more women journalists . . . but a fundamental change in news as a narrative form' (Rakow and Kranich, 1991, p. 9). Similarly, Bird and Dardenne (1988) conclude that the journalist-storyteller is 'indeed using culturally embedded story values,' but they believe it is also within the journalist's power to 'actively reshape' patterns in news and thereby to 'repair the paradigm' (p. 81). Their stress on individual influence differs from Rakow and Kranich's (1991) narrative structural approach.

Critical scholars like Tuchman (1978), Hall (1980), Gitlin (1980), and Herman and Chomsky (1988) have been more concerned with structural influences on news content, such as those posed by the filters of news organization's corporate goals and values, the journalistic routines of newsmaking, and the knowledge and philosophies that individual journalists have acquired through hegemonic educational systems steeped in elite values. Through structural influences, news stories are *framed*, or given perspective and interpretation.

Like other marginalized groups, women have not been able simply to ignore the import of news. There is evidence that for marginalized groups to gain greater power, they must have greater visibility and public voice – they must be able to frame their own issues and then communicate them, not just through interpersonal channels or their own specialized media, but also through mainstream news and other media channels that reach larger audiences. Kielbowicz and Scherer (1986) have shown that the press has long been essential to Western social movements, both in the early stages to mobilize public interest and membership, and in the later stages to maintain momentum. Socialist feminists have been particularly vocal in their insistence that the media can be one site of struggle between dominant and oppressed classes (Steeves and Arbogast, 1993). O'Connor (1990) has pointed out that the active use of the mass communications media by marginalized groups can help in the formation of their own identities and cultural agendas. An active effort to co-opt media channels represents, in fact, an intervention in the status quo. For example, Anand (1983, p. 7), a development specialist, maintains that information is useless to women unless it helps

to raise their consciousness about the oppressive structures that keep them in positions of powerlessness. . . . [What a woman] craves is knowledge of why she must bear so many children, work endless hours without respite, be beaten and raped, have an alcoholic husband, and go hungry.

Female journalists have been in a potentially central position to contribute to gender advancements by including women's perspectives and achievements in news stories. For example, Kate Abbam, editor of the women's magazine *Obaa Sima* (*Ideal Woman*) in Ghana, found that 'Women in media professions are at the forefront of bringing about women's emancipation in Ghana' (in *Media Report to Women*, August 1 1975).

This interventionist philosophy permeated the *World Plan of Action*, passed by 1000 female and male delegates attending the UN Decade for Women conference in México City in June 1975. The plan named the mass media as the central mechanism through which women's roles would be changed, their social participation accelerated, and discrimination against them ended: 'the mass communication media ... could exercise a significant influence in helping to remove prejudices and stereotypes, accelerating the acceptance of women's new roles in society and promoting their integration into the development process as equal partners' (*Decade for Women: World Plans of Action*, 1975, paragraphs 161–162).

But the plan went on to note the inadequacy of the media to carry out the task: 'At the present time, the media tend to reinforce traditional attitudes, often portraying an image of women that is degrading and humiliating and fails to reflect the changing role of the sexes' (*Decade for Women: World Plan of Action*, 1975, paragraph 162). As such the Women's Feature Service was designed to address this gap between potential and reality.

Intervention through women's feature services

The present-day Women's Feature Service (WFS), headquartered in New Delhi, has its roots in the 'women's feature service project,' which was envisioned by its creators to be a partial solution to these problems. The original umbrella project – which operated between 1978 and 1983 under the direction of the UN Educational, Scientific, and Cultural Organization (UNESCO), with funds from the UN Fund for Population Agency (UNFPA) – was proposed by journalists and feminist leaders attending a special media workshop after the México City conferences. The project contained elements of several feminist philosophies. On the one hand, the project aimed to interrupt or intervene in hegemonic news systems, where women and their concerns had been marginalized, underrepresented, and misrepresented, by making a place for female journalists and news about women in 'the existing information networks and systems that might operate in promoting a regular service of news, information, and background on women's issues' (*UNFPA Project Request*, July 1 1976).

Although it might be argued that this was a liberal reformist strategy, there also are clear signs of intent to create a space for oppositional (feminist) personnel and ideas in a previously closed male system. Moreover, the project was designed to guarantee feminist control of both the individual feature service programs (see below) and the content of the stories they produced. In other words, the individual programs maintained a strong degree of autonomy and separation from their sponsor agencies. There was, in addition, a stated mission of independence in the UNESCO program. Women's Feature Service project administrator Yvette Abrahamson make it clear from the outset that UN funds would end in 1983 and that individual programs needed to work toward self-sufficiency from their respective beginnings (Byerly, 1990b). Women's informational needs, lives, views, achievements, and creative control were top priorities for both the umbrella project and its five individual programs. Male sponsorship was approached as a necessary but temporary measure in the programs' self-determination.

Those five services and their sponsors included: (a) the *Oficina Informativa de la Mujer* (OIM), sponsored by the Inter Press Service, in San José, Costa Rica, to serve the Latin American region; (b) the *Caribbean Women's Feature Syndicate*, sponsored by the Caribbean News Agency, in Barbados, to serve the Caribbean region; (c) the *Depthnews Women's Service*, sponsored by Press Foundation of Asia, in Manila, the Philippines, to serve Southeast Asia; (d) the *African Women's Feature Service*, sponsored by Inter Press Service, in Nairobi, Kenya, to serve both Anglophone and Francophone Africa; and (e) the *Arab States Women's Feature Service*, sponsored by the Federation of Arab News Agencies, in Beirut, to serve the Middle Eastern region. UNFPA's start-up and operation funds, which ranged in annual amounts from $5000 (for the Caribbean Women's Feature Service) to $30,000 (for IPS's adminis- tration of the OIM and African Women's Feature Service) were set to end in 1983, when sponsoring agencies were to have found other financing to continue their operations.

UNESCO's women's feature service project personnel also approached the major international news services – based in North America and Europe – to be sponsors, but found them uninterested. Gallagher (1981, p. 146) reported that these agencies

> had their own established networks of correspondents (mainly male), a primarily Western orientation in coverage, and an emphasis on 'spot' news rather than features or background information, [so] there was no real perception for the need for the kind of material called for by the [WFS] project.

Gallagher suggests that these agencies' refusal to participate signified a fundamental incompatibility between the project's goals of increasing women's access and self-determination and the news industries' vested interest in keeping their structures and policies intact.

The project had emerged in the context of the globally turbulent 1970s, during which gendered struggles coincided with newly defined interna- tional political and economic struggles. Third World nations' proposals for both a New World Information and Communication Order (NWICO) and a New International Economic Order (NIEO), which UNESCO supported, were seen by Western governments and news enterprises as fundamentally anti-Western, anti-free press, and anti-capitalist. The WFS project's goals to intervene in the order of things, with women in developing nations being the primary benefactors and UNESCO again the advocate, provided yet another occasion for a clash between developed Western and Third World Nations. Roach (1990) notes the essential irony in this conflict in her assessment of why the NWICO and NIEO failed: women had had little relationship to either of these, because they had been denied a voice in both formulating and debating the NWICO and NIEO proposals. Had women been allowed participation by Third World male elites, the proposals would have had a broader base of support, Roach insists. Instead, women's concerns about both development and communication were relegated to a separate international public arena in the form of UN Decade for Women events.

The women's feature service project met with mixed success in its five years of operation. The project generated an estimated 100 or more new female journalists in developing nations over a 5-year period. The project also strengthened the visibility of issues related to women and to both community and national development processes. Using the development news format, these stories revealed not just women's problems but the historical circumstances out of which problems grew, as well as how women were addressing them. Exemplary was one story filed in Cotonou, Benin, for the African Women's Feature Service in 1980, explaining why women in rural Benin could not get loans to finance farming cooperatives: 'In most cases rural women take part in the production process, but [they] do not own what [they] produce. A woman has no right to own property and she is considered, once married, as an asset for her husband's personal belongings' (Gisele, 1980).[2] The story went on to report on a new program being set up in all six counties of Benin to teach literacy to and initiate community development projects for women. Some groups of men and women would teach new information about the role of women in rural development (Gisele, 1980).

Overall, the project increased the number of stories about women in news by about 1200 during its 5-year operation. This increase was seen most strongly in Latin America and Southeast Asia, where the respective women's feature service programs had been most productive and well received (Byerly, 1990b; Rush and Ogan, 1989). Higher literacy rates, a longer tradition of womens participation in public affairs, and the established credibility of Inter Press Service (OIM's sponsor agency) in Latin America are possible reasons that OIM showed particular success in this region (Byerly, 1990b). The Caribbean area produced fewer stories and encountered less enthusiasm among male editors, who preferred to run stories reflecting women's traditional roles and problems (Gordon, 1981; Rush and Ogan, 1989).

Sexist attitudes in news selection by male gatekeepers had also been a problem in Africa, where the media were so reluctant to use stories about women that UNESCO's Yvette Abrahamson organized a series of meetings with African leaders and media representatives to confront the problem. Similarly, in the Middle Eastern region, the Arab States Women's Feature Service had trouble producing its required number of stories, in part because male journalists in some nations had blocked the work of Arab Women's Feature Service correspondents (Abrahamson, 1982; Byerly, 1990a). Technical and logistical difficulties prevented timely distribution of stories in some areas of Africa and the Middle East, which still relied on mail for delivery. And unforeseen political difficulties, such as the bombing of the Federation of Arab News Agencies (and its Arab Women's Feature Service) headquarters in Beirut had interrupted news production (Abrahamson, 1982).

When UNESCO sponsorship of the women's feature service project ended in 1983, only the Rome-based Inter Press Service and the Press Foundation of Asia, in Manila, had succeeded in finding the means to continue their programs. Of these, Inter Press Service (IPS), with media, government, and other subscribers in 80 nations, adopted a long-range plan to support a global news service for women. In 1986, IPS Director Roberto Savio hired development specialist Anita Anand to head the 'Women, Communication and Development' project, with Anand's primary duties being to merge the flagging remains of the Latin American and African women's feature services and then to expand these services' operations around the world (Byerly, 1990a). The original project, the product of global feminism, had laid the foundation for a new generation of women-defined and women-controlled news.

Strengthening organization and news directions

By 1986, women's feature programs under IPS sponsorship had been through two developmental stages – an original organizational and experimental stage, with UN funding, and a transitional stage, with IPS Funding. IPS's women's news component entered its third phase in 1986, one characterized by a consolidated identity as Women's Feature Service (WFS) and by mobilization aimed at independence. Between 1986 and 1989, under Anand's direction, WFS established a global administrative structure, strengthened its regional journalistic personnel, and secured funds for independent operation. WFS also identified its new headquarters as New Delhi, an important symbolic step that would, in 1990, move it from Europe to the developing world it primarily served (Anand, 1983).

This was a period of rapid change in many respects; however, WFS remained fairly constant in several ways. The agency continued to circulate its stories both in English and Spanish, with IPS as its distributor. Many stories continued to be translated into local languages at regional IPS offices around the globe. In addition, WFS maintained its commitment to the feminization of development news, with particular emphasis on the development news feature story. This commitment to include feminist perspectives within the development news format, refined by nearly a decade's practice, represented (and continues to represent) a substantial contribution to world news.

Recent research continues to show that, on the whole, women remain marginalized in most news from and about the developing nations, in terms of the number of women writers and female subjects in news content (Giffard *et al.*, 1991; Rush and Ogan, 1989). Statistical findings derived from counting the number of women in bylines, story themes, attribution, and photos are useful in revealing the work yet to be done, but they should not overshadow the significant efforts of agencies to expand the amount of news about women as well as to reframe news using women's views and daily experiences. Although more difficult to measure, the aspect of framing holds perhaps the greatest potential for assessing how feminism has influenced world and local news. In their study of the news from the Caribbean News Agency (CANA), Rush and Ogan (1989) demonstrate one way of assessing news frames within a more traditional quantitative analysis. The authors identified stories within their sample that might have included a woman's perspective (or angle) and did not. More familiar treatment of news frame analysis by Tuchman (1978) and Gitlin (1980) provides additional models, though both are concerned with U.S. news.

Byerly's (1990b) analysis of WFS stories utilized both statistical and qualitative methods to reveal that WFS stories make a particular effort to frame their content using 'a progressive woman's perspective' (*Women's Feature Service*, 1992b). Issues like politics, economics, war, peace, environmental destruction, religion, social customs, families, health, and all other topics related to Third World culture and development become the stuff of WFS news features. However, issues are developed within the context of women's daily lives, questions, and social participation. One 1988 story from Bihar, India, for example, concerned police brutality, a common problem in industrial and Third World nations alike. But this story, which focused on the long-standing practice of police rape of village women, was framed by a feminist analysis of rape. Village women were allowed to speak of their outrage in the article, as well as to outline their efforts to have policemen who assaulted women fired from their state-paid jobs (Dasgupta, 1988). The story foregrounded women's right to fight back and to interrupt the patriarchal practices of using violence against women as a means of control. This story was also typical in providing a history of police rape of Indian women and a status report on women's efforts to respond through organized resistance and local services for victims.

Byerly's analysis also revealed that WFS stories expanded the numbers of women at all levels of the socioeconomic scale to be heard. In a sample of 105 stories, from 1986 through 1989, the author found that 78% of all primary sources were female, and, of those, 56% were nonelite women, whose occupations ranged from mothers to agricultural and unskilled workers (Byerly, 1990b). The aforementioned study suggests that individual journalists have more power to reshape news codes (Bird and Dardenne, 1988) in favour of marginalized groups when they operate in structures controlled by those groups (Rakow and Kranich, 1991). WFS stories illustrate the ways in which women journalists, using a progressive perspective, have been able to embed new cultural codes favourable to women in their news features.

It is important to grasp the contribution that this new kind of news agency structure and the news stories it produces has already made to world news. As production of stories increased, WFS stories found favourable reception among their largely mainstream subscribers. One analysis of publication rates revealed that 60% of the approximately 500 stories disseminated for the months March, April, and May between 1986 and 1989 were published at least once and as many as eight times. Publication rates continued to be highest in Latin America, particularly in Venezuela, México, and Bolivia. Demand also has grown steadily in Europe, where 23 Finnish and eight Dutch publications printed WFS stories on a regular basis in the years surveyed (Byerly, 1990b).

WFS presently centralizes the final editing and distribution of features and manages its overall financial and administrative affairs from its new headquarters. The agency receives and recirculates news features regularly among nations in Latin America, Africa, South Asia, the Philippines, the United States, and Japan, with intermittent service from Southeast Asia, the Pacific, the Middle East, and Europe. News features are written by paid part-time correspondents, many of whom are employed as full-time journalists at mainstream media organizations. The service was extended to Japan in 1992. Located in Tokyo, this operation has become the first in WFS network to meet its own expenses (Women's Feature Service, 1993).

Since 1990, WFS has produced about 500 stories annually (from all regions), with major languages still English and Spanish; translations to other languages are still performed at regional levels. The service reports that 70% of its stories are published or broadcast annually, indicating stable and reasonably high demand for its materials. Since WFS relocated to New Delhi, the publication rate in India has increased 100% in the mainstream media, with all major dailies now carrying the women's features (Women's Feature Service, 1993).

All this is accomplished on an annual budget of well under $1 million. Major sources of income include grants from UN agencies such as UNIFEM, Dutch and Swiss development cooperation agencies, both large and small nongovernmental organizations, and subscriber fees. There are also a number of minor sources of revenue, such as UNICEF, which provide funds according to the number of features produced. Fundraising is a major part of the director's work (Anand, 1993; Rebecca Foster, personal communication, July 1993).

The agency ended its arrangement with IPS for telex distribution in 1992 and has since established its own multichanneled dissemination. This has made distribution more versatile but not entirely adequate to reach the broad IPS audience in the 80 nations of earlier years. In the U.S., for instance, where WFS has expanded its marketing push, clients can access news features through regular mail, fax, or through subscription to the WFS *Bulletin*, and through the Internet (PeaceNet News, Institute for Global Communication). In addition, the agency tries to provide commissioned stories, on request (Margaret Bald, personal communication, July 1993). Still, financial constraints, together with long-standing difficulties finding markets for products in some areas, have meant some streamlining of services. After years of unsuccessful attempts both to produce and market the stories in the Caribbean region, WFS closed its Caribbean operation in Jamaica in 1992 (Women's Feature Service, 1992a).

On the other hand, WFS has continued to cover major world meetings, such as the UN Conference on Environment and Development in Rio de Janeiro in 1992 and the UN Conference on Human Rights in Vienna in 1993. WFS staff are working with Asian women's groups to develop a regional media strategy for news coverage of the next UN Decade for Women follow-up meeting, to be held in Beijing in 1995 (Women's Feature Service, 1993). In an effort to reach nonreading publics, WFS has begun to experiment with news feature videos. One 25-minute segment on literacy campaigns for women in India was distributed in India in 1993, for instance (Rebecca Foster, personal communication, July 1993).

Conclusion

Status quo social practices must be interrupted if new ones are to be introduced and eventually to replace them. Such interruptions, or interventions, stand the best chance of succeeding when they are institutionalized, either through existing structures or new ones. The original women's feature service project – and its descendant, the New Delhi WFS – was the first intentionally organized effort to interrupt global news practices that had historically ignored and marginalized women's concerns and achievements. Under UNESCO funding and administration, the original five services took an important symbolic step to assert greater control over the creation of messages and representations in news. The project had limited success, in terms of the numbers of stories it produced over its 5-year life and in the degree to which mainstream print media used them.

But first steps are not necessarily final steps. In this project's case, two of the feature services have continued on, still serving both specialized and mainstream media and nonmedia organizations throughout the world. This could signal the coming of a new era, one in which woman-controlled news agencies can become viable in the competitive world of global newsmaking.

Still primarily concerned with women's participation in development processes, WFS challenges traditional definitions of not only Western (event-oriented) news, but development (process-oriented) news as well. WFS news features make gender central as they foreground the daily experiences, views, activities, and analyses of their female subjects and sources. News features make no particular effort to 'balance' these with more traditional (male-oriented) interests. In this way, WFS stories may recognize that women in developed and developing nations are divided by material differences in their daily lives, as well as cultural and political histories, while at the same time sharing important elements in their paths toward self-determination.

Other issues related to women's suffering and progress cross national boundaries: new diasporas of refugees escaping war, persecution, and economic hardship – many of these women with children seeking asylum in industrial Western nations; the dramatic spread of AIDS, first among heterosexual African women and, more recently, heterosexual female populations in North America and Europe; the persistence of men's rape and battering of women in nations at war, like Bosnia, as well as in other nations ostensibly at peace; and, of course, women's unflagging determination to address these situations.

Any woman's news service would be challenged to tackle the enormity of what remains to be done in bringing women more soundly into world journalism and, by extension, women's problems, efforts, interpretations of events, and accomplishments into public consciousness. And yet there is a compelling case to be made for efforts in this direction, not just by the Women's Feature Service – which provides an obvious prototype – but for other organizations that might spring from need and opportunity. But where to begin?

The difficulties that first the parent WFS project and, more recently, the successor Women's Feature Service of New Delhi, had in reaching literate publics with information about women in the Arab, African, and Caribbean regions would give pause to the most determined of leaders. But neither cultural inhibitors, such as predominantly oral traditions in many African states and the Caribbean, nor persistent lower literacy rates should represent permanent barriers to future initiatives to reach large, diverse populations with new ideas about women's roles in society. As women's movements gain momentum in these areas, there may be a wider opening for renewed efforts to bring these regions (particularly the Caribbean) into WFS activities, or for other women's news systems to emerge and carry out the task.

Arab women's forceful entrance onto the world stage in recent years suggests new possibilities for informational linkage among women-owned networks. Such invitation seems implied in statements like this one by Syrian academic Bouthaina Shaaban (1993), who was reflecting on a long (but relatively unknown) tradition of Arab feminist journals when she wrote:

A stream of articles that appeared in a number of these journals established an interesting link between the emergence of political movements for national independence and the awakening of a feminist consciousness in the Arab world, arguing that no country can be truly free so long as its women remain shackled (p. 76).[2]

Shaaban articulates the quintessential case for informational mechanisms committed to helping women's voices to be heard, both among each other and in the general population. News production under the control of and in the service of women assures the best guarantee of achieving this task, as ample stores of data demonstrate.

Notes

1. From Inter Press Services African Women's Feature Service wire story. Reprinted by permission of IPS-Women's Feature Service.
2. Reprinted by permission of *Ms.* Magazine © 1993.

References

Abrahamson, Y. (1982) Minutes of Women, Development and Communication Meeting, Libreville, Gabon, February 1982. (*UNESCO Archives, Registry No. 307:392:2-055.2,* Paris.)

Anand, A. (1983) Rethinking women and development. In Isis International Information and Communication Service (ed.) *Women in development: A resource guide for organization and action,* ISIS, Geneva, pp. 5–11.

Anand, A. (1992) Introduction. In Women's Feature Service (ed.) *The power to change: Women in the Third World redefine their environment,* Kali Press for Women, New Delhi, pp. 1–21.

Anand, A. (1993) The clothesline goes up at the Human Rights Conference. *WFS Bulletin,* Vol. 3, No. 3, p. 2.

Bird, S. E., and Dardenne, R. W. (1988) Myth, chronicle, and story: Exploring the narrative qualities of news. In Carey J. W. (ed.) *Media, myths, and narratives: Television and the press,* Sage, Newbury Park, CA, pp. 67–86.

Byerly, C. M. (1990a) Taking a stronger hand: The Women's Feature Services and the making of world news. *Development,* Vol. 2, pp. 79–85.

Byerly, C. M. (1990b) *The Women's Feature Services and the making of world news,* unpublished doctoral dissertation, University of Washington.

Charlton, S. E. M. (1984). *Women in Third World development,* Westview, Boulder, CO.

Dasgupta, R. (1988, Fall) *India: Abusing the uniform* (wire story), Inter Press Service, Parraria, Bihar, India.

Decade for women: World plan of action (1975) Washington, DC: Women's Equity Action League Educational and Legal Defense Fund (WEAL Fund). (Condensed version of the World Plan of Action and Related Resolutions adopted at México City in July 1975 by the United Nations World Conference of the International Women's Year.)

Gallagher, M. (1981) *Unequal opportunities: The case of women and the media,* UNESCO, Paris.

Giffard, C. A. (1984, Autumn) Inter Press Service: News from the Third World. *Journal of Communication,* Vol. 34, No. 4, pp. 41–59.

Giffard, C. A., Byerly, C. M., and Van Horn, C. (1991). *The world of Inter Press Service,* unpublished report prepared for the International Association for Mass Communications Research (IAMCR), The Hague, the Netherlands.

Gisele, A. (1980, September 7) *Benin: Toward improving rural women's lives* (wire story), Inter Press Service – African Women's Feature Service.

Gitlin, T. (1980) *The whole world is watching: The making and unmaking of the New Left*, University of California Press, Berkeley.

Gordon, L. (1981) The portrayal and participation of women in the Caribbean mass media: A socio-economic perspective. In Cuthbert M. (ed.) *Women and media decision-making in the Caribbean*, CARIMAC, Kingston, Jamaica.

Hall, S. (1980) Encoding/decoding. In Hall S. *et al.* (eds.) *Culture, media, language: Working papers in cultural studies*, Hutchinson, London, pp. 128–132.

Herman, E. and Chomsky, N. (1988) *Manufacturing consent: The political economy of the mass media*, Pantheon, New York.

Kielbowicz, R. and Scherer, H. (1986) The role of the press in the dynamics of social movements. *Research in Social Movements, Conflict and Change*, Vol. 9, pp. 71–96.

Mohanty, C. T. (1991) Introduction: Cartographies of struggle: Third World women and the politics of feminism. In Mohanty, C. T., Russo, A. and Torres L. (eds.) *Third World women and the politics of feminism*, Indiana University Press, Bloomington, pp. 1–47.

O'Connor, A. (1990) Culture and communication. In Downing, J., Mohammadi, A. and Sreberny-Mohammadi A. A. (eds.) *Questioning the media*, Sage, Newbury Park, CA, pp. 27–41.

Rakow, L. and Kranich, K. (1991) Woman as sign in television news. *Journal of Communication*, Vol. 41, No. 1, pp. 8–23.

Roach, C. (1990) The movement for a New World Information and Communication Order: A second wave? *Media, Culture and Society*, Vol. 12, No. 3, pp. 283–307.

Rush, R. R. and Ogan, C. L. (1989) Communication and development: The female connection. In Rush R. R. and Allen D. (eds.) *Communication at the cross roads*, Ablex, Norwood, NJ, pp. 265–278.

Shaaban, B. (1993, May–June) The hidden history of Arab feminism: Women's networks and journalism have flourished since 1982. *Ms.*, pp. 76–77.

Steeves, H. L. and Arbogast, R. (1993) Feminism and communication in development: Ideology, law, ethics, practice. In Dervin B. and Hariharan U. (eds.) *Progress in communication sciences*, Vol. 11, Ablex, Norwood, NJ, pp. 229–277.

Tuchman, G. (1978) *Making news: A study in the construction of reality*, Free Press, New York.

UNFPA Project Request, (1976, July 1) UNESCO, Paris.

Women's Feature Service (1992a) *Annual report 1992*, Women's Feature Service, New Delhi.

Women's Feature Service (1992b) *The power to change: Women in the Third World redefine their environment*, Kali Press for Women, New Delhi.

Women's Feature Service (1993) *Women's Feature Service: Reporting on change* (core proposal for the period January 1993–December 1995). [Available from: Women's Feature Service, 49 Golf Link, New Delhi, 110 003, India].

22

China turned on (revisited): television, reform and resistance

James Lull

San Jose State University, U.S.A. (1995).

Anthony Giddens has described modernity not as a 'monster' (which he claims was Marx' way of understanding it) or an 'unfinished project' (attributed to Habermas), but as a 'juggernaut – a runaway engine of enormous power which human beings can drive collectively to some extent, but which also threatens to rush out of control' (Giddens 1990, p. 139). Furthermore, Giddens suggests that the juggernaut 'is not an engine made up of integrated machinery, but one in which there is a tensionful, contradictory, push-and-pull of different influences' (p. 139). This metaphor of a powerful, contradictory, essentially uncontrollable machine effectively brings to mind not only the condition of global modernity (or even postmodernity), but also the historically specific processes of *modernizing*. It applies especially well to the hugely ambitious project initiated by communist authorities in the People's Republic of China two decades ago.

If the memorable television images emanating from Beijing June 4 1989 indicated to viewers that China's revolutionary activity had been effectively extinguished, nothing could be further from the truth. Although the military show of force at Tiananmen Square preserved the political authority of Deng Ziaoping and the Chinese Communist Party (CCP) for the short term, the events of Beijing Spring have in fact profoundly accelerated the pace of China's striking cultural and economic transformation, and in this epoch it is culture and economics that define and propel modernization. The popular media images we see of China today only hint at the deep structural changes which infiltrate all aspects of life on the mainland. The careening juggernaut of Chinese modernization has brought with it everything from the production, display, and consumption of seemingly superficial, but deeply symbolic cultural markers like cheeseburgers, lipstick, and MTV to a staggering economic metamorphosis that includes an ever-widening division of social classes, astounding economic growth accompanied by rapid inflation, and the development of a convenient 'Chinese socialist market economy.'

Such remarkable consequences of the Chinese modernization reflect confusions and contradictions that have characterized the entire history of the Asian nation's attempt at reform. China's unsteady march toward modernity is a product of the instruments and processes of modernization itself. In particular, the rapid development and massive deployment of telecommunications technology is key to understanding the dynamics of conflict and change. Following the historic Third Plenum of the Eleventh Central Committee meeting of the CCP in December, 1978 – wherein the fundamental contours of the modernization were officially prescribed – a satellite-based national television system was made a top priority for achieving a wide range of propagandist objectives. Such plans for information dissemination and persuasion have not been fulfilled, however, despite the fact that the television system grew quickly and TV sets were made easily available to nearly everyone, especially urban families, as early as the mid-1980s. Ironically, the ultimately uncontrollable social institution of television (and other media), together with the ability and willingness of audiences to interpret TV content in unintended and often resistant ways, has undermined the ideological and cultural aspects of the modernization plan. What I argue in this chapter is that the social stresses China has experienced since 1978 have resulted from implacable contradictions existing in the popular consciousness, many of which predate the introduction of television there, but have been accelerated to dramatic proportions because of the rapid spread and influence of the medium. Television's democratizing and agitating mediations have interacted in the public mind with the harsh realities imposed by an unstable economy, the desire for more personal freedom, and with a collective depression that has descended over the country as the people confront a mean and sluggish bureaucratism that punishes them concretely as they negotiate the most basic routines of everyday life. Some variation of this story reveals what has happened in the tremble and fall of communist governments around the world (Lull, 1995). Indeed, 'Modern broadcasting devices, once the perfect instruments for capturing loyalties and maintaining the state, are becoming consummate devices for undermining the established order' (Price, 1994, p. 704).

Television was peaking as a communications medium in China during the troubled 1980s and had itself become a significant symbol of the national modernization. By the middle of the decade nearly every urban family had bought a television receiver, many had colour models, and some owned more than one set. Journalistic practices, entertainment fare, and cultural developments in general were more liberal and exciting than ever before. But when push came to shove, televised reports of the military invasion of the student-worker encampment at Tiananmen Square were not transmitted in China. While the rest of the world tuned in to pictures of courageous students, intellectuals, and workers standing up to the brute force of tanks and the political power of ageing bureaucrats, Chinese television viewers saw very different visuals and accounts of the tragic events in the capital city, and even those images came late. Television had been forcibly restored to its original place as a blatant propaganda device.

By managing television coverage of the brutal crackdown and subsequently constructing a massive propaganda onslaught, Chinese government officials hoped to re-establish social stability, reassert the place of the CCP as the nation's legitimate political authority, and minimize ideological damage brought by the economic, political, cultural, and social stresses that China experienced in the late 1980s. But it's too late for that now. Television does not just serve the government in China and the manipulation of program content certainly does not guarantee that the people will interpret messages as they are intended to be understood. This was clear long before the conflict in 1989.

Although the Chinese government has attempted to use television to unify the people, preserve the authority of the party, and fulfill the promises of the reformation, the medium has also become a central agent of popular resistance against a political and economic system that many loyal Chinese feel has become hopelessly inefficient and out of touch with the people. Television demarcates the current period of Chinese history – an era of technological growth and cultural adaptation that includes the rapid spread of telecommunications technology and the formation of the world's largest television audience.

The ethnographic analysis presented here was developed from systematic, in-depth interviews that my research partner, Se-wen Sun, and I had with nearly 100 urban Chinese families and with television executives in 1986, and from similar encounters I had with scholars, students, citizens, and broadcasters in the fall of 1989, four months after the standoff at Tiananmen Square. The material presented in this chapter is distilled from a much larger and more encompassing original account (Lull, 1991).

The electronic amplification of contradiction

Beginning with the absolutist dictates of Qin Shi Huang, China's first feudal emperor, the idea of a supreme authority – one who stands above the people and guides them to their destiny – has been a fundamental trait of Chinese society. While forms of government ranging from the extreme right to the extreme left have ruled the country, Chinese people have always placed their trust in this notion of a central authority, personified by a national leader, to whom they are fiercely loyal. Cast in terms of unity of purpose and of total devotion to ideological principles, one need not go back further in history than the Cultural Revolution to see clearly the lengths to which this passionate faith can be taken and the consequences it can bring. But today history may be catching up with itself. Perhaps more than anything else, the resistance movement in China, with its twin emphases of freedom and democracy, has strongly challenged the tradition of autocratic rule. It could not have happened without television.

Television, of course, is itself an authoritarian institution of sorts, one that articulates confidently and widely. Critics in societies all over the world complain that the medium has the power to serve the political and economic interests of its owners and managers by creating a narrow agenda and monopolizing public opinion, that it debases culture, and that it nearly mesmerizes viewers psychologically. Precisely because it is so influential, television seems to be the perfect communications medium for the perpetuation of autocratic rule in a restrictive environment such as China. Certainly the perceived potential for doing so encouraged officials in Bejing to develop the television system as a mechanism to promote national modernization. But despite their intentions, a 'single leader, single voice' complementary of communist politics and modern communications technology, wherein official mandates are diffused efficiently and unproblematically through the electronic wizardry of television, has not taken place.

Lightning-fast and ultimately uncontrollable, television has instead given rise to a diversity of cultural and political sentiments in China at a speed that disrupts stability and control. Furthermore, the often conflicting perspectives that television articulates do not simply stand alongside one another in the popular consciousness, unanalyzed and uncriticized by viewers. Television exaggerates and intensifies each stream of information in the ideological flood that it cumulatively delivers to its audiences, producing an electronic amplification of contradiction that has dramatically altered the nation's cultural contours.

Since 1978 China has desperately tried to develop its economy while at the same time promising to repair its internal political difficulties, especially the widespread corruption, and to modernize technologically while judiciously expanding its cultural horizons. The immense magnitude and ill-defined nature of such an undertaking has led to the formulation of policies and practices that are often in conflict with one another, creating a kind of national schizophrenia. As Orville Schell noted two years before the blowup in Beijing in 1989, 'On the one hand [China] continues to protest against despoilers of its socialist revolution, while on the other hand it promotes crypto-capitalism. The country often appears to be going in opposite directions at the same time' (Schell, 1987, p. 13–14). It is exactly contradictions such as this, manifest not only in economic policy but in virtually all aspects of life – highlighted, legitimated, and popularized by television – that have stimulated alternative, competing visions of China's collective future and the personal dreams of millions of Chinese citizens.

This is not what Deng Xiaoping had in mind in 1978. Above all else, the Chinese government has tried to act as a unified body. According to the principle of democratic centralism, Deng (the *de facto* supreme leader until death), as well as the general secretary of the CCP, the premier, and the politburo are supposed to demonstrate unity and solidarity by acting in full agreement. National objectives, as decided by the top leadership are to be carried out at all levels within the society – a charge that is to be facilitated in part by television. There is, therefore, a chain of agents of authority designed to promote unity: the nation (including especially its history and many cultural traditions), the supreme ruler, the CCP, the current government, and, with its own type of influence owing mainly to technological capabilities, television. [. . .]

The unity ground to a halt late in the last decade. When the economy took a dramatic downward turn, the people strongly criticized the government's utopian visions as unrealistic while they still clung to their own dreams. [. . .]

The fundamental economic contradiction – a fast-developing class difference in a society that promises and promotes equality, but does not provide equal opportunity for financial success, produced extreme negative reactions from those who felt they were losing ground. Economic restructuring had come to a standstill. The old system would continue to prevent them from ever utilizing their potential, while other people – private unit merchants often engaged in less demanding work – would still benefit from the partial, undemocratic restructuring. The dilemma was magnified by television. Commercials and imported films and dramas celebrated the individualism and materialism of a consumer society at the very time the people could not break out of their monotonous routines or prosper from their own initiative. [. . .]

The people began to realize that other political and economic systems function far better than their own and that their personal freedoms are few. The moralizing and sacrificing lifestyle that is demanded of the citizenry was widely known not to be practised even by high-ranking communist officials. The economic crisis of the late 1980s served to increase reliance on *guanxi wang* (personal connections), leading to even more corruption, years after the government promised to reduce or eliminate the problem. In the name of solving the financial crisis, the CCP strongly reasserted its political authority. In fall 1989, Jiang Zemin promised 'no total Westerniza-tion' of China and Li Peng called for greater political control of ideology and the economy. Yet, at the same time, many television programs and commercials kept serving up attractive alternatives to the tiresome political rhetoric and the hard reality of everyday life.

The most fundamental contradictions in China, then, are glaring dispar-ities within the idealized, unified voice of the CCP that was first raised by Mao Zedong as he shouted into the public address microphone at Tianenmen Gate in 1949, alternative realities that are made known primarily by television, and what has been a worsening state of everyday life under communism. Coming to realize the discrepancies, contradictions, and broken promises, the people have felt not only frustrated, they feel betrayed. The shift in their thinking has been fundamentally influenced by television which has acted like a two-edged sword piercing the armor of the CCP. Some television programming has sparked deep criticism and the imagination of a better life, while the doctrinaire and strident propaganda that still appears on the very same channels has, for many viewers in the cities especially, crystallized resistance and undercut cultural and political hegemony in the process.

Political television, polysemy, and the demise of the mass audience

In order to further understand how television has decisively stimulated the revolutionary change of consciousness that has taken place in China, we must consider specific institutional practices of the medium, the pro-gramming that is transmitted by the television system, and the particular ways that Chinese TV viewers interpret and use this symbolic material. To begin with, it is a mistake to try to determine what '*the* government' or '*the* system' is doing in China. Doing so presumes a singularity of purpose and an administrative efficiency that simply does not exist. Although in principle television should reflect and advocate a coherent political philosophy and suggest conforming social practices, what we find instead at all three analytical domains mentioned above – the institution of television, the programs it transmits, and audience activity – is diversity and contradiction. What I will now argue is that, first of all, the Chinese television system articulates a multiplicity of competing cultural and political visions that is the product of the carrying out of workplace routines by media professionals. Second, television programs, even when they are produced and selected under tightly-controlled circumstances, are not semantically homogenous. Finally, viewers frequently interpret and use television symbolism in a manner that is not intended by the government. What makes these variations and divergences so significant in China is that they occur in circumstances where ideological unity and social conformity are promoted as keys to national stability, and where they are essential to the long-term maintenance of political power by the CCP. Television makes it impossible for the government successfully to promote but one cultural or political system. The Chinese people no longer know or care what is *ru* (the official culture). The unchallengeable authority of the CCP has been strongly challenged. [. . .]

Television a cultural and ideological forum

The principle of television as a cultural forum certainly applies in China. The men and women who occupy the offices, studios, newsrooms, editing booths, and every other quarter of the Chinese television industry represent a heterogeneity that has led to a diversity in what that system transmits. These media specialists make the day-to-day decisions that introduce, emphasize, interpret, shade, and downplay the content of television. Their decisions are often self-consciously political and reflect the oppositional sentiment that has grown so precipitously in the cities since the mid 1980s. [. . .]

The likelihood that diverse views, some of them quite subversive, can find their way onto the airwaves in China is further increased by the inability of the bureaucracy to manage state ideology well. This was the case most remarkably in the controversial airing in the late 1980s of the TV series. *New Star* and *River Elegy* – cultural and political events in China that further reveal the unique and compelling role of television as a communications medium, and the television series as a storytelling format, as interacting ideological fields of force. These television series articulated the Chinese 'subject in crisis,' stimulating all kinds of people throughout the broad and diverse nation to commune emotionally in repeated, ritualistic experiences of political resistance. Ideological contrasts are also reflected in the incredible contradictions that exist between the blatant materialism and individualism that are allowed to be promoted on television and the content of other programming that advocates traditional socialist values. Also, the desire of TV station officials to attract large audiences has encouraged them to take the interests and desires of their viewers more into account in recent years, creating another institutional shift of emphasis away from the sanctity and uniformity of official positions. Furthermore, the rapidly-expanding size of the television system in China, wherein more and more channels are added, each of which requires programs to fill airtime, likewise contributes to the diversity.

These specific conditions – multiple visions and intentions held by employees at every level within the TV industry, an inefficient and confused bureaucracy that cannot manage or control, contradictory values expressed in programs and commercials, a trend toward trying to attract and please larger audiences, and the appetite of a growing television system, have all made the medium a potent cultural and ideological forum in China. In fact, the government finally admitted during the stressful summer of 1989 that it had lost control if its own media, that the plethora of perspectives had assumed a dangerous life of its own.

Some steps have been taken to exercise greater control over television content since the period of martial law in 1989. Two of CCTV's most popular personalities – prime-time news anchorwoman Du Xian and anchorman Xue Fei – have been reassigned to non on-air positions after they dressed in black and tearfully read the news on the night of June 4th. By late 1990, the term 'comrade' (*tongzhimen* was once again being used by the news-casters to address their audiences. The government also tried to use television to directly counteract the influence of the TV program that is commonly thought to have contributed greatly to the unrest – *River Elegy*. In the wake of the 1989 military crackdown, CCTV produced a series of short programs titled *One Hundred Mistakes of River Elegy*. Each instalment was designed to refute one major historical claim or cultural criticism that had been made in the original production. *River Elegy* was popular and controversial precisely because it dared to dishonor Chinese culture. Like *New Star*, it stood out conspicuously on the TV system, influencing viewers in ways that thou-sands of hours of propagandistic television programs could never do. The remedial program, *One Hundred Mistakes of River Elegy*, may have actually extended the influence of the original by calling attention to *River Elegy* once again. It also confused viewers. The perplexity was perhaps best articulated by the young daughter of one of my narrators in 1989, when she said: 'Daddy, how come *River Elegy* was 100 per cent right before June 4th, and 100 per cent wrong after?' The bewilderment was exacerbated by the spate of commercials which often appeared immediately after an episode of the corrective program, advocating behaviour that directly conflicts with the moral lessons that had just been given. Contradictory juxtapositions of imagery such as this are commonplace on Chinese television contributing to its role as a cultural and ideological forum.

Television's messages and meanings

Even in the most controlled television systems, programs can never foster a single understanding or response on the part of the audience. [. . .] Tele-vision programs do not have a single meaning, connotation, or objectively definable significance. Television's images are, instead, polysemic. [. . .] This is not to say that TV programs are completely open texts that encourage limitless or wholly unguided interpretations. We must be careful not to overstate or romanticize the role of the viewer in the reception and use of television content. The specific images, framing, format, the internal structure of any specific program, and the program's relation to other symbolic material on the medium, all help establish cues for preferred 'readings' by audiences (Hall, 1980). [. . .]

Certainly television does have its intended effects, in some ways, for some of the audience, some of the time. Nonetheless, even in cases where program producers are clear in their own minds about what a program should say, they cannot, ultimately, control the way audiences will respond to their creations. Even the most seemingly uncomplicated attempts to 'transfer meaning' greatly oversimplify the nature of viewers' negotiations with television. This has certainly been the case in China. [. . .]

Polysemy does not simply open up the possibility of subversive, alternative readings, however. One of the most memorable images ever to appear on Chinese television, and on TV all over the world, is the famous video footage of the lone man standing in front of a line of tanks near the Beijing Hotel. This image has been widely celebrated outside China as the definitive representation of defiance and courage – the personification of resistance to political and military repression. [. . .]

The very same video footage was played many times in propaganda programs on Chinese television too. But the propagandists framed the famous incident quite differently, as the narration reveals: 'If the soldiers had not exercised restraint, how could this man, hailed as a hero by some Western media, have been able to show off in front of these tanks?' For advocates of the military measures that were taken to 'restore order to the capital' in China, the exact same image that to some viewers symbolized bravery in the face of violent military repression, was used as evidence to argue that the military 'acted with full restraint.'

Chinese television viewers saw this footage in programs that featured many other forms of disobedience. Viewers saw hundreds of young Chinese men and women throwing rocks and sticks at military vehicles, apparently attacking and beating the drivers, torching some of the vehicles with the men still inside, and so on. Despite the gravity of their surfaces, all these images are richly polysemic. Television does many things at the same time; propaganda and resistance can spring simultaneously from precisely the same source. [. . .] Furthermore, how viewers come to interpret messages such as these are influenced greatly by the economic, political, and cultural conditions that impinge upon their living situations, the macrosocial factors – which by spring of 1989 had become intolerable. But semiotic negotiations that take place between viewers and programs must also be considered in relation to the interpretive work of audience members who occupy individualized contexts – their microsocial worlds.

The Chinese TV audience at work

While the government has tried to use television to unify China, in the cities, at least, just the opposite has happened. The Chinese audience is not a mass. It does not respond to television in a uniform way. Viewers interact with television's symbols and semiotic structures to create their own meanings, promote their own understandings, and develop their own ideological coalitions. Though television surely has the ability to influence viewers in ways that benefit its controllers, the role of the viewer as an agent in the construction of his or her own experience with the medium should not be underestimated.

The political contexts of many communist countries (past and present) throughout the world have stimulated television viewers in those nations to become masters of interpretation, reading between the lines in order to pick up the less obvious messages. This was common in Eastern Europe, for instance, and it has certainly been the case in China. Many of my narrators describe not only what they watch, but how they watch television. Because viewers know that the government often bends and exaggerates its reports, they become skilled at imagining the true situation. What is presented, what is left out, what is given priority, how things are said – all these modes are noticed and interpreted sensitively. Changes in consciousness brought on by television in China, therefore, are stimulated not just by exposure to new information and ideas, but by the inventive ways that viewers critically interpret and use TV's symbolic content. The often taken-for-granted activity, 'watching television', signifies something in China that is very different from that to which most of us are accustomed.

Certain basic characteristics of Chinese culture and communication invite distinctive interpretive practices. It begins with language. The people must listen very attentively in spoken interaction and read print messages carefully and creatively in order to decode messages. In spoken Chinese, for instance, each sound can be expressed in four tones: flat, ascending, descending, and a combination of ascending and descending. The meaning of the utterance depends greatly on the inflection, so listeners become very good at carefully picking up the most subtle shifts of emphasis. Written Chinese characters likewise require skill in interpretation as they are individually far less denotative than are the basic symbols of other language groups. The characters are uniquely meaningful in relation to the linguistic structure in which they are embedded, a circumstance that requires the reader 'correctly' to infer the meaning from the *associations* of the characters, a challenging and imprecise activity. Hence, Chinese language is more 'aesthetic' – metaphorical and poetic – than it is 'efficient,' in the purely functional sense of the world. Because the language is so inexact in this way, it encourages playful articulations and interpretations, which, in a repressive political environment, enhances the opportunity for communicating subversive messages. Nonverbal forms of communication – gestures, body movement, facial expressions, paralanguage – are also extremely subtle and sensitively read in Chinese cultural. These intricate communications are not limited to unmediated interpersonal exchanges. An unacknowledged, strategic co-ordination between sources of public messages in China – the journalists, TV producers, and filmmakers, for instance – and the audience, make it possible to represent unofficial commentaries and views in the Chinese media. In this way, the television system has been appropriated by the people for purposes of resistance to the very authority which, theoretically, controls them.

Chinese people also readily deconstruct institutional pronouncements by means of their alert and ambitious involvement with television. The country's depressed economic status, its broadening culture, and the stinging political turmoil all encourage critical interpretations of the public face and voice of government. These critical interpretations include disbelief of news items, hatred of the government's constant self-promotion, mocking of the 'model worker' programs, disgust with misleading commercials, and so on. The turmoil in 1989 sharpened critical viewing even more.

Audiences for television are not constituted solely in acts of watching programs. 'The audience' is also formed at times when television's symbolic agenda is recognized, reconstructed, and transformed in the routine discourses of viewers' everyday lives. Political sentiments often develop more clearly and firmly in these moments of social interpretation – ideological editing that takes place in the minds of viewers as they talk about and reflect further upon what they see on TV. In an environment like China, this type of public dialogue confirms individual viewers' political sentiments and socially validates their feelings through the formation of constituencies of resistance. But television's agenda is reproduced, reconstructed, and transformed even in the most routine talk about programs in any political environment. The medium is a resource that, because of its sweeping presence, appeal, and social utility, expands an ideological agenda in a way that no other form of communication can, sometimes in accord with the intentions of its controllers, sometimes not. This is by no means an entirely imposed or predictable process. The ideological consequences of television rest as much with the audience as they do with the producers and presenters of programs.

China turned on

When students and workers took to the streets of Beijing in 1989, the government self-righteously disparaged them as 'counterrevolutionaries' – enemies of the people. This loaded term is habitually invoked to promote the idea that the government still spearheads a heroic communist revolution against the evils that confronted China before 1949 and continue to threaten her stability and progress today. In truth, of course, the real revolution in China now is a struggle against the 'revolutionary' government that nearly 50 years after its founding has become far more a force of repression than of liberation. Resistance to totalitarian rule in China is not simply a cry for change in the political structure. More than anything else, what the people want is freedom – to choose and change jobs, to travel, to chart one's own destiny. While these issues have political and economic origins and consequences, they are profoundly cultural matters. Modifications in the cultural identities and visions of China's urban population have interacted with economic realities and perceived political possibilities to provoke widespread discontent. Television is the eye of the cultural storm, its presence influencing the future of China in ways that no other technology or human agency can.

References

Giddens, A. (1990) *The Consequences of Modernity*, Stanford University Press, Stanford, CA, (1991), Polity Press, Cambridge, U.K.

Hall, S. (1980) Encoding/decoding. In Hall, S., Hobson, D., Lowe, D. and Willis, P. (eds.) *Culture, Media, Language*, Hutchinson, London.

Lull, J. (1991) *China Turned On: Television, Reform, and Resistance*, Routledge, London.

Lull, J. (1995) *Media, Communication, Culture: A Global Approach*, Polity Press, Cambridge, U.K.

Price, M. (1994) The market for loyalties: Electronic media and the global competition for allegiances. *The Yale Law Journal*, Vol. 104, No. 3, pp. 667–704.

Schell, O. (1987) Serving the people with advertising: From propaganda to PR in the 'new China' *This World*, June 7, pp. 13–14.

Section 6

Transnational media texts and audiences

23

Global harmonies and local discords: transnational policies and practices in the European recording industry

Keith Negus

From Negus, K. (1993) *European Journal of Communication*, Sage, London, Vol. 8, No. 3, pp. 295–361.

This article focuses on processes of globalization in the music industry by examining the transnational practices of the major record companies in Europe. Outlining various pan-European repertoire policies and working arrangements, it describes how tensions arise between staff in different national divisions of record companies; over the unequal exchange of musical products and due to the way in which locally produced music is deprioritized in favour of material produced by artists from Britain and the U.S.A. It also describes how various local state and community interests attempt to support musical activity, assuming a position explicitly in opposition to that of the major entertainment corporations. In general, this article argues that a complex series of nation-state, commercial market and civil society relationships concretely mediate processes of 'globalization', intervening as the global strategies of corporations are actively translated into specific local cultural practices.

During the latter half of the 1980s the entertainment corporations that own the major record companies began describing themselves as global organizations and projecting images of the planet Earth in their annual reports and advertising literature. [. . .]

This article is about how the recording divisions of these entertainment groups, the major record companies, are pursuing avowedly global policies in Europe.[1] Europe is now one of the most important markets for 'information and entertainment', and the attentions of these transnational corporations are becoming increasingly focused on both the EC and non-EC nations of Western Europe, and on the potential markets emerging in the previously inaccessible states of Eastern Europe. My aim is to describe how these vaguely stated 'global' intentions are actively translated into specific policies and working practices in particular regional contexts. I argue that the 'transnational practices' (Sklair, 1991) initiated by music companies generate a number of local tensions and reactions, both within the corporations and outside them. In the process I highlight how a complex series of nation-state/market/civil society relationships and reactions concretely mediate processes of 'globalization' and intervene as these global intentions are translated into specific local activities.

Globalization and popular music

In very general terms, 'globalization' indicates a shift in thinking and directs attention away from viewing the world as a series of discrete nation-states and towards a consideration of the relationships between geographical regions. It is an attempt to conceptualize the economic, social and cultural movements across conventional boundaries, and to highlight various similarities and convergences which are becoming a feature of the world capitalist economy; what Levitt, in an influential rallying call to big business, referred to as the 'homogenisation of the world's needs and desires' (Levitt, 1983, p. 93).

Globalization is not, as has sometimes been glossily implied in popular journalism and corporate literature, about the spontaneous unifying of the world into a cosy 'global village'. As Robins (1991, p. 25) has pointed out: ' "Globalisation" is about the organization of production and the exploitation of markets on a world scale'. In its current form it signifies the latent stage of a long historical trend towards the concentration of industrial and finance capital, and the concomitant attempts by capitalist corporations to expand by overcoming geographical and political boundaries. Modern companies seek to operate in all markets simultaneously, rather than sequentially, targeting and actively constructing consumers in multiple regions on the basis of demographics and lifestyles, rather than national identities. This has been facilitated by the technologies of the mass media and telecommunications which have enabled corporations to impose what Robins (1991, p. 28) has called 'an abstract electronic space' over and across pre-existing physical and social geographies.

This is particularly noticeable in the music industry where the videos and recordings of major artists such as Michael Jackson and Madonna are consumed simultaneously throughout the world; their sounds and images rapidly communicating across linguistic frontiers and cultural boundaries. Robins has argued that globalization breaks the link between culture and territory, dissolving distances and creating new imaginary spaces and identities. Popular music – less dependent for its comprehension upon language, education and the acquisition of a sophisticated body of knowledge – is one of *the* forms of mass communication which has been able to globalize most dramatically; constructing audiences around the commonly shared experience of a cultural event (such as Live Aid and the Nelson Mandela Freedom Concert), or an artist's lifestyle and identity, rather than a purely local experience in a discrete time and place.

However, while sounds, images and information may be moving across cultural borders more rapidly than in the past, the ability to transmit and receive these messages is dependent upon access to the means of information production and telecommunication and the distribution of technologies of reception. Globalization might break the link between culture and territory for the hegemonic transnational corporations, whose cultural products and information cannot be identified with their national origins in any straightforward way. But globalization makes the relationship between culture and territory more acute in those regions where these products and messages are perceived as coming from 'outside'. Here processes of globalization and the spread of 'global mass culture' (Hall, 1991) heightens the awareness of local territories and particularities. This tension is particularly noticeable in the recording industry. Here the transnational corporations are attempting to impose very specific spaces across existing cultural divisions. The discussion of Europe here, therefore, should be taken as an example of just one region in the world where transnational practices initiated by major entertainment corporations are generating a number of tensions and reactions among individuals and groups in particular local and regional contexts.

The recording industry and the (re)construction of Europe

Since the 1950s the U.S. has been the most important source of both revenue and repertoire for the recording industry. However, in 1988 the income generated from the sales of recorded music (vinyl LP's, tapes and CDs) in the EC taken as a whole (31 per cent) crept above those of North America (30 per cent) for the first time. Two years later retail sales in the EC had climbed to 35 per cent while those of the U.S. remained at 31 per cent of the world total (IFPI, 1989, 1991). [. . .]

Some commentators have viewed such figures as an indication of a significant shift in the relative importance of the U.S. within the world recording industry, an opinion which has been given added weight by the moves towards greater European integration and by the emergence of potential new markets in Eastern Europe. [. . .]

There is no doubt that Europe, as both a market and cultural space, is becoming increasingly important to the recording industry. Already various satellite operators – most notably MTV – are attempting to construct a distinctive pan-European identity as part of their broadcasting policies. MTV's aims are avowedly global,[2] and they have moved across the Atlantic in recognition that this continent provides greater opportunities than are currently available in the U.S. Managing Director Bill Roedy explained that North America has a proliferation of channels, whereas in Europe the company has 'the opportunity to fill a much bigger entertainment void' (Davis, 1991, p. 27). In making this move, MTV has introduced a broadcasting system based on its tried and tested formula of seeking large audiences by transmitting the sounds and visions of the major superstars. But at the same time, Roedy has evangelically emphasized: 'Our mission is not to make music homogeneous but to take advantage of local music. We expose music to audiences who would not previously have been able to see it, so audiences in Greece, for example, can see French music' (Davis, 1991, p. 27).

Like MTV, a number of major record companies have publicly espoused an approach to Europe which promotes the culture-crossing music and images of the global superstars, but maintains an interest in local particularities. Rudi Gassner, the President of BMG Music International, outlined his company's policy as an attempt to 'regionalise local repertoire and, in some cases, to globalise local repertoire' (Dalton, 1992, p. 15): the economics of recouping investment and generating further capital in the music industry demand that the appeal of the local is widened to include surrounding regions, and if possible 'crossed-over' to achieve global status. At the same time, however,

Gassner has referred to the diversity of cultural traditions throughout Europe and spoken of the company's 'cultural obligations' to sign artists in specific territories where the cost of recording, manufacturing and marketing their music exceeds the revenue that can be derived from local sales (White and Dalton, 1989). Gassner is not, of course, being philanthropic. As a senior executive of a multimedia enterprise that has itself developed from a European base, he is recognizing the very specific conditions within which the global strategies of his corporation are being implemented; acknowledging the need to support the local in its purely specific context, where pressures come from musicians, audiences and various workers within the industry, who all want some kind of local recognition or representation. However, Gassner's approach, like that being put forward by a number of recording industry executives, is based on a perception of the increasingly fluid boundaries within Europe and the potential for selling music across these formal barriers.

Uneven global change

Many staff within the recording industry are sceptical about the claims being made on behalf of Europe. There is a belief that the language and cultural differences, coupled with the different media and promotion systems that are currently in place, will continue to mark out very distinct boundaries for the foreseeable future. Processes of globalization are clearly operating unevenly in the recording industry, and it is important to make a distinction between:

- The construction of Europe as an identifiable market, involving the integration and harmonization of retail practices, prices, trade agreements, distribution systems and copyright law. This process is proceeding quite rapidly. And:
- The emergence of Europe as a distinctive cultural region and undivided repertoire source. Such an identity is occurring somewhat clumsily across the existing national boundaries which historically have informed how the recording industry has been organized. Here the dominance of Britain and the U.S. is likely to continue for some time, as it has become deeply embedded in the relations between record companies and label divisions throughout the world, and is decisively informing the way in which pan-European policies are being introduced, as I highlight below.

Existing tensions within the corporations

When promoting artists abroad, record company staff who are based in the U.K. have developed and employed a system that has become common around the globe. This has involved staff based in record company offices in London contacting personnel working in nationally based label subdivisions, or at licensed companies around the world, with the aim of persuading them to release the recordings of a British artist. Having achieved this, the personnel in Britain then assist local staff by supplying information and providing any material required for promotion. At the same time, representatives from these sister companies have been trying to negotiate the release of their own artists' products in Britain. This practice has become well established, but it does not involve an equal exchange of acts. One director at a British label who had been in the industry for over 15 years explained that:

> It's a real imbalance, and it causes a certain amount of frustration. Particularly with the French. I think the Germans are much more pragmatic about it. The Scandinavians are probably more like the French. They've all got some local acts that they've done very well with. And, they all want us to release stuff here – because it's very important for all those guys to have hits in the UK.[3]

France is exceptional in Europe as it is one of the few countries, along with Italy, to have consistently sustained a recorded music market which has regularly included a high percentage of domestic repertoire, rather than one being based predominantly on Anglo-American recordings (Shore, 1983; Hung and Morencos, 1990).[4] The German Federal Republic, prior to the unification of Germany, was a more typical example of how the national record markets of Europe have developed over the last 30 years. Recent figures showed that British artists accounted for 33–40 per cent of the sales of all recordings in Germany between 1985 and 1988 (BPI, 1988, 1989), with acts from the U.S.A. taking a further third (Hennessey, 1991).

This dominance of 'imported' styles and fashions, which gained momentum throughout continental Europe during the rock era, has been reinforced by the way in which the British sales charts have set the programming agendas at radio stations and influenced the acquisition policies of record labels across the continent for a number of years (Wallis and Malm, 1984). Because of this the U.K. has been of strategic importance as a point of entry into Europe for North American artists, and further pressure is exerted as companies based in the U.S. seek British success as an integral part of their global marketing strategies.

The dominance of Anglo-American repertoire around the world, and the adoption of business practices and promotional techniques derived from models developed in the U.K. and U.S., has provided a series of opportunities for successful British and North American artists to generate additional income through retail sales, performances and copyright revenue. At the same time, it has severely restricted the opportunities for local artists.

The frustrations among staff in different European countries, detected by the British director quoted above, have long been a source of tension across the continent. [. . .] Similar concerns have been voiced about MTV's programming policies and business practices in Europe. Despite MTV's pan-European public stance, Helmut Fest, EMI's Regional Managing Director for Germany, Austria and Switzerland has complained that continental repertoire accounts for only five per cent of MTV's European transmissions. [. . .]

From the perspective of Anglo-American record industry personnel there seem to be two main reasons why they remain unconvinced that artists from countries other than the U.K. or U.S.A. have much to offer. One of these is based on a critical, and occasionally sneering, aesthetic judgement which perceives many countries to be 'behind' the 'trendsetting', 'superior' and more 'authentic' sounds coming out of the U.S.A. and U.K. The other reason is simply an uncritical acceptance of established traditions and working practices as *the* way of doing things. [. . .] Despite the fact that continental acts have occasionally achieved success when promoted in Britain, staff in the U.K. tend to be more comfortable when dealing with genres and artistic conventions they are familiar with.[. . .] Continental acts are considered an unpredictable proposition, and there is only a sporadic tradition of working with them. Hence, it is presumed that the market in the U.K. will not sustain acts from continental Europe.

However, when attempting to persuade sister companies, licensees and labels to release material in other territories, it is tactically advantageous for staff in Britain to agree to release a number of recordings from other regions rather than to block every release. In order to get a recording by an Anglo-American act released abroad (particularly if it is by a relatively unknown artist), the British staff will agree to accept recordings from another country in return. These are then released simply to maintain relations with staff in another territory; no effort is expended on their marketing or promotion. Recordings are merely scheduled as 'courtesy' releases. The failure of continental acts in Britain then becomes a self-fulfilling prophecy.

Inevitably, staff in different regions start asking questions and want to know what is happening to their recordings. Soon they become aware that little effort is being expended on their artists. So they reciprocate by accepting the recordings of British artists and put little energy into their promotion or marketing. For established artists this is often not a problem, but for the newer acts who rely on a building process involving press coverage, radio promotion, advertising and strategic marketing, this can severely hamper their prospects.

This reciprocal exchange of acts and the resulting mutual torpor reigns not only between labels in Britain and other nations in continental Europe, it also affects each territory throughout the world to a greater or lesser degree. Over the years, a vast number of recordings have been released by record labels in different countries purely in order to get their own material distributed in another territory. [. . .]

Pan-European restructuring and global ordering

As the costs of recording, manufacturing and marketing popular music have increased, and various acquisitions and licensing agreements have drawn numerous production companies and minor record labels into the webs of a global entertainment industry, the major corporations have started to restructure in order to acquire artists in a less arbitrary manner. Companies have begun setting priorities for regions, rather than allowing them to arise as a consequence of the cacophony of independent decision-making in each territory.

One way they have done this is by curtailing local acquisition activity and concentrating resources in each region on the marketing and promotion of Anglo-American recordings. In many countries the balance of power within the offices of the major record companies has been firmly structured through investment, policy decisions and by the appointment of particular senior executives to favour the promotion of 'international' acts, rather than the acquisition and development of local artists. [. . .] It goes without saying that these policies restrict the potential for local artists even further; their recordings are not even available for mutual exchange with their counterparts in Britain and the U.S.A.

In conjunction with this policy and as part of a strategy of dividing the world into a series of global blocs, the major record companies have been setting up pan-European repertoire divisions which will operate across national boundaries. The aim is to focus the decision-making and invest- ment in a single division which is responsible for acquiring artists across the continent. For example, in July 1991 Sony Music announced the formation of a new label called Sony Music Soho Square which was to operate as the 'first ever pan-European repertoire source'.[5] Not only is the title of this label decidedly English, being named after the company's base in London, the brief of this 'pan-European' operation is restricted to signing only English- speaking artists in Europe. Such policies immediately impede the prospects for local performers who do not sing in English, and reinforces the assumption that English is the lingua franca of pop.[6] Although Muff Winwood, the Director of Sony's new label, proudly announced that he had scouts in Germany, Scandinavia, France and Belgium in search of acts, this pan-European operation is firmly centred in London. Winwood explained that when artists were found he intended 'to bring them over to the U.K. and develop them from there'.[7]

Warner Music International has developed a very similar system and introduced the Magnet label to operate much like Sony Music Soho Square. Prior to the formation of this label, Kick van Hengel, who was the Vice- President of International Marketing and Artist Development, elaborated the company's policy by explaining: 'The German and French speaking markets are large enough to support local acts. But when the advances are over a certain amount they have to be cleared in London' (Laing, 1989, p. 15).[8] Record company divisions in Germany and France are allowed to operate with a degree of local autonomy in instances when they are able to sign and sustain artists based on national sales alone. However, what van Hengel referred to as the 'smaller countries' do not have the same market potential and are not accorded this autonomy. As he added when describing the 'artist development' side of his work across Europe: 'We're talking to a band in Norway right now and if we sign them they will be placed with our Norwegian company' (Laing, 1989, p. 15). Here the international executive – who spends most of the marketing part of his job in New York, and ensures that key artist development decisions across the continent are cleared by London – can survey what is going on across continental Europe and then sign up an act and 'place' them with the company's local office, who have little say in the acquisition.

In a similar way, the 'practical resources' of BMG's International Marketing in Europe are co-ordinated from Britain. In 1989 Chris Stone was running the operation from London. As Heinz Henn, BMG Senior Vice-President of Marketing, explained:

> On a practical level, if the American company were to get a call from Spain, it may not even take the call. But if it's Chris calling from London, they know it's important and are more likely to take notice. (Dalton, 1989, p. 7)

So the Spanish executive who wants to place his or her artist in the U.S. – a country with a large Spanish-speaking population – is required to mediate through London merely to gain access to companies and label divisions in North America.

These examples give some indication of the way in which the major companies have been rationalizing their repertoire operations in order to set agendas and priorities across existing national divisions, and to co-ordinate the placement of local acts on a regional and global scale.

Hence a system is being established whereby the key decisions about acquiring and marketing local acts across continental Europe have to be negotiated through the priorities and prejudices of executives in London and then New York, with only a degree of regional autonomy accorded to the larger local markets in Germany and France. Such a strategy clearly overcomes the internal conflict and mutual passivity which is endemic when the recordings of a number of locally signed acts are exchanged between national labels and company subdivisions. But it reinforces the dominance of Anglo-American and English-speaking pop, re-emphasizing the importance of London and New York, thereby further restricting the opportunities for local artists who might wish to break into global markets.[9]

One implication of such policies is that performers and musicians who wish to establish themselves internationally (or even those who simply wish to communicate with audiences beyond their immediate locality), will come under increasing pressure to migrate to these centres. [. . .]

Local responses

So far I have described how tensions occur between staff in the national divisions of record companies over the unequal exchange of musical products, and the way in which the recordings which *are* exchanged have been deprioritized when judged by Anglo-Americans. The resulting conflicts have been partially overcome by corporations forming pan-European and global operating divisions and hence setting priorities *across* different regions. I now want to conclude by briefly highlighting three analytically distinct, but practically interconnected, local responses to this process; responses indicating that a complex series of state/civil society/market relationships intervene between the global strategies of the corporations and their local realization in particular regions.

The first response involves national governments supporting their music industry in an international context. An example here is the work of the French Music Office in the U.S. which was launched in November 1990. The office is a non-profit-making body funded by French music industry organizations and the French Ministry of Culture. It was set up to promote all types of French music in the U.S.A., and to support artists by providing information, offering assistance with touring and advice about the complex visa and immigration laws. The general aim is to enable French music to establish a presence and help individual French acts build a reputation in North America. One particular objective is to obtain recording contracts directly with U.S.A. labels by creating a demand locally rather than by relying on a series of transatlantic mediations (often via London). However, artists with material already released have an advantage. As Christian Dalbavie, Director of the Office explained:

> I'm not supposed to give any artistic criticism on the project; whatever the project's musical grounds are it doesn't matter. If they want to come to the United States and tour I can't stop them. I do recommend to an artist not to tour if an album is not out . . . There's more motivation for a promoter to work when he knows there's a record which is in the store. (Felder, 1991, p. 21)

Hence, despite the attempts to promote all types of French music and although Dalbavie is concerned not to make artistic judgements, the work of the French Music Office is being conducted according to the dominant commercial criteria of the recording industry, where 'the market is the principle force shaping production and distribution . . . irrespective of the specific qualities of each individual musical piece' (Rutten, 1991, p. 295/6). As Dalbavie has remarked, 'We work the American market like any other company – the only thing is that we work with French catalogue' (Felder, 1991, p. 21).

Like the French Music Office, the government-funded Danish Rock Council (Rosa) gives assistance to artists who are attempting to attract the attention of the transnational record companies, and was instrumental in helping Miss B. Haven obtain a recording contract with Warner Music International. A co-council composed of an alliance of different organizations and interests, Rosa's main operations are conducted locally in Denmark which is an indication of a second response: state support for the local rather than the national. Rosa promotes and sponsors live events and tours, provides finance to assist record production and is explicitly concerned with supporting sounds that are of no interest to the major corporations.

Governments in the Netherlands and Scandinavia have been supporting local popular music in various ways since the 1970s, in a concerted effort to provide an alternative to the Anglo-American sounds of global pop. Many of these state initiatives have grown out of community-based activities and 'grassroots' musical movements (the third response I am identifying here). In 1975 the Stichting Popmuziek Nederland (The Netherlands Pop Music Foundation) was established as a pressure group explicitly opposed to 'commercialized pop.' Through concerted lobbying, the foundation eventually obtained grants from the Dutch Ministry of Culture in order to establish a series of community practice rooms, information centres and workshops, and to give financial support to live music in smaller venues which would otherwise be unable to put on performances (van Elderen, 1985). In a similar way the Contact Network for Non-Commercial Music (Kontaktnätet) was established in Sweden during 1974 in order to support a number of local 'music clubs' (Fornäs, 1992). As a result of pressure from this 'music movement' the Swedish government began attempting to balance the major corporations' 'unrestrained pursuit of profit' by providing finance for 'collective' and non-market-oriented forms of music making (Malm, 1982).

In recent years, urban councils in Britain have been taking tentative steps towards developing local music policies. Like those referred to above, these have been for economic and commercial reasons: to assist urban regeneration, to promote a city as a tourist attraction, and to generate revenue from signing and marketing local artists. And, also for social and community reasons: to provide jobs, to give musicians access to equipment and facilities and to support music that will 'benefit the local community' and maintain indigenous musical traditions that are not catered for elsewhere (Cohen, 1991).

Hence, a series of commercial market/nation-state/civil society relationships and associated activities can actively intervene and interrupt the global goals of the corporations, and shape the way in which the 'global' is actively translated and transformed into and by the local.

Conclusion: local traces in global spaces

In this article I have described some of the ways in which corporate dreams of world domination are being translated into specific regional repertoire policies and creating a number of local tensions in the process. I have argued that the current global strategies of the music corporations are firmly oriented towards gaining the maximum revenue from the sounds and images of Anglo-American artists and musical styles, and based on working practices concentrated in and co-ordinated from the U.S. and Britain. I am not, however, suggesting that this influence can be explained by reference to the 'cultural imperialism' thesis. There are two main reasons for this.

Firstly, this argument too easily portrays the Anglo-American as a homogeneous sound. Anglo-American pop contains many divisions – from thrash metal through acoustic folk ballads to slickly crafted love songs. This category also contains a significant African-American dimension. It is worth noting that the influential hip-hop and rapping styles of the 1980s emerged as a result of a complex meeting and synthesis of elements from European electro-pop, African-American rhythm and blues and Caribbean sound system toasting. There is not, therefore, simply one undifferentiated North American (or Anglo-American) musical culture that dominates the world (although further research might reveal the extent to which certain artists and genres are more dominant than others).

Secondly, the cultural imperialism model tends to propose a straightforward correspondence between a culture and the territory associated with it (Laing, 1986). In an era of 'polycentric corporations' (Robins, 1991), owned and financed through an alliance of Japanese, European and North American interests (Robinson *et al.*, 1991), it becomes increasingly difficult to locate the 'source' of this culture, other than as an abstract Anglo-American cultural space floating over the triadic manufacturing and communication grids of European, Japanese and U.S.A. capital. [. . .]

Having noted these points, however, the musical information currently 'feeding the world' *is* that of Anglo-American North Atlantic pop – euphemistically called 'international repertoire' by staff working in the recording industry. This is the 'dominant particular' (Hall, 1991) against which other sounds are assessed and around which the world production and consumption of music is currently organized.

However, this dominant particular has provoked a number of reactions. Tensions over musical production and cultural identity (often theorized in the past by reference to an antagonistic dynamic between major and

independent companies) are becoming increasingly focused around conflicts between the national and international. There are indications of an
increasing shift among the producers and consumers of popular music
throughout continental Europe; a movement away from the Anglo-American
towards local repertoire. This has been particularly noticeable in the recorded
music markets of France, Germany, Belgium and Italy. Recognizing that local
artists may 'lose out' within the context of pan-European policies,
recording industry staff are beginning to make greater efforts to support
their own national artists, reacting against and attempting to redefine the
global priorities of their parent corporations (Pride, 1992). An explicit
challenge to the hegemonizing practices of the corporations has been posed
by the formation of the European Music Network – an alliance of music
industry personnel and organizations from France, Germany, Ireland,
Belgium, the Netherlands and Denmark brought together under the
chairmanship of Mikael Hoejris (of the Danish Rock Council). The aim of
this self-supporting network is to assist artists who would not otherwise
have the opportunity to gain exposure in other countries (Clark-Meads, 1992).
Further south, a complex history of colonialism and migration links Spain
to the Hispanic populations of Latin America and the U.S. Spanish music
business organizations have begun formally organizing to take account of
this. As a consequence, major acts such as Mecano and Julio Iglesias have
achieved considerable success in such areas, while remaining more or less
invisible to many audiences in Northern Europe.

In addition to these tensions and reactions 'within' the record industry,
a local counterpoint has started filling out the gaps and cultural spaces
vacated by the major corporations as they pursue narrow repertoire policies
and global priorities. A number of community-generated and state-supported
musical practices are emerging and being actively encouraged, explicitly
defined through their connection with local experiences. As Cohen
concluded from her research in Britain: 'In this age of global mobility,
opportunity, expanding markets, and European integration, cultural
producers are still defining themselves and their social space in terms of
their particular localities' (Cohen, 1991, p. 345). However, just as we should
be wary of caricaturing the global sounds of 'international pop' as a
homogenized mass culture, we should also be careful about extolling the
virtues of local music. The predicament of local music is more ambiguous.
Support for 'local culture' often sits uneasily alongside the resurgence of
petty nationalism and ethnic absolutism that has been occurring in many
European regions in recent years.

Within this context there is a further division emerging at the point where
the global meets the local. Two strands of local music making can be detected,
themselves part of a wider set of social and cultural tensions. One involves
dynamic and changing forms of musical practice which engage with and
explore eclectic, syncretic forms of acculturated expression brought about
by the meeting of various musical techniques, technologies and traditions.
The other is characterized by stasis and a retreat into nostalgia and restoration,
with attempts to narrowly define local music as an authentic expression of
lived folk culture, or to preserve the imagined purity of the past by
constructing idealized 'heritage' cultures. If either of these cultural

practices has the potential to participate in the reconstruction of Europe as a 'new mythical space' – a space within which many voices speak in a constant dialogue with the surrounding world – it is surely the former rather than the latter.

Notes

1. Current estimates suggest that six major recorded music/entertainment groups account for about 80–85 per cent of the music that is legally produced, manufactured and distributed in the world; EMI (Thorn-EMI), Sony Music (Sony), Polygram (Philips), Warner Music (Time Warner), BMG (Bertelsmann) and MCA (Matshushita). For further details see Burnett (1990, 1992), Laing (1992) and Negus (1992).
2. Music Television (MTV), a round-the-clock service of pop music, was launched through the cable television network in the United States on 1 August 1981 and rapidly expanded its operations in North America during the 1980s. In August 1987 MTV began broadcasting in Western Europe, and moved into Eastern Europe by setting up a service in Hungary during March 1989. Through its company Viscom, MTV has established networks in Japan, Latin America and Australia, and in August 1991, on its tenth anniversary, MTV claimed to be broadcasting in 41 countries and reaching 204 million homes (*Billboard*, 31 August 1991, p. 28).
3. Personal interview May 1989.
4. During 1988 and 1989 the publication *Europe Etc* (*Music Week*) ran a series of market profiles on different countries. Local repertoire was reported as highest in France – 44 per cent (January 1989) and Finland – 45 per cent (November 1989). Foreign, predominantly Anglo-American, repertoire is highest in Belgium – 95 per cent (July 1989), Portugal – 85 per cent (October 1989), the Netherlands – 74 per cent (February 1989) and Norway – 74 per cent (September 1989). Domestic repertoire figures reported for Italy (in various sources) were inconsistent, oscillating from anything between 30 and 51 per cent; Laing (1992) puts the figure at 46 per cent. There are indications that the percentage of airplay time devoted to locally produced repertoire on radio stations across Europe is even smaller than the sales figures (Teller, 1990). In February 1992 it was reported that approximately 70 per cent of music publishing revenues in Europe were currently derived from material created by Anglo-American artists (*Music Week*, 1 February 1992, p. 23). Thus, various indicators point to similar trends.
5. *Music Week* (27 July 1991: 1).
6. This raises a very interesting point about the nature and influence of 'global English' that is beyond the scope of this article: Stuart Hall (1991) has pointed out that English is the language of 'global mass culture', but stresses that this is not exactly the 'Queen's English' but it is 'English as an international language which is quite a different thing'. It is 'English as it has been invaded, and as it has hegemonized a variety of other languages without being able to exclude them from it. It speaks Anglo-Japanese, Anglo-French, Anglo-German . . . It is a new form of international language, not quite the same old class-stratified, class-dominated, canonically-secured form of standard or traditional highbrow English' (Hall, 1991, p. 28).
7. 'A & R World is Forced to Broaden Horizons' (*Music Business International*, 1992, Vol. 2, No. 1, p. 22.
8. In 1990 Germany was, along with the U.K., the third largest market for recorded music in the world (behind the U.S.A. and Japan) and accounted for nine per cent of the total world retail sales revenue derived from recordings (the same as the U.K.), France was just behind at seven per cent.

9. It is perhaps too early to tell whether the recent acquisitions of record companies (Sony, MCA) by Japanese hardware manufacturers is adding a further dimension to this and shifting certain key decisions to Tokyo.

References

BPI (1988) *Annual Report*, British Phonographic Industry Ltd, London.

BPI (1989) *Annual Report*, British Phonographic Industry Ltd, London.

Burnett, R. (1990) Concentration and Diversity in the International Phonogram Industry, University of Gothenburg.

Burnett, R. (1992) Dressed for Success: Sweden from Abba to Roxette. *Popular Music*, Vol. 11, No. 2, pp. 141–50.

Clark-Meads, J. (1992) 6 Euro Firms Band to Expose Talent. *Billboard*, 8 February, p. 33.

Cohen, S. (1991) Popular Music and Urban Regeneration: The Music Industries of Merseyside. *Cultural Studies*, October, pp. 332–46.

Dalton, D. (1989) BMG Pieces Mecano into Language Puzzle. *Europe Etc* (Music Week Publication), October, pp. 6–7.

Dalton, D. (1992) 1992: How The Giants Line up in the Sales Battle, *Music Business International*, Vol. 2, No. 1, pp. 15–19.

Davis, S. (1991) Uniting Europe with a Sight and Sound Assault. *Music business International*, August, pp. 26–7.

Felder, R. (1991) France Looks to Conquer the US. *Music Business International*, May, pp. 20–1.

Fornäs, J. (1992) Play it Yourself, Swedish Music in Movement. Working Paper, Department of Journalism, Media and Communication (JMK), Stockholm University.

Hall, S. (1991) Old and New Identities, Old and New Ethnicities. In A. King (ed.), *Culture, Globalization and the World System*, Macmillan, London.

Hennessey, M. (1991) International Spotlight; Germany, Austria and Switzerland. *Billboard*, 29 June.

Hung, M. and Morencos, E. (1990) World Record Sales 1969–1990. International Federation of the Phonographic Industry, London.

IFPI (1989) World Sales of Recordings 1988 and World Sales Trends 1981–1988, International Federation of the Phonographic Industry, Press Information, 5 December.

IFPI (1991) World Sales 1990, International Federation of the Phonographic Industry, Press Information, 1 October.

Laing, D. (1986) The Music Industry and the 'Cultural Imperialism'. Thesis. *Media, Culture and Society*, Vol. 8, pp. 331–41.

Laing, D. (1989) Moving Away From US Influence. *Europe Etc* (Music Week Publication), January, pp. 14–15.

Laing, D. (1992) 'Sadeness', Scorpions and Single Markets: National and Transnational Trends in European Popular Music. *Popular Music*, Vol. 11, No. 2, pp. 127–39.

Levitt, T. (1983) The Globalization of Markets. *Harvard Business Review*, May–June, pp. 92–102.

Malm, K. (1982) Phonograms and Cultural Policy in Sweden. In K. Blaukopf (ed.) *The Phonogram in Cultural Communication*, Springer-Verlag, Vienna.

Negus, K. (1992) *Producing Pop: Culture and Conflict in the Popular Music Industry*, Edward Arnold, London.

Pride, D. (1992) Markets Face Shocks in Brave New Europe. *Music Business International*, Vol. 2, No. 1, p. 21.

Robins, K. (1991) Tradition and Translation: National Culture in its Global Context. In J. Corner and S. Harvey (eds.) *Enterprise and Heritage*, Routledge, London.

Robinson, D., Buck, E. and Cuthbert, M. (1991) *Music at the Margins. Popular Music and Global Cultural Diversity*, Sage, London.

Rutten, P. (1991) Local Popular Music on the National and International Markets. *Cultural Studies*, Vol. 5, No. 3, pp. 294–305.

Shore, L. (1983) The Crossroads of Business and Music, PhD Thesis, Stanford University, CA.

Sklair, L. (1991) *Sociology of the Global System*, Harvester Wheatsheaf, Brighton.

Teller, A. (1990) European Radio Can Avoid US Mistakes. *Billboard*, 23 June, p. 11.

Van Elderen, P. (1985) Pop and Government Policy in the Netherlands. In Frith, S. (ed.) *World Music, Politics and Social Change*, Manchester University Press, Manchester.

Wallis, R. and Malm, K. (1984) *Big Sounds From Small Peoples*, Constable, London.

White, A. and Dalton, D. (1989) Running the World. *Europe Etc* (Music Week Publication), March, pp. 13–15.

24

Distinguishing the global, regional and national levels of world television

Joseph D. Straubhaar

Department of Communications, Brigham Young University, Utah, U.S.A. (1996).

From cultural imperialism to globalization

One of the enduring problems in international communication has been how to theorize and explain the international flow and impact of television across cultures. Unequal television (Nordenstreng and Varis, 1974) and news flows (Boyd-Barrett, 1980) were two of the most crucial issues driving the New World Information and Communication Order discussions in the 1970s, in which developing countries criticized the inequities of the existing world order in media (McPhail, 1989; Nordenstreng and Schiller, 1979).

Critical scholars in the 1960s–1980s often analysed problems of unequal television flows and structural inequalities of television production in the world in terms of media imperialism (Lee, 1980), transnationalization (Roncagliolo, 1985, 1986) and dependency (Fox, 1992), but more recently these approaches have fallen under critique as overly simplistic. In seeing the major industrialized countries as dominant and Third World countries as dependent, these theories have missed much of the complexity of change in industries, genres and audience reception in the Third World or periphery.

The current discussion tends to focus on the globalization of cultures within a world economy (Featherstone, 1990; Wallerstein, 1991). The globalization approach in general posits that the world is becoming a single world society, 'more uniform and standardized, through a technological, commercial and cultural synchronization emanating from the West, and that globalization is tied up with modernity' (Pieterse, 1995, p. 45). There is a great deal of discussion about the globalization of television, particularly as it is being driven by the spread of satellite and cable television technologies around the world. There is a fear of a renewed cycle of one way television flows out from the United States, adding complete U.S. television channels, such as CNN, MTV, Nickelodeon and the Cartoon Channel to the already large export of U.S. film, television programs and music.

The discussion on globalization focuses less on dominant and dependent nation-states, more on globalized cultural actors, corporations and governments, as well as globalized audiences. This approach does build on the older idea of transnationalization (Lins da Silva, 1986; Roncagliolo, 1986) in its focus on multi- or transnational corporations who act increasingly globally, but diminishes the focus on the relative dependency of the peripheral nation states. In our view, this view of globalization diminishes too much the continuing importance of national identity among communication audiences in selecting and interpreting cultural products and messages. In much of the world, such as Eastern Europe or the Middle East, we currently see a rise of ethnic nationalism that reflects a search for identity and seems to extend to cultural consumption. The globalization discussion may also overlook the rise of a new level of television flow and impact, that within regions of the world.

Globalization and regionalization

This chapter argues that although some level of globalization is taking place, it often tends to be overstated. Ferguson's excellent discussion of the myths of globalization raises several key problems: the idea that the world is becoming one homogeneous culture, largely fed by the U.S. culture industries; that big cultural industries, like those of the U.S., have an automatic advantage due to economies of scale and the polish of their products; and that differences of time, space and geography are eroded by technology (1992). This chapter will critique the ideas of globalization as the worldwide homogenization of television, the erosion of national and cultural differences, and domination of all by U.S. productions.

We propose that, in terms of media and media flows, a more significant phenomenon than this idea of globalization, *per se*, may well be the 'regionalization' of television into multi-country markets linked by geography, language and culture. These might more accurately be called the geo-cultural markets, rather than regional markets, since not all these linked populations, markets and cultures are geographically contiguous.

For example, the U.S. is clearly the main media exporter in the world. However, the 'global' flow of television outward from the U.S. is probably strongest among the Anglophone nations of the world, such as the U.K., Anglophone Canada, Australia, and the English-speaking Caribbean, where U.S. television exports tend to be most popular, and best understood (Straubhaar *et al.*, 1992). These are also among the few countries which manage to export television, film or music back to the Anglophone U.S. market.

There are a number of other geo-cultural markets emerging: Western Europe, where the European Community has been trying to create a region-wide cultural market; Latin America, linked also to other 'Latin'-based language markets in Italy and France: a Francophone market linking France and its former colonies: an Arabic world market; a Chinese market: and a Hindi or South Asian market.

Multi-level approach

This chapter will focus on the importance of regional or geo-linguistic cultures (and television markets). However, this focus on regions needs to be placed within a context that includes several levels of television flow and impact. There is a level that is truly global, one that is regional or geo-linguistic, one that is national, and others that are sub-national or 'regional' (within the nation), and even local. In fact, the most current theorizations of globalization recognize that 'what globalization means in structural terms, then, is the *increase in the available modes of organization*: transnational, international, macro-regional, national, micro-regional, municipal, local.' (Pieterse, 1995, p. 50, emphases in original). [. . .] While the main argument of this chapter is that the role of geo-cultural regions need to be emphasized more, that can be fitted into the more sophisticated interpretations of globalization that are emerging, such as Pieterse (1995).

The global level of analysis is increasingly crucial. There are several kinds of globalization relevant to television. Some of the new cable and satellite channels, such as CNN or the Cartoon Channel, take the same content to world-wide audiences, although some 'global' channels are creating regionally or locally adapted versions. Some television programs, such as 'Dallas' or 'Baywatch' still are syndicated to flow globally to be broadcast nationally or locally. Quite a few national and local productions derive from formats or genres that have spread globally beyond their places of origin. Even more basically, the models for broadcasting are being spread globally as private, commercial, entertainment-oriented stations and networks continue to spread into more nations. [. . .]

While globalization increasingly dominates current discussion of television flows and impacts, Tomlinson (1991, pp. 23–24) observes that most of the media imperialism and cultural imperialism discussion assumes that the primary actors are nations. Many of the studies done on media flows, media models, etc. are national case studies. [. . .]

However, the view of the nation as a cultural unit is changing. Very few nations are ethnically homogeneous, Portugal, Greece, Iceland, Norway, Malta and, perhaps, Germany and Japan. Most have fairly large minorities (Smith, 1981). If language is a primary characteristic of culture, then most nations are multilingual and not homogeneous nation-states (Schlesinger, 1987). This opens up a large area of interest in media, including television in many areas, which address media audiences of smaller than national scope. Many local audiences would like to see programming in their own languages, addressing their own cultures. If this local audience shares a language, like the Chinese minority in Malaysia, with a larger geo-linguistic group, then they might import programming in their language and culture, as did the Malaysian Chinese, first with VCRs, then DBS, particularly Star TV (Chan, 1994; McDaniel, 1994).

In many countries, broadcast television had been seen as too expensive to direct toward groups smaller than nations. Even countries like Brazil, a large middle income country with an extensive commercialized television system, have only recently begun to address television programs toward regional and local audiences. However, in many countries, including Brazil again, local use of alternative video, outside broadcast television, has been growing, as have local television news, local educational stations and local religious stations.

Modernity

In much recent work on globalization, there has been a tendency to try to more fully consider both temporal and spatial aspects of international change (Giddens, 1991), including culture and media (Friedman, 1994). Several theorists, including Giddens (1991), Friedman (1994) and Robertson (1995) have raised the need to consider modernity as a crucial aspect of globalization. [. . .]

Globalization can be seen as both spatial, the outward geographic spread of ideas and forms, particularly those related to capitalism, and temporal, changes over time within many locales. 'One way to attempt to simplify the level of complexity which the intensification of global flows is introducing in the figuration of competing nation-states and blocs, is to regard globalization as an outcome of the universal logic of modernity.' (Featherstone, 1995, p. 2) [. . .]

Current academic debates are reviving modernity as a key concept. Tomlinson (1991) argues that much of what was labeled cultural imperialism is in fact a broader spread of a globalized pattern of modernity. This new discourse argues, in particular, that much of what was seen as Americanization or Westernization was a more general, deeper globalization of capitalism.

> We can make a distinction between two possible discourses of cultural imperialism as they have emerged . . . The first [. . .] is the familiar discourse of cultural imperialism as the attack on national/cultural identity, a discourse conducted around the binary opposition of 'us' and 'them' and on the 'synchronic-spatial' plane. It is the discourse of 'Americanization' and so on. [. . .]
>
> But underlying this is the broader discourse of cultural imperialism as *the spread of the culture of modernity itself*. This is a discourse of historical change, of 'development', of a global movement towards, among other things, an everyday life governed by the habitual routine of commodity capitalism. One reason for calling this discourse a broader one is that the 'imaginary' discourse of cultural identity only arises *within* the context of modernity. [. . .] (Tomlinson, 1991, pp. 89–90).

Global spread of market capitalism

For many writers from the neo-Marxist and dependency traditions, globalization is essentially the world-wide spread, over both time and space, of a world capitalist market or, in Wallerstein's formulation, a world capitalist system (1979). Economically, globalization is seen as the spread of capitalism as a system, of consumerism and commercialism as social ethics (often referred to as McDonaldization or CocaColanization), and of the growing penetration and power of international corporations. Culturally, it is still seen by many as Westernization, a variation on or updating of the idea of cultural imperialism and synchronization (Tomlinson, 1991). While economics are a basis issue, various critics of globalization see overly simplistic assumptions being made about the causality of economics, particularly the global spread of capitalism, in globalization and fear a new wave of economic reductionism which might oversimplify cultural phenomena (Boyne, 1990; Ferguson, 1992).

International processes produce national and local identities

In television and in other cultural industries as well, people use globally distributed forms to create cultural products which define and redefine what the national and the local are. Robertson observes that 'globalization has involved the reconstruction, in a sense the production, of "home", "community" and "locality" ' (1995, p. 30). Cultural producers use forms and genres that have spread globally to express ideas of what home is like. There is a subtle interplay between the global and local in television form and content.

For example, the soap opera has distinct roots in both English and French serial novels, which were carried over time in magazines and newspapers. U.S. radio and later television took this idea and developed a particular form of soap opera, to entertain and draw loyal audiences over time, but explicitly also to sell soap. In fact, for quite a long time, the shows were produced for radio and television networks by advertising agencies on behalf of soap manufacturers. Soap companies and advertising agencies took this successful genre abroad, particularly to Latin America. Latin American radio and television producers adapted the genre to their cultures and needs, moving it into prime time, aiming it at both men and women, changing the form of story telling, and using local motifs, characters, humour, etc.

In a sense, then, a global form is being localized, both for purposes of global capitalist development and for expression of local identity. The soap opera genre is still used to sell soap and, even more basically, to show local people an ethic or goal of consumption. For example, in one Brazilian soap opera in the late 1970s (Fernandes, 1982), a high point in the plot came when a man asked his wife if she would like a refrigerator and she burst into tears of joy. This consumption ethic is itself localized, with a refrigerator being an almost supreme ambition, compared to, say, an automobile. [. . .]

While such a local soap opera is delivering an adapted underlying global message about joining the lower ranks of an emerging global consumer economy, it is primarily carrying messages about the local culture. In fact, in Brazil and India, among others, the soap opera became a prime vehicle for creating elements of a 'national' culture and spreading them among localized and regionalized audiences that had not always shared a great deal of common culture between them despite being within common national boundaries (Fadul, 1993; Mitra, 1993). [. . .]

In this example, the local adaptation of an increasingly global form of television illustrates that '. . . the concept of globalization has involved the simultaneity of what are conventionally called the global and the local . . .' (Robertson, 1995, p. 30). In particular, we see a diffusion of some basic global forms related to the expansion of the world economy, but those globalized forms co-exist and even promote local adaptations and the expression of unique local content. With this kind of example, we can also see that globalization is not equal to global homogenization. While cultural forms, particularly those related to consumption within capitalist societies, diffuse globally, they tend to be adapted locally. In fact, global diffusion of certain elements of consumer culture may well be more effective when those consumer elements are cast in local terms and adapted to local economic realities.

There is also a process of active resistance to globalization in some places. The example of popular rejection of cultural Westernization, mobilized effectively by Islamic clerics in Iran, was one of the first clear signals that not all cultures were going to easily adapt Western cultural elements. Barber speaks of two opposing trends, a 'McWorld' of global homogenization versus the 'Jihad world' of localizing or particularizing 'Lebanonization' (1992). [. . .]

Film and television as global phenomena

In the current era of globalization, the audiovisual media loom very large. The presence of television now builds upon patterns laid down by film in the early part of the 20th Century.

The U.S. has dominated international film production and distribution since World War I. During both World War I (1914–1918) and World War II (1939–1945), a number of the other major world film producers, such as Italy, Germany, Japan, France and Great Britain, had their industries destroyed, or at least disrupted and cut off from world trade in films. Hollywood stepped in to occupy world film markets both times. [. . .]

Film has also become somewhat regionalized. Shohat and Stamm (1994) note:

> "Third World cinema', taken in broad sense, far from being a marginal appendage to First World cinema, actually produces most of the world's feature films. If one excludes made-for-TV films, India is the leading producer of fiction films in the world, releasing between 700 and 1,000 feature films a year. Asian countries, taken together, make over half of the annual world total.' (p. 29). [. . .]

However, Hollywood has had a substantial indirect impact by defining film genres, which other countries then used as a basis for creating their own productions.

American television built on this base of film production and distribution controlled by Hollywood. In the late 1950s, when the U.S. film studios also began to produce for television, these studios could use their existing channels of distribution to start selling television programs worldwide with the same economic and even cultural advantages that American films had enjoyed. That coincided with a need by many new television networks around the world to find something cheap to put on the air to fill up the hours of broadcast time (Tunstall, 1977).

Starting in the early 1960s, American films, sitcoms, action-adventures, and cartoons flooded into many other countries. Television production was expensive and new, and not many countries had the equipment, people or money to produce enough programming to meet their own needs (Katz and Wedell, 1976). A few countries decided to limit broadcast hours to what they could fill themselves, but most countries responded to audience demands for more television by importing (Tunstall, 1977).

A 1972 study for the U.N. Educational, Scientific and Cultural Organization found that over half of the countries studied imported over half of their television, mostly entertainment and mostly from the U.S. [. . .]

More recently, however, there is some debate and questioning about whether U.S. dominance is slipping in world television markets. American television programs are facing increased competition at a variety of levels: regional, national, and local. More countries are also competing to sell programs to others. Some, like Brazil and Hong Kong, compete world-wide (Marques de Melo, 1988).

What has happened to replace American programming in a number of countries is the local adaptation of the American commercial model and American television program formats (Oliveira, 1990). In the process of diffusion, the 'American' model has been generalized and adapted in a global model for commercial media. This fits the model of Robertson (1995) and others that a number of current transformations may be described as glocalization, the oftentimes deliberate adaptation of a foreign or global model to fit national circumstances. Robertson observes that Japan is in some ways the prototype for this approach and in fact developed the term 'glocalization.'

In some countries, the process of adaptation of global genres or formats is more formal. Some nations, particularly in Europe, have been legally licensing specific U.S. television program formats, like 'Wheel of Fortune,' since the local adaptation of even a specific format is more popular than the simple importation of the program. This is most true of genres and formats which are talk or language intensive, supporting the idea that languages form a natural barrier to the straightforward importation of programs. [. . .]

Global cable-satellite channels

While cable TV has been familiar to most Americans, Canadians and some Europeans for years, it is now expanding in many countries of the world. While direct satellite broadcasting (DBS) is still new to most Americans, however, Japanese and British audiences have had it available for several years, and DBS is also growing quickly in many other countries, frequently spanning borders of neighbouring countries.

By the 1990s, however, cable systems and private satellite TV channels to feed them were growing fast in Europe, Latin America and Asia. Some of the new cable and satellite channels constitute truly global channels in the strictest sense of being almost simultaneously available to a world-wide audience. This global layer of cable and satellite television is dominated by U.S. cable channels who have expanded into this new market. CNN, MTV, HBO, ESPN, TNT, Nickelodeon, the Cartoon Channel, Discovery, Disney and others began to sell their existing channels in these countries. However, this market is more limited than some optimistic early industry estimates originally predicted. While a few of the middle income countries, such as Taiwan, Argentina and Venezuela, have a relatively high penetration of pay TV (over 25 per cent of TV households), associated with cable and satellite TV (Katz and Liebes, 1984), other major potential markets, like Brazil, have fewer than one per cent of the television audience signed up for some foreign channel pay service (Katz and Liebes, 1984). Audiences are limited by income, since pay TV (or satellite or cable TV) often cost $25 a month or more. The potential audience is also limited by cultural capital, since few speak foreign languages or have extensive interest in international news, sports, documentaries, etc. To achieve greater popularity among local audiences, some channels have begun to translate and adapt their U.S. channels to the languages and cultures of regional audiences.

Regional media and cultures

A major trend of the last 20 years has been the 'regionalization' of television into multi-country markets linked by geography, language and culture. As stated earlier, these might more accurately be called the geo-cultural markets, rather than regional markets, since not all these linked populations, markets and cultures are geographically contiguous.

Efforts to define cultural markets, particularly for television, by geographic regions have met with very mixed success. There is the hope for some regions that old common cultural traditions will bind diverse nations into a common cultural region that would welcome common television programming. Huntington (1993) has hypothesized that there are a limited number of 'civilizations' based on underlying religious, language and cultural divisions. If his analysis extends to culture as represented on television, then we might expect to see the Chinese market broaden to a 'Confucian' cultural influence area market, the Arabic language market broaden to an Islamic market, and a Slavic-Orthodox market emerging out of the ex-USSR and Eastern Europe (Huntington, 1993). [. . .]

Geo-cultural markets are unified by language (even though different accents and dialects may divide countries somewhat). However, they go beyond language to include history, religion, ethnicity (in some cases), and culture in several senses: shared identity, gestures and non-verbal communication; what is considered funny or serious or even sacred; clothing styles; living patterns; climate influences and other relationships with the environment. Geo-cultural markets are often centred in a geographic region, hence the tendency to call them regional markets, but they have also been spread globally by colonization, slavery, and migration.

There are waves of creation of regional or geo-linguistic cultures and effects on local cultural identity from early recorded history (and before). Greek colonies spread Greek culture through the Mediterranean and Asian world during the Hellenistic era. The Roman empire spread its systems and influences even further into Northern Europe and the Mediterranean. Christianity spread via the empire in its latter stages. Chinese, Hindu and other Asian civilizations also spread both political systems, economic forms, and culture in early recorded history. Somewhat later, the spread of Islam reached from southern Europe to India and Southeast Asia. These empires had very strong impacts, often spreading religion and culture beyond the reach of any boundaries of conquest, as with the spread of Buddhism well beyond India into much of Asia or with the spread of Chinese customs through much of Asia. [. . .]

At about this point, we have the bases for the great civilizations that Huntington (1993) talked about. Although they exerted globalizing influences, these empires turned civilizations also form the basis for the major geo-linguistic and geo-cultural regions. Some of these regions are supranational, such as the widespread Chinese speaking population of the Pacific Rim. Others are subnational or regions within countries. For instance, Francophone Canada was created by French colonization (plus new waves of immigrants from Africa, Italy, Spain and Asia), while the Hispanic U.S. population results both from the original Spanish colonization and more recent migrations from Mexico and Latin America.

These cultural similarities and common histories come together to define cultural markets to which television responds. Populations defined by these kinds of characteristics tend to seek out cultural products, like television programs or music, which are most similar or proximate to them. [. . .]

The cultures reflected in these geo-cultural markets are not static, they reflect the adaptation of European languages and cultures to colonialized populations, as well as an ongoing cultural hybridization between multiple elements. For instance, for Mexico, Garcia Canclini (1990) discusses the ongoing hybridization of culture between several indigenous cultures, the Spanish heritage, other European cultures, the U.S. culture, the experience of migrant and immigrant workers in the U.S., and the influence within Mexico of the border and Hispanic American cultural blends. [. . .]

Regional television markets

[. . .] Major regional TV markets are developing in Spanish, Arabic, Chinese, Hindi, English and French. These are often called regional because they are focused around a world region tied together by common language, culture, religion, and a history of being colonized by the same country (usually Great Britain, France or Spain). Increasingly, though, these cultural markets extend beyond neighbouring countries to follow populations that have migrated throughout a larger region or even the world. For instance, the Chinese audience is centred on China and nations near it (Hong Kong, Singapore and Taiwan) but extends slightly further away to Chinese populations mixed in with others (Singapore, Malaysia) and further to Chinese speakers around the world. Such world spanning populations are not so much 'regional' as they are defined by language and culture. They are reached and united through a variety of new technologies: video, satellite television, and cable TV.

It seems that languages and cultural differences (particularly cultural cues about what is funny, what is politically correct, what is outrageous or sacrilegious) are both uniting and dividing world television audiences. For instance, the attempt to produce programming for a Europe-wide television market, promoted hard by the European Economic Community, is proving very difficult because Europeans are divided by language and culture (Schlesinger, 1994). French audiences prefer not to listen in either German or English, and vice versa. [. . .]

On the other hand, language and cultural cues, where they are shared across borders, can help build cross-national markets. For instance, Latin American countries used to import American situation comedies whose jokes were not always particularly clear in translation, but have largely stopped doing so. They now tend to import comedy shows, whether comedy ensembles, sitcoms or soap operas, from each other because the cultural proximity of Latin American Spanish speaking nations to each other makes slang, jokes and references easier to understand. Even Brazilian programs, which have to be translated from Portuguese to Spanish, are funnier and more comprehensible because the languages, styles and cultures are still much more similar to Spanish speakers than are U.S. programs. [. . .]

Regional cable-satellite channels

A number of channels and DBS services have been started with a more specific language or regional focus. A number of European channels have been started in news, music, sports, films, children's, etc. At least one of the new satellite television services in Asia, Star TV, has American (MTV, film), European (BBC news) and Chinese language channels, which have been the most popular with Chinese audiences in Taiwan and China.

Satellite TV and cable or multichannel television are beginning to expand in the Third World, the less developed economies of Asia, Latin America and the Mid-East. Again, industrialized nations' export channels (CNN, BBC, MTV, etc.) are popular but several nations (Brazil, Hong Kong, Mexico, Egypt, Saudi Arabia) are developing their own satellite television channels. The Mexican and Saudi channels are also aimed at regional markets in Spanish and Arabic. Increasingly, cable systems in various regions are reflecting the availability and attraction to audiences of regional and local channels. [. . .]

National and local television production

[. . .] Television genres have developed remarkably over the last 20–30 years. For example, a number of people have remarked on the change in the soap opera/serial/*telenovela* over time and the variety of forms it has taken in various settings (Allen, 1995). More importantly, in some ways, is that a number of very low cost genres have evolved which can be produced almost anywhere with the simplest and cheapest of equipment: news, talk, variety, live music, and games. More and more nations are producing an increasing proportion of their own programming using such genres. Table 24.1 from a study by Straubhaar *et al.* (1992) shows that a significant number of countries are doing over half of their own programming, both in the total broadcast day and during prime time, where audience viewing is concentrated and the most popular programs are usually placed.

Some genres also lend themselves to more localized programming on provincial level or municipal stations. There seems to be some tendency in Latin America, for example, for an increase in local news and discussion programs on television stations. For public stations, such programs are a natural line of programming, if resources from public or state sources allow. For private stations, the viability of such local programming depends on costs of production balanced against audience demand and advertiser willingness to pay. Indications from a recent study in one fairly poor Latin American country, Bolivia, by Huesca (1985), is that local programming in new and public affairs varied considerably, particularly depending on who owned and controlled the station, and what their resources were, but that

Table 24.1. Percentage of nationally-produced programming in prime time and total broadcast day

	1962		1972		1982		1991	
	Prime	Total	Prime	Total	Prime	Total	Prime	Total
Asia								
Japan	81%	92%	95%	90%	96%	95%	92%	94%
South Korea	73	76	80	79	89	87	89	86
Hong Kong	23	26	64	62	92	79	95	83
India			98	80	89	88	97	78
Latin America								
Dominican R	38	45	33	55	21	32		
Chile	63	65	54	52	58	48	58	44
Brazil	70	69	86	55	64	63	72	64
Colombia	65	77	81	75	83	66		
Hispanic US			3	66	14	43	0	43
Mexico	63	59	68	62	58	57	46	67
Anglo US	99	98	98	98	98	93	98	99
Mid-East								
Israel			63	69	72	71	67	57
Lebanon	66	60	46	38	37	34	34	24
Caribbean								
Trinidad	26	24	46	42	31	18		
Jamaica	17	30	30	29	37	20		
Barbados	16	16	13	51	10	16		

Note: This table is based on samples of one week of programming for each year, which was categorized by expert coders from each country by genres and country or region or origin (Straubhaar *et al.*, 1992).

quite a bit was being done by many stations. Furthermore, he found that stations were able to draw on some resources and programs produced by alternative producers. Bolivia, like Brazil and a number of other countries, has had a growing tradition for several years of alternative video production by non-governmental organizations, activist groups, church groups, unions, etc. (Alvarado, 1988). As one of the main alternative video producers in Brazil, Luiz Santoro (1989, 1992) has observed, many such groups see alternative video as a means toward producing materials for television as local, provincial or even national opportunities open up. [. . .]

Conclusions

Current formulations of globalization are becoming more sophisticated and more adequate for explaining the complexity of international television production, flow and impact. There is less economic reductionism, less tendency to assume a monolithic and homogenizing globalization, more awareness that there is an active interplay between global, national and local (Friedman, 1994; Robertson, 1995). Some previous assertions about the role of globalization in cultures, that it leads to homogenization, the more or less automatic erosion of national and cultural differences, and domination of all by U.S. productions, have been modified by recent theorization (Featherstone and Lash, 1995).

However, even the current work on globalization may still underplay somewhat the role and force of regional or geo-linguistic cultural pheno-mena, like television. Recent work does recognize the existence of separate layers of global, supranational/regional, national, subnational/regional, and local (Featherstone and Lash, 1995; Pieterse, 1995). One of the strengths of recent work is pointing out the long history and current intensity of interaction between these levels. Robertson (1995) asserts, with some logic and evidence, that most of the cultures we now think of as national or local have been touched and often partially shaped over the centuries by contact with other cultures at 'national,' regional and global levels. He argues that there is a certain pattern now of what we expect national and local cultures to look like that is an aspect of what he calls glocalization. We might be able to extend that same analysis to geo-linguistic or geo-cultural regions. Certainly in television production, there is good evidence that regional or geo-linguistic area productions of major genres are influenced by global developments in those genres, such as the global evolution of the soap opera, in which global, regional and national experiences interplay.

From the brief reviews we have made of empirical trends in film, television, and new television technologies, such as cable and satellite TV, it seems clear that while flows in these media are strong at the global level, that by no means overwhelms the regional and national levels. Evidence for mono-polization of the flow at a global level by a few producers is strongest in film, where the U.S. does tend to dominate global cultural markets. Even there, though, strong producers exist in certain regional markets, particularly in South and East Asia, primarily within the Hindi and Chinese geo-linguistic markets, but crossing into other markets as well. In television, regional and national strength seems much clearer. There we see a pattern of certain producers tending to dominate their geo-linguistic markets, such as the U.S. within the English-speaking world, Hong Kong within the extended Chinese market, Egypt in the Arab world, Mexico within the Spanish-speaking, etc. However, in several of those, such as the Spanish geo-linguistic market, we do see considerable competition, by country producers or sometimes even by subnational geo-linguistic groups, like the Hispanic producers within the U.S.

One of the strengths of the new globalization theorization is that it is more historically nuanced than much of the cultural imperialism debate. As Tomlinson (1991) pointed out, the cultural imperialism debate was often primarily concerned with the current geographic or spatial spread of media exports, which sometimes had the effect of neglecting complex histories of development prior to the advent of the medium under discussion. Tomlinson and others (Featherstone and Lash, 1995; Pieterse, 1995; Robertson, 1995) observe that it is necessary to add a historical dimension, which has been manifested as an analysis of modernity as part of globalization and vice-versa. This permits us to see, overall, that different countries have distinct paths to 'modernity'. Theoretically, this makes it easier to see how countries may have very distinct developments of certain kinds of 'modern' television genres, like the soap opera or the variety show. Even more basically, it helps us understand that a commercial network employing modern advertising and cultivating audiences as consumers may be operating within a distinct capitalist modernity of its own. Japanese or Brazilian or Indian capitalism may all employ globalized, modern television advertising, which we can profitably compare across countries for common origins, commonalities, similarities and differences, but the national adaptation of advertising will be made quite distinct by their own historical development. If we wish to look for commonalities, one logical place would be within geo-linguistic regions, like Latin America, where some commonalities within a genre like the *telenovela* or within approaches to advertising are evident.

Tomlinson and others have pointed out that globalization seems to be occupying the theoretical and explanatory ground that cultural and media imperialism had held (Featherstone and Lash, 1995; Peterse, 1995; Tomlinson, 1991). Certainly a number of useful contrasts in assumptions can be shown between the two sets of theories. The media imperialism and cultural synchronization theories assumed an epochal change in the power of media to affect cultures. Earlier generations of anthropologists had seen change in cultures from contact with other cultures as constant and normal. Friedman (1994), for example, documents a long history of empires, migrations and other strong forms of contact leading to cultural change. Current globalization theorists seem to be reverting more to this mode of thinking, seeing mass media as one recent wave in a very long series of cultural interactions on a global or nearly global scale (Friedman, 1994; Robertson, 1995). [. . .]

Overall, within an increasingly internationalized world of television, we find a fairly compelling argument for looking at global, regional and national levels fairly equally. Much of the development of the 1970s–1990s has been the development of more national production by almost all countries. However, in several regions, particularly Latin America and the Arab world, regional trade in television has grown rapidly as well. Now the new technologies of cable and satellite television present a new level of globalization, simultaneous global exposure to some channels delivered by satellite. These media also present an equal if not larger opportunity for a new level of regionalization, channels targeted at geo-linguistic groups across national borders. Both these new global and new regional channels will impact on nation states' sovereignty and control, but perhaps no more than earlier waves of cultural change that preceded most of the current nation states and will be absorbed by local cultures in much the same way.

References

Allen, R. C. (1995) *To be continued – soap operas around the world*, Routledge, London, New York.

Alvarado, M. (1988) *Video World-Wide*, John Libbey, London.

Barber, R. R. (1992) Jihad vs. McWorld. *The Atlantic*, p. 3.

Boyd-Barrett, O. (1980) *The international news agencies*, Sage Publications, Beverly Hills.

Boyne, R. (1990) Culture and the World System. *Theory, Culture and Society*, Vol. 7, pp. 57–62.

Chan, J. M. (1994) National Responses and Accessibility to STAR TV in Asia. *Journal of Communication*, Vol. 44, No. 3, pp. 70–88.

Fadul, A. (1993) *Serial Fiction in TV: The Latin American Telenovelas*, Escola de Communações e Artes. University of São Paulo, São Paulo, Brazil.

Featherstone, M. (1990) *Global Culture – National Globalization and Modernity*, Sage Publications, Newbury Park, CA.

Featherstone, M. and Lash, S. (1995) An Introduction. In Featherstone, M., Lash, S. and Robertson R. (eds.) *Global Modernities*, Sage, Thousand Oaks, CA.

Ferguson, M. (1992) The Mythology about Globalization. *European Journal of Communication*, Vol. 7, pp. 69–93.

Fernandes, I. (1982) *Memoria da telenovela brasileira*. Proposta Editorial, São Paulo.

Fox, E. (1992) Cultural Dependency Thrice Revisited, presented at International Association for Mass Communication Research, Guarujá, Brazil.

Friedman, J. (1994) *Cultural Identity and Global Process*, Sage, Thousand Oaks, CA.

Garcia Canclini, N. (1990) *Culturas hibridas: estrategias para entrar y salir de la modernidad*, Grijalbo: Consejo Nacional para la Cultura y las Artes, Mexico, D.F.

Giddens, A. (1991) *Modernity and Self-Identity*, Polity, Oxford.

Huesca, R. (1985) Popular Radio in Bolivia. Conference paper, International Communcation Association.

Huntington, S. (1993) The Clash of Civilizations. *Foreign Affairs*, Vol. 72, No. 3, pp. 22–9.

Katz, E. and Liebes, T. (1984) Once upon a Time in Dallas. *Intermedia*, Vol. 12, No. 3, pp. 28–32.

Katz, E. and Wedell, G. (1976) *Broadcasting in the Third World*, Harvard University Press, Cambridge.

Lee, C. (1980) *Media Imperialism Reconsidered*, Sage Publications, Beverly Hills, CA.

Lins da Silva, C. E. (1986) Transnational Communication and Brazilian Culture. In Atwood R. and McAnany E. G. (eds.) *Communication and Latin American Society – Trends in Critical Research, 1960–1985*, University of Wisconsin Press, Madison.

Marques de Melo, J. (1988) *As telenovelas da Globo: Produção e exportação*, Summus, São Paulo.

McDaniel, D. O. (1994) *Broadcasting in the Malay World*, Ablex, Norwood, NJ.

McPhail, T. (1989) *Electronic Colonialism* (second edn), Sage, Newbury Park.

Mitra, A. (1993) *Television and Popular Culture in India: A Study of the MAHABHARAT*, Sage, New Delhi.

Nordenstreng, K. and Schiller, H. I. (1979) *National Sovereignty and International Communications*, Ablex Publishing Corp, Norwood, NJ.

Nordenstreng, K. and Varis, T. (1974) *Television Traffic – A One-Way Street*, UNESCO, Paris.

Oliveira, O. S. (1990) Brazilian Soaps Outshine Hollywood: Is Cultural Imperialism Fading Out? Paper at International Communication Association, Intercultural and Development Division, Dublin.

Pieterse, J. N. (1995) Globalization as Hybridization. In Featherstone, M., Lash, S. and Robertson R. (eds.) *Global Modernities*, Sage, Thousand Oaks, CA, pp. 45–68.

Robertson, R. (1995) Glocalization: Time-Space and Homogeneity-Heterogeneity. In Featherstone, M. Lash, S. and Robertson R. (eds.) *Global Modernities*, Sage, Thousand Oaks, CA, pp. 25–44.

Roncagliolo, R. (1985) Information and Transnational Culture: directions for policy research. *Media, Culture and Society*, Vol. 7, pp. 369–83.

Roncagliolo, R. (1986) Transnational Communication and Culture. In Atwood R. and McAnany E. (eds.) *Communication and Latin American Society: Trends in Critical Research, 1960–1985*, University of Wisconsin Press, Madison, WI.

Santoro, L. F. (1989) *A Imagem nas Maos – O Video Popular no Brasil*, Summus Editorial, São Paulo.

Santoro, L. F., and Festa, R. (1992) Experiments on audiovisual co-productions (cinema, video and TV) in Latin America: the Brazilian case. In Marques de Melo J. (eds.) *Brazilian Communication Research Yearbook*, University of São Paulo Press, São Paulo, pp. 69–88.

Schlesinger, P. (1987) On National Identity: Some Conceptions and Misconceptions Criticized. *Social Science Information*. Vol. 26, No. 2, pp. 219–264.

Schlesinger, P. (1994) Europe's Contradictory Communicative Space. *Daedalus*, Spring, pp. 25–52.

Shohat, E. and Stamm, R. (1994) *Unlinked Eurocentrism: Multiculturalism and the Media*, Routledge London.

Smith, A. D. (1981) *The Ethnic Revival in the Modern World*, Cambridge University Press, Cambridge.

Straubhaar, J., Campbell, C., Youn, S.-M., Champagnie, K., Elasmar, M., and Castellon, L. (1992) The Emergence of a Latin American Market for Television Programs. Paper at International Communication Association, Miami.

Tomlinson, J. (1991) *Cultural Imperialism*, Johns Hopkins Press, Baltimore, MD.

Tunstall, J. (1977) *The media are American*, Columbia University Press, New York, NY.

Wallerstein, I. (1979) *The Capitalist World Economy*, Cambridge University Press, Cambridge.

Wallerstein, I. (1991) *Geopolitics and Geoculture – Essays on the Changing World System*, Cambridge University Press, Cambridge.

25

Neighbourly relations? Cross-cultural reception analysis and Australian soaps in Britain

Stuart Cunningham and Elizabeth Jacka

From Grossberg, L. and Radway, J. (eds.) (1994) *Cultural Studies*, Routledge, London, Vol. 8, No. 3, pp. 509–26.

This article, part of a longer study of the increasingly international orientation of Australian television, outlines first some of the methodological issues that must be considered in cross-cultural and reception analysis of peripheral nations' television export activity, particularly soap opera. Then we focus, as a case study, on modes of explanation of the popularity of Australian soaps on British television.

Cross-cultural reception analysis of soap opera

[. . .] In different markets Australian television programmes have very different levels of exposure and different potentials for audience acceptance. Thus they have a substantial profile in the U.K., are less well established in continental Europe, barely emerging in Asia, and in the U.S. there is a relatively large number of Australian programmes shown but they are lost in the contextless flood of the multichannel environment that lies outside network and syndication television.

Given this, we shall argue that both the global explanatory schemata of political economy (with its subset the cultural imperialism thesis) and micro-situational audience use models of analysis are in themselves inadequate to track the fortunes of the television export activity of a peripheral nation like Australia. Instead we posit a middle-range methodology that looks at the important role played in the acceptance of Australian television by the 'gatekeepers' of the television industry, such as commissioning editors and programme buyers. We also look at the context of reception set by relevant media, notably tabloid newspapers and television guides.

The U.K. is the territory where Australian material, and most spectacularly Grundy's serial *Neighbours*, has achieved its greatest levels of penetration and popularity so far. But even in this case, factors other than those which are usually captured by textual and audience analysis are necessary and partially sufficient reasons for the success of Australian drama.

Explanations for the popularity and success of imported television drama range from arguments about textual form and content to their fortuitous placement in the schedules. There is also the approach, most closely associated with John Fiske, which focuses on the use to which particular programmes might be put by audiences – the pleasures they might gain and the cognitive, intersubjective and intersocial experiences that might be generated around particular programmes (Fiske, 1987). [. . .]

There are also methodological protocols central to audience use studies that are not central to our approach. Researchers have often been most interested in the atypical or subculturally specific responses to programmes, and to achieve the depth of qualitative analysis desired, they have had to sacrifice breadth of audience coverage. Such studies rarely weigh the relative importance of non-textual factors in explaining the impact and use of programmes by audiences. By limiting themselves to the reporting and analysis of the self-understanding of selected audience respondents, wider factors impinging on the impact of programmes are often bracketed out or treated more superficially.

Liebes and Katz's *The Export of Meaning* is arguably the best-known study of cross-cultural audience response. It is an account of the audience decodings of *Dallas* on three continents and in it the authors argue that the key reasons for the international popularity of U.S. prime-time television, and especially serial/soap formats like *Dallas*, line in

> (1) the universality, or primordiality, of some of its themes and formulae, which makes programs psychologically accessible; (2) the polyvalent or open potential of many of the stories, and thus their value as projective mechanisms and as material for negotiation and play in the families of man; and (3) the sheer availability of American programs in a market-place where national producers – however zealous – cannot fill more than a fraction of the hours they feel they must provide. (1990, p. 5)

However, it is clear that universality and primordiality are more features of the genre as a whole rather than peculiar to U.S. soap operas; even a cursory examination of telenovelas or, for example Malaysian soap opera, makes this clear. Thus they cannot account for the international success of U.S. serials. The third reason that Liebes and Katz adduce to account for global popularity is the one they least explore, yet it is far more significant than they allow. 'Vigorous marketing', they say, is certainly a reason for the international success of *Dallas* (1990, p. 4), but there is almost no attention paid to this level in the book.

The intriguing chapter on the reasons for the failure of the programme in Japan includes no discussion of the scheduling, promotional, marketing and purchase practices involved in the (short-lived) introduction of *Dallas* into the Japanese market.

This should be compared to the analyses of the introduction of *Dallas* into foreign markets as presented by Jean Bianchi (1984) and the *East of Dallas* research team led by Alessandro Silj (1988, p. 36–8) which indicate that factors like scheduling, programme philosophy and cultural environment prior to programme reception militated against its success in countries such as Peru or, for unexpected and surprising reasons, enhanced it in countries such as Algeria. [. . .]

Bianchi's and Silj's conclusions are that reception is a dynamic process governed by the cultural identities of audiences and the 'sedimentation of other social practices' (Silj, 1988, p. 40), which we can take to mean, amongst other factors, the industrial and institutional conditions obtaining prior to any audience seeing any foreign programme. [. . .]

It can be assumed that viewing audiences will interact with popular programmes from a range of foreign sources in culturally complex and dynamic ways, provided there is sufficient opportunity to do so, given the prior contingencies of production, purchasing, programming and promotion. [. . .]

The success or otherwise of peripheral export nations (like Australia) is far more contingent than for the U.S., which explains why so little reception research has been able to be conducted on their product in international markets, and equally why such analysis must take the middle range course outlined here. It is because of our concern with this wider industrial environment that our attention is directed toward what we shall call the 'primary audience' for Australian material – producers and (often international) co-producers of the material itself, regulatory officials and trade papers and newspaper and journal commentary overseas and in Australia and, most crucially, buyers, programmers and schedulers. These are the prime sources of expert or informed 'gatekeeping' which regulate (in the widest sense) the flow of Australian programming in international markets. For these reasons, our approach can be understood as a close analysis of the industrial and cultural *preconditions* for the success or failure of Australian programmes internationally. All these factors embody legitimate, indeed central, aspects of cultural exchange, as virtually all the significant research on non-dominant nations' television production and reception highlights (Lee, 1980; Hjort, 1985; Silj, 1988; de la Garde *et al.*, 1993).

The nature and structure of major international television trade markets have to be considered. There is an ever wider variety of modes of contracting for international programme exchange: off-shore, co-production, official co-production, co-venture, including predominantly presales, and straight purchase of territorial rights for completed programmes in the major trade markets (MIP-TV, etc.) which run on annual cycles suited to the programming and scheduling patterns of the major northern hemisphere territories. Here, programming is bought or not bought often sight unseen, in job lots, and based on company reputation or distributor clout. [. . .]

This study traverses a wide range of cross-cultural scenarios and the methodology of the analysis must reflect this variety. At one extreme, there is the North American market. While the U.S. market is by far the biggest in the world, it is also the most resistant to foreign programming, particularly in the commercial broadcast sector. About 98 per cent of commercial broadcast television is American; while Australian programming ranks with Mexican, Latin American and Canadian imports on a second tier behind British imports in the U.S. market, this still represents an extremely marginal fraction of total overall programme content. [. . .]

Thus, there is a negligible place for Australian programming, as for all non-U.S. programming, on U.S. commercial broadcast television. Those very few programmes which have been screened on network are either culturally indistinguishable in origin, hard-action genre flicks, or have some definite U.S. angle, either through co-production, narrative content or U.S. actors (preeminently the *Crocodile Dundee* films and *Mad Max Beyond Thunderdome*). [. . .]

While one-shot drama (especially children's) and documentaries have been purchased, the biggest absence is series and serial drama, which preeminently builds an audience over time. [. . .]

The case of Canada is, in some respects, the strangest and least promising of all territories. Despite strong similarities between the two countries and shared political and historical heritages that produce much interchange at these levels, the Canadian television market's potential interest in Australian product is affected, not only by the domination actual U.S. signals enjoy in the country, but because the effects of Canadian regulatory policy – in placing strong emphasis on minimum levels of local programming in response to this dominance – means that virtually no other 'foreign' other than U.S. material finds its way onto Canadian screens. And what little that does is 'screened' through horizons of expectation also dominated by U.S. models of mainstream programming. Thus, the Canadian resembles many other 'minimum penetration' scenarios for Australian product – scope for standard international formats such as children's and nature documentary, but considerable resistance to any other mainstream television fare, particularly long-form drama with ratings-building potential. The possibilities for turning this situation around reside at the margin, in short-form, high budget co-production development.

At the moment Australian programmes have a similar status in Asia but the potential for further penetration there of both programmes and services is quite high though as yet rather hard to predict. [. . .]

Australian programming is best established and has the highest profile as specifically Australian in Europe although of course each individual territory represents significantly different industrial and cultural mediascapes and thus different reception conditions for them. [. . .]

The fact that Australian programmes are perceived as imitations of U.S. formats constitutes a problem for both commentators and regulators in Europe. Australian exports are written up in the same language that is used for discussion of U.S. programming – in terms of an invasion. A recent European study (de Bens *et al.*, 1992) which updates Nordenstreng and Varis' and other studies of international television content flows, shows Australia as a leading supplier of series material into Western European markets. [. . .]

To be sure, the structure of content and the form of internationally popular serial drama are widely shared and may even be 'borrowed' from U.S. practice. But the 'surface' differences almost always make a difference, and this can contribute to the acceptance or rejection of non-U.S. material, depending on whether the primary audience and the viewing audience respond positively or negatively to that difference. As Anne Cooper-Chen (1993) has shown, even that most transparently internationalized of television formats, the game show, contains significant differences in the widely variant cultures in which it is popular. [. . .]

Australian soaps in Britain

Australian drama has been seen on British screens for many years (including, since the late 1970s, serial drama such as *A Country Practice, The Sullivans,*

The Flying Doctors, Richmond Hill, and *Prisoner: Cell Block H*). In the mid 1980s Australian soaps achieved a breakthrough by appearing in early evening prime-time slots and winning very large audiences. This provided a platform for a range of Australian programmes, produced a wide range of social response, and helped foster the development of new and more organic co-production arrangements between the British and Australian industries. The U.K. is by far the most significant market for the Australian television industry.

Neighbours began on BBC 1 in October 1986, stripped in the early afternoon Monday to Friday. Its sleeper success led to the day's episode being rescreened in the early evening, allowing it to capture a far greater proportion of young viewers and leading to runaway popularity. By 1988, it had become the most popular children's and young adults' programme on British television and remained in the top 10 most-watched programmes in Britain for several years. In an effort to counter, the ITV network similarly strip-scheduled *Home and Away* from 1990 to immediately follow *Neighbours* in the early evening. These were the two major Australian serials which attracted considerable attention and popularity, but a large number of other serial dramas achieved longevity and/or notoriety in the schedules of the terrestrial networks as well as on satellite services for several years in the late 1980s and early 1990s – *Prisoner: Cell Block H, Sons and Daughters, The Young Doctors, Chances, The Flying Doctors.* By 1993, there were signs that the Australian cycle had waned somewhat, with the ratings of *Neighbours* slipping, and with a greater degree of industry resistance to foreign programmes dominating key parts of the schedules.

The reasons for the popularity of soaps like *Neighbours* and *Home and Away* were tested in 1992 under standard audience appreciation protocols established by the Broadcasters' Audience Research Board (BARB), which are regularly analysed by research staff at the Independent Television Commission (ITC) (Wober, 1993). The difference, in this case, was that reasons for the popularity of whole series were tested, rather than single episodes, which are the normal units used to compile the audience Appreciation Indexes (AIs) in Britain. The survey sample was a nationally representative group who were surveyed by standard questionnaire method. The survey analysts claimed that such testing of popularity among viewers has direct relevance to the industry in providing some systematic findings which might guide programming decisions.

An interesting difference in this audience survey was that the views offered for success by professional critics were used as the qualitative control hypotheses which were then tested on viewers. It was clear from surveying journalistic commentary that the most public and popularized mode of explanation for the success of soaps like *Neighbours* or *Home and Away* in Britain rested on speculations about the mythological content and serial formats of the programmes (speculations which closely resemble Liebes and Katz's findings). The soaps are seen as filling a need in the public imagination once occupied by mediaeval morality plays and preaching for models of behaviour directly relevant to their particular audiences. The serial format allows the consequences of such behaviour to be followed and also allows for varying means, times and degrees of involvement and several points of association with and 'reading' of character.

The results of the viewer survey also provide interesting conclusions relevant to the question of consumption of non-domestic material. There was some evidence bearing out one of the *East of Dallas* team's dictums that a moderate foreignness (what one critic called the soaps' 'slight foreignness' [Marin, 1989]) engendered more involvement and enjoyment among some viewers. This idea is expanded by the critic in these terms: 'characters outside our class system . . . can speak to us more freely than any well-defined character in an English soap, whose very definition would risk provoking all the class antagonisms which are so easily aroused here.' The 'morality tale' element put forward by critics for the appeal of soaps, which parallels so closely Liebes and Katz's findings, needs to be framed within this sense of slight foreignness. That is, the exotic or foreign elements – that 'Australians get into each others' lives and homes more than British people do', that there is a, to some, pleasing degree of 'old-fashioned' verbal cliché in the scripting, that overall the most widely noticed characteristic is an inference about life in Australia (that social interaction is more fluid) – carry with them a sense of attractive difference which is read in the act of viewing as a commentary on British life. Again, this correlates well with critics who point to

> a complete alternative universe, one ruled by goodwill, common sense and a faith in the power of hard work. It is . . . sunny, decent, fair, not preachy, not guilty . . . nobody is rich but everyone has a nice big kitchen. When one job falls through there is always another . . . with *Neighbours* that dream is of ordinary people in a land of opportunity . . . it is optimism with a bright shiny package. (Reynolds, 1988)

As an attempt to test critical hypotheses and as the only nationally representative survey of opinion about Australian soaps, the ITC research is valuable but partial. The method used, a delivered questionnaire asking for nothing more than single responses on a Likert scale to a small set of simple questions, is hardly the most likely to be able to draw out the complex responses required to address cross-cultural issues of general likes and dislikes about whole series.

Gillespie's (1991) ethnographic study of south London Punjabi communities' use of *Neighbours* is arguably the most in-depth audience-use study yet conducted of Australian soaps in Britain. It is deliberately narrowly focused where the ITC research is broad. Gillespie studied groups of teenagers' use of *Neighbours* in negotiating the relations between parental and peer cultures in an environment where much of their knowledge of white Anglo society perforce comes from television. Whereas many of the key cultural audience studies of the 1980s focused on variables of class along with gender, Gillespie focuses on ethnicity, age and gender. With regard especially to her focus on a youth demographic, Gillespie's research performs a particularly useful function in illuminating that age group which has allowed *Neighbours* to perform so strongly in Britain.

The Australianness of the serial is reported to be of little importance compared to its being about a white society (1991, p. 29). But this should not be taken at face value. Several indications in the research lead to the conclusion that the degree of interaction and association with *Neighbours* could not be readily substituted for any other serial at the same slot in the schedule. *Neighbours* outranked all other soaps among Gillespie's cohort by far in terms of popularity, with the other major Australian serial *Home and Away* second – there is strong circumstantial evidence that it is something about Australian serials specifically that provoke interest. The 'social text' created around *Neighbours*, with its stars Kylie Minogue, Jason Donovan and Craig McLaughlan enjoying considerable extra-televisual exposure in British youth culture, cemented the specific attractions of the serial.

The character networks of *Neighbours* are based around a set of extended families in a single locale, Ramsey Street. This is a fictional space which corresponds at times quite literally to the living conditions of Gillespie's Southall cohort, where gossip and rumour have the potential to conflict strongly with both family honour and the aspirations for peer acceptance among the teenagers studied. Gillespie notes the effortless ability that one of her cohort has in producing a detailed map of human relationships over time in the serial. Given that a recent Social Trends analysis (1990, quoted in Gillespie, 1991, p. 35) states that 82 per cent of the surveyed British population claim they would never have moved into their home if they had known who their neighbours were, the attractions of a fictional space in which scenarios for dealing with 'far from ideal' neighbourly relations in social life are routinely played out are obvious. One of Gillespie's key findings is that her teenage cohort construct associations (rather than identifications) between their social world and the fictional world of the serial, creatively 'misreading' the fiction by folding it into their realities of high-density urban extended family and community life.

This is the point at which perceptions of a distinctly 'Australian' social space, intertwined with aspects of the format of *Neighbours*, might come into play, although it is not a drawn-out feature of Gillespie's analysis. The fluidity of the (fictional) social life portrayed, that 'Australians get into each others' lives and homes more than British people do', facilitates perceptions of the serial's usefulness in the participation in and negotiation of gossip and rumour for the Punjabi teenagers. Moreover, the format, including the production values, of the series (low cost, cheap sets, naturalistic camera-work), which differs markedly from popular U.S. soaps like *Dallas* and *Dynasty*, places an emphasis on dialogue, on the verbal over the visual. This observation allows Gillespie to make a series of connections between her cohort's social reality and a fiction based to a larger degree than most soaps on young people and a narration of 'proximity, intimacy and intensity' dealing with the central themes of family and kinship, romance and community relations.

These textual and audience response and use examinations of the success of Australian television in Britain can only be partial explanations, however. In all the foregoing textual and audience modes of explanations, perhaps what may seem to be the most missing is any sense of the 'sharp end' of the social intertext created around Australian soaps, any ideological evaluation of their impact in the industrial circumstances of British television in the late 1980s. A case can be made (Copley, 1991, on whose study some of the following paragraphs rely) for *Neighbours* (and at least some of the other high-rating Australian drama) fitting all too well into the dual trajectories of deregulation and reregulation of British television in the late 1980s. On the one hand, it was cheaply and readily available soap that answered a need for the BBC to respond, in an increasingly constrained financial environment, to attacks on its élitism and the challenges of the new commercialism. On the other, it was clean, morally unproblematic soap, well suited to the moral reregulations that proceeded apace with structural deregulation and the skew toward commercialism. What bolsters this argument is the evidence that what *Neighbours* could be construed as representing in terms of a moral universe was mobilized by opinion leaders like the tabloid press in campaigns against 'degenerate' values in British television.

Fuelled by a history of U.S. dominance in cinema and other popular arts and a strong, if aggrieved, sense of rightful cultural leadership, there has long been an entrenched anti-Americanism in official British culture of both the left and right. The drive to further commercialize and deregulate British television in the 1980s therefore needed alternative models of such a media culture. [. . .]

It is in this general context that the BBC was, by the mid 1980s, desperate for popular but relatively low-cost serial drama that would begin to recapture some of the audience lost to both the ITV network and especially the new Channel Four, which began in 1982. *East Enders* was launched in 1985, the first continuing serial the BBC had produced since 1969 (Buckingham, 1987, p. 2). During the same time period, the popularity of U.S. soaps in Britain, such as *Dallas* and *Dynasty*, had begun to wane considerably. Substituting for U.S. programming, paralleling the need for alternative commercial media models, became a priority.

Buckingham (1987, p. 10) argues that *East Enders'* ratings success was financially and politically crucial to the BBC, caught in the pincer thrust between government determination to streamline and reposition public service broadcasting and the growing threat of expanded commercial services. But its high production costs meant that it was only a partial solution; the BBC could pay reputedly in the vicinity of only £27,000 for a week's *Neighbours* (five episodes stripped twice a day, amounting to 5 hours of high rating programming), as against £40,000 production costs for one half hour of *East Enders* (Kingsley, 1988, p. 363).

Buckingham's (1987) study of the first two years of *East Enders* notes prominent themes of unemployment, urban deprivation, nervous break-downs, infidelity and divorce, prostitution, illiteracy, drugs and alcoholism, and conflict between the generations leading to breakdowns of the extended family. *East Enders* was the first English soap to feature Afro-Caribbean, Asian, Greek and gay and lesbian characters, attempting to show the multicultural composition of the inner city community and examine racial and sexual stereotyping. Those elements of the press which mobilized against the soap argued its 'bleak realism' was 'squeezing out' moral standards.

Often, the press rated the appeal of *Neighbours* against the 'bad' models of soap: 'not high life like *Dallas,* not low life like *East Enders,* just everyday life' (*Trader,* 6 April 1987). Hilary Kingsley (1987) argued that 'one of the reasons for *Neighbours'* success is people have tired of the low life, working class themes of *East Enders.' East Enders* was written up as threatening, polemic, difficult; *Neighbours* was cosy, unopinionated, ordinary. Its stars [. . .] were model WASPs: 'perfect Anglo-Saxon good looks, blonde haired, blue eyed, 5' 11' Scott Robinson', 'Petite blonde haired blue eyed Kylie', 'Blond bombshell Jason Donovan'. Germaine Greer's withering commentary highlighted the values the tabloids and other elements of the press saw fit to lionize:

> There are no Asian characters in *Neighbours*, the only Southern Europeans are ridiculous stereotypes. There is not even a Jew, let alone a Muslim, or a Buddhist. Religion is never discussed, sexual orientation is always heterosexual . . . If a group of Aborigines were to camp on the manicured lawns the good neighbourliness would evaporate immediately. (Greer, 1989)

The 'moral crusade' which elements of the press mounted around its constructed opposition between *Neighbours* and *East Enders* demonstrates the degree to which Silj's 'sedimentation of other social practices' particular to a host country can inflect dramatically the reception of popular imported television material. However, this is further complicated by the dissonances between the press crusade and the fact of the continuing high popularity of *East Enders*. The press's stance (and the brief flurry in May 1991 when British junior Education Minister Michael Fallon and his Labour shadow Jack Straw both attacked *Neighbours* for 'dulling the senses' of schoolchildren and being 'pretty trashy') reveals more of the deep structure of cultural and moral élitism which can be mobilized within the British polity (and indeed much about the tone and content of *Neighbours*) than it tells us much about the audience uses of the soap. Instead, the most intriguing aspects of audience response to *Neighbours* may lie in the fantasy projections the soap may fortuitously generate in a particular host society with historically close ties to Australia. Copley (1991, p. 39–40), in a small survey of opinions about *Neighbours* amongst mothers at a south-east London play centre, found that Australia can be projected onto as an alternative utopic admixture of exotic holiday brochure and cinema images creatively pitted against that which is seen as inferior in the British 'lifestyle': 'They do work, but the pace of life is slower, like when you're abroad and people slow down because of the climate and spend less time worrying.' Regardless of whether viewers 'believe' the fantasies or not, this form of engagement evidently provides much pleasure and defies any simple correlation between the moral cause espoused at a public level and viewer reception. It is hard not to see this conception of Australian soaps as an influence on the ill-fated BBC serial, *El Dorado*.

These aspects of *Neighbours* as a 'social text' are complemented by necessary prior television industry decision-making regarding scheduling and marketing. Both industry (e.g. Wober, 1993) and some journalist commentators regard such factors as a necessary and even partially sufficient recipe for success. Kate Bowles (in Taylor, 1993, p. 13) argues against the 'common mythology' that 'open plan housing, beautiful people and hot weather' in *Neighbours* and *Home and Away* are the key ingredients. It was the prior factor of their placement in the schedules – stripped and in the late afternoons, as well as, with *Neighbours*, in the early afternoons – that laid the base for their fantastic Australianness (like Pauline Kael's famous summation of the appeal of Australian period film from the 1970s in the U.S., that it had the 'Good Housekeeping Seal of Approval'), to become a featured factor. Indeed, it was supremely good timing that *Neighbours* became the first programme to be stripped across the weekdays in Britain; the leading edge of a scheduling revolution within the commercializing thrust both BBC and ITV have pursued strongly since the mid 1980s. (The second programme to be similarly stripped was *Home and Away*.) Another strategy that worked as an influence prior to content was their being marketed to young audiences. This set them apart from the majority of established popular soaps which featured mostly middle-aged and older characters and themes appropriate to them, such as *Coronation Street*. This is borne out in the BARB Appreciation Index measurement of reasons for viewers watching the Australian material, which show a very markedly skewed youth demographic (BBC, 1989, 1990, 1991).

Conclusion

The point of this exercise in reviewing modes of explanation for international success is to demonstrate that middle-range factors – factors which focus on the mediating role of 'gatekeepers' and the role of the media in creating a reception context – are necessary and prior explanations for the careers of especially peripheral export countries' product in international markets, and that primordiality and seriality – the structure of the content and the form of the drama – cannot operate as a generalizable mode of explanation.

That the mode of explanation offered by Liebes and Katz is overly textual is underlined by the fact that there can be no general set of explanations for the career of whole categories of exported national production. The category 'Australian soap operas' and even more the category 'Australian drama' on British television embraces a range of material that is far from uniform – the very successful *Neighbours* and *Home and Away* in key network timeslots; those screened in much more limited slots such as *Prisoner* which nevertheless drew a dedicated cult following; those which were bought for satellite transmission such as *Chances*; and those which were only ever screened as daytime soaps (*Sons and Daughters, The Young Doctors*). In the case of *Prisoner*, while in economic terms for the copyright holder (Grundys) the returns are now negligible and the prestige of the show is minimal, the cult following it has generated makes it a *cause célèbre* for subcultural audience-use models of international reception. And, as we have seen in considering the mediascapes of major territories for Australian programming, preconditions for success may vary widely from those which may obtain in Britain.

The cycle of acceptance of foreign serial drama is also typically shorter than the life cycle for a programme in its domestic market. The high point of the cycle of acceptance for Australian serials in the British market is certainly finished. This waning cannot be attributed simply to viewer preference. The 'invasion' of Australian soaps became an industrial issue, with concerns being expressed that they were squeezing potential local production off the schedules. It is in part for this reason that the successful exporter of soaps and game and quiz shows, Grundys, realizing that exporting from Australia into foreign territories is at best a hit and miss affair, with long-term prospects for stability of sales dependent on others' readings of viewer preferences and a relatively accommodating regulatory and industry environment together with a preparedness to dub or subtitle material into several European languages, set up wholly owned local production companies in Europe under the strategy dubbed 'parochial internationalism' (Smith, 1992; Gerrie, 1992).

The success of Australian programming in international markets cannot be explained by any one factor. As we have argued, the level of penetration varies widely in different territories and depends on a variety of factors like the nature of the media landscape it is entering, the attitudes and perceptions of viewer preferences by gatekeepers, the regulatory 'culture', perceptions that Australian programming is like, or on the other hand, unlike, U.S. programming and a variety of other more cultural and even mythic factors which come into play in a country like Britain with very close historical and ethnic ties to Australia.

The success of the cycle of Australian soaps in Britain seems to be partly due to the fact that they opened up a new market among young people for serial drama, an audience segment not entirely satisfied by *Coronation Street* and *East Enders*. The particular mythic role that 'Australia' plays in the British psyche seems also to be a factor but in other markets the Australianness of a programme is much less of a factor, although there is some evidence that in Europe the fascination with 'the outback' could play a role in the popularity of programmes like *The Flying Doctors*. Finally, in more 'culturally distant' markets like those in the Asian region, even in France, Italy and Germany, and certainly in the U.S., the Australian origin of the programme plays little or no role; the programmes are simply 'schedule fodder', helping because of programme type and cost factors to fill up empty television time.

The implications for Australia in developing a cultural and industrial strategy for this new multi-channel world would seem to be to continue to produce largely for the home market and with local cultural relevance to the fore, but at the same time to be aware of some of the strengths of Australian programme styles and production methods in the international arena. Any wholesale attempt to water down cultural aims for the audio-visual sector in favour of pursuing the chimera of international fame and fortune would seem to be as doomed for television as it was for film before it.

Note

The research for this article was supported by an Australian Research Council Large Grant 1992–4 entitled 'Global Trends in Audiovisual Media – Effects on Australian Industrial and Cultural Development'. We would like to thank Jason Copley, Maree Delofski, Amanda Hickie and Julie Morrison for research support.

References

BBC (Broadcasting Research Department) (1989) *Annual Review of BBC Broadcasting Research Findings*, John Libbey, London.

BBC (Broadcasting Research Department) (1990) *Annual Review of BBC Broadcasting Research Findings*, John Libbey, London.

BBC (Broadcasting Research Department) (1991) *Annual Review of BBC Broadcasting Research Findings*, John Libbey, London.

Bianchi, Jean (1984) *Comment comprendre le succès international des séries de fiction à la télévision? – Le cas 'Dallas'*, Laboratoire CNRS/IRPEACS, Lyon, July.

Buckingham, David (1987) *Public Secrets: Eastenders and its Audience*, British Film Institute, London.

Cooper-Chen, Anne (1993) Goodbye to the global village: entertainment TV patterns in 50 countries, paper delivered at the Association for Education in Journalism and Mass Communication Annual Convention, Kansas City, August.

Copley, Jason (1991) The road that leads to Ramsey Street: Towards the study of soap opera's popularity in its imported context, BA Hons dissertation, Goldsmiths' College, University of London.

de Bens, Els, Kelly, Mary and Bakke, Marit (1992) Television content: Dallasification of culture. In Siune Karen and Treutzschler Wolfgang (eds for the Euromedia Research Group) *Dynamics of Media Politics: Broadcast and Electronic Media in Western Europe*, Sage, London.

de la Garde, Roger, Gilsdorf, William and Wechselmann, Ilja (eds.) (1993) *Small Nations, Big Neighbour: Denmark and Quebec/Canada Compare Notes on American Popular Culture*, John Libbey, London.

Fiske, John (1987) *Television Culture*, Routledge, London.

Geraghty, Christine (1991) *Women and Soap Opera: A Study of Prime Time Soaps*, Polity Press, London.

Gerrie, Anthea (1992) Teaching the US to suck soap. *The Bulletin* 9 June, pp. 98–100.

Gillespie, Marie (1991) Soap viewing, gossip and rumour among Punjabi youth in Southall, paper presented to the Fourth International Television Studies Conference, London, July. A shorter version is published in Drummond, P., Paterson R. and Willis J. (eds.) (1993) *National Identity and Europe: The Television Revolution*, BFI Publishing, London, pp. 25–42.

Greer, Germaine (1989) Dinkum? No bunkum, *Radio Times*, 11–17 March.

Hjort, Anne (1985) When women watch TV – how the Danish female public sees *Dallas* and the Danish serial *The Daughters of War*. In *Medieforskning*, Denmark Radio.

Kingsley, Hilary (1987) *Daily Mirror*, 7 July.

Kingsley, Hilary (1988) *Soap Box*, Papermac, London.

Lee, Chin-Chuan (1980) *Media Imperialism Reconsidered: The Homogenizing of Television Culture*, Sage, London.

Liebes, Tamar and Katz, Elihu (1990) *The Export of Meaning: Cross-Cultural Readings of 'Dallas'*, Oxford University Press, New York.

Marin, Minette (1989) *Daily Telegraph*, 10 March, p. 18; quoted in Wober (1993).

Reynolds, Gillian (1988) *Daily Telegraph*, 14 December, p. 15.

Silj, Alessandro (1988) *East of Dallas: The European Challenge to American Television*, British Film Institute, London.

Smith, Roff (1992) I am 68. I live in the Bahamas. I am Australia's biggest TV star. Who am I?, *Sunday Age*, 26 July, Agenda 1, 2.

Taylor, Catherine (1993) Squeaky-clean soap, export quality, *The Australian*, 28 May, p. 13.

Wober, Mallory (1993) Neighbours at Home and Away: viewers perceptions of soap operas in Britain and overseas, *Media Information Australia*, forthcoming.

26

Finding a place for Islam: Egyptian television serials and the national interest

Lila Abu-Lughod

From Breckenridge, C. A. (ed.) (1993) *Public Culture*, University of Chicago Press, Chicago, IL, Vol. 5. No. 3, pp. 494–512.

I want to explore here the relationship of Egyptian television serials to national political contests as a way of engaging the methodological and theoretical challenges that studies of the politics of media pose. The crucial importance of television serials is obvious to anyone who has been to Egypt. [. . .] Easily the most popular of television genres, these Egyptian serials, usually lasting 15 days, seem to set the very rhythms of national life. [. . .]

If the serials produce a national community and television in Egypt, as in most countries, is state-controlled, one needs to ask how the entertainment provided to these large audiences that cross boundaries of class, gender, and region articulates with national politics, policies, and cultural identities. [. . .] The kinds of questions that must be addressed are: What are the internal politics of these national productions? Meant to entertain, are the serials free of political messages? Who controls these messages and who is excluded? Concerns about global inequalities and domination should not lead us to forget the existence of domestic forms of inequality and political control.

On the basis of an analysis of several key serials of the late 1980s, I will argue that although the writers and producers of the most sophisticated Egyptian television serials have a certain independence from the government that is reflected in the social criticism characteristic of their productions, they nevertheless participate in a shared discourse about nationhood and citizenship that manifests itself most directly these days in their treatment of religion. Their television dramas thus play an important part in the most pressing political contest in Egypt (and other predominantly Muslim countries): the contest over the place of Islam in social and political life.

I also want to argue, however, that this vividly drawn contest over the proper place of Islam in national life may not be perceived as such by many of the communities that constitute the audiences for these serials. Nearly all mass-media cultural production takes place in Cairo, the capital and major city of Egypt.[1] Moreover, those professionals responsible for producing the entertainment are urban and educated, part of the national cultural and intellectual elite, and civil servants. Although they self-consciously direct their products to their imagined audience – the Egyptian people – their perspectives as urban professionals living in the political centre of the country can be quite different from those of their viewers, whether in the regional or class 'peripheries.' In at least two rural regions, for example – the Bedouin area in the northwest of Egypt and the agricultural area in the south – people view the two positions that are so at odds in the capital as merely the twin faces of modernity. This raises the question of the effectiveness of the government-sanctioned political messages of these serials against the actualities of people's particular situations within the nation-state.

The view from the centre

Questions about the place of Islam are at the centre of public life in Egypt. Among the more educated and the professionals, especially in Egypt's cities, with occasional assassinations (including that of former President Sadat) making news, periodic government crackdowns on Islamic groups alternating with attempts at co-optation and accommodation, and signs of a self-consciously Islamic cultural identity growing, the contest is sharply drawn. The contest is reflected and managed in the mass media, especially television, in subtle ways. [. . .]

One of the best ways to explore how this opposition between the secular television producers and the forces of 'religious extremism' plays itself out is to examine several popular serials. Analysis of a few successful serials of the last few years provides a sense of the way television is working in contemporary Egypt to assert a particular place for Islam. With one important exception (a controversial serial called 'Hilmiyya Nights'), these television serials maintain a noticeable silence on the Islamic movements and deliberately ignore the alternative vision these movements offer of Islam's place in Egypt's future – that is, as the solution to many of its problems – for specific political reasons.

The two works I consider first are directed by Muhammad Fadil, arguably Egypt's foremost television director, and scripted by Usama Anwar 'Ukasha, a thoughtful writer with a mission to provide high-quality fare for television. Their collaboration has resulted in the most noteworthy serials of the past few years – programs of immense popularity that have also generated intense debate in the press and at public meetings around the country. Both works can be seen as critical commentaries (skilfully embedded in an entertaining mix of melodrama and comedy) on Egypt in the post-Nasser period – the period beginning in the mid-1970s known as that of the *infitah* or 'opening' to the West and to capitalist development. The first serial, 'The White Flag,' was aired finally in 1989 after several years of trouble with the censors; the second, titled 'The Journey of Mr. Abu al-'Ela al-Bishry' and subtitled 'A Comedy about People and the Morals of These Times' was broadcast several years earlier.

The protagonists of both serials are dignified, cultured, and highly moral men in their late fifties or early sixties who have spent their lives in public service, one as an ambassador in Europe and the other as an irrigation inspector in provincial Egypt. The ambassador returns to Alexandria after a long stint abroad; the engineer returns to the Cairo he has not visited for

years. Both find a changed Egypt and are forced to confront the contemporary forces of corruption threatening Egyptian society. [. . .]

These serials deplore the moral state of the nation in modern times; they
ask whether the harsh but all-too-familiar circumstances of inadequate
housing, low wages, and rising prices must lead people to abandon their
principles. Especially in 'The Journey' we hear a good deal about
manners, principles, morality, and values. [. . .]

The serials directed by Fadil and written by 'Ukasha are cleverer, more
subtle, and complex than the works produced by most other television professionals. But they differ little in the catalogue of social ills they associate with
the times. Other recent serials show individuals and families struggling
against bureaucratic red tape, the near impossibility of getting anything done
without connections and/or bribes, the corruption of government officials,
the fallout of the housing crisis, and high prices. [. . .] The serials, in other
words, are often about the struggles of good, decent people and families
to remain so in these trying times.[2]

What may be unique about these two popular serials is that they personify
morality and immorality not by the contrast between tradition and modernity
or the local versus the Western but by two social classes. One class consists
of those who took advantage of the economic liberalization and 'opening'
that President Sadat initiated in the 1970s and President Mubarak has
continued: people portrayed in the serials as fat cats who drive around in
late-model Mercedes while others cannot afford to marry, wear fancy suits
and sit in glass-and-steel office buildings, deal in construction, take and offer
bribes, and embezzle while others are unemployed. The younger generation is represented as spoiled and self-centred, dazzled by the allure of money
and glamour and trying to become movie stars, pop singers, and boutique
owners.[3]

The other class consists of educated professionals – not just irrigation
engineers and diplomats but lawyers, architects, doctors, medical students,
university students, philosophy teachers, school principals, responsible
journalists, serious artists, and translators. Some have risen from the bottom
of society through their education; others have been comfortable all their
lives. The quality they share is that they are honest and care about others
and their society.[4]

No opposition is set up between Westernization and an authentic indigenous identity, however defined. Both classes are presented as having
appropriated much that could be considered modern and Western; the
difference lies in what they have incorporated into their lives. [. . .]

What is startling in these works, in the context of the current situation
in Egypt, is the absence of religion as a source of morality and the avoidance
of overt signs of Muslim piety and identity in the protagonists. The silence
on the Islamic movement as a modern alternative is broken only to mock.
The villain in 'The White Flag' wears clothes that are a travesty of the new
Islamic modest dress that has become a fashionable sign of piety in the cities
and towns of Egypt. [. . .]

While the everyday forms of piety that are so much a part of life in Egypt
are occasionally reflected in the popular serials – older characters or simple
peasants are sometimes shown praying or using religious phrases – the new

forms of piety are never portrayed. One never sees the young in the cities asserting an Islamic identity in the serials. The obscuring of this crucial group can be tracked through dress. There is a stark contrast between what the fashionably outfitted bareheaded actresses wear in the serials and what real urban women depicted in television documentaries wear. These educated and semi-educated women on the streets, in schools, in health clinics, and in offices (including those of the Union of Television and Radio itself) are more often than not wearing the head covering known as the *higab* and the full-length clothing of new Islamic modest dress.[5]

This is not to say that religious programming on television does not exist; there is an increasing amount of it.[6] [. . .] But such religious programming is generally kept segregated from the more popular shows, especially the serials.

Exclusions

Why these exclusions and segregations? A look at who is involved in television gives some indication. Television was introduced to Egypt in 1960 under President Nasser and used, along with radio, as an instrument of national development and political mobilization.[7] This ideology of mass communication in the service of national development, common enough in the Third world, persists for some like the director whose serials I have been describing. He diagnoses the problem of citizens of this 'developing nation' as 'cultural illiteracy' and sees television drama as the best instrument for eliminating such illiteracy.[8] The discourse of other influential figures in television is a somewhat patronizing one of the guidance and education of the Egyptian masses.[9] [. . .]

Many urban intellectuals within the television industry, people like Fadil and 'Ukasha who came of age during the Nasser period, see their vision of modernity and progress under threat today from both the newly wealthy and the religious groups. Their serials uphold the secular national institutions of the post colonial state, promote the ideals of informed citizenship, and deplore what they view as abuses of basically good institutions like the law, government, education, and the family.[10] Although somewhat controversial, the social criticism they offer remains within the bounds of the familiar paradigms of the official political parties.

Such is not the case for the self-proclaimed radical Islamic reformists who are ignored in the serials. They speak directly to the same corruption and consumerism the serials deplore. In their meetings, pamphlets, magazines, and Friday sermons in the thousands of private mosques for which the Ministry of Religious Endowments cannot provide preachers, they offer an alternative path to modernity – a path that rejects the West and the secular nationalist vision that derived from it, as well as those Egyptians who have associated themselves with the West.[11] This alternative vision of a self-consciously Islamic path has a widespread appeal because it seems to offer people a moral way to deal with the times.

What Fadil and 'Ukasha, as well as other television professionals seem to be contesting, in excluding this vision for the future from the serials, is not the value of religious faith and piety but the place where Muslim discourse is relevant. The segregation of religious and popular programming produces a sense of the separation of spheres, declaring the *irrelevance* of religion, except as a moral guide, to the public domain of political development, economic progress, and social responsibility. The same television professionals who refuse or are unable to portray the appeal of the Islamist vision or to criticize it openly may be personally pious.[12] But they carefully set up boundaries that are rejected by the Muslim activist groups who assert that Islam, referring to sources like the Koran and the model of the Prophet and his first community, can and should provide a blueprint for society and government and should inform every aspect of life; there is no distinction made between 'public' and 'private.'

If the short pieces published on the back page of *Al-I'tisam*, the magazine of the Muslim Brotherhood, are any indication, these groups resent this exclusion and are quick to condemn television.[13] [. . .]

The magazine is even critical of the voice of official Islam in Egypt, Shaykh Jad-al-Haq, rector of Al-Azhar University. [. . .]

Shaykh Jad-al-Haq does take a more moderate stance on television entertainment. In a *fatwa*, or legal opinion, on the arts, written on July 5 1988, and published by *Al-Azhar Magazine* he states that 'Islam does not forbid entertainment or enjoyment.' [. . .] The Shaykh recognizes the importance of ends. Unlike those in *Al-I'tisam* who attack actors and actresses, he notes that 'acting can be used as a tool to educate society through discussing issues that are threatening to the harmony of a successful society – issues such as family ties and how they have weakened, or how selfishness, betrayal and dishonesty are widespread in modern societies' (Jad-al-Haq, 1988–89, pp. 10–23).

This latter judgement would condone the work of the socially conscious television drama producers I have been describing whose central themes were exactly those the religious leader valued. Here, as in many other arenas, the position of the highest official in the religious establishment in Egypt does not challenge the government, in so far as television represents the position of the government that controls it.

But the relationship between government and television production is complex. Since some of the best directors can and do fund most of their productions through independent financing, the state television bureaucracy has at its disposal only the power of censorship together with the preemptive self-censorship that accompanies this in the case of culture producers like Fadil and 'Ukasha.[14] Unlike many other serials, their works are often controversial because they are so critical of social conditions in Egypt and, by implication, government policy. Fadil has always been known and respected for this political criticism. His first serial, aired in the days after the 1967 defeat and called 'Cairo and People,' focused on cases of corruption and the abandoning of national ideals in the Nasser period. [. . .]

With the significant shifts in government policy pursued by Nasser's successors, Sadat and Mubarak, this socially concerned director and the writer with whom he often collaborates seem to have become even more critical. In their productions they now nostalgically invoke, through charged symbols of the Nasser era like the great singer Umm Kulthum or the Aswan High Dam, the period of socialist ideals and nationalist vision. In fact, an upsurge of interest in the Nasser period is noticeable in a number of the popular serials aired during the last few years. One [. . .] was an extraordinarily popular serial called 'Ra'fat al-Haggan,' whose first two instalments were shown during the months of Ramadan in 1989 and 1990. Based on a book by Salih Mursy, it claimed to tell the true story of an Egyptian spy successfully planted in Israel for 20 years beginning in the 1950s.[15] [. . .] Unlike most Egyptian television serials this was a political rather than a family drama. It offered, however, only the simple message of identity politics, which guaranteed its appeal to a wide constituency.

The opening scene sets the terms. Shown writhing in pain, the protagonist is dying of cancer in his home in Germany. He confesses to his German wife: 'I'm not an Israeli, I'm an Egyptian. I'm not a Jew, I'm a Muslim,' His widow then goes to Egypt in search of the truth about her husband. The rest of the serial unfolds the story of his life, through flashbacks accompanying the narrative his handler recounts to her. What matters in this opening scene and another in the same episode is that our hero, Ra'fat al-Haggan, although initially a small-time crook, is a patriotic Egyptian who has sacrificed himself for his country. [. . .] Other kinds of politics besides this general love of country are noticeably absent. There is nothing to indicate what Egypt's internal politics were at the time although one hears some of Nasser's emotional radio broadcasts about the 1956 war. More intriguing, neither the politics nor history of the Palestine conflict is presented even though our hero is living in Israel.[16] [. . .]

In the context of Islam and national television, however, the most fascinating aspect of the serial is the way it asserts that Islam is an essential part of our hero's Egyptian identity even though he is not living a religious life. In Israel he is regularly shown drinking wine over meals and gambling (to obtain secrets); moreover, since he is passing himself off in Israel as an Egyptian Jew, he even attends temple. Yet two moving scenes claim for him his Muslim identity. The first occurs in the first episode, right after Ra'fat's death. His body has been prepared for burial and lies in a casket. The Egyptian Intelligence Officer who has taken special charge of him cannot bear the thought that he will have a Jewish burial and that no Egyptians will attend to honour him. So he flies to Europe and, disguised as a rabbi, manages to get into the house while everyone is away. As he stands before the casket he slips off his shoes, as one would do to pray in a mosque, and pulls out from his breast pocket a copy of the Koran. With tears in his eyes, he recites over the corpse of the hero the proper verses for praying over the dead.

We see this officer cry in another episode as well, the one in which, late one night, he first discovers the file of Agent 313 and thus the existence of Ra'fat in Israel. Although others in the Intelligence Service have lost faith in Ra'fat because he is not sending worthwhile information, this young officer in training is moved by what he finds when he looks through the file; he decides to take responsibility for the young spy. When he opens the folder, he finds an envelope marked, 'To be opened after my death.' It begins (and we hear Ra'fat's voice repeating after him), 'In the Name of God the Merciful the Compassionate. Truly we are God's and to Him we return.' This is our hero's will, to be executed, he says, if he does not return alive to the land of his beloved Egypt. In a broken voice, with mournful music playing in the background, Ra'fat goes through, one by one, the sums to be given to each of the members of his family, even those brothers who mistreated him after the death of his father. He ends, by now practically sobbing, with the Muslim profession of faith: 'Thus I will have cleared myself of all guilt in front of God, after I sacrificed everything in the service of the cherished homeland. God is Great, and for the glory of Egypt, I testify that there is no god but God and that Muhammad is his prophet.'

The protagonist has, in this document, neatly linked Egyptian patriotism with Islamic identity. The serial can be interpreted as asserting that those in the more militant Islamic movements today – and by implication perhaps their brethren jailed during the Nasser era – have no grounds for accusing their secular government of being less than fully identified with Islam. This program can thus be seen as part of a struggle to reappropriate Islamic identity for secular nationalists, a struggle in which the state-controlled mass media, as in much else, are instrumental.

Peripheral visions: regionalism

In the cities of Egypt the secular visions purveyed by television dramas and the Islamists' assertions of Islam's relevance to national political and social life are clearly opposed. But is this opposition viewed in the same way in rural areas? To suggest how differently the contest might be viewed, I want to sketch in the surprising interplay between the forces of mass-media entertainment and Islamic activism in two communities outside Cairo with which I am familiar. I had initially become interested in television and radio dramatic serials while working with the Awlad 'Ali Bedouin of the Western Desert because these figured in generational conflicts. Resistance to the authority of elders was beginning, in the mid-1980s, to take the form of a slight shift on the part of the younger generation toward identification with a national Egyptian culture based in the Nile Valley. The irony was that while the radio soap operas and Egyptian popular music inspired in some young people a tentative desire to emulate certain aspects of middle-class urban Egyptian life-styles – romantic love, companionate marriage, and education and careers for women – the same avid consumers were those whose involvement in national schooling was putting them in contact with the growing urban trend toward public religiosity.

The attitude of one young Bedouin woman I call Kamla, the only girl in the community in which I lived to have graduated from high school, illustrate this seemingly strange confluence. Over the 10 years I knew her, Kamla had come more and more to chafe against the restrictions facing Bedouin girls and women. [. . .]

Her attitudes towards the new Islamic activists were more positive than the older generation's. Because most of the older people in the Bedouin community are secure in their identities as Muslims, they have mixed reactions to the sanctimonious Egyptians they are beginning to encounter and the assertions of some moderately educated Awlad 'Ali from the towns and cities who are becoming, as they called them, 'followers of the traditions' (meaning the model of the Prophet). The older women are not cowed. They argue that they had always worn modest clothing and covered their hair with a head cloth – unlike urban Egyptians who had until recently preferred Western clothes. They resent being told that some of the ways they have been devout Muslims are wrong.

Kamla was less certain. Sometimes she defended these Muslim sisters and brothers, as they called them, and sometimes she went along with the old Bedouin women as they made fun of them. [. . .] Kamla defended the new Islamists, as she would defend ordinary Egyptians when her sisters criticized them for their stinginess or their immorality compared to Awlad 'Ali Bedouin. Her involvement in school had developed in her a patriotism that her parents did not share, a national identification that extended from the love stories of the non-Bedouin soap operas to the piety of the urban Islamists.[17]

In brief research visits in 1990 to a village at the opposite end of Egypt I saw further evidence of this association between mass-media values and the new Islamic identity as twin aspects of a national urban identity, an identity distinct from the local regional identity of villagers. Although their assertions of separate identity are less pronounced than the Awlad 'Ali's, people in Upper Egypt (in the south) do claim they are different from northern Egyptians, drawing, like the Awlad 'Ali, on a distinctive origin. [. . .]

Television was more widely available in this village than among the Awlad 'Ali Bedouin, many of whom still had no electricity. Most households owned a television set, and there were said to be five colour-television sets in the village. [. . .] As in Cairo, the most popular programs were films and the dramatic serials. Some adults were as enthusiastic about television as their children; others were less interested in television and worried that it was interfering with their children's schoolwork. The influence of the Cairo-based national mass media, however, was present in such phenomena as the distinction between the dialect of the younger people and the older and the fact that, at the celebrations for brides, the young women tended to sing songs learned from movies and the radio rather than the traditional songs of the region.[18]

As with the Awlad 'Ali, however, those going to school were also adopting some of the accoutrements of the new Islamic piety. All the girls past puberty who went to school were required to wear the new veil. At home they went back to their ordinary head scarves. Their female schoolteachers, all from Luxor, the town across the river, also wore the *higab*, except the Coptic (Christian) assistant. The young male teachers, by and large a dogmatic group with strong sympathies with the new Islamic movements, were strict with the girls and sometimes quite insulting. [. . .] New linguistic practices were also imposed on the local children. They were forbidden to use, in school or on the schoolgrounds, many of the ordinary words of greeting from the local dialect. Instead they were told they had to use the more conventional Islamic Arabic greetings.[19]

The two experiences of urban or educated sophistication these young villagers encountered were contrary in their messages and intents, as we saw above. Yet like the Awlad 'Ali, these villagers on the margins of the dominant national culture did not perceive the contradictions between the new Islamic pious activism and the dramas of secular television because the people involved were equally associated with the nonlocal – with the major cities of Cairo and Alexandria or even the provincial cities and towns closer to home.

Television as a national medium

In many parts of the world, television is the most popular and ubiquitous public medium, offering diverse fare and available to a wider range of people than print media. Because programs are fleeting, repeated only occasionally in reruns, and part of a daily 'flow', as Raymond Williams has noted, their impact is hard to assess. Yet if we can determine which programs do seem to capture the imaginations of audiences we can begin to ask why and to what effect. In so far as popular programs deal with national social and political issues, as I have argued about Egyptian serials, they cannot be analysed at the general level of cultural difference but must be treated as historically specific. For the anthropologist this means not just describing and analysing the texts of the programs or the responses of the audience but also relating these to the complex dynamics of political life in the country concerned. [. . .]

Television can be a powerful national cultural force, as it is in Egypt, but it never simply reflects or produces the interests of the nation-state. Even if the medium is state-controlled, the producers are not necessarily puppets. In Egypt they have some freedom of expression and respond creatively to many of the restrictions in place. And though the political and moral issues that the most sophisticated of these producers engage may seem clear to them – living in the capital where the political debates about Egypt's future are part of a daily conversation and take a certain familiar form due to the structure of a press organized along political party lines – their programs can be received quite differently in outlying areas. The case I discussed here concerned the hostile relation between the popular television soap operas and the ideologies of the Islamic groups: for the people I knew in the Awlad 'Ali Bedouin community, as for those in the Upper Egyptian village who may have found it difficult to see themselves in either the secular and sophisticated vision of the television serials or the Islamist vision of a rigid, textually based Islamic identity that seeks to transform society, both visions were compelling because associated with superior education and cosmopolitanism.

The case of Egyptian television reminds us of the continuing importance of regional identities within nation-states. As we become increasingly sophisticated in attending to global or transnational cultural processes (Appadurai, 1990; Hannerz, 1989) we must not lose sight of the internal dynamics of the nation-states that participate in these flows. When we speak of centre and periphery, we need to recall that it is not just Western capitalism and Third World peripheries in question but, equally important, centres and peripheries within countries. This is especially true in countries with cities that tend to dominate other regions – politically, economically, and culturally. Where groups in outlying regions have distinct identities and are not well integrated into the centre or are integrated at the bottom of the hierarchy, any consideration of national cultural productions must explore differential reception of mass-media products. This project – of examining regional variation and asking how, in particular places, the people who form the imagined audience of the culture producers respond to and appropriate what is broadcast to them – must be part of any study of television as a national medium.

Notes

1. Alexandria is involved with some theatre and film, and many television serials are now filmed abroad in the superior studios of Jordan and the Gulf states.
2. A study conducted in 1981–82 that included a content analysis of all television dramas, interviews about current social problems with members of the Writers' Union, and a survey of problems reported in major newspapers suggested that most television drama was based on stories about Egyptian problems. The major foci were quite similar to those I noted in 1989–90: class conflict and the gap between rich and poor; economic problems such as housing, price inflation, poverty, and Byzantine bureaucracies; family problems; the persistence of traditional attitudes and rejection of modern practices. Confirming one of the points of this article, the study noted that 87.7% of the works were concerned with urban, as opposed to rural, problems. See Ali (1984).
3. Significantly, the critique of this class of *nouveau riche* entrepreneurs and the linking of the deterioration of family ties with the business opportunities of the 'opening up' are themes common to what Malkmus (1988) has labelled the 'new' Egyptian cinema, a more realistic and socially conscious cinema that emerged in the late 1970s and 1980s.
4. For a more detailed treatment of 'The White Flag' that differs in some respects from mine, see the dissertation in progress on Egyptian popular culture by Walter Armbrust, Department of Anthropology, University of Michigan.
5. The only exception of which I am aware to this exclusion of the Islamics from serials is the highly critical portrayal of 'religious extremists' in the fourth instalment of 'Hilmiyya Nights,' the controversial serial written by 'Ukasha. The serial is so unusual that it merits a separate study, which is forthcoming. For the first full-length study of the new veiling among lower-middle-class women in Cairo, see MacLeod (1990). See also Abaza (1987), El Guindi (1981), Hoffman-Ladd (1987), and Stowasser (1987b) for excellent discussions of the ideology of the new veiling and its relation to larger political trends in Egypt.
6. Abaza (1987, p. 20–23) sees the increase in religious programming as a strategy for assertions by the state of its religiosity to counter the religious opposition groups so popular in the early 1980s.
7. For an outline of the history of television and radio in Egypt, see CEDEJ (1987). Karthigesu (1988) explores the common development aims of television in the post colonial world.
8. Interview with Muhammad Fadil by the author, April 15, 1990.
9. This is consistent with Rugh's observations in the late 1970s (1984, p. 250).
10. A telling scene is one in 'The Journey' in which a young woman is reassured by a lawyer that justice will be done. He tells her, 'The law isn't just texts and we aren't just machines for putting them into effect. The law is based on values and morality.'
11. The literature on the Islamic movements around the Arab world is vast. Some important studies are Dessouki (1982), Ibrahim (1980), Kepel (1985), Kramer (1987–88), and Stowasser (1987a).
12. When I interviewed them during the month of Ramadan they were observing the religious fast – just as Egyptian presidents like Sadat and Mubarak are televised praying at the mosques on religious holidays.
13. A book critical of the negative effects of television on Muslim family life even draws on research by Western social scientists to bolster its claims. See Kashak (1986).
14. In recent years, an even more powerful force for self-censorship has been the economic necessity of selling programs to the morally conservative wealthy Arab nations of the Gulf.

15. For a review of the press concerning this serial, see the dossier in CEDEJ (1988).
16. For a discussion of the way the Egyptian serials, even when presenting social criticism, are depoliticized, see Abu-Lughod (1991).
17. For more discussion of Kamla and the issues of generational conflict see Abu-Lughod (1989, 1990, 1993).
18. Slyomovics (1987) has studied the traditional epic poetry performed by male poets in this region, but I am not aware of studies of women's traditional song in the region.
19. For example, a schoolteacher told me that they did not allow children to use the local word for goodbye – '*adiiila* – but instead had to use *ma' as-salama*.

References

Abaza, Mona (1987) *The Changing Image of Women in Rural Egypt*. Cairo Papers in Social Science, Vol. 10, No. 3, America University in Cairo Press, Cairo.
Abu-Lughod, Lila (1989) Bedouins, Cassettes, and Technologies of Public Culture. *MERIP Middle East Report*, 159, Vol. 19, No. 4, pp. 7–11.
Abu-Lughod, Lila (1990) The Romance of Resistance: Tracing Transformations of Power through Bedouin Women. *American Ethnologist*, Vol. 17, pp. 41–55.
Abu-Lughod, Lila (1991) Public Culture in Contemporary Egypt. *Newsletter of the American Research Center in Egypt*, Vol. 154, pp. 9–12.
Abu-Lughod, Lila (1993) *Writing Women's Worlds: Bedouin Stories*. University of California Press, Berkeley and Los Angeles.
'Ali, Samya Ahmad (1984) Television Drama and the Problem of Egyptian Society. (In Arabic.) Thesis, Faculty of Communication, Cairo University.
Appadurai, Arjun (1990) Disjuncture and Difference in the Global Cultural Economy. *Public Culture*, Vol. 2, No. 2, pp. 1–24.
CEDEJ (1987) Anciens et nouveaux médias en Egypte: radio, télévision, cinéma, vidéo. *Bulletin de CEDEJ*, Vol. 21, Premier semestr.
CEDEJ (1988) Renseignements égyptiens: le héros, la pécheresse et l'agent double. *Revue de la presse egyptienne*, Vol. 32/33, 2ème semestre, pp. 109–54.
Dessouki, Ali E. Hillal (1982) *Islamic Resurgence in the Arab World*, Praeger, New York.
El Guindi, Fadwa (1981) Veiling Infitah with Muslim Ethic. *Social Problems*, Vol. 28, pp. 465–85.
Hannerz, Ulf (1989) Notes on the Global Ecumene. *Public Culture*, Vol. 1, No. 2, pp. 66–75.
Hoffman-Ladd, Valerie (1987) Polemics on the Modesty and Segregation of Women in Contemporary Egypt. *International Journal of Middle East Studies*, Vol. 19, pp. 23–50.
Ibrahim, Saad Eddin (1980) Anatomy of Egypt's Militant Islamic Groups. *International Journal of Middle East Studies*, Vol. 12, pp. 423–53.
Jad al-Haq, Jad al-Haq Ali (1988–89) Characteristics of the Lawful and the Forbidden. (In Arabic.) *Al-Azhar Magazine*, Vol. 61 [suppl.].
Karthigesu, Ranggasamy (1988) Television as a Tool for Nation-Building in the Third World: A Post-colonial Pattern, Using Malaysia as a Case-Study. In Drummond, Phillip and Paterson, Richard (eds.) *Television and Its Audience*, British Film Institute, London, pp. 306–26
Kashak, Marwan (1986) *The Muslim Family in Front of Video and Television*. (In Arabic.) Dar al-Kalima al-Tayyiba, Cairo.
Kepel, Gilles (1985) *The Prophet and Pharaoh: Muslim Extremism in Egypt*. Al-Saqi, London.
Kramer, Gudrun (1987–88) The Change of Paradigm: Political Pluralism in Contemporary Egypt. *Peuples mediterraneens*, Vol. 41–42, pp. 283–302.

MacLeod, Arlene (1990) *Accommodating Protest: Working Women, the New Veiling, and Change in Cairo*, Columbia University Press, New York.

Malkmus, Lizbeth (1988) The 'New' Egyptian Cinema: Adapting Genre Conventions to a Changing Society. *Cineaste*, Vol. 3, pp. 30–3.

Rugh, Andrea (1984) *Family in Contemporary Egypt*, Syracuse University Press, Syracuse, NY.

Slyomovics. Susan (1987) *The Merchant of Art*, University of California Press, Berkeley and Los Angeles.

Stowasser, Barbara (ed.) (1987a) *The Islamic Impulse*, Center for Contemporary Arab Studies, Georgetown University, Washington DC.

Stowasser, Barbara (1987b) Religious Ideology, Women, and the Family: The Islamic Paradigm. In Stowasser, Barbara (ed.) *The Islamic Impulse*, Center for Contemporary Arab Studies, Georgetown University, Washington, DC.

27

Local uses of the media: negotiating culture and identity

Marie Gillespie

From Gillespie, M. (1995) *Television, Ethnicity and Cultural Change*, Routledge, London, pp. 76–108.

TV offers powerful representations of both Indian and British culture for the youth of Southall who, though British citizens, do not always feel themselves to be part of the British nation and, though of Indian heritage and Punjabi background, are often less than willing to embrace all aspects of their cultural heritage. One of this chapter's key arguments is that [. . .] the consumption of an increasingly transnational range of TV and films is catalysing and accelerating processes of cultural change among London Punjabi families. But it will also be argued that Punjabi cultural 'traditions' are just as likely to be reaffirmed and reinvented as to be challenged and subverted by TV and video viewing experiences. [. . .]

Technology and tradition

The video cassette recorder (VCR) has been appropriated by many parents and grandparents ('elders') in Southall as a means of recreating cultural traditions in Britain; but their efforts are both subverted and 'diverted' by young people. [. . .]

Viewing Hindi films on video is the main, regular, family-centred leisure activity. The weekend family gathering around the set is a social ritual where notions of togetherness take precedence. The weaving of conversation around the film is facilitated by the episodic structure of the narrative which moves the viewer through successive modes of song, dance action and affect, providing breaks for the discussion of issues raised by a member of the family in response to the film. While fathers are generally seen to control access to the main TV screen when at home, mothers, and females in the family more generally, are seen to exert more influence over the choice of what is watched. [. . .]

As gender differences are important to understanding parental control over viewing, they are also a significant factor in understanding young people's viewing preferences and behaviour. Boys experience greater freedom in deciding how to use their leisure time and spent more of it in public leisure pursuits. In contrast, girls are expected to remain at home where strong and supportive female cultures are strengthened by collectively viewing and discussing Hindi films. Female-only viewing sessions which span three or four generations are common. One of the dominant themes of Hindi movies is the 'clash of tradition and modernity' in Indian society, which is normally resolved at the expense of the latter. Films, or young viewers' interpretations of them, which affirm 'modernity' as against 'tradition' provoke discussion with female elders, many of whom, as their children or grandchildren say, 'are living in the India which they left 20 years ago' and are unwilling to embrace change. Thus the viewing of Hindi films is often accompanied by an airing of views and intense debates on tradition and modernity; indeed there is evidence that the content of Hindi films is discussed far more, by viewers in India and Britain alike, than is the content of Western films (Pfleiderer and Lutze, 1985). [. . .] Conversely, the family is often fragmented by British and American films: 'When it's Indian films it's all of us together but when it's English films it's just me and my brother.' This is partly due to the texts of such films themselves and, given parental reservations about their morality, or lack of it, the values they are seen to endorse, and sexual explicitness, young people often prefer to view them on their own to escape parental censure.

The avid consumption of VCR films largely conforms to this dichotomy: Hindi films are viewed in large family gatherings and accompanied by intense social interaction, while the viewing of most British and American films on the part of young people constitutes a more or less assertive circumvention of parental control and rejection of their cultural preferences. But young people's viewing of Hindi films raises further ethnographic questions about perceptions of India and Britain and what it is to 'be Indian' or 'be British'. [. . .]

Representations of/from India

For young people in Southall, Indian films are invariably an important influence on their perceptions of the subcontinent. This is especially true of those with little or no direct experience of India but, even for those who have spent long periods there, the films provide a counterpoint to their lived experience. A series of related binary oppositions structure interviewees' accounts of how India is perceived through the films:

Tradition . . . . . . .Modernity
Village/rural . . . . City/urban
Poverty . . . . Wealth
Communality . . . Individualism
Morality . . . . .Vice

This pattern of social, political and moral discourse is indeed prevalent in Hindi films, where a pristine, moral, rural India is conventionally constructed in opposition to its exotic, decadent 'other', signified by symbols of city life and the West (Thomas, 1985). [. . .] But the 'unrealistic' portrayal of village life was also much criticized, and the interviewees were well aware of the selective and ideological nature of such representations. [. . .]

Striking gender differences emerged in the way accounts of the films were framed. Girls often expressed their perceptions of India by drawing out the social and moral values inherent in films through a retelling of the narratives.

Boys seemed much more concerned with representational issues, particularly 'negative images', and in many cases rejected Hindi films *per se* on that basis. Several male informants saw the films' emphasis on poverty and corruption as offensive: 'They shouldn't portray India as if it's really poor and backward even though they're Indians themselves, it's degrading'. One boy vehemently rejected the films, wishing to dissociate himself both from the films and from India, with the ironic comment: 'I didn't learn anything from the films apart from the fact that India is one of the most corrupt countries in the world', and later: 'That country has nothing to do with me any more'.

In discussions of this topic, representations of India in the British media were also often commented upon. These are seen as reinforcing an 'uncivilized', poverty-stricken image: 'documentaries shown in this country degrade India badly as well'. Strong resentment is felt at the circulation in the West of images of poverty, underdevelopment, death and disease, images which are seen to be linked to the 'degradation' of Indians in Britain where they 'get racist harassment'. Experiences of racism in Britain undoubtedly influence the range of meanings projected on to Hindi films, as they underpin responses to constructions of Indian society in all media. Boys especially show an understanding of how 'outsiders', for example their white peers, may rebuke Hindi films as 'backward' and 'ludicrous', but they also clearly feel estranged themselves from the sense of 'Indianess' and the 'India' represented in the films. There is an underlying awareness that the films, when viewed in the 'West', may function to confirm dominant racist discourses on India and Indian/'Asian' people. Apparently, experiences of racism as well as such readings of the films are gender specific.

Western critics – academics and film enthusiasts alike – have either reviled or ignored Hindi films for nearly a century. This disdain and ignorance both springs from and feeds into racism. The fierce rejection of Hindi films as a 'genre', especially among boys, echoes Western critical discourses. One 18-year-old boy's condemnation of Indian films was particularly eloquent:

> With the standards of media appreciation in the West it's hard to understand the sort of psyche that would appreciate these kinds of film again and again and again [. . .] it's like driving a Morris Minor after you've driven a Porsche.

This coincidence of views does not confirm a 'truth' about the Hindi cinema. Rather it exposes a common frame of reference based on dominant Western (Hollywood) film-making practices. Even where language presents no barrier, popular Hindi films subvert the generic conventions of Western cinema and disorientate spectators whose expectations have been formed by Western genres. [. . .]

One of the commonest assertions made by interviewees was that the films all have the same type of stories, and that they are therefore 'totally predictable' and not worth watching. Three basic narrative themes, popular in the late 1970s and 1980s, were repeatedly identified: (1) 'Dostana', where a bond of male friendship overcomes the desire for a woman; (2) 'lost and found', where parents and children are separated and reunited years later following a revelation of mistaken identities; and (3) 'revenge', where villains get their just desserts at the hands of wronged heroes (Thomas, 1985, pp. 125). [. . .]

But interviewees who enjoy Hindi films reject the narrative structure typical of Western films which are seen as 'continuous all the way [. . .] they just continue, no songs, no dances [. . .] that's why I find them boring'.

Pleasure is taken in the non-linear narratives, and the intricate and convoluted nature of storytelling in the Hindi cinema becomes apparent in attempts at narrative reconstructions. [. . .] Viewers expect to become emotionally involved with characters and this is a crucial part of the pleasure. Affective engagement is ensured not only by cinematic techniques which encourage identification but also through the songs which heighten the emotional impact of the film: 'The songs back everything up [. . .] they have real feeling in them and it's not just any old songs, they relate to the actual situations in the films, they get you emotionally involved and influence you'.[. . .]

Fantasy, particularly romantic fantasy, is a chief source of pleasure for those who enjoy Hindi films. The songs and dances and their settings provide discrete 'dream-like' sequences and a 'moment of escape from reality'. [. . .]

Others take a more critical view of such fantastical scenes. They are seen as exploitative and reactionary by more politically minded informants who compare recent films with the social-realist films of the 1950s:

> I think people could identify their immediate life with them [. . .] if they showed a farmer losing his crops after years of hard labour that was a reflection of life [. . .] there was nothing magical about it as it is now. After this period people didn't want tragedies they wanted fantasies, they wanted a means of escape, they wanted to break out of reality.

Many, however, even if they make such criticisms, reorganize the cathartic and therapeutic aspects of these cinematic opiates. They are seen as enabling a temporary release from the tensions of everyday life and as helping viewers to discharge distressful emotions vicariously. One girl revealed:

> I'm scared of my parents finding out that I have a boyfriend but after I've watched a film, and listened to a few songs and calmed myself down, I'm not scared of my parents any more – so they give you courage in a way.

Some girls find the films provide a source of support and encouragement, affirming their ideology of romantic love and legitimizing their 'illicit' romantic liaisons through the power of feeling expressed by the lovers in the films. Some girls who are concerned about their own love and future marital relationships appear to seek confirmation in the movies that 'true love' can really be found. 'Sometimes we just sit there and wonder if there's a thing called love, you hear so many terrible stories of broken relationships and marriages [. . .] whereas in an Indian film you're so convinced that love is real [. . .] that it's true.'

Then again, Western conventions of heightened realism are often contrasted with what are seen to be ludicrously unrealistic action and fight sequences in Hindi films. Anachronism is not easily tolerated. However, the criteria of verisimilitude proper to Hindi cinema appear to be based primarily on the skill exercised in manipulating the rules of the film's moral universe. Among regular viewers, accusations of implausibility are more likely to occur if the ideal codes of kinship duty are flouted than if the hero performs an outrageously unrealistic feat (cf. Thomas, 1985).

Despite the contradictory evaluations of Hindi films, most young people are encouraged to view and discuss the issues they raise with parents. [. . .]

Grandparents use the films to convey a sense of their past in India to their grandchildren, to tell stories of their youth and to describe what life was like for them. Elders regard most Hindi films as a powerful resource for educating their children in the values and beliefs that are seen to be deeply rooted in Indian culture and traditions: 'they teach not only the language but how 'to be' in an Indian environment'. Young adults enjoy films which encourage discussion: 'films which bring out the contradictions in families, the arranged marriage system, the caste system and moral conflicts'. Thus the films serve both youth and their elders as tools for eliciting views on salient themes, especially the issues of kinship duty, courtship and marriage, the most intensely debated of all issues among children and parents. It would appear that Hindi films are used to legitimate a particular world-view but also to open up its contradictions. So, while young people use Indian films to deconstruct 'traditional culture', many parents use them to foster cultural and religious traditions. Some remain sceptical of parental attempts to 'artificially maintain a culture through film' but, successful or not, it is clear that the VCR is being used for the purposes of reformulating and 'translating' cultural traditions in the Indian diaspora.

Devotional viewing: 'sacred soaps'

As I indicated, films serve the purpose of language learning, and elders also use them to impart religious knowledge. [. . .] Religious or 'mythological' films are viewed for devotional purposes, particularly (but not only) in Hindu families, and their viewing is often integrated into daily acts of worship.

In recent years India's government monopoly TV channel, Doordarshan, has screened serial versions of sacred texts of Hinduism, the *Ramayana* and the *Mahabharata*. They have enjoyed unprecedented popularity not only in India, where some 650 million viewers regularly tune in, but also in the Indian diaspora where they are followed on cable TV, on video or, as with the *Mahabharata* in Britain, on broadcast TV. [. . .]

During my fieldwork in Southall, I was fortunate enough to be welcomed into the home of the Dhanis – a Hindu family – in order to watch the Channel 4 broadcast of Peter Brook's stage adaptation of the *Mahabharata*, which occupied six hours on a Saturday evening in November 1990. A few weeks later BBC2 began broadcasting Doordarshan's 91-part serialized version of the *Mahabharata*. So over a two-year period I visited them regularly on Saturday afternoons to watch it. The juxtaposition of the two versions, one Indian and the other 'Western', led the Dhanis to perform a contrastive analysis. [. . .]

The *Mahabharata* and the *Ramayana* are the foundation myths of Indian society. They are said to permeate every aspect of Indian social life and to enshrine the philosophical basis of Hinduism and for centuries have served as an *ithisa* or a fundamental source of knowledge and inspiration for all the arts. In Sanskrit, *maha* means great; '*Bharat*' is the name of a legendary family, which in an extended sense means 'Hindu', or – extended further – 'mankind'. The *Mahabharata* is thus variously translated 'The Great History of India' or 'The Great History of Mankind'. [. . .]

The devotional viewing of religious films involves taboos, prohibitions and rituals, similar to those surrounding sacred places and objects. It is incorporated into the Dhanis' everyday lives as are their domestic acts of worship. For example, at the start of a religious film, incense is lit and when a favourite god such as Krishna appears, the mother will encourage her children to sit up straight and make a devout salutation. An extra *puja* (an act of worship which is generally performed three times a day; before dawn, at noon and in the evening) may be performed before or after viewing. Once a religious film has been switched on it must be viewed until the end out of respect. Food should not be eaten whilst viewing, except *prasad* or holy food that has been blessed. Viewing religious films is seen as a pleasurable act of devotion in itself and devotional viewing is arguably a mark of transformations in religious practices. However, these 'new' modes of TV consumption are nevertheless deeply rooted in Indian religious and cultural traditions, especially the iconographic conventions associated with the representation of deities (Guha-Thakurta, 1986), and devotional modes of looking, seeing and worshipping images deemed sacred (Appadurai and Breckenridge, 1992).

My first visit to the Dhanis to watch Peter Brook's production of the *Mahabharata* was marked by confusion and a crisis. From the outset confusion reigned as the international casting and bleak, sackcloth costumes had the immediate effect of rendering their dearly loved gods unrecognizable:

Ranjit: That's Ganesha!
Sefali: No it isn't, be quiet.
Lipi: That's Vishnu!
Malati: Don't be silly, that's Vyasa.
Ranjit: But Vyasa is Vishnu.
Sefali: No he's not, he's Krishna.

After 20 minutes or so Mr Dhani and his elder son went out proclaiming: 'It's no good, it doesn't carry the meaning'. Mrs Dhani, her five daughters, youngest son and myself continued watching half-heartedly. A sullen and solemn atmosphere reigned and their lack of interest in the programme was evident. [. . .]

It is difficult to convey the sense of relief and change of atmosphere that occurred the moment the set was switched off. I was troubled that they had been putting up with it because of my presence and, as I later discovered, indeed they had. [. . .]

Brook's production was so distasteful to the Dhanis because, firstly, it flouted the iconographic conventions associated with the representation of Hindu deities. Certain visual codes, such as the use of colour to symbolize the personal and moral qualities of the gods, had not been respected in their eyes:

Sefali: You can't even recognize Krishna, normally he's blue.
Malati: Gunga and Bhisma normally wear white because it's a symbol
            of purity and truth.
Ranjit: Duryodhana should wear red shouldn't he because of his
            anger and the blood that gets shed.

Such systems of colour classification and symbolism are to be found in many ancient religions; according to Turner (1966) they provide a kind of primordial classification of reality. [. . .]

However, for the Dhanis, more disturbing than the flouting of visual codes in Brook's production was the transgression of yet more deeply rooted cultural codes, such as the primary distinction between gods and humans. In their view the gods were not portrayed with due dignity or respect. [. . .]

In contrast, in the Indian version, the representation of the Hindu deity conforms to traditional iconographic conventions and therefore can be worshipped on the screen, as are the gods in the popular prints which adorn every room in their home. Thus, for devotional viewing to occur, the image must be perceived as sacred, as entitled to and worthy of veneration. Brook's production violated the sacred aura of the gods as represented by conventional iconography.

The dramatic composition and weighting must also be correctly balanced in order to satisfy the requirements of devotional viewing. Clearly, the experience of viewing a 91-part serialized drama with many of the generic ingredients of the conventional melodrama or soap opera is quite different to that of viewing a six-hour televised theatrical production. Doordarshan's production is aimed at mass popular audiences whilst Brook's is targeted at middle-class theatre-going élites. [. . .] Yet more profoundly, the serial narrative form is able to represent the specific, epic and cyclical notions of time which constitute the philosophical core of the *Mahabharata* – which is seen to convey one cycle of birth, destruction and rebirth – the circle in which humans are caught until they reach spiritual union with the gods.

The role of the narrator also differs between the two versions in a culturally significant way. In Brook's production the story is narrated by Vyasa (an incarnation of Vishnu, one of the principal deities) who appears on screen. In the Indian version the narrator is Vishnu himself, but he is invisible and thus given a divine and mystical quality. [. . .]

The Dhanis highlighted moments in which the narrative weighting was markedly different in the two versions. [. . .]

It is interesting that the Dhanis' criticisms of Brook's production coincide with those of several Indian critics, such as Barucha (1991). Brook's production, according to both, lacks a clearly defined religious and moral frame of reference and is not contextualized within the social and ritual processes of Hindu culture and society; as a result, divine characters undergo a loss of sanctity. [. . .]

In many aspects of their everyday lives the Dhanis apply religious ideas and beliefs which were undoubtedly developed and refined by their viewing of the *Mahabharata*. Specific notions of time, fate and free will, destiny and reincarnation frame their everyday perceptions but, in their contrasted analysis of the two versions of the *Mahabharata*, the Dhanis explicitly articulated their understanding of the Hindu philosophical and religious tradition in a way which illuminated, for them perhaps as much as for me, key aspects of this tradition and so contributed to a further shaping of their values and beliefs. [. . .]

Watching 'Western' soaps

If the viewing of 'sacred soaps' sustains and enhances a commitment to religious and cultural traditions in some families, in others the viewing of 'white', 'Western' soaps such as the Australian *Neighbours*, the favourite soap among young people in Southall, is another domestic ritual, one involving both intimacy and censure. The distinction between the reception of 'sacred soaps' and that of secular, 'Western' soaps, between 'devotional viewing' and what might be called 'devoted viewing', is indeed less sharp than might be thought. The reception of 'Western' soaps too is governed by a moral framework and implicated in informal didactic practices which expose the cultural dynamics of family life – though the issues involved concern the pragmatic ethics of everyday life, lacking any cosmic dimension, and are more likely to provide inter-generational conflict. For young people in Southall, the regular viewing of soaps encourages a sense of participating in a daily activity shared simultaneously with youth audiences nationally and internationally. In fact they feel themselves to belong to a wider youth culture shaped by, among other things, watching *Neighbours*. At the same time their immediate, local concerns are projected on to such soaps and the cultural specificities of Punjabi family life inflect their readings, especially because of the ways in which their elders, in many cases, tend to censure *Neighbours* and their viewing of it.

Viewing soaps with siblings and, in many cases, with mother is by far the most common arrangement. It would appear that most mothers condone their children's regular viewing of *Neighbours* because it is a time, structured into the day, when they know their children will be settled down in front of the TV. Many young people recognize that mothers need a rest from domestic chores. 'Watching with mother' becomes a pretext for intimacy and conversation. But intimacy may be heightened by the act of sharing an experience regardless of what is shared. Given that some mothers understand and speak very little English, it may be the relaxed atmosphere of the viewing situation and the desire to be together, more than the soap itself, which is appreciated. [. . .]

But viewing with mother may just as easily lead to argument and censure as to intimacy. Translation is often necessary which some find tedious and difficult. Others claim that they find it very difficult to communicate with their mothers, as they simply do not understand young people's values. Amrit, a 16-year-old girl, claims that she prefers to watch *Neighbours* without her mother. Moral issues feature prominently in family discussions about soaps. In some families the channel is switched over as soon as kissing or more explicitly sexual behaviour appears on screen. It is often younger members of the family, rather than parents, who quickly grasp the remote control in order to avoid embarrassment or a row. Fathers are seen to be much more censorious than mothers. [. . .]

Diljit, a 17-year-old boy, is expected to speak Punjabi at home and when he and his siblings speak in English together, their father blames the television for influencing them to become 'more English'. He also believes that his children will eventually copy the behaviour they watch on screen and is outraged when young people are shown being disrespectful to their elders, kissing or arguing with siblings. Diljit disagreed with his father, dismissing as absurd his fears about the potential of soaps to inspire imitative behaviour; yet he does admire the way in which young people in *Neighbours* assert themselves to their elders:

> If there are arguments in *Neighbours* with parents and that, then I'll sit there and get even more involved [. . .] I'll sit there thinking, yeah I should have done that [. . .] I should learn to talk back to my dad, but you know, it's very bad to show disrespect like that to your father [. . .] we're not allowed to backchat and argue with our dad but it's good to see how someone else can.

Many parents feel that their values are undermined by soaps like *Neighbours*; the only virtue of such programmes in their eyes is that they alert them to the temptations and traps that their children may fall into. Those commonly mentioned are squandering money in games arcades, smoking, drinking or taking drugs, dating and getting pregnant, and running away from home. Such potential threats make parents more vigilant and lead to censoriousness during soap viewing or, as in several cases I came across, to an absolute injunction against viewing *Neighbours*. In all these cases young people managed to subvert paternal structures with impressive cunning. But neither parents nor their children wish to remain locked in battle, and mothers often act as mediators in such family disputes, alleviating tensions and pacifying the different parties. Thus 'watching with mother' frequently functions as a pretext for intimacy and communication, in which the reaffirmation of shared values negotiates with the articulation of aspirations towards cultural change.

Television as an object and a social experience is embedded in family life, and family relationships are expressed in and through the viewing situation. Soaps bring alternative sets of social behaviour and moral values into the heart of domestic life. In Southall, soap viewing has become a domestic agonistic ritual which involves defining and redefining relationships with 'others' both absent and present: from the characters on the screen, who constitute a televisual presence, to the wider audience, an absent but implied cultural referent; from parents and the local 'community', to siblings and peers. But if soaps are a domestic ritual mediating, shifting and (in some senses) dissolving the boundaries between the public and private, then viewing broadcast news implicates viewers in a further, national daily ritual, addressing them as citizens and members of the British nation.

Local news media

British national press and TV news coexists in Southall with a particular range of both local and international news media. The widespread availability and consumption of newspapers and current affairs magazines from or about the Indian subcontinent is a distinguishing feature of Southall's news culture. But whilst reading newspapers in Punjabi, Hindi or Urdu is rare among young people, listening to news and discussions about current affairs in a variety of South Asian languages, as well as in English, on the local radio station Sunrise is almost inescapable. Sunrise addresses its audience as British 'Asians' and aims, in the words of its chief executive, Avtar Lit, to 'preserve their unique cultural identity and keep them in touch with their mother country'. Sunrise is played continuously in most cafés, restaurants and shops, as well as in most 'Asian' homes. Local folklore emphasizes its ubiquitous quality: a common tale is that one can hear the same song or even a whole programme while walking the length of Southall Broadway. [. . .] News bulletins and current affairs programmes are transmitted in English, Punjabi, Hindi, Urdu and Gujarati. The primary emphasis is on news from the Indian subcontinent, local news stories and news concerning 'Asians' in Britain. It aims to appeal as much to a Glaswegian Sikh as to a Muslim from Bradford or a Gujarati in Wembley. It is often referred to by young people as a 'lifeline' or a 'voice' for the parents. Others, though, see Sunrise as a further index of their 'ghettoization' in an 'Asian community' in London, in much the same way as the local Hindi video culture is held to cut the 'community' off from British society. By and large, young people prefer to listen to London's various independent radio stations, such as Kiss FM and Capital Radio, which target youth audiences. Even though most young people do not share their parent's enthusiasm for Sunrise radio, it is nevertheless their major source of news apart from national TV. [. . .]

But young people's main interest in radio as a medium is in pop programmes and phone-ins, and it is only a matter of contingency that news stories are consumed. Patterns of radio consumption confirm the general tendency towards a preference for British and 'Western', as opposed to Indian or Pakistani, media among Southall youth. However, it is also clear that, whilst few young people would tune into Sunrise voluntarily, many are in fact regular consumers due to their parents' interest, as with Hindi films.

If exposure to news stories through the local press and radio seems inescapable, the extent of broadcast TV news, equally, gives it an ineluctable quality. Survey figures, to my surprise at first, revealed that TV news is the genre most frequently watched and discussed in families in Southall (see Appendix). [. . .] The sheer quantity of hours devoted to news and the strategic positioning of news bulletins in the schedules, as well as parental interest in the news, suggest that it would be difficult for most young people to avoid some news consumption, at least without making a wilful and conscious effort to do so. But these facts alone do not suffice to explain the survey results. Fieldwork research revealed that young people have compelling reasons of their own for watching news programmes with their families. Participation in the domestic ritual of news viewing is perceived to function as a kind of 'rite of passage' both to adult status and to effective British citizenship, particularly when young people are called upon by their parents to act as translators and interpreters of the national news agenda.

News viewing, like soap viewing, helps to structure daily routines and has become a domestic ritual in most homes. [. . .] News is generally seen as the chief source of information about the world, a necessary link to the world outside the local community, and a prerequisite to functioning as a citizen in Britain. National news broadcasts address viewers as citizens, inform them of their rights and responsibilities, and foster a sense of national identity. So it is often in the sphere of news consumption and TV news talk that young people most clearly articulate the complexities and ambivalences of their relation to dominant, national modes of identification – complexities and ambivalences which are closely bound up with teenagers' ambiguous status, on the margin between childhood and adulthood.

'Not the turkey type': Christmas and TV

[. . .] Annual 'British' rituals – notably Christmas, to a lesser extent Easter, and also key events in the sports calendar – are key arenas for the construction of a sense of British national identity. The significance of this function of broadcasting for cultural minorities, who may otherwise have little access to mainstream British culture, is evident.

Belonging to the British nation and participating in national rituals, such as Christmas, are marked by a sense of ambivalence or most Southall families. [. . .] Families in Southall incorporate different aspects of its rituals and customs to varying degrees and in diverse ways. The following account was written by Kuljit, a 17-year-old Sikh girl, on her family's Christmas in 1989:

> Christmas is a Christian festival though my family does not follow the exact Christian way. We do have a party, not the turkey type, but one with food that we all like. We also give presents and cards and we invite family and friends over. We put a Christmas tree up and hang decorations on walls and ceiling. At Christmas we don't watch anything religious, us kids watch English films while our parents watch plenty of Indian movies which we hate because we find them so boring [. . .] we did watch some family films together like *Indiana Jones* and *Crocodile Dundee*. They also watched a programme called *Follow that Star* about an Indian actor named Amitabh Bachan who talked about his life, his family and his career.

Alibhai (1987) sees Christmas as posing particular problems for parents in Southall. She argues that the impetus to celebrate, to buy trees, lights and wrap and exchange presents comes primarily from children, who are the dupes of commercial interests, and she sees participation in Christmas by Southall youth and their families as a manifestation of oppressive, post-colonial, white power – a form of cultural racism. [. . .]

Participation in Christmas can indeed be seen as yet another way in which the dominant culture exercises its power over the minority – a festival for the majority 'other' which simultaneously entices but excludes the minority. However, such views are not shared by many Sikh and Hindu families in Southall, many of whom now celebrate Christmas rituals in their own manner. For some, Christmas is an occasion for extended family gatherings and viewing popular American 'family' films. [. . .]

A more insightful analysis of the significance of Christmas for Punjabi families in Southall is offered by Baumann (1992). He argues, and my data would support his arguments, that Christmas is a domestic ritual which is centrally concerned with defining and redefining relationships with 'others'. To the children these 'others' are their peers and school friends, with whom they discuss and compare their own family's celebrations. To parents and elders the 'others' are fellow Punjabis, kin or neighbours, 'who assess the merits of going too far, or not far enough, in replicating an originally 'alien ritual''. There are further 'others': the 'English' or *gori* whom both adults and children know as the minority locally and the majority nationally. Thus, through Christmas rituals, not least patterns of watching TV, youth and their

parents negotiate their subtly differing relationships to surrounding 'others'.
[...]

The religious and national rituals of Christmas, through the mediation of TV, both incorporate and are incorporated into Punjabi family life in London. Youth and their parents selectively adopt and adapt a range of customs and practices associated with Christmas, redefining their relations to a range of significant 'others', both present and absent. Such cultural interactions and transformations are typical in plural societies. [...] In many respects the differences between peer and parental cultures, and various kinds of attempt to negotiate between 'Indian' or 'Asian' and 'British' or 'Western' systems of representation, values and beliefs, structure the viewing patterns reported by young people in Southall. Certainly this process can be conflictual. But as the aspects of the local media culture which I have outlined in this chapter indicate, outright confrontation is much rarer – certainly in domestic settings – than processes of debate, accommodation and adaptation, in which young people, mothers, fathers and grandparents take up contextually variable positions in response to their viewing. What can be discerned overall is a complex process of many-sided negotiation between the cultures actually and televisually present in Southall, a negotiation which is reflected in patterns of TV talk in youth culture.

Appendix

TV and video use

(a) Family viewing patterns
(A)   'Which types of programme do you often watch with the family?'
(B)   'Which types of programme do you talk about with your parents?'
(C)   'Which types of programme did you actually watch in the last week?'
(D)   'Which types of programme do you prefer to watch without older people?'

For the results to all four questions (shown in 10a–e below), $N = 217$, of which 104 males, 113 females.

	% (A)	%(B)	%(C)	%(D)
News	76	43	64	0
Comedy	74	19	78	43
Crime	56	17	64	34
Soaps	54	13	59	37
Cartoons	51	7	72	36
Game show	51	10	65	0
Quiz	48	10	61	0
Pop	38	5	71	63
Children's	38	5	69	0
Nature	33	13	37	0
Documentary	25	9	39	0
Science	22	4	30	0
Sci-fi	20	3	36	0
Current affairs	20	4	28	28	0

(b) Gender breakdown: (A)
'Which type of programme do you often watch with the family?'

	% males	% females
News	74	78
Comedy	72	75
Crime	57	55
Soaps	48	58
Cartoons	47	55
Quiz	42	54
Game show	51	44
Pop	31	45
Children's	33	42
Nature	35	39
Documentary	28	22
Science	28	16
Sci-fi	29	12
Current affairs	21	18

(c) Gender breakdown: (B)
'Which type of programme do you talk about with your parents?'

	% males	% females
News	34	50
Comedy	17	20
Crime	13	21
Soaps	7	20
Nature	12	13
Game show	10	11
Quiz	7	13
Documentary	10	8
Cartoons	4	10
Pop	3	7
Children's	5	4
Science	4	4
Sci-fi	3	3

(d) Gender breakdown (C)
'Which types of programme did you actually watch in the last week?'

	% males	% females
Comedy	78	79
Cartoons	66	79
Pop	66	76
Children's	59	78
Crime	67	63
Game show	63	67
News	61	66
Quiz	57	66
Soaps	56	62
Documentary	42	36
Nature	49	26
Sci-fi	51	22
Science	41	21

(e) Gender breakdown (D)
'Which types of programme do you prefer to watch without older people?'

	% males	% females
Pop	54	70
Cartoons	72	36
Comedy	47	40
Soaps	32	40
Crime	43	25
All others	0	0

(f) Favourite programmes
'Which programme do you try to watch every week?'

	% total (N = 118)
Neighbours	67
The Bill	28
The Cosby Show	27
East Enders	24
Dallas	22
Home and Away	20
Dynasty	20
Top of the Pops	18
Miami Vice	7
Grange Hill	6
Brookside	6
Prisoner Cell Block H	3

(g) Preferred TV channel

	% family (N = 188)	% self
BBC1	82	64
ITV	76	45
Channel 4	16	21
BBC2	7	13

(h) Preferred video type
(A)   'often watch with whole family'.
(B)   'often talk about with father or mother'.

	% (A) (N = 217)	% (B)
Indian video	66	32
English video	55	15
American video	51	10

(j) Judgements about Indian films

	% females (N = 213)	% males
I enjoy them	48	24
They bring the family together	33	33
They help me with the language	39	23
They tell me something about Asia	37	25
They tell me about my religion	19	28
My parents like me to watch them	21	24
They teach me about Asian culture	26	15
I can watch them with friends	18	4
I like watching the stars	64	22
I like the songs and dance most	61	21
I like the action most	18	31
I like the dialogue most	25	17
They do not show the real Asia	30	24
I find them too slow	18	26
I don't like any of it	14	30

References

Alibhai, Y. (1987) A White Christmas. In *New Society*, 18 December 1987, pp. 15–17.

Appadurai, A. and Breckenridge, C. A. (1992) Museums are Good to Think: Heritage on View in India. In Karp, I. and Lavine, S. D. (eds.) *Museums and Communities: The Politics of Public Culture*, Smithsonian Institute, Washington.

Baumann, G. (1992) Ritual Implicates 'Others': Re-reading Durkheim in a Plural Society. In De Copet, D. (ed.) *Understanding Ritual*, Routledge, London, pp. 97–117.

Bharucha, R. (1991) A View From India. In Williams, D. (ed.) *Peter Brook and the 'Mahabharata': Critical Perspectives*, Routledge, London.

Guha-Thakurta, T. (1986) Artisans, Artists and Mass Picture Productions in Late 19th and Early 20th Century in Calcutta. Paper presented at the South Asia Research Conference, School of Oriental and African Studies, University of London, May 1986.

Pfleiderer, B. and Lutze, L. (eds.) (1985) *The Hindi Film: Agent and Re-agent of Cultural Change*, Manohar Publications, New Delhi.

Thomas, R. (1985) Indian Cinema: Pleasures and Popularity. In *Screen*, Vol. 26/3, No. 4, pp. 116–32.

Turner, V. (1966) Colour Classification in Ndembu Ritual. In Banton, M. (ed.) *Anthropological Approaches to the Study of Religion*, Tavistock, London, pp. 47–83.

Author index

Abaza, M. 320
Abbam, K. 249
Abrahamson, Y. 252
Abu-Lughod, L. ix, xvii, 311–22, 321
Addy, G. xxiv
Adorno, T. W. 238
Ahmed, A. S. 75
Alexandre, L. xvi, 108–12
Alger, C. 9
Ali, S. A. 320
Alibhai, Y. 333
Allen, R. C. 293
Alvarado, M. 294
Anand, A. 248, 249, 253, 255
Anderson, B. xiv, 7, 31, 58–66, 58
Ang, I. xxvii
Antonielli, C. 185
Appadurai, A. 319
Arbogast, R. 249
Archer, M. S. 4
Armbrust, W. 320

Bagdikian, B. 154
Bakke, M. 302
Bald, M. 255
Balibar, E. 70
Bangemann, M. 163
Baran, S. 146
Barber, R. R. 289
Barbrook, 240
Barendt, E. M. 216, 217
Barlow, W. 237, 238, 240, 242, 244
Barnouw, E. 238
Barucha, R. 329
Bassets, 230
Bauman, Z. 69
Baumann, G. 333
Beck, U. 165
Bell, M. 159, 180
Benjamin, W. 60
Bentham, J. 6
Bergesen, A. 3
Bergson, C. 41
Berrigan, F. 237
Bianchi, J. 300
Bill, J. 224
Bird, S. E. 249, 254
Blumer, J. G. 71
Booth, J. 239, 238, 244
Booz-Allen, 219
Boserup, E. 39
Boyd-Barrett, O. iv–xxx, xvi, xix, xxi, xxv, 131–44, 131, 133, 142, 284
Boyle, M. 100

Boyne, R. 287
Braman, S. xiv
Braslavsky, C. 57
Brecht, B. 221, 245
Breckenridge, 328
Browne, 240
Bryant, C. G. A. 4
Buck, E. 279
Buckingham, D. 306
Bull, H. 2, 32
Burnett, R. 281
Byerly, C. M. xviii, 248–56, 248, 250, 252, 253, 254
Byram, M. 221

Campbell, C. 285, 293
Canada, government of xxiii, 162, 173
Canclini, G. 292
Carver, B. 183
CEC, xix, xxii, xxiii, xxiv
Chan, J. M 98, 103, 286
Cheng, J.-C. 78
Wen, S.-C. 78, 79, 83, 85
Chesnais, F. 180
Chin, S. xiv, xv, xx, 78–93
Chirico, J. 3
Chomsky, E. 249
Clark-Meads, J. 280
Clarke, S. 145
Cohen, A. 131, 146, 149, 158, 159
Cohen, I. J. 4
Cohen, S. 279, 280
Cole, J. 42
Collins, R. 68, 73, 98, 101
Commission of the European Communities, 71
Comor, E. xv, xvi, xix, xxi, 194–206
Cooper-Chen, A. 302
Copley, J. 305, 307
Corominas, M. 72
Cox, R. W. 162, 163, 194, 195, 202, 203, 204
Cunningham, S. xxvi, xxvii, 142, 299–310
Curran, J. 217
Cuthbert, M.
Cuthbert, M. xvi, xix, xxi, 162–76, 171, 279
Cutts, P. 186

Dahrendorf, R. 75
Dalton, D. 272, 273
Dardenne, R. W. 249, 254
Darnton, R. 220

Dasgupta, 254
Davies, S. 105
Davis, 272
de Bens, E. 302
de la Garde, R. 301
de Witte, B. 216
Deas, M. 50
Delcourot, X. 72
Der Derian, J. 3, 6
Dessouki, A. E. H. 320
DeSwaan, 73
Dillinger, B. 160
Dobash, R. E. 73
Dobash, R. P. 73
Dombey, xxii
Dominick, J. R. 147
Donald, D. C. 149
Douglas, 244
Douglas, S. J. 238
Dowmunt, T. 233
Downing, J. 221, 223, 225, 226, 240
Drake, W. 205
Dunning, J. H. 179
Dykes, J. 100
Dyson, K. 71

Edwards, C. 40
El Guindi, F. 320
Elliot, P. 149, 158
Elliot, T. S. 75
Enzensberger, H. M. 221
Estes, R. 43

Fadul, A. 288
Falkenberg, K. F. 205
Fang, J. S. 102
Fathi, A. 221
Featherstone, M. 30, 284, 287, 295
Febvre, L. 60
Felder, R. 278
Fentress, J. 68
Ferguson, M. 145, 285, 287
Fernandes, I. 288
Festa, R. 294
Findahl, O. 99
Fisher, D. 104
Fiske, J. 300
Fornäs, J. 278
Foster, R. 255
Fox, E. 284
Fredenburg, P. 94
Freud, S. 52
Friedland, J. 138
Friedman, M. 287, 295, 296

340   *Author index*

Furchtgott, R. H. 204

Gail, B. 41
Galeano, 52
Gallagher, M. 248, 251
Galtung, J. 163, 164, 169, 171
Gans, H. 143
Garitaonandia, C. 153
Gellner, E. 59, 68
Gerrie, A. 309
Giddens, A. ix, xi, 3, 4, 5, 6,
    19–26, 29–30, 163, 166, 169,
    226, 259, 286
Giffard, C. A. 248, 253
Gifreu, J. 72
Gill, S. R. 202, 204, 205
Gillespie, M. xxvi, xxvii, 304,
    305, 323–37
Gilsdorf, W. 301
Giorgi, L. 69
Gisele, A. 252
Gitlin, T. xxvii, 249, 253
Goel, M. L. 229
Golding, P. 149, 158, 169, 205,
    219
Gong, G. W. 2
Gonzalez, A. 43
Gordon, L. 252
Gore, 172
Gowing, N. 151, 159
Graham, R. 228
Gramsci, A. 52
Green, J. 226
Greer, G. 307
Gregg, R. 169
Grossberg, L. xxvii
Guha-Thakurta, T. 328
Gurevitch, M. 131, 146, 149, 158,
    159

Habermas, J. 162, 164, 165, 166,
    167, 168, 173
Haggard, S. 180
Hall, S. 149, 237, 249, 265, 272,
    279, 281
Halliday, F. 205
Hamelink, C. T. 14, 162
Hamilton, 219
Hannerz, U. ix, xi, 11–18, 319
Harrison, P. 159
Harvey, D. 69
Hawkins, 182
Hawkins, R. xiii, xvi, 175–93, 189
Hay, J. xxvii
Hayek, F. 164
Headrick, D. 184
Heath, R. 105
Hegel, F. 5
Hein, K. J. 238, 244
Held, D. 163, 164, 166

Helland, K. 160
Hennessey, M. 274
Herman, E. S. 205, 249
Hicks, N. 43
Hills, J. xviii
Hitchens, L. P. xvi, xix, xxi, xxii,
    xxiii, 207–18
Hjort, A. 301
Hobday, M. 185, 189
Hobhouse, L. T. 4
Hobsbawm, E. 68, 69
Hochheimer, J. L. xvii, xviii,
    236–47, 237, 243, 244, 245
Hoffman-Ladd, V. 320
Hoffman-Riem, W. 71, 103
Holmes, P. 172
Hood, S. 238, 244
Horst, T. 41
Horwitz, R. 205
Hsiung, 87
Hsueh, C.-H. 79
Hu, Y.-S. 179
Huesca, R. 293
Hughes, O. 104
Hung, M. 274
Huntington, S. 164, 291
Husseini, S. 154

Ibrahim, S. E. 320
Iida, 184
Inglehart, R. 9
Intercom, 52

Jacka E. xxvi, xxvii, 142, 299–310
Jackson, T. xxii
Jakubowicz, K. 239, 239, 240, 241
Jankowski, N. 221, 233, 240
Jary, D. 4
Johnstone, C. B. 131
Jones, A. xv
Jouet, J. 237, 240

Kakabadse, M. A. 173
Kapur, J. xv
Karthigesu, R. 320
Kashak, M. 320
Katz, E. 73, 73, 290, 300, 303,
    304, 308
Kavoori, A. P. 155, 160
Keane, J. xxiv, 164, 169
Kelly, M. 302
Kepel, G. 320
Kern, S. 2
Kielbowicz, R. 249
Kindleberger, C. 179
Kingsley, H. 306
Kohn, H. 4
Kosicki, G. xxvii
Kottak, C. P. xxvi
Kramer, G. 320

Kranich, K. 248, 249, 254
Kwan, M. 82

Laing, D. 276, 279, 281
Lash, S. 295, 296
Lau, T. Y. 102, 104
Lechner, F. J. 3, 5, 7
Lee, C. 284
Lee, C.-C. 79, 86, 300
Lee, P. 102
Lee, T.-L. 87
Levitt, 271
Levy, M. 131, 146, 149, 158,
    159
Lewis, P. M. xviii, 239, 238, 244
Li, H.-L. 88
Liebes, T. 73, 290, 300, 303, 304,
    308
Lins da Silva, 285
Liu, M. T.-L. 231
Lockwood, D. 29
Luhmann, N. 9
Lull, J. xxvi, xxvii, 260, 259–68,
    261
Luther, M. 61
Lutze, L. 324
Luyten, J. M. 56

MacLeod, A. 320
Mader, R. xxi
Maffesoli, M. 69
Malik, R. 146, 154
Malkmus, L. 320
Malm, K. 278
Man Chan, J. xiv, 94–106
Mann, M. 3
Mansell, R. 74, 172, 184
Marin, M. 304
Marques de Melo, J. 290
Martin, H.-J. 60
Martin, J. xxi
Martin-Barbero, J. xiv, 50–7
Mattelart, A. 72, 223, 224,
    230
Mattelart, M. 72
McClear, R. 238
McCombs, M. E. 149
McDaniel, D. O. 286
McKenna, J. iv–xxx
McLeod, J. xxvii
McMahan, J. 205
McNeill, W. H. 7
McPhail, T. 284
Mead, G. H. 162, 165, 166, 168,
    173
Mele, M. 72
Melody, W. H. 205
Melucci, A. 68
Mendler, C. 183
Michael, J. 71

Milbraith, L. W. 229
Mills, C. W. 162, 165, 166, 167, 168, 169, 171, 173
Mitra, A. 288
Mittleman, J. H. 179, 180
Mohammadi, A. xviii, 220–35, 226
Mohanty, C. T. 248
Mol, A.-L. 240
Molina, G. G. 158
Molnar, H. 240
Monsivais, C. 52, 53, 54
Moore B. 223
Moore, W. E. 5
Moran, T. 41
Morencos, E. 274
Morgan, K. 172
Morin, E. 52
Morley, D. 73
Morris, M. 43
Morumpei, O. R. xv
Murdoch, R. 154
Murdock, G. 169, 205, 219

Naficy, H. 230
Nairn, T. 58
Namer, G. 68
Negrine, R. 72, 103, 153
Negus, K. xvii, 270–83, 281
Nettl, J. P. 3, 6
Nicolaidis, K. 205
Noam, E. 162
Nordenstreng, K. 284
Nott, S. 101

O'Connor, A. 238, 244, 249
Ogan, C. L. 252, 253
Oliveira, O. S. 290
Ong, 232
Østergaard, B. S. 71
Ottosen, R. 152

Palmer, M. 131
Palmer, R. 159
Pan, Z. xxvii
Panitch, L. 205
Papathanassopoulos, S. 72, 103, 153
Pareja, R. 51
Parker, I. 205
Parsons, T. 2 , 9
Patel, P. 179, 191
Paterson, C. xix, xvi, xx, 131, 135, 145–60, 152
Pavitt, K. 179, 180
Pendakur, M. xv
Perlmutter, T. xx, xxv
Pfleiderer, B. 324
Pieterse, J. N. 284, 286, 295, 296
Pohoryles, R. 71

Polybius, 4
Pool, I. xxiii
Pratrap, A. 97
Prehn, 240
Prehn, O. 221, 233
Preston, W. 205
Price, M. 260
Pride, D. 280
Pye, 164

Rakow, L. 248, 249, 254
Ranganath, H. K. 230
Ranger, T. 68
Rantanen, T. 131, 132
Read, D. 131, 138, 149
Reich, R. 179
Renan, E. 59
Reynolds, G. 304
Richeri, G. 73
Rivera, J. B. 56
Roach, C. 251
Robbins, xxv
Robertson, R. ix, xi, 2–10, 3, 6, 7, 31, 287, 288, 290, 295, 296
Robins, 271, 279
Robins, K. 73
Robinson, D. 279
Roche, D. 220
Roeh, I. 131, 146, 149, 158, 159
Roncagliolo, R. 284, 285
Rosenblum, M. 151
Rosencrance, R. 5
Rothschild-Whitt, J. 242, 243, 244
Ruggie, J. G. 180
Rush, R. R. 252, 253
Rutten, P. 278

Salter, L. 189
Santoro, L. F. 294
Sapper, A. 238
Sauvant, K. 45
Sauvant, K. P. 205
Schaffer, B. 101
Schell, O. 262
Scherer, H. 249
Schiller, H. I. xvii, 153, 205, 284
Schiller-Lerg, S. 238, 239
Schlesinger, P. xiv, 67–77, 68, 71, 73, 149, 158, 286, 292
Schmoch, U. 179
Schnöring, T. 179
Schramm, W. 221
Schudson, M. 143
Schulman, M. 238, 242, 244
Seton-Watson, H. 58
Shaaban, B. 256
Shain, Y. 226
Shapiro, M. J. 3

Shaw, D. L. 143
Shaw, M. ix, xii, 27–36
Shefrin, I. A. 186
Shinar, D. 233
Shohat, E. 289
Shore, L. 274
Siegelaub, S. 230
Silj, A. 72, 300, 301
Sinclair, J. 142
Siwek, S. E. 204
Sklair, L. ix, xii, xv, 37–47, 270
Skogerbo, E. 237, 240
Slater, J. 185
Slyomovics, S. 321
Smith R. 309
Smith, A. D. 3, 6, 30, 31, 74, 286
Snoddy, xxii, xxv
Soley, L. 226
Solomon, J. 199, 205
Spero, J. E. 205
Splichal, S. 74
Sreberny-Mohammadi, A. iv–xxx, xiv, xvii, xviii, xix, 220–35, 226
Staff, 100
Stamm, R. 289
Stappers, J. 221, 233
Steeves, H. L. 249
Stewart, L. 100
Stowasser, B. 320
Straubhaar, J. D. xv, xvi, xvii, xx, 284–98, 285, 293
Streeten, P. 43, 180
Sun, P.-Y. 78, 79
Sung, M.-C. 82
Sunkel, G. 55, 56, 57
Sweeney, T. 183

Tarjanne, P. 163
Taylor, C. 307
Taylor, M. 101
Tedesco, J. C. 57
Teller, A. 281
Thomas, R. 324, 325, 326
Tilly, C. 223
Tiryakian, E. 231
Trade Negotiations Committee, xxiii, 162
Tomlinson, J. 68, 142, 286, 287, 295, 296
Tuchman, G. 149, 249, 253
Tunstall, J. 131, 135, 142, 205, 289
Turner, J. 3
Turner, V. 329

Van Horn, C. 248
van Elderen, P. 278
Varis, T. 284
Vartanova, E. 131

Vincent, R. C. 172
Vreg, F. 237, 239

Wade, G. 221
Wagar, W. W. 4
Waite, T. L. 147
Wallerstein, I. 22, 29, 284, 287
Wallis, R. 148
Wang, G. 79, 97, 103
Wartella, E. xxvii
Warwick, W. 190
Wasko, J. xvi, xix, xx, xxiv,
    113–30
Watson, A. 2

Weaver, C. K. 73
Weber, M. 164, 241
Webster, xxv
Wechselmann, I. 310
Westcott, T. 153, 155, 159
White, A. 273
White, R. A. 237, 238, 239
Wickham, C. 68
Widlok, P. 238
Williams, R. 55, 319
Winseck, D. iv–xxx, xvi, xix, xxi,
    xxiii, xxiv, 135, 162–76,
    163, 171, 173
Wober, M. 303, 307

Wolton, D. 72
Woodrow, R. B. 205
Wuggenig, U. 71
Wuthnow, R. 4

Yang, C.-C. 87, 88
Youn, S.-M. 285, 293
Yücel, F. 189

Zeldin, T. 55
Zonis, M. 224, 229
Zubaida, S. 231

Subject index

access
  by-product of competition
    xxiv
Amnesty International 230
  function of 227

blocs
  capitalist 44
  capitalism vs communism 43
  communism 44
  EC 44
  global capitalist system 45
  Group of 77 45
  Non-Aligned Movement
    (NAM) 45
  oil exporters 44
  socio-political blocs 43
book-publishing
  basis for national
    consciousness 63
  birth of administrative
    vernaculars 61, 62
  history of 60
  impact of Reformation 61
  print-languages 63
  Protestantism and,61
  decline of use of Latin 60-3
broadcasting
  government broadcasting
    xvi, xvii
  Direct Broadcasting Satellite
    (DBS) 87
  European TV market,
    barriers
    (linguistic/cultural) 153
  Taiwan, history of 78-91
broker states 190
  Brazil 189
  Singapore/Korea 189
  India 189
  Turkey 189-90

cable-satellite
  global 290
  regional 293
capitalism
  expansion opportunities
    200-1
  global spread of market 287
capitalist
  block 44
  military alliance 44
centrally-planned economies 38
centre-periphery relationship
  asymmetry 13
  defined by input/scale 11

influence of culture 12
influence on economy 17-18
tier structure 13
civil societies
  global, emergence of 34
cold war 8, 68
  capitalism vs communism 43
  end of 8
  influence on modernity 2, 3
  national society, and 28
collective identity 70, 75
  communication, and 67
  characteristics 68
  European 67, 68, 69
  xenophobia 69
communication
  attempts to create new
    relations xiv
  civil society and 168
  changing regulatory practise
    xxiii
  constitutional protection 169
  contributions of xiv
  competition law xxiv
  commodity, as a xxiv
  decentralization xxi
  democratization xxii, xxv
  economic and technological
    convergence xxi
  emergence of multicultural
    centres xvii
  flows xiii
  globalization and
    internationalization 145
  historical xv
  historical relationships xiv
  horizontal integration xiii,
    xiv, xxiv
  international xvi, xvii
  Internet xviii
  nature of xxii
  new technologies xiv, xv,
    224-6
  marketing xiii
  mergers and acquisitions
    xxi
  ownership and control xix,
    74
  patterns xiii
  political xiii, xix, 226-7,
    228-9
  and political upheaval 226-7
  processes xiii, xxvi, 220
  public 165, 166, 167, 169, 173
  regulatory frameworks xxii
  restrictions on xiv

social interaction xiv
telecommunications xxi
Taiwan, difficulties in
  developing policy 89
vertical integration xxiv
communication goals
  formation of common
    markets xxiv
  international
    competitiveness
    xxiv
  technological innovation
    xxiv
communication networks
  standards setting xvi
communication system
  analysis of 167
  limited democracy 164
communication technologies
  143
  effect on discourse 166
  innovation 141
  regulation debate 172
communication policy xxii, xxiii,
  xxiv
  commitment to pragmatic
    democracy 171
  communicative democracy
    168
  democratic dilemmas 171,
    172
  development of global
    information infrastructure
    163
  General Agreement on Trade
    and Tariffs (GATT) 162,
    171, 173, 174
  International
    Telecommunications
    Union (ITU) 162, 163, 164,
    165, 169, 171, 172, 173,
    174
  INTELSAT 171
  limited democracy approach
    163
  Maitland Report 172
  North American Free Trade
    Agreement (NAFTA) 162,
    171, 173, 174
  politics of 174
  regulation and protection
    172-3
  rise of private sector 163
  trends 162-3
  UNESCO 162, 163, 169, 171,
    173, 174

communism 2, 9
  bloc 44
  centrally-planned economies
    43
  collapse implications 200, 203
  developing economies 43
  demise of communist bloc 67
  East European non-market
    economies 43
  military alliance 44
  v capitalism 43
community radio
  audience integration, control
    of 239
  community centre 238
  community, issues of 238
  consolidation of 8
  homogeneity 243
  ideal dimensions 241-2
  identification of target
    audience 238
  management of decision
    making 240
  mediation over segments
    and generations 239-40
  problems of emotional
    intensity 243
  reflection of traditional
    media 240
  societal segmentation 239
  versus traditional stations
    240-1
cultural alarmism
  anecdotes 16
  benefits of transnationalism
    14-15
  influence of West 14
cultural homogenization 103
cultural identities 74
  Greek 291
  Roman 291
  Islam 291
  examples of 291
cultural imperialism 286, 299
cultural influence
  colonial powers 12
  historical ties 12
  language 12
cultural management
  problems with 74
cultural markets 291
cultural production
  subordinate to cultural
    distribution xxvi
cultural purity vs creative
    interaction 15
cultural transfer
  artifacts 13
  effect to indigenous culture
    15

example, Nigeria 15, 16,
    17
  knowledge 14
  literature 13
  music 13
  products 13
  transnational 14
culture
  individuals and 12
  national centres of 12, 13
  oral/aural, roots of 232
  restriction of flow 13

democracy 242
  basic presupposition 165
  citizen participation 174-5
  communicative 168, 170, 173,
    237
  communicative dimension
    165
  communicative, theory 166-8
  defining 236
  'free flow of information'
    doctrine 173, 174
  global information age, and
    175
  limited 164, 166, 167, 168,
    170, 172, 174, 175
  pragmatic 170, 171, 172, 173
  public communication and,
    165, 169
  public sphere 167-8, 169, 171,
    173
  representative 165, 168
  role of state in
    communication rights 169
  technical 173
  technical dimension 164, 166
  technical vs communicative
    163-4
  universal right to
    communicate 167
democratic capitalism 2
democratic feminist socialism
    46
developing economies 43
dynamism of modernity
  time-space distinction 19
  disembedding 19
  reflexivity 19

East European non-market
    economies 43
Egypt
  rural attitudes to Islam
    317-18
Egyptian television
  absence of religion 313
  development of television
    315

government relationship
    with 316-17
  Islam and 311, 312
  personification of class 313
  producers of serials 311-12
  regionalism 317-18
  segregation of religion 316
  serials 312-13
    example, 'Ra'fat al-
      Haggan 316-17
    subject exclusion 315-18
ethnic exclusivism 46
ethnic nationalism 29
Euro-state 70
Europe
  audiovisual space 70, 71, 72,
    74
  common culture, core values
    74
  ethno-nationalist revival 69
  Europeanization resistance
    75
  integration, decline in 74, 75
  political union, decline in 73
  xenophobia 69
European Community (EC) 70
  Bangemann Report 214
  changing media
    environment 213-14
  EC Competition Law 211
  EC Treaty, Article 59 207
  EC Green Paper (1992) 208,
    217
  General Agreement in Trade
    and Tariffs (GATT) xvi,
    xxiii, xxiv
  income from music 272
  information society 214-16
  internal market regulation
    issues 212
  internal market protection
    211-12
  media concentration 210, 212
  media ownership and
    control 208, 210, 212
    constraints of existing
      regulation 215-16
  media ownership regulation
    208, 209-15, 216
  mergers, study of 213
  pluralism and economic
    objectivity 210-11
  television regulation 208
  Television Without Frontiers
    Directive 207, 208
  terrestrial vs satellite TV
    213
Europeanism
  see global society, identity
    35, 74-5

export-led industrialization
(ELI) 41

facism 2
film
American dominance 295
cinema of Mexico 52, 53
commodification 114
degradation 53
global phenomena 289
Hindi, and tradition 323–4
Hindi, criticism of 325–6
Hindi, enjoyment of 326
Hindi, narrative themes 325
Jurassic Park, success of 124
licensing 122
merchandising 122
melodrama, key to success 53
Mexican, development of 54
modernization 53
national identity 53
nationalism 53
product advertising 113–14,
120
product placement 114–17
regionalization 289
representation of India 324–5
tie-ins 118–22
theatrical 53
free trade
implications 203–4
free trade institutionalization
implications 200–2
key developments 201

geo-cultural markets 291
global
and local, relationship
between xiv
capitalism 46, 47
communication, increase in
means of 8
communication, societies
and 30
culture, news agencies and
143
ecumene 11
interdependence, move
towards 5
marketing 101
media system, dominance of
U.S. xvii
standard 39
system, rich/poor gap 46
global communication
infrastructure
(information
superhighway)
classification of accumulation
180–1

domination by G7 countries
177–8
locational advantage 190
R&D 179
regional power centres 178
technical infrastructure, lack
of 178, 190
global network infrastructure
development
Brazil 189
China 190
European infrastructure
184–5
global telecommunication
system 187
India 189
ITU 184
ITU and regional standards
bodies 183
national objectives 184
OAS/CITEL mechanism
185–6
R&D investment 190
regional articulation 187
regional centres 187, 189
regionalization 181–2, 183
example, Economic Union
181
Singapore/Korea 189
standards and computer
vendor involvement 183
standards definition 182, 183
sub-regions 188, 189, 191
technological regions 182
Turkey 189–90
U.S. infrastructure 185–6
global society
and anarchy 32, 33
civil 34, 35
cohesion 30
concept 31
constraints of cultural system
33
differences from national
societies 32
economic system 32, 33
homogenization 31
horizontal integration xiii
identity 35
issues of development 30
political conflict 31
political system 33
social relations 31
structural complexities 32
vertical integration xiii
global system classification 45–7
bloc-based 37, 43–5, 45
income-based 37, 45
quality of life based 37, 42–3,
45

resource based 37, 41–2, 45
state-centred categories,
problems with 45
trade-based 37, 40–1, 45
world 37
global telecommunication
system
ITU 182
standards definition 182
global-local nexus 4
globalism 178
globalization 21, 287, 295
abstract systems 30
access to news 226
affect on labour 25
affect on political
communication 226–7
American state as mediator
194–5
association with global state
system 6
cable-satellite 290–1
capitalism xv
centralization vs sovereignty
23
communication of news 26
components 7
conception of 3
counter-hegemonic
challenges 203, 204
cultural development 30, 34
current theory 295–6
debate 284–5
defining of social relations 31
definition 19, 179, 180, 271
development of central
reference points 8
diffusion of nationalism 31
European 273
extent of 285
global ordering 276
growth of 19
implementation of world
time 8
implications of free flow 203
importance of 6
industrial development 25
influence of capitalism 21, 22
influence of societal
participation 8
information revolution 201
innovation activity indicator
179
local transformation 19
microeconomics indicators
180
modernity 284, 287
national society, aspect of 7
national-station system 22
new technologies and, 296

globalization (*contd*)
   news agencies and, *see* news
      agencies
   news homogenization, threat
      of 155
   communications 145
   opposition to xiv
   pattern of 11
   patterns of production 142
   production of national, local
      identities 288
   reflexive modernization 169
   relationship to modernity 4
   resistance to 289
   restriction of 6
   rise of local nationalism 20
   role of state 195
   sociological debate 29
   state, importance of 203
   structural 286
   survival of transnational
      corporations (TNC's) 201
   technologies of
      communication 25
   transformation of state role
      179
   uneven change 273
   use of term 3
   variation in nations and
      cultures 142
   vertical integration xiii
   world capitalist economy 22
   world military order 24
   world wars 24
   world-wide homogenization
      xvii
globalization mapping
   germinal phase 7
   incipient phase 7
   take-off phase 7, 8
   struggle for hegemony phase
      8
   uncertainty phase 8
glocalization 290

hegemony
   concept of 202
Human Rights Watch 227

identity
   cultural xv, xiv
   European xiv
ideology of consumption xv
import substitution
      industrialization (ISI) 40–1
income-based classification 37
   assumptions 38
   exclusions 39
   problems 38, 39
   women, invisibility of 39

industrialism
   labour 25
   diffusion of technology 25
   communication 25
information, public good 173
information society
   Bangemann Report 214
   EC and, 214
   EC and Acting Plan 214
infrastructures
   technological xxiii
   services or contents xxiv
international
   as an expression 6
   development of conventions
      and relations 7
   development of society 8
   of law of nations 6
   relations, concept 35
   relations, variants of 3
   trade structure 187
International
      Telecommunications
      Union (ITU) xvi
   World Administrative
      Telegraph and Telephone
      Conference (1988) 199
   GATT process and free flow
      to free trade 198–9
internationalization 3
   news agencies and, 143
   television news 145
Internet 135, 139
   and newsflow xxi
   new markets and, 140
interregional articulation 187

Korean Airline (KAL 007)
      tragedy xvii, 108
   anti-Soviet campaign 108,
      110–11
   broadcasting output 109
   broadcasting program 109–10
   disinformation 111, 112
   propaganda operation
      108–12
   role of U.S.A. (broadcasting)
      109–10
   U.S.A. editorials 110

languages, authority control of
      64
licensing
   benefits of 126
   definition 122
   licensees 125
   owners 125
   research companies 125
   retailers 125
   risks of 126

royalties 125
   trade magazines 125
local-global nexus 9
low-income economies 38

markets, defining xv
mass communication
   vertical integration xviii
mass culture
   formation in Latin American
      51, 52
   sensationalist press, and 57
   transformation of
      nationhood idea 51
mass media
   accessibility 54
   appropriation by popular
      masses 51
   cinema of Mexico 52, 53
   cultural sphere 50
   European identity 71
   example of, Columbia 51
   expression of popular
      demands 51
   historical perspective 50
   political sphere 50
   press 54
media
   alternative organizations
      241–2
   alternative xvii, xviii
   and industry xix
   as a 'virtual space' 223
   audiences
   benefits to U.S. xv
   media boundaries xxi, 213,
      216
   British representations of
      India 325
   censorship xxi
   commercialization xx
   convergence xxi
   corporations xix
   development trends xv, xvi
   economic role 214
   emancipatory use 221
   global flow 295
   globalization 142
   horizontal integration xxii
   importance of xv
   integration into power
      centres xx
   local news 331–3
   low-cost technologies xviii
   media flows 285
   mergers and acquisitions xxii
   mergers xix, xx
   multi-media environment
      xxii
   news networks xvi

New World Information and
   Communication Order
   (NWICO) 284
one-way flow xvii
relationship with youth xxvii
setting agenda for TV news
   149
texts xvii
trends xvii, xix, xxv
variety xxv
vertical integration xviii, xxii,
   xxv
vertically dis-integrated xxv
Western examples of
   participatory forms 221
women in 249, 251, 257
media (dis-) integration xxiv
affect on social relations of
   communication xxiv
media convergence
economic, role of xxi
media ownership, xiii
internal market regulation
   212
EC regulation issues 208
media power
conceptualization xxvi, xxvii
influence xxvi
media production
globalization of xxv
media corporations xxv
subordinate to xxv
media system
allows exploration of
   alternative lives xxvi
China xxvi
development of popular
   culture xxvi
relationships and influence
   on socio-economic
   merchandizing
definition 123
future, reasons for 126–7
generic movie studio
   products 123
Hollywood, history of 124–5
importance of marketing
   campaigns 124
product range 123
television, and 125
tie-in to Hollywood stars 123
trends 123
mergers and acquisitions
EC and increased activity 213
effect of xxii, 211
examples of mergers 213
horizontal mergers 213
MCI Communications and
   News Corporation 213
vertical mergers 213

middle class
rise of xv
modernity 2, 3, 284
Allies v. the Axis 8
definition 259
modernization 259–60
China 261
globalization 142
news agencies and, 142
Murdoch, Rupert 154, 155
music industry xvii
abstract electronic space 271
Anglo-American dominance
   274, 277
community-based activities
   278–9
cultural imperialism 279
emergence of 'local music'
   280–1
European Music Network
   280
globilization, impact on
   271–2
importance of Europe 270,
   272–3
national government
   support 277–8
national/international
   conflicts 280
pan-European restructuring
   275–7
popular music 271
recording companies, global
   aims 272–3
Sony Music 276
state support for local 278
uneven global change 273
Warner Music International
   276
working practice tensions
   274–5, 279

nation
bases for 64
definition 59–60
nationalism, roots of 60
problems of defining 58
nation-state 20, 22, 28, 46, 70
global system 20
homogeneous 7
media policy process 74
national societies, and 27
regional identities 319
relationships with each other
   20
sovereign 23, 24, 69
unification 21
national consciousness, rise of
   60

national identity
political xii
cultural xii
national society 7
national symbolism 16
nationalism 31
cultural roots of 60
development of 28, 29
ethnic 29
ethno-nationalism 70
rebirth 68
resurgence 34
Neo-facism 2
neo-tribalism 69
network infrastructure, concept
   of 184
new technologies 295
effect on production costs
   xxv
regulation and 213–14
New World Information and
   Communication Order
   (NWICO) xviii, 197, 198,
   203, 251
news
development, definition 248
female journalists 249, 251
framing, example 253–4
Ghana 249
local, impact on domestic
   ritual 332–3
marginalized groups 249, 254
representation of women
   248–50, 252, 256–7
sexist attitudes 252
structure of content
   (framing) 249, 253
UN Decade for Women
   conference (1975) 249–50
UNESCO and 250, 251
Women's Feature Service
   250–5
women's marginalization 253
news agencies
Agence France Press (AFP)
   132, 133
agency strength 135
Anglo-American dominance
   135
as retailers, 134, 135
as transnational media
   systems 132
as wholesalers 131, 134, 135
Associated Press (AP)
   (U.S.A.) 131, 133
benefits of 131–2
'Big 4' 133
challenge of information
   superhighway 141
characteristics of 133

news agencies (*contd*)
  client participation 138
  collaborations between
    companies 134
  competition 140
  communications technology
    and, 141
  continuing independence
    135
  corruption and, 140
  distribution channels,
    growth in 135, 139, 140–1
  diversification 138
  examples of, xvi, xx, xxiii, xxv
  financial television news
    services 135
  global 137, 142, 143
  global agency, conditions for
    development of 136
  global culture 143
  global identities and, 143
  globalization and 132–9, 143
  importance of domestic
    market 137
  internationalization and
    143
  modern communicational
    needs 142, 143
  objectives 142
  previous debates 133
  problems of market entry
    136
  relationship with
    governments 132, 133, 138
  Reuters xvi, 131, 133, 134,
    135, 136, 137, 138, 140, 143,
    153
  satellite and, 134
  services 139–40
  television 134
  UNESCO and, 132
  United Press International
    (UPI) 133–4
  video 134, 137
  vehicles for 132
  Western-based, criticism of
    132
  western origins 143
North American Free Trade
    Agreement (NAFTA) xvi,
    xxiii, xxiv
North Atlantic Treaty
    Organization
    and Warsaw Pact 44

oil imports, significance on
    development 41
OPEC
  oil exporter block 44
  power of 41

organization
  value-rational orientation
    241
Organization for Economic
    Cooperation and
    Development (OECD) 44
ownership and control xxiii
  relaxation of U.S.A.
    ownership restrictions
    xxiv

Peoples Republic of China 43
  aesthetic language 267
  economic contradiction 262
  electronic amplification of
    contradiction 261–3
  low-income economy 43
  modernization 259, 262–3
  television as a cultural forum
    264–5
  television, control of 265
  television, loss of mass
    audience 266–8
  television, polysemic 265–6
pluralism
  competition and, xxiv, 210,
    211
  economic objectives and
    210–11
  European Commission and,
    209–10
  Fininvest 210
  media concentration and 210
  media regulation and 214
political mobilization
  culture and 230
popular culture
  and the Third World 15
press
  Chilean 55, 56
  development of popular
    journalism in Latin
    America 56
  historical analysis of popular
    54, 55
  prototypes for popular
    journalism 56
  sensationalism 57
  sensationalist in U.S., Europe
    55
print-capitalism 63, 64
print-languages
  bases for national
    consciousness 64
printing 25
product advertising 113–14
  example, Jack Daniels 113,
    114
  Fortune 500 companies 114
  rise in sophistication 114

product placement
  audience 115
  example, Pepsi-Cola 114
  family deals 117
  lawsuit example, Black and
    Decker 117
  other media types 117
  placement fees 114, 115
  placement firms 114
  placement procedure 115
  pressure in scripts 116–17
  production costs vs
    advertiser intrusion
    116–17
  regulation, lack of 117
  revenue 114, 115
  successfulness, examples 115,
    116
  verbal mentions 115
production
  contracting out process xxv
programme reduction
  quantitative vs qualitative xx
  affect of budget cuts xx
public communication
  participatory media and 221
public sphere
  defining 224
  Iran and 224

quality of life classification
  basic needs theory 43
  controversy 43
  economic indicators 43
  index of social progress 43
  social welfare indicators 42

radio
  community radio and
    democratic structure 237
  development of 236
  foundation of
    media/audience
    relationship 236
radio
  Sunrise, Southall local station
    331–2
regionalization 181–2, 188
  geo-linguistic/cultural 292
  regional centres 187
  sub-regions 188, 189, 191
  television 285, 291
regulation
  impact of relaxed restrictions
    in U.S.A. xxiv
  harmonization xiii
  liberalization xvi, xvii
  media industry xix
regulatory systems
  limitations for emerging
    technology xxiii

exclusions from tax xxiv
restriction on convergence
and competition xxiii
relationships
centre-periphery of culture
12
religious identity and political
power 231
resource-based classification 41
resource dependence of U.S.
41
oil imports, significance on
development 41
Reuters 154, 155, *see also* news
agencies
client links 138
client numbers 139
diversification 138–9
financial television 135
Internet and 135, 141
links to satellite 134
networks 141
new markets 140
Reuters Television 146, 147,
148
revenue 139
services 139, 140
staff levels 139
television news 147
vertical link with U.K.
136–7
revolution
communicative process 220
Iranian 220
French 220
revolutionary mobilization 222
China 259
communication and
participation 228–9
contemporary model 233
exile communication 227
small media and, 223–33
Iran 223, 224, 226, 227, 228,
229, 230, 230, 231, 232, 233,
234
Nicaragua 224, 229, 231
Poland 225–8, 229, 230, 231
reconstruction of collective
memory/identity 232–3
religion 230–1, 232
religious identity and
political power 233
repoliticizing popular culture
229–30
reproductive power of small
media, and 225, 226
social authority 232
revolutionary movements
impact of new technologies
225

importance of small media
222
Iranian 222, 223
contemporary model 222
rituals, British 333–4
national rituals, impact on
minorities 333–4

satellite
competition from terrestrial
TV 98
future problems of policing
99, 103, 104
global 290–91
linguistic barriers 99
link to nation's affluence 101
programming 100
regional 293
regulation problems 207
revenue 100, 101
technological innovations 99
television news and, 147
satellite communications
AsiaSat 1: 94
small media
cultural power 230
defining 221
ease of production 225
indigenous culture 229
political mobilization 224
political participation 227–31
religious networks 230–31
revolutionary mobilization
222
samizdat 223, 225
social authority 231–32
magnetizdat 223
supporting popular
mobilization 220
soap opera
Asian market 302
as social text 305, 307
Australian, development in
Britain 303
Australian, reasons for
popularity 302–4, 306, 309
Canadian market 302
cross-cultural reception
analysis 299–300
Dallas, studies of 300
devotional viewing 327–9
East Enders 306–7
European market 302
financial importance of 306
Gillespie study (1991) on
Neighbours 304–5
impact on cultural values
330–1
importance of scheduling
303, 308

imported, reasons for success
299–300, 301
Independent Television
Commission (ITC) 1992
Survey 303–4
Neighbours 330
Neighbours, reasons for
success 304–5, 307
primary audience
(gatekeepers) 301, 308
television market structure
301
Southall youth 'devote
viewing' 330
study methodology 300–1
U.S. market 301
weekday stripping 308
social authority
secondary orality 232
small media, and 231–2
social indicator 42 *see also*
quality of life classification
social relations
global society 31
societies
discrete 28
divisions 30
national 30, 32
tribal 28, 30
society 30
definitions 27
discrete 27
historical development 28
international 32
multicultural/polyethnic 8
problems 8
society-state relationships 32
STAR TV 153
accessibility, determinants of
98
advertising and, 101
Asian restrictions, reasons for
98
AsiaSat 1 97
China and, 97–8, 102–3
competitive position 98, 99,
100, 102
cultural homogenization 103
cultural policy 100
Hong Kong and 102, *see also*
television
illegal openness 96–7
impact on national media-
culture 104
importance of Mandarin
audience 99
language diversity, problems
of 99, 100
operating costs 101
penetration 94–6, 99, 100, 102

STAR TV (*contd*)
'prior consent' principle
breakdown 103–4
programming 100
regulation 95, 98
regulated openness 96–7
service 94–5, 99, 103
subscriptions 101
suppression 96, 97
Taiwan and, 102
target markets 101
technological innovations
and, 99
state
relations, powers and limits
6
sovereignty and relations vs
statehood conceptions 6
structural autonomy, reduction
of xix, xx
censorship, privatization of
xx
emphasis on profitability xx
investing national
competition xx
loss of cultural specificity xx
structuration, concept 4
super powers
influence of world
movement 11

Taiwan broadcasting system
84
Broadcasting and Television
Law (1976) 79, 81, 82, 83
Broadcasting Development
Fund for Chinese Public
Television (CPTV) 85
Cable Television Association
(1990) 84
Cable Law (1993) 85, 84
cable TV 82, 84, 90
Common Antennas
Television (CATV) 82, 83
deregulation 89, 90
Direct Broadcasting Satellite
(DBS) 86
Fourth Channel 81, 82
future challenges 91
Green television station 80–1
history of 78
'one area five systems' 84
political influence 79, 86,
90–1
public television, rise of 85–6,
91
quality of programs 91
radio broadcasting 89, 90
rise of cable TV 81
rise of illegal TV 80–1, 83

satellite broadcasting 86, 87,
90
satellite, collaboration with
other countries 89
satellite deregulation 86, 87
satellite projects 87, 88, 89
STAR TV 99
Taiwan Democratic Cable
Television (TOCATU) 81
Taiwan Television Enterprise
(TTV) 78, 79
television, local 90
technological confusion xxiv
technologies, new xvii
effect on production costs
xxv
introduction of
technology
globalization and, 25
specific measures of xxiii
telecommunications
information society 214
interactive communication
xviii
increase in flows xviii
development of horizontal
communication xviii
GATT agreement xxiii, xxiv
NAFTA agreement xxiii,
xxiv
Internet xxiv
telephone
declining costs xviii
television
American dominance 289–90
Australian soaps 299–309
authoritarian power 261
Brazilian soap 288
British, late 1980's 306
Canadian market 302
China, amplification of
contradiction 262–3
China, growth of system 260
China, loss of mass audience
266–8
China, propaganda device
260–1
constraints on European
distribution 73
control of 265
cultural forum 264–5
cultural markets 292
Egypt, importance of serials
311
Egyptian 311–19
Egyptian serials xvii
European market and soaps
302
European programming 72
fallacy of distribution 73

global phenomena 289–90,
295
identity-conferring 71
implications for Australian
strategy 309
importance of, to Southall
youth 323
internationalization 72, 103
limitations of European
programs 72
local 293–4
market structure and soaps
301
markets, multi-level
approach 285–6, 295
MEDIA 92: 72
MEDIA 95: 72
media ownership and
control 210
national 293–4, 319
parochial internationalism
309
pluralism and economic
objectivity 212–13
polysemy 265–6
public perception of crisis
coverage 150–1
regional markets 292–3
regionalization 285, 291
satellite 213
satellite and cable, problems
of regulation 207
satellite vs terrestrial 98,
104
shape western view of world
148
soap opera 288
social experience in Southall
families 331
STAR TV (Hong Kong) 88,
94–105
Taiwan, rise of public
television 85
Television Directive (EEC)
(1989) 207, 208
terrestrial 213
threat of Americanization 72
traditional regulation 207
U.S. market resistance to
foreign imports 301
use of, figures 334–7
television company ownership
quality of programs 79–80
standardization of dialects 79
television news
affiliations 147–8
agencies influence on news
actually seen 148–9, 150–2
agenda setting by other
media 149

Anglo-American dominance 148
client interest 152
CNN 145
competition 145
coverage 152
crisis coverage 151–2
    example, Rwanda 151–2
    public perception of, 149–50
Disney Corporation 145
Euronews 153
European market, problems with 153
fees 147
history of 147
homogeneity 146, 154–5, 156
ideological neutrality argument 148–9
importance of illustrations 145
influence of costs 152
interaction of audience 155
internationalization 145
London, seat of 145
ownership 153
packagers and distributors (retailers) 146
profits 153
resource allocation 152, 154
Reuters/Murdoch alliance 154
rise in global coverage 152–3
service 147
single language news channels 153–4
two-tier structure 146–7
video images 146
war coverage 150–1
    example Bosnian 150–1
wholesalers 146
television visuals
wholesalers 146
territory
corporations vs states control of 22–3
Third World development
foreign debt 41
import substitution industrialization (ISI) 40–1
tie-ins
benefits of 119, 121
definition 118
disadvantages of 121–2
example, *An American Tail* 120
example, *Kraft Inc.* 119
example, *Pizza Hut* 118
example, *Quaker* 118–19
importance of film release

schedule 120, 121
Land Before Time 119, 120
    marketing strategy 120–1
Oliver & Company products tied-in 119, 120
other examples 119
promotional arrangements 122
Willow products, tied in 118
Time Warner xix, xxii, xxiii
time–space distanciation
local involvement's 19
interaction across distance 19
trade-based classification 40
consumption patterns 42
export-led industrialization 41
food imports, indicator of dependence 42
foreign trade patterns 40
import substitution industrialization (ISI) 40–1
oil import, significance of development 42
tradition
use of video cassette recorder 323
transnational capitalism 44
transnational consumption communities xv
transnational cultural flow
commodity flow 17
long-term effects 17
importance of time 16
international comprehension of 16
saturation vs maturation 17

United States
corporation dominance 195–6
disinformation 108, 111, 112
free flow to free trade 194
industries 195–6
reassertion of hegemony 197–9
withdrawal from UNESCO 197–8, 199
United States foreign communication policy
American state as mediator 202, 204
crisis 197
emergence of free trade of information-based systems 196–7
emergence of free trade solution 198–9
First Amendment 197
foreign corporations 198

free flow of information
crisis 195–7
free trade institutionalization 199–200
free trade opposition weakened 200
GATT Uruguay Round negotiations 199–200, 202, 209
exemptions 199
hegemony 202–4
implications of free flow 203
trade regimes 198–9
USTR (Office of the United States Trade Representative) 199
United Nations 24
establishment of 8
United Nations Education, Scientific and Cultural Organization (UNESCO) xvi, 197, 198, 250, 251, 252, 255

vertical disintegration
casual employment xxv
bypass of unions xxv
vertical integration xxv
video
use of, figures 334–7
video agencies
development from parent infrastructure 137–8
independence from government 138

Warsaw Pact
and NATO 44
women
understatement of economic significance 39
Women's Feature Service 250–5
example 251–2
framing, example 253–4
multichanneled dissemination 255
publication rates 254
service 250, 254–5, 255–6, 256
UNESCO and, 250, 252, 255
world
capitalist economy 21, 23
cultural flow 13
economics 21
homogenization 11
order 3
system 3, 4, 6, 21, 22
study of 3
organization of whole 4
singular system, creation of 5

world development indicators
 GNP per capita 37, 38
World Development Report 37
world economy
 capitalist states 22
 corporations 23
world politics
 conception of 2
World Trade Organization xvi

World War I 2, 5, 8, 236
 and modernity 2
 postwar development of
  nation-states 5
World War II
 establishment of orders 2
 legacy of cynicism 9